AF836097

IRISH TAX REPORTS

2006 Cases, Cumulative Tables and Index (1922–2006)

IRISH TAX REPORTS

2006 Cases,
Cumulative Tables
and Index (1922–2006)

Editor

Kelley Smith BCL, LLM, AITI, BL

Tottel
publishing

Published by
Tottel Publishing Ltd
Maxwelton House
41-43 Boltro Road
Haywards Heath
West Sussex
RH16 1BJ

Tottel Publishing Ltd
Fitzwarren Business Centre
26 Upper Pembroke Street
Dublin 2
Ireland

ISBN 13: 978-1-84766-040-4
ISBN 10: 1-84766-040-1
Complete set ISBN 13: 978-1-84766-044-2
ISBN 10: 1-84766-044-4
Formerly published by LexisNexis Butterworths

1922-2006 edition published 2007

British Library Cataloguing-in-Publication Data
A catalogue record for this book is available from the British Library

These reports should be cited thus: [Year] (Volume) ITR (Page)

Typeset by Marlex Editorial Services Ltd., Dublin, Ireland
Printed and bound in Great Britain by
Athenæum Press Limited, Gateshead, Tyne & Wear

Introduction

This book contains the 2006 tax cases. As with previous editions of this book, it also serves as a cumulative tables and index volume for the six volumes of Irish Tax Reports. These tables and this index should ensure that the required cases are easily and quickly located. If you have any comments or suggestions for improvements, please contact the editor or Tottel Publishing.

1. **Contents 2006** vii
   This outlines cases and determinations contained in the 2006 volume.

2. **Contents 1922–2006** 1
   This is a *chronological* list of all the cases reported, which also shows key words relating to each case and references indicating where the case was previously reported.

3. **Cases 2006** 55
   These are all the relevant cases since the 2005 publication.

4. **Cases reported** 107
   This is an *alphabetical* list of the cases reported.

5. **Cases considered** 117
   This is an *alphabetical* list of the cases referred to in judgments or cases cited in the cases reported in full.

6. **Statutes considered** 161
   This table lists, in *alphabetical and numerical* sequence, the statutory provisions considered by the courts.

7. **Destination table (Taxes Consolidation Act 1997)** 187
   This table enables the reader to trace the present location of legislation between 1967 and 1997.

8. **Index** 281
   This is an *alphabetical* subject index which sets out the subject matter of each case in the six volumes.

Tottel Publishing

February 2007

http://www.tottelpublishing.com

Contents 2006

Campus Stadium Ireland Development Ltd v Dublin Waterworld Ltd............................55

Electricity Supply Board v The Minister for Social Community and Family Affairs & Others..63

The Revenue Commissioners v O'Flynn Construction Co Ltd, John and Michael O'Flynn...81

Contents 1922–2006

Arthur Guinness Son & Co Ltd v Commissioners of Inland Revenue
1 ITC 1, [1923] 2 IR 186 .... Vol I p 1

Income tax and excess profits duty – liability in respect of transactions under DORA requisition orders – trade or business – ITA Sch D – FA 1915 (No 2) s 38.

McCall (Deceased) v Commissioners of Inland Revenue
1 ITC 31 .... Vol I p 28

Excess profits duty – purchase of whiskey in bond by a publican – whiskey in bond could be sold to best advantage – whether sale at cost plus interest constituted a trade – whether an investment with capital gains – whether a trade is carried on as a question of law and fact – whether facts found by Special Commissioners can be reopened.

Boland's Ltd v Commissioners of Inland Revenue
1 ITC 42 .... Vol I p 34

Excess profits duty – whether profits to be ascertained by actual profits or a percentage standard – percentage standard based on 6 per cent of company's net capital – whether proper deduction for wear and tear and capital expenditure on replacements of capital items – whether assessment can be reopened – doctrines of res judicata and equitable estoppel – whether inspector entitled to recompute percentage basis – whether appellants precluded from introducing new grounds of appeal.

Evans & Co v Phillips (Inspector of Taxes)
1 ITC 38 .... Vol I p 43

Income tax – Schedule D – obsolescence of assets – ITA 1918 Sch D Cases I & II rule 7.

Irish Provident Assurance Co Ltd (In Liquidation) v Kavanagh (Inspector of Taxes)
1 ITC 52, [1930] IR 231 .... Vol I p 45

Income tax – Schedule D – interest on money – ITA 1918 Sch D Case III.

The King (Harris Stein) v The Special Commissioners
1 ITC 71 .... Vol I p 62

Confirmation of assessment – request for case stated by taxpayer – allowance of expenses where assessment has been confirmed

Phillips (Inspector of Taxes) v Keane
I ITC 69, [1925] 2 IR 48 .... Vol I p 64

Income tax – Schedule E – deduction – travelling expenses – ITA 1918 (8 & (Geo V, Ch 40)), Sch E, rule 9.

Phillips (Inspector of Taxes) v Limerick County Council
1 ITC 96, [1925] 2 IR 139 .... Vol I p 66

Income tax – Sch D Case III – interest – deduction.

Commissioners of Inland Revenue v The Governor & Company of The Bank of Ireland
1 ITC 74, [1925] 2 IR 90 .... Vol I p 70

Corporation profits tax – the Governor and Company of the Bank of Ireland incorporated by letter patent – Act of Irish Parliament 1783 – whether a company within the meaning of FA 1920 s 52(3) – unpaid debts of bank – whether personal liability of members unlimited.

Boland's Ltd v Davis (Inspector of Taxes)
1 ITC 91, [1925] ILTR 73 .... Vol I p 86

Income tax – Schedule D – discontinuance – distance trades – set-off for losses – ITA 1918 Sch D Cases I and II and miscellaneous rules.

Fitzgerald v Commissioners of Inland Revenue
1 ITC 100, [1926] IR 182, 585 .... Vol I p 91

Excess profits duty – deductions – expenditure on temporary premises – restoration of destroyed premises under covenant to repair.

The Alliance & Dublin Consumers' Gas Co v Davis (Inspector of Taxes)
1 ITC 114, [1926] IR 372 .... Vol I p 104

Income tax – Schedule D – profits of trade – deduction – capital loss – ITA 1918 Sch D, Cases I & II, rule 3.

The City of Dublin Steampacket Co v The Revenue Commissioners
1 ITC 118, [1926] IR 436 .... Vol I p 108

Corporation profits tax – company formed mainly for purpose of trading by use of steam vessels – cargo business and carriage of mails between Dun Laoghaire and Liverpool and Holyhead – cargo business ceased 1919 – mails contract terminated 1920 – whether running down of business constituted a trade or business – whether collection of debts a business undertaking – periodic payments on foot of an earlier debt and acquisition of profits – whether carrying on a business.

Donovan (Inspector of Taxes) v Crofts
1 ITC 214, [1926] IR 477 .... Vol I p 115

Income tax – husband and wife living apart – "married woman living with her husband" – ITA 1918 rule 16 of general rules.

Commissioners of Inland Revenue v The Dublin and Kingstown Railway Co
1 ITC 285, [1930] IR 317 .... Vol I p 119

Corporation profits tax – The Dublin and Kingston Railway Co was incorporated in 1831 to make and maintain a railway between Dublin and Kingston – railway lines leased to another company at an annual rent – all the property of owning company (except offices) passed to lessee company – whether collection of rents and dividends and distribution of profits thereout to shareholders constituted a trade or business – whether company has a corporate existence.

Green & Co (Cork) Ltd v The Revenue Commissioners
1 ITC 142, [1927] IR 240 .... Vol I p 130

Excess profits duty – stock relief claim – "trading stock in hand" – FA 1921, Sch 2 Pt II, rule 1.

Wing v O'Connell (Inspector of Taxes)
1 ITC 170, [1927] IR 84 .... Vol I p 155

Income tax – Schedule E – vocation – professional jockey – whether present from employer taxable emolument or gift.

The Executors and Trustees of A C Ferguson (Deceased) v Donovan (Inspector of Taxes)
1 ITC 214, [1927] ILTR 49, [1929] IR 489 .... Vol I p 183

Income tax – Sch D Case 1 – business carried on abroad – control by trustees.

Hayes (Inspector of Taxes) v Duggan
1 ITC 269, [1929] IR 406 .... Vol I p 195

Income tax – Schedule D – profits on sweepstakes – illegal trades not assessable to tax – ITA 1918 Sch D Cases II & VI.

The Alliance and Dublin Consumers' Gas Co v McWilliams (Inspector of Taxes)
1 ITC 199, [1928] IR 1 .... Vol I p 207

Income tax – profits of trade – compulsory detention of ships by government – compensation payment – capital or trading receipt – ITA 1918.

MacKeown (Inspector of Taxes) v Roe
1 ITC 206, [1928] IR 195 .... Vol I p 214

Income tax – public office or employment of profit – solicitor to local authority – ITA 1918 Sch E, rules 1 & 5 – profits not received in the year of assessment.

The King (Evelyn Spain) v The Special Commissioners
1 ITC 227, [1934] IR 27 .... Vol I p 221

Mandamus – finality of Special Commissioners' decision on claim for relief -income tax – income accumulated for minor – benefit taken by way of capital – ITA 1918 ss 25 & 202.

Conyngham v The Revenue Commissioners
1 ITC 259, [1928] ILTR 57, 136 .... Vol I p 231

Super tax – total income – trust deed – trust for expenditure of moneys upon property beneficially occupied by life tenant – ITA 1918 s 5.

The Revenue Commissioners v Latchford & Sons Ltd
1 ITC 238 .... Vol I p 240

Excess profits duty – loss in trade – forward purchase contracts – fall in market value of goods before delivery – FA 1915 (No 2) Fourth Schedule Pt I rule I.

Prior-Wandesforde v The Revenue Commissioners
1 ITC 248 .... Vol I p 249

Income tax – Schedule D – domicile and ordinary residence – foreign possessions – ITA 1918 Case V rule 3, FA 1925 Sch D (No 28) s 12.

Earl of Iveagh v The Revenue Commissioners
1 ITC 316, [1930] IR 386, 431 .... Vol I p 259

Income tax – Schedule D – super tax – domicile and ordinary residence, foreign securities and possessions – ITA 1918 Sch D Case IV rule 2(a) & Case V rule 3(a) – FA 1925 (No 28) s 12.

Kennedy (Inspector of Taxes) v The Rattoo Co-operative Dairy Society Ltd
1 ITC 282 .... Vol I p 315

Corporation profits tax – The Rattoo Co-operative Dairy Society Ltd – registered under the Industrial and Provident Societies Act 1893 – milk supplied by members and non-members – whether monthly surpluses retained by the society arose from trading – whether surpluses arose from trading with its own members – whether exemption under FA 1921 s 53 applied.

The City of Dublin Steampacket Co (In Liquidation) v The Revenue Commissioners
1 ITC 285, [1930] IR 217 .... Vol I p 318

Corporation profits tax – company's contract to carry mails between Ireland and England terminated in 1920 – petition to wind up the company filed on 11 August 1924 – income from company's investments continued after winding up application – business – whether during a period of winding up a company may earn income – whether winding up order prevents carrying on business for tax purposes.

The Cunard Steam Ship Co Ltd v Herlihy (Inspector of Taxes) and
The Cunard Steam Ship Co Ltd v Revenue Commissioners
1 ITC 373, [1931] IR 287, 307 .... Vol I p 330

Income tax – Schedule D – non-resident company – exercise of trade within Saorstat Eireann – ITA 1918 Sch D, rule 1(a)(iii).

The Great Southern Railways Co v The Revenue Commissioners
1 ITC 298, [1930] IR 299 .... Vol I p 359

Corporation profits tax – The Great Southern Railways Co – Railways Act 1924 – absorbed the Dublin and Kingston Railway Co – lessor of railway line – whether a railway undertaking – whether precluded from charging any higher price or distributing any higher rate of dividend – whether lessor company carries on a railway undertaking – whether prices under control of lessee company.

McGarry (Inspector of Taxes) v Limerick Gas Committee
1 ITC 405, [1932] IR 125 .... Vol I p 375

Income tax – deduction – expenses of promoting bill in Parliament – ITA 1918 (8 & 9 Geo V, Ch 40), Sch D, Cases I & II, rule 3.

Beirne (Inspector of Taxes) v St Vincent De Paul Society (Wexford Conference)
1 ITC 413 .... Vol I p 383

Income tax – exemption – trading by charity – work done by beneficiaries – FA 1921 (11 & 12 Geo V, Ch 32) s 30(1)(c).

Davis (Inspector of Taxes) v The Superioress, Mater Misericordiae Hospital, Dublin
2 ITC 1, [1933] IR 480, 503 .... Vol I p 387

Income tax – Schedule D – Hospital – whether carrying on a trade – profits derived from associated private nursing home – ITA 1918 Sch D.

Hughes (Inspector of Taxes) v Smyth and Others
1 ITC 418, [1933] IR 253 .... Vol I p 411

Income tax – disposition of income – deed of trust in favour of charitable objects with provision for re-vesting of income in settlor in certain contingencies – FA 1922 (12 & 13 Geo V c 17) s 20(1)(c).

Robinson T/A James Pim & Son v Dolan (Inspector of Taxes)
2 ITC 25, [1935] IR 509 .... Vol I p 427

Income tax – Sch D Case 1 – ex gratia payment by British government – recommendation by Irish Grants Committee – whether income of appellant assessable to income tax.

Howth Estate Co v Davis (Inspector of Taxes)
2 ITC 74, [1936] ILTR 79 .... Vol I p 447

Income tax – family estate company – claim for relief in respect of expenses of management – "company whose business consists mainly in the making of investments, and the principal part of whose income is derived therefrom" – ITA 1918 s 33(1).

The Agricultural Credit Corporation Ltd v Vale (Inspector of Taxes)
2 ITC 46, [1935] IR 681 .... Vol I p 474

Income tax – Schedule D – profits on realisation of investments – whether trading profits.

Estate of Teresa Downing (Owner)
2 ITC 103, [1936] IR 164 .... Vol I p 487

Income tax – Land Purchase Acts – arrears of jointure – ITA 1918 rule 21 of general rules.

Cloghran Stud Farm v A G Birch (Inspector of Taxes)
2 ITC 65, [1936] IR 1 .... Vol I p 496

Income tax – Schedule D – profits from stallion fees.

Davis (Inspector of Taxes) v Hibernian Bank Ltd
2 ITC 111 .... Vol I p 503

Income tax – Schedule D – banking company – change effected by Railways Act 1933, in company's holdings of railway stock – whether equivalent to sale or realisation.

Birch (Inspector of Taxes) v Delaney
2 ITC 127, [1936] IR 517, 531 .... Vol I p 515

Income tax – Schedule D – builder's profits – whether fines and capitalised value of ground rents are assessable to tax.

The Trustees of the Ward Union Hunt Races v Hughes (Inspector of Taxes)
2 ITC 152 .... Vol I p 538

Income tax – exemption – Agricultural Society – FA 1925 s 4.

The Pharmaceutical Society of Ireland v The Revenue Commissioners
2 ITC 157, [1938] IR 202 .... Vol I p 542

Income tax – exemption – charitable purposes – ITA 1918 s 37(1)(b) – FA 1921 s 30(1)(a) – trade – ITA 1918 s 237.

Mulvey (Inspector of Taxes) v Kieran
2 ITC 179, [1938] IR 87 .... Vol I p 563

Income tax – husband and wife living together – husband's income from securities – additional assessment on husband in respect of first year of wife's income from securities etc – ITA 1918 General Rule 16 – FA 1929 ss 10 & 11 and Sch 1 Pt.

The State (at the prosecution of Patrick J Whelan) v Smidic (Special Commissioners of Income Tax)
2 ITC 188, [1938] IR 626 .... Vol I p 571

Income tax – Schedule D – assessment of builder's profits – ruling of Special Commissioner on question of discontinuance – variation of ruling before figures agreed upon or fixed – determination of an appeal – ITA 1918 (8 & 9 Geo 5, c 40) ss 133, 137 & 149, FA 1929 (No 32 of 1929) s 5.

Connolly v Birch (Inspector of Taxes)
2 ITC 201, [1939] IR 534 .... Vol I p 583

Income tax, FA 1935 Sch D s 6 – assessment of builders profits – inclusion in 1935-36 assessment of amounts received in respect of fines and capitalised value of surplus ground rents created prior to the coming into operation of the section.

O'Reilly v Casey (Inspector of Taxes)
2 ITC 220, [1942] IR 378 .... Vol I p 601

Income tax – provisions in codicil to a will charging the rents of the testator's real and leasehold property with the payment of 10 per cent, thereof to a named son so long as that son continued to manage the property – whether such payment was remuneration chargeable upon the recipient under ITA 1918 Sch E – ITA 1918 Sch E – Charging Rule: FA 1922 s 18.

Mulvey (Inspector of Taxes) v Coffey
2 ITC 239, [1942] IR 277 .... Vol I p 618

Income tax – Schedule E – emolument of office – grant to a President of a college on retirement – whether chargeable to income tax – ITA 1918 Sch E rule 1 – FA 1929 s 17.

O'Dwyer (Inspector of Taxes) and The Revenue Commissioners v Irish Exporters and Importers Ltd (In Liquidation)
2 ITC 251, [1943] IR 176 .... Vol I p 629

Income tax and corporation profits tax – whether or not a sum of money payable and paid to a limited liability company under a prior agreement by the Minister for Agriculture in the event of his having terminated, within a prescribed period, a supply of the raw material of the trade of another company, (promoted by the first company at the request of said Minister), is or is not a receipt of the first company's trade – ITA 1918 Sch D Case 1 – FA 1920 s 53.

Kealy (Inspector of Taxes) v O'Mara (Limerick) Ltd
2 ITC 265, [1942] IR 616 .... Vol I p 642

Income tax – deductions – whether expenses preliminary to, and in connection with, the formation of a "holding company" were admissible as part of trading expenses of a bacon manufacturing company – ITA 1918 ss 100(2), 209 and Sch D, rule applicable to Case I, and rules 1(1) & 3 of Cases I & II.

Dolan (Inspector of Taxes) v "K" National School Teacher
2 ITC 280, [1944] IR 470 .... Vol I p 656

Income tax – Schedule E – professed nun employed as national school teacher but bound by constitutions of her order to hand over all her earnings to the order – whether or not assessable Schedule E as having earned or exercising an office or employment, as national school teacher – ITA 1918 Sch E rule 1.

McGarry (Inspector of Taxes) v Spencer
2 ITC 297, [1946] IR 11 .... Vol II p 1

Nurseries and market gardens – ITA 1918 Sch B rule 8 ss 186 & 187 – whether rule 8 applies in Eire, that is, whether the income is chargeable with reference to annual value or upon profits estimated according to the rules of Schedule D.

Gilbert Hewson v Kealy (Inspector of Taxes)
2 ITC 286 .... Vol II p 15

Income tax – Sch D Case III – interest and income from securities and possessions – execution of document under seal in the Isle of Man – contention that beneficial interest in the said securities and possessions had been transferred – original document not produced – secondary evidence of its terms not admissible.

The Revenue Commissioners v Switzer Ltd
2 ITC 290, [1945] IR 378 .... Vol II p 19

Excess corporation profits tax – company on "substituted standard" – portion of issue of debenture stock bought back by company – whether in computing substituted standard such portion of the issue should be taken into account – FA 1941 s 39 as amended by FA 1942 s 16.

Property Loan & Investment Co Ltd v The Revenue Commissioners
2 ITC 312, [1946] IR 159 .... Vol II p 25

Corporation profits tax – company incorporated under the Companies Acts 1908 to 1917 – business consisting of the advancement of moneys to persons not members of the company for the purpose of enabling them to acquire dwelling-houses – whether company carries on "the business of a building society" – FA 1929 s 33(1)(d), as amended.

Vale (Inspector of Taxes) v Martin Mahony & Brothers Ltd
2 ITC 331, [1947] IR 30, 41 .... Vol II p 32

Income tax – Schedule D – deduction – expenditure upon mill sanitation.

Davis (Inspector of Taxes) v X Ltd
2 ITC 320, [1946] ILTR 57, [1947] ILTR 157 .... Vol II p 45

Income tax – Schedule D – profits of trade – deductions – new factory in course of erection – interference with rights as regards light and air claimed by tenants of adjoining houses – settlement of action – sums paid to tenants as compensation and for legal costs.

AB v Mulvey (Inspector of Taxes)
2 ITC 345, [1947] IR 121 .... Vol II p 55

Income tax – Schedule D – business carried on by sole trader – partner admitted at beginning of year – business sold later in year to private company – whether assessment on sole trader for the previous year can be reviewed – ITA 1918 Sch D Cases I & II rule 11 – FA 1929 s 12.

A and B v Davis (Inspector of Taxes) 2 ITC 350 .... Vol II p 60

Income tax, Schedule D – appeal to High Court by way of case stated from decision of Circuit Judge – failure of appellants to send to respondent, at or before the required date, notice in writing of fact that case had been stated etc – ITA 1918 s 149(1)(e).

O'Sullivan (Inspector of Taxes) v O'Connor, as Administratrix of O'Brien, (Deceased)
2 ITC 352, [1947] IR 416 .... Vol II p 61

Income tax – Schedule D – compulsory sale to Minister for Finance, in return for sterling equivalents, of dollar balances consisting of income from securities, etc, in the USA – whether moneys so received assessable – FA 1929 Sch 1 Pt II.

Tipping (Inspector of Taxes) v Jeancard
2 ITC 360, [1948] IR 233 .... Vol II p 68

Income tax – Schedule E – office of profit within the State – director, resident abroad, of a company incorporated in the State but managed and controlled abroad.

Ua Clothasaigh (Inspector of Taxes) v McCartan
2 ITC 367, [1948] IR 219 .... Vol II p 75

Income tax – husband and wife- "married woman living with her husband" – ITA 1918 general rule 16.

O'Dwyer (Inspector of Taxes) v Cafolla & Co
2 ITC 374, [1949] IR 210 ....Vol II p 82

Income tax – dispositions of income – father taking his elder children and his mother-in-law into partnership – subsequent assignment of mother-in-law's interest to his younger children – whether income of children to be deemed to be income of father – FA 1922 s 20 – FA 1937 s 2.

The Attorney-General v Irish Steel Ltd and Crowley
2 ITC 402 ....Vol II p 108

Income tax and corporation profits tax – company in hands of a receiver – preferential claim – Companies (Consolidation) Act 1908 ss 107 and 209.

O'Dwyer (Inspector of Taxes) v The Dublin United Transport Co Ltd
2 ITC 437, [1949] IR 295 ....Vol II p 115

Income tax – Schedule D – cessation – deduction of corporation profits tax and excess corporation profits tax in computing profits for income tax purposes – ITA 1918 Sch D, Cases I & II, rule 4 – FA 1929 s 12.

The Revenue Commissioners v R Hilliard & Sons Ltd
2 ITC 410 ....Vol II p 130

Corporation profits tax (including excess corporation profits tax) – accounting period – accounts made up half-yearly – yearly account for general meeting prepared from half-yearly accounts – whether Revenue Commissioners required to determine the accounting period – FA 1920 s 54(1).

CD v O'Sullivan (Inspector of Taxes)
2 ITC 422, [1949] IR 264 ....Vol II p 140

Income tax – Schedule D – bad debts – executor carrying on trade – recovery by executor of debts allowed as bad debts in lifetime of deceased – whether a trading receipt.

O'Loan (Inspector of Taxes) v Noone & Co
2 ITC 430, [1949] IR 171 ....Vol II p 146

Income tax – Schedule D – fuel merchants – whether a new trade of coal mining set up or commenced – FA 1929 ss 8(1) & 9(2).

Moville District Board of Conservators v Ua Clothasaigh (Inspector of Taxes)
3 ITC 1, [1950] IR 301 ....Vol II p 154

Income tax – Schedule D – surplus revenue of Board of Conservators – whether annual profits or gains – ITA 1918 Case VI.

Corr (Inspector of Taxes) v Larkin
3 ITC 13, [1949] IR 399 ....Vol II p 164

Income tax – Schedule D – sum recovered under loss of profits policy – whether a profit or gain arising from the trade – year in which assessable.

Associated Properties Ltd v The Revenue Commissioners
3 ITC 25, [1951] IR 140 .... Vol II p 175

Corporation profits tax -"the shareholders" – whether a "post-appointed day company" was a subsidiary of the appellant company – whether appellant company director-controlled and, if so, whether its managing director was the beneficial owner of, or able to control more than 5 per cent of its ordinary shares – FA 1944 s 14 – FA 1941 s 36(4).

The Revenue Commissioners v Y Ltd
3 ITC 49 .... Vol II p 195

Corporation profits tax (including excess corporation profit tax) – Industrial and Provident Societies – society trading with its own members and with non-members – investments and property purchased out of trading profits – whether the dividends and rents form part of the profits or surplus arising from the trade – additional assessments – FA 1920 s 53(2)(h) – FA 1921 s 53 – FA 1946 s 24.

The Veterinary Council v Corr (Inspector of Taxes)
3 ITC 59, [1953] IR 12 .... Vol II p 204

Income tax – body corporate performing statutory functions – surplus of receipts over expenditure – whether annual profits or gains – ITA 1918 Sch D Case VI.

The Exported Live Stock (Insurance) Board v Carroll (Inspector of Taxes)
3 ITC 67, [1951] IR 286 .... Vol II p 211

Income tax – Sch D Case 1 – statutory body set up to carry into effect a compulsory insurance scheme – whether statutory body was carrying on a trade within the meaning of Sch D Case I and whether the surpluses arising from the carrying on of its statutory activities were taxable as profits of such a trade – ITA 1918 Sch D Case I.

Flynn (Inspector of Taxes) v John Noone Ltd, and
Flynn (Inspector of Taxes) v Blackwood & Co (Sligo) Ltd
3 ITC 79 .... Vol II p 222

Income tax, Schedule D – capital or revenue – lump sum paid on execution of lease – whether capital payment and receipt or rent paid in advance – ITA 1918 Sch D Case III rule 5 and Cases I & II, rule 3(a).

L v McGarry (Inspector of Taxes)
3 ITC 111 .... Vol II p 241

Income tax – Schedule B – whether rule 8 applicable where the lands occupied as gardens for the sale of produce comprise part only of a unit of valuation – power to apportion valuation and land purchase annuity – ITA 1918 ss 186 & 187 and Sch B rule 8.

McGarry (Inspector of Taxes) v E F
3 ITC 103, [1954] IR 64 .... Vol II p 261

Income tax – general manager of company "Y" – professional services rendered to company "X" without agreement as regards remuneration – payment made by company "X" on termination of services – whether chargeable as income – ITA 1918 Sch E rule 7 and Sch D Case VI.

Hodgins (Inspector of Taxes) v Plunder & Pollak (Ireland) Ltd
3 ITC 135, [1957] IR 58 .... Vol II p 267

Income tax – Schedule D – deduction in computing profits – cost of replacement of weighbridge house – ITA 1918 Sch D Cases I & II, rule 3(d) and (g).

The Revenue Commissioners v L & Co
3 ITC 205 .... Vol II p 281

Corporation profits tax – foreign company trading in this country – expenditure attributable to Irish trading not transferred from company's Irish resources to head office in the USA – devaluation of sterling – deduction from profits.

Collins and Byrne and Power v Mulvey (Inspector of Taxes)
3 ITC 151, [1956] IR 233 .... Vol II p 291

Income tax – Schedule D – profits from illegal trade – admissibility of evidence of illegality – ITA 1918 Sch D Case I.

O'Conaill (Inspector of Taxes) v R
3 ITC 167, [1956] IR 97 .... Vol II p 304

Income tax – Schedule D – trade carried on wholly in England – basis of assessment under Case III – "single source" – ITA 1918 Sch D Case III rule 2 (FA 1922 s 17) – FA 1926 Sch 1 Pt II s 2(2) & 1(3) – FA 1929 ss 10, 11 & 18 and Sch 2 para 3.

Mac Giolla Riogh (Inspector of Taxes) v G Ltd
3 ITC 181, [1957] IR 90 .... Vol II p 315

Income tax – Schedule D – company trading in bloodstock – animal bought in course of trade, sent to stud after successful racing career and subsequently sold to a syndicate – whether amount realised on syndication a trading receipt – ITA 1918 Sch D Case I and FA 1939 Sch B s 7.

The Revenue Commissioners v Orwell Ltd
3 ITC 193 .... Vol II p 326

Corporation profits tax and excess corporation profits tax – whether excess corporation profits tax is exigible for accounting periods in respect of which no corporation profits tax (other than excess corporation profits tax) is payable – FA 1941 s 37.

Colclough v Colclough
[1965] IR 668 .... Vol II p 332

Income tax-funds in court – (a) whether rules 19 and 21 of the general rules applicable to ITA 1918 Sch A, B, C, D and E apply to the court when paying interest on debts out of funds in court and – (b) whether tax deductible from income accrued to funds in court for years prior to 1922/23.

EG v Mac Shamhrain (Inspector of Taxes)
3 ITC 217, [1958] IR 288 .... Vol II p 352

Income tax – Sch D Case III – Settlement of income – deed of appointment by parent in favour of child – power of revocation – FA 1922 s 20(1), FA 1937 s 2(1) – rule 16, general rules applicable to all Schedules.

Curtin (Inspector of Taxes) v M Ltd
3 ITC 227, [1960] IR 59 .... Vol II p 360

Income tax – Schedule D – profits of trade – deduction – expenditure on rebuilding of business premises – whether portion thereof deductible in computing profits.

O'Broin (Inspector of Taxes) v Mac Giolla Meidhre
O'Broin (Inspector of Taxes) v Pigott
3 ITC 235, [1959] IR 98 .... Vol II p 366

Income tax – Schedule E – deductions – expenses – ITA 1918 Sch E rule 9.

Bourke (Inspector of Taxes) v Lyster & Sons Ltd
3 ITC 247 .... Vol II p 374

Income tax – Schedule D – profits of a trade – sum received in part payment of a debt previously treated as bad-res judicata – jurisdiction of Circuit Court Judge when hearing on appeal against an assessment.

Milverton Quarries Ltd v The Revenue Commissioners
3 ITC 279, [1960] IR 224 .... Vol II p 382

Corporation profits tax – deduction from profits – expenses of removing top soil from surface of quarry – whether capital or revenue expenditure – ITA 1918 Sch D Cases I & II rule 2 – FA 1920 s 53.

McHugh (Inspector of Taxes) v A
3 ITC 257, [1958] IR 142, [1959] ILTR 125 .... Vol II p 393

Income tax – Schedule D – pension, annuity or other annual payment – payments made by a British company to a person resident in the State – whether income from a foreign possession – ITA 1918 Sch D Case III, FA 1922 s 18, FA 1929 s 11, FA 1932 s 4.

The Revenue Commissioners v Associated Properties Ltd
3 ITC 293 .... Vol II p 412

Corporation profits tax – Interest paid to a person having controlling interest – FA 1920 s 53(2)(b).

AB Ltd v Mac Giolla Riogh (Inspector of Taxes)
3 ITC 301 .... Vol II p 419

Income tax – Schedule D – finance company dealing in stocks and shares – whether investments should be valued at cost or market value.

Casey (Inspector of Taxes) v The Monteagle Estate Co
3 ITC 313, [1962] IR 106 .... Vol II p 429

Income tax – estate company – claim for relief in respect of expenses of management – "company whose business consists mainly in the making of investments and the principal part of whose income is derived therefrom" – ITA 1918 s 33(1).

Connolly (Inspector of Taxes) v McNamara
3 ITC 341 ....Vol II p 452

Income tax – Schedule E – emolument of employment – rent paid by employing company for house occupied voluntarily by employee – ITA 1918 Sch E, FA 1922 s 18.

Kelly (Inspector of Taxes) v H
3 ITC 351, [1964] IR 488 ....Vol II p 460

Income tax – Schedule E – deductions – expenses – ITA 1918 Sch E rule 9.

O'Sullivan (Inspector of Taxes) v P Ltd
3 ITC 355 ....Vol II p 464

Income tax – Schedule D – payment in advance on the signing of a lease – whether a capital receipt (ie a fine or premium) or rent paid in advance assessable to income tax – ITA 1918 Sch D Case III, FA 1929 s 11 and Sch 1 Pt II.

Swaine (Inspector of Taxes) v VE
3 ITC 387, [1964] IR 423, 100 ILTR 21 ....Vol II p 472

Income tax – Schedule D – builder's profits – whether fines and capitalised value of ground rents are assessable to tax.

Molmac Ltd v MacGiolla Riogh (Inspector of Taxes)
3 ITC 376, [1965] IR 201, 101 ILTR 114 ....Vol II p 482

Income tax Schedule D – carry forward of losses – managing of "six following years of assessment" – FA 1929 s 14.

Forbes (Inspector of Taxes) v GHD
3 ITC 365, [1964] IR 447 ....Vol II p 491

Income tax – Schedule D – pensions payable under the British National Insurance Act 1946, as amended or extended, to persons resident in the State – whether income from foreign possessions – ITA 1918 Sch D Case III, FA 1926 Sch 1 Pt II, FA 1929 s 11.

Casey (Inspector of Taxes) v AB Ltd
[1965] IR 575 ....Vol II p 500

Income tax – Schedule D – legal costs in defending action in High Court for balance alleged to be due to a building contractor in respect of the construction of cinema – whether the costs were incurred in earning the profits assessed, and whether they were capital or revenue expenditure – ITA 1918 Sch D Case I.

Dolan (Inspector of Taxes) v AB Co Ltd
[1969] IR 282, 104 ILTR 101 ....Vol II p 515

Income tax – Schedule D – petrol marketing company-whether expenditure incurred under exclusivity agreements with retailers deductible – ITA 1918 s 209 and Sch D Cases I & II rule 3 – FA 1929 s 9.

Bedford (Collector-General) v H
[1968] IR 320 .... Vol II p 588

Aggregate of monthly payments made in year on account of remunerations less than tax-free allowances-no tax deducted under PAYE – balance of remuneration for year voted and paid in following year – tax deducted under PAYE – assessment made in respect of full remuneration for earlier year – whether tax so deducted under PAYE from balance of remuneration in following year should be treated as covering tax charged in assessment – FA (No 2) 1959 s 13(1) (ITA 1967 s 133(1)), IT(E)R 1960 clause 45(1) (SI 28/1960).

Cronin (Inspector of Taxes) v C
TL 106 .... Vol II p 592

Income tax – Schedule D – personal pension and other assets assigned to company – pension continued to be paid to pensioner – whether pensioner ceased to receive pension as a source of income for himself beneficially – ITA 1918 Sch D, Case III of miscellaneous rules applicable to Schedule D and FA 1929 s 10

Pairceir (Inspector of Taxes) v EM .... Vol II p 596

Income tax – Schedule D – income from the leasing of premises – whether such activity constitutes a "trade" the income from which would qualify for earned income relief – FA 1920 s 16 – replaced by FA(No 2) 1959 s16 – amended by FA 1961 s 3.

S Ltd v O'Sullivan........ Vol II p 602

Income tax – Schedule D – payments made under an agreement for the supply of technical information.

HH v Forbes (Inspector of Taxes) .... Vol II p 614

Income tax – whether profits of a bookmaker from certain transactions in Irish Hospital Sweepstakes tickets should be included as receipts for purposes of assessment to tax under Schedule D.

W Ltd v Wilson (Inspector of Taxes)........ Vol II p 627

Income tax – Schedule D and corporation profits tax, FA 1920 – whether the inspector of taxes had made a "discovery" on finding that inadmissible deductions had been allowed in the computation of the company's tax liability for certain years and whether he was entitled to raise additional assessments for those years – ITA 1967 s 186.

O Conaill (Inspector of Taxes) v Z Ltd .... Vol II p 636

Income tax – whether the appellant company was in occupation of lands, forming part of a military establishment, for the purposes of ITA 1918 Sch B or ITA 1967.

S W Ltd v McDermott (Inspector of Taxes) .... Vol II p 661

Income tax – whether the capital allowances to be apportioned in accordance with the provisions of ITA 1967 s 220(5), in computing the appellant's liability under Sch D Case I were to be confined to the allowances outlined in Part XVI of that Act.

Mara (Inspector of Taxes) v GG (Hummingbird) Ltd
[1982] ILRM 421 .... Vol II p 667

Income tax – Sch D Case I – whether the surplus arising to the company from the sale of certain property was profit of a trade of dealing in or developing land, or the profit of a business which was deemed by F(MP)A 1968 s 17, to be such a trade.

MacDaibheid (Inspector of Taxes) v SD .... Vol III p 1

Income tax – whether a deduction should be allowed under ITA 1967 Sch 2(3) in respect of incidental expenses.

O hArgain (Inspector of Taxes) v B Ltd
[1979] ILRM 56 .... Vol III p 9

Property company – income tax – trade – trading stock – farm land – company letting land to partners on conacre – area zoned for development – land transferred to new company – whether land trading stock of company – F(MP)A 1968 (No 7) s 17.

De Brun (Inspector of Taxes) v Kiernan
[1981] IR 117, [1982] ILRM 13 .... Vol III p 19

Income tax – whether the taxpayer was a "dealer in cattle" within the meaning of ITA 1918 Sch D Case III rule 4 and ITA 1967 s 78.

Revenue v ORMG
[1984] ILRM 406 .... Vol III p 28

Club to promote athletics or amateur games or sports – whether legitimate avoidance of payment of tax – funds provided by one person – total control in two trustees – whether bona fide club – whether established for sole purpose of "promoting sport" – whether two persons can constitute a "body of person" – ITA 1967 ss (1), 349.

MacDermott (Inspector of Taxes) v BC .... Vol III p 43

Income tax – Schedule E – whether the taxpayer was engaged under a contract of service or a contract for services – ITA 1967 s 110.

O'Laoghaire (Inspector of Taxes) v CD Ltd .... Vol III p 51

Corporation profits tax – company engaged in manufacture and erection of prefabricated buildings – deposit of 15 per cent of total cost paid on execution of contract – whether a payment on account in respect of trading stock – whether security for contracts – whether value of stock for stock relief be reduced – FA 1975 s 31.

K Co v Hogan (Inspector of Taxes)
[1985] ILRM 200 .... Vol III p 56

Appellant unlimited investment company – whether dividends arising from sales of capital assets liable to corporation profits tax – whether profits shall be profits and gains determined on the same principles as those on which the profits and gains of a trade are determined – whether company carrying on a trade – whether similar distributions previously charged to corporation profits tax – whether statutory provision can become obsolete on the basis of past practice – whether FA 1920 s 53(2) ambiguous in meaning –

whether words of a taxing statute must be clear and unambiguous – whether s (2) is purely for purpose of determining profits for income tax purposes – whether question of distinguishing capital and income arises – whether proceeds of sale of capital assets may be capital in hands of companies selling the assets and income in the hands of the shareholders to whom paid in the form of dividends.

O'Conaill (Inspector of Taxes) v JJ Ltd .... Vol III p 65

Income tax – whether a building which housed offices, a showroom, a canteen, computer department and utilities qualified for industrial building allowance under ITA 1967 s 255.

Doyle v An Taoiseach
[1986] ILRM 522 .... Vol III p 73

Excise duty – levy of 2 per cent of value of bovine animals imposed on the farmer producer – whether ultra vires the enabling provisions of FA 1986 – imposed on proprietors of slaughter houses and exporters of live animals – whether levy operated arbitrarily and unreasonably – whether levy passed on to the prime producer – whether end result untargeted indiscriminate and unfair – FA 1966 – SI 152/1970 and 160/1979 – Treaty of Rome Article 177 – FA 1980 s 79.

GH (Stephen Court) Ltd v Browne (Inspector of Taxes)
[1984] ILRM 231 .... Vol III p 95

Income tax – whether letting fees and legal expenses incurred by the company in respect of first lettings of property qualified as deductions under ITA 1967 s 81(5)(d).

BKJ v The Revenue Commissioners
[Not previously reported] .... Vol III p 104

Family settlement dated 22 December 1955 – discretionary trust – income to beneficiary on attaining thirty years of age until 31 December 1985 and thereafter to the beneficiary absolutely – whether beneficiary took an absolute interest on attaining thirty years of age – whether vested interest subject to contingency of favour of children and remoter issue – appointment dated 4 April 1978 in favour of beneficiary – whether gift of a contingent interest – whether liable to gift tax – CATA 1976 ss 2, 4, 5, 6.

Breathnach (Inspector of Taxes) v McCann
[1984] IR 340 .... Vol III p 113

Income tax – Sch D Case 11 – profession – capital allowances – whether barrister's books are plant.

In Re HT Ltd (In Liquidation) and Others
[1984] ILRM 583 .... Vol III p 120

Income tax – corporation profits tax – corporation tax – court liquidation – whether deposit interest earned on monies held by the official liquidator liable to tax – whether tax payable a "necessary disbursement" under court winding-up rules – whether tax payable ranks as a preferential payment or an unsecured debt – Companies Act 1963 ss 244, 285 – FA 1983 s 56, Winding Up Rules 1966 r 129.

The State (FIC Ltd) v Ó Ceallaigh.. Vol III p 124

Capital gains tax clearance certificate on sale of bonds – whether statutory requirements satisfied – whether applicant is the person making the disposal – whether applicant is the owner of the property and ordinarily resident in the state – whether statutory provision mandatory – whether inspector of taxes is entitled to investigate applicant's title to the property – whether applicant as owner and ordinarily resident in the state is entitled to a clearance certificate.

Madigan v The Attorney General, The Revenue Commissioners and Others
[1986] ILRM 136.. Vol III p 127

Residential property tax – whether unconstitutional – whether unjust attack on property and family rights – whether invidious discrimination – whether unreasonable or arbitrary – whether taxation statutes presumed to be unconstitutional – locus standi – FA 1983 – Constitution of Ireland 1937 Articles 40(1), 40(3), 41, 43.

JB O'C v PCD and A Bank
[1985] IR 265.. Vol III p 153

Income tax – particulars of taxpayers bank accounts – bond of confidentiality between banks and customers – strict compliance with statutory provisions – whether reasonable grounds for court application – discretion of court – particulars of accounts – dealings in accounts – name(s), nature of account and dates of opening and closing – whether costs of bank to be borne by Revenue – FA 1983 s 18.

The State (Multiprint Label Systems Ltd) v Neylon
[1984] ILRM 545.. Vol III p 159

Practice – Revenue case – statutory provision requiring person to express dissatisfaction with the determination of a point of law "immediately after the determination" – whether "immediately" to be interpreted strictly – whether provision directory or mandatory – ITA(No 6) 1967 ss 428, 430.

Ó Cléirigh (Inspector of Taxes) v Jacobs International Ltd Incorporated
[1985] ILRM 651.. Vol III p 165

Corporation tax – whether a training grant paid to the company was a capital or revenue receipt.

McElligott & Sons Ltd v Duigenan (Inspector of Taxes)
[1985] ILRM 210.. Vol III p 178

Stock relief – whether the company was carrying on a single trade, or several different trades, for the purposes of a claim under FA 1975 s 31 (as amended by FA 1977 s 43).

Muckley v Ireland, The Attorney General and The Revenue Commissioners
[1985] IR 472, [1986] ILRM 364.. Vol III p 188

Constitution validity of taxing statute – personal rights of citizens – unauthorised exactions – married persons – statute with retrospective effect – enacted in consequence of decision that portion of income tax legislation unconstitutional – whether lawful for the State to collect arrears of tax due under the unconstitutional provisions – FA 1980 s 21 – Constitution of Ireland 1937, Articles 40.1, 40.3, 41

Cronin (Inspector of Taxes) v Cork & County Property Co Ltd
[1986] IR 559 .... Vol III p 198

Corporation tax – property company dealing in land – interest in land acquired and disposed of within one accounting period – whether ordinary principles of commercial accounting apply – whether artificial method of valuation pursuant to F(MP)A 1968 s 18(2) prevails.

Mac Giolla Mhaith (Inspector of Taxes) v Cronin & Associates Ltd
[Not previously reported] .... Vol III p 211

Corporation tax – advertising agency – whether its business consisted of or included the carrying on of a profession or the provision of professional services for the purposes of the corporation tax surcharge provided for in CTA 1976 s 162

Ó Srianain (Inspector of Taxes) v Lakeview Ltd .... Vol III p 219

Capital allowances – machinery and plant – whether applicable to the provision of a deep pit poultry house.

Cronin (Inspector of Taxes) v Youghal Carpets (Yarns) Ltd
[1985] IR 312, [1985] ILRM 666 .... Vol III p 229

Corporation tax – whether the expression "total income brought into charge to corporation tax" for the purposes of CTA 1976 s 58(3) meant income before or after the deduction of group relief.

The Revenue Commissioners v HI .... Vol III p 242

Income tax – whether an individual was entitled to repayment of tax deducted from payments made under an indenture of covenant pursuant to ITA 1967 s 439(1)(iv).

Murphy (Inspector of Taxes) v Asahi Synthetic Fibres (Ireland) Ltd
[1985] IR 509, [1986] IR 777 .... Vol III p 246

Irish subsidiary company and Japanese parent company – interest on loan by parent company – whether tax chargeable under Schedule D or Schedule F – Double Taxation Relief (Taxes on Income)(Japan) Order 1974 SI 259/1974, CTA 1976 ss 83/84.

MacCarthaigh (Inspector of Taxes) v Daly
[1985] IR 73, [1986] ILRM 24, 116 .... Vol III p 253

Income tax – whether the taxpayer was entitled to claim a share of capital allowances on the basis of a leasing transaction, involving a purported limited partnership, against his personal income tax liability.

The Attorney General v Sun Alliance and London Insurance Ltd
[1985] ILRM 522 .... Vol III p 265

Excise duty – deed of bond – principal and surety – payment of excise duty deferred – whether creditor to resort to securities received by creditor from principal before proceeding against surety – Excise Collection and Management Act 1841 (4 & 5 Vict c 20) s 24.

O'Connlain (Inspector of Taxes) v Belvedere Estates Ltd
[1985] IR 22 .... Vol III p 271

Trading company dealing in and developing – tax avoidance scheme – series of transactions with associated companies – aggregate of costs of stock in trade – artificial method of valuation under F(MP)A 1968 s 18 – legal consequences of transaction – whether s 18 can be construed to alter legal consequences.

The State (Melbarian Enterprises Ltd) v The Revenue Commissioners
[1985] IR 706 .... Vol III p 290

State side – mandamus – requirement of tax clearance certificate with tenders for Government contracts – refusal to issue by Collector General – whether Revenue Commissioners can have regard to tax default of previous "connected" company – whether Collector General's decision amenable to judicial review – duty to act judicially – requirement not based on statutory provisions.

Heron and Others v The Minister For Communications
[1985] IR 623 .... Vol III p 298

Liability for capital gains tax – compulsory acquisition – tax arising on disposal – compensation determined without regard to the liability of landowner for tax on chargeable gain – Acquisition of Land (Assessment of Compensation) Act 1919 s 2.

McCann Ltd v Ó Culacháin (Inspector of Taxes)
[1985] IR 298, [1986] IR 196 .... Vol III p 304

Corporation tax – exports sales relief – whether process of ripening bananas constituted manufacturing – no statutory definition of word manufacture – interpretation of taxation statute – ordinary meaning or strict construction – scheme and purpose of statute – test to be applied – matter of degree – CTA 1976 s 54 and Pt IV.

Knockhall Piggeries v Kerrane (Inspector of Taxes)
[1985] ILRM 655 .... Vol III p 319

Income tax – whether the activity of intensive pig rearing constituted farming for the purposes of FA 1974 s 13(1).

Maye v The Revenue Commissioners
[1986] ILRM 377 .... Vol III p 332

Value added tax – installation of fixtures subject to low rate of value added tax – whether or not television aerials attached to roof of a house are fixtures – test based on mode and object of annexation – VATA 1972 s 10(8).

Belville Holdings Ltd (In Receivership and Liquidation) v Cronin (Inspector of Taxes)
[1985] IR 465 .... Vol III p 340

Corporation tax – case stated on question of losses incurred by a holding company, whether notional management fees deductible – whether evidence required to determine the amount of such fees – whether Appeal Commissioner in error – whether a High Court order can be subsequently amended by a further High Court order – whether High Court has jurisdiction to amend order – whether jurisdiction limited to Order 28 rule 11 of Superior Court rules and judgments incorrectly drawn up – whether certainty of

administration of law can be breached – whether discretion under ITA 1967 s 428 applied by judge – whether discretion "implicit" in judgment – whether application of s 428(b) an additional remedy – whether amending order be set aside.

Warnock and Others practising as Stokes Kennedy Crowley & Co v The Revenue Commissioners
[1985] IR 663, [1986] ILRM 37 .... Vol III p 356

Income tax – tax avoidance – transfer of assets to offshore tax havens – statutory notice requesting information – whether from of accountants could be requested to furnish relevant particulars in respect of all their clients – ten named territories over a six year period – whether a limit to extent of particulars sought – whether cost of compliance excessive – whether notice ultra vires *the section – FA 1974 s 59.*

Cronin (Inspector of Taxes) v Lunham Brothers Ltd
[1986] ILRM 415 .... Vol III p 363

Corporation tax – relief – losses forward – cessation of company's trade – major change in nature of conduct of trade – change of ownership – CTA 1976 ss 16(1), 27(1), 182 184.

Guinness & Mahon Ltd v Browne (Inspector of Taxes) .... Vol III p 373

Corporation tax – whether a sum which arose to the company on the liquidation of a wholly owned subsidiary was part of its trading profits.

McLoughlin and Tuite v The Revenue Commissioners and The Attorney General
[1986] IR 235, [1986] ILRM 304, [1990] IR 83 .... Vol III p 387

Income tax returns – whether penalties for failure to make returns are punitive – whether proceedings for recovery of penalties are criminal trials – whether unconstitutional – ITA 1967 s 500 – Constitution of Ireland Act 1937 s 34.

Navan Carpets Ltd v Ó Culacháin (Inspector of Taxes)
[1988] IR 164 .... Vol III p 403

Corporation tax – interest on repayment of tax – no provision for interest in Taxes Act – whether or not award on interest applicable under Courts Act 1981.

Curtis and Geough v The Attorney General and The Revenue Commissioners
[1986] ILRM 428 .... Vol III p 419

Customs duties – locus standi evasion of customs duties on specified goods – whether District Court authorised to determine value of goods – criminal case – whether disputed issue of fact a matter for jury – whether statutory provisions unconstitutional – whether unappealable finding unjust – FA 1963 ss 34(4)(d)(i), 34(4)(d)(iii) – Constitution of Ireland 1937, Articles 34.3.4, 38.1, 38.2, 38.

Williams Group Tullamore Ltd v Companies Act 1963 – 1983 .... Vol III p 423

Petition under Companies Act 1963 s 205 – oppression of ordinary minority shareholders – voting and non voting shares – whether preference shareholders entitled to receive a portion of issue of new ordinary shares – whether preference shareholders entitled to participate in capital distribution – whether proposal burdensome harsh and wrongful –

whether isolated transaction can give rise to relief – whether for benefit of company as a whole – whether in disregard of interests of ordinary shareholders.

Bairead (Inspector of Taxes) v Maxwells of Donegal Ltd
[1986] ILRM 508 .... Vol III p 430

Corporation tax – whether a company, resident and trading in Northern Ireland was an associated company of a company resident and trading in the State for the purposes of CTA 1976 s 28.

Kinghan v The Minister for Social Welfare .... Vol III p 436

Social welfare – benefits – whether entitled to old age contributory pension – whether issue open to appeal – true construction of statute – jurisdiction of High Court – meaning of entry into insurance – definition of contribution year – Social Welfare (Consolidation Act 1951 s 299).

Cronin (Inspector of Taxes) v Strand Dairy Ltd .... Vol III p 441

Corporation tax – whether the processing of and sale of milk in plastic bottles produced by the company constituted the manufacture of goods for the purposes of the reduction in corporation tax provided for in FA 1980 Pt I Ch VI.

Cronin (Inspector of Taxes) v IMP Midleton Ltd .... Vol III p 452

Corporation profits tax – export sales relief – sale of meat into intervention within the EEC – conditional contracts – when does property in goods pass – sold in course of trade – exporter need not be owner at time of export – F(MP)A 1956 s 13(3).

Director of Public Prosecutions v McLoughlin
[1986] IR 355, [1986] ILRM 493 .... Vol III p 467

Income tax (PAYE) and Social Welfare (PRSI) regulations – whether contract for services between skipper of fishing vessel and crew members – whether a partnership existed – no wages – rights to share of profits and to decide on division of profits but not to share in losses.

Moloney (Inspector of Taxes) v Allied Irish Banks Ltd as Executors of the Estate of Doherty (Deceased)
[1986] IR 67 .... Vol III p 477

Income tax – liability of personal representatives – income on estate in course of administration – trustees under Succession Act 1965 – ITA 1967 s 105.

Ó Coindealbháin (Inspector of Taxes) v Gannon
[1986] IR 154 .... Vol III p 484

Income tax – fees due to a barrister prior to his appointment to the bench – fees refused but could be paid to a family company if solicitors so wished – whether or not received within the meaning of FA 1970 s 20 – interpretation of taxing act.

Healy v Breathnach (Inspector of Taxes)
[1986] IR 105 .... Vol III p 496

Income tax – exemption of earnings from original and creative works of artistic or cultural merit – whether newspaper articles and journalism qualify – tests for exemption – grounds for setting aside a Circuit Court decision on a Revenue case stated – FA 1969 s 2.

The Minister for Labour v PMPA Insurance Co Ltd (Under Administration)
[1990] IR 284 .... Vol III p 505

Contract of service or contract for services – temporary employee engaged through employment agency – agreement between employee and agency – agreement between agency and defendant hirer – whether defendant liable for employee's holiday pay – nature of contractual relationship between employee and defendant – whether a contract of service between employee and agency – Holidays (Employees) Act 1973.

The Companies Act 1963–1983 v Castlemahon Poultry Products Ltd
[1986] IR 750, [1987] ILRM 222 .... Vol III p 509

Social Welfare Acts – employer's contribution in respect of "reckonable earnings" of employees – when payable – liability of liquidator – preferential status under Companies Act 1963 s 285.

Rahinstown Estates Co v Hughes (Inspector of Taxes)
[1987] ILRM 599 .... Vol III p 517

Corporation tax – surcharge on undistributed income of close company – extension of period for making distribution of dividends – shorter period allowed for making distributions of share capital in a winding up – whether distinction absurd or unjust. CTA 1976 ss 84(1), 100 & 101.

Noyek & Sons Ltd (In Voluntary Liquidation) v Hearne (Inspector of Taxes)
[1988] IR 772 .... Vol III p 523

Voluntary liquidator – interest earned on deposit interest after date of liquidation – whether corporation tax on such interest is a charge within the meaning of Companies Act 1963 s 281 – whether liability of voluntary liquidator is different to that of court liquidator.

Orr (Kilternan) Ltd v The Companies Act 1963-1983, and
Thornberry Construction (Irl) Ltd v The Companies Act 1963-1983
[1986] IR 273 .... Vol III p 530

Liquidation – High Court fees on funds realised by liquidator in course of liquidation – whether applicable to monies payable to secured creditors or to proceeds of sale of property subject to a fixed charge – Supreme Court and High Court (Fees) Order 1984 (SI 19/1984 as amended by SI 36/1985).

Deighan v Hearne (Inspector of Taxes), Fitzgerald, Murphy, Ireland, The Attorney General and The Minister for Finance
[1986] IR 603, [1990] IR 499 .... Vol III p 533

Income Tax Acts – constitutionality -estimated assessments – incorrect description of taxpayer – material enactments and statutory instruments not available – invalid seizure of

goods – exercise of judicial function – Courts bypassed – personal rights of citizen violated – constitutional right to have recourse to High Court denied – ITA 1967 as amended.

Masser Ltd (In Receivership) and Others v The Revenue Commissioners .... Vol III p 548

Charge on book debts by deed of mortgage – whether a fixed or floating charge – essential distinction – when is charge effected – test is whether unrestricted use of property is permitted – conflict in terms of deed – determining restriction in prevention of charging, assigning or otherwise disposing of book debts and other debts.

Wayte (Holdings) Ltd (In Receivership) v Hearne (Inspector of Taxes)
[1986] IR 448 .... Vol III p 553

Liability of receiver appointed by a debenture holder to corporation tax provisions of CTA 1976 – company is chargeable and tax assessed on company – whether provisions of ITA 1967 are adopted into corporation tax code – role of company secretary – adoption heavily qualified – whether permissible to adopt paying provision while ignoring charging provisions.

Murphy (Inspector of Taxes) v The Borden Co Ltd .... Vol III p 559

Case stated – whether a dividend declared on 11 December 1980 was received by related company not later than 12 December 1980 – whether payment of cheque required – whether payment through inter-company account was sufficient evidence of actual payment – whether making of journal entries after 23 December 1980 material evidence – whether making of accounting entry a mere record of underlying transaction.

Cronin (Inspector of Taxes) v C
[1968] IR 148 .... Vol III p 568

Income tax – Schedule D – Personal Pension and other assets assigned to company – pension continued to be paid to pensioner – whether pensioner ceased to receive pension as a source of income for himself beneficially – ITA 1918 Sch D Case III, rule of miscellaneous rules applicable to Schedule D and FA 1929 s 10.

Rowan (Deceased) v Rowan and Others
[1988] ILRM 65 .... Vol III p 572

Domicile – Irish domicile of origin – tests for acquisition of domicile of choice – whether determined by Irish law – whether domicile of origin restored – whether intention without residence sufficient.

The State (Calcul International Ltd and Solatrex International Ltd) v The Appeal Commissioners and The Revenue Commissioners .... Vol III p 577

Corporation/income/value added tax – concurrent determination of tax liability by High Court and Appeal Commissioners – whether mutually exclusive – conditional order of prohibition against Appeal Commissioners – application to make order absolute – tax code only permissible procedure – Appeal Commissioners powers and functions unconstitutional – nature of powers – limited or unlimited – ITA 1967 Pt XXVI and s 488. Articles 34 and 37 of the constitution.

Kennedy v Hearne, The Attorney General and Others
[1987] IR 120, [1988] IR 481, [1988] ILRM 53, 531 .... Vol III p 590

PAYE regulations – whether procedures unfair and unconstitutional – whether Revenue Commissioners involved in administration of justice – enforcement order issue to city sheriff after payment of tax – whether defamatory of plaintiff – question of damages.

Irish Agricultural Machinery Ltd v Ó Culacháin (Inspector of Taxes)
[1987] IR 458, [1990] IR 535 .... Vol III p 611

Stock relief under FA 1975 s 31 – trade consisting of the manufacturing of goods or sale of machinery or plant to farmers – whether assembly of agricultural machinery constitutes manufacturing – raw materials manufactured goods – changes in appearance but assembly not understood as manufacturing by well informed laymen – whether sales operations constitute a trade under s 31 – sales must be direct to farmers.

Kerrane (Inspector of Taxes) v Hanlon (Ireland) Ltd
[1987] IR 259 .... Vol III p 633

Export sales relief – ambulances manufactured in the State and exported – payments in advance lodged in deposit account – income not "immediately derived" from a trade of business – income received on foot of an obligation with bank – CTA 1976 ss 58 and 59.

Director of Public Prosecutions v Downes
[1987] IR 139, [1987] ILRM 665 .... Vol III p 641

Prosecution for payment of a Revenue penalty – whether criminal or civil proceedings applicable – no indicia of a criminal offence – ITA 1967 ss 17, 127, 128 & 500.

Browne (Inspector of Taxes) v Bank of Ireland Finance Ltd
[1987] IR 346, [1991] 1 IR 431 .... Vol III p 644

Business of banking – government stocks purchased to comply with Central Bank requirements – whether carrying on trade of dealing in securities – whether liable as profits under Schedule D or exempt capital gains on Government stocks – tests to be applied in a case stated by High Court – whether true and only reasonable conclusion to be drawn – Corporation Tax Act.

Patrick Monahan (Drogheda) Ltd v O'Connell (Inspector of Taxes)................. Vol III p 661

Capital allowances – industrial building or structure for the purposes of a dock undertaking – whether bonded transit sheds qualify – nature of business -sheds used as clearing house and not for storage – meaning of undertaking – ancillary to business of dock undertaking – ITA 1967 s 255.

Pandion Haliaetus Ltd, Ospreycare Ltd, Osprey Systems Design Ltd v The Revenue Commissioners
[1987] IR 309, [1988] ILRM 419 .... Vol III p 670

Corporation income tax – hot car wash invention – whether income from patent rights disregarded for income tax purposes – where payable to a non-resident – effect of interpretation of FA 1973 s 34 as given by Revenue Commissioners – whether particular scheme disclosed – whether interpretation binding on Inspector of Taxes – tax avoidance

scheme within Furniss v Dawson *principle – declaration by way of application for judicial review.*

The Diners Club Ltd v The Revenue Commissioners and The Minister for Finance
[1988] IR 158 .... Vol III p 680

Value added tax – interpretation of statutory instrument – charge card scheme – method of conducting business – purpose of a charge or credit cards – to facilitate sales by retailer to a purchaser – retailer paid by credit card or charge card company – described in statutory instrument as reimbursement – accepted as meaning paid for – whether debt due to retailer purchased – whether part of overall agreement between credit card company, retailer and purchaser – whether an individual transaction to be looked at in isolation.

McGrath and Others v McDermott (Inspector of Taxes)
[1988] IR 258, [1988] ILRM 181, 647 .... Vol III p 683

Capital gains tax – tax avoidance scheme – scheme technically valid – allowable loss – s 33 of Act plain and unambiguous meaning – whether provision to be disregarded unless a real loss – no equity in taxation – separation of powers – functions of courts and legislature – Superior Courts alone review court decisions – no general anti-avoidance legislation.

Kill Inn Motel Ltd (In Liquidation) v The Companies Acts 1963–1983 .... Vol III p 706

Disposal of assets at an undervalue by a company – granting of a preferential mortgage – creditors prejudiced – application by liquidator – gifts made by a company – Fraudulent Conveyances Act 1634 (10 Charles 1).

Ó Coindealbháin (Inspector of Taxes) v Price
[1988] IR 14 .... Vol IV p 1

Capital gain on sale of lands – absent landowner – proceeds of sale reinvested in acquisition of further lands – absent owner returns to take on active farming – whether rollover relief on transfer of a trade applies – FA 1974 ss 13, 15, 17 & 21, FA 1975 s 12 and CGTA 1975 s 28.

Murphy (Inspector of Taxes) v Dataproducts (Dublin) Ltd
[1988] IR 10 .... Vol IV p 12

Non resident company – carries on a manufacturing business through a branch in the State – tax free profits from Irish branch paid into a Swiss bank account – whether interest earned on Swiss bank account is chargeable to corporation tax on the Irish branch.

McNally v Ó Maoldhomhniagh .... Vol IV p 22

Income tax – capital allowance – plant and machinery used in a designated area – whether used exclusively in designated area – whether allowance extends to plant and machinery used under a hire contract – FA 1971 s 22.

Ó Culacháin (Inspector of Taxes) v Hunter Advertising Ltd .... Vol IV p 35

Corporation tax – manufacturing relief – advertising company – production for sale of advertising materials such as TV videos – word manufacture not defined – creative concept formed into a film – printing and processing in UK – tangible physical product -

whether manufacturing process applied by respondent – nature and complexity of process – view of ordinary man – test of change brought about by process – characteristics and value – chemical reaction – matter of degree – purpose of legislation – promotion of manufacturing industry.

Ó Coindealbháin (Inspector of Taxes) v Mooney
[1990] IR 422 .... Vol IV p 45

Income tax – a contract of employment – whether a contract of service or a contract for services – branch manager of local employment office of Dept of Social Welfare – income tax assessed on PAYE basis – whether respondent a self employed independent contractor – whether Court should look beyond terms of written contract – tests to be applied, essential conditions of a contract of service.

Mooney v Ó Coindealbháin and The Revenue Commissioners .... Vol IV p 62

Income tax – whether interest recoverable on foot of overpaid income tax – whether basis of assessment under Schedule E or Schedule D – whether branch manager of employment exchange to be taxed as an employee or as a self employed person – whether interest recoverable under FA 1976 s 30 – whether appeal to nil assessments to tax rules out interest on overpayments on tax – whether appeal of assessments under wrong Schedule rules out interest on overpayments of tax – whether implied agreement applies between the parties in regard to years of assessment not appealed.

Dunnes Stores (Oakville) Ltd v Cronin (Inspector of Taxes) .... Vol IV p 68

Capital allowance against corporation tax – plant – expenditure on installation of suspended ceiling in supermarket – whether suspended ceiling constitutes plant – nature of trade – functional test – question of degree – goods distinguished from services.

The Racing Board v Ó Culacháin .... Vol IV p 73

Levies on course betting by bookmakers – whether an activity analogous to a trade – whether income taxable as profits – scheme of Act – development of horse breeding and racing, statutory body whether to Racing Board and Racecourse – Act 1945 ss 4, 15, 27(1) – ITA 1967 s 537.

The Companies Act 1963–1983 v MFN Construction Co Ltd (In Liquidation) on the application of Patrick Tuffy (Liquidator) .... Vol IV p 82

PAYE/PRSI – company insolvent – Bank of Ireland a secured creditor and revenue debts due to collector general – winding up deferred by reason of scheme of arrangement approved by High Court – collector general agreed to deferral of revenue debt pending completion of contracts by company – unsecured creditors promised 40p in £1 and voted to accept scheme – a third party paid off the unsecured creditors by way of subrogation agreements – whether third party bound by terms of scheme of arrangement.

Cusack v O'Reilly and The Collector General .... Vol IV p 86

This interpleader summons arose out of the seizure by the applicant in his role as Revenue sheriff of goods and chattels claimed to be the property of the claimant in the action. The sheriff on being challenged, issued the interpleader summons to have his claim determined by the court whether or not the chattels in question are:

Texaco Ireland Ltd v Murphy (Inspector of Taxes)
[1989] IR 496, [1991] 2 IR 449 .... Vol IV p 91

Corporation tax -whether petroleum exploration constitutes scientific research – whether such scientific research qualifies for tax relief by way of an allowance under ITA 1967 s 244 – whether proximate sections are relevant to the interpretation of the particular section – whether Act as a whole should be construed – whether proviso to s 244(3) applies – the principles of construction of taxing statutes – whether there is any equity about taxation, whether in imposition, exemption or manner of application – whether capital expenditure herein comes within the application of the proviso – whether the claim for relief comes within the express wording of the proviso.

United Bars Ltd (In Receivership), Walkinstown Inn Ltd (In Receivership) and Jackson v The Revenue Commissioners
[1991] IR 396 .... Vol IV p 107

Company – debentures creating fixed and floating charges – receiver appointed by debenture holder – fixed charges paid off leaving surplus – preferential creditors – priority – whether surplus to be paid to preferential creditors or to company – Companies Act 1963 (No 33) s 98.

Hearne (Inspector of Taxes) v O'Cionna (t/a Kenny & Partners) .... Vol IV p 113

Employer's liability to deduct PAYE and PRSI from employee's emoluments – deductions to be paid to the collector general – loan arrangement between partnership and limited company – whether partnership liable for PAYE and PRSI of employees of company – special meaning of word employer under Income Tax Acts – no similar meaning under social welfare legislation – whether employer's liability different in respect of PRSI.

Bourke (Inspector of Taxes) v Bradley & Sons
[1990] IR 379 .... Vol IV p 117

Value added tax – service supplied by solicitor on instructions of Insurance underwriter – in relation to insured litigant – whether supplied to underwriter or to the defendant – services to a non-resident in the State but resident within EEC – no establishment in the state – where services are deemed to be supplied.

McMahon (Inspector of Taxes) v Murphy .... Vol IV p 125

Capital gains tax – market value on 6 April 1974 of holding of 73 acres of land – agricultural land situate outside town of Macroom – appeal on value of land as determined in Circuit Court – whether subsequent planning permission for milk processing plant relevant – whether development potential attached to the lands on 6 April 1974 – whether agricultural value the sole determining factor.

Carroll Industries Plc v S Ó Culacháin (Inspector of Taxes)
[1988] IR 705 .... Vol IV p 135

Appellant company's accounts, based on current cost accounting convention (ie replacement cost) – whether acceptable for tax purposes as a basis for accountancy – whether historical cost accounting convention is the only method of commercial accountancy for tax purposes – Whimster *decision and its two "fundamental commonplaces" – true profits for tax purposes based on difference between receipts and*

expenditure laid out to earn those receipts and the accounts framed consistently with ordinary principles of commercial accounting – profits and gains for tax purposes not defined in Tax Acts – no particular basis of accountancy stipulated by statute – appropriate accounting method may not give "true profits" – whether provision for inflation applicable – stock relief allowed by Finance Acts – different methods of costing stock – basic premise that profits is the difference between receipts and expenditure laid out to earn those receipts.

McDaid v Sheehy, The Director of Public Prosecutions and Others
[1991] IR 1 .... Vol IV p 162

Whether applicant validly convicted of an offence and fined for keeping in the fuel tank of his motor vehicle hydrocarbon oil on which custom or excise duty had not been paid – whether Imposition of Duties Act 1957 Constitutional – whether order empowering the government to impose, terminate or vary duties invalid – where delegation of powers is permissible – whether test of coming within principles and policies of Act applies – whether subsequent statutory provision validates order – whether reasonable interpretation to be applied.

Wiley v The Revenue Commissioners
[1989] IR 351 .... Vol IV p 170

Excise duty – what persons may be authorised by order of the Minister for Finance to import goods such as motor vehicles free of excise duties – to what extent must such persons be suffering from disability – whether such persons must be wholly without the use of each of his legs – doctrine of legitimate expectation – whether refunds of excise duty on two previous occasions constitutes a practice – whether expectation is a legitimate one – whether a regular practice can be discontinued or altered without notice.

Waterford Glass (Group Services) Ltd v The Revenue Commissioners
[1990] IR 334 .... Vol IV p 187

Stamp duty – agreement for sale granting immediate possession on payment of deposit followed by agreement for sale of residual interest – whether the transfer of the residual interest stampable on the value of the residual interest or on the value of the entire property – what constitutes a conveyance for sale under Stamp Act of 1891 – whether courts will look at legal effect and legal rights of a transaction – whether FA 1986 s 96(1) applies – whether a contract for sale of legal estate is a contract for sale of property – whether contract conferred a benefit within the meaning of F(1909-10)A 1910 s 74(5).

The Hammond Lane Metal Co Ltd v Ó Culacháin (Inspector of Taxes)
[1990] IR 560 .... Vol IV p 197

Corporation tax – whether an agreement between the taxpayer and the inspector of taxes in relation to an assessment of tax under appeal is binding and conclusive – whether full disclosure – whether "discovery" applies – whether unappealed assessment and compromised appeal are subject to the same interpretation – whether discovery constitutes unfair procedure – whether tax avoidance scheme under ITA 1967 Ch VI tax effective – whether premium under lease allowable under ITA 1967 s 91 – whether election under s 83(6) alters lessee's entitlement to deduction for entire premium – whether lessee to be

treated as paying an amount according to a formula – whether s 83 is dealing with actualities – whether general rules on deductions overruled.

Bank of Ireland Finance Ltd v The Revenue Commissioners .... Vol IV p 217

Disposal of property by mortgagee – disposal as nominee for mortgagor – whether payment of capital gains tax by purchaser was in accordance with CGTA 1975 – whether absence of a clearance certificate entitled Revenue Commissioners to return the payment – whether mortgagee entitled to a refund of tax paid.

Ó Coindealbháin (Inspector of Taxes) v O'Carroll
[1989] IR 229 .... Vol IV p 221

Garda Siochana Pensions Order 1981 – widows contributory pension and children" contributory pensions granted – whether children's pension income of the widow or income of the children for income tax purposes – widow's pension payable to the widow whereas children's pension payable to widow for children – children's pension not mandatory when widow's pension not payable – rate of tax related to tax status of payee – whether children's pension the beneficial property of children in all circumstances.

Purcell v Attorney General .... Vol IV p 229

Whether implementation of Farm Tax Act constituted unfair procedures – effect of repeal in budget statement in March 1987 – consequences of absence of amending legislation – locus standi of applicant – legislation based on will of Oireachtas – if legislation interfered unlawfully then what remains cannot be enforceable in the future or past.

O Cahill (Inspector of Taxes) v Harding .... Vol IV p 233

Income tax – whether lump sum payments to disabled employees exempt from income tax – closure of assembly works made most of work force redundant – compensation package agreed but no distinction between disabled and other employees – whether disabled employees whose jobs were lost because of redundancy were entitled to claim relief from income tax – whether a distinction to be made between disabled employees whose jobs continued and disabled employees whose jobs ceased.

Frederick Inns Ltd, The Rendezvous Ltd, The Graduate Ltd, Motels Ltd (In Liquidation) v The Companies Acts 1963-1983 .... Vol IV p 247

Recovery of outstanding taxes from a group of companies – whether Revenue Commissioners may appropriate payments between separate companies within the group – company law in regard to gratuitous alienation of assets by a company – whether insolvency of a company is relevant to gratuitous alienation of assets – whether Revenue disregarded rights of creditors of individual companies within the group.

O'Grady v Laragan Quarries Ltd
[1991] 1 IR 237 .... Vol IV p 269

Whether lorry owners carrying sand and gravel were engaged in the haulage for hire of materials within the meaning of FA 1970 s 17 – whether the payments to the lorry owners were for subcontracting under a construction contract – whether the lorry owners became the proprietors of the quarry materials – whether any ambiguity attached to the agreements – whether parties are free to enter into form of contract which is tax effective.

Murphy v District Justice Brendan Wallace..Vol IV p 278

Excise duty – bookmaker convicted and fined in the District Court of offences under the Betting Acts – arising out of non-payment of fines distress warrants issued to Garda Superintendent to distrain against defaulter's goods – return of no goods – penal warrants for imprisonment of defaulter sought by Revenue Authorities under provisions of Excise Management Act 1827 s 90 (as amended) – discretion to Revenue under s 90 to release or retain defaulter in prison for six months – whether such power constitutional and whether s 90 invalid.

Ó Culacháin v McMullan Brothers
[1991] 1 IR 363 ....Vol IV p 284

Whether forecourt canopies at petrol filling stations constitute plant for tax purposes – competition between petrol companies has led to major changes in the design and facilities at petrol stations – whether a canopy is essential to provide advertising, brand image and attractive setting – whether canopies provide no more than shelter from rain and wind or play a part in carrying on the trade of selling petrol – market research has proven the sales effectiveness of canopies – principles upon which the court approaches a case stated in relation to findings of primary fact, conclusions or inferences and interpretation of the law – test to be applied in deciding whether disputed object is apparatus or not – whether canopy creates an ambience and has a function in the carrying on of the business.

Irish Nationwide Building Society v The Revenue Commissioners.................Vol IV p 296

Whether a conveyance to a building society was exempt from stamp duty by virtue of the Building Societies Act of 1976 – certain categories of instruments relating to the internal affairs of a society were specifically exempted by the Act of 1976 – whether the general provision of the exempting provision contained in s 91 of the Act extended to a conveyance or transfer of a premises to a society for the purpose of conducting its business – ejusdem generis rule – intention of legislature – whether the internal affairs of a society are distinguishable from its commercial dealings.

Murnaghan Brothers Ltd v Ó Maoldhomhnaigh
[1991] 1 IR 455 ....Vol IV p 304

Whether lands the subject matter of a contract for sale entered into during an accounting period constitute trading stock for the year ending in that accounting period – trading stock and trade as defined in the Finance Acts – appellant company carrying on trade of building contractors – whether absence of possession, conveyance of legal estate and planning permission fatal to taxpayer's claim for relief – whether inclusion of the lands in the accounts by accountant in accordance with good accounting procedure was the best evidence of the commercial reality of the transaction.

Phonographic Performance (Ireland) Ltd v Somers (Inspector of Taxes)
[1992] ILRM 657 ....Vol IV p 314

Value added tax – whether corporate body exploiting copyrights supplying service within meaning of the Value Added Tax Act – Copyright Act 1963 (No 10), ss 7(1), 7(3) & 17(4) – VATA 1972 (No 22) ss 2(1), 5.

Browne and Others v The Revenue Commissioners and Others
[1991] 2 IR 58 .... Vol IV p 323

Sales representative – motor car "a tool of his trade" – whether in position of tax on benefit accruing from private use of employer's motor car is constitutional – whether legislation impinges on individuals' right to earn a livelihood – whether an unjust attack on property rights in breach of Article 40 of the Constitution – whether legislation impinges on individuals' rights to be held equal before the law – whether any constitutional right infringed – whether tax limited to availability of car for private use – whether tax avoidable – Constitution of Ireland Art 40 – ITA 1967 ss 117, 118, 119, 120 – FA 1958 ss 23, 24, 25, 26 – FA 1982 s 4.

Quigley (Inspector of Taxes) v Burke
[1991] 2 IR 169 .... Vol IV p 332

Whether the inspector of taxes is entitled to call for production of a taxpayer's nominal ledger – whether the inspector required the nominal ledger to satisfy himself on the adjustments made in the accounts and the reasons for such adjustments made in the accounts – whether the accountant was acting as agent to the taxpayer or as a professional person and client – whether the nominal ledger formed part of the accountant's working papers – whether the nominal ledger was "within the power or possession" of the taxpayer – whether a reasonable person could be satisfied on the income tax computation in the absence of the nominal ledger.

Crowe Engineering Ltd v Lynch and Others
In the Matter of The Trustee Act 1893 s 36 .... Vol IV p 340

Superannuation scheme – whether trustees have absolute discretion on the distribution of the fund following the death of a member – whether trustees are bound by a direction in the member's will – whether a separated wife, a common law wife and children are entitled as defendants or relatives to be considered as beneficiaries – whether renunciation under a separation deed rules out entitlement under the superannuation scheme – whether discretion of trustees is absolute – whether court can be called on for guidance.

Forde Decision by Appeal Commissioners .... Vol IV p 348

This appeal was brought by Michael Forde against the refusal of the inspector of taxes to grant him exemption under FA 1969 s 2 in respect of the books written by him on the Constitutional law in Ireland, Company law in Ireland and Extradition law in Ireland. Section 2 grants an exemption from income tax in respect of original and creative works which are generally recognised as having cultural or artistic merit. Subsection 5(b) provides a right of appeal as if it were a right of appeal against an assessment subject to all the appeal provisions of ITA 1967.

Brosnan (Inspector of Taxes) v Cork Communications Ltd .... Vol IV p 349

Cork Communications Ltd providing a cable television system – whether company supplying electricity – whether company transmitting TV and radio signals – whether liable to vat on sales to customers – whether company's system consists of immovable goods and exempt from value added tax.

O'Leary v The Revenue Commissioners .... Vol IV p 357

This application for judicial review was made on the grounds that the interest and penalty provisions for stamp duties which were introduced by FA 1991 s 100 did not take effect until 1 November 1991 and that the previous provision for interest and penalties under Stamp Act 1891 s 15 was repealed on 29 May 1991, the date of the passing of FA 1991.

Ó Laochdha (Inspector of Taxes) v Johnson & Johnson (Ireland) Ltd [1991] 2 IR 287 .... Vol IV p 361

Corporation tax – case stated as to whether the production of J Cloths and nappy liners from bales of fabric is a manufacturing process – whether manufacturing relief under FA 1980 s 42 applies – whether use of a sophisticated and expensive machine constitutes manufacturing – whether absence of change in raw material is relevant – whether product is a commercially different product – what is manufacturing – whether appearance, utility, qualities and value are the characteristics of manufacturing – whether question is one of degree – whether use of expensive and sophisticated machinery is relevant – how product is perceived by an ordinary adequately informed person – whether quality of and product is commercially enhanced by process.

VIEK Investments Ltd v The Revenue Commissioners [1991] 2 IR 520 .... Vol IV p 367

Stamp duty – proper amount of stamp duty chargeable on a deed of transfer – contracts and consideration structured to minimise stamp duty – substance of transactions – Stamp Act 1891 s 13.

The Minister for Social Welfare v Griffiths .... Vol IV p 378

Whether a member of the crew of a fishing vessel can be an "employee" – whether Social Welfare (Consolidation) Act 1981 applies to self employed persons – whether Act is limited in its application to the traditional relationship of employer/employee – whether there can be an "employee" without there being a corresponding employer – whether scheme of Act and regulations is limited to employer/employee circumstances – whether Minister has unlimited power to make regulations enabling any person to be treated as an employee.

McCrystal Oil Co Ltd v The Revenue Commissioners .... Vol IV p 386

Customs duties – action for damages for retinue and conversion arising out of the seizure by the Revenue Commissioners of an oil tanker – marked gas oil found in one of the tanker's compartments – outlet from the compartment not indelibly marked as required by statutory regulations – tanker seized and gas oil sold – whether there was a breach of the statutory regulation – what constitutes a conveyance under the legislation – whether outlet distinguished from container – whether defendants' case confined to breach in respect of the outlet – whether regulations must be construed strictly – whether court restricted to consideration of the breach of the regulations as pleaded – issue of damages.

Louth v Minister for Social Welfare .... Vol IV p 391

Appeal on a point of law under the social welfare code – whether deepsea dockers working under a pooling arrangement have a right to sign on for social welfare benefit as being unemployed when they are not occupied in unloading ships – whether dockers had a contract of employment with their association – whether level of earnings material to

question of employment – whether a contract of service or a contract for services – whether separate contracts with dockers on each occasion of their employment.

The Director of Public Prosecutions v Boyle .... Vol IV p 395

Excise duty – case stated – complaints of non-payment of excise duty payable on bets entered into by the defendant as a registered bookmaker – whether recovery of an excise penalty a criminal matter – whether use of words guilty of an offence and summary conviction indicate a criminal matter – whether amount of penalty is relevant – what is a crime – whether a crime can be defined – whether the act is prohibited with legal consequences – what are the indicia of a crime – whether any words of prohibition – whether option of making a payment as alternative to compliance – whether words such as fine, offence, summary conviction disigrate a criminal offence.

The Revenue Commissioners v Arida Ltd .... Vol IV p 401

Income tax – case stated by Circuit Court Judge pursuant to ITA 1967 ss 428 and 430 – whether or not a Circuit Court Judge hearing an appeal pursuant to ITA 1967 s 429 has jurisdiction to award costs – whether a tax appeal constitutes proceedings under the Circuit Court rules – whether the Circuit Court Judge's jurisdiction is limited to the powers and duties of the Appeal Commissioners – whether the principle "expressio unius exclusio alterius" applies – whether s 428(b) granting power to High Court to award costs is superfluous – whether exception to Circuit Court rule expressly or impliedly stated – extensive jurisdiction of Circuit Court – normal practice on costs.

Ó Síocháin (Inspector of Taxes) v Morrissey .... Vol IV p 407

Eleanor Morrissey commenced employment with the Bank of Ireland 27 March 1972 – she married respondent 14 May 1977 and resigned employment 10 May 1985 – whether "marriage gratuity" received on resignation was a retirement payment under ITA 1967 s 114 or was a perquisite of her office under ITA 1967 s 110 – whether a conflict between agreement of March 1974 with bank officials and bank superannuation scheme – whether real issue of liability under s 100 considered by Circuit Court Judge.

In the matter of Stamp (Deceased) v Noel Redmond .... Vol IV p 415

Succession – construction of will – whether "issue" included adopted children – whether Adoption Acts changed scope and meaning of family to include adopted as well as legitimate children – whether court bound by words used in will – intention of testator – whether issue restricted to children of marriage – Adoption Act 1952 ss 4, 26(2).

Connolly v The Collector of Customs and Excise .... Vol IV p 419

Excise duty – judicial review – publican's licence – whether new licence obtainable – whether application within six year period – meaning of year immediately preceding.

O'Grady (Inspector of Taxes) v Roscommon Race Committee .... Vol IV p 425

Expenditure on racecourse stand – whether deductible repairs or non deductible capital expenditure or expenditure qualifying as plant – trade of promoting and organising horse races – long established stand used for viewing races – what is function of stand – provides shelter and creates atmosphere of excitement – categories of work carried out – whether works on retained part of stand constitutes repairs – whether new bar and extension to old

bar non-deductible capital improvements – whether stand or racecourse is the entirety – whether expenditure on roof a repair – whether word done to walls a repair – whether re-design or lower terracing an improvement – whether stand as renewed and repaired is plant – agreed test – whether stand is part of the means by which trade is carried on or merely part of the place where at which trade is carried on.

JW v JW .... Vol IV p 437

Domicile – constitutional rights – whether common law rule of dependent domicile of a wife constitutional – recognition of foreign divorces – wife's separate domicile.

McGurrin (Inspector of Taxes) v Champion Publications Ltd.......................... Vol IV p 466

Respondent is a newspaper publisher – newspapers are "goods" for the purpose of manufacturing relief from corporation tax – whether income from advertising qualifies for such relief – whether indirect income from advertising can be treated equally with direct income from newsagents – whether advertising income is receivable in respect of the sale in the course of the trade of goods – whether advertising income is from a separate trade or providing a service – whether the matter to be considered from aspect of commercial reality – whether proper construction of words of s 41 brought advertisements within definition of goods – whether advertising revenue is received in respect of the sale of newspapers.

Bairead v McDonald .... Vol IV p 475

Appeal against judgment for income tax and interest – what constitutes a proper return of income for the assessment of income tax – whether a return of income equalling income tax exemption limits a valid return – whether lack of records justifies such a return – whether taxpayer treated unfairly by the Revenue – whether practice of allowing late returns amounts to promissory estoppel – whether taxpayer has availed of opportunity to make later returns after assessments had become final – whether treated unfairly by the Revenue – whether adjournment be granted to allow taxpayer to make proper returns – whether counterclaim for damages for harassment untenable.

O'Callaghan v Clifford... Vol IV p 478

Income tax – appeal against a decision of the High Court to refuse on a judicial review application to quash three convictions with six months imprisonment for each offence imposed in the District Court on the appellant for failure to make income tax returns – inspector of taxes empowered to require of an individual by notice a return of income – civil offence rendered a criminal offence by FA 1983 s 94(2) – whether a certificate by the inspector of non compliance is sufficient proof – whether in absence of accused in court the certificate contains the necessary mens rea – whether refusal in District Court to grant an adjournment denied the appellant the opportunity to defend himself – whether such refusal was unconstitutional – whether limits to District Judge's discretion to refuse an adjournment – whether extra degree of caution called for a criminal matter – whether appellant's right to instruct his counsel denied – whether audi alteram partem *rule and fair administration of justice applies – whether absence of due process on foot of certificate.*

Manning v Shackleton and Cork County Council .... Vol IV p 485

Capital gains tax compulsory acquisition of land – whether property arbitrator obliged to give details of his findings of facts and law and a breakdown of his award – whether applicant is unable to formulate an appeal without being given the reasons for the award – whether breakdown required for capital gains tax purposes – whether award could be justified on the evidence – whether any obligation imposed on arbitrator by the Acquisition of Land (Assessment of Compensation) Act 1919 – whether the giving of reasons necessary for the proper exercise of a judicial or administrative function – whether failure by applicant at the hearing to request an apportionment of the award under the several heads of claim or to request a case stated rules out any further relief – whether failure to advance further arguments of unfairness amounted to acceptance of the normal practice – whether undertakings affected the amount of the arbitrator's award.

Carbery Milk Products Ltd v The Minister for Agriculture .... Vol IV p 492

Classification of milk products – EC regulations – milk protein powder – whether a whey or skimmed milk product – whether export refunds on consignments from EC countries to non EC countries – whether Revenue Commissioners responsible for classification – whether Revenue Commissioners and state chemist negligent and in breach of duty – whether re-classification renders products liable for repayment of export refunds – whether principle of legitimate expectation applies – whether Minister for Agriculture agent for European Commission – whether Minister entitled to counterclaim against plaintiff – whether plaintiff entitled to indemnity against Revenue Commissioners – EEC Regulations 804/68 and 2682/72.

Bairead v Carr .... Vol IV p 505

Summary summonses served on the defendant in respect of tax liabilities the subject matter of earlier appeals – whether dissatisfaction expressed at the Circuit Court appeal hearings – whether dissatisfaction must be expressed immediately after determination by the Circuit Court Judge – whether notice to county registrar must be lodged within 21 days together with the £20 fee – whether requirements are directory or mandatory – whether tax must be paid before the case stated is determined – whether time lapse after expression of dissatisfaction is fatal – whether payment of tax denies access to the courts – whether Circuit Court judge has discretion to accept late filing of notice and fee.

Keller v The Revenue Commissioners .... Vol IV p 512

Importation of used motor vehicles from a Member State – interpretation of excise duties payable under SI 422/1983 – applicant a German citizen residing with his family in Ireland for upwards of twenty years – a collector of vintage Mercedes Benz motor cars – whether his normal residence in Germany – whether requirements for normal residence in Germany satisfied – whether importation for temporary purpose and for transport for private use – interpretation of the expression "a new motor vehicle of a similar or corresponding type" – whether regulations provide guidance on the retail price as may be determined by the Revenue Commissioners – whether regulations contrary to Article 95 of Treaty of Rome – whether excise duties fall more unfairly on imported used cars than on used cars sold on the Irish market – whether credit of German value added tax allowable – whether onus of proof discharged – whether value added tax charged on value added tax

contrary to Sixth Council Directive – whether penalty of seizure and forfeiture disproportionate to offence – whether legitimate expectation infringed.

Kelly (Inspector of Taxes) v Cobb Straffan Ireland Ltd.................................. Vol IV p 526

Case stated on question of manufacturing relief – respondent company carries on business of producing day old chicks – whether day old chicks are goods within the meaning of FA 1980 – whether use of extensive plant machinery and skilled workers constitute a process of manufacturing – whether goods are required to be inanimate – whether question is one of degree – whether raw material in process was not the egg but twenty years of research – whether process is similar to fish farming which required a specific statutory exemption – whether respondent was producing as opposed to manufacturing day old chicks – whether chick is a product that could not be produced by a natural process – whether process constitutes manufacturing.

Hussey (Inspector of Taxes) v Gleeson & Co Ltd.. Vol IV p 533

Case stated on question of manufacturing relief – respondent company a wholesaler of beers and stouts as part of its trade conditions bottled Guinness stout – whether conditioning of bottled Guinness constitutes manufacturing process – chemical change in contents, carbon dioxide added and alcohol level increased – whether plant and equipment sufficiently sophisticated – whether process no more than keeping the stout in an even temperature for fourteen days – whether process of such a degree as to be classified as manufacturing.

Pine Valley Developments Ltd, Healy v The Revenue Commissioners............ Vol IV p 543

Award by European Court of Human Rights for pecuniary and non-pecuniary damages and costs lodged in High Court on foot of a claim by the plaintiffs – part of the award amounting to £273,000 held pending determination of the tax liabilities of the third plaintiff – conceded that £209,250 out of the £273,000 was in respect of income tax on interest accruing in the year 1993/94 – income tax liability would not arise prior to January 1995 – consequently £209,250 released on consent – balance of £63,750 relates to capital gains tax – third plaintiff is resident in the State and entitled to tax clearance certificate from capital gains tax – whether the sum of £63,750 should be withheld.

Dilleen (Inspector of Taxes) v Kearns.. Vol IV p 547

Abandonment of an option within the meaning of CGTA 1975 s 47(3) – tax avoidance scheme – respondent and his wife grant each other options over their separate shareholdings in a private company – series of transactions through a chain of companies including the abandonment by the respondent and his wife of their respective options for sums totalling £2,532,500 – whether abandonment of options for a cash consideration constitutes an abandonment of the option or a chargeable disposal of assets – what is true meaning of term abandonment of an option – whether it means non-exercise – whether ordinary meaning applies – whether the entire and the substance of the transaction to be considered – whether tax avoidance exercise relevant – whether substantial payment for non-exercise can be said to be an abandonment within the meaning of the Act.

Allied Irish Banks plc v Bolger .... Vol V p 1

Stamp duty – mortgage deeds – whether property stamped – whether admissible in evidence – whether admissible on foot of undertaking – whether possession of a premises can be obtained by way of special summons or summary procedure – whether ejectment proceedings required – whether procedure question raised in course of hearing

Airspace Investments Ltd v Moore (Inspector of Taxes) .... Vol V p 3

Corporation tax – whether company carrying on a trade – whether capital expenditure – series of agreements – whether a tax avoidance scheme – whether agreements to be viewed as a composite transaction – whether loan repayable – whether transactions can be considered with the benefit of hindsight.

Brosnan (Inspector of Taxes) v Leeside Nurseries Ltd .... Vol V p 21

Corporation tax – case stated – manufacturing relief – dwarfed potted chrysanthemum plants – whether McCann v Ó Culacháin properly decided – whether sophisticated process of cultivation constitutes manufacturing – whether a question of change in appearance, quality and value – whether a question of degree – whether "goods" capable of being manufactured – whether goods are inanimate – whether growing plants can be manufactured – whether manufactured or cultivated

In the Matter of Davoren (Deceased); O'Byrne v Davoren and Coughlan........... Vol V p 36

Trust – Discretionary – interpretation of residuary bequest – whether a valid charitable gift trust for education of children at discretion of trustees – class consisting of children, grandchildren and descendants of specified persons – meaning of the term "descendants" – whether capital of fund to be preserved – whether rule against perpetuities – whether bequest failed for uncertainty.

The Governor & Co of the Bank of Ireland v Meeneghan .... Vol V p 44

Value added tax – UK liability – UK court order restraining the taxpayer from disposing of his assets – whether bank account in Ireland subject to court order – whether foreign revenue debt recoverable in Ireland – whether effect of UK court order prevents the taxpayer from withdrawing the monies – whether principle of international law relating to revenue debts applies – whether value added tax subject to laws of European Union

Travers v Ó Síocháin (Inspector of Taxes)... Vol V p 54

Income tax – case stated – appellant's wife employed as a nurse by a Health Board in Northern Ireland – wife's remuneration taxed in Northern Ireland – whether appellant entitled to double taxation relief in Ireland – whether Article 18(2) of Double Taxation Relief (Taxes on Income and Capital Gains) [UK] Order 1976 grants relief.

WLD Worldwide Leather Diffusion Ltd v The Revenue Commissioners........... Vol V p 61

Value added tax – judicial review – non resident company registered in the State – single trading transaction – whether entitled to be registered for value added tax – whether Revenue Commissioners have discretion to refuse registration – whether applicant a taxable person – fiscal advantage – whether application bona fide – whether transaction a trading transaction.

Orange v The Revenue Commissioners .... Vol V p 70

Judicial Review application – applicant dependent upon criminal legal aid work – all legal aid fees due by Minister for Justice attached by respondents pursuant to FA 1988 s 73 whether procedure constitutional – whether court order required -whether constitutional right to earn a livelihood infringed – whether an unfair attack on applicant' s property rights – whether attachment of value added tax element of legal aid fees unconstitutional applicant offered reasonable terms of payment by respondents – whether attack on property rights to be viewed in the light of surrounding circumstances – whether legislation requires amendment.

Erin Executor and Trustee Co Ltd v The Revenue Commissioners..................... Vol V p 76

Value added tax – properties leased for ten or more years – VAT incurred on expenditure on leasehold properties – whether credits for VAT allowable – whether reversionary interest outside VAT net.

McAuliffe v The Minister for Social Welfare .... Vol V p 94

Social welfare appeal – appeal as to whether a contract of services or a contract for services – wholesale distributor of newspapers – deliveries of newspapers subcontracted to two individuals – individuals own delivery vehicles and pay all overheads – provide relief drivers – accept liability for losses or delays – time and reliability essence of contracts – whether contracts contain distinctive features of contracts for services – whether differences with contracts of service.

The Revenue Commissioners v Ó Loinsigh... Vol V p 98

Income tax – case stated – series of books known as "Pathways to History" whether original and creative – whether within the meaning of FA 1969 s 2

McCabe (Inspector of Taxes) v South City & County Investment Co Ltd .... Vol V p 107

Corporation Tax – whether periodic payments subject to Corporation Tax – annuity contract – annual payments off £500 plus share of profits in return for capital sum – whether correctly described as annuities – whether income receipts – whether return of capital – whether case law overturns logic of transactions – interpretation of tax statutes and documents – whether content of agreement conforms with its purpose
Additional judgment 1998 p 183

Fennessy (Inspector of Taxes) v McConnellogue .... Vol V p 129

Income tax – respondent resides with his wife in Northern Ireland – respondent employed in Co Donegal and chargeable to Irish tax in his salary – respondent's wife employed in Northern Ireland and because of her residence there her salary not chargeable to Irish tax – whether respondent entitled to a full married allowance and double rate income tax bands – whether allowances restricted to a single person's allowance and single rate bands.

O'Shea (Inspector of Taxes) v Mulqueen... Vol V p 134

Income tax – lump sum payment on retirement – whether liable to income tax – whether received on account of illness – whether a redundancy payment – whether payment made on grounds of retirement – whether payment made on grounds of ill health.

Brosnan (Inspector of Taxes) v Mutual Enterprises Ltd .... Vol V p 138

Case Stated – Corporation Tax – purchase of trading premises financed by foreign borrowings – losses incurred annually by reason of fluctuations in currency rates – whether allowable against trading profits – whether losses a revenue or capital item – whether a means of fluctuating and temporary accommodation – whether conflicting views of UK courts to be distinguished – whether monies borrowed to be used for purchase of a capital asset – whether monies so used – whether repayable on demand – whether a question of fact or law – whether grounds for setting aside findings of primary facts.

Mooney (Inspector of Taxes) v McSweeney .... Vol V p 163

Capital Gains Tax – loan to company – loan agreement with right to convert loan into shares – whether a mere debt – whether a debt on a security – whether an allowable loss for Capital Gains Tax purposes – whether characteristics of a debt on a security exist – whether synonymous with secured debt – whether marketable – whether loan had potential to be released at a profit – whether difficulty in finding a purchaser relevant – whether right to repayment and right to convert can co-exist -whether right to convert distinguishing factor – whether proviso to s 46 of Capital Tax Act 1975 applies.

In re Cherry Court v The Revenue Commissioners .... Vol V p 180

Stamp duty – deed of release – whether or not a sale – whether liable to ad valorem stamp duty – series of transactions – whether release of option constituted a sale – meaning of sale – reality of transaction – whether phrases used imply a transfer of property.

In re Private Motorists Provident Society Ltd (In Liquidation) and Horgan v Minister for Justice .... Vol V p 186

Court fees payable by official liquidator – court liquidation fees prescribed by statutory instrument – whether monies received in realisation of assets of a company – meaning of assets – meaning of realisation – whether assets can be realised more than once – whether accrual of interest a realisation – whether assets vested in liquidator – whether monies received from associated companies in liquidation constitute a realisation – whether interpretation of realisations a matter of debate.

In re Hibernian Transport Companies Ltd .... Vol V p 194

Court liquidation – fees payable by official liquidator – fees prescribed by statutory instrument – monies received in realisation of assets of a company – interest earned from monies on deposit – capital gains from disposals of exchequer bills – whether a realisation – whether an investment – rate of court duty – yearly accounts – whether rate in force for accounting period applicable – whether rate at date of certification applies.

Ó Culacháin (Inspector of Taxes) v McMullan Brothers Ltd .... Vol V p 200

Corporation tax – principles to be applied in a case stated – whether canopies in forecourts of petrol filling stations constitute plant – whether part of the premises – whether part of setting in which business carried on – whether function is to provide shelter and light – whether function is to attract customers – whether view of law correct – whether correct tests applied – whether "setting" and "plant" mutually exclusive – whether conclusion is one which a reasonable judge could not have arrived at.

Irwin v Grimes .... Vol V p 209

Income tax – summary summons issued on 4 October 1989 – whether certificates under Waiver of Certain Tax, Interest and Penalties Act 1993 apply – whether proceedings initiated prior to 1993 Act – whether defendant non resident in the State up to 1992 – whether defendant liable for any taxes.

Daly v The Revenue Commissioners & Ors .... Vol V p 213

Income tax – judicial review – fees paid by Health Board – applicant a medical doctor – payments subject to withholding tax – scheme of withholding tax amended by FA 1990 – self employed taxed on profits and gains of actual year of assessment – windfall gain to established taxpayers – amendment to eliminate gain – effect on new entrants to system – effect of interim refunds – financial hardship – property rights infringed – proportionality test – whether unconstitutional.

Revenue Commissioners v Arida Ltd .... Vol V p 221

Circuit Court rehearing of tax appeal – whether Circuit Court judge has jurisdiction to award costs – whether a tax appeal constitutes "proceedings" – whether statutory authority required – whether court has inherent jurisdiction to award costs – whether award of costs ultra vires the rules of the Circuit Court – whether jurisdiction of Circuit Court to award costs extends to cases vested in the Circuit Court since the passing of the Courts of Justice Act 1961.

In re Sugar Distributors Ltd .... Vol V p 225

High Court application – whether share issue invalid – whether meetings took place or resolutions passed – whether backdating of transactions invalid – whether acts of company binds company – whether consent of corporators sufficient – whether s 89 be given a liberal "just and equitable" meaning – whether discretion of court under s 89 restricted – whether underlying policy of s 89 to be considered – whether remedy limited to defective title to shares – whether any proprietary interest in shares acquired by "innocent" persons – whether remedy available without court assistance – whether court can accede to a fiction.

Henry Denny & Sons (Ireland) Ltd T/A Kerry Foods v Minister for Social Welfare
.... Vol V p 238

Social Welfare appeal – PRSI – whether demonstrator engaged under a contract of service or contract for service – whether on insurable person as an employee or insurable as a self-employed person – whether written contract the determining factor – whether facts and realities govern the relationship – whether Circuit Court decision relevant – whether decision of Appeals Officer incorrect in law – whether control the deciding factor – whether in business on one's own account decisive – whether written agreement the sole source of the relationship – whether agreement fully considered by Appeals Officer – whether each case to be considered on its particular facts – whether Appeals Officer was entitled to conclude that there was a contract of service.

Quigley (Inspector of Taxes) v Maurice Burke .... Vol V p 265

Income tax – whether an accountant acting in the preparation of accounts and computations of taxable income on behalf of a taxpayer is acting as an agent of the

taxpayer – whether the relationship is that of a professional person and client – whether nominal ledger drawn up by the accountant is a document within the possession or power of the taxpayer – whether nominal ledger is part of accountant's working papers – whether accountant acting as auditor or agent.

Lynch v Burke & AIB Banks plc .... Vol V p 271

Succession – joint bank deposit account – whether survivor entitled – whether presumption of resulting trust – whether immediate gift to joint holder – whether true joint tenancy – whether provider retained a life interest – whether intention in favour of survivor – whether trust on death in favour of survivor – whether a testamentary disposition – whether in contravention of Wills Act 1837.

Purcell v The Attorney General of Ireland & The Minister for the Environment
.... Vol V p 288

Farm tax – Farm Tax Act 1985 repealed in March 1987 – whether legislation lawfully amended – whether application of Act resulted in prejudicial discrimination – whether Act validly imposed – whether tax imposed in disregard of the intention of the Oireachtas – whether classification of farms had first to be completed – whether Act intended to discriminate between farmers according to the acreage of their farms – whether provisions of Act open to more than one construction – whether constitutional construction to be upheld – whether Minister obliged to bring farm tax into operation in the year 1986 – whether statutory instrument made under powers conferred and for purposes authorised by the Oireachtas – whether statutory instrument ultra vires.

The Revenue Commissioners v Young .... Vol V p 294

Case Stated – Capital acquisitions tax – valuation of shares in a private non trading investment company – whether method of valuation of shares governed by CATA 1976 s 17 – whether s 17 subject to the market value rules comprised in s 15 – whether artificial method governed by commercial reality – whether voting rights held by Ordinary Shares could be used to redeem the Preference Shares – whether the application of s 17 mandatory.

O'Grady (Inspector of Taxes) v Roscommon Race Committee .... Vol V p 317

Case stated – whether a stand at Roscommon Racecourse was plant-trade of promoting and organising horse races at the racecourse for viewing by the public – raised stand gives better views and generates an atmosphere of excitement for patrons – provides shelter and a meeting place – work undertaken provides a new and enlarged stand giving shelter, additional viewing space and bars – test is whether the stand is part of the means whereby the trade is carried on or whether it is merely part of the place where the trade is carried on.

O'Rourke v The Revenue Commissioners.. Vol V p 321

Income tax – repayment of overpaid PAYE tax – whether taxpayer entitled to interest – whether FA 1976 s 30 applied – whether requirements for assessments and appeals satisfied – whether implied agreement – whether constructive trust – whether statutory possession required – whether common law right to interest – appropriate rate of interest – Woolwich doctrine of common law rights – whether repayment of tax as a matter of right

whether defendants unjustly enriched at expense of plaintiff – whether plaintiff acquiesced without protest in payment of tax – recovery of money paid in mistake of law – development of law of restitution – money paid without consideration – Murphy's case – whether fiscal problem for State – whether present case can be distinguished – small number of affected taxpayers and minimal fiscal consequences – whether taxpayer entitled as of right to interest – whether rate of interest under Courts Acts applicable.

In the Matter of G O'C & A O'C (Application of Liston (Inspector of Taxes)) .... Vol V p 346

Income tax – appeal to Supreme Court – application by inspector of taxes for High Court order – order to bank to furnish particulars of accounts of taxpayers and their children – whether discrepancy between returns of income and assets owned by taxpayers – whether discovery of illegal export of £500,000 by taxpayers a matter for further investigation – whether inspector had reasonable grounds for application – whether pre-condition of a request to deliver a return of income satisfied – whether findings of High Court erroneous in point of law – whether taxpayers deemed to have made returns of income – whether deeming provision confined to ITA 1967 s 172(4) – whether unjust, anomalous or absurd result would follow.

McMahon and Others v Rt Hon Lord Mayor Alderman & Burgess of Dublin .... Vol V p 357

Residential development – tax benefits for holiday cottages – planning permission for private residential purposes – whether holiday homes a change of use – whether use specified – purpose for which the homes designated – whether exempted development – complaints by permanent residents – appeal against the decision of An Bord Pleanala.

Kenny v The Revenue Commissioners, Goodman & Gemon Ltd (Notice Parties) .... Vol V p 363

Stamp duty – judicial review – instruments incorrectly stamped – whether instrument a promissory note – whether an assignment of a debt fully stamped – whether Revenue adjudication correct – whether taxpayer is entitled to challenge administrative decisions relating to another taxpayer's affairs – defendant is entitled to question the stamping of documents in the course of court proceedings – whether judicial review is an appropriate remedy – whether court has jurisdiction to make declaratory orders against notice parties – whether court has jurisdiction to issue declaratory orders relating to admissibility of documents in proceedings in which the admissibility has been raised.

In Re Estates of Cummins: O'Dwyer & Charleton v Keegan .... Vol V p 367

Capital Acquisitions Tax – Succession Act 1965 – legal right share – husband survived by wife twelve hours – no children – wife in a coma and unaware of husband's death – whether widow's estate acquired a half share in husband's estate – whether legal right share vests on death – whether legal right share has the same meaning as a share under a will or intestacy – whether intentions of deceased husband and surviving spouse frustrated – law should be certain

Saatchi & Saatchi Advertising Ltd v McGarry (Inspector of Taxes)................. Vol V p 376

Corporation tax – case stated – manufacturing relief for film production – proper construction of FA 1990 s 41 – relief deemed to apply prior to FA 1990 where relief was sought – whether application for relief a pre-requisite – whether scheme and purpose of a statutory enactment relevant – whether procedure irrelevant to taxing statutes – whether equitable principles operate – whether principles of construction of taxing statutes must be applied.

In the Matter of Williams (Tallaght) (In Receivership) and Companies Act 1963-1990 .... Vol V p 388

Revenue debts – company in receivership – property subject to floating charge – Revenue as preferential creditors for PAYE and PRSI – company in liquidation – whether Revenue a preferential creditor for corporation tax liability of company – whether double preference claims precluded – no statutory authority to deny double preference claims – whether Revenue debt statute barred – six months limitation period – whether notified – whether known to liquidator – whether actual knowledge required – whether extended to include constructive knowledge – whether statutory time limit can be extended by court.

Action Aid Ltd v The Revenue Commissioners .... Vol V p 392

Income tax – payments under deeds of covenant in favour of named children in Third World countries – whether entitled to exemption limits under FA 1980 s 1 – appellant a registered corporate charity in Ireland and a trustee for the named children – whether withdrawal of relief from 1984 onwards justified – whether payments applied for benefit of covenantees – whether payments made into fund for a group – whether payment must be made direct to covenantee – whether exemption restricted to persons aged over 65 years – whether exemption applies to non residents.

Taxback Limited v The Revenue Commissioners .... Vol V p 412

Value Added Tax – judicial review – goods transported to a destination outside EC member states exempt from VAT – whether foreign tourists to Ireland can claim VAT refunds on goods purchased in Ireland – whether refunds obtainable through refunding agencies – whether accounts of refunding agency in order – whether Revenue justified in withholding refunds

Burke & Sons Ltd v The Revenue Commissioners, Ireland and the Attorney General .... Vol V p 418

Value Added Tax – Judicial review – VAT scheme for retailers – interpretation of scheme – whether scheme based on sales or purchases – alcoholic liquors purchased out of bonded warehouse – whether payment of excise duty to be treated as zero rated – whether applicant's interpretation correct – whether scheme retrospectively altered – whether Revenue acted in breach of natural justice – whether Revenue bound by accepted applicant's interpretation over a period of years

Gilligan v Criminal Assets Bureau, Galvin, Lanigan and The Revenue Commissioners .... Vol V p 424

Income Tax – husband and wife – joint assessment – whether husband is liable for tax on wife's income – whether wife is separately liable on her income – whether both living

together for chargeable period – whether wife is obliged to make a return in respect of her own income – whether "Special Provisions" in relation to married couples prevail in all circumstances.

Ó Síocháin (Inspector of Taxes) v Neenan.. Vol V p 472

Case Stated – Income Tax – increase in Widows Social Welfare Contributory Pension granted in respect of dependent children – whether the income of the widow or the child – whether beneficiary distinguished from qualified child – whether additions to pension for benefit of children – whether a residence relationship applies – whether rate of pension or entitlement attracts chargeability to tax – whether trust in favour of children read into Act – whether purposeful construction to be applied – whether additional payment 'travels' with child – whether payments to qualified children exempt from income tax

Proes v The Revenue Commissioners.. Vol V p 481

Case Stated – Income Tax – domicile of appellant – Irish domicile of origin – English domicile of choice – holiday house in Ireland – death of appellant's husband – whether new domicile of choice acquired – whether existing domicile of choice abandoned – whether wrong test applied – when was domicile of choice abandoned – whether appellant's intention in regard to her permanent home retained.

Hibernian Insurance Company Limited v MacUimis (Inspector of Taxes) .... Vol V p 495

Corporation tax – case stated – investment company – whether expenses of management tax deductible – interpretation of expenses of management – whether management implies regular expenditure – whether expenses of acquisition are capital expenditure – whether expenses of management and expenses by management can be distinguished – whether expenses an integral part of costs of purchaser – whether phrase expenses of management has a technical or special meaning.

Kearns v Dilleen (Inspector of Taxes)... Vol V p 514

Capital Gains Tax – tax avoidance scheme – options to purchase shares in the same company granted by husband to wife and by wife to husband – 98% of the purchase price paid for the option and 2% payable on the exercise of the option – commercial reality of transactions – meaning of word abandonment – substance of transactions – principles of construction of taxing statutes – whether rights and obligations of parties to the transaction to be considered – whether an abandonment when consideration is received – whether receipt of capital sum a separate taxable disposal

The Attorney General v Power.. Vol V p 525

Estate duty – FA 1894 (57 & 58 Vict c 30), s 5(3) – interest in possession – whether conveyancing form determines liability.

Smyth v The Revenue Commissioners.. Vol V p 532

Estate duty – valuation of private company shares – restriction on transfer of shares – whether dividends paid represented profit earning capacity of the company – whether profit earning capacity is proper test of value of shares – whether remuneration of

directors exceeded commercial level – return on monies invested by purchasers – whether a sale of entire shareholding.

The Revenue Commissioners v Doorley .... Vol V p 539

Legacy duty – charitable bequest – whether to be expended in Ireland – construction of will – interpretation of taxing statute – exemption from legacy duty – whether charitable bequest had to be expended in Ireland.

Byrne v The Revenue Commissioners.. Vol V p 560

Revenue – stamp duty – deed of conveyance – exemption from stamp duty – deed executed by grantors and delivered as escrow – subsequent execution by grantees – inadvertent stamping – repayment of duty – date of execution of deed – whether claim for repayment within two years of date of execution – Poor Relief (Ireland) Act 1838 (1 & 2 Vict c 56) s 96 – Stamp Duties Management Act 1891 (54 & 55 Vict c 38) s 10 – Revenue Act 1898 (61 & 62 Vict c 46) s 13.

In re Swan (Deceased); Hibernian Bank Ltd v Frances Stewart Munro
.... Vol V p 565

Will – construction – annuity "free of income tax" – annuitant entitled to refunds in respect of tax borne by testator's estate – whether annuitant entitled to retain such refunds or bound to account for them to testator's estate – ITA 1918 (8 & 9 Geo, 5, c 40) ss 16 and 29, All Schedules Rules, r 19.

O'Sullivan v The Revenue Commissioners .... Vol V p 570

Stamp duty – case stated – whether a lease assessable as a conveyance or transfer on sale – money consideration in addition to rent – whether words and scheme of FA 1947 s 13 are appropriate to leases – whether doubt in a Stamp Act construed in favour of the taxpayer – whether a tax upon the citizen must be stated in clear language.

In re Estate of McNamee v The Revenue Commissioners .... Vol V p 577

Estate duty – valuation of private company shares – minority shareholding – principles of valuation – profit earning capacity – preservation of assets – dividend policy – past sales – actual sale – imaginary open market.

The Revenue Commissioners v Moroney.. Vol V p 589

Estate duty – whether receipt clause in a deed binding – whether stated consideration recoverable – whether extrinsic evidence admissible to contradict statement of consideration – whether doctrine of promissory estoppel applies – whether a question of mistake or rectification.

In Re the Estate of Urquhart (Deceased) and The Revenue Commissioners v AIB Ltd
.... Vol V p 600

Revenue – Estate duty – legal right – whether surviving spouse competent to dispose of statutory share in estate – election – FA 1894 (57 & 58 Vict c 30) ss 2, 22 – Succession Act 1965 (No 27) ss 111, 115.

Murphy v The Attorney General .... Vol V p 613

Income tax – incomes of husband and wife aggregated – tax payable by a married couple in excess of the amounts payable by a husband and wife if taxed as separate persons – whether in breach of constitutional rights – ITA 1967 ss 138, 192-198 – income tax – recovery of tax overpaid – tax improved by statute deceased to be invalid – whether money paid under mistake of law can be recovered.

Stephen Court Ltd v Browne (Inspector of Taxes)
[3 ITR 95] .... Vol V p 680

Corporation tax – auctioneer's commission and solicitor's costs – whether expenses of a revenue or capital nature – ITA 1967 ss 81(5)(d), 81(6)(a)(i) – FA 1969 s 22 – CTA 1976 s 15

AE v The Revenue Commissioners .... Vol V p 686

Revenue – capital acquisitions tax – gift of farm to niece – whether niece worked substantially full-time on the farm – whether herding of cattle under a letting agreement constituted a business – meaning of business – CATA 1976 (No 8) 2nd Schedule, Pt 1, para 9.

Director of Public Prosecutions v Cunningham .... Vol V p 691

Betting duty – whether Inland Revenue Regulation Act 1890 complied with – whether court proceedings preceded by order of the Revenue Commissioners – whether onus on prosecution to prove existence of order of the Commissioners.

McDaid v Sheehy .... Vol V p 696

Excise duties – judicial review – whether applicant entitled to an order of certiorari – whether order validated by confirmation and re-enactment in subsequent legislation – whether court should rule on constitutional validity of legislation when pronouncement of no benefit to applicant.

Parkes (Roberta) v David Parkes .... 1998 p 169

Stamp Duty – Husband purchasing property in wife's name – Presumption of advancement rebutted – whether resulting trust – Husband procuring wife to make false declaration in conveyance – Husband subsequently seeking court's aid to enforce trust – Whether husband entitled to relief in equity

In the matter of The Sunday Tribune Limited (in Liquidation)
.... 1998 p 177

Company – Winding up – Creditors – Preferential payments – Test applicable – Unpaid wages of employees or contractual payments Whether employee engaged under a contract of service or a contract for services journalists – Claimants entitled to be paid as creditors preferential – Companies Act 1963 s 285.

B McCabe (Inspector of Taxes) v South City & County Investment Co Ltd [Vol V p 107] .... 1998 p 183

Corporation Tax – whether periodic payments subject to Corporation Tax – annuity contract – annual payments of £500 plus share of profits in return for capital sum – whether correctly described as annuities – whether income receipts – whether return of capital – whether case law overturns logic of transactions – interpretation of tax statutes and documents – whether content of agreement conforms with its purpose

Re Coombe Importers Ltd (In Liq) and Re the Companies Acts 1963–1990 .... Vol VI p 1

PAYE/PRSI – payments to employees without deduction of PAYE/PRSI – Company in examinership – estimated assessments by Inspector of Taxes – Company in liquidation – Revenue debt – whether super-preferential status – interpretation of Social Welfare Consolidation Act 1981, s 120(2) – whether Court obliged to look at things done or failing to be done Social Welfare (Consolidation) Act 1993, s 301.

The Revenue Commissioners v Sisters of Charity of the Incarnate Word .... Vol VI p 7

Income Tax – Case stated – foreign charity with a branch in Ireland – whether Irish branch entitled to exemption from income tax on its profits – whether "established" in Ireland – interpretation of ss 333/334 Income Tax Act 1967 – whether geographical limitation contained in the statute – charitable activities in Ireland – whether facts distinguished from Camille case in UK – meaning of word established – whether a sufficient Irish establishment to justify exemption.

Byrne (John Oliver) v Noel Conroy .... Vol VI p 19

Extradition Order – appeal on grounds of a revenue offence – Monetary Compensation Amounts – agricultural levies under EEC regulations – fraudulent charges – whether agricultural levies constitute a tax – question to be determined by Irish law – whether a tax in normal concept of taxes – whether part of revenue of any particular country.

Saatchi & Saatchi Advertising Ltd v Kevin McGarry (Inspector of Taxes) .... Vol VI p 47

Corporation Tax – case stated – manufacturing relief for film production – whether relief applies to short advertising films produced for use on television – retrospective application of s 41 Finance Act 1990 – whether claim for relief prior to assessment a pre-requisite – whether strict interpretation of a taxing statute prevails – whether scheme and purpose of a statute relevant.

Sean Ó Síocháin (Inspector of Taxes) v Bridget Neenan .... Vol VI p 59

Income Tax – Case stated – social welfare benefits – increases in widow's contributory pension by reason of dependent children – whether liable to income tax – whether increases the property of the children or the widow – whether widow liable for income tax on the benefits for dependent children – proper interpretation Chapter II of Social Welfare (Consolidation) Act 1981.

Haughey v Attorney General .... Vol VI p 67

Tribunal of Inquiry – jurisdiction of Oireachtas and Taoiseach – whether Tribunal of Inquiry Evidence Act 1921 applies – whether Tribunal constitutionally valid – whether powers of Tribunal unlimited – grounds of appeal – whether personal rights infringed – right to equality of treatment, privacy and fair procedures – whether powers of Tribunal exceeded

Criminal Assets Bureau v Gerard Hutch .... Vol VI p 125

Income tax – appeal against judgment – assessment made in absence of income tax returns – tax appeal procedures – late appeal – assessment becoming final and conclusive – Collector General's certificate as proof of amount due

Patrick J O'Connell (Inspector of Taxes) v Fyffes Banana Processing Ltd
.... Vol VI p 131

Corporation tax – case stated – company providing banana ripening services – process of maturation of foodstuffs – whether goods manufactured within the State – strict interpretation of taxing statutes – whether any doubt or ambiguity in the statutory provisions – services rendered deemed to be the manufacture of goods – goods manufactured within the State to be distinguished from services rendered in a process of manufacture of goods

Simple Imports Ltd and Another v Revenue Commissioners.......................... Vol VI p 141

Customs law – books or documents, transactions contravening customs laws – whether search warrants invalid – whether reasonable cause – whether exercise properly conveyed on face of warrant – whether exercise of warrant challenged – whether entry refused – whether within jurisdiction of district judge.

Hibernian Insurance Company Ltd v MacUimis (Inspector of Taxes) .... Vol VI p 157

Corporation Tax – case stated – investment company – expenses of management deductible – interpretation of expenses of management for corporation tax purposes – expenses incurred in respect of investment appraisals and advices with a view to acquisitions of investments – whether expenses incurred prior to the date on which a decision was made to acquire the particular investment – whether character of expenditure alters depending upon whether the investment was purchased or not – whether expenses were of a revenue or capital nature – Corporation Tax Act 1976, s 15

In the Matter of Millhouse Taverns Ltd and the Companies Act
1963–1999 .... Vol VI p 191

VAT, PAYE and PRSI – unpaid taxes, interest and penalties – petition to wind up company – whether a substantial and reasonable defence to petition – whether company insolvent

Beverly Cooper-Flynn v RTÉ, Charlie Bird and James Howard .... Vol VI p 195

Tax evasion – whether James Howard sought to evade his obligation to pay tax by not availing of the tax amnesty – whether he failed to return for tax his investment in the CMI Personal Portfolio – whether Beverly Cooper-Flynn ("the plaintiff") had induced him and others to invest in the CMI Personal Portfolio for the purpose of evading tax – issue of costs – whether plaintiff's reputation had suffered – whether costs should follow the

decision – whether special causes apply – whether plaintiff obtained something of value – whether inconsistencies in evidence of defendants amounted to a special cause.

Patrick J O'Connell (Inspector of Taxes) v Thomas Keleghan .... Vol VI p 201

Case stated – Income Tax (IT) – service contract of sale of shares – binding contract to serve as sale director of Siúcra Éireann ("the purchaser") – inducement payment of £250,000 – whether taxpayer ever became an employee – whether purchaser had an interest direct or indirect in the performance of the contract of employment – whether inference of acceptance of agreement – whether payment taxable under ITA 1967 s 110.

Capital Gains Tax (CGT) – sale of shares in Gladebrook Ltd by shareholders in 1990 for a consideration in the form of loan notes – loan notes not transferable or assignable – whether CGT chargeable on redemption of loan notes for cash in 1993 – whether loan notes constitute debenture stock – "paper for paper" transaction and exempt under CGTA 1975 Sch 2 para 4 – whether statutory fiction treats loan notes as shares – whether legislation so provides – whether exemption on disposal of a debt applies – whether loan notes a debt on a security – whether marketable and capable of increasing in value.

Sean MacAonghusa (Inspector of Taxes) v Ringmahon Company .... Vol VI p 327

Corporation Tax – case stated – redeemable preference shares issued to satisfy borrowings- Ringmahon Company redeemed £6 million redeemable preference shares and raised a bank load for this purpose – whether the annual interest on the loan is a deductible expense – whether the loan was related to the capital restructuring of the company – whether the interest on such a loan was stamped with the character of capital expenditure and therefore was deductible – whether non deductibility an anomaly in tax code – whether interest on borrowings used for purposes of trade allowable.

Francis Griffin v Minister for Social, Community and Family Affairs, William Deasy v The Minister for Social, Community and Family Affairs .... Vol VI p 371

PRSI – share fisherman – whether employed on a contract of service or engaged in a joint venture with boat owner – whether liable to PRSI as a self employed person – whether agreement whereby net proceeds of catch divisible between boat owner and crew constitutes a partnership – optimal social welfare scheme for self employed share fishermen – whether losses carried forward – whether leading Irish judgment disregarded – whether relationship between parties is one of employment or one of partnership – whether each voyage a separate venture – whether Minister has unlimited power to make regulations – whether High Court decisions are binding on Appeals Officer – whether tests of control, enterprise integration remuneration or economic reality apply – whether conclusions based on evidence – whether capital investment essential for a partnership – whether equality among partners required – whether same mistake of law made in decisions by both Appeals Officers.

Michael F Murphy v GM, DB, PC Ltd and GH John Gilligan v Criminal Assets Bureau, Revenue Commissioners & Others .... Vol VI p 383

Proceeds of Crime Act 1996 – provisions relating to proceeds derived from criminal activities – non-constitutional and constitutional issues- whether defendants can be prohibited from disposing of a sum of £300,000 – whether defendants obliged to give details of all property and income therefrom in their possession or control over past 10

years – whether High Court has jurisdiction to impose orders of restraint and appropriation over property situate within and outside the State – whether plenary summons procedure seeking interim and interlocutory relief appropriate – whether provisions of Act retrospective – whether hearsay evidence sufficient to satisfy onus of proof on the balance of probabilities – whether provisions of Act formed part of the criminal law and not of the civil law – whether persons affected deprived of safeguards under criminal code – whether presumption of innocence ignored – whether standard of proof based on reasonable doubt rather than balance of probabilities – whether provision for trial by jury required – whether purposes and mens rea punitive and deterrent – whether forfeiture of property and mens rea indicative of crime – whether Revenue case precedents apply – whether delays under Act oppressive – whether provisions unfair and retrospective – whether in breach of European Convention on Human Rights.

Criminal Assets Bureau v P McS .... Vol VI p 421

Income tax – Notice of Appeal – interpretation of TCA 1997 s 933 and s 957(2) – computation of appeal periods – right to a late appeal – reasonable cause saver – anonymity of CAB officers – whether certificates have presumption of regularity – fair procedures – locus standi – hearsay evidence.

Criminal Assets Bureau v H(S) and H(R) .... Vol VI p 441

Garnishee order – High Court practice and procedure – whether CAB empowered to execute a judgment – interpretation of TCA 1997 s 58 – taxation of costs on solicitor and client basis – corporation incorporated by an Act of the Oireachtas.

Criminal Assets Bureau v D(K) .... Vol VI p 445

Income tax – Notice of appeal – interpretation of TCA 1997 s 933(7) – whether taxpayer had invoked his right to appeal – right to a late appeal – reasonable cause saver – assessment becoming final and conclusive.

Patrick J O'Connell (Inspector of Taxes) v John Fleming .... Vol VI p 453

Capital Gains Tax – case stated – non-competition agreement – whether consideration for disposal of shares – approach to a case stated – bargain at arm's length – interpretation of documents – subsequent stamping of documents.

Criminal Assets Bureau v PS and PS .... Vol VI p 465

Income tax – mareva injunction at interim stage – delay in interlocutory hearing – whether interim order against notice party should be discharged.

Oliver Masterson v Director of Public Prosecutions .... Vol VI p 471

Excise duty – case stated – whether the importation of kerosene oil with coumarin contravened Article 28 of Council Directive 92/12/EEC – quantative restrictions on imports between Member States – whether the Hydrocarbon (Heavy) Oil Regulations 1991 were a measure restricting trade.

Cyril Forbes v John Tobin and Jeanette Tobin .... Vol VI p 483

Value Added Tax – specific performance – contract for sale of garage premises – VAT Act 1972 – whether building was developed – whether VAT was exigible – failure to furnish details of development – contractual obligation to supply details of development.

Patrick J O'Connell (Inspector of Taxes) v Thomas Keleghan .... Vol VI p 497

Income tax – whether correct year of assessment – inducement payment to enter into service contract – consideration by way of loan note – loan notes not transferable or assignable.

Criminal Assets Bureau v John Kelly .... Vol VI p 501

Income tax – appeal against judgment – tax appeal procedure – whether assessments pursuant to TCA 1997, s 922 – access to monies held under "freezing order" – whether appellant deprived of access to appeal – locus standi.

Bank of Ireland Trust Services Ltd v The Revenue Commissioners .... Vol VI p 513

Value added tax – whether repayments of VAT should carry interest – whether the provisions of the Income Tax Acts regarding payment of tax are implied into the VAT Acts – law of restitution – unjust enrichment.

Patrick O'Connell (Inspector of Taxes) v Tara Mines Ltd .... Vol VI p 523

Corporation tax – mining company – whether carrying on mining operations – whether mining operations is confined to underground activities – whether categorisation as manufacturing precludes the activity from being a mining operation – factors to be considered in determining whether activity is a mining operation.

Criminal Assets Bureau v Sean and Rosaleen Hunt (nee Maher) Also known as Jean Hunt and Jean Maher .... Vol VI p 559

Income tax – Value added tax – Mareva injunction – appropriate summons under TCA 1997 s 966 – assessments not "final and conclusive" – prerequisite of a prior demand – ultra vires – suspected criminal activity – whether assessments were arbitrary and unreasonable – hearsay evidence – admissibility of documents – fraudulent preference – beneficial ownership of funds.

P O'Muircheasa (Inspector of Taxes) v Bailey Wastepaper Ltd .... Vol VI p 579

Corporation tax – case stated – manufacturing relief – recycling wastepaper – was there a significant change in raw materials – whether raw materials were acquired in bulk – whether decision of Appeal Commissioners was unreasonable.

Bank of Ireland Trust Services Ltd (formerly Erin Executor and Trustee Company Limited) (as Trustee of the Irish Pension Fund Property Unit Trust) v The Revenue Commissioners .... Vol VI p 587

Value Added Tax – which rate of interest applies to repayments – what period does the repayment apply to – judicial discretion pursuant to TCA 1997 s 941(9) – performance rate of interest – interest under Courts Act 1981.

DA MacCarthaigh, Inspector of Taxes v Cablelink Ltd, Cablelink Waterford Ltd & Galway Cable Vision Ltd .... Vol VI p 595

Value Added Tax – case stated – refusal of repayment – whether findings by an Appeal Commissioner were law or fact – whether package of services was a single supply or two separate services – whether connection at premises was integral to the provision of telecommunication signals – immovable goods.

Ó Culacháin (Inspector of Taxes) v Stylo Barratt Shoes Ltd .... Vol VI p 617

Value Added Tax – findings of fact of an Appeal Commissioner – whether sale agreement was chargeable to VAT – transfer of a business exception – test to be applied – whether exception applied to transfer of assets only.

Terence Keogh v Criminal Assets Bureau, Revenue Commissioners and the Collector General .... Vol VI p 635

Income Tax – Statutory Appeal Procedure – Taxpayers' Charter of Rights – duty to provide appeal information to taxpayer – legitimate expectation – when assessments became final and conclusive – interpretation of TCA 1997 ss 933 and 957.

The Attorney General v Charles Ashleigh Nicholson and Ruth Ellen Ashleigh Nicholson .... Vol VI p 667

Extradition – order of rendition – corresponding offence – revenue offence – additional sentences of imprisonment.

Castleisland Cattle Breeding Society Ltd v Minister for Social and Family Affairs .... Vol VI p 673

Income tax – social welfare appeal – PRSI – master and servant – whether a cattle inseminator performed services under a contract of service or a contract for service – whether appeals officer was entitled to conclude that a contract of service existed.

Donal Crowley (Inspector of Taxes) v Nuala Forde .... Vol VI p 685

Income tax – case stated – chargeable person – gains realised on share options – self-assessment – surcharge – emoluments – interpretation of TCA 1997 Part 42, Chapter 4.

Sean Neeson (Inspector of Taxes) v Longford Timber Contractors Ltd .... Vol VI p 691

Corporation tax – manufacturing relief – whether timber harvesting constituted the manufacture of goods pursuant to TCA 1997, s 443 – case stated.

Kevin McGarry (Inspector of Taxes) v Harding (Lord Edward Street) Properties Ltd .... Vol VI p 699

Corporation tax – industrial buildings allowance – case stated – construction of a taxation statute – whether hostel qualified as "trade of hotel-keeping" within TCA 1997, s 268.

The Attorney General v Anthony Karl Frank Baird Hilton .... Vol VI p 711

Extradition – rendition – appeal – test for corresponding offence – revenue offence exception – whether offence of cheating the public revenue exists in Ireland.

The Criminal Assets Bureau v PS .... Vol VI p 719

Income tax – statutory appeal procedure – whether assessments were unreasonable, irrational and ultra vires – when assessments become final and conclusive – CAB estopped from admitting notice of appeal – expiry of appeal period – anonymity of witnesses – constitutionality of certificates – whether onerous appeal conditions infringe fair procedures and separation of powers.

The Revenue Commissioners v Bus Éireann .... Vol VI p 743

Excise duty – appeal – availability of excise duty rebate on fuel purchased in the State but combusted outside the State – statutory interpretation – extra-territorial application of laws.

Séamus Lynch (The Inspector of Taxes) v Neville Brothers Ltd .... Vol VI p 757

Income tax – case stated – master and servant – whether a merchandiser was performing services under a contract of service or a contract for service.

BD v JD .... Vol VI p 763

Family law – appeal – division of assets on judicial separation – whether the court should consider the tax implications post litigation – mechanisms for extraction of funds from company – tax as a realisation cost – valuation of company – costs.

Philip Kirwan v Technical Engineering and Electrical Union .... Vol VI p 771

Income tax – PRSI – master and servant – whether a trade union official had a contractual relationship with a trade union – whether a trade union official was performing services under a contract of service or a contract for service.

CG v The Appeal Commissioners and Others .... Vol VI p 783

Income tax – judicial review – appeal – power and function of Appeal Commissioners – whether appeal should be adjourned pending outcome of criminal proceedings – risk of prejudice or injustice – Constitution – right to a fair trial – right to silence and privilege against self incrimination.

PO Cahill (Inspector of Taxes) v Patrick O'Driscoll, Michael O'Driscoll and William F O'Driscoll .... Vol VI p 793

Income tax – case stated – Appeal Commissioner – rate of income tax applicable to interest earned on clients' funds – monies held in trust – fiduciary duty – duty to account.

AS v Criminal Assets Bureau .... Vol VI p 799

Income tax – judicial review – ultra vires – execution against assets where assessment based on criminal activity – proceeds of crime – chargeable person – whether assessments were arbitrary and unreasonable – statutory appeal procedure – time limits – notice of attachment.

PV Murtagh (Inspector of Taxes) v Samuel Rusk .... Vol VI p 817

Income tax – case stated – situs of speciality debt – loan stock certificates issued under seal – interest paid on foreign securities – whether income arising from loan notes is

chargeable to Irish tax – Ireland United Kingdom Double Taxation Agreement – remittance basis.

Brendan Crawford (Inspector of Taxes) v Centime Ltd .... Vol VI p 823

Value Added Tax – case stated – taxable person pursuant to Value Added Tax Act 1972 – investment incurred for the purpose of intended economic activity – conditions required by guidelines for the treatment of property developer as a taxable person – deductibility of input tax on investment expenditure.

Robert Harris v JJ Quigley and Liam Irwin .... Vol VI p 839

Income tax – repayment of overpaid tax – statutory interpretation – whether taxpayer entitled to repayment pending outcome of case stated – restitution – unjust enrichment.

Campus Stadium Ireland Development Ltd v Dublin Waterworld Ltd .... 2006 p 55

Value Added Tax – whether arbitrator's award should be set aside on basis of misconduct – valuation of interest in immovable property – VAT on capitalised value of lease – economic value test

Electricity Supply Board v The Minister for Social Community and Family Affairs & Others .... 2006 p 63

Social welfare appeal – remit of court in an appeal on a point of law – whether a contract meter reader performed services under a contract of service or a contract for services – whether appeals officer was entitled to conclude that a contract of service existed – provision of substitute – control test

The Revenue Commissioners v O'Flynn Construction Co Ltd, John and Michael O'Flynn .... 2006 p 81

Case stated – income tax – advance corporation tax – Schedule F – general anti-avoidance provision – statutory interpretation – export sales relief – whether impugned transaction was a tax avoidance transaction pursuant to TCA 1997, s 811 – primary objective – business profits exclusion – misuse or abuse of relief exclusion

Campus Stadium Ireland Development Ltd v Dublin Waterworld Ltd

High Court
Gilligan J
26 September 2005

Value Added Tax – whether arbitrator's award should be set aside on basis of misconduct – valuation of interest in immovable property – VAT on capitalised value of lease – economic value test

This case concerned the enforcement of an arbitration award and whether the arbitrator had misconducted himself in respect of the method of valuation of the interest being disposed of.

Section 4(3A) of the Vat Act 1972 defines the economic value of an interest in property as the expenditure incurred in the acquisition and development of the property. For a lease to be subject to VAT, the capitalised value of the lease has to equal or exceed the economic value.

Campus and Stadium Ireland Development Limited ('the plaintiff') entered into a lease with Dublin Waterworld Limited ('the defendant') of the National Acquatic Centre ('the property'). It was accepted by both parties that the lease would be subject to VAT on its capitalised value subject to the economic value test. The plaintiff obtained a valuation report for VAT purposes from the Valuation Office. This report provided a capitalised value of the lease below the economic value. The plaintiff preferred to use one of the prescribed formulae under the VAT Acts. This formula provided a capitalised value in excess of the economic value. On the basis of the alternative formula, the plaintiff charged VAT on the lease of the property. The defendant contended that this VAT was not properly charged. The issue of whether the plaintiff was obliged to rely on the report from the Valuation Office and was prevented from relying on the alternative formula was referred to arbitration. The arbitrator confirmed that VAT was correctly charged.

The defendant argued that the arbitrator departed from the usual practice and procedure in relation to VAT principles when he disregarded the Valuation Office report. The arbitrator had concluded that as the property was unique in the State the Valuation Office report was merely an estimate. The defendant contended that this was unfair and unjust as it did not have the opportunity to address this issue at the arbitration. The defendant also contended that there was an error of law on the face of the award when the arbitrator stated that the VAT system could not function effectively if a supplier's VAT charge was subject to review by his customer.

Held by Gilligan J in refusing to set aside the arbitrator's award:

i. To interfere with an arbitrator's award a court would have to be satisfied that the award showed on its face an error of law so fundamental that the court could not allow it to remain unchallenged or the arbitrator misconducted himself so that the arbitration was tainted by a substantial injustice or unfairness.
Keenan v The Shield Insurance Company [1988] IR 89 followed.

ii. There was evidence available for the arbitrator to come to the conclusion that the Valuation Office report merely provided an estimate of the open market value of the property. It was not necessary for the arbitrator to signal this conclusion in advance of the award as the issue had been raised during the course of the arbitration.

iii. The arbitrator made an incorrect statement of law when he indicated that the VAT system could not function effectively if a supplier's VAT charge was subject to review by his customer. However, this did not constitute a fundamental error on the face of the award nor did it have any significant impact on the arbitrator's decision.
Forbes v Tobin VI ITR 483 confirmed.

Legislation

Arbitration Act 1954, ss 38, 41
Rules of the Superior Courts 1986, Ord 56, r 4F
Value Added Tax Act 1972, s 4(3A)
Value Added Tax Regulations 1979, reg 19

Cases referred to in the judgment

Doyle v Kildare County Council [1995] 2 IR 424
Re Enoch and Zaretzky, Bock & Co's Arbitration [1910] 1 KB 327
Forbes v Tobin VI ITR 483
Keenan v Shield Insurance Company Ltd [1988] IR 89
London Export Corporation Ltd v Jubilee Coffee Roasting Co Ltd [1958] 1 Lloyd's Rep 367
McCarthy v Keane & Others (16 December 2004, unreported) SC
McStay v Assicurazioni Generali SpA [1991] ILRM 237
Port Sudan Cotton Co v Govindaswamy Chettiar & Sons [1971] 1 Lloyd's Rep 166
Power Securities Limited v Daly (27 February 1984, unreported) HC (Murphy J)
Pratt v Swanmore Builders Ltd and Baker [1980] 2 Lloyd's Rep 504
Williams v Wallis and Cox [1914] 2 KB 478

High Court – 26 September 2005

Gilligan J, On the 3 June, 2005, in proceedings entitled Campus and Stadium Ireland Development Limited and Dublin Waterworld Limited, Record No 2005 No 1466P, an order was made by Kelly J in the Commercial Court directing that the issue between the parties in relation to a claim for €10,254,600 relating to a VAT payment on a lease as entered into between the parties on the 30th day of April, 2003, be referred to arbitration.

The agreed arbitrator Mr Dermot O'Brien, a recognised VAT expert, gave his award on 1st July, 2005, finding that the amount of VAT of €10,254,600 charged by Campus and Stadium Ireland Development Limited (CSID) on the capitalised value of the lease of 30th April, 2003, to Dublin Waterworld Limited (DWL) was correctly charged. By letter dated 7 July, 2005, solicitors for CSID wrote to DWL seeking payment of the aforesaid sum and no payment has been forthcoming. These proceedings were issued on 14 July, 2005, between the parties seeking an order granting the plaintiff leave pursuant to s 41 of the Arbitration Act, 1954 and Order 56, rule 4F of the Rules of the Superior Courts, 1986, as amended to enforce the arbitration award of 1 July, 2005, in the sum of €10,254,600 as made by the arbitrator Dermot O'Brien in favour of the plaintiff as against the defendant and further the plaintiff claims interest pursuant to the Courts Act, 1981 and such further or other order as to this Honourable Court shall deem fit in addition to the costs of the proceedings.

The defendants, DWL, seek to set aside the order of the arbitrator pursuant to s 38 of the Arbitration Act, 1954, as amended on the basis that the arbitrator misconducted himself.

McCarthy J in *Keenan v Shield Insurance Company Ltd* [1988] IR 89 succinctly summed up the appropriate approach of the courts to arbitration awards wherein, at p 96, he states:

> 'Arbitration is a significant feature of modern commercial life; there is an International Institution of Arbitration and the field of international arbitration is an ever expanding one. It ill becomes the courts to show any readiness to interfere in such a process; if policy considerations are appropriate as I believe they are in a matter of this kind then every such consideration points to the desirability of making an arbitration award final in every sense of the term. *Church and General Insurance Company v Connolly and McLoughlin* (Unreported, High Court, Costello J, 7th May, 1981) itself is an example of the type of fine-combing exercise which courts should not perform when it is sought to review an arbitration award. There may be incidents in which an award which shows on its face an error of law so fundamental that the courts cannot stand aside and allow it to remain unchallenged.'

This approach was reiterated again by the Supreme Court in *McStay v Assicurazioni Generali SpA* [1991] ILRM 237 where Finlay CJ stated, at p 242 that:

> 'A fundamental ingredient of the concept of arbitration, as contained in the common law, is the finality of the decision of the arbitrator, subject, of course, to certain qualifications and precautions. Broadly speaking, however, as one might expect, the law appears to acknowledge that where two parties agree to refer a particular question which is in dispute between them to the decision of a particular individual by way of arbitration, they are taken to have abandoned their right to litigate that precise question.'

In *Doyle v Kildare County Council* [1995] 2 IR 424 the Supreme Court followed the previous decisions in *Keenan* and *McStay.* Furthermore, Hamilton CJ at p 444 approved Murphy J's statement in *Power Securities Limited v Daly* (27 February, 1984, unreported) HC (Murphy J) to the effect that:

> 'The Courts should be slow to usurp the functions of the chosen tribunal by intervening whether by way of setting aside an award, remitting an award or directing a case to be stated.'

I take the view that it follows from the decision of the Supreme Court in *Doyle v Kildare County Council* [1995] 2 IR 424 that this court has no statutory jurisdiction to set aside an award of an arbitrator in the absence of a finding that the arbitrator has misconducted himself or the proceedings pursuant to s 38(1) of the Arbitration Act 1954 as amended.

Atkin J in *Williams v Wallis and Cox* [1914] 2 KB 478, at p 485, refers to the meaning of the expression misconduct of an arbitrator where he stated:

> 'That expression does not necessarily involve personal turpitude on the part of the arbitrator, and any such suggestion has been expressly disclaimed in this case. The term does not really amount to much more than such a mishandling of the arbitration as is likely to amount to some substantial miscarriage of justice, and one instance that may be given is where the arbitrator refuses to hear evidence upon a material issue'.

In *London Export Corporation Ltd v Jubilee Coffee Roasting Co Ltd* [1958] 1 Lloyd's Rep 367, [1958] 1 WLR 661 at pp 369 and 665, Jenkins LJ (as he then was) referred to 'misconduct' as 'used in the technical sense in which it is familiar in the law relating to arbitrations as denoting irregularity, and not any moral turpitude or anything of that sort.' Of course, it would be stretching the meaning of the term misconduct to say that it included mistakes. As Donaldson J (as he then was) pointed out in *Port Sudan Cotton Co. v Govindaswamy Chettiar & Sons* [1977] 1 Lloyd's Rep 166 at p 178:

> '... there is a distinction between error and misconduct. To err in fact or law is not only human but an occupational hazard. Unless it is so often repeated as to give rise to some suggestion of incompetence it happily involves absolutely no reflection upon the person concerned, whether Judge, umpire or arbitrator.'

In the case of *Pratt v Swanmore Builders Ltd and Baker* [1980] 2 Lloyd's Rep 504, in deciding whether or not the arbitrator had misconducted himself, Pain J applied the test set out by Cozens-Hardy, MR, in *Re Enoch and Zaretzky, Bock & Co's Arbitration* [1910] 1 KB 327. In that case the learned judge had said at p 331:

> '... I wish to make it clear that I am not suggesting fraud on the part of Mr Von Lymburg, [who is the umpire] but I do say his conduct as umpire, as manifested by the particulars which I have given, is such that it would not be satisfactory, it would not be fair, it would not be just, to leave the rights of the parties, as they necessarily would be, in his sole hands.'

Fennelly J in *McCarthy v Keane and Others* (16th December, 2004, unreported) SC deals very fully with the meaning of misconduct in the context of the actions of an arbitrator in and about the conduct of the arbitration when he states at p 12 of the judgment:

> 'Real cases of misconduct may arise in the conduct of the arbitration, where the arbitrator acts unfairly either by clear acts of favouritism towards a party or adopts procedures which place one or other party (perhaps even both) at a clear disadvantage.
>
> It seems to me that the standard or test of misconduct of such a nature would be something substantial, something that smacks of injustice or unfairness. One of the cited examples is of an arbitrator inspecting the farm he was to value in the presence of one party and in the absence of the other or of any representative of the other ... there is a sharp distinction between acts committed in the course of the arbitration and its result. Mere error is not misconduct. Parties submit disputes, including disputes as to the law to arbitration. They expect the arbitrator to rule on all matters in dispute, but they do not have any guarantee that the arbitrator will reach the correct result. An arbitrator may err in his interpretation of the law or of the facts, without being guilty of misconduct'.

The arbitration in question was conducted by way of a review of documents furnished by representatives of both parties and by an oral hearing held at the office of the arbitrator on 28 June, 2005. It was accepted by both parties that the lease of the 30 April, 2003, by CSID to DWL is a lease which would be subject to VAT at 13.5% on its capitalised value subject to the provisions of s 4(3A) of the Value Added Tax Act, 1972, as amended. These provisions are commonly referred to as the economic value test.

The economic value of the lease is the amount of money excluding VAT incurred by the landlord in acquiring and developing the property and in this case it was accepted by both sides that the economic value was a figure of approximately €62 million. In order for the lease of the National Aquatic Centre to be subject to VAT the capitalised value of the lease determined in accordance with the provisions of the Value Added Tax Act, 1972 would have to equal or exceed the economic value.

CSID obtained a valuation report for VAT purposes from Mr Cahill of the Valuation Office which came to the conclusion that the value of the unencumbered rent per annum was €3.376 million and that the open market price of the interest being disposed of by CSID was €35 million.

CSID did not rely on Mr Cahill's valuation for VAT purposes in relation to the open market price but instead preferred to use one of the prescribed formulae in Regulation 19 to multiply the unencumbered rent figure of €3.376 by 75% by 30 years thereby giving a capitalised value of the lease of €75,960,000, a value in excess of the economic value of

the lease, it being clear that if CSID had relied on Mr Cahill's valuation of €35 million then the capitalised value of the lease would not have equalled or exceeded the economic value and VAT would not be payable on the lease nor would CSID be entitled to recover the VAT expenditure it occurred on the cost of developing the property.

On the basis of the calculation used by CSID an invoice was issued to DWL on 15th May, 2003, charging VAT of €10,254,600 on the lease.

In contending that this VAT was not properly chargeable, DWL accepted neither Mr Cahill's valuation of €3.376 million in respect of the unencumbered rent nor his open market price in the sum of €35 million and they in turn engaged the services of the firm of valuers Hamilton Osborne King who in a report gave a substantially lower rental figure and consequently a figure which if accepted and used on the same basis of calculation as that proposed by CSID would not yield a figure which would meet or exceed the economic value of €62 million.

An issue then centered on an interpretation of the relevant VAT regulation and as to whether or not CSID were obliged to rely on the valuation as obtained from Mr Cahill and were prevented from relying on the alternative formula which were available to calculate the open market value, because of the valuation obtained from Mr Cahill.

The arbitrator in his award proceeded as follows.

> 'The issues to be resolved are as follows:
>
> 1. If the valuer has given his opinion as the market value of the interest being disposed of, is CSID then entitled to rely on one of the other formula based methods of capitalising the lease set out in Regulation 19?
> 2. Is CSID entitled to rely on the opinion of its appointed valuer or does it need to question his method of valuation?'

Mr Sanfey on the defendants' behalf submits that for the arbitrator to disregard the opinion of Mr Cahill is a radical departure of a unique nature from the standard practice and that his clients did not have an opportunity to address this issue at the arbitration. He accepts that Mr O'Brien is an expert arbitrator who knows the VAT code inside out but says there is a basic unfairness in the arbitrator coming to a conclusion that the expert opinion of Mr Cahill, in respect of the €35 million valuation as the open market price of the property the subject matter of the lease, is an estimate and does not provide evidence because the nature of the property is unique with no close comparison in the state. Mr Sanfey argues that the point was not flagged and in effect the arbitrator found a way not to answer the very question he had posed for himself to the effect that if the valuer has given his opinion as to market value of the interest being disposed of was CSID then entitled to rely on one of the other formula based methods of capitalising the value of the lease as set out in Regulation 19. He submits that the attitude adopted by the arbitrator was virtually unprecedented, unfair, and took his clients utterly by surprise.

Mr Sanfey refers to paragraph 22 of the affidavit of Mr Broderick wherein he deposed;

> 'I say and believe also that the arbitrator, given his particular expertise in VAT matters, would be aware that it has been established and accepted in principle and practice since the introduction of VAT in 1972 that a valuation by a competent valuer is regarded as evidence of OMP for VAT purposes. In this regard I beg to refer to the guide to the Value Added Tax produced in July 1972 by the Revenue Commissioners ... that if the arbitrator was of this view it should have been communicated to the parties. Not to do so was unjust and unfair to the defendant.'

Mr Sanfey makes the case on his clients behalf that the arbitrator should have advised both parties that in view of the unique nature of the property he was of a mind that contrary to the usual practice and procedure in relation to VAT principles he would not regard Mr Cahill's opinion as the opinion of a competent valuer as in his view it was only an estimate.

He further relies on the inconsistency of the arbitrator, instancing the situation whereby on the one hand the arbitrator declined to accept the evidence of Mr Cahill as regards his valuation of the open market price but praised his evidence as regards the unencumbered rent of the property to the extent of stating that he believed that CSID were entitled to rely on that opinion and that it would be absurd to expect a non-qualified person to question the professional judgment of a qualified valuer. Mr Sanfey argues that this is further evidence of an unfair approach.

Mr Sanfey further relies on an error of law on the face of the award wherein the arbitrator stated that the VAT system could not function effectively if a supplier's VAT charge was subject to review by his customer. He contends that this is a misstatement of the law and a purchaser can question any charge in relation to VAT as demonstrated in the Supreme Court decision of *Forbes v Tobin* VI ITR 483.

Mr Sanfey urges on the court that in the circumstances of this case there is particular disquiet as to the arbitrator's approach and his decision is fatally flawed.

Mr Sanfey did have to accept that his clients were at all times aware that it was the intention of CSID to use the formulae and not to rely on the open market price valuation of Mr Cahill.

Mr McDonald, on the plaintiffs' behalf, submits that it was a matter for the arbitrator either to accept or reject Mr Cahill's view as regards his opinion of €35 million as the open market price. He contends that it is an essential part of the defendants argument that Mr Cahill's opinion not be regarded as evidence of the open market value. He refers specifically to the cross examination of Mr McCarthy, the valuer from Hamilton Osborne King, who conceded that where two valuations were to hand and they are so wide apart it was perfectly proper to adopt a different approach and this, Mr McDonald submits, was part of the evidence and was clearly flagged as a central part of the case and no objection was taken and there was no reference to the defendants requiring any further time to consider the matter. He further refers to the fact that both valuers in giving evidence before the arbitrator accepted that this particular property was unique, Mr Cahill stating the nature of the property was a once off totally unique specialised property whose main function was to hold major sporting events on an international and national basis and that there was no comparator. Mr McCarthy from Hamilton Osborne King accepted that he had carried out many valuations but nothing quite like this particular building as it was unique in nature. In particular Mr McDonald refers to Mr O'Keeffe's summing up and in particular to the point he made in respect of the wording of Regulation 19 that if there is evidence of an open market value that should be relied on and he submitted, at the time to the arbitrator, that the evidence would have to be clear and adequately established and that this was not the case in the circumstances that pertained and there was no clear evidence and in the circumstances the far more appropriate approach was to move to a more mathematical method of calculation which was the 'multiplier method'.

Mr McDonald submits that clearly the defendants were not taken by surprise as to the argument being advanced during the course of the arbitration on the plaintiffs behalf.

Insofar as Mr Sanfey relied on inconsistency on the part of the arbitrator Mr McDonald submits that this frequently occurs where a trial judge accepts part of the evidence of a witness but rejects some other aspect and that is what occurred in the circumstances of this

case in that the arbitrator disregarded part of Mr Cahill's evidence as he was fully entitled to do so and also accepted part of his evidence as regards the value of unencumbered rent. He was, Mr McDonald urges fully and clearly, entitled to adopt this approach.

As regards the alleged error of law Mr McDonald relies on the judgment of the Supreme Court in *Keenan v The Shield Insurance Company* [1988] IR 89 that any error of law would have to be fundamental. He draws a distinction between the facts of the present case and those in *Forbes v Tobin* and that in the present case the only issue was conflicting opinions and the arbitrator came to a conclusion that the nature of the property was unique with no close comparison and in his view the figure of €35 million was an estimate and did not provide evidence of its open market price thereby enabling CSID to use an unencumbered rent figure to calculate the capitalised value of the lease by means of one of the prescribed formulae in Regulation 19.

Mr Sanfey in reply accepts that there is no doubt but that Mr O'Keeffe did refer to the argument in his summing up and he accepts that this also appears from certain notes that were taken on his clients' behalf. He emphasises however that in circumstances where the practice and principle of VAT law is applied, and is well known to this particular arbitrator, and was to regard the opinion of a competent valuer as being synonymous with evidence, if there was to be a departure from that practice such a departure should have been flagged to the parties and in particular the parties prejudiced by such a view and on behalf of his clients he says it was unfair of the arbitrator not to do so.

In coming to a decision in this matter I take the view that this Court has to be mindful of the clear statement of law as laid out by the Supreme Court in *Keenan v The Shield Insurance Company* as regards interference with an arbitrator's award. In my view it follows that for this Court to interfere with the award of Mr O'Brien it would have to be satisfied that the award showed on its face an error of law so fundamental that this Court could not stand aside and allow it remain unchallenged or alternatively Mr O'Brien misconducted himself or the arbitration to such an extent that it was tainted by a substantial injustice or unfairness.

The defendants were at all times aware that CSID was not relying on Mr Cahill's valuation of the open market price being €35 million and was instead going to rely on one of the alternative formula as set out in Regulation 19 of the Value Added Tax Act, 1972, which brought about a situation whereby the open market price was valued at a sum in excess of €75 million. There was evidence before the arbitrator that the particular property was unique with no close comparison in the State and at the hearing before him the defendants queried that valuation of €35 million suggesting a lower open market figure. Mr McCarthy, the valuer from Hamilton Osborne King, was cross examined by Mr O'Keeffe, Barrister at Law, on behalf of the plaintiffs in relation to the position pertaining if there were two valuations and in summing up it is clear that Mr O'Keeffe indicated that if there was no clear evidence as regards the open market value you go the unencumbered rent formula and that the question for the arbitrator was as to what CSID was entitled to do. He submitted, during the course of the arbitration, to the arbitrator that there was no evidence of the open market value of the lease and that the plaintiffs then proceeded to do what the legislation required of them and what the Revenue Commissioners had advised them to do and on the basis of the evidence adduced before him and clearly taking into account the submissions of counsel for the plaintiff the arbitrator arrived at a decision whereby in his view because of the unique nature of the property with no close comparison in the state he did not consider Mr Cahill's opinion in respect of the figure of €35 million

to be evidence of the property's open market price. He took the view that the opinion of Mr Cahill was an estimate of the open market price of the property.

I come to the conclusion that on the evidence available, having regard to the submissions as made by Mr O'Keeffe, during the course of the arbitration the decision arrived at was available to the arbitrator and was one of the possible conclusions that he could have arrived at in respect of the issues before him. I accept that this brought about a situation whereby the arbitrator did not have to decide the central issue which he posed for himself as regards the situation of Mr Cahill 'having given his opinion as to the market value of the interest being disposed of were CSID then entitled to rely on one of the other formula based methods of capitalising the lease set out in Regulation 19' but in the circumstances of the decision the arbitrator came to the conclusion that there was not evidence of the property's open market price before him and thus it was not necessary for him in the circumstances to answer the very issue that he proposed for himself.

I do not consider that it was necessary for the arbitrator to have flagged to the defendants in advance of making his award the view he was considering adopting as it was not something new and had been the subject matter of cross examination and submissions by counsel before him during the course of the arbitration.

I do not accept the submission advanced on the defendants' behalf that the arbitrator was inconsistent in his approach. I take the view that insofar as he was referring to 'CSID being entitled to rely on the opinion of Mr Cahill and that it would be absurd to expect a non qualified person to question the professional judgment of a qualified valuer' he was at all times referring to Mr Cahill's evidence in respect of the unencumbered rent and quite clearly he was entitled to accept part of Mr Cahill's evidence and to reject that part of his evidence which did not find favour with him.

I am satisfied that the arbitrator made an incorrect statement of the law when he indicated that the VAT system could not function effectively if a supplier's VAT charge was subject to review by his customer having regard to the judgment of the Supreme Court in *Forbes v Tobin* VI ITR 483 but in my view this statement cannot be regarded as a fundamental error of law on the face of the award, or of having any significant impact on the decision of the arbitrator.

In these circumstances I come to the conclusion that no basis is laid out to set aside the award of the arbitrator as delivered on 1 July 2005, and I refuse the defendants application for relief in this regard.

I will hear the submissions of counsel as to the form of the order to be made.

Electricity Supply Board v The Minister for Social Community and Family Affairs & Others

High Court
Gilligan J
21 February 2006

Social welfare appeal – remit of court in an appeal on a point of law – whether a contract meter reader performed services under a contract of service or a contract for services – whether appeals officer was entitled to conclude that a contract of service existed – provision of substitute – control test

This was an appeal on a point of law from the decision of an Appeals Officer of the Department for Social, Community and Family Affairs ('the first respondent'). The appeal considered whether contract meter readers were engaged under a contract of service or a contract for services for the purposes of social welfare contributions.

The Electricity Supply Board ('the applicant') engaged contract meter readers. Their written contract labelled a meter reader as an independent contractor. The meter reader was paid a fee for each customer visit completed. The contract permitted the use of a substitute provided he was suitably instructed and trained to do the work. The meter reader was responsible for his own income tax and social welfare payments and was obliged to provide his own transport and public liability insurance. The applicant provided each meter reader with a schedule of the date each meter should be read but if this was unsuitable an alternative was accommodated. To perform the work, each meter reader was provided with a handheld meter reading device by the applicant.

The applicant also engaged 'network technicians', and as part of their functions, they carried out, *inter alia*, meter reading work. It was accepted that the technicians were employed under a contract of service.

The status of the contract meter readers had been adjudicated by the first respondent on a number of occasions in the past. All of these adjudications confirmed that the contract meter readers were engaged under a contract for services. The Appeals Officer found that since the last adjudication there were two fundamental changes in the employment of a meter reader. Firstly, any substitute meter reader had to be approved by the applicant and was issued with an identity card by the applicant. This was held to remove the freedom of the meter reader to send a substitute. Secondly, historically meter readers manually entered their readings on a paper-based system, but meter readers were now supplied with a handheld meter reading device, essentially a portable computer which provided the applicant with daily data. The Appeals Officer held that this resulted in the Applicant being in greater control of a meter reader's work pattern.

Held by Gilligan J in refusing the appeal:

i. Primary findings of fact of an administrative tribunal cannot be set aside by a court unless there is no evidence whatsoever to support such findings. Inferences drawn from such facts should not be disturbed unless they are such that no reasonable tribunal could arrive at the inferences drawn. If the court is satisfied that a conclusion arrived at is based on an incorrect view of the law then this conclusion should be set aside.
   Deely v Information Commissioner [2001] 3 IR 439 followed.

ii. There was evidence of a change in the level of control exercised where the freedom to provide a substitute was limited and electronic data logging equipment was introduced. The Appeals Officer was entitled to conclude that the contract meter readers were employed by the applicant pursuant to a contract of service.

Legislation

Social Welfare (Consolidation) Act 1993, ss 263, 271

Cases referred to in the judgment

Brides v Minister for Agriculture [1998] 4 IR 250
Cassidy v Ministry of Health [1951] 2 KB 343
Castleisland Cattle Breeding Society Limited v Minister for Social and Family Affairs VI ITR 673
Deely v Information Commissioner [2001] 3 IR 439
Express and Echo Publications Limited v Tanton (Ernst) [1999] IRLR 367
Henry Denny and Sons (Ireland) Limited v Minister for Social Welfare [1998] 1 IR 34, V ITR 238
Mara (Inspector of Taxes) v Hummingbird Limited [1982] ILRM 421, II ITR 667
Narich Property Limited v Commissioner of Payroll Tax [1984] ICR 286
O'Coindealbháin (Inspector of Taxes) v Mooney [1990] 1 IR 422
Premier Periclase v Valuation Tribunal (24 June 1999, unreported) HC
Queensland Stations Property Limited v Federal Commissioner of Taxation [1945] 70 CLR 539
Readymix Concrete (South East) Limited v Minister of Pensions and National Insurance [1968] 2 QB 497
Ryanair v The Labour Court (14 October 2005, unreported) HC
Tierney v An Post [2000] 1 IR 536

High Court – 21 February 2006

Gilligan J, The appeal of the ESB is on a point of law against the decision of the Appeals Officer of the first named respondent to classify six contract meter readers as being engaged under a contract of service rather than a contract for services for the purposes of social welfare contributions. The appeal is brought pursuant to section 271 of the Social Welfare (Consolidation) Act 1993. The summonses were issued by way of appeal against the decisions of the Appeals Officer of 23 January, 2002, and the Chief Appeals Officer of the 15 April, 2002. By Order of this Court on the 15th November, 2004, [Kelly J] the proceedings were consolidated.

The ESB engages the services on a contractor basis of approximately 300 persons who are engaged in the task of reading electricity meters. This practice has been ongoing since in or about 1955. The contract meter reader is paid a fee at a rate agreed between the ESB and the meter reader in respect of the number of customer visits completed by the contract meter reader. A higher fee has been agreed for such meter readings in rural areas as against urban areas. The ESB also engages under contracts of employment, employees described as 'Network Technicians' and as part of their duties and functions, such employees carry out *inter alia* meter reading work. It is accepted that they are employed under a contract of service.

The status for social welfare purposes of the contract meter readers has been the subject of adjudication by Appeals Officers of the Department of Social Community and Family Affairs on six occasions since 1955. All of these decisions confirmed their status as engaged under a contract for services. In August, 2000, six contract meter readers (the second to seventh named respondents herein) referred the matter of their classification for

social welfare insurability purposes to the first named respondent for a decision. A report was prepared by a social welfare inspector of the first named respondent and forwarded to a Deciding Officer. The Deciding Officer on the 15th November, 2000, issued a decision confirming that the six contract meter readers were engaged under a contract for services and not a contract of service.

The decision of the Deciding Officer was appealed by the six contract meter readers to an Appeals Officer of the first named respondent. An appeal hearing was held before the Appeals Officer on 9th August, 2001. The Appeals Officer reversed the decision of the Deciding Officer in all six cases and found that for the purposes of social welfare insurability, the six contract meter readers were engaged under a contract of service.

By letter of 13 February, 2002, the ESB sought a revision of the decision of the Appeals Officer by the Chief Appeals Officer (CAO) pursuant to section 263 Social Welfare (Consolidation) Act, 1993. By letter of 15th April, 2002, the ESB was notified of the decision of the CAO refusing to revise, and, affirming the decision of the Appeals Officer.

The matter of the status of personnel engaged by the ESB as contract meter readers has been the subject of numerous decisions by Appeals Officers of the first named respondent over the years. There are six such decisions of Appeals Officers which confirm the status of meter readers as being engaged under a contract for services. These comprise two decisions in 1955, a decision in 1968, two further decisions in 1976 and a decision in 1994. These decisions have been accepted and relied upon by the ESB and the contractors (save these six in 2000) and the position adopted for over 50 years has been upheld by all decisions of Appeals Officers and the Deciding Officer in these six cases. One of those decisions which confirms the status of contract meter readers as being engaged under a contract for services is a decision in 1994 concerning the status for social welfare insurance purposes of Eamonn Sheridan, the second named respondent in the proceedings herein.

The six contract meter readers have been engaged by the ESB as meter readers for periods ranging respectively from 1966 (in respect of Eamonn Sheridan) through to 1998 (in respect of John McAleer). During the period of their engagement, the only reference made by any of these six contract meter readers regarding their status for social welfare insurance purposes was that made by Eamonn Sheridan which, as previously referred to herein, resulted in a decision of an Appeals Officer of the first named respondent in 1994 confirming his status as engaged under a contract for services. Since 1994, no other contract meter reader has referred the matter of their status to the first named respondent for a decision save for the present reference by the second to the seventh named respondents.

The appellant being the Electricity Supply Board seeks an order setting aside, reversing and/or quashing the decision of the Appeals Officer. The appellants also seek a declaration that the contract meter readers are insurable under Class S and are engaged under a contract for services.

The appellant claims that:

i. The Appeals Officer erred in law in failing to have regard for the written terms of the contract between the parties.

ii. The Appeals Officer wrongly held that there were new facts or evidence which justified a revised decision on the insurability of the meter readers to those arising from previous appeals.

iii. The Appeals Officer erred in her analysis of the distinction between contract meter readers and the full time meter readers and also as to the significance to be attached to the introduction of hand held devices for the purposes of data logging. The Appeals

Officer misconstrued the terms of the contracts in concluding that there is a requirement for the meter readers to provide personal service and in ignoring the express terms which permit the use by the contract meter readers of substitutes and subcontractors to undertake the work.

iv. The Appeals Officer applied the incorrect legal principles. In particular, the Appellants place particular emphasis on the Appeals Officer's consideration of the right to sub-contract the task, the extent to which the meter reader may profit from the activity and the failure of the Appeals Officer to attach weight to the requirement for meter readers to carry insurance and provide an indemnity and provide their own transport. The Appeals Officer was also misdirected in her application of the law in considering matters extraneous to the terms of the contract in circumstances where the contract regulates and governs all aspects of the contractual relationship.

Background

The respondent meter readers are all employed pursuant to a contract for meter reading services with the Electricity Supply Board. The contract specifically states that the meter reader is an independent contractor and shall not be an employee of the ESB.

The meter reader is entitled to use other persons in the provision of services under the contract and in these circumstances he shall ensure that such persons are suitably instructed and trained to do the work required. The 'independent contractor' shall be responsible for making appropriate income tax and social welfare contributions from the remuneration he pays his personnel (if any) and any other levies required by law to be paid by an employer in respect of such persons and no responsibility shall lie with the ESB in this regard.

The meter reader is not the agent of the ESB and shall not make any contracts on behalf of the ESB or bind the ESB to any obligations or in any way act as an agent of the ESB.

The contract provides for summary termination of the meter readers contract in certain circumstances and also that the contract may be terminated by either party subject to 30 days notice in writing being given and in such a situation the meter reader shall be paid such amount as may be necessary to cover the work actually undertaken to the satisfaction of the ESB at that time. The extent of the liability of the ESB in the carrying out of the contract shall be limited to the settlement of that amount.

The contract provides for the allocation of meter reading equipment and certain required standards. The meter readers are provided with a handheld terminal described as a portable computer and certain associated communication equipment and a procedure is set out for the reporting of the relevant readings taken by the portable computer. The meter reader is required to report in detail on all matters found on reading a meter such as *inter alia* broken seals, faulty meters, damaged meters.

There are six two monthly billing periods for each customer and the meter reader is obliged under his contract to ensure at least one official reading per annum on all meters. He is also obliged to estimate the reading at least once per annum on all meters. Payment is only provided for the meter reader if he actually carries out a reading so that his payment conditions in effect are governed by the number of times he actually reads each meter and the maximum number of readings for any meter is five allowing for the one obligatory estimation. The meter reader conversely can estimate the meter five times thereby only necessitating one reading but it follows that he is then on an annual basis only paid for the one reading.

The contract provides that when the meter reader is carrying out his duties reading the meter he is responsible for all loss, damage or injury caused by himself and his employees,

agents or sub-contractors in the course of or arising out of the provision of meter reading services.

The contract sets out the rates that are to be paid differentiating between urban rates and rural rates.

The meter reader is responsible pursuant to his contract for ensuring that any vehicle used by him has adequate and full insurance cover for the purpose of his employment with the ESB.

The meter reader is obliged to maintain comprehensive public liability insurance cover in amounts acceptable to the ESB for such liabilities.

The meter reader agrees to keep confidential any information obtained by him in the course of carrying out his contractual duties on behalf of the ESB.

Since the issue as regards the nature of the employment of persons in a similar position to that of the second to seventh named respondents employed pursuant to the contract for meter reading services with the ESB was previously decided by the Department of Social, Community and Family Affairs, the Appeals Officer found in her decision that two fundamental changes had occurred with regard to the employment of the meter readers. The first is that the relevant substitute employed by the meter reader must have ESB approval and must carry an ESB ID card and that an ID document supplied by the meter reader does not suffice. The second change is that the meter readers are provided with a handheld terminal which in effect is a portable computer whereas previously meter readers entered their readings on meter sheets in meter books.

With regard to the necessity for the substitute to have an ESB identity card, the factual situation appears to be that the meter reader has to apply to the ESB for approval of a nominated substitute who is then provided with an ESB identification card. The procedure accordingly in place allows the ESB to veto a nominated substitute and it appears that this has happened on an occasion. It is understandable that the procedure in place has been adopted for security purposes. The identification card itself carries the wording that the particular person is 'authorised to read meters for billing purposes on behalf of the ESB' and on the card itself it is stated that it is 'the property of the ESB'.

The situation pertaining to the introduction of data loggers is that the data obtained during the day is downloaded daily and provides the ESB with instant information as regards the days meter readings. All the necessary equipment is provided by the ESB. The ESB do employ, pursuant to a contract of service, a number of full time meter readers and they too adopt the same procedure arising from the use of the data logger. The meter reader is obliged to enter the relevant reading in the data logger at the time when the reading is taken and the reader is not allowed to take manual readings and enter them later in the data logger. The meter reader is given instructions as to what date each meter is to be read. The meter readers are prohibited for both practical and security reasons from taking meter readings after dark. If a meter reader is unavailable on a particular day, the procedure in place is that the reading would probably be estimated unless it was possible for the ESB to provide a substitute meter reader.

The ESB makes out the relevant daily schedules for meter reading purposes and it was clarified on behalf of the ESB before the Appeals Officer that meter readers are not consulted in the setting up of schedules but if a particular schedule time did not suit a meter reader, he would be free to explain the reason to the ESB and an alternative would be accommodated.

In her judgment, delivered on 23rd January, 2002, the Social Welfare Appeals Officer reviewed the submissions made to her on behalf of the relevant parties and then 'commented' as follows:

> 'The issue in this case has already been decided on by Appeals Officers on numerous occasions over the years. In fact one of those involved in this case ie, Eamonn Sheridan, had his employment status decided by an Appeals Officer in 1994 (Ref AP93/16838) What I must discern, therefore, is whether there are new facts or evidence which would warrant alteration of the decisions taken over the years.
>
> Having examined reports of the previous appeals (copies placed on file) a number of significant points of difference arise in a situation which was always finely balanced.
>
> It has been submitted, and accepted in the past that part-time meter readers were not required to give personal service, but were free to send a substitute, and the case of Mr Eamonn Sheridan who has substituted for his wife seemed to support the submission. It has now emerged however, that the 'Substitute' must have ESB approval, and must carry an ESB ID card. An ID document supplied by the meter reader does not, apparently, suffice. This evidence has not been challenged. It has been submitted to me that this limits, and indeed removes, the freedom of the individual meter reader to send substitute in his place. This is, I consider, a valid contention, and one which does not appear to have emerged in previous cases. ['She did not as a matter of routine, engage other people to assist her in her work. Where she was unable to do the work herself she had to arrange for it to be done by someone else, but the person in question had to be approved by the Appellants.' Ref Supreme Court Judgment, *Henry Denny and Sons* 1997].
>
> At the time of consideration of the earlier appeals, the meter readers were still entering readings on meter sheets in meter books. The[y] were not therefore in on-going contact with the ESB, and were operating free from supervision or control. Since the introduction of the 'Data logger' however, this situation has been significantly altered. The extensive data is down-loaded daily and provides the ESB with a very effective monitoring mechanism. The control of his work pattern previously enjoyed by the meter readers has significantly diminished. In some cases, though very few, the meter reader has to report to ESB Offices to down-load the data. On this point, there has been a notable change in circumstances (more than the mere replacement of a manual by an electronic recording system) since the earlier decisions.
>
> There is uncertainty as to whether the meter readers are free to engage in other work while under contract to the ESB. It may well be that at different hours or days, other work could be carried out by them, but the level of control exercised indirectly by the ESB would, I consider, preclude carrying out other business on meter reading visits. Even if such work were possible, I do not consider that the case would turn on the issue.
>
> As regards holiday arrangements, the meter readers are allowed to estimate one bill per consumer, per annum. They are not paid for this estimated 'Reading'. I doubt if such an arrangement would have been proposed or accepted, unless the payment rates for actual reading took account of this 'Free' period. If this is the case, then there is effectively, a holiday allowance. This however, is purely speculative, and the issue is not defining of, but rather a consequence of the nature of the employment contract. The same could be said to apply to the non-provision for paid sick leave. The non-provision for payment of travel expenses could suggest a Contract for Service, but again, is not necessarily defining of such Contract.
>
> On the question of the "Entrepreneurial Test", it was contended that these meter readers have potential to be in business on their own behalf if meter reading is in the future contracted out by enterprises such as Bord Gais. At the moment, however, I am examining a situation where

these men are engaged by the ESB to read ESB meters. They did not ply for hire, nor do they take financial risk, or stand to make a profit other than their earnings.

Full-time meter readers (located in the bigger urban centres) have always been employed under a Contract of Service. Given the alterations in the working conditions of the part-time meter readers, the distinction between them in relation to meter reading duties is now rather blurred. The authority given, or affirmed, by the *Denny* case to look at the actual operation of an employment contract has enabled me to look beyond the stipulation that the part-time meter readers are engaged on a contract which 'Is not an employment contract'. The details before me suggest very strongly that they are in fact in a master/servant relationship with the ESB, and I therefore consider that they are engaged under a Contract of Service. I further consider that this has been the position since the introduction of the "Data Logger" technology, said at the hearing to be in 1994. I must emphasise, however, that while I attach great importance to it, the introduction of this technology, with its inherent control mechanism, is not the only factor to have persuaded me to the view I have taken. I have carefully considered the overall picture, and the significance of all the new facts which have emerged since this issue was last examined by an Appeals Officer.

My decisions are on the individual files.'

The law

In *Deely v Information Commissioner* (11 May 2001, unreported) HC, McKechnie J noted at p 17 that the remit of the Court in an appeal on a point of law encompassed the following:

(a) it cannot set aside findings of primary fact unless there is no evidence to support such findings,

(b) it ought not set aside inferences drawn from such facts unless such inferences were ones which no reasonable decision making body could draw,

(c) it can however reverse such inferences, if the same were based on the interpretation of documents and should do so if incorrect, and finally,

(d) if the conclusion reached by such bodies shows that they have taken an erroneous view of the law, then that also is a ground for setting aside the resulting decision. See for example *Mara (Inspector of Taxes) v Hummingbird Limited* [1982] ILRM 421, *Henry Denny and Sons (Ireland) Limited v Minister for Social Welfare* [1998] 1 IR 34 and *Premier Periclase v Valuation Tribunal* HC (24 June, 1999 U/R) HC.'

Budd J in *Brides v Minister for Agriculture* [1998] 4 IR 250 dealt with the position of the examining role of the High Court in an appeal such as this wherein he stated at pp 274–275:

'Since this is an appeal on a point of law, it is not a rehearing. Accordingly, the facts as found by the Labour Court are binding on this court where those facts are supported by credible evidence and this court should be slow to disregard the inferences drawn by the Labour Court from its findings of fact unless the inferences drawn are wholly unwarranted on the findings of fact made. The role of this court has been explained by Kenny J in the Supreme Court in *Mara (Inspector of Taxes) v Hummingbird* [1982] ILRM 421 at p 426 in a case stated where the Income Tax Appeal Commissioners found, as a fact, that Hummingbird purchased premises in Baggot Street, Dublin, as an investment and so its sale was not in the course of trade.

At page 426 Kenny J said:

> 'A case stated consists in part of findings on questions of primary fact, e.g. with what intention did the taxpayer purchase the Baggot Street premises. These findings on primary facts should not be set aside by the courts unless there was no evidence whatever to support them. The commissioner then goes on in the case stated to give his conclusion or inferences from these primary facts. These are mixed questions of fact and law and the court should approach these in a different way. If they are based on the interpretation of documents, the court should reverse them if they are incorrect for it is in as good a position to determine the meaning of documents as is the commissioner. If the conclusions from the primary facts are ones which no reasonable commissioner could draw, the court should set aside his findings on the ground that he must be assumed to have misdirected himself as to the law or made a mistake in reasoning. Finally, if his conclusions show that he has adopted a wrong view of the law, they should be set aside. If however they are not based on a mistaken view of the law or a wrong interpretation of documents, they should not be set aside unless the inferences which he made from the primary facts were ones that no reasonable commissioner could draw. The ways of conducting business have become very complex and the answer to the question whether a transaction was an adventure in the nature of the trade nearly always depends on the importance which the judge or commissioner attaches to some facts. He will have evidence some of which supports the conclusion that the transaction under investigation was an adventure in the nature of trade and he will have some which points to the opposite conclusion. These are essentially matters of degree and his conclusions should not be disturbed (even if the court does not agree with them, for we are not retrying the case) unless they are such that a reasonable commissioner could not draw them or they are based on a mistaken view of the law.'

Hamilton CJ in his judgment in *Henry Denny and Sons (Ireland) Limited v Minister for Social Welfare* [1998] 1 IR 34 at p 37 dealt with the role of the court in an appeal such as this and succinctly stated at pp. 37–38 of the judgment:

> '…I believe it would be desirable to take this opportunity of expressing the view that the courts should be slow to interfere with the decisions of expert administrative tribunals. Where conclusions are based upon an identifiable error of law or an unsustainable finding of fact by a tribunal such conclusions must be corrected. Otherwise it should be recognised that tribunals which have been given statutory tasks to perform and exercise their functions, as is now usually the case, with a high degree of expertise and provide coherent and balanced judgments on the evidence and arguments heard by them it should not be necessary for the courts to review their decisions by way of appeal or judicial review.'

Keane J in his judgment in *Denny* dealt with a number of relevant significant factors. At p 48 of his judgment, he deals with the significance of the written agreement such as exists in this case wherein he stated:

> 'In the present case, both the appeals officer and the learned High Court Judge were of the view that the fact that Ms Mahon was described in the written agreement as being employed as an "independent contractor" was not conclusive. It is accepted that they were correct in so holding. It is correct to say that the appeals officer appears to have taken the view that the importance of the terms of the written contract was somewhat diminished by the fact that Ms. Mahon wanted the job and accordingly had no option but to sign the contract. However, it is also clear from his report that he considered in some detail the actual terms of the written contract and also had regard to the manner in which the work was done by Ms. Mahon.
>
> If the appeals officer had erred in law in his construction of the written contract, then, in accordance with the principles explained by Kenny J, his decision would be liable to be set aside by the High Court. In the present case, however, it has not been shown that the appeals officer in any way misconstrued the written contract: he was, on the contrary, entirely correct

in holding that he should not confine his consideration to what was contained in the written contract, but should have regard to all the circumstances of Ms Mahon's employment. Equally, the High Court Judge was correct in the view she took that she should not interfere with his findings in this regard unless they were incapable of being supported by the facts or were based on an erroneous view of the law.'

Keane J goes on to state that there is a consensus to be found in the authorities that each case must be considered in the light of its own particular facts and of the general principles which the courts have developed.

Keane J deals with the significance of the extent and degree of the control which is exercised by one party over the other in the performance of the work and states that at one stage this was regarded as decisive. He goes on to state at p. 49 of his judgment:-

'However, as later authorities demonstrate, that test does not always provide satisfactory guidance. In *Cassidy v Ministry of Health* [1951] 2 KB 343, it was pointed out that, although the master of a ship is clearly employed under a contract of service, the owners are not entitled to tell him how he should navigate the vessel. Conversely, the fact that one party reserves the right to exercise full control over the method of doing the work may be consistent with the other party being an independent contractor: see *Queensland Stations Property Ltd v Federal Commissioner of Taxation* [1945] 70 CLR 539.'

Keane J at p 50 of the judgment summarises the approach to be taken by the court in the following terms:

'It is, accordingly, clear that, while each case must be determined in the light of its particular facts and circumstances, in general a person will be regarded as providing his or her services under a contract of service and not as an independent contractor where he or she is performing those services for another person and not for himself or herself. The degree of control exercised over how the work is to be performed, although a factor to be taken into account, is not decisive. The inference that the person is engaged in business on his or her own account can be more readily drawn where he or she provides the necessary premises or equipment or some other form of investment, where he or she employs others to assist in the business and where the profit which he or she derives from the business is dependent on the efficiency with which it is conducted by him or her.'

The legal principles at issue in this matter were further discussed in the decision of the Supreme Court in *Castleisland Cattle Breeding Society Limited v Minister for Social and Family Affairs* VI ITR 673, wherein both the judgments in *Denny* and *Mara* were followed, Geoghegan J stating at p 13 of the judgment that the principles as outlined by Keane J in *Henry Denny* ought to have been applied by the Appeals Officer in the *Castleisland* case and in his view if they had been, there would have been a different result.

Submissions

The appeal in this case is brought pursuant to section 271 of the Social Welfare (Consolidation) Act, 1993. Section 271 provides:

'Any person who is dissatisfied with—

(a) the decision of an appeals officer, or

(b) the revised decision of the Chief Appeals Officer,

on any question, other than a question to which section 265 applies, may appeal that decision or revised decision, as the case may be, to the High Court on any question of law.'

It is submitted on behalf of the second named respondents that the tribunal's conclusions should not be disturbed (even if the Court does not agree with them as the Court is not retrying the case) unless they are such that a reasonable tribunal could not possibly draw such conclusions, or they are based on a mistaken view of the law: *Mara (Inspector of Taxes) v Hummingbird Limited* [1982] ILRM 421.

Counsel for the Minister submits that the role of the High Court in considering appeals on a point of law from expert tribunals has been carefully circumscribed by case law as set out in *Henry Denny & Sons (Ireland) Limited t/a Kerry Foods v Minister for Social Welfare* [1998] 1 IR 34.

It is submitted on behalf of the Minister that thus the Court is confined to a consideration of whether the Appeals Officer erred in law in reaching her determination.

The appellant claims that the respondents have sought to confine the scope of the Court in adjudicating an appeal on a point of law in a manner that is not consistent with the well established authorities. It is submitted that this is an overly restrictive position. The appeal is provided for by the Act of 1993.

The appellant contends that the Appeals Officer has fallen into error in the adjudication in respect of all four facets of the test as outlined in *Deely v Information Commissioner* (11th May, 2001, unreported) HC (McKechnie J).

When this matter resumed hearing on 26 October 2005, counsel for the individual respondents referred to the decision of Hanna J in *Ryanair v Labour Court* (14 October, 2005, unreported) HC (Hanna J) wherein he stated at page 27 that:

> 'if the applicant fails to establish that a decision of the Labour Court was irrational in the sense that there was no relevant material upon which it could ground such a decision or that such material could not properly be relied on or that the material and evidence offered by the appellant so conclusively and overwhelmingly trumped such case as was offered by the notice party to such an extent as to render a decision in its favour perverse then, in such circumstances, this aspect of the applicant's case would have to fail….The question is whether or not I am satisfied that there was no or no sufficient material or evidence before the Labour Court which would enable it to come to the conclusion which it did.'

The respondents submit that the Court should adopt a similar approach in the instant case. The fact that the Court might not take the same view as the original decision-maker is not of itself enough. Only if there is no relevant material on which such a decision could be grounded should the court intervene.

Misconstruction and misinterpretation of the written contract

It is submitted on the appellants behalf that the Appeals Officer has not adequately or appropriately considered the actual terms of the contract between the ESB and the contract meter readers. Since 1995, the ESB and the contract meter readers have concluded annual written contracts setting out and regulating the terms, arrangements, nature and scope of the services to be provided by the meter readers. The only references to the written contract contained in the decision of the Appeals Officer are at pages 3 and 6 of her decision. It is claimed that an examination of the decision discloses that there has been a complete failure by the Appeals Officer to have regard for the terms of the contract and the manner in which they regulate and govern the relationship between the parties.

The appellant claims that in determining the nature of the contractual relationship between the parties, the Appeals Officer failed to have due regard to the intention of the parties which is reflected in the written contractual documents which they have executed.

The appellant refers to *Narich Property Ltd v Commissioner of Pay-Roll Tax* [1984] ICR 286 at p 291 where the Court stated in relation to the importance of the written contract terms in the context of determining whether a relationship is one of employer/employee engaged under a contract or contract engaged under a contract for services:

> 'In the present case, where there is no reason to think that the clause is a sham, or that it is not a genuine statement of the parties' intentions, it must be given its proper weight in relation to other clauses in the agreement.'

In *Henry Denny*, Keane J stated at p 48:

> 'If the appeals officer had erred in law in his construction of the written contract, then, in accordance with the principles explained by Kenny J, his decision would be liable to be set aside by the High Court.'

In the Supreme Court decision in *Castleisland Cattle Breeding Society Limited v Minister for Social and Family Affairs* VI ITR 673, Geoghegan J stated at p 680:

> '[T]he wording of a written contract still remains of great importance. It can, however, emerge in evidence that in practice the working arrangements between the parties are consistent only with a different kind of contract or at least are inconsistent with the expressed categorisation of the contract.'

The appellant submits that in applying these principles, the Appeals Officer has clearly erred in law to the approach adopted. No regard or weight has been afforded to very important terms of the contract, in particular, those terms which clearly do not oblige the meter reader to provide personal service and which do require the meter reader to make an investment in their business by way of the provision of transport, indemnity and insurance.

The respondents argue that there is no doubt that the Appeals Officer had the contract before her when considering the question posed and she conducted a lengthy oral hearing. Although she did not carry out a clause by clause analysis of the contract, her decision records a summary of the arguments made and the essential conclusions reached in respect of the contract. It is clear that the Appeals Officer took considerable care in coming to the conclusion that she did. Both sides were legally represented. It was a matter wholly within her discretion to decide what if any weight to attach to the various matters set before her. The fact that the appellant does not agree with her conclusion is not sufficient to set her decision aside. Nor is it appropriate for the Court to substitute its views for hers unless the Court comes to the conclusion that no reasonable tribunal could come to the conclusion which she did.

In the circumstances the fact that the written document describes meter readers as 'independent contractors' cannot be regarded as determinative. Such a term purports to express a conclusion of law as to the consequences of the contract between the parties. In this regard it is submitted on behalf of the second to seventh named respondents that the decision in *Henry Denny & Sons (Ireland) Limited v Minister for Social Welfare* [1998] 1 IR 34 is of considerable assistance in this case.

The importance of the requirement to provide personal service

The appellants claim that the Appeals Officer misconstrued the terms of the contract of the contract meter reader in concluding that the contract meter reader's freedom to use subcontractors is limited or removed. In her decision, the Appeals Officer found that the meter readers 'do not have to render personal service and can send a substitute who would be paid by the reader themselves'. The Appeals Officer noted that any substitute must have

ESB approval and must carry an ESB ID card. She records at page 9 of her decision that 'an ID document supplied by the meter reader does not, apparently suffice. This evidence has not been challenged'. The Appeals Officer then noted that this limits and indeed removes the freedom of the individual meter reader to send substitutes in his place.

With regard to the requirement to provide personal service, the appellant claims that there is absolutely no ambiguity in the terms of the contract. Clearly, the contract meter reader is permitted to use other persons to carry out the work. The only prerequisite is that the person is suitably instructed and trained to do the work. The terms of the contract make it clear that the contract meter reader shall be responsible for tax and social welfare contributions in respect of such personnel and that no responsibility shall lie with the ESB in this regard.

The appellant claims that if the contract meter reader requests the ESB to supply an ID card, the ESB will do so. The introduction of an ID card for contract meter readers arose because of concerns for consumer safety and security.

The appellants refer to *Express and Echo Publications Limited v Tanton (Ernest)* [1999] IRLR 367, UK Court of Appeal (Civil Division) 11/3/99, where Gibson LJ emphasised the importance of a contractual provision which allowed the contractor to assign the work to be performed by another party and referred to the decision of McKenna J in *Ready Mix Concrete (South East) Ltd v Minister of Pensions and National Insurance* [1968] 2 QB 497. Gibson LJ stated at p 5 of his judgment:

> 'In the *Ready Mix Concrete* case, McKenna J regarded the freedom of the owner/driver to choose a competent driver to take his place at other times as a significant feature leading to the conclusion that the contract in that case was a contract for services and not a contract of service.'

In this jurisdiction a similar approach to the importance of a requirement to provide personal service was adopted by Blayney J in his decision in *Ó Coindealbháin (Inspector of Taxes) v Mooney* [1990] 1 IR 422 where he stated at p 431:

> '[I]n my opinion these features are inconsistent with the contract being one of service – they all point rather to its being one for services, in particular the absence of any requirement to perform the work personally and the obligation to provide and furnish the premises in which the work is to be performed. Both these features suggest that the respondent is an independent contractor.'

It is submitted that the only basis for the conclusion of the Appeals Officer that the entitlement of the meter reader to send substitutes to do the work is limited was information tendered on behalf of the appellants at the hearing of the appeal regarding the requirement for the substitute to carry an ID card. It is submitted that such a finding flies in the face of the weight and preponderance of evidence, material and information that was before the Appeals Officer and in particular is in complete disregard of the express contractual provision and the evidence of the use of substitutes or subcontractors (including family members) that was before the Appeals Officer.

The appellant submits that in all of the leading cases in this area, the Court focused on the contractual relationship between the parties and its operation and not on whether there was freedom to carry out work for someone else or to do other work whilst engaged in the work in question. The ability to work for someone else is but one factor to be considered.

The evidence before the Appeals Officer was that one of the meter readers had acted as a substitute for his wife who was contracted to the ESB as a meter reader. This is expressly acknowledged by the Appeals Officer at page 7 of her decision. The meter readers in their

submissions acknowledge that the contract meter readers can use a substitute to carry out the work. The conclusion of the Appeals Officer that the requirement for a substitute to carry an ESB ID and to be approved by the ESB limits and indeed removes the freedom of the individual meter reader to send substitutes in his place is an inference that no reasonable decision maker could draw from the evidence, material and information available. None of the meter readers at the appeal hearing denied that they could use substitutes. Their submission rather was that the requirement for the substitute to carry ID and the notification procedure to the ESB in relation to the use of substitutes affected their flexibility in relation to the use of substitutes. A requirement for prior notification or even approval for the use of a substitute or the right to subcontract to another person does not nor can it logically justify the conclusion reached by the Appeals Officer that it limits or removes the freedom to use substitutes.

In *Tierney v An Post* [2000] 1 IR 536, there was a clear and unambiguous provision in the written contract for the Postmaster to obtain approval for the use of substitutes. Keane J in the Supreme Court stated at p 545:

> 'the fact remains that it is not normal to find in a contract of service that the employee can hire assistants to perform the work which he or she is employed to do.'

However, it is submitted on behalf of the Minister that on a true construction of the relevant contractual provision, the contract meter reader is not permitted to subcontract but only permitted to use other people for assistance.

The respondents submit that the production of the identification card is a matter for the ESB. Indeed the ESB decides which information should be included in the ID card. They require details to be sent to them of the proposed substitute before the ESB can approve and authorise such a substitute.

The respondents claim that in effect the request for an ID card for a substitute triggers an opportunity to exercise a veto on the part of the ESB. It is clear that in requiring such information to be supplied the ESB are monitoring who attends the houses of ESB customers. In effect this is an acknowledgement that the person who arrives to read the meter is the 'public face of the ESB'. Indeed, the card itself provides that it is 'the property of ESB'.

Entrepreneurial test

In considering the entrepreneurial test in her decision, the Appeals Officer has done so by reference to whether the contract meter reader is precluded from carrying out other business while on meter reading business.

At page 10 of her decision, the Appeals Officer states that the contract meter reader 'did not ply for hire nor do they take financial risk or stand to make a profit other than earnings'. The appellant claims that this approach is unreasonable and illogical. The appropriate issue in relation to this aspect of the matter is not whether the contract meter reader is or is not precluded from carrying out any other business at an ESB customer's home while on meter reading visits but rather, whether the contract meter reader makes investment and carries risk and can regulate and influence his profit, earnings and turnover by reference to the manner in which the work (*any other work*) is planned, carried out and conducted. It is claimed that the Appeals Officer has misunderstood the entrepreneurial test and misapplied same. The written contract provides for an investment to be made by the contract meter reader in insurance, indemnity and transport and furthermore allows the meter reader to manage their own time and regulate their earnings by reference to the use

of employees, sub-contractors, substitutes or agents to carry out the work for them. The contract meter reader may be offered additional 'grounds' that have been relinquished by another meter reader within their immediate area and can decline or accept the additional 'grounds'.

The appellant refers to the fact that there are six billing periods in the contract year for the contract meter reader. In the six billing periods, the only obligation on the contract meter reader is to estimate once and to read once. As to the other four potential customer readings, the contract reader can choose to estimate all four, read all four or estimate and read as he chooses. He does not get paid for estimates and the number of readings he chooses to carry out has a direct impact on his earnings.

In *Castleisland Cattle Breeding Society Limited v Minister for Social and Family Affairs* (15 July 2004, unreported) SC, Geogheghan J emphasised the importance to be attached to provisions in the inseminators contract and evidence before the Appeals Officer in that case which allowed the inseminator 'to make his own timetable'.

In *Tierney v An Post* [2000] 1 IR 536, the Court concluded that even a modest capacity to regulate or influence earnings or profit was a vital factor in determining that the contract in question of the postmaster was a contract for services.

The contract meter readers in their submissions have contended that the volume of work carried out by the meter reader is in reality determined by the ESB and that the meter reader is restricted in the amount of work they carry out by virtue of the control exercised by the ESB. The income earned by a meter reader is effectively capped by the number of 'grounds' allocated to the meter reader by the ESB.

The fact that the contract contained a requirement for the meter reader to provide public liability insurance is noted by the Appeals Officer but she did not consider this to be a decisive factor in determining the relationship. The Appeals Officer noted that as a matter of fact the ESB had provided a group insurance scheme option to the meter readers.

The appellant submits that the group scheme is irrelevant and that the key point is that the contract obliges the meter reader to maintain their own public liability insurance. This requirement was deemed an extremely significant factor in *Castleisland* and is wholly consistent with a contract for services. Clearly the contract meter reader has to make an investment in the business. In *Ready Mix Concrete (South East) Ltd v Minister of Pensions and National Insurance* [1968] 2 QB 497, the company insured the contractors vehicle and mixing unit and subsequently deducted the amounts paid from the charges made by the contractor. This was deemed to be consistent with a contract for services. In the case of the contract meter reader, the requirement to make an investment and provide the indemnity is in stark contrast to an employee who carries out meter reading work. Moreover, the meter reader may choose or not choose to avail of the ESB group scheme.

Control test

The matter of the status of personnel engaged by the ESB as contract meter readers has been the subject of numerous decisions by Appeals Officers of the first named respondent over the years. The Appeals Officer states that these decisions 'do have standing and cannot be lightly set aside'.

The question posed by the Appeals Officer in determining this appeal is 'whether there are new facts or evidence which would warrant alteration of the decisions taken over the years'. The Appeals Officer relied upon alterations in the working conditions for the contract meter readers as a basis for her conclusions that the distinction between the six meter readers and the full-time permanent staff of the ESB who are also engaged in meter

reading is 'rather blurred' such as to justify a departure from all previous decisions of Appeals Officers. This finding is based on the introduction of data logger technology and also the fact that any relevant substitute employed by the meter reader must have ESB approval and must carry an ESB ID card and an ID document supplied by the meter reader does not apparently suffice.

It is well established in *Henry Denny* that the control test, as set down in *Ready Mix Concrete (South East) Ltd v Minister of Pensions and National Insurance* [1968] 2 QB 497, once thought to be the dominant test in determining the status of a relationship is an important but not a decisive factor. The Appeals Officer considered how the introduction of the data logger technology together with the means through which recordings on that device are transmitted to the appellant increased the degree of control which the appellant exercised in fact over the functions of the meter readers.

The appellant submits that the introduction of data logger technology did not create any new distinction between the respective categories or any new conditions. The distinctions between those engaged in meter reading work for the ESB who are full time permanent employees and contract meter readers who are also engaged in meter reading work remain the same as they were when all previous decisions of the Appeals Officers were made. This is purely modernising technology adopted for the same end and purpose as the filling out of meter sheets and in all material respects is the same as if the meter reader was writing on paper.

If anything, this technology affords the meter reader greater flexibility in their working arrangements in terms of planning and scheduling the work by virtue of speedier transmission of information regarding the customer meters to be read and allows the contract meter reader to have a greater influence over the regulation of their earnings and profit.

It is submitted on behalf of the respondents that the use of this equipment by both groups brings the two groups of meter readers much closer together and thus blurs the distinction. The appellant submits that this view is erroneous.

The respondents claim that the introduction of the data logging equipment is rightly regarded by the Appeals Officer as a matter of considerable significance. The equipment itself belongs at all times to the ESB. The time period within which information collected must be passed on to the ESB is dictated by the ESB, and the method of transmission (by modem into a telephone line) is also dictated by the ESB.

Conclusion

I take the view that the approach of this Court to an appeal on a point of law is that findings of primary fact are not to be set aside by this Court unless there is no evidence whatsoever to support them. Inferences of fact should not be disturbed unless they are such that no reasonable tribunal could arrive at the inference drawn and further if the Court is satisfied that the conclusion arrived at adopts a wrong view of the law, then this conclusion should be set aside. I take the view that this Court has to be mindful that its own view of the particular decision arrived at is irrelevant. The Court is not retrying the issue but merely considering the primary findings of fact and as to whether there was a basis for such findings and as to whether it was open to the Appeals Officer, to arrive at the inferences drawn and adopting a reasonable and coherent view, to arrive at her ultimate decision.

I take the view that the issue which the Appeals Officer had to decide in this case is to be approached on the basis that the written agreement existing between the parties is of considerable importance and has to be given due consideration but is not conclusive in its

own right and therefore, following Keane J in *Henry Denny & Sons (Ireland) Limited t/a Kerry Foods v Minister for Social Welfare* [1998] 1 IR 34, the particular facts and circumstances of the case have to be considered.

In general, a person will be regarded as providing his or her services under a contract of service and not as an independent contractor where the person is performing the services for another person and not for himself. The degree of control exercised over how the work is to be performed is a factor to be taken into account but is not decisive. Factors to be considered include who provides the necessary premises and equipment or some other form of investment, whether others are employed to assist in the business, and whether the profit derived is dependent on the efficiency of the person concerned.

I take the view that the Appeals Officer adopted a reasoned approach in deciding the issue before her. She was entitled to look beyond the contract and in particular the stipulation as contained therein that part-time meter readers were engaged in a contract which is not 'an employment contract'. The Appeals Officer comes to the conclusion that it was not necessary for her to consider in depth as to whether or not meter readers were free to engage in other work while under contract to the ESB and she accepts that it may well be that at different hours of the day, other work could be carried out by the meter readers, however the level of control exercised indirectly by the ESB would in her opinion preclude carrying out other business on meter reading visits. She concludes this aspect by stating that even if such work were possible she does not consider that the case would turn on this issue.

The Appeals Officer gave consideration to the entrepreneurial test indicating that the meter readers were engaged by the ESB to read ESB meters and did not ply for hire nor did they take financial risk or stand to make a profit other than their earnings.

As regards the aspect of holiday arrangements, the Appeals Officer did not come to any definite conclusion merely indicating that the non provision for payment of travel expenses could suggest a contract of service but again in her view the situation was not necessarily defining of a contract of service.

The Appeals Officer clearly considered the contract in some detail and while she may not have carried out an in depth analysis of the contract her judgment records at length, a summary of the arguments made and the essential conclusions reached arising from the content of the contract. The Appeals Officer accepted that there were elements of the contract more consistent with a contract for services than a contract of service but took the view that the relevant features were not conclusive in determining the nature of the relationship.

The Appeals Officer indicated that she had to discern whether there were new facts or evidence which would warrant an alteration of the decisions taken over the years by previous appeals officers. She decided that two significant points of difference arose in the situation as presented before her and she quite reasonably describes the central issue as having always been finely balanced. The Appeals Officer bases her decision on the change brought about by the ESB in the procedure relating to substitutes being retained by the meter readers and the fact that they now have to be approved by the ESB and provided by the ESB with an identity card. She considers in the circumstances that it is a valid contention that this limits and indeed removes the freedom of the individual meter reader to send a substitute to do the work. I take the view that there was evidence of a change in the control element relating to the meter reader relying on a substitute and it was open to the Appeals Officer to have come to a conclusion that there has been a change in the level of

control exercised in this regard and that the freedom of the meter reader in relation to the use of a substitute has been limited.

The Appeals Officer has also taken the view that the introduction of the data logger equipment has altered the level of control exercised by the ESB in relation to the meter readers working arrangements. The Appeals Officer noted the degree of control exercised and considered that the introduction of the data logger device together with the means through which recordings on that device are transmitted to the appellant increase the degree of control which the appellant exercised in fact over the functions of the meter readers. In my view it was open to the Appeals Officer to scrutinise the introduction of the data logging equipment and it does appear that this aspect was regarded by the Appeals Officer as a matter of considerable significance. The data logging equipment itself remains the property at all times of the ESB, any data obtained by the meter reader on the logging equipment is to be kept strictly confidential and not disclosed to any third party. The time period within which the information collected must be passed on to the ESB is a matter to be dictated solely by the ESB and the method of transmission by modem into a telephone line is also chosen by the ESB. It is also noted that the data logging equipment is now used by all meter readers engaged by the ESB both full time and those described as contract meter readers being the various individual respondents in this matter. In my view, there was evidence available to the Appeals Officer to enable her to draw the inference arrived at, having regard to the facts and circumstances surrounding the introduction and use of the data logger equipment, that the level of control exercised by the ESB had altered and was more representative of a master/servant relationship between the contract meter reader and the ESB.

It does appear that the Appeals Officer did carefully consider the overall picture and the significance of all the new facts which had emerged since this issue was last examined by an Appeals Officer.

I am satisfied that there are significant arguments to be made for and against the proposition that the individual respondent meter readers are employed pursuant to a contract of service. There are significant factual situations pertaining to the manner in which the contract meter reader carries out the prescribed duties which will tend to support the arguments for and against employment pursuant to a contract of service but as previously indicated the situation has probably always been finely balanced and I take the view that on the evidence available to her, the Appeals Officer was entitled to draw the inference that there was a change in the level of control that was exercised by the ESB over the individual respondent meter readers which entitled her to come to a conclusion that the individual meter readers were employed by the ESB pursuant to a contract of service.

In these circumstances I decline to set aside the decision as arrived at by the Appeals Officer and dismiss the application.

The Revenue Commissioners v O'Flynn Construction Co Ltd, John and Michael O'Flynn

High Court
Smyth J
25 April 2006

Case stated – income tax – advance corporation tax – Schedule F – general anti-avoidance provision – statutory interpretation – export sales relief – whether impugned transaction was a tax avoidance transaction pursuant to TCA 1997, s 811 – primary objective – business profits exclusion – misuse or abuse of relief exclusion

This was an appeal by way of case stated by the Appeal Commissioners at the request of the Revenue Commissioners. The question for determination was whether the impugned transaction was a tax avoidance transaction pursuant to s 811 of the Taxes Consolidation Act ('TCA') 1997.

Section 811 of TCA 1997 provides that, subject to two exclusions in sub-s (3), a transaction is a tax avoidance transaction where the Revenue Commissioners form the opinion that the transaction gives rise to a tax advantage and the transaction was not undertaken for purposes other than to give rise to a tax advantage. The first exclusion applies where a transaction was undertaken to realise profits in a business and not primarily to give rise to a tax advantage (the 'business profits exclusion'). The second exclusion arises where the transaction was undertaken to benefit from a relief and would not result in a misuse or abuse of that relief (the 'misuse or abuse of relief exclusion').

The first respondent was a company engaged in the construction business. The second and third respondents were shareholders in the first respondent. An unrelated company was engaged in the manufacture of goods for export and as a result had accumulated export sales relief ('ESR') reserves. The tax code relieved such reserves from corporation tax and dividends derived from such reserves were also relieved of a Schedule F income tax charge in the hands of the shareholder. The impugned transaction was designed to allow the second and third respondents access to the accumulated ESR reserves of the unrelated company. A series of steps were undertaken whereby the first respondent purchased the unrelated company's ESR reserves and ultimately paid tax-free dividends out of those reserves to the second and third respondents.

The Revenue Commissioners contended that the first respondent avoided the imposition of advance corporation tax on a distribution of its assets and the second and third named respondents avoided a Schedule F charge on the distribution. The respondents argued that, pursuant to s 811, the onus was on the Revenue Commissioners to prove that the impugned transaction was a tax avoidance transaction. The respondents also contended that the impugned transaction was a commercial transaction which created an enduring economic effect and the use of tax efficient structuring did not render it a tax avoidance transaction. It was also submitted that for s 811 to be operable there must be a charge to tax or a significant probability of a charge to tax which is then avoided.

The Appeal Commissioners concluded that the transaction was undertaken to obtain the benefit of ESR relief which resulted in a tax advantage but held that the misuse or abuse of relief exclusion applied and accordingly the transaction was not a tax avoidance transaction pursuant to TCA 1997, s 811.

Held by Smyth J in allowing the appeal:

i. In considering whether a tax avoidance transaction exists, regard should be had to objective considerations only. A taxpayer's motivation in entering into a transaction is irrelevant.

ii. Pursuant to the wording of s 811(1), a tax advantage arises where any 'potential or prospective charge or assessment' to tax is reduced, avoided or deferred.

iii. The Appeal Commissioners are obliged on the evidence to determine whether a tax avoidance transaction has taken place. The burden of proof is on the taxpayer to satisfy the Revenue Commissioners that he has availed of the business profits exclusion or that he has availed of a relief without misuse or abuse.

iv. In construing a word used in a statute, the court may look to the scheme and purpose of the statute or the relevant parts thereof.
McGrath v McDermott [1988] IR 258 and *Charles McCann Ltd v Ó Cualacháin (Inspector of Taxes)* III ITR 304 followed.

v. Section 811(3) specifically requires the Revenue Commissioners to have regard to the substance of the relevant transaction. Payment of ESR profits to a company not engaged in the manufacture of goods for export amounts, directly or indirectly, to a misuse of the relief having regard to the purposes for which such relief was enacted and to the nature of the relief afforded to those dividends. Accordingly, the impugned transaction is a tax avoidance transaction.

Legislation

Taxes Consolidation Act 1997, s 811 (formerly s 86 of Finance Act 1989)

Cases referred to in the judgment

Ashbourne Holdings Ltd v An Bord Pleanála [2003] 2 IR 114
Charles McCann Ltd v O'Culacháin (Inspector of Taxes) III ITR 304
Cronin (Inspector of Taxes) v Strand Dairy Limited III ITR 441
De Brun (Inspector of Taxes) v Kiernan (No 1) [1981] IR 117, III ITR 19
Furniss v Dawson [1984] STC 153
IRC v Duke of Westminster 19 TC 490
McCausland v Ministry of Commerce [1956] NILR 36
McGrath v McDermott III ITR 683
O'Sullivan v P Ltd III ITC 355, II ITR 464
Revenue Commissioners v Doorley [1933] IR 750, V ITR 539
WT Ramsay Ltd v IRC [1981] STC 174

The High Court – Smyth J

Smyth J, This is an appeal by way of case stated (the full text of which is set out in the appendix to this Judgment) from a decision of the Appeal Commissioners and the relevant questions of law in which the opinion of the Court is requested are set out at paragraph 13 (in the case of the Revenue Commissioners) and in paragraph 15 (in the case of the taxpayers) of the case stated dated 13 July 2005.

The Appeal Commissioners accepted that the transaction outlined in the notice of opinion issued on behalf of the Revenue Commissioners did not consider the transaction, as so defined, required any amendment (paragraph 9(ii) of the case stated). No evidence

was adduced at the appeal hearing by the taxpayers. The component steps of the transaction are not in issue in the case before the Court: the question is whether it is a tax avoidance transaction that is the subject of section 86 of the Finance Act, 1989.

The scheme may be briefly stated to be one whereby two companies, the Appellant company (O'Flynn Construction Company Limited) and another company, (O'Brien & O'Flynn Limited) was designed to allow each companies' shareholders to access the export sales relief reserves of a member of the Dairygold Group. Mitchelstown Export Company Limited, a member of the Dairygold Group, had accumulated export sales relief reserves in a number of subsidiaries. This meant that tax free dividends could be paid out of those reserves to individual shareholders. A structure involving a number of steps was designed and carried out so that these reserves were sold to an unconnected non-export sales relief company – O'Flynn Construction Limited – for cash consideration. Appendix 3 to the case stated clearly indicates that the total cost of the acquisition of the export sales relief (ESR) from the Dairygold Group was IR£ 117,668, which cost was shared equally between O'Brien & O'Flynn Ltd. And O'Flynn Construction Company Ltd. The total amount of the ESR reserves utilised was IR£1,200,000.After taking into account accountancy fees of IR£10,000, the shareholders in O'Brien and Flynn Ltd received tax free dividends of IR£590,000. After taking into account accountancy fees of IR£4,000, the shareholders of O'Flynn Construction Company Ltd – the individual taxpayers – received tax free dividends of IR£596,000. Again, which was paid by O'Flynn Construction Company Ltd to them as its shareholders.

In short, the effect of the scheme (which is not disputed by the taxpayers) was that the shareholders of a non-ESR company (O'Flynn Construction Company Ltd) ultimately received tax free, export sales relief dividends originally earned by an ESR company (Mitchelstown Export Company Limited) but funded by O'Flynn Construction Limited.

It was contended by the Revenue Commissioners that the taxpayers had entered into the scheme or arrangement for the purpose of extracting funds from the non-ESR company – O'Flynn Construction Ltd – in a manner which avoided a liability to Advance Corporation Tax (ACT) by the company and avoided income tax by Michael O'Flynn and John O'Flynn on receipt of the dividends funded by the said company. A 'tax advantage' was secured by the company in avoiding liability to ACT on a distribution of its assets to its members and a tax advantage was secured by Michael O'Flynn and John O'Flynn by the avoidance of a Schedule F charge on a distribution of funds by the company. The scheme involved three different phases, to wit:

1. The isolation within the Dairygold Group of ESR reserves of IR£1,200,000.
2. The utilization of IR£6,000,000 of the reserves by unconnected parties.
3. The utilization of the balance of the ESR reserves of £600,000 by Michael O'Flynn and John O'Flynn.

(Each phase is also detailed in Appendix 3 to the case stated and is found at paragraphs 1(a) and 3(m) of the Notices of Opinion).

By notices of 12 August 1997, a nominated officer of the Revenue Commissioners concluded that the transactions specified were each a tax avoidance transaction within the meaning of section 86 of the Finance Act 1989. It was contended by the Revenue Commissioners that various transactions of steps in the overall transaction have little or no commercial basis as identified at paragraph 6(ii) of the case stated and that the transaction which is caught by the general anti-avoidance provision of the Irish Tax Code, section 86 of the Finance Act 1989.

The Appeal Commissioners (at paragraph 9(x) of the case stated) stated that they were not satisfied that the transaction was undertaken or arranged with a view to the realisation of profits in the course of the business activities of the business.

Section 86 of the Finance Act 1989 (now section 811 of the Taxes Consolidation Act, 1997) provides specific anti-avoidance measures which are clearly intended to block particular schemes that are considered unacceptable by the legislature. The general anti-avoidance provisions are intended to counteract 'artificial schemes', ie transactions which have little or no commercial reality but are carried out primarily to create an artificial tax deduction or to avoid or reduce a tax charge.

Throughout the course of the hearing, I have had the benefit of elaborate detailed written submissions from both parties which were spoken to by Counsel for the parties engaged. It was common case that whether or not a tax avoidance transaction existed, such must be determined objectively. Accordingly the taxpayers' motivation in entering into the transaction is absolutely irrelevant. Mr McCann on behalf of the taxpayers submitted that under section 86, the onus of proof is on the Revenue and that it was for Mr Ó Laoghaire who determined whether the transaction is a tax avoidance transaction must prove the matter before the Appeal Commissioners. In my judgment, the Appeal Commissioners are the parties obligated on the evidence to come to a view as to whether a tax avoidance transaction has taken place. He submitted that for section 86 to apply, the primary purpose of the transaction (as defined), is determined on an objective basis, must have been a tax avoidance one and that the object here was a purely economic/business one, i.e. the transference of a sum of money in undistributed profits of the construction company to the directors of that company. The submission was that the receipt of cash by John and Michael O'Flynn in the amount of IR£600,000 was exclusively a commercial transaction which creates an enduring economic effect; the method whereby the cash was received was as a result of tax structuring.

Section 86 contains a number of definitions which are of importance to which I now refer. The expression 'transaction' is defined in very wide terms and includes any series of or combination of circumstances specifically referred to, whether entered into or arranged by one person or by two or more persons:

1. whether acting in concert or not, or
2. whether or not entered into or arranged wholly or partly outside the State, or
3. whether or not entered into arranged as part of a larger transaction or in conjunction with any other transaction or transactions (emphasis added).

Tax advantage means:

'(1) a reduction, avoidance or deferral of any charge or assessment to tax, including any potential or prospective charge or assessment, or

(2) a refund of or a repayment of an amount of tax or an increase in the amount of tax, refundable or otherwise, payable to a person including any potential or prospective amount so refundable or payable,

Arising out of, or by reason of, a transaction, including a transaction where another transaction would not have been undertaken or arranged to achieve the results, or any part of the results, achieved or intended to be achieved by the transaction.'

In my judgment the word 'potential' in (1) above means what it says, and I do accept the contention of the taxpayer that a charge must exist before the provisions of the section become operable.

Subsection 1(b) provides that:

> 'In subsections (2) and (3) (for the purposes of the hearing or rehearing under section 8 of an appeal made under subsection 7) for the purposes of the determination of a question of law arising on the statement of a case for the opinion of the High Court, the references to the Revenue Commissioners shall, subject to any necessary modifications, be construed as references to the Appeal Commissioners or to a Judge of the Circuit Court or, to the extent necessary, to a Judge of the High Court as appropriate.'

It is expressly provided for in subsection (2) of section 86 as follows:

> 'For the purposes of this section and subject to subsection (3), a transaction is a '**tax avoidance transaction**' if, having regard to any one or more of the following, that is to say:
>
> (a) the result of the transaction,
>
> (b) its use as a means of achieving those results, and
>
> (c) any other means by which the results or any part of the results could have been achieved, the Revenue Commissioners formed the opinion that:
>
> (1) it gives rise to, or but for this section, would give to a tax advantage, and
>
> (2) the transaction was not undertaken or arranged primarily for purposes other than to give rise to a tax advantage,
>
> and references in this section to the Revenue Commissioners forming an opinion that a transaction is a tax avoidance transaction shall be construed as references to them forming an opinion with regard to the transaction in accordance with the provisions of this subsection.'

The foregoing has to be considered on its own terms and not merely in the context of the provisions of subsection 3. Subsection 3 of section 86 provides as follows: 'without prejudice to the generality of the provisions of subsection (2), in forming an opinion in accordance with that subsection and subsection (4), as to whether or not the transaction is a tax avoidance transaction, the Revenue Commissioner shall not regard the transaction as being a tax avoidance transaction if they are satisfied that:

> '(A) (2) Notwithstanding that the purpose of the transaction could have been achieved by some other transaction which would have given rise to a greater amount of tax being payable by the person, the transaction:
>
> (1) was undertaken or arranged by a person with a view, directly or indirectly, to the realisation of profits in the course of the business activities of a business carried on by the person,
>
> (2) was not undertaken or arranged *primarily* to give rise to a tax advantage, or
>
> (B) the transaction was undertaken or arranged for the purpose of obtaining the benefit of any relief, allowance or other abatement, provided by any provision of the acts and that transaction would not result, directly or indirectly, in a misuse of the provision or an abuse of the provision having regard to the purposes for which it was provided:'

Before considering the proviso that follows, I note with particularity the expression 'without prejudice to the generality of subsection (2)', accordingly the provisions of subsection 2 are not limited by subsection 3. The decision in *Ashbourne Holdings Ltd v An Bord Pleanála & Anor* [2003] 2 IR 114 to which reference was made, is a decision arising under the Local Government Planning and Development Act 1963, section 26(1) and 26(2). Subsection (1) of the said Act provides in general terms the restrictions on the granting of planning permission, subsection (2) which provides that 'without prejudice to the generality of the foregoing section, certain other conditions may be attached.' However, there is a clear distinction in the instant case from that in Ashbourne Holdings in that the

words in the Planning Act to which I have referred are to the effect that 'insofar as' occur, such restriction is not imposed in the instant case before the Court. 'The purpose of' referred to in (B) from the citation earlier made must have been determined and this has been determined by the Appeal Commissioners, correctly in my view, on opinion. However, the subsection further provides as follows:

> 'Provided that, in forming an opinion as aforesaid ....'
>
> [ie in accordance with subsection 4]
>
> '....in relation to *any* transaction, the Revenue Commissioners shall have regard to
>
> (1) the form of that transaction,
>
> (2) the *substance* of that transaction (emphasis added),
>
> (3) the *substance* of any other transaction or transactions which that transaction may reasonably be regarded as being directly of indirectly related to or connected with (emphasis added),
>
> (4) the final outcome and result of that transaction and any combination of those other transactions which are so related or connected.'

I shall return to the expression 'the substance of the transaction' later in this judgment for a considerable number of submissions were made arising from the case of *Patrick McGrath & Others v McDermott* III ITR 683. Subsection 4 of section 86 provides that subject to the provisions of the section, the Revenue Commissioners with respect to any transaction may at any time form the opinion that the transaction is a tax avoidance transaction and, furthermore, subsection 5(A) provides that where, in the opinion of the Revenue Commissioners, a transaction is a tax avoidance transaction is formed, it becomes final or conclusive and it may, notwithstanding any other provisions of the Acts, make such adjustments and do all such acts as are just and reasonable. The expression in subsection 5(a): 'notwithstanding any other provisions of the Acts', in my judgment means that the legislature acknowledged the primacy of section 86 but enabled any other provisions of the Acts to be taken into account where appropriate. Furthermore, in paragraph (A), the Revenue Commissioners may re-characterise for tax purposes the nature of any payment or other amount. Furthermore, as provided for in paragraph (e)(ii) of subsection 5, the opinion of the Revenue Commissioners that a transaction is a tax avoidance transaction shall be final and conclusive is expressed thus:

> '(ii) as and when all appeals made under the said subsection (7) against any such matter or matters have been finally determined and none of the appeals has been so determined by an order directing that the opinion of the Revenue Commissioners to the effect that the transaction is a tax avoidance transaction is void.'

While it is true to say that tax benefit cannot be derived from re-characterisation, it is necessary, nonetheless, to return to the main plank of the contention of the taxpayers that the provisions of the section have to be viewed in the light of the *McGrath* decision. The first point to note concerning the *McGrath* case is that it considered different statutory provisions. Furthermore, Carroll J in the High Court allowed an appeal of the taxpayer that in determining whether a liability to tax arose from a transaction it was necessary to look not at the substance of the transactions or financial results but the actual legal effect of each transaction and the rights of the parties thereunder. She expressly determined that if the legislature had failed to legislate against a tax avoidance scheme, it was not the function of the Courts to intervene. This reference to the absence of tax avoidance legislation and looking at the substance of the transaction are in marked contrast to the facts of the instant

case. The decision of Carroll J was appealed to the Supreme Court who dismissed the appeal. The Respondent had no difficulty in accepting the dictum of Lord Tomlin in *IRC v Duke of Westminster* 19 TC 490, [1936] AC 1 that:

> 'Every man is entitled, if he can, to order his affairs so that the tax attaching under the appropriate Acts is less than it otherwise would be.'

It is clear in *McGrath's* case that the High Court refused to follow that approach of ignoring the legal position and regarding simply 'the substance of the matter.' A difficulty in the consideration of the Duke of Westminster's case in the case of *O'Sullivan v P Ltd* 3 ITC 355 by Kenny J was considered by Carroll J at first instance and she did so as follows:

> 'It seems to me, therefore, that the principle in the Duke of Westminster's case as approved by Kenny J can be stated thus; in determining whether liability to tax arises, the Court does not look at the substance or financial results of a transaction. It looks at the actual legal effect and legal rights of the parties according to legal ideas and concepts. The rights are not necessarily determined by the words used by the parties.

An exemption from tax is governed by the same considerations as a liability to tax. In this regard, liability to tax (see *Revenue Commissioners v Doorley* [1933] IR 750) where Kennedy CJ stated at page 766:

> 'It is clear that a tax is imposed by the Acts under consideration, then exemption from that tax must be given expressly and in clear and unambiguous terms, within the letter of the statute as interpreted with the assistance of the ordinary canons for the interpretation of statutes'
>
> This arises from the nature of the subject matter under consideration and is complimentary to what I have already said in this regard. The Court is not, by greater indulgence in delimiting the area of exemption, to enlarge their operation beyond what the statute clearly stated and beyond doubt and in express terms except for some good reason from the burden of tax thereby imposed generally on that description of subject matter. It is the imposition of, to the exemption from, that tax must be brought within the letter of the Taxing Act as interpreted by the established canons of construction so far as applicable.'

Carroll J considered in great detail the decisions of *WT Ramsay Ltd v IRC* [1981] STC 174, [1982] AC 300 and *Furniss v Dawson* [1984] STC 153, [1984] AC 474 and stated the issue in the McGrath case thus:

> '....whether the new development which emerged from the House of Lords decisions in *WT Ramsay v IRC* and *Furniss v Dawson* should be applied in this jurisdiction. It certainly represents a new approach.'

The learned Judge considered that the legislature as at the time of her determination had not enacted a general prohibition of tax avoidance schemes such as has been done in Australia and Canada and that 'if the legislature has failed to plug a hole' in advance or has failed to pass a law which strikes generally at tax avoidance schemes, then I am strongly of the opinion that this is not the function of the Court to intervene. The judge held that in the absence of a general power conferred by Statute to disallow tax avoidance schemes, the scheme involved in *McGrath* succeeded.

On the matter being appealed to the Supreme Court, Finlay CJ expressed himself in full agreement with the reasoning of the decisions of the learned trial Judge and in conclusion he noted:

> 'In some jurisdictions such as Canada and Australia, general statutory provisions against tax avoidance have been enacted, which in cases they would apply would, of course, affect the interpretation of specific provisions of taxation laws. In the absence of any such general

provisions in our law, there are no grounds for departing from the plain meaning of these sections.'

The provisions of the section which are at the centre of this action, followed upon the decision in *McGrath v McDermott*. In the course of his decision in *McGrath v McDermott*, Finlay CJ stated at [1988] IR 258 at 276 as follows:

> 'The function of the courts in interpreting a statute of the Oireachtas is, however, strictly confined to ascertaining the true meaning of each statutory provision, resorting in cases of doubt or ambiguity to a consideration of the purpose and intention of the legislature to be inferred from other provisions of the statute involved, or even other statutes expressed to be construed with it. The courts have not got a function to add to or delete from express statutory provisions so as to achieve objectives which to the courts appear desirable. In rare and limited circumstances, words or phrases may be implied into statutory provisions solely for the purposes of making them effective to achieve their expressly allowed objective.'

That is the approach I am taking to the provisions of section 86. In my judgment, the Appeal Commissioners were correct in their determination to the extent that they determined the appeal in favour of the Revenue Commissioners. In relation to that part of balance of the appealed decision, against which the Revenue have appealed, ie the misuse or abuse of the provisions of the Taxation Code, there has been a focus on the belief by the Appeal Commissioners that the decision of the Supreme Court (delivered by McCarthy J) in *Charles McCann Ltd v S Ó Culacháin, Inspector of Taxes* III ITR 304 was not of assistance. The case was concerned with Corporation Tax and the application or otherwise of export sales relief. In that case, Carroll J at first instance disallowed an appeal, but when referred to the Supreme Court, it determined that one must also, in aid of construction of a particular word used in a particular statute, look to the scheme and purpose as disclosed by the statute or the relevant parts thereof.

In the instant case, the company were a construction company and were not in any way carrying on business of either providing for or manufacturing or otherwise dealing in goods for export. The acquisition of the export sales relief in the manner earlier referred to in my judgment was considerably outside the ambit of their business. In considering the three rules referred to by Henchy J in *Inspector of Taxes v Kiernan (No 1)* [1981] IR 117 at 121, McCarthy J considered in particular the second rule, i.e. if a word or expression is used in a statute creating a penal or taxation liability, and there is looseness or ambiguity attaching to it, the word should be construed strictly so as to prevent a fresh imposition of liability from being created unfairly by use of oblique or slack language. Delivering the judgment of the Supreme Court, McCarthy J stated:

> 'Its application upon there being ambiguity or doubt as to the meaning of the word, and certainly there is that, since the decision in the High Court, Murphy J in construing somewhat like legislation, FA 1980 s 41(2) (as amended by FA 1982 s 26) and Sch 2 thereof) in *M Cronin (Inspector of Taxes) v Strand Dairy Limited* unreported judgement delivered 18th December 1985, having adverted to the judgment of Carroll J in that case and that of Lord McDermott LCJ in *McCausland v Ministry of Commerce* [1956] NILR 36 expressed his own view as follows:
>
> > 'It seems to me, therefore, that one must look at the goods alleged to have been manufactured to consider what they are, how they appear, what qualities they possess, what values attach to them. One then looks at the process and seeks to identify to what extent the process conferred on the goods the characteristics which they are found to possess.

> It is obvious, as indeed Lord McDermott pointed out (at page 43) that the question is to a large extent one of degree. Nobody would doubt that well made and fully finished furniture would constitute manufactured goods but it is unlikely that the ordinary man would accept that the trunk of a tree which had been felled and provided a convenient seat constituted a manufactured article.'

> 'I agree with the approach as so stated subject to the qualification that one must also, in aid of construction of the particular word as used in the statute, look to the scheme and purpose as disclosed by the statute or the relevant part thereof.'

McCarthy J further stated as follows:

> 'The scheme and purpose of the relevant part of the statute appear to me to be the very context within which the word is used and the requirements of which must be examined in order to construe it. It is manifest that Part IV of the Act of 1976 was, by tax incentives, to encourage the creation of employment within the State and the promotion of exports, naturally outside the State, objectives of proper, social and economic kind which the State would be bound to encourage. Employment is created by labour intensive processes and exports by the creation of saleable goods. The operation described in the case stated clearly comes within both categories, in my judgement. It is then a matter of degree, itself a question of law, as to whether or not what the company has done to the raw material makes it goods from the definition in section 84.'

The export sales relief purchased in the instant case was relief granted and intended by the legislature for a particular purpose and not as a commercially available product, as occurred in the instant case. *The Revenue Commissioners v Doorley* earlier referred to establishes that the taxpayer seeking to avail of an exemption from tax must show that the exemption is given in clear and unambiguous terms. In short, the onus of proof is on the taxpayer to show that the exemption applies. In a section 86 context, it was submitted that the onus of proof similarly falls on taxpayers seeking to establish that they have availed of relief 'without misuse or abuse' and they must do so having regard to the express wording of section 86(3)(b) and *satisfy* the Revenue Commissioners that they are entitled to avail of the 'relief without misuse or abuse' exclusion. The same principle applies as applies to a taxpayer seeking to avail of the business profits exclusion.

Under the 'relief without misuse or abuse' exemption, a transaction is not regarded as a tax avoidance transaction if the Revenue Commissioners are satisfied that:

> '(a) the transaction was undertaken or arranged to obtain the benefit of any relief, allowance or other abatement from tax available under any provision of the Taxes Acts;
>
> (b) the same transaction does not directly or indirectly result in a misuse or abuse of the relief allowance or abatement having regard to the purposes for which that relief, allowance or abatement was intended.'

As in the case of Business Profits Exclusion, the onus in on the taxpayer to establish the matters necessary to *satisfy* the Revenue Commissioners (or, on appeal, the Appeal Commissioners or the Court, as the case may be). Although the terms 'misuse' and 'abuse' are not defined, there are some comments of the Supreme Court of Canada in the recent case of *Canada Trustco Mortgage Company v Canada* [2005] SCC 54 at paragraph 60 which are of assistance wherein it is stated as follows:

> 'Abuse of tax avoidance may be found where the relationships and transactions as expressed in the relevant documentation lack a proper basis relative to the object, spirit or purpose of the provisions that are purported to confer the tax benefit, or where they are wholly dissimilar to the relationships contemplated by the provisions.'

In my judgement, the transaction the subject of these proceedings – whereby export sales relieved reserves in the Dairygold Group were transferred to a company that was not engaged in the manufacture of goods for export to enable fully tax relieved dividends to be paid to the shareholders of the construction company, it is completely at odds with the purpose for which the export sales relief was provided.

The Revenue Commissioners (by their nominated officer) in reaching an opinion do so on the basis of the documentation before them and, as in this case, they have to do so in the absence of any other evidence. An Inspector may ask for explanations and may get explanations or may not get explanations, in which case the officer may have to simply, on an objective analysis of documents and their surrounding circumstances, in order to decide whether or not in his opinion there is a tax avoidance transaction. On the appeal, the taxpayer has the option and right to give evidence in support of the case that he is making. In the absence of such evidence, it is necessary to infer, solely from objective considerations, for what purpose the transaction has been undertaken or arranged. An evaluation of such evidence is necessary for the determination as to whether the transaction is a tax avoidance transaction. Section 86(2) refers to the result of the transaction, its use as a means of achieving those results and any other means by which the results could have been achieved, all of which are objective results-based criteria. In my judgment, there is more than a reasonable basis for considering that the transaction not undertaken or arranged primarily for non-tax purposes, in which event the onus rests on the taxpayer to establish what the primary was other than to give rise to tax advantage. Considerable time was devoted by Counsel to a consideration of a range of decisions made in other jurisdictions. In my judgment, such were of interest and general assistance but were no substitute for the provisions of the Statute and, in particular, for the express wording of section 86(3)(b) where the onus is on the taxpayer to ensure that the Court is satisfied that the transaction would not result in the misuse or abuse of any provision of the acts granting relief, allowance or other abatement having regard to the purposes for which the provision was enacted. On the authority of *Doorley's* case, the onus of proof is on the taxpayers to establish that they have availed of a relief 'without misuse or abuse' and to satisfy the Revenue Commissioners that they are entitled to such 'relief without misuse or abuse' and fall within the exclusion. The same principle applies to a taxpayer seeking to avail of the business profits. There is an undoubted tax advantage in the instant case; no issue is taken that the actual export sales relieved profits of Mitchelstown Export Co. Ltd which were distributed in this case were derived from anything other than bona fida export sales or that those profits had been improperly calculated, accordingly there was o real dispute concerning what the Appeal Commissioners determined in paragraph 9 (xxii) that is the first component of the export sales relief scheme. However, I am unable to accept the determination of the Appeal Commissioners that the scheme and purpose disclosed by the Statute of the export sales relief attributable to or derived from manufacture can be equated to or embraced by what was essentially a building or construction company. Whatever argument might be advanced in respect of a company that carried on business purely intended to be embraced by the export sales relief provisions, such do not exist in the instant case. In my judgment, payment of the export sales relieved profits in the present case does amount if not directly, certainly indirectly, to a misuse of the relief having regard to the purposes for which such relief was enacted and to the nature of the relief afforded to those dividends. The Appeal Commissioners concluded at paragraph 9(xxix) of the case stated as follows:

> 'To conclude that there had been a misuse of the export sales relief provisions would, in our view, be to ignore the statement of the law laid down in *McGrath v McDermott*. While it is necessary to look at the purpose for which section 86 was enacted, in our opinion section 86, in itself, cannot be used to abandon the clear principles of statutory construction laid out in this case. These principles of statutory interpretation set out in McGrath – v- McDermott prohibit us from adopting such a purposive approach.'

In my judgment, that final determination is to disregard the provisions of section 86 and a particular proviso of subsection 3 which specifically indicates that the Revenue Commissioners shall have regard to the substance of the transaction. Prior to the introduction of that provision in section 86, the determination of ignoring a purposive approach would be correct.

In my judgment, the answer to question 13 of the case stated is no. In my judgment, the transaction is a tax avoidance transaction by virtue of section 86(3)(b) of the Tax Act 1989 on the ground that the transaction did result, directly or indirectly, in a misuse of the ESR provisions having regard to the purpose/s for which they were enacted. In regard to the questions raised in paragraph 15 of the case stated by the taxpayer, I am satisfied that the Appeal Commissioners were correct in holding that the transaction gave rise to a tax advantage for O'Flynn Construction Limited and likewise gave rise to a tax advantage for John O'Flynn and Michael O'Flynn and furthermore that the transaction was not undertaken or arranged primarily for purposes other than to give rise to a tax advantage. Further, that the transaction was arranged with a view to the realisation of the profits in the course of the business activities of O'Flynn Construction Limited pursuant to section 86(3)(a) of the Finance Act 1989.

Case stated

Case stated pursuant to section 941 Taxes Consolidation Act 1997 as adopted by section 811(8) Taxes Consolidation Act 1997 by John O'Callaghan and Ronan Kelly, Appeal Commissioners.

1. This matter came before us for hearing at the Irish Life House, South Mall, Cork on 18 May, 5 July, 23 and 24 November 1999 pursuant to appeals submitted by O'Flynn Construction Co Ltd, Michael O'Flynn and John O'Flynn (hereinafter referred to collectively as 'the taxpayers') under section 86(7) Finance Act 1989 against notices of opinion issued on 12 August 1997 by Mr PC Ó Laoghaire, and officer of the Revenue Commissioners nominated under the provisions of s 86(12) Finance Act 1989.

2. The question for determination was whether section 86 Finance Act 1989 applied to the transaction entered into by the taxpayers and thus whether it was a tax avoidance transaction thereby securing a tax advantage. The terms 'transaction', 'tax avoidance transaction' and 'tax advantage' were defined in section 86(1) and (2) Finance Act 1989.

3. Evidence

The following person gave evidence before us:
Mr Paul Walsh, Inspector of Taxes.

4. Facts proved or admitted

(A) The following facts were submitted as proved:

(i) Mr Padraig Ó Laoghaire issued Notices of Opinion under section 86(6) Finance Act 1989 to O'Flynn Construction Company Limited, John O'Flynn and Michael O'Flynn (Exhibit 1). It was found as a fact that each of

the steps set out at paragraphs 1A to 3M inclusive of the said Notices had taken place as set out in the said Notices.

(ii) The issued share capital of O'Flynn Construction was, at all relevant times, held equally by Mr John O'Flynn, Pinewood, Kilcrea, Ovens, Co Cork and Mr Michael O'Flynn, Kilcrea, Ovens, Co. Cork.

(iii) O'Flynn Construction Company Limited never paid a dividend and there was no evidence or indication that it ever had the intention of doing so.

(iv) In mid 1995 and Inspector carried out Revenue audits of the taxpayers. These audits were carried out by Cork Tax District in conjunction with the Anti-Avoidance Unit of the Office of the Chief Inspector of Taxes. Mr Padraig C Ó Laoghaire, the nominated officer who formed the Opinions, had no involvement with these audits.

(B) In drafting this Case Stated we have had several meetings with the parties and a considerable amount of correspondence has been involved. We have been pressed by agents for the taxpayer to included as specific findings of fact various matters such as that the trade of Mitchelstown Export Company Ltd consisted of the manufacture and export of goods. We did not take evidence upon these matters, although they may have been referred to indirectly. However, we did point out, and we maintain, that implicit in the assessment raised under section 86 Finance Act, 1989, is the assumption that the 'scheme' which is the subject of the Notice of Opinion is effective in achieving a 'tax advantage' as defined by the section. We therefore held that these matters have been accepted by the Revenue Commissioners and that, in the absence of any specific provisions of the tax code, there was no need for us to refer specifically to procedural issues in our findings of fact in this case except insofar as we decide that they had relevance to the argument in relation to section 86.

5. Documents

The following documentary evidence was admitted or proved:

(i) Copies of the Notices of Opinion which issued under s 86(6) Finance Act 1989 are annexed hereto as Exhibit 1 and form part of the Case Stated

(ii) Accounts and tax computations for O'Flynn Construction Co Ltd for the accounting period ended 31st March 1992. These documents are annexed hereto as Exhibit 2 and form part of the Case Stated.

(iii) A schedule of documentation made available to the Revenue Commissioners in respect of the details of the transaction set out in the Notices of Opinion is attached hereto as Exhibit 3 and forms part of the Case Stated.

6. Revenue Submissions

The Revenue Commissioners made the following contentions. These contentions are elaborated upon in the Revenue Commissioners' submission to the Appeal Commissioners which are attached to this Case Stated as Exhibit 4.

(i) The taxpayers had entered into a scheme or arrangement the purpose of which was the extraction of funds from O'Flynn Construction Co Ltd in a manner which avoided a liability to Advance Corporation Tax by the company and the avoidance of income tax by Michael O'Flynn and John O'Flynn on the receipt of dividends funded by the said company. A tax advantage was secured by O'Flynn Construction Co Ltd in avoiding a liability to Advance Corporation Tax on a

distribution of its assets to its members and a tax advantage was secured by Michael O'Flynn and John O'Flynn by the avoidance of a Schedule F charge on a distribution funded by O'Flynn Construction Co. Ltd.

On the 27th January 1992 Michael O'Flynn and John O'Flynn each received income of 298,000 in the form of tax-free Export Sales Relieved (ESR) dividends. The dividends were funded by the write-off of a loan of £650,000 by their company O'Flynn Construction Co Ltd at the same time, resulting in a depletion of the assets of the company. The dividends were received by Michael O'Flynn and John O'Flynn as a result of a scheme or arrangement, not undertaken to legitimately avail of tax reliefs but involving an abuse and misuse of law. Through the use of this scheme:

(a) O'Flynn Construction Co Ltd did not suffer any charge to Advance Corporation Tax under s 38 Finance Act 1983 (s 159 of the Taxes Consolidation Act 1997) in paying a dividend to Michael O'Flynn and John O'Flynn, and

(b) Michael O'Flynn and John O'Flynn did not suffer any charge to Income Tax (Schedule F) under s 83 Corporation Tax Act 1976 (s 20 of the Taxes Consolidation Act 1997) on the receipt of dividends from their company O'Flynn Construction Co. Ltd.

The scheme circumvented the provisions of:

(I) Section 84 of the Corporation Tax Act 1976 (s 130(2) Taxes Consolidation Act 1997)

(II) Section 84(3) of the Corporation Tax Act 1976 (s 130(3) Taxes Consolidation Act 1997) which treats as distributions any distribution our of assets of a company in respect of shares in the company, and the amount or value of any benefit received where assets are transferred to members for less than market value, respectively,

(III) Section 39 of the Finance Act 1983 (s 159 Taxes Consolidation Act 1997) which charges payers of distributions to Advance Corporation Tax, and

(IV) Section 83 of the Corporation Tax Act 1976 (s 159(1) Taxes Consolidation Act 1997) which charges distributions to Income Tax

In essence, the capital contribution made by O'Flynn Construction Co. Ltd. and the write-off of a large proportion of that contribution resulted in the assets of O'Flynn Construction Co. Ltd. being depleted. The case extracted from the company was ultimately received by its shareholders in the guise of ESR dividends.

(ii) The scheme or arrangement as set out in paragraphs IA to 3M in the Notices of Opinion which issued to the taxpayers contained three distinct phases. The first phase, set out in paragraph 1 of the notices, related to the isolation within the Dairygold group of ESR reserves of £1,200,000. The second phase, set out in paragraph 2 of the notices, related to the utilisation of £600,000 of the reserves by unconnected persons and the third phase, set out in paragraph 3 of the notices related to the utilisation of the balance of the ESR reserves of £600,000 by Michael O'Flynn and John O'Flynn.

(iii) The following transactions had little or no commercial basis:

(a) The subscription by Dalemount Investments Ltd. and Gatesvale Investments Ltd on 10 December 1991 for share capital in

Mitchelstown Export Company Ltd. The share capital was issued at a premium of £99 per share and on 18 December 1991 the shares were redeemed at par, each company thereby suffering a loss of £658,845.

(b) The payment of a dividend of £1,200,000 by Mitchelstown Export Company Ltd to Twingrove Investments Ltd on 16 December 1991 following the subscription for share capital on 10 December 1991,

(c) The write-off by O'Flynn Construction Co. Ltd in the accounts for the period ended 31 March 1992 of £650,000 relating to its investment in Dalemount Investments Ltd.

(iv) In forming an opinion as to whether a transaction falls to be treated as a tax avoidance transaction the Appeal Commissioners are required to have regard to:

(a) the form of that transaction

(b) the substance of the transaction

(c) the substance of any other transaction or transactions which that transaction may reasonably be regarded as being directly or directly related to or connected with, or

(d) the final outcome and result of that transaction and any combination of those other transactions which are so related or connected (S 86(3) Finance Act, 1989)

The substance of the transaction was that the profits of O'Flynn Construction Co Ltd were used to fund an ESR dividend payment to its shareholders. The transaction took the form of a complicated and unusual series of steps including the write off of capital contribution and the final outcome and the result was that the reserves of O'Flynn Construction Co. Ltd had been depleted to the benefit of its shareholders.

(v) In considering whether a transaction should fall to be treated as a tax avoidance transaction the provisions of s 86(3)(a) Finance Act 1989 specify that the Appeal Commissioners shall not regard a transaction as being a tax avoidance transaction if they are satisfied that –

'(a) notwithstanding that the purpose or purposes of the transaction could have been achieved by some other transaction which would have given rise to a greater amount of tax being payable by the person, the transaction

(i) was undertaken or arranged by a person with a view, directly or indirectly, to the realisation of profits in the course of the business activities of a business carried on by the person, and

(ii) was not undertaken or arranged primarily to give rise to a tax advantage

or

(b) the transaction was undertaken or arranged for the purpose of obtaining the benefits of any relief, allowance or other abatement provided by the provision of the Acts and that the transaction would not result directly or indirectly in a misuse of the provisions or an abuse of the provisions having regard to the purposes for which it was provided'.

It was submitted on behalf of the Revenue Commissioners that the transaction outlined in the Notices of Opinion was not carried out with a view to the realisation of profits in the course of the business activities of a business. A business is defined in subsection (I) as 'any trade, profession or vocation'. The activities identified in the Notice are not trading activities

with a view to the realisation of profits. The activities, in fact, resulted in substantial losses having been incurred by O'Flynn Construction Co Ltd, Dalemount Investments Ltd and Gatesvale Investments Ltd. In addition, it was submitted that the transaction was undertaken primarily to give rise to a tax advantage. There was no evidence that the purpose of the transaction was to realise profits or that there was any other commercial motive or purpose for the transaction.

In relation to the provision of s 86(3)(b) it was submitted that the transaction identified in the Notices of Opinion resulted in a misuse or, in the alternative, an abuse of the ESR provisions having regard to the purposes for which it was provided. In determining whether there had been an abuse or misuse the Appeal Commissioners are required by the provisions of s 6(3) Finance Act 1989 to have regard to the form, substance and final outcome of the transaction.

The scheme and purpose of the ESR provisions was to encourage investment in the manufacture within the State of goods for export by relieving from Corporation Tax the profits arising from that trade (See McCarthy J in *McCann v Ó Culacháin*). In addition, it was provided that on a distribution to shareholders these profits would be fully relieved in the hands of shareholders. It was submitted on behalf of the Revenue Commissioners that neither Michael O'Flynn nor John O'Flynn nor O'Flynn Construction Co Ltd had invested monies for the purpose of funding the manufacture within the State of goods for export, and the money paid by way of dividend to Michael O'Flynn and John O'Flynn were not the profits of Mitchelstown Export Company Ltd per se but the profits of O'Flynn Construction Co Ltd As the profits of O'Flynn Construction Co Ltd did not qualify for export sales relief there has an abuse, or in the alternative, a misuse of the ESR provisions where these profits qualified for export sales relief.

It was further submitted that the provision of s 54 Finance Act 1974 were introduced to curb a particular abuse of the ESR provisions. The Oireachtas, in seeking to curb an abuse can introduce specific legislation to deal with that abuse. However, the introduction in 1989 of general anti-avoidance legislation in s 86 Finance Act 1989 provides that all abuses or misuses of relief are now subject to the restrictions set out in these provisions.

The form of the transaction was an important feature and itself indicated that the transaction was far from being a normal or usual use of the ESR provisions. The fact that the complicated and unusual form of the transaction contrasted with the substance and net effect or result achieved also indicated abuse, or, at the least misuse.

(vi) The taxpayers had entered into a transaction which was a tax avoidance transaction and which secured a tax advantage to the taxpayers as set out in the Notices of Opinion. The scheme adopted resulted in the profits of O'Flynn Construction Co Ltd being distributed to Michael O'Flynn and John O'Flynn in the guise of ESR dividends. Arising from the scheme, O'Flynn Construction Co. Ltd had avoided a liability to Advance Corporation Tax and Michael O'Flynn and John O'Flynn had received dividends which were fully relieved from income tax.

Accordingly, it was submitted that:

(a) the transaction specified in the Notice of Opinion was a tax avoidance transaction,

(b) the amount of the tax advantage specified in the Notice of Opinion which would be withdrawn from or denied to the taxpayers was correct.

(c) the tax consequences specified in the Notice of Opinion were just and reasonable in order to withdraw or to deny the tax advantage specified in the Notice of Opinion.

7. Taxpayers Submissions

The taxpayers made the following submissions. These contentions are elaborated upon in the taxpayers' written Submissions to the Appeal Commissioners which are attached to and form part of the Case Stated at Exhibit 5.

(i) The onus is on the Revenue Commissioners to prove that the procedures outlined in the section 86 Opinions are 'tax avoidance transactions' within the meaning of the section. The Authorised Officer formed the Opinion that the Taxpayers were involved in 'tax avoidance transactions'. The onus is therefore on the Revenue Commissioners to prove that the Opinions are correct. There is no onus on the Taxpayers to prove that the Revenue Commissioners were not correct.

(ii) In relation to O'Flynn Construction Company Ltd, the Opinion is void because the Revenue Commissioners have not taken into account the mandatory offset of Advance Corporation Tax against mainstream Corporation Tax. Advance Corporation Tax is not referred to at all in the Opinion issued to the company. The reason why Advance Corporation Tax was not referred to in the Opinion was that the Revenue Commissioners misconstrued the relevant legislation in that they erroneously believed that the set-off of Advance Corporation Tax against mainstream Corporation Tax was elective as opposed to a mandatory statutory procedure.

The Opinion which issued to O'Flynn Construction Ltd states that the 'tax advantage' accruing to the company is in the amount of £189,666 and describes that amount as 'being advance corporation tax attributable to a distribution of £596,000 for the accounting period ending 31 March 1992'. It is submitted that the definition of 'tax advantage' in section 86(1) means a real and actual reduction in taxation, not an illusory one. The Opinion does not advert at all to the offset of Advance Corporation Tax against mainstream Corporation Tax. Under section 39 Finance Act, 1983, this set-off is mandatory. Section 39 sets out the rules which apply to the off-set of Advance Corporation Tax. Any unutilised Advance Corporation Tax in an accounting period may, by election within two years, be carried back against mainstream corporation tax of the previous accounting period. Any remaining surplus Advance Corporation Tax must be carried forward against mainstream Corporation Tax of subsequent years. This carry forward is not by way of an election but rather is a mandatory statutory procedure.

It is submitted by the Taxpayers that this failure to deal with Advance Corporation Tax is a fatal flaw in the Opinion and means that the Opinion is void. Section 86 is about the collection of real tax. Evidence was given before the Appeal Commissioners on behalf of the Appellant that if the Appeal Commissioners

upheld the Opinion issued to O'Flynn Construction Company Ltd no tax would become payable by the company.

Under section 86(2) Finance Act, 1989, a transaction will only fall within the definition of a 'tax avoidance transaction' if, having regard to the three criteria set out in that sub-section, the transaction gives rise to a 'tax advantage' and was not undertaken or arranged primarily for purposes other than to give rise to a 'tax advantage'. Subsection (2) sets out the only criteria which can be taken into account when issuing an Opinion. These criteria must be applied objectively. It is submitted by the Taxpayers that it is impossible to conclude on an objective basis that O'Flynn Construction Company Ltd derived a 'tax advantage' from the transaction or that the primary purpose of the transaction was the avoidance of tax. Aside from the fact that O'Flynn Construction Company Ltd did not actually pay a dividend and that there is no evidence to suggest that the company ever intended to pay a dividend, even if a dividend had been declared, the Advance Corporation Tax would have been off-set against mainstream Corporation Tax with the result that, as the Revenue Commissioners witness stated in evidence, no net tax would become payable by the company.

(iii) The Revenue Commissioners did not produce Mr Padraig C Ó Laoghaire, the Authorised Officer who formed the Opinions, to give evidence before the Appeal Commissioners. A different Inspector of Taxes, who was not an Authorised Officer and who did not issue the Opinions gave evidence instead. It is submitted that in the absence of evidence from Mr Ó Laoghaire the Appellants' case is void. It is submitted that the only person who can give evidence is Mr Ó Laoghaire. He, and he alone, is the person who formed the Opinion that the transaction was a tax avoidance transaction.

For instance, one of the Taxpayers' submissions is that the Opinion issued to O'Flynn Construction Company Ltd is void because the mandatory offset of Advance Corporation Tax against mainstream Corporation Tax was not taken into account in the Opinion. The only person who can give an explanation (if there is one) as to how a 'tax advantage' arose to O'Flynn Construction Company Ltd when, as the other Inspector admitted in evidence, the upholding of the Opinion would not give rise to any net tax liability is Mr Ó Laoghaire. He, and he alone, formed the Opinion that a *'tax advantage'* arose in these circumstances.

(iv) Section 86 Finance Act, 1989 has not changed the approach to the interpretation of tax legislation. The analytical, non-interventionalist approach enunciated in *Revenue Commissioners v Doorley* [1933] IR 750, *Inspector of Taxes v Kiernan* [1982] 1 ILRM, and reaffirmed in *McGrath v McDermott* III ITR 539 continues to apply. Section 86 is to be interpreted in the same manner as every other provision of the tax code.

(v) Section 86 does not contain the words: '*notwithstanding any other provision of this Act*'. These, or word to similar effect, are used frequently elsewhere in the tax code. This indicates that section 86 has no particular priority over other taxing sections. Rather, taxing sections containing those words prevail over section 86.

(vi) For a tax advantage to occur in relation to O'Flynn Construction Company Ltd there must be a pre-existing liability to tax. No such liability to tax existed here. There must be some *'standard'* against which the alleged tax avoidance is measured. In this case, no such standard exists. O'Flynn Construction Company

Ltd did not and there is no evidence to suggest it ever contemplated paying a dividend. In effect, the Opinion withdraws from the company an alleged tax advantage in respect of a tax liability which never existed in the first place.

(vii) The '*tax avoidance transaction*' as determined by the nominated Inspector cannot be extended by either the Inspector, the Appeal Commissioners or any appellate Court to create a liability which would not otherwise arise within text of the initially defined '*transaction*'. It is not the Appeal Commissioners' role to extend the original assessment or determination beyond its original scope. Under subsection (8) of section 86, the Appeal Commissioners' role in relation to appeals against Opinions issued under section 86 is no different. Further, a proper analysis of subsection (9) of section 86 leads to the conclusion that the Appeal Commissioners cannot extend the '*transaction*'. Once the '*transaction*' has been defined by the Inspector, it is against that transaction only that the appeal lies.

Section 86(9)(a)(i)(II) allows the Appeal Commissioners to make such additions to the '*transaction*' as they consider necessary. It is submitted that subsection 9(a) allows the Appeal Commissioners to add to the transaction, but only to the extent that this benefits the taxpayer.

(viii) The nominated Inspector cannot amend his Opinion during the appeal process. Aside from the inherent unfairness which would result if the Inspector could continually amend his Opinion during the appeal process, administrative absurdities would be produced.

(ix) Subsection 2 of section 86 sets out the only criteria to be applied (and these criteria must be applied objectively) in determining whether a '*tax avoidance transaction*' exists. For a '*tax avoidance transaction*' to exist, the nominated Inspector must objectively reach the conclusion that the transaction was not undertaken or arranged primarily other than to give rise to a '*tax advantage*'.

The procedures in this case were not carried out primarily for the purposes of avoiding tax. Firstly, there was not tax to avoid. Secondly, real commercial effects resulted and that was the primary purpose here.

(x) If it is held that the opinions are valid in the context of sub-section (2) of section 86, then it is necessary to validate the opinions against the criteria set down in sub-sections 3(a) and (b) of section 86.

Under section 86(3)(a) a transaction is not a tax avoidance transaction if it was not undertaken or arranged primarily to give rise to a tax advantage and it was undertaken or arranged with a view to directly or indirectly to the realisation of profits in the course of a business. Regarding the former test, the procedures created an enduring economic effect. The fact that tax did not become payable on that cash did not confer on the transaction tax avoidance as its primary purpose. Regarding the latter test, O'Flynn Construction Company Ltd was carrying on a business. The profits of that business enure for the benefit of the shareholders. Any cash they receive ultimately relates to those business activities. The Taxpayers are within section 86(3)(a) and the opinions are therefore void.

(xi) Subsection 3(b) of section 86 provides an exception to subsection (2) in respect of transactions which would not result in an abuse or misuse of the relevant relieving provisions. The intention of any legislative provision must be derived from the words actually used. If a taxpayer has satisfied the detailed statutory provisions, as

has occurred in this case, then at a minimum he must be deemed to have satisfied the perceived purpose of the legislation.

The Legislature was careful to ensure that the tax attributes of an ESR sourced dividend retained their characteristic at all stages right through to the ultimate recipients of the dividend. This policy was a deliberate and considered aspect of the legislation which was carried on continuously throughout the 36 year period of the ESR legislation was in existence. For example, section 56 Finance Act, 1958 amended a flaw in section 15 Finance (Miscellaneous Provisions) Act, 1956. Section 15 limited the tax attributes of ESR dividends to the exporting companies within a chain of companies. The amendment ensured that the tax characteristics of ESR dividends were retained no matter what number of companies through which the dividend flowed.

Further, the use of ESR dividends became an instrument of economic policy when promoted by the State in connection with 'Section 84 loans'. This promotion resulted in the conversion of otherwise taxable interest in the hands of a bank into tax free distributions. The tax attributes of ESR dividends also extended to various double taxation treaties negotiated by the State. The State ensured that recipients of dividends out of ESR relieved profits resident in Japan, Norway, Germany, etc. would benefit from export sales relief in respect of those dividends.

For over thirty years the legislature provided a particular way of taxing dividends ultimately sourced from ESR profits. It cannot therefore be said that a taxpayer who arranged his affairs in a way that the legislature deliberately made the most attractive can be deemed to be in some vague and undefined way not acting in conformity with the object and spirit of the legislation. A taxpayer is entitled to create a situation by entry into procedures which will attract the tax consequences for which the legislature has made specific provision. The mere fact that the taxpayer may have organised the various transactions and entered into them in order to produce a beneficial tax result does not necessarily mean that the transaction falls within section 86.

(xii) There is nothing in the tax code which provides that all payments, of whatever nature, out of a company must be taxable. There is legislation on the definition of 'distributions' and if a particular payment falls within such a definition it is taxed as such. Section 88 Finance Act, 1989 introduced legislations in relation to what is described as 'schemes to avoid liability to tax under Schedule F'. Nowhere in the legislation is there any indication that payments out of a company which are not taxed under Schedule F as distributions or fall within section 88 are to be taxed in any particular way or are liable to taxation at all. There can therefore be no presumption that the legislation even intended that all payments of whatever nature from a company to its shareholders directly or indirectly are liable to taxation. Absent the existence of such a statutory intention no question can even arise as to its misuse or abuse.

8. Cases

The following cases were referred to in the course of the hearing:

W T Ramsay Ltd v IRC [1981] STC 174
Furniss v Dawson 55 TC 324
Craven v White [1988] STC 476
Brebner v CIR 43 TC 705

CIR v Parker 43 TC 396
CIR v Challenge Corp [1986] STC 548
Ashton v IRC [1975] STC 471
FCT v Peabody 123 ALR 451
FCT v Spotless Services Ltd 141 ALR 92
Cridland v FCT 77 ACT 4538
WP Keighery Pty Ltd v The Queen [1984] CT 294
Stubart Investments Ltd v The Queen 1997 DTC 111
McNichol et al v The Queen 1997 DTC 111
The Revenue Commissioners v Doorley [1933] IR 750, V ITR 539
Inspector of Taxes v Kiernan [1982] ILRM 13
Charles S McCann Ltd v O'Culachain III ITR 304
Calcul International Ltd v The Appeal Commissioners III ITR 577
McGrath v McDermott III ITR 683

9 Decision

Having adjourned the matter for consideration we gave out decision on 27 April 2000 in the following terms:-

(i) We decided that the role of the Appeal Commissioners under section 86 was not to review the opinion of the Revenue Commissioners but to form our own opinion on the basis of the evidence and the facts before us and on the basis on the evidence and facts to determine, on the balance of probabilities, whether the section applies. We accepted that the test to be met in construing the legislation was an objective test.

(ii) We accepted the 'transaction' as outlined in the Notice of Opinion issued on behalf of the Revenue Commissioners and we considered that the transaction as do defined did not require any amendment.

(iii) In order to determine whether the transaction was a tax avoidance transaction, we were required, by the provisions of s 86(2) Finance Act 1989, to establish whether the transaction gave rise to a tax advantage. These provisions provide that if having regard to one or more of the following:

(a) the results of the transaction
(b) its use as a means of achieving those results and
(c) any other means by which the results or any part of the results could have been achieved

[We] form the opinion that:

(i) [the transaction] gives rise to ... a tax advantage, and
(ii) the transaction was not undertaken or arranged primarily for purposes other than to give rise to a tax advantage

then the transaction shall be a tax avoidance transaction (subject to subsection (3) see below)

(iv) Regarding (a), '*The results of the transaction*', we concluded that the critical features of the transaction were that the assets of the company had been depleted and its shareholders had been enriched as a result of that depletion. Further, this event occurred without any incidence of tax either upon the company or upon the shareholders.

(v) Regarding (c), 'any other means by which the results or any part of the results could have been achieved', we considered that by far the most analogous 'other

means' was a dividend paid by the company. The reasons for this conclusion were that there was no evidence adduced that any consideration was given by the shareholders for the company arranging that a substantial part of its assets would be transferred to its shareholders. Further, there was no evidence given to the effect that the depletion of the company's assets was in substitution for any salary payable to the shareholders and, consequently, there was no question of the company having the right to claim the reduction in its assets as a deduction for the purposes of Corporation Tax, again analogous to a dividend.

(vi) Regarding (b), '*its use as means of achieving those results*', those '*other means*' as referred to in (c), namely the payment of a dividend by the company, would have resulted in the company incurring an obligation to pay Advance Corporation Tax (see below re. company's argument as to the quantum, if any, of such a liability) and in the shareholders incurring a liability to income tax in respect of the receipt of the dividend paid by the company (which did not have any tax exempt ESR reserves).

(vii) Concerning the question of whether the transaction gave rise to a 'tax advantage' within the meaning of subsection 2(i) we noted the terms of section 86(1) 'Tax advantage means (i) a reduction, avoidance or deferral of any charge or assessment to tax, including any potential or prospective charge or assessment.....arising out of or by reason of a transaction.....' and we determined that the company had avoided a potential charge to ACT and that the shareholders had avoided a potential charge to income tax under Schedule F (Section 83 Corporation Tax Act 1976) by reason of the transaction with the consequence that the transaction gave rise to a 'tax advantage' for the company and for both of the shareholders.

(viii) It was admitted by the company that the transaction was a prearranged sequence of events and on foot of this and following a consideration of all the evidence we determined that the transaction was entered into solely for the purpose of obtaining a tax advantage with the consequence that we were satisfied that the transaction 'was not undertaken or arranged primarily for purposes other than to give rise to a tax advantage' as specified in subsection (2)(ii).

(ix) Therefore, but for subsection (3), we would have concluded that the transaction was a tax avoidance transaction.

(x) The provisions of section 86(3)(a) provide that we shall not regard a transaction as a tax avoidance transaction if we are satisfied that 'the transaction was undertaken or arranged with a view to the realisation of profits in the course of the business activities of a business and [the transaction] was not undertaken or arranged primarily to give rise to a tax advantage.'

(xi) Section 86(3) commences 'Without prejudice to the generality of the provisions of subsection (2)'. Subsection (2) defines a 'tax avoidance transaction' and sets out the matters to be considered in forming an opinion that a transaction is a tax avoidance transaction. Subsection (3) excludes certain transactions from that definition. It would appear, therefore, that subsection (3) does not have a bearing on the generality of subsection (2). However, for the purposes of our decisions in this case, we did not consider that the phrase had any applicability

(xii) The subsection goes on to provide that '... [we] shall not regard the transaction as being a tax avoidance transaction if ... [we] ... re satisfied that ... (b) the

transaction was undertaken or arranged for the purpose of obtaining the benefit of any relief, allowance or other abatement provided by any provision of the Acts and that transaction would not result directly or indirectly in a misuse or the provision or an abuse of the provisions having regard to the purpose for which it was provided....'.

Clearly it was undertaken to obtain the benefit of the Export Sales Relief.

(xiii) Regarding the second part of subsection 3(b), the subsection distinguishes between misuse and abuse. The context in which section 86 applies is one in which a tax advantage has been achieved through the use of some arrangements which are, considered without reference to section 86, effective in avoiding or reducing a tax charge. Therefore, we conclude that the word 'abuse' cannot be used in the context of a fraudulent tax scheme, such as claiming to export good that were sold within the State. We consider that the word 'abuse' must be construed with careful reference to the phrase '... having regard to the purpose for which it [i.e. the relief] was provided'.

(xiv) We have some guidance from the courts in relation to the purpose for which the scheme providing for a reduced rate of tax to apply to profits derived from the manufacture of certain goods was enacted: 'It is manifest that Part IV of the Act of 1976 was, by tax incentives, to encourage the creation of employment within the State and the promotion of exports, naturally, outside the State, objectives of proper, social and economic kind which the State would be bound to encourage.' (McCarthy J in *Charles S McCann v S Ó Culacháin* at III ITR 318)

(xv) It is obvious that, however helpful such judicial dicta might be to us, we are not confined to them in determining the purposes for which a particular provision was provided. However, the words of McCarthy J, while not specific to Export Sales Relief, are, in our opinion, of relevance to this case

(xvi) Export Sales Relief was the precursor to the more general scheme of relief for profits from manufacturing activities and can be said to have had two essential components so far as tax relief is concerned. The first was that certain profits of companies were entirely free of tax. The second was that distributions of those profits in the form of dividends were completely free of Irish tax in the hands of the recipients of those dividends.

(xvii) In determining the purpose for which the provision was provided the words of McCarthy J are of direct relevance to the first of these components. He did refer to the export of goods but not in relation to the scheme for Export Sales Relief. However, it seems entirely reasonable to adopt his approach and to conclude that the statute within the country from tax was enacted for the same purposes as identified by the learned judge.

(xviii) We are of the view that a consideration of the purpose for which the relief was provided must have regard to the restrictions to which the relief was subject.

(xix) We are of the opinion that one of the main purposes of confining the relief to profits derived from exports was to protect the existing tax revenue which the exchequer derived from companies which were manufacturing and selling within Ireland.

(xx) Having considered the aforementioned matters we concluded that a scheme which had the effect of transferring goods outside the territorial waters of Ireland and then importing them for sale within the country would be an example of an abuse

of the relief having regard to the purposes for which it was provided; namely, to encourage bona fide exports and to maintain the existing tax base.

(xxi) The word '*misuse*' is not as strong as the word '*abuse*' although it seems reasonable to suggest that their meanings overlap to some extent. As an example of a misuse of the Export Sales Relief provisions we considered that a company which was manufacturing goods and exporting them and was also selling manufactured good on the Irish market might be misusing the relief to the extent that the profits from 'home sales' were diverted to the export side of the business by, for example, charging no management salaries on the export side and arranging for those expenses to be paid out of profits derived from local sales. The relief was not provided to enable companies to minimise profits on such home sales. (These comments are made without reference to the specific anti-avoidance provisions the Export Sales legislation itself.)

(xxii) As we have already stated, there was no evidence that the export sales relieved profits which were distributed in this case were derived from anything other than bone fide export sales not that those profits had been improperly calculated. So, in regard to the first component of the Export Sales Relief scheme, we cannot find that there was any abuse or misuse of the relief having regard to the purposes for which it was enacted.

(xxiii) In considering the second component of the Export Sales Relief Scheme, the exemption of tax dividends, we do not have the guidance of McCarthy J. We can, however, make some fairly straightforward comments on the issue.

(xxiv) The complete exemption of a company's profits from tax was a radical proposal. The fact that the exemption was confined to exported goods was highly likely to, and in fact did, lead to foreign-based companies coming to Ireland to establish manufacturing and exporting operations. The exemption from tax to which recipients of dividends from qualifying companies were entitled was, arguably, more radical than the exemption of the underlying profits from tax in that there were no restrictions imposed on the shareholders in those companies. Some of the possible distinctions between shareholders that could have been made in connection with the exception of the dividends from tax are as follows:

The exception to apply only to:

- Shareholders with a percentage holding of above or below a certain threshold
- Dividends paid subject to a certain maximum level
- Dividends paid out prior to a particular date subsequent to the generation of the profits
- Either corporate or individual shareholders
- Shareholders living in Ireland or living abroad
- Those shareholders who were either employees or directors of the company
- Those persons who were shareholders at the time the profits were earned by the company
- Those persons who were shareholders at the time of the actual manufacture and/or export of goods
- Dividends paid by a company prior to it ceasing to trade
- Those non-resident shareholders who were resident in a country with which Ireland had concluded a double taxation agreement

(xxv) In view of the fact that such restrictions were enacted we conclude that the comprehensive and entirely unencumbered nature of the exemption can only be considered as intentionally buttressing the total exemption of the corporate profits from tax.

(xxvi) The above comments may need qualification in connection with an ESR Dividend that was paid in substitution for some other legal entitlement foregone by the recipient; e.g. if a salary entitlement were waived and an equivalent amount was paid in the form of an ESR dividend to an employee or director, that might in our view, be considered a misuse of the relief having regard to the fact that the belief was not enacted to enable employees to avoid tax on their salaries. The specific anti-avoidance legislation introduced in the 1971 Act can be taken as a confirmation of this point but, even in the absence of that legislation we would not be of this point of view. To generalise, it may be that the use of the tax free nature of the dividends to avoid a specific tax charge that otherwise would have arisen could be said to be a misuse, whether direct or indirect, of the relief.

(xxvii) In this context the agent for the taxpayers emphasised and we found as a fact that there was no evidence of any intention to pay a dividend which would have been liable to Advanced Corporation Tax.

(xxviii) In regard to the second component of the Export Sales Relief scheme insofar as the shareholders are concerned we are of the view that the payment of bona fide Export Sales Relief relieved profits in the present case does not amount directly or indirectly to a misuse or abuse of the relief having regard to the purposes for which the said second component was enacted and to the nature of the relief afforded to those dividends.

(xxix) To conclude that there had been a misuse of the export sales relief provisions would, in our view, be to ignore the statement of the law laid down in *McGrath c McDermott*. While it is necessary to look at the purpose for which section 86 was enacted, in our opinion section 86, in itself, cannot be used to abandon the clear principles of statutory construction laid out in that case. These principles of statutory interpretation set out in *McGrath v McDermott* prohibit us from adopting such a purposive approach.

(xxx) Accordingly, for the reasons set out above, we are precluded from forming the view that the transaction was a tax avoidance transaction by virtue of the terms of s 86 (3)(b) Finance Act 1989.

10. Determination

We determined in accordance with s 86(9)(a)(i)(III) Finance Act 1989 that the opinions dated 12 August 1999 are void.

11. Advance Corporation Tax

The agent for the taxpayer urged us at several hearings to hold that the quantum of the 'tax advantage' was either nil or negligible given the fact that any Advance Corporation Tax (ACT) would have been offsettable against 'mainstream' Corporation Tax payable in respect of periods subsequent to that in which 'the transaction' was carried out. This submission was made to deal with the possibility that the High Court might find that we had been wrong in finding that the quantum of the 'tax advantage' was not at issue because of our principal findings. We determined that the question of the quantum of the 'tax advantage' was a moot point given our conclusion that the provisions of section 86(3)(b)

Finance Act, 1989 applied. Notwithstanding this determination we were and remain of the opinion that we had not heard sufficient evidence to enable us to make a decision on the Taxpayers' arguments in relation to Advance Corporation Tax.

We respectfully suggest that, in the event of the Court finding that the quantum of the 'tax advantage' is relevant, the matter be referred back to us to enable us to hear further argument and, if necessary, evidence so that we can determine the quantum, if any, of the said 'tax advantage'.

12. Request for Case Stated by Revenue Commissioners

Immediately on giving our determination, dissatisfaction was expressed by the Revenue Commissioners with our determination as being erroneous in law and, in due course, a formal request was received by us from the Revenue Commissioners that we should state and sign a case for determination by the High Court which we now do.

13. Question of Law – Revenue Commissioners Request for Case Stated.

The question of law for determination by the High Court is whether on the foregoing facts and evidence, we were correct in holding that the transaction is not a tax avoidance transaction by virtue of s 86(3)(b) Finance Act 1989 on the ground that the transaction did not result, directly or indirectly, in a misuse or an abuse of the ESR provisions, having regard to the purpose/s for which they were enacted.

14. Request for Case Stated by Taxpayers

Immediately on giving our determination, the Taxpayers also expressed dissatisfaction with our determination and cross-appealed our determination as set out at paragraphs 9(iii) and 9(x) of this Case Stated.

15. Questions of Law – Taxpayers' Request for Case Stated

In relation to the cross-appeal, the questions of law for determination by the High Court are whether on the foregoing facts and evidence we were correct in holding that:

(a) the transaction gave rise to a 'tax advantage' for O'Flynn Construction Company Ltd,

(b) the transaction gave rise to a 'tax advantage' for John O'Flynn and Michael O'Flynn,

(c) the transaction was not undertaken or arranged primarily for purposes other than to give rise to a 'tax advantage'.,

(d) the transaction was not arranged with a view to the realisation of profits in the course of the business activities of O'Flynn Construction Company Ltd pursuant to section 86(3)(a) Finance Act, 1989.

Cases reported

A

A & B v WJ Davis (Inspector of Taxes) .... Vol II p 60
AB Ltd v Mac Giolla Riogh (Inspector of Taxes) .... Vol II p 419
AB v JD Mulvey (Inspector of Taxes) .... Vol II p 55
Action Aid Ltd v Revenue Commissioners .... Vol V p 392
AE v The Revenue Commissioners .... Vol V p 686
Agricultural Credit Corporation Ltd, The v JB Vale (Inspector of Taxes) .... Vol I p 474
Airspace Investments Ltd v M Moore (Inspector of Taxes) .... Vol V p 3
Alliance & Dublin Consumers' Gas Co, The v Davis (Inspector of Taxes) .... Vol I p 104
Alliance and Dublin Consumers' Gas Co, The v McWilliams (Inspector of Taxes) .... Vol I p 207
Allied Irish Banks plc v James Bolger & Joan Bolger .... Vol V p 1
AS v Criminal Assets Bureau .... Vol VI p 799
Associated Properties Ltd v The Revenue Commissioners .... Vol II p 175
Attorney General, The v Anthony Karl Frank Baird Hilton .... Vol VI p 711
Attorney General, The v Charles Ashleigh Nicholson and Ruth Ellen Ashleigh Nicholson .... Vol VI p 667
Attorney General v Power .... Vol V p 525
Attorney General v Sun Alliance & London Insurance Ltd .... Vol III p 265
Attorney General v Irish Steel Ltd and Vincent Crowley .... Vol II p 108

B

Bairead, MA (Inspector of Taxes) v Martin C Carr .... Vol IV p 505
Bairead, MA (Inspector of Taxes) v Maxwells of Donegal Ltd .... Vol III p 430
Bairead, MA (Inspector of Taxes) v M McDonald .... Vol IV p 475
Bank of Ireland Finance Ltd v The Revenue Commissioners .... Vol IV p 217
Bank of Ireland Trust Services Ltd (formerly Erin Executor and Trustee Co Ltd) (as Trustee of the Irish Pension Fund Property Unit Trust) v The Revenue Commissioners .... Vol VI p 587
Bank of Ireland Trust Services Ltd v The Revenue Commissioners .... Vol VI p 513
BD v JD .... Vol VI p 763
Bedford (Collector-General) v H .... Vol II p 588
Beirne (Inspector of Taxes) v St Vincent De Paul Society (Wexford Conference) .... Vol I p 383
Belville Holdings Ltd (in receivership and liquidation) v Cronin (Inspector of Taxes) .... Vol III p 340
Birch (Inspector of Taxes) v Denis Delaney .... Vol I p 515
BKJ v The Revenue Commissioners .... Vol III p 104
Boland's Ltd v Davis (Inspector of Taxes) .... Vol I p 86
Boland's Ltd v The Commissioners of Inland Revenue .... Vol I p 34
Bourke (Inspector of Taxes) v Lyster & Sons Ltd .... Vol II p 374
Bourke (Inspector of Taxes) v WG Bradley & Sons .... Vol IV p 117
Breathnach (Inspector of Taxes) v MC .... Vol III p 113
Brosnan (Inspector of Taxes) v Mutual Enterprises Ltd .... Vol V p 138
Brosnan (Inspector of Taxes) v Leeside Nurseries Ltd .... Vol V p 21
Brosnan, TJ (Inspector of Taxes) v Cork Communications Ltd .... Vol IV p 349

Browne, JA (Inspector of Taxes) v Bank of Ireland Finance Ltd .... Vol III p 644
Browne Paul and Others v The Revenue Commissioners & Ors .... Vol IV p 323
Burke & Sons Ltd v Revenue Commissioner, Ireland and
Attorney General ....Vol V p 418
Byrne (John Oliver) v Noel Conroy .... Vol VI p 19
Byrne (Terence) v The Revenue Commissioners ....Vol V p 560

C

Cahill (PO) (Inspector of Taxes) v Patrick O'Driscoll, Michael O'Driscoll and
William F O'Driscoll .... Vol VI p 793
Campus Stadium Ireland Development Ltd v Dublin Waterworld Ltd .... 2006 p 55
Carbery Milk Products Ltd v The Minister for Agriculture & Ors .... Vol IV p 492
Carroll Industries Plc (formerly PJ Carroll & Co Ltd) and
PJ Carroll & Co Ltd v S Ó Culacháin (Inspector of Taxes) .... Vol IV p 135
Casey (Inspector of Taxes) v AB Ltd ....Vol II p 500
Casey (Inspector of Taxes) v The Monteagle Estate Co ....Vol II p 429
Castleisland Cattle Breeding Society Ltd v Minister for Social and
Family Affairs .... Vol VI p 673
CD v JM O'Sullivan (Inspector of Taxes) ....Vol II p 140
CG v The Appeal Commissioners and Others .... Vol VI p 783
Cherry Court v The Revenue Commissioners ....Vol V p 180
City of Dublin Steampacket Co, The (In liquidation) v The Revenue
Commissioners .... Vol I p 318
City of Dublin Steampacket Co, The v Revenue Commissioners .... Vol I p 108
Cloghran Stud Farm v Birch (Inspector of Taxes) .... Vol I p 496
Colclough v Colclough ....Vol II p 332
Collins, Daniel & Ors (as executor of the will of Michael Byrne (Deceased))
and Daniel Collins v J D Mulvey (Inspector of Taxes) ....Vol II p 291
Commissioners of Inland Revenue v The Governor and Company of The
Bank of Ireland .... Vol I p 70
Commissioners of Inland Revenue v The Dublin and Kingstown
Railway Co .... Vol I p 119
Companies Act 1963-1983, The v Castlemahon Poultry
Products Ltd .... Vol III p 509
Companies Act 1963-1983, The v M F N Construction Co Ltd
(in liquidation) .... Vol IV p 82
Connolly (Inspector of Taxes) v Denis McNamara ....Vol II p 452
Connolly (Inspector of Taxes) v WW ....Vol II p 657
Connolly, Edward v Birch (Inspector of Taxes) .... Vol I p 583
Connolly, Peter v The Collector of Customs and Excise .... Vol IV p 419
Coombe Importers Ltd (In Liq) and Re the Companies Acts 1963–1990, Re ...... Vol VI p 1
Cooper-Flynn (Beverly) v RTE, Charlie Bird and James Howard .... Vol VI p 195
Corr, F (Inspector of Taxes) v FE Larkin ....Vol II p 164
Crawford (Brendan) (Inspector of Taxes) v Centime Ltd .... Vol VI p 823
Criminal Assets Bureau v D(K) .... Vol VI p 445
Criminal Assets Bureau v Gerard Hutch .... Vol VI p 125
Criminal Assets Bureau v H(S) and H(R) .... Vol VI p 441

Criminal Assets Bureau v Sean and Rosaleen Hunt (nee Maher)
Also known as Jean Hunt and Jean Maher .... Vol VI p 559
Criminal Assets Bureau v John Kelly .... Vol VI p 501
Criminal Assets Bureau v Patrick A McSweeney .... Vol VI p 421
Criminal Assets Bureau v PS .... Vol VI p 719
Criminal Assets Bureau v PS and PS .... Vol VI p 465
Cronin (Inspector of Taxes) v C .... Vol II p 592
Cronin (Inspector of Taxes) v Cork & County Property Co Ltd .... Vol III p 198
Cronin (Inspector of Taxes) v IMP Midleton Ltd .... Vol III p 452
Cronin (Inspector of Taxes) v Lunham Brothers Ltd .... Vol III p 363
Cronin (Inspector of Taxes) v Strand Dairy Ltd .... Vol III p 441
Cronin (Inspector of Taxes) v Youghal Carpets (Yarns) Ltd .... Vol III p 229
Crowe Engineering Ltd v Phyllis Lynch and Others .... Vol IV p 340
Crowley (Donal) (Inspector of Taxes) v Nuala Forde .... Vol VI p 685
Cummins (Decd), In Re Estates of, O'Dwyer & Charleton v Keegan
& Ors .... Vol V p 367
Cunard Steam Ship Co Ltd, The v Herlihy (Inspector of Taxes), and
The Cunard Steam Ship Co Ltd v The Revenue Commissioners .... Vol I p 330
Curtin (Inspector of Taxes) v M Ltd .... Vol II p 360
Curtis, Gerard and Brendan Geough v The Attorney General and
The Revenue Commissioners .... Vol III p 419
Cusack, Patrick v Evelyn O'Reilly and The Collector General .... Vol IV p 86

D

Daly, Michael v The Revenue Commissioners & Ors .... Vol V p 213
Davis (Inspector of Taxes) v Hibernian Bank Ltd .... Vol I p 503
Davis, RG (Inspector of Taxes) v The Superioress, Mater Misericordiae
Hospital, Dublin .... Vol I p 387
Davis, WJ (Inspector of Taxes) v X Ltd .... Vol II p 45
Davoren, Estate of Mary Davoren, Thomas O'Byrne v Michael Davoren
& Anne Coughlan .... Vol V p 36
De Brun (Inspector of Taxes) v K .... Vol III p 19
Deighan, Michael v Edward N Hearne, Attorney General & Ors .... Vol III p 533
Denny & Sons (Ireland) Ltd T/A Kerry Foods v Minister for
Social Welfare .... Vol V p 238
Dilleen, TA (Inspector of Taxes) v Edward J Kearns .... Vol IV p 547
Diners Club Ltd, The v The Revenue and The Minister for Finance .... Vol III p 680
Director of Public Prosecutions v Martin McLoughlin .... Vol III p 467
Director of Public Prosecutions v Michael Cunningham .... Vol V p 691
Director of Public Prosecutions v Robert Downes .... Vol III p 641
Director of Public Prosecutions v Seamus Boyle .... Vol IV p 395
Dolan (Inspector of Taxes) v AB Co Ltd .... Vol II p 515
Dolan, JD (Inspector of Taxes) v "K" National School Teacher .... Vol I p 656
Donovan (Inspector of Taxes) v CG Crofts .... Vol I p 115
Downing, Estate of Teresa (Owner) .... Vol I p 487
Doyle & Ors v An Taoiseach & Ors .... Vol III p 73
Dunnes Stores (Oakville) Ltd v MC Cronin (Inspector of Taxes) .... Vol IV p 68

E

EG v Mac Shamhrain (Inspector of Taxes)....................Vol II p 352
Electricity Supply Board v The Minister for Social Community and Family Affairs
.... 2006 p 63
Erin Executor and Trustee Co Ltd (as trustee of Irish Pension Fund Property Unit Trust) v the Revenue Commissioners ....Vol V p 76
Evans & Co v Phillips (Inspector of Taxes).................... Vol I p 43
Executors and Trustees of AC Ferguson (Deceased) v Donovan (Inspector of Taxes) .... Vol I p 183
Exported Live Stock (Insurance) Board, The v TJ Carroll (Inspector of Taxes) ....Vol II p 211

F

Fennessy (Inspector of Taxes) v John McConnellogue ....Vol V p 129
Fitzgerald, Martin v Commissioners of Inland Revenue .... Vol I p 91
Flynn, W (Inspector of Taxes) v (1) John Noone Ltd, and Flynn, W (Inspector of Taxes) v (2) Blackwood & Co (Sligo) Ltd....................Vol II p 222
Forbes (Cyril) v John Tobin and Jeanette Tobin.................... Vol VI p 483
Forbes (Inspector of Taxes) v GHD....................Vol II p 491
Forde, Michael; Decision by Appeal Commissioners.................... Vol IV p 348
Frederick Inns Ltd, The Rendezvous Ltd, The Graduate Ltd, Motels Ltd (In Liquidation) v The Companies Acts 1963–1983 .... Vol IV p 247

G

GH Ltd v Browne (Inspector of Taxes) .... Vol III p 95
Gilbert Hewson v JB Kealy (Inspector of Taxes) ....Vol II p 15
Gilligan v Criminal Assets Bureau, Galvin, Lanigan & Revenue Commissioners ....Vol V p 424
Governor & Co of the Bank of Ireland v MJ Meeneghan & Ors....................Vol V p 44
Great Southern Railways Co, The v The Revenue Commissioners.................... Vol I p 359
Green & Co (Cork) Ltd v The Revenue Commissioners.................... Vol I p 130
Griffin (Francis) v Minister for Social, Community and Family Affairs William Deasy v The Minister for Social, Community and Family Affairs.................... Vol VI p 371
Guinness & Mahon Ltd v Browne (Inspector of Taxes).................... Vol III p 373
Guinness, Arthur Son & Co Ltd v Commissioners of Inland Revenue Arthur Guinness Son & Co Ltd v Morris (Inspector of Taxes) .... Vol I p 1

H

Hammond Lane Metal Co Ltd, The v S Ó Culacháin (Inspector of Taxes) .... Vol IV p 197
Harris (Robert) v JJ Quigley and Liam Irwin .... Vol VI p 839
Haughey v Attorney General .... Vol VI p 67
Hayes, C (Inspector of Taxes) v RJ Duggan.................... Vol I p 195
Healy, John v SI Breathnach (Inspector of Taxes) .... Vol III p 496
Hearne, EN (Inspector of Taxes) v O'Cionna & Ors t/a JA Kenny & Partners .... Vol IV p 113
Heron, Peter C & Ors v The Minister For Communications .... Vol III p 298
HH v MJ Forbes (Inspector of Taxes).................... Vol II p 614

Hibernian Insurance Company Limited v MacUimis (Inspector of Taxes) .... Vol V p 495, Vol VI p 157
Hibernian Transport Companies Ltd, In re .... Vol V p 194
Hodgins, JT (Inspector of Taxes) v Plunder & Pollak (Ireland) Ltd .... Vol II p 267
Howth Estate Co v WJ Davis (Inspector of Taxes) .... Vol I p 447
HT Ltd, In re (In Liquidation) & Ors .... Vol III p 120
Hughes, HPC (Inspector of Taxes) v Miss Gretta Smyth (Sister Mary Bernard) & Ors .... Vol I p 411
Hussey, J (Inspector of Taxes v M J Gleeson & Co Ltd .... Vol IV p 533

I

Irish Agricultural Machinery Ltd v Ó Culacháin (Inspector of Taxes) .... Vol III p 611
Irish Nationwide Building Society v The Revenue Commissioners .... Vol IV p 296
Irish Provident Assurance Co Ltd (In Liquidation) v Kavanagh (Inspector of Taxes) .... Vol I p 45
Irwin, Liam J v Michael Grimes .... Vol V 209

J

JW v JW .... Vol IV p 437

K

K Co v Hogan (Inspector of Taxes) .... Vol III p 56
Kealy, J B (Inspector of Taxes) v O'Mara (Limerick) Ltd .... Vol I p 642
Kearns (Edward J) v Dilleen (Inspector of Taxes) .... Vol V p 514
Keller, Karl v The Revenue Commissioners & Ors .... Vol IV p 512
Kelly, HF (Inspector of Taxes) v H .... Vol II p 460
Kelly, JF (Inspector of Taxes) v Cobb Straffan Ireland Ltd .... Vol IV p 526
Kennedy (Inspector of Taxes) v The Rattoo Co-operative Dairy Society Ltd .... Vol I p 315
Kennedy, Giles J v EG Hearne, the Attorney General & Ors .... Vol III p 590
Kenny, J v Revenue Commissioners, Goodman & Gemon Ltd (Notice Parties) .... Vol V p 363
Keogh (Terence) v Criminal Assets Bureau, Revenue Commissioners and the Collector General .... Vol VI p 635
Kerrane, JG (Inspector of Taxes) v N Hanlon (Ireland) Ltd .... Vol III p 633
Kill Inn Motel Ltd (In Liquidation) v The Companies Acts 1963/1983 .... Vol III p 706
King (Evelyn Spain), The v The Special Commissioners .... Vol I p 221
King (Harris Stein), The v The Special Commissioners .... Vol I p 62
Kinghan, Albert v The Minister for Social Welfare .... Vol III p 436
Kirwan (Philip) v Technical Engineering and Electrical Union .... Vol VI p 771
Knockhall Piggeries v JG Kerrane (Inspector of Taxes) .... Vol III p 319

L

Louth, James & Ors v Minister for Social Welfare .... Vol IV p 391
Lynch, Mary v Moira Burke & AIB Banks plc .... Vol V p 271
Lynch (Séamus) (The Inspector of Taxes) v Neville Brothers Ltd .... Vol VI p 757

M

MacAonghusa (Inspector of Taxes) v Ringmahon Company .... Vol VI p 327
MacCarthaigh, DA (Inspector of Taxes) v Francis Daly .... Vol III p 253
MacCarthaigh (Inspector of Taxes) v Cablelink Ltd, Cablelink Waterford Ltd
& Galway Cable Vision Ltd.. Vol VI p 595
MacDaibheid (Inspector of Taxes) v SD .... Vol III p 1
MacDermott (Inspector of Taxes) v BC.. Vol III p 43
MacGiolla Mhaith (Inspector of Taxes) v Cronin & Associates Ltd............... Vol III p 211
MacGiolla Riogh (Inspector of Taxes) v G Ltd ....Vol II p 315
MacKeown (Inspector of Taxes) v Patrick J Roe .... Vol I p 214
Madigan, PJ & Or v The Attorney General, Revenue Commissioners
& Ors... Vol III p 127
Manning, David v John R Shackleton & Cork County Council .... Vol IV p 485
Mara (Inspector of Taxes) v GG (Hummingbird) Ltd ....Vol II p 667
Masser, AH Ltd (In receivership) & Ors v Revenue Commissioners.............. Vol III p 548
Masterson (Oliver) v Director of Public Prosecutions..................................... Vol VI p 471
Maye, John v Revenue Commissioners .... Vol III p 332
McAuliffe, Tony v The Minister for Social Welfare ....Vol V p 94
McCabe (Inspector of Taxes) v South City & County Investment Co Ltd
....Vol V p 107, 1998 p 183
McCall (Deceased) v Commissioners of Inland Revenue .... Vol I p 28
McCann, Charles Ltd v S Ó Culacháin (Inspector of Taxes) .... Vol III p 304
McCrystal Oil Co Ltd v The Revenue Commissioners & Ors......................... Vol IV p 386
McDaid, Charles v His Honour Judge David Sheehy, DPP & Ors.................. Vol IV p 162
McDaid, Charles v His Honour Judge Sheehy & Ors ....Vol V p 696
McElligott p & Sons Ltd v Duigenan (Inspector of Taxes)............................ Vol III p 178
McGarry (Inspector of Taxes) v Limerick Gas Committee .... Vol I p 375
McGarry (Inspector of Taxes) v Harding (Lord Edward Street)
Properties Ltd, Re .... Vol VI p 699
McGarry, L v W S (Inspector of Taxes) ....Vol II p 241
McGarry, W S (Inspector of Taxes) v EF ....Vol II p 261
McGarry, WS (Inspector of Taxes) v JA Spencer ....Vol II p 1
McGrath, Patrick & Ors v JE McDermott (Inspector of Taxes)...................... Vol III p 683
McGurrin, L (Inspector of Taxes) v The Champion Publications Ltd............. Vol IV p 466
McHugh (Inspector of Taxes) v A ....Vol II p 393
McLoughlin, Edward and Thomas Marie Tuite v Revenue
Commissioners and The Attorney General... Vol III p 387
McMahon,T & Ors v Rt Hon Lord Mayor Alderman & Burgess of Dublin .....Vol V p 357
McMahon, J (Inspector of Taxes) v Albert Noel Murphy .... Vol IV p 125
McNally, Daniel v S O Maoldhomhniagh .... Vol IV p 22
McNamee, Estate of Thomas & Or, v The Revenue Commissioners.................Vol V p 577
Millhouse Taverns Ltd and the Companies Act 1963–1999, Re .... Vol VI p 191
Milverton Quarries Ltd v The Revenue Commissioners ....Vol II p 382
Minister for Labour, The v PMPA Insurance Co Ltd
(Under administration).. Vol III p 505
Minister for Social Welfare v John Griffiths .... Vol IV p 378
Molmac Ltd v MacGiolla Riogh (Inspector of Taxes).......................................Vol II p 482

Moloney (Inspector of Taxes) v Allied Irish Banks Ltd as executors of the estate of Francis J Doherty (Deceased) .... Vol III p 477
Monahan, Patrick (Drogheda) Ltd v O'Connell (Inspector of Taxes)............ Vol III p 661
Mooney, TB v EP Ó Coindealbháin and The Revenue Commissioners .... Vol IV p 62
Mooney (Inspector Of Taxes) v McSweeney .... Vol V p 163
Most Honourable Frances Elizabeth Sarah Marchioness Conyngham, The v Revenue Commissioners............ Vol I p 231
Moville District Board Of Conservators v D Ua Clothasaigh (Inspector of Taxes) .... Vol II p 154
Muckley, Bernard and Anne, v Ireland, Attorney General & Revenue Commissioners............ Vol III p 188
Mulvey, JD (Inspector of Taxes) v Denis J Coffey .... Vol I p 618
Mulvey, JD (Inspector of Taxes) v RM Kieran .... Vol I p 563
Murnaghan Brothers Ltd v S O'Maoldhomhnaigh............ Vol IV p 304
Murphy (Inspector of Taxes) v Asahi Synthetic Fibres (Ireland) Ltd .... Vol III p 246
Murphy, Frances & Mary Murphy v The Attorney General .... Vol V p 613
Murphy, John B v District Justice Brendan Wallace & Ors .... Vol IV p 278
Murphy (Michael F) v GM, DB, PC Ltd and GH John Gilligan v Criminal Assets Bureau, Revenue Commissioners............ Vol VI p 383
Murphy, S (Inspector of Taxes) v Dataproducts (Dublin) Ltd .... Vol IV p 12
Murphy, Sean (Inspector of Taxes) v The Borden Co Ltd .... Vol III p 559
Murtagh (PV) (Inspector of Taxes) v Samuel Rusk .... Vol VI p 817

N

Navan Carpets Ltd v S Ó Culacháin (Inspector of Taxes)............ Vol III p 403
Neeson (Sean) (Inspector of Taxes) v Longford Timber Contractors Ltd............ Vol VI p 691
Noyek, A & Sons Ltd (In voluntary liquidation) v Edward N Hearne .... Vol III p 523

O

Ó Broin, SP (Inspector of Taxes) v (1) Mac Giolla Meidhre, and O'Broin, SP (Inspector of Taxes) v (2) Finbar Pigott............ Vol II p 366
O'C, JB v PCD and A Bank .... Vol III p 153
O'C (G) & A O'C, In the Matter of, (Application of Liam Liston (Inspector of Taxes))............ Vol V p 346
O'Cahill (Inspector of Taxes) v Albert Harding & Ors............ Vol IV p 233
O'Callaghan, Thomas v JP Clifford & Ors............ Vol IV p 478
Ó Cleirigh (Inspector of Taxes) v Jacobs International Ltd Inc .... Vol III p 165
Ó Coindealbháin (Inspector of Taxes) v Breda O'Carroll............ Vol IV p 221
Ó Coindealbháin (Inspector of Taxes) v KN Price............ Vol IV p 1
Ó Coindealbháin (Inspector of Taxes) v TB Mooney .... Vol IV p 45
Ó Coindealbháin, EP (Inspector of Taxes) v The Honourable Mr Justice Sean Gannon .... Vol III p 484
Ó Conaill (Inspector of Taxes) v JJ Ltd............ Vol III p 65
Ó Conaill (Inspector of Taxes) v R............ Vol II p 304
Ó Conaill (Inspector of Taxes) v Z Ltd .... Vol II p 636
O'Connell (Patrick) (Inspector of Taxes) v Fyffes Banana Processing Ltd............ Vol VI p 131
O'Connell (Patrick) (Inspector of Taxes) v John Fleming .... Vol VI p 453
O'Connell (Patrick) (Inspector of Taxes) v Tara Mines Ltd .... Vol VI p 523

O'Connell (Patrick J) (Inspector of Taxes) v Thomas Keleghan
.... Vol VI p 201, 497
Ó Connlain (Inspector of Taxes) v Belvedere Estates Ltd.............. Vol III p 271
Ó Culacháin , S (Inspector of Taxes) v Hunter Advertising Ltd .... Vol IV p 35
Ó Culacháin (Inspector of Taxes) v McMullan Brothers Ltd ....Vol V p 200
Ó Culacháin, S v McMullan Brothers.............. Vol IV p 284
Ó Culacháin (Inspector of Taxes) v Stylo Barratt Shoes Ltd.............. Vol VI p 617
O'Dwyer (Inspector of Taxes) and the Revenue Commissioners v Irish Exporters and Importers Ltd (In Liquidation).............. Vol I p 629
O'Dwyer, JM (Inspector of Taxes) v Cafolla & Co..............Vol II p 82
O'Dwyer, JM (Inspector of Taxes) v The Dublin United Transport Co Ltd ....Vol II p 115
O'Grady (Inspector of Taxes) v Laragan Quarries Ltd.............. Vol IV p 269
O'Grady (Inspector of Taxes) v Roscommon Race Committee .... Vol IV p 425
..............Vol V p 317
Ó hArgain, L (Inspector of Taxes) v B Ltd.............. Vol III p 9
Ó Laochdha, (Inspector of Taxes) v Johnson & Johnson (Ireland) Ltd.............. Vol IV p 361
Ó Laoghaire (Inspector of Taxes) v CD Ltd .... Vol III p 51
O'Leary, Edward v The Revenue Commissioners.............. Vol IV p 357
O'Loan, HA (Inspector of Taxes) v Messrs M J Noone & Co ....Vol II p 146
O'Muircheasa (Inspector of Taxes) v Bailey Wastepaper Ltd.............. Vol VI p 579
O'Reilly, Gerald v W J Casey (Inspector of Taxes) .... Vol I p 601
O'Rourke v Revenue Commissioners ....Vol V p 321
O'Shea (Inspector of Taxes) v Michael Mulqueen ....Vol V p 134
Ó Síocháin, Sean (Inspector of Taxes) v Bridget Neenan .... Vol V p 472, Vol VI p 59
Ó Síocháin, S (Inspector of Taxes) v Thomas Morrissey .... Vol IV p 407
Ó Srianáin (Inspector of Taxes) v Lakeview Ltd.............. Vol III p 219
O'Sullivan (Inspector of Taxes) v p Ltd ....Vol II p 464
O'Sullivan JM (Inspector of Taxes) v Julia O'Connor, as Administratrix of Evelyn H O'Brien (Deceased)..............Vol II p 61
O'Sullivan v The Revenue Commissioners ....Vol V p 570
Orange, James G v The Revenue Commissioners ....Vol V p 70
Orr, Michael (Kilternan) Ltd v The Companies Act 1963-1983, and Thornberry Construction (Irl) Ltd v The Companies Act 1963-1983.... Vol III p 530

P

Pairceir (Inspector of Taxes) v EM..............Vol II p 596
Pandion Haliaetus Ltd, Ospreycare Ltd & Or v Revenue Commissioners....... Vol III p 670
Parkes (Roberta) v David Parkes .... 1998 p 169
Pharmaceutical Society of Ireland, The v Revenue Commissioners .... Vol I p 542
Phillips (Inspector of Taxes) v Keane.............. Vol I p 64
Phillips (Inspector of Taxes) v Limerick County Council .... Vol I p 66
Phonographic Performance (Ireland) Ltd v J Somers (Inspector of Taxes)...... Vol IV p 314
Pine Valley Developments Ltd & Ors v Revenue Commissioners.............. Vol IV p 543
Prior-Wandesforde, Captain RH v Revenue Commissioners .... Vol I p 249
Proes v Revenue Commissioners..............Vol V p 481
Property Loan & Investment Co Ltd v Revenue Commissioners..............Vol II p 25

Private Motorists Provident Society Ltd & WJ Horgan v Minister for Justice .... Vol V p 186
Purcell v Attorney General .... Vol IV p 229
Purcell, Joseph v Attorney General Ireland & The Minister for the Environment .... Vol V p 288

Q

Quigley, JJ (Inspector of Taxes) v Maurice Burke .... Vol IV p 332, Vol V p 265

R

Racing Board, The v Ó Culacháin .... Vol IV p 73
Rahinstown Estates Co v M Hughes, (Inspector of Taxes) .... Vol III p 517
Revenue Commissioners v ORMG .... Vol III p 28
Revenue Commissioners v Arida Ltd .... Vol IV p 401, Vol V p 221
Revenue Commissioners v Associated Properties Ltd .... Vol II p 412
Revenue Commissioners v Bus Éireann .... Vol VI p 743
Revenue Commissioners v Colm O Loinsigh .... Vol V p 98
Revenue Commissioners v Daniel Anthony Moroney & Ors .... Vol V p 589
Revenue Commissioners v Edward Doorley .... Vol V p 539
Revenue Commissioners v Henry Young .... Vol V p 294
Revenue Commissioners v HI .... Vol III p 242
Revenue Commissioners v L & Co .... Vol II p 281
Revenue Commissioners v Latchford & Sons Ltd .... Vol I p 240
Revenue Commissioners v O'Flynn Construction Co Ltd, John and Michael O'Flynn .... 2006 p 81
Revenue Commissioners v Orwell Ltd .... Vol II p 326
Revenue Commissioners v R Hilliard & Sons Ltd .... Vol II p 130
Revenue Commissioners v Sisters of Charity of the Incarnate Word .... Vol VI p 7
Revenue Commissioners v Switzer Ltd .... Vol II p 19
Revenue Commissioners v Y Ltd .... Vol II p 195
Right Hon Earl of Iveagh v The Revenue Commissioners .... Vol I p 259
Robinson, WA T/A James Pim & Son v JD Dolan (Inspector of Taxes) .... Vol I p 427
Rowan, In the Goods of Bernard Louis (Deceased) Joseph Rowan v Vera Agnes Rowan & Ors .... Vol III p 572

S

S Ltd v O'Sullivan .... Vol II p 602
S W Ltd v McDermott (Inspector of Taxes) .... Vol II p 661
Saatchi & Saatchi Advertising Ltd v McGarry (Inspector of Taxes) .... Vol V p 376, Vol VI p 47
Simple Imports Ltd and Another v Revenue Commissioners and Others .... Vol VI p 141
Smyth EA & Weber Smyth v The Revenue Commissioners .... Vol V p 532
Stamp (Deceased) In the matter of, v Noel Redmond & Ors .... Vol IV p 415
State, The (at the Prosecution of Patrick J Whelan) v Michael Smidic (Special Commissioners of Income Tax) .... Vol I p 571
State, The (Calcul International Ltd and Solatrex International Ltd) v The Appeal Commissioners and The Revenue Commissioners .... Vol III p 577
State, The (FIC Ltd) v O'Ceallaigh (Inspector of Taxes) .... Vol III p 124

State, The (Melbarian Enterprises Ltd) v The Revenue Commissioners .... Vol III p 290
State, The (Multiprint Label Systems Ltd) v The Honourable Justice Thomas Neylon .... Vol III p 159
Stephen Court Ltd v JA Browne (Inspector of Taxes) .... Vol V p 680
Sugar Distributors Ltd v The Companies Acts 1963–90 .... Vol V p 225
Sunday Tribune Limited (in Liquidation) .... 1998 p 177
Swaine (Inspector of Taxes) v VE .... Vol II p 472
Swan (Deceased), In re Hibernian Bank Ltd v Frances Munro & Ors .... Vol V p 565

T

Taxback Limited v The Revenue Commissioners .... Vol V p 412
Texaco Ireland Ltd v S Murphy (Inspector of Taxes) .... Vol IV p 91
Tipping, WJ (Inspector of Taxes) v Louis Jeancard .... Vol II p 68
Travers, John v Sean Ó Síocháin (Inspector of Taxes) .... Vol V p 54
Trustees of The Ward Union Hunt Races, The v Hughes (Inspector of Taxes) .. Vol I p 538

U

Ua Clothasaigh, D (Inspector of Taxes) v Patrick McCartan .... Vol II p 75
United Bars Ltd (In receivership), Walkinstown Inn Ltd (In receivership) and Raymond Jackson v Revenue Commissioners .... Vol IV p 107
Urquhart D (Decd), In Re the Estate of, & The Revenue Commissioners v AIB Ltd .... Vol V p 600

V

Vale, JB (Inspector Of Taxes) v Martin Mahony & Brothers Ltd .... Vol II p 32
Veterinary Council, The v F Corr (Inspector of Taxes) .... Vol II p 204
Viek Investments Ltd v The Revenue Commissioners .... Vol IV p 367

W

W Ltd v Wilson (Inspector of Taxes) .... Vol II p 627
Warnock & Ors practicing as Stokes Kennedy Crowley & Co v The Revenue Commissioners .... Vol III p 356
Waterford Glass (Group Services) Ltd v The Revenue Commissioners .... Vol IV p 187
Wayte (Holdings) Ltd (In Receivership) v EN Hearne (Inspector of Taxes) ... Vol III p 553
Wiley, Michael v The Revenue Commissioners .... Vol IV p 170
Williams Group Tullamore Ltd v Companies Act 1963-1983 .... Vol III p 423
Williams (Tallaght) (In Receivership and Liquidation) and the Companies Act 1963-1990, In the Matter of .... Vol V p 388
Wing v O'Connell (Inspector of Taxes) .... Vol I p 155
WLD Worldwide Leather Diffusion Ltd v Revenue Commissioners .... Vol V p 61

Cases considered

A

AB v JD Mulvey (Inspector of Taxes) 2 ITC 345, [1947] IR 121 .... Vol III p 373
Abbey Films Ltd v Ireland [1981] IR 158 .... Vol III p 533
Abbot Laboratories Ltd v Carmody 44 TC 569 .... Vol III p 65
Abbot v Philbin 39 TC 82 .... Vol VI p 498
Aberdeen Construction Co Ltd v Commissioners of Inland Revenue [1978] 52 TC 281 .... Vol V p 163, Vol VI p 203
Absalom v Talbot 26 TC 166, [1944] AC 204 .... Vol II p 281
Adams, Re [1967] IR 424 .... Vol III p 572
Addie, Robert & Sons' Collieries v Commissioners of Inland Revenue 8 TC 671 [1924] SC 231 .... Vol I p 91, Vol II p 32, 382
Administration des Douanes v Societe Anonyme Gondrant Freres and Sociéte Anonyme Garancini (Case 169/80) [1981] ECR 1931 .... Vol VI p 20
Agricultural Credit Corporation Ltd, The v JB Vale (Inspector of Taxes) 2 ITC 46 [1935] IR 681 .... Vol I p 629, Vol III p 1, 373
Aikman v Aikman 3 Macq HL 877 .... Vol I p 259
Ainsworth v Wilding [1896] 1 Ch 673 .... Vol III p 340
Ajayi v RT Briscoe (Nig) Ltd [1964] 1 WLR 1326 .... Vol V p 589
Alianze Co Ltd v Bell 5 TC 60, 172 [1904] 2 KB 645, [1905] 1 KB 184, [1906] AC 18 .... Vol II p 515
Allchin v Coulthard 25 TC 430, [1943] AC 607 .... Vol II p 332
Alliance and Dublin Consumers' Gas Co v Davis (Inspector of Taxes) 1 ITC 114, [1926] IR 372 .... Vol I pp 474, 629
Alliance and Dublin Consumers' Gas Co v McWilliams 1 ITC 199, [1928] IR 1, 1 LTR 201 .... Vol I p 164, 207
Allied Irish Banks Ltd v Ardmore Studios International [1972] .... Vol V p 226
Allingham, Re (1886) 32 Ch D 36 .... Vol VI p 441
Almeida-Sanchez v US [1973] 413 US 266 .... Vol V p 614
Amalgamated Engineering Union v Minister of Pensions and National Insurance [1963] 1 WLR 441 .... Vol VI p 771
Amalgamated Meat Packers Ltd, Re .... Vol III p 452
Amalgamated Property Co v TENAS Bank [1982] QB 84 .... Vol IV p 492
American Thread Co v Joyce 106 LT 171, 29 LTR 266, 6 TC 1 & 163 .... Vol I pp 28, 583 .... Vol II p 68
Ammonia Soda Co v Chamberlain [1918] 1 Ch 266 .... Vol II p 515
Anderson v Laneville 9 Moo PC 325 .... Vol I p 259
Anderton and Halstead Ltd v Birrell (Inspector of Taxes) [1932] I KB 271 .... Vol II pp 195, 627, Vol IV p 505
Anderton v Lambe [1981] 43 Ch D .... Vol IV p 1
Andrews v Astley .... Vol I p 64
Andrews v Partington [1791] 3 Bro CC 401 .... Vol V p 37
Anglo Persian Oil Co Ltd v Dale 16 TC 253, [1932] 1 KB 124 .... Vol I p 642 .... Vol II p 515
Anheuser Busch v The Controller of Patents Design and Trade Marks [1987] IR 329 .... Vol IV p 485
Anisimova v Minister for Justice [1998] 1 IR 186 .... Vol VI p 636

Antelope, The, 10 Wheaton 66 .... Vol V p 45
Aplin v White (HM Inspector of Taxes) [1973] 1 WLR 1311 .... Vol VI p 794
Appenroot v Central Middlesex Assessment Committee [1937] 2 KB 48 .... Vol II p 515
Archer-Shee v Baker 11 TC 749, 759, [1927] 1 KB 109, [1927] AC 844 .... Vol II p 393
.... Vol III p 477
Archibald Thomson Black and Co v Betty 7 TC 158 .... Vol VI p 328
Article 26 and the Employment Equality Bill 1996, Re [1997] 2 IR 321 .... Vol VI p 720
AS v RB, WS and Registrar General [1984] ILRM 66 .... Vol IV p 437
Ashbourne Holdings Ltd v An Bord Pleanála [2003] 2 IR 114 .... 2006 p 82
Ashbury Railway Carriage and Iron Co v Riche .... Vol IV p 247
Ashcroft, Clifton-V-Strauss, Re (1927) 1 Ch 313 .... Vol V p 295
Ashton Gas Co v Attorney General [1906] AC 10 .... Vol V p 565
Ashwander v Tennessee Valley Authority 297 US 288 .... Vol V p 696
Associated Portland Cement Manufacturers Ltd v Kerr 27 TC 103, [1945] 2 All ER 535, [1946] 1 All ER 68 .... Vol II p 515
Associated Portland Cement Manufacturers Ltd v The Prices Commission [1975] 119 So 30, 63, [1975] ICR 34 .... Vol IV p 135
Athenaeum Life Assce Society, Re [1858] Ch 4 Kay & J 304 .... Vol V p 226
Atherton v British Insulated & Helsby Cables Ltd 10 TC 155, [1925] 1 KB 421, [1926] AC 205 .... Vol I p 642, Vol II pp 32, 45, 222, 267, 360, 500, 515, 602
.... Vol III p 95, Vol IV p 425, Vol V p 496
Atkinson, Re 31 Ch D 577 .... Vol V p 526
Attorney General (New South Wales) v Quin [1990] 170 CLR 1 .... Vol IV p 170
Attorney General for Manitoba v Attorney General for Canada [1925] AC 561
.... Vol III p 73
Attorney General of Hong Kong v NG Yuen Shiu [1983] 2 AC 629 .... Vol IV p 170
.... Vol VI p 636
Attorney General of Jamaica v Williams [1998] AC 357 .... Vol VI p 142
Attorney General of New Zealand v Ortiz [1984] AC 1 .... Vol V p 45
Attorney General v Black IR 6 Ex 308 .... Vol II pp 154, 204
Attorney General v Carlton Bank (1899) 2 QB 158 .... Vol VI p 422, 636
Attorney General v Casey [1930] IR 163 .... Vol III p 387, Vol VI p 386
Attorney General v De Preville [1900] 1 QB 223 .... Vol V p 539
Attorney General v Delaney [1876] IR 10 CL 125 .... Vol I p 542, Vol V p 539
Attorney General v Great Eastern Co 5 AC 473 .... Vol II p 241
Attorney General v Hamilton [1993] 2 IR 250 .... Vol VI p 68
Attorney General v Hope IR 2 CL 308 .... Vol V p 539
Attorney General v Irish Steel Ltd and Vincent Crowley 2 ITC 402 .... Vol II p 108
Attorney General v Jameson [1905] 2 IR 218 .... Vol V p 532, 577
Attorney General v London County Council No 1 4 TC 265, [1901] AC 26
.... Vol I pp 447, 487, 515
Attorney General v London County Council No 2 5 TC 242, [1907] AC 131
.... Vol I p 487
Attorney General v Metropolitan Water Board 13 TC 294, [1928] 1 KB 833
.... Vol II p 332
.... Vol III p 229
Attorney General v Pettinger 6 H & N 733 .... Vol I p 259
Attorney General v Power [1906] 2 IR 272 .... Vol III p 104

Attorney General v Southern Industrial Trust (1960) 94 ILTR 161 .... Vol VI p 386
Attorney General v Southern Industrial Trust Ltd [1947] ILTR 174 .... Vol III pp 127, 387
Attorney General v Till 5 TC 440 .... Vol III p 229
Austin v United States 509 US 602 .... Vol VI p 386
Ayerst v C & K (Construction) Ltd [1974] 1 All ER 670 .... Vol IV p 247
Aylmer v Mahaffy 10 TC 594 & 598, [1925] NIR 167 .... Vol II p 374

B

Bach v Daniels 9 TC 183, [1925] 1 KB 526 .... Vol 1 p 515, Vol II pp 315, 636
Bagge v Whitehead .... Vol III p 387
Balgownie Land Trust Ltd v Commissioners of Inland Revenue 14 TC 684 .... Vol III p 1
Balkan-Import-Export GmbH v Hauptzollamt Berlin-Packhof (Case 118/76) [1977] ECR 1177 .... Vol VI p 20
Banbury Union (Guardians of) v Robinson 4 QB 919 .... Vol V p 560
Bank of Ireland v Caffin [1971] IR 123 .... Vol IV p 437
Bank of Ireland v Kavanagh [Judgment delivered 19 June 1987] .... Vol IV p 407
Bank of Ireland v Rockfield Ltd [1979] IR 21 .... Vol V p 226
Bankline Ltd v Commissioners of Inland Revenue 49 TC 307 .... Vol III p 633
Barclays Bank v Siebe Gorman [1979] 2 Lloyd's Rep 142 .... Vol III p 548
Barker (Christopher) & Sons v Commissioners of Inland Revenue [1919] 2 KB 222 .... Vol III p 211
Barnardo's Homes v Commissioners of Inland Revenue 7 TC 646, [1921] 2 AC 1 .... Vol III p 477
Baroness Wenlock v River Dee Co [1885] 10 AC .... Vol II p 241
Barrington's Hospital v Commissioner of Valuation [1975] IR 299 .... Vol II p 661
Bartlett v Mayfair Property Co [1898] 2 Ch 28 .... Vol II p 130
Baxendale v Murphy 9 TC 76 [1924] 2 KB 494 .... Vol I p 601
Baytrust Holdings Ltd v Inland Revenue Commissioners [1971] 1 WLR 1333 .... Vol III p 661
Beak v Robson 25 TC 33, [1943] AC 352 .... Vol II p 515
Bean v Doncaster Amalgamated Collieries 27 TC 296, [1944] 2 All ER .... Vol II p 515
Beatty (Earl) v Commissioners of Inland Revenue 35 TC 30 .... Vol II p 627
Beauchamp v FW Woolworth Plc [1989] STC 510 HL .... Vol V p 138
Beaumont, Re, deceased [1980] Ch 444, [1979] 3 WLR 818 .... Vol V p 614
Bebb v Bunny 8 TC 454, 1 K & J 217 .... Vol II p 332
Bede Steam Shipping Co Ltd, Re [1917] 1 Ch 123 .... Vol V p 532
Beechor v Major [1865] BLT 54 .... Vol V p 271
Beke v Smith (1836) 2 M & W 191 .... Vol VI p 21
Belgian State and Grand Duchy of Luxembourg v Martens (Cases 178, 179 and 180/73) [1974] ECR 383 .... Vol VI p 21
Bell Bros Ltd v Shire of Serpentine-Jarrahdale [1969] 121 CLR 137 .... Vol V p 614
Bell Bros Ltd, Re, ex p Hodgson (1) 65 TLR 245 .... Vol V p 532
Bell v Kennedy LR 1 SC Appeal p 307, I S & D 307, LRIA SC 441 .... Vol I p 259
Belmont Farm v Minister for Housing 60 LGR 319 .... Vol V p 357
Belmont Finance Corporation Ltd v Williams Furniture Ltd (No 2) [1980] 1 All ER 393 .... Vol IV p 247
Beni Felkai Mining Co Ltd, Re [1934] 1 Ch 406 .... Vol III p 523

Bennet v Marshall 22 TC 73, [1938] 1 KB 591 .... Vol II pp 68, 393
Benson (Inspector of Taxes) v Yard Arm Club Ltd 53 TC 67, [1979] STC 266 .... Vol III p 219, Vol IV p 284
Benyon & Co Ltd v Ogg 7 TC 125 .... Vol I p 629
Beresford (Lady) v Driver [1851] 2 OLJ (Ch) 476 .... Vol IV p 332
Berkeley v Edwards [1988] IR 219 .... Vol VI p 142
Berry v Farrow [1914] 1 IR 358 .... Vol II p 332
Berry v Fisher [1903] IR 484 .... Vol IV p 415
Best v Samuel Fox & Co Ltd [1952] AC 716 .... Vol IV p 437
Beynon and Co Ltd v Ogg 7 TC 125 .... Vol I pp 1, 28
Bickerman v Mason per Reps TL 2976 .... Vol IV p 22
Biddell Brothers v Clemens Horst Co [1911] 1 KB 934 .... Vol I p 130
Birch (Inspector of Taxes) v Denis Delaney 2 ITC 127, [1936] IR 517, 531 .... Vol I p 583, Vol II pp 315, 429, 472, 596, Vol III pp 1, 9
Birmingham Mosque Trust Ltd v Alavi [1992] ICR 435 .... Vol VI p 771
Birmingham v District Land Co v London & North Investment Railway Co [1888] 40 Ch D 268 .... Vol V p 589
Blake v Attorney General [1982] IR 117, [1981] ILRM 34 .... Vol III p 127 .... Vol IV pp 187, 323
Blakiston v Cooper 5 TC 347, [1907] 1 KB 702, 2 KB 688, [1909] AC 104 .... Vol I p 155
Bolam v Regent Oil Co Ltd 37 TC 56 .... Vol II p 515
Boland v An Taoiseach [1974] IR 338 .... Vol V p 614
Boland's Ltd v Davis (Inspector of Taxes) 1 ITC 91, [1925] ILTR 73 .... Vol I p 86 .... Vol III p 363
Bolson J & Son Ltd v Farrelly 34 TC 161 .... Vol III p 253
Bomford v Osborne [1942] AC 14, 23 TC 642 .... Vol II pp 241, 515
Bonner v Basset Mines Ltd 6 TC 146 .... Vol II p 382
Bord na gCon v Stokes (November 1975) .... Vol IV p 73
Boulton v Bull (1795) .... Vol III p 441
Bourne and Hollingsworth v the Commissioners of Inland Revenue 12 TC 483 .... Vol II p 429
Bowers v Harding 3 TC 22 .... Vol II p 366
Bowlby, Re [1904] 2 Ch 685 .... Vol V p 526
Bowles v The Attorney General TC 685, [1912] 1 Ch 123 p 135 .... Vol I p 583
Boyd v Shorrock .... Vol III p 332
BP Australia Ltd v Commissioner of Taxation of the Commonwealth of Australia [1966] AC 224 .... Vol II p 515
Bradbury v The English Sewing Cotton Co Ltd 8 TC 481, [1923] AC 744 .... Vol I p 583
Bradbury v United Glass Bottle Manufacturers Ltd 38 TC 369 .... Vol II p 515
Bradshaw v Blundon 36 TC 397 .... Vol III p 373
Bray (Inspector of Taxes) v Best (1989) STC 167 .... Vol IV p 407, Vol VI p 498
Breathnach v McCann 3 ITR 112, [1984] ILRM 679 .... Vol V p 200
Breathnach, SI (Inspector of Taxes) v MC [1984] IR 340 .... Vol III p 219
Breen v The Minister for Defence (20 July 1990) SC .... Vol IV p 170
Brennan v Attorney General [1984] ILRM 355 .... Vol IV pp 229, 323
Brennan v Attorney General and Wexford Co Co [1983] ILRM 449 (HC) [1984] ILRM 355 (SC) .... Vol III p 127
Brett, ex p [1897] 1 IR 488 .... Vol I p 28

Brice v The Northern Association Co [1911] 2 KB 577, [1912] 2 KB 41
[1913] AC 610, 6 TC 327 .... Vol I p 474
Brickwood & Co v Reynolds 3 TC 600, [1898] 1 QB 95 .... Vol I p 642
Brides v Minister for Agriculture [1998] 4 IR 250 .... 2006 p 64
Brighton College v Marriott 10 TC 213, [1925] 1 KB 312, [1926] AC 192
.... Vol I pp 387, 542, Vol II p 211
Bristow (Inspector of Taxes) v Dickinson and Co Ltd 27 TC 157, 62 TLR 37,
[1946] KB 321 .... Vol II pp 140, 374
British Airways plc v Customs and Excise Commissioners [1990] STC 643
.... Vol VI p 596
British Airways v C & E Commissioners [1989] STC 182 .... Vol IV p 349
British American Tobacco Co v The Inland Revenue Commissioners [1943] AC 335,
[1941] 2 KB 270 .... Vol II p 175
British Broadcasting Corporation v Johns 41 TC 471 .... Vol IV p 73
British Insulated & Helsby Cables Ltd v Atherton [1926] AC 205 .... Vol V p 680
British Legion peterhead Branch v Commissioners of Inland Revenue
35 TC 509 .... Vol III p 253
British Mexican Petroleum Co v Jackson 16 TC 570 .... Vol II p 281
British Railways Board v Customs and Excise Commissioners [1977] STC 221
.... Vol IV p 349, Vol VI p 596
British Sugar Manufacturers Ltd v Harris (Inspector of Taxes) [1938] 2 KB 220
.... Vol II p 195, Vol IV p 505
British Transport Commission v Gourley [1955] 3 All ER 796, ... 2000 p 269
Briton Ferry Steel Co Ltd v Barry 23 TC 414, [1940] 1 KB 463 .... Vol II p 315
Brocklebank, Re 23 QBD 461 .... Vol II p 130
Broken Hill Property Co Ltd v Commissioners of Taxation 41 ALJR 377
.... Vol III pp 113, 120, 219, Vol IV p 284
Brosnan (Inspector of Taxes) v Cork Communications Ltd Vol IV ITR 349
.... Vol VI p 596
Brosnan (Inspector of Taxes) v Leeside Nurseries Ltd [1998] 1 IR 304 .... Vol V p 21
.... Vol VI p 691
Brosnan (Inspector of Taxes) v Mutual Enterprise Ltd [1997] 3 IR 257 .... Vol V p 138
.... Vol VI p 328, 524, 596
Brown & Co v Commissioners of Inland Revenue 12 TC 1256 .... Vol I p 427
Brown v Donegal County Council [1980] IR 132, 146 .... Vol III p 19
Brown v Inland Revenue Commissioners [1965] AC 244 .... Vol VI p 794
Browne & Bank of Ireland Finance Ltd [1991] 1 IR 431 .... Vol III p 644, Vol V p 139
Browne Paul v Inland Revenue Commissioners [1991] 2 IR 58 .... Vol IV p 125
Browne v Burnley Football & Athletic Co Ltd 53 TC 357, [1980] STC 424
.... Vol IV p 425, Vol V p 317
Browns Transport Ltd v Kropp (1958) 100 CLR 263 .... Vol III p 73
BSC Footwear Ltd v Ridgeway 47 TC 495 .... Vol IV p 135
Buchanan Ltd, Peter v McVey [1954] IR 89 .... Vol V p 45, 226, Vol VI p 21
Buckley v Attorney General [1950] IR 67 .... Vol V p 696
Bucks v Bowers [1970] Ch D 431 .... Vol III p 633
Bula Ltd v Tara Mines Ltd [1994] ILRM 111 .... Vol V p 266
Bullcroft Main Collieries Ltd v O'Grady [1932] 17 TC 93 .... Vol II p 267, 360
Bullimore v C & E Commissioners MAN/86/145 .... Vol IV p 349

Burmah Steamship Co Ltd v Commissioners of Inland Revenue [1931] SC 156, [1931] SLT 116, 16 TC 67 .... Vol I p 427
Burman v Thorn Domestic Appliances (Electrical) Ltd [1982] STC 179 .... Vol III p 165
Button v West Cork Railway [1883] 23 Ch D .... Vol III p 706
Byrne v Grey [1988] IR 31 .... Vol VI p 142
Byrne v Ireland [1972] IR 241 .... Vol V p 614

C

Cadwalader 12 SC LTR 499, 5 TC 101 .... Vol I p 259
Café Brandy Syndicate v Commissioners of Inland Revenue 12 TC 358 .... Vol VI p 48
Cafolla v Attorney General [1985] IR 486 .... Vol IV p 323
Cahill v Harding .... Vol IV p 233, Vol V p 134
Cahill v Sutton [1980] IR 269 .... Vol III p 127, 419, Vol VI p 502
Calcul v Appeal Commissioners III ITR 577 .... Vol VI p 561
Caledo-Toledo v Pearson Yacht Leasing Co (1974) 416 US 663 .... Vol VI p 386
California Copper Syndicate v Harris 5 TC 159, [1904] 41 SLR 691, 6F 894 .... Vol I pp 474, 503, 629, Vol III p 644
Campbell v Hall [1774] 1 Cowp 204 ([1558-1774] All ER Rep 252 .... Vol V p 322
Cannon Industries Ltd v Edwards 42 TC 265, [1966] 1 All ER 456 .... Vol II p 614
Cape Brandy Syndicate v Inland Revenue Commissioners 12 TC 358, [1921] 1 KB 64 .... Vol I pp 1, 28, Vol III pp 56, 477 .... Vol IV p 91, Vol V p 376, 472, Vol VI p 744
Capital and National Trust Ltd v Golder 31 TC 265 .... Vol III p 95, ... Vol V p 496, 680, Vol VI p 158
Card Protection Plan Ltd v Commissioners of Customs and Excise Case C–349/96 (25 February 1999) ECJ .... Vol VI p 596
Carlisle and Silloth Golf Club v Smith 6 TC 198, [1912] 2 KB 177, [1913] 3 KB 75 .... Vol I pp 387, 515
Carr v Commissioners of Inland Revenue [1944] 2 All ER 163 .... Vol III p 211
Carroll Group Distributors Ltd v GAJF Bourke Ltd .... Vol V p 108
Carroll Industries Plc (formerly PJ Carroll & Co Ltd) and PJ Carroll & Co Ltd v Ó Culacháin (Inspector of Taxes) [1988] IR 705 .... Vol IV p 304
Carroll v Mayo County Council [1967] IR 364 .... Vol II p 636
Carson v Cheyney's Executor 38 TC 240, [1959] AC 412, [1958] 3 All ER 573 .... Vol III p 484, Vol IV p 135
Cary v Cary 2 Sch and Lef 173 .... Vol I p 601
Casdagli v Casdagli [1919] AC 177 .... Vol I p 259
Cassidy v Ministry of Health [1951] 2 KB 343 .... 2006 p 64
Cassidy v Minister for Industry and Commerce [1978] IR 297 .... Vol III p 73, Vol V p 288
Cassidy v Minister of Health (1978) IR 207 .... Vol V p 239
Castleisland Cattle Breeding Society Ltd v Minister for Social and Family Affairs .... Vol VI p 673, 2006 p 64
Caudron v Air Zaire [1985] IR 716 .... Vol VI p 386
Cavan Co-Operative Society, Re [1917] 2 IR 608 .... Vol III p 319
Cayzer Irvine & Co Ltd v Commissioners of Inland Revenue 24 TC 491 .... Vol II p 472
CCSV v Minister for the Civil Service [1984] 3 All ER 935 .... Vol IV p 170
CD v JM O'Sullivan (Inspector of Taxes) 2 ITC 422, [1949] IR 264 .... Vol II p 140
Cecil v Commissioners of Inland Revenue [1919] 36 TLR 164 .... Vol III p 211

Cenlon Finance Co Ltd v Ellwood 40 TC 176, [1961] 2 All ER 861, [1961] Ch 634, [1962] AC 782, [1974] ITC No 10 .... Vol II p 627, Vol III p 56, Vol IV p 187
Central London Property Trust Ltd v High Trees House Ltd [1947] KB 130 .... Vol V p 589
Chambers v Fahy [1931] SC .... Vol V p 472
Chamney v Lewis [1932] 17 TC 318 .... Vol II pp 393, 491
Chancery Lane Safe Deposit and Office Co Ltd v Commissioners of Inland Revenue 43 TC 83 .... Vol II p 627
Chantrey Martin & Co v Martin [1952] 2 All ER 691 .... Vol IV p 332, Vol V p 266
Charente Steamship Co v Wilmot 24 TC 97, [1941] 2 KB 386 .... Vol II p 602
Charge Card Services Ltd, Re .... Vol III p 680
Charleston Federal Savings and Loan Assn v Alderson [1945] 324 US 182 .... Vol III p 127
Charterbridge Corporation v Lloyds Bank [1969] 2 All ER .... Vol IV p 247
Chaulk v R [1990] 3 Scr 13 .... Vol V p 213
Chetwode (Lord) v Inland Revenue Commissioners [1977] 1 WLR 248 .... Vol III p 403
Chevron Oil Co v Huson [1971 404 US 97 .... Vol V p 614
Chibett Robinson 9 TC 48, 132 LTR 31 .... Vol I p 155
Chicago, Indianapolis & Louisville Railway Co v Hackett [1931] 228 US 559 .... Vol V p 614
Chicot County Drainage District v Baxter State Bank [1940] 308 US 371 .... Vol V p 614
Chinn v Collins [1981] AC 533, [1981] 2 WLR 14, [1981] 1 All ER 189 [1980] 54 TC 311 .... Vol III p 683
Cipriano v City of Houma [1969] 395 US 701 .... Vol V p 614
Cityview Press Ltd v An Chomhairle Oiliuna [1980] IR 381 .... Vol III p 127 .... Vol IV p 162
Clancy v Ireland [1988] IR 326 .... Vol VI p 386
Clerical, Medical and General Life Assurance Society v Carter 2 TC 437, 22 QBD 444 .... Vol I p 45
Cleveleys Investment Trust Co v Commissioners of Inland Revenue 47 TC 3000 .... Vol VI p 203
Clifford & O'Sullivan, Re [1921] 2 AC 570 .... Vol III p 290
Clinch v Inland Revenue Commissioners [1974] IQB 76 .... Vol III p 356
Clitheroes Estate, Re 31 Ch D 135 .... Vol V p 526
Clover Clayton & Co v Hughes [1910] AC 242 .... Vol I p 427
CM v TM (No 2) [1990] 2 IR 52, [1991] ILRM 268 .... Vol IV p 437
CM v TM [1987] IR 152, [1988] ILRM 456 .... Vol IV p 437
Coates v Holker Estates Co [1961] 40 TC 75 .... Vol II p 657
Codman v Hill [1919] .... Vol III p 253
Cole Bros Ltd v Phillips (Inspector of Taxes) [1981] STC 671, [1982] STC 311 .... Vol IV pp 68, 284
Cole Bros v Phillips [1980] Ch D 518, 55 TC 188 .... Vol III p 219
Cole Bros v Phillips [1981] STC 671 .... Vol V p 200
Coleman's Depositaries Ltd and Life and Health Assurance Association, Re [1907] 2 KB 798 .... Vol III p 159
Collco Dealings Ltd v Inland Revenue Commissioners 39 TC 509, [1961] 1 All ER 762 .... Vol III p 246
Collins v Adamson 21 TC 400, [1937] 4AE 236, [1938] 1 KB 477 .... Vol II p 515

Collins v Inland Revenue Commissioners 12 TC 773, [1925] SC 151 .... Vol I p 240
Collyer v Hoare & Co Ltd [1931] 1 KB 123, 17 TC 169, [1932] AC 407
.... Vol I pp 447, 515
Colquhoun (Surveyor of Taxes) v Heddon (1890) 2 TC 621 .... Vol VI p 744
Colquohoun v Brooks 2 TC 490, (1889) 14 AC 493 .... Vol I p 183
.... Vol II pp 393, 491, Vol VI p 818
Coltness Iron Co v Black 1 TC 287 .... Vol II p 382
Colville v Commissioners of Inland Revenue 8 TC 422, [1923] SC 423,
60 SCLR 248 .... Vol I p 601
Combe v Combe [1951] 2 KB 215 .... Vol V p 589
Commercial Structures Ltd v Briggs 30 TC 477, [1948] 2 All ER 1041
.... Vol II pp 195, 627
Commission of European Communities v Hellenic Republic [1989] ECR 2965
.... Vol VI p 21
Commission of the European Communities v Council of the European Communities
[1973] ECR 575 .... Vol IV p 170
Commission of the European Communities v Denmark C47/88 .... Vol IV p 512
Commission of the European Communities v France and UK (Cases 92and 93/87)
[1989] ECR 405 .... Vol VI p 21
Commissioner of Stamps v Hope [1891] AC 476 .... Vol VI p 818
Commissioner of Taxes v Nchanga Consolidated Copper Mines [1964] 2 WLR 339
1 All ER 208 .... Vol II pp 515, 602
Commissioners for Special Purposes of Income Tax v Pemsel 3 TC 53,
[1891] AC 531 .... Vol I pp 221, 387, 542, Vol II p 661
Commissioners of Customs and Excise v Madgett and Baldwin
[1998] ECR 1–0000 .... Vol VI p 597
Commissioners of Inland Revenue v Alexander von Glehn & Co
[1920] 2 KB 553 .... Vol II p 515
Commissioners of Inland Revenue v Anderstrom 13 TC 482,
[1928] SC 224 .... Vol II pp 393, 491
Commissioners of Inland Revenue v Barclay Curle and Co Ltd 45 TC 221
.... Vol III pp 113, 120, 219, Vol IV pp 68, 425
Commissioners of Inland Revenue v Birmingham Theatre Royal Estate Co Ltd
12 TC 580 .... Vol I p 447, Vol III p 253
Commissioners of Inland Revenue v Brender and Cruickshank
46 TC 574 .... Vol IV p 45
Commissioners of Inland Revenue v Buchanan 37 TC 365,
[1957] 3 WLR 68 .... Vol II p 352
Commissioners of Inland Revenue v Budderpore Oil Co Ltd 12 TC 467 .... Vol I p 629
Commissioners of Inland Revenue v Burrell 9 TC 27, [1924] 2 KB 52 .... Vol I p 318
Commissioners of Inland Revenue v Carron Co 45 TC 18 .... Vol VI p 328
Commissioners of Inland Revenue v Cock Russel & Co Ltd 29 TC 387 .... Vol IV p 135
Commissioners of Inland Revenue v Cola 38 TC 334, [1959] SLT 122 .... Vol II p 515
Commissioners of Inland Revenue v Dalgety & Co 15 TC 216 .... Vol III p 403
Commissioners of Inland Revenue v Dowdall O'Mahony & Co Ltd
33 TC 259 .... Vol VI p 8
Commissioners of Inland Revenue v Edinburgh and Bathgate Railway Co
12 TC 895, [1926] Sess Cas 862 .... Vol I p 359

Commissioners of Inland Revenue v Forrest 3 TC 117, 15 AC 334 .... Vol I p 542
Commissioners of Inland Revenue v Forsyth Grant 25 TC 369, [1943] SC 528 .... Vol II p 636, Vol IV p 1
Commissioners of Inland Revenue v Forth Conservancy Board [1930] SC 850, [1931] AC 540, 47 TLR 429, 16 TC 103 .... Vol I p 656, Vol II p 154, Vol IV p 73
Commissioners of Inland Revenue v Fraser 24 TC 498 .... Vol III p 178, 253
Commissioners of Inland Revenue v Gas Lighting Improvement Co Ltd [1922] KB 381, 12 TC 503 .... Vol I p 447
Commissioners of Inland Revenue v George Burrell and William Burrell 9 TC 27, [1924] 2 KB 52, 129 LTR 542 .... Vol I p 45
Commissioners of Inland Revenue v Governor & Co of Bank of Ireland 1 ITC 74 [1925] 2 IR 90 .... Vol I p 70
Commissioners of Inland Revenue v Granite City Steamship Co [1927] Sess Cas 705, 13 TC 1 .... Vol II p 515, Vol III p 165
Commissioners of Inland Revenue v Granite City Steamship Co Ltd 13 TC 1 .... Vol V p 496
Commissioners of Inland Revenue v Gribble [1913] 3 KB 212 .... Vol III p 611
Commissioners of Inland Revenue v Gull 21 TC 374 .... Vol VI p 8
Commissioners of Inland Revenue v Hendersons Executors 16 TC 282 .... Vol III p 477
Commissioners of Inland Revenue v Hyndland Investment Co Ltd 14 TC 694 .... Vol III p 1
Commissioners of Inland Revenue v Kingston Railway Co 1 ITC 131 .... Vol I p 387
Commissioners of Inland Revenue v Korean Syndicate Ltd [1920] 1 KB 598 12 TC 181 p 205 .... Vol I p 447
Commissioners of Inland Revenue v Lambhill Ironworks Ltd 31 TC 393 .... Vol III p 65
Commissioners of Inland Revenue v Land Securities Investment Trust Ltd 45 TC 495 .... Vol III p 95, Vol V p 139
Commissioners of Inland Revenue v Land Securities Investment Trust Ltd 45 TC 495 Vol V p 680
Commissioners of Inland Revenue v Livingston 11 TC 538 .... Vol III pp 1, 253, 373
Commissioners of Inland Revenue v Lysaght 13 TC 511, [1928] AC 234 .... Vol I p 259, Vol II p 32
Commissioners of Inland Revenue v Mackinlay's Trustees 22 TC 305, [1938] SC 765 .... Vol II p 627
Commissioners of Inland Revenue v Maxse 12 TC 41 .... Vol III pp 178, 211
Commissioners of Inland Revenue v Metrolands 54 TC 679 .... Vol VI p 203
Commissioners of Inland Revenue v Morton [1941] SC 467, 24 TC 259 .... Vol II p 82
Commissioners of Inland Revenue v Newcastle Breweries 12 TC 926, 95 LJ, KB 936, 97 LJ, KB 735 .... Vol II p 515, Vol III p 165
Commissioners of Inland Revenue v Orion Caribbean Ltd (in voluntary liquidation) [1997] STC 92 .... Vol VI p 818
Commissioners of Inland Revenue v Payne 110 LJKB 323, 23 TC 610 .... Vol II p 82
Commissioners of Inland Revenue v Peebleshire Nursing Association 11 TC 335 [1927] SC 215 .... Vol I p 387
Commissioners of Inland Revenue v Pullman Car Co Ltd 35 TC 221 .... Vol VI p 328
Commissioners of Inland Revenue v Ramsay [1935] 154 LT 141 20 TC 79 .... Vol II p 222, 464, 602

Commissioners of Inland Revenue v Ransom (William) & Son Ltd
12 TC 21 .... Vol III p 178
Commissioners of Inland Revenue v Reinhold 34 TC 389 .... Vol III p 1
Commissioners of Inland Revenue v Robins Brothers Ltd 43 TC 266 .... Vol IV p 425
Commissioners of Inland Revenue v Saunders & Pilcher 31 TC 314 .... Vol III p 304
Commissioners of Inland Revenue v Scott Adamson 17 TC 679
[1933] SC 23 .... Vol II p 482
Commissioners of Inland Revenue v Scottish & Newcastle Breweries Ltd
55 TC 252 .... Vol III pp 113, 120, 219
Commissioners of Inland Revenue v Scottish Automobile & General Insurance Co Ltd
[1932] SC 87, 16 TC 381 .... Vol I p 474, 629
Commissioners of Inland Revenue v Scottish Central Electric Power Co
13 TC 331, [1930] SC 226, 15 TC 761 .... Vol II p 32, Vol III p 403
Commissioners of Inland Revenue v Sneath 17 TC 149, [1932] 2 KB 362
.... Vol I p 571, Vol II p 326, 374
Commissioners of Inland Revenue v South Behar Railway Co Ltd 12 TC 657
[1925] AC 476 .... Vol I p 387
Commissioners of Inland Revenue v Sparkford Vale Co-operative Society Ltd
133 LT 231, 12 TC 891 .... Vol I p 315
Commissioners of Inland Revenue v Toll Property Co Ltd 34 TC 13 .... Vol III p 1
Commissioners of Inland Revenue v Trustees of Joseph Reid, Deceased
30 TC 431, [1947] SC 700, [1949] LJR 701 .... Vol II p 464
Commissioners of Inland Revenue v Tyre Investment Trust Ltd 132 LT 59
12 TC 646 .... Vol I p 447
Commissioners of Inland Revenue v Von Glehn & Co Ltd 12 TC 232
[1920] KB 553 .... Vol I p 195
Commissioners of Inland Revenue v Wilsons Executors 18 TC 465 .... Vol V p 496
Commissioners of Inland Revenue v Yorkshire Agricultural Society 13 TC 58
[1928] 1 KB 611 .... Vol I p 542
Commissioners of Taxes v Melbourne Trust Ltd [1914] AC 1001, 84 LJPC 21
30 TLR 685 .... Vol I p 474
Companies Act 1908 v Ross & Boal Ltd [1924] 1 IR 129 .... Vol III p 332
Compton, Re [1945] Ch 123; [1945] 1 All ER 198; 114 LJ Ch 99; 172 LT 158;
61 TLR 167; 89 SJ 142 .... Vol V p 37.
Connolly, Edward v AG Birch (Inspector of Taxes) 2 ITC 201, [1939] IR 534
.... Vol II p 472, Vol III p 9
Construction Industry Training Board v Labour Force Ltd [1970] 3 All ER 220
.... Vol III p 505, Vol IV p 391
Cook, Exp, 29 LJQ B 68 .... Vol I p 221
Cooke v Beach Station Caravans Ltd [1974] 49 TC 514, [1974] STC 402
.... Vol IV pp 68, 425, Vol V p 317
Cooke v Walsh [1984] IR 710 .... Vol V p 696
Cookson v Lee 23 LJ Ch NS p 473 .... Vol II p 241
Cooper v Stubbs 10 TC 29, [1925] 2 KB 753 .... Vol I p 629, Vol II pp 204, 614
Cooper, Re [1911] 2 KB 550 .... Vol II p 332
Co-operative Insurance Society v Richardson [1955] CLY 1365 .... Vol III p 43
Copeman v Coleman 22 TC 594, [1939] 2 KB 484 .... Vol II p 82

Cormacs Trustees v The Commissioners of Inland Revenue [1924] SC 819 .... Vol V p 181
Corporation of Birmingham v Barnes 19 TC 195 .... Vol III pp 165, 253
Corporation of Dublin v Building and Allied Trades Union [1996] 1 IR 468 .... Vol VI p 513
Corr, F (Inspector of Taxes) v F E Larkin 3 ITC 13, [1949] IR 399 .... Vol II p 164
Costa Rica Railway Co Ltd v Commissioners of Inland Revenue 29 TC 34 .... Vol II p 429
Costa v ENEL [1964] ECR 585 .... Vol VI p 21
Cottin v Blane [1975] 2 ANSTR 544 .... Vol III p 265
Coughlan v Ireland and the Attorney General (12 July 1995) HC .... Vol VI p 502
Council for Civil Services Union v Minister for the Civil Service (1985) 1 AC 374 .... Vol VI p 636
Courtauld v Leigh LR 4 Ex at 149 .... Vol V p 570
Cowan v Seymour 7 TC 372, [1920] 1 KB 500 .... Vol I pp 155, 618
Cox v Glue 5 CB 533 .... Vol II p 636
Cox v Hickman 8 HCL 268 .... Vol III p 467
Cox v Ireland [1992] 2 IR 503 .... Vol VI p 386
Cox v Murray [1919] 1 IR 358 .... Vol II p 332
Cox v Rabbits 3 AC 478 .... Vol I p 601
Craddock v Zevo Finance Co Ltd 27 TC 267, [1944] 1 All ER 566, 174 LT 385 .... Vol II p 419
Craignish, Re [1892] 3 Ch 192 .... Vol I p 259
Craven's Mortgage, Re 8 TC 651, [1907] 2 Ch 448 .... Vol II p 332
Criminal Assets Bureau v Craft (12 July 2000) .... Vol VI p 422
Criminal Assets Bureau v Hunt VI ITR 559 .... Vol VI p 720
Criminal Assets Bureau v KB (15 May 2001) HC .... Vol VI p 422, 636
Criminal Assets Bureau v Kelly VI ITR 501 .... Vol VI p 422
Criminal Assets Bureau v McDonnell (20 December 2000) SC .... Vol VI p 422, 502, 636, 840
Criminal Assets Bureau v McSweeney VI ITR 423 .... Vol VI p 561,636,720
Criminal Assets Bureau v PS VI ITR 719 .... Vol VI p 800
Criminal Law (Jurisdiction) Bill 1975, Re [1977] IR 129 .... Vol VI p 744
Croft v Sywell Aerodrome 24 TC 126, [1942] 1 All ER 110 .... Vol II p 315
Cromwell (Lord) v Andrews Cro Eliz 15 .... Vol II p 222
Cronin (Inspector of Taxes) v Cork & County Property Co Ltd [1986] IR 559 .... Vol III p 271, Vol IV p 135
Cronin v Strand Diary Ltd III ITR 441 .... Vol III p 611 .... Vol IV p 35, 533, 526, Vol V 21, Vol V p 21, Vol VI p 524, 691, 2006 p 82
Cronk, John & Sons Ltd v Harrison [1936] 120 TC 112 .... Vol III p 683
Crosby v Wadsworth [1805] 6 East 602 .... Vol II p 636
Crowley v Ireland [1980] IR 102 .... Vol V p 614
Cullen v Attorney General LR 1 HL 190 .... Vol V p 539
Cullen v Cullen [1962] IR 268 .... Vol V p 589
Currie v Commissioners of Inland Revenue & Durant v Commissioners of Inland Revenue [1921] 12 TC 245 .... Vol III p 211
Custom & Excise Commissioners v Zinn [1988] STC 57 .... Vol IV p 349
Customs & Excise Commissioners v Dearwood Ltd [1986] STC 327 .... Vol VI p 618

Customs and Excise Commissioners v United Biscuits (UK) Ltd (t/a Simmers) [1992] STC 325 .... Vol VI p 597
Cyprus (Republic of) v Demetriades [1977] 12 JSC 2102 .... Vol V p 615
Cyril Lord Carpets Ltd v Schofield 42 TC 637 .... Vol III p 165

D

D & GR Rankine v Commissioners of Inland Revenue 32 TC 520, [1952] SLT 153 .... Vol II p 429, Vol IV p 135
Dagnall, Re 12 TC 712, [1896] 2 QB 407 .... Vol I p 108
Dale v Commissioners of Inland Revenue [1953] 34 TC 468 .... Vol II p 596
Dale v Johnson 32 TC .... Vol III p 661
Daphne v Shaw [1926] 11 TC 256 .... Vol II p 602, Vol III pp 113, 120
Dassonville [1974] ECR 837 .... Vol VI p 472
Date v Mitcalfe [1928] 1 KB 383, 13 TC 41, [1927] WN 271 .... Vol I p 221
Davies v Presbyterian Church of Wales [1986] ICR 280 .... Vol VI p 771
Davis (Inspector of Taxes) v Hibernian Bank Ltd 2 ITC 111 .... Vol II p 419 .... Vol III p 373
Davis (Inspector of Taxes) v The Superioress, Mater Misericordiae Hospital Dublin [1933] IR 481, 1 ITR 387 .... Vol V p 6
Davis v Adair [1895] 1 IR 379 .... Vol I p 259
Davis v Johnson [1978] 1 All ER 841, CA 1132 HL (E) .... Vol III p 113, 120
Davis v M 2 ITC 320, [1947] IR 145 .... Vol II p 500, 515
Dawson v Dawson 11 Jur 984 .... Vol II p 332
De Brun (Inspector of Taxes) v K [1981] IR 117, [1982] ILRM 13 .... Vol III pp 56, 113, 120, 304, 319, 441, 477, 533, 611, 683 .... Vol IV pp 91, 349, 526, 547, Vol VI p 524, 686, 2006 p 82
De Burca v The Attorney General [1976] IR 38 .... Vol V p 614
Deely v Information Commissioner [2001] 3 IR 439 .... 2006 p 64
De Nicolls v Saunders LR 5, CP 589 .... Vol II p 222
Deane, Re [1936] IR 556 .... Vol VI p 818
Dearle v Hall 15 TC 725, 3 Russell Reports 1 .... Vol II p 592
Deaton v Attorney General [1963] IR 170, [1962] 98 ILTR 99 .... Vol III pp 419, 533, Vol IV p 278
Defrenne v Sabena [1976] 2 CMLR 98 .... Vol V p 614
Deighan, Michael v Edward N Hearne, Attorney General [1986] IR 603, [1990] IR 499, III ITR 533 .... Vol III p 590 .... Vol IV p 505, Vol VI p 126, 422, 446, 561, 720, 800
Dennehy v Minister for Social Welfare (26 July 1984) HC .... Vol IV p 437
Denny and Sons (Ireland) Ltd v Minister for Social Welfare [1998] 1 IR 34, V ITR 238 .... Vol VI p 373, 674, 757, 771, 2006 p 64
Depoix v Chapman 28 TC 462, [1947] 2 All ER 649 .... Vol II p 241
Derby (Earl of) v Aylmer 6 TC 665 .... Vol III p 113, 120
Derry v Inland Revenue [1927] SC 714 Vol V p 614
Derry v The Commissioners of Inland Revenue [1927] Sess Cas 714, 13 TC 30 .... Vol II p 75
Deuchar v Gas Light & Coke Co [1925] AC .... Vol II p 241
Deutsche Bank Aktiensgesellschaft v Murtagh [1995] 1 ILRM 381 .... 2000 p 216
Deutsche Morgan Grenfell Group plc v Inland Revenue Commissioners [1996] 2 IR 1 .... Vol VI p 840

Dewar v Inland Revenue Commissioners 19 TC 561 .... Vol III p 484
Dickinson, ex p (1856) 44 ER 542.. Vol VI p 442
Dickson v Fitch's Garage [1975] STC 480 .... Vol V p 200
Diggines v Forestal Land, Timber and Railways Co Ltd 15 TC 630,
[1931] AC 380..Vol II p 304
Dillon v Dunnes Stores [1966] IR 397 .... Vol VI p 784
Dinning v Henderson 3 de G & S 702 ....Vol II p 332
Diplock v Wintle [1948} Ch 465 .... Vol IV p 247
Director of Public Prosecutions v Humphrys [1977] AC 1, [1976] 2 WLR 837,
[1976] 2 All ER 497 .... Vol III p 419
Director of Public Prosecutions v Luft 2 All ER 569, [1976] 3 WLR 32............ Vol III p 28
Director of Public Prosecutions v Lynch [1982] IR 64, [1981] ILRM 389....... Vol III p 419
Director of Public Prosecutions v McLoughlin [1986] IR 355, [1986] ILRM 493
.... Vol IV p 378, Vol VI p 373
Director of Public Prosecutions v Ottewell [1970] AC 642, 649......................... Vol III p 19
Director of Public Prosecutions v Robert Downes [1987] IR 139, [1987] ILRM 665
.... Vol IV p 395
Director of Public Prosecutions v Walsh [1981] IR 412.................................. Vol IV p 437
Directory Public Prosecutions v Shaw [1982] IR 1 .... Vol VI p 784
Directory Public Prosecutions v Ward (27 November 1998) SCC .... Vol VI p 784
Ditcher v Denison 11 Moore PC 325 p 337...Vol II p 108
Diver v McCrea [1908] 42 ILTR 249 .... Vol V p 271
Dixon v Fitch's Garage Ltd 50 TC 509, [1975] STC 480, [1975] 3 All ER 455
....Vol III p 219, Vol IV pp 68, 284, 425
Dixon, Heynes v Dixon, Re [1900] 2 Ch 561 .... Vol III p 265
Dolan (Inspector of Taxes) v AB Co Ltd [1969] IR 282, 104 ILTR 101 ....Vol II p 602
Dolan v Corn Exchange [1975] IR 315 .... Vol V p 322
Dolan v Joyce and Kirwan [1928] IR 559 ....Vol II p 1
Dolan v Neligan [1967] IR 247 .... Vol III p 403, Vol V p 322, 614, Vol VI p 840
Dolan, JD (Inspector of Taxes) v "K" National School Teacher 2 ITC 280,
[1944] IR 470 .... Vol II p 592, Vol III p 484, Vol IV p 221
Donald v Thomson 8 TC 272, [1922] SC 237 ....Vol II p 636
Donovan (Inspector of Taxes) v CG Crofts 1 ITC 214, [1926] IR 477
.... Vol I p 183, Vol II p 75
Douglas v Douglas CR 12 Eq 643 .... Vol I p 259
Downing's Estate, Re 1 ITC 103, [1936] IR 164 ....Vol II p 332
Doyle v An Taoiseach [1986] ILRM 522 .... Vol IV p 162
Doyle v Kildare County Council [1995] 2 IR 424 ....2006 p 56
Doyle v Government of Ireland [1981] ECR 735 .... Vol III p 73
Doyle, In Re Evelyn (SC) 21 Dec 1955 .... Vol V p 614
Draper v Attorney General [1984] IR 277, [1984] ILRM 643 .... Vol IV p 437
Drexl, Re No 299/86 .... Vol IV p 512
Dreyfus (Camille and Henry) Foundation v Commissioners of Inland Revenue
(1955) 36 TC 126 .... Vol VI p 8
Drummond v Commissioners of Inland Revenue 32 TC 263,
[1951] SC 482 ....Vol II p 636
DTE Financial Services Ltd v Wilson (Inspector of Taxes)
[2001] STC 777 .... Vol VI p 686

Dublin Corporation v Building and Allied Trade Union
(24 July 1996)SC .... Vol V p 322
Dublin Corporation v Flynn [1980] IR 357 .... Vol III p 419
Dublin Corporation v M'Adam 20 LR IR 497 .... Vol II p 211
Dublin Steampacket Co v Inland Revenue Commissioners 1 ITC 118,
[1926] IR 436 .... Vol I p 387
Duggan v An Taoiseach [1989 ILRM 710] .... Vol IV pp 170, 229, Vol VI p 636
Duncan v O'Driscoll [1997] ELR 38 .... Vol VI p 373
Duncan's Executors v Farmer [1909] Sess Cas 1212, 46 SCLR 857,
5 TC 417 .... Vol I p 618
Dunn Trust (In Voluntary Liquidation) v Williams 31 TC 477 .... Vol III p 373, 644
Dunne v Hamilton [1982] ILRM 290 .... Vol III p 356
Duple Motor Bodies Ltd v Inland Revenue Commissioners [1961] 1 WLR 739
.... Vol III p 198
Duple Motor Bodies Ltd v Ostime 39 TC 537 .... Vol IV p 135
Durbeck's, Re [1981] ECR 1095 .... Vol IV p 492
DWS Corporation v Minister of National Revenue [1968] 2 Ex CR 44 .... Vol VI p 328

E

Eadie v Commissioners of Inland Revenue 9 TC 1, [1924] 2 KB 198
.... Vol I p 115, Vol II p 75
East Cork Foods v O'Dwyer Steel [1978] IR 103 .... Vol V p 322, 614, Vol VI p 513
East Donegal Co-operative Livestock Marts Ltd v Attorney General [1970] IR 317,
104 ILTR 81 .... Vol III pp 73, 127, 590, Vol V p 614, Vol VI p 68, 386, 784
East India Trading Co Inc v Carmel Exporters and Importers Ltd
[1952] 1 All ER 1053 .... Vol II p 281
East Realty and Investment Co v Schneider Granite Co [1916] 240 US 55 .... Vol III p 127
Eastend Dwellings Co Ltd v Finsbury Borough Council [1953] AC 109 .... Vol VI p 203
Eastmans Ltd v Shaw 43 TLR 549, 14 TC 218 .... Vol II pp 32, 515
.... Vol III p 95, Vol V p 680
Ebrahimi v Westbourne Galleries Ltd [1973] AC 379 .... Vol V p 226
Edinburgh Life Assurance Co v Lord Advocate 5 TC 472 .... Vol IV p 135
Educational Co v Fitzpatrick No 2 [1961] IR 345 .... Vol VI p 68
Edwards (Inspector of Taxes) v Bairstow 36 TC 207, [1956] AC 14
.... Vol II pp 515, 614, 636, Vol III pp 1, 178, 211, 219, 253, 644
.... Vol IV p 135, Vol V p 139, 200, Vol VI p 579, 597
Eglinton Silica Brick Co Ltd v Marrian [1924] Sess Cas 946, 61 SC LR 601,
9 TC 92 .... Vol II p 115
Egyptian Delta Land and Investment Co Ltd v Todd 14 TC 119,
[1929] AC 1 .... Vol I p 259
Egyptian Hotels Ltd v Mitchell 6 TC 542, CA [1914] 3 KB 118,
[1915] AC 1022 .... Vol I p 359, Vol II p 68
Eisher v Macomber 252 US 207 .... Vol IV p 135
Ellerker v Union Cold Storage Co Ltd 22 TC 195 .... Vol III p 304
Elliott v Elliott 9 M & W 23 .... Vol I p 130
Elmhirst v The Commissioners of Inland Revenue 21 TC 381,
[1937] 2 KB 551 .... Vol I p 563
Emery, John & Sons v Commissioners of Inland Revenue 20 TC 213,
[1935] SC 802, [1937] AC 91 .... Vol I p 515, 583, Vol II pp 429, 472

Emery's Investment Trusts, Re [1959] 1 Ch 410 .... 1998 p 169
English Crown Spelter Co Ltd v Baker 5 TC 327, 99 LTR 353 .... Vol I p 642
Ensign Tankers (Leasing) Ltd v Stokes (Inspector of Taxes) [1989] STC 705, [1992] 2 All ER 275 .... Vol V p 6
Enoch and Zaretzky, Re, Bock & Co's Arbitration [1910] 1 KB 327 .... 2006 p 56
Equal Status Bill, Re [1997] 2 IR 387 .... Vol VI p 720
Erichsen v Last 4 TC 422, 8 QBD 414 .... Vol I p 330, 387
Essex County Council v Ellman (1989) STC 31T .... Vol V p 108
Evans & Co v Phillips (Inspector of Taxes) 1 ITC 38 .... Vol I p 43
Evans Medical Supplies Ltd v Moriarty 37 TC 540, [1956] 1 WLR 794 .... Vol II p 602
Evans v Wheatley 38 TC 216 .... Vol II p 515
Exham v Beamish [1939] IR 336 .... Vol II p 154
Exported Live Stock (Insurance) Board, The v TJ Carroll (Inspector of Taxes) 3 ITC 67, [1951] IR 286 .... Vol IV p 73
Express and Echo Publications Limited v Tanton (Ernst) [1999] IRLR 367 .... 2006 p 64

F

Faccini Dore v Recreb [1995] All ER European Cases .... Vol VI p 21
Fakih v Minister for Justice [1993] 2 IR 406 .... Vol VI p 636, 720
Falcke v Scottish Imperial Insurance Co 34 Ch D 234 .... Vol I p 601
Fall v Hitchen 49 TC 433 .... Vol III p 43, Vol IV p 45
Farmer v The Juridicial Society of Edinburgh [1914] Sess Cas 731, 6 TC 467 [1914] .... Vol I p 542
Farmer v The Scottish North American Cross Ltd .... Vol V p 139
Farrell v Alexander [1975] 3 WLR 642, 650-1, [1977] AC 59 .... Vol III p 19, 229
Federal Commission of Taxation v Broken Hill Proprietary Co (1967–1969) 120 CLR 241 .... Vol VI p 524
Federal Commission of Taxation v Henderson (1943) 68 CLR 29 .... Vol VI p 524
Federal Commission of Taxation v Northwest Iron Co Ltd (27 March 1986), Federal Court of Australia .... Vol VI p 524
Federal Commissioner of Taxation v Utah Development Co (1976) 76 ATC 4119 .... Vol VI p 524
Federal Commissioner of Taxation v Westraders Pty Ltd [1980] 114 CLR 35 .... Vol III p 683
Federal Commissioners of Taxation v ICI Australia Ltd [1972] 127 CLR 529 3 ATR 321 .... Vol IV p 68, Vol VI p 524
Fee v Collendars Trustees [1927] SLT (Sh Ct) 17 .... Vol II p 32
Feeny v Pollexfen and Co Ltd [1931] IR 589 .... Vol III p 661
Ferguson v Dawson & Partners CA [1976] .... Vol V p 239
Ferguson v Noble [1919] 2 SC LT 49, 7 TC 176, [1919] SC 534 .... Vol I p 231
Ferguson, Re [1935] IR 21 .... Vol II p 332
Figgis Deceased, Re [1969] 1 Ch 123, [1968] 2 WLR 1173, [1968] 1 All ER 999 .... Vol V p 272
Finden v Stephens 2 Ph 142 .... Vol I p 601
Findlay's Trustees v Inland Revenue Commissioners [1938] 22 ATC 437 .... Vol V p 577
Finlay v Murtagh [1979] IR 249 .... Vol IV p 117
Finucane v McMahon [1990] 1 IR 165 .... Vol V p 272
Firma A Racke v Hauptzollamt Mainz (Case 98/78) [1979] ECR 69 .... Vol VI p 21
Firman, Re .... Vol III p 387

First National Commercial Bank plc v Anglin [1996] IR 75 .... Vol VI p 126
Fitzgerald v Persse Ltd [1908] IR 279 .... Vol II p 130
Fitzgerald, Martin v Commissioners of Inland Revenue 1 ITC 100, [1926] IR 182, 585 .... Vol II pp 32, 45, 222, 267, 360, Vol IV p 425
Flanagan v University College Dublin [1988] IR 724 .... Vol VI p 784
Fleming v Wilkinson 10 TC 416 .... Vol II p 393, 491
Floor v Davis (Inspector of Taxes) [1978] STC 436 .... Vol VI p 203
Flynn, W (Inspector of Taxes) v (1) John Noone Ltd, and Flynn, W (Inspector of Taxes) v (2) Blackwood & Co (Sligo) Ltd 3 ITC 79 .... Vol II pp 222, 464, 515, Vol III p 683
Foley v Fletcher [1858] 3 H & N 769 .... Vol V p 108
Food Controller v Cork [1923] AC 647 .... Vol I p 45
Forbes v Forbes Kay 341 .... Vol I p 259
Forbes v Tobin VI ITR 483 .... 2006 p 56
Forsyth v Thompson 23 TC 374 .... Vol I p 164
Foster v Elsley 19 Ch D 419 .... Vol I p 601
Fraikey v Charlton (1920) 1 KB 147 .... Vol VI p 386
Franconini v Franconini 11 Jur NS 124 .... Vol I p 427
Fraser (Inspector of Taxes) v London Sportscar Centre Ltd [1985] STC 688, [1985] 59 TC 63 .... Vol III p 611, Vol IV p 304
Frasers (Glasgow) Bank Ltd v Commissioners of Inland Revenue 40 TC 698 .... Vol III p 373
Freidson v Glynn Thomas [1922] WN 251 .... Vol I p 64
Fry v Burma Corporation Ltd 15 TC 113, [1930] 1 KB 249, [1930] AC 321 .... Vol I p 571,
Fry v Inland Revenue Commissioners [1959] Ch 86 .... Vol III p 56
Fry v Salisbury House Estate Ltd [1930] 1 KB 304, 143 LT 77, [1930] AC 432 .... Vol II p 429, 596, Vol V p 680
Furniss v Dawson [1984] AC 474, [1984] 2 WLR 226, [1984] 1 All ER 530, [1984] 55 TC 324, [1984] STC 153 .... Vol III p 670, 683, Vol IV p 547 .... Vol V p 6, 108, 163, 515, 2006 p 82
Furse, Re (1980) 3 All ER 344 .... Vol V p 481
Furtado v Carndonald Fening Co [1907] SC 36, 20 TC 223 .... Vol I p 515

G

G v An Bord Uchtála [1980] IR 32, [1979] 113 ILTR 25 .... Vol IV p 437
G v Director of Public Prosecutions [1994] 1 IR 374 .... Vol V p 362
Gaffney v Gaffney [1975] IR 133 .... Vol IV p 437
Gallagher v The Revenue Commissioners [1991] 2 IR 370 .... Vol VI p 784
Garforth v Tankard Carpets Ltd 53 TC 342 .... Vol III p 340
Gartside v Inland Revenue Commissioners [1968] 2 WLR 277 .... Vol III p 104
Garvey v Ireland [1981] IR 75 .... Vol V p 696
Gascoigne v Gascoigne [1918] 1 KB 223 .... 1998 p 169
Gason v Rich 19 LR (Irl) 391 .... Vol V p 272
Gatien Motor Co v Continental Oil [1979] IR 406 .... Vol IV p 269
General Medical Council v Commissioners of Inland Revenue 13 TC 819, [Reported 139 LTR 225] .... Vol I p 542
General Nursing Council for Scotland v The Commissioners of Inland Revenue 14 TC 645, [1929] SC 664 .... Vol I p 542

General Reversionary Interest and Investment Co Ltd v Hancock 7 TC 358,
[1939] 1 KB 25 .... Vol II p 515
George Ingelfield Ltd, Re [1933] Ch 1 .... Vol V p 515
Germyn Street Turkish Baths Ltd [1971] 3 All ER 184 .... Vol III p 423
Gibbon v Pearse [1905] 1KB 816 .... Vol IV p 332
Gibbs v Mersey Docks Trustees [Not reported] .... Vol II p 241
Gilbert v Commissioners of Inland Revenue [1957] 248 F 2d 399 .... Vol III p 683
Gilli v Andres [1980] ECR 2071 .... Vol VI p 472
Gillies v Commissioners of Inland Revenue 14 TC 329, [1929] SC 131 .... Vol I p 411
Gilroy v Flynn (3 December 2004) SC .... Vol VI p 824
Gisbourne v Gisbourne [1877] 2 AC 300 .... Vol IV p 340
Glamorgan Quarter Sessions v Wilson 5 TC 537, [1910] 1 KB 725 .... Vol II p 332
Glanely (Lord) v Wightman 17 TC 634, [1933] AC 618 .... Vol I p 496
Glanely v Wightman 17 TC 634, [1933] AC 613 .... Vol II p 315
Glasgow Corporation v Inland Revenue [1959] SLT 230 .... Vol V p 614
Glenboig Union Fireclay Co Ltd v Commissioners of Inland Revenue 12 TC 427,
[1922] Sess (HL) 112 .... Vol I p 1, 427, Vol II p 515
Glencar Exploration Plc v Mayo County Council [2001]1 IR 112 .... Vol VI p 636
Gliksten 14 TC 364 .... Vol I p 164
Global Plant Ltd v Secretary of State for Health and Social Security
[1971] 3 All ER 385, [1971] 2 WLR 269, [1972] 1 QB 139 .... Vol III p 43
.... Vol IV p 45
Gold Coast Selection Trust v Humphrey 30 TC 209, [1948] AC 459, [1946] 2 All ER 742,
[1948] 2 All ER 379 .... Vol II p 419
Golden Horse Shoe Ltd v Thurgood [1934] 1 KB 548 .... Vol II p 515
Golder v Great Boulder Proprietary Gold Mines Ltd 33 TC 75, [1952] 1 All ER 360
.... Vol II p 500
Golding (Inspector of Taxes) v Kaufman [1985] STC 152 .... Vol IV p 547, Vol V p 515
Goldstein v Commissioners of Inland Revenue [1966] 364 F 2nd 734 .... Vol III p 683
Goodman International v Hamilton (No 1) [1992] 2 IR 542 .... Vol VI p 68, 720
Gordon and Blair Ltd v Cronin 40 TC 358 .... Vol III p 363
Gordon v Dunleavy [1928] IR 595 .... Vol II p 291
Goslar v Breitsol [2001] STC 355 .... Vol VI p 824
Goslings and Sharpe v Blake 2 TC 450, 23 QBD 324 .... Vol II p 332
Gould v Curtis 6 TC 293, [1913] 2 KB 84 .... Vol II p 661
Governors of Rotunda Hospital v Coman 7 TC 517, [1921] 1 AC 1, 36 TLR 646
.... Vol I p 387, 515
Gowers v Walker 15 TC 165, [1930] 1 Ch 262 .... Vol II p 108
Graham v District Justice Carroll (9 December 1987) HC .... Vol IV p 278
Graham v Greene [1925] 9 TC 309 .... Vol II p 614, Vol III p 363
Graham v Minister for Industry and Commerce [1933] IR 156 .... Vol III p 43
Vol IV p 45, Vol V p 239
Grainger v Gough 3 TC 462, [1896] AC 325 .... Vol I p 330
Granite Supply Association Ltd Kitton 5 TC 168, 43 SCLR 65, [1905] 8F 5
.... Vol I p 91, Vol II pp 32, 45, 382, 515
Granville Building Co Ltd v Oxby 35 TC 245 .... Vol III p 1
Gray & Co Ltd v Murphy 23 TC 225 .... Vol I p 164
Gray and Gillet v Tiley 26 TC 80 .... Vol III p 1

Gray v Formosa [1963] P 259 .... Vol IV p 437
Gray v Holmes 30 TC 467, [1949] TR 71 .... Vol II p 452
Great Northern Railway Co v Sunburst Oil & Refining Co [1932] 287 US 358 .... Vol V p 614
Green v Favourite Cinemas Ltd 15 TC 390 .... Vol II p 464
Green v Inland Revenue Commissioners ITC 142, [1927] IR 240 .... Vol I p 240
Green v J Gliksten & Sons Ltd [1928] 2 KB 193, [1929] AC 381, 14 TC 364 .... Vol I p 427
Green v Minister for Agriculture [1990] ILRM 364 .... Vol IV p 323
Green, JW & Co Ltd v the Inland Revenue Commissioners [1927] IR 240, [1927] ILTR 145 .... Vol IV p 304
Greene v Louisville and Interurban Railway Co [1917] 244 US 499 .... Vol III p 127
Greenhalgh v Arderne Cinemas Ltd [1950] 2 All ER 1120 .... Vol III p 423
Greenore Trading Co Ltd (28 March 1980) .... Vol III p 423
Gresham Life Assurance Society Ltd v Bishop 4 TC 464, [1903] 2 KB 171 .... Vol III p 484
Gresham Life Assurance Society v Attorney General [1916] 1 Ch 228 .... Vol I p 34
Gresham Life Assurance Society v Styles 3 TC 185, [1892] AC 309 .... Vol I pp 1, 515 .... Vol IV p 135
Griffin v Illinois [1956] 351 US 12 .... Vol V p 614
Griffiths (Inspector of Taxes) v Harrison (Waterford) Ltd, JP [1962] 1 All ER 909 .... Vol V p 6
Griffiths v Mockler 35 TC 135; [1953] 2 All ER 805 .... Vol II p 366
Grimes v Wallace (4 March 1994) .... Vol V p 210
Grocock v Grocock [1920] 1 KB 1 .... Vol I p 629
Groome v Fodhla Printing Co [1943] IR 380 .... Vol II p 360
Grove v Young Men's Christian Association 88 LT 696, 4 TC 613 .... Vol I p 387
Grundstuckgemeinschaft Schlosstrasse [2000] ECR 1 (Case C–396/98) .... Vol VI p 824
Guildford Corporation v Brown [1915] 1 KB 256 .... Vol III p 441, 611
Guinness & Mahon Ltd v Browne (Inspector of Taxes) .... Vol III p 644
Gulbenkian Settlement Trusts, Re [1970] AC 508; [1968] 3 WLR 1127, [1968] 3 All ER 785 .... Vol V p 37
Gutrani v Governor of Mountjoy Training Unit, Mountjoy Prison [1993] 2 IR 427 .... Vol VI p 636

H

Haegeman (R & V) v Commission (Case 96/71) [1972] ECR 1005 .... Vol VI p 21
Hafton Properties Ltd v McHugh [1987] STC 16 .... Vol VI p 818
Hall v Inland Revenue Commissioners 12 TC 382, [1921] LJ 1229 .... Vol I p 240
Hallett's Estate, Re [1879] 13 Ch D 696 .... Vol IV p 247
Hallstrooms Pty Ltd v Federal Commissioners of Taxation [1946] 72 CLR 634 .... Vol II p 515
Hamerton v Overy 35 TC 73 .... Vol II p 366
Hamilton v Commissioners of Inland Revenue 16 TC 28 .... Vol III p 229
Hamilton v Hamilton [1982] IR 466, [1982] ILRM 290 .... Vol III p 73, Vol IV p 162
Hamilton v Linaker [1923] IR 104 .... Vol II p 332
Hammond Lane Metal Co Ltd, The v Ó Culacháin (Inspector of Taxes) [1990] IR 560 .... Vol V p 6

Hampton (Inspector of Taxes) v Fortes Auto-Grill Ltd [1980] STC 80, 53 TC 691 .... Vol IV pp 68, 284
Hanbury, Re 38 TC 588 .... Vol V p 108
Hancock v General Reversionary and Investment Co 7 TC 358, [1919] 1 KB 25 .... Vol II p 32
Hanlon v North City Milling Co [1903] 2 IR 163 .... Vol V p 532
Hann v Darby [1979] ECR 3795 .... Vol VI p 472
Harling v Celynen Collieries Workmen's Institute 23 TC 558, [1940] 2 KB 465 .... Vol II p 482
Harrision, JP (Watford) Ltd v Griffith 40 TC 281 .... Vol III p 373
Hartland v Diggines 10 TC 247, [1926] AC 289 .... Vol II p 452
Harvey v Caulcott 33 TC 159 .... Vol II p 472, Vol III p 1, 9, 373
Harvey v Minister for Social Welfare [1990] ILRM 185 .... Vol V p 696
Haughey, Re [1971] IR 217 .... Vol III p 590, Vol V p 614, Vol VI p 68
Hay v O'Grady [1992] IR 210 .... Vol VI p 597
Hayes, C (Inspector of Taxes) v RJ Duggan 1 ITC 269, [1929] IR 406 .... Vol II p 291
Healy, John v SI Breathnach (Inspector of Taxes) [1986] IR 105 .... Vol V p 98
Heaney v Ireland [1994] 2 ILRM 420 .... Vol V p 213
Heather v PE Consulting Group Ltd 48 TC 293 .... Vol IV p 135
Helby v Matthews [1895] AC 471 .... Vol V p 515
Helby v Rafferty [1979] 1 WLR 13 .... Vol V p 614
Henderson v Folkestone Waterworks Co [1885] 1 TLR 329 .... Vol V p 614
Henley and Co 1 TC 209, 9 Ch D 469 .... Vol I p 45
Henriksen v Grafton Hotels Ltd 24 TC 453, [1942] 1 KB 82, [1942] 2 KB 184 .... Vol II p 515
Herbert v McQuade 4 TC 489, [1902] 2 KB 631 .... Vol I pp 155, 427, 618, Vol II p 261
Heydon's Case 3 Rep 75 .... Vol V p 539
HH v MJ Forbes (Inspector of Taxes) .... Vol III p 178
High Wycombe Squash Club Ltd v C & E Commissioners [1976] VAT TR 156 .... Vol IV p 349
Highland Railway Co v Balderston 26 SC LR 657, 2 TC 485 .... Vol II p 32
Hill v East and West India Dock Co 9 AC 448 .... Vol II p 130
Hill v Gregory 6 TC 39, [1912] 2 KB 70 .... Vol I p 515
Hill v Mathews 10 TC 25 .... Vol II p 115
Hinchcliffe (Inspector of Taxes) v Crabtree 47 TC 419 .... Vol IV p 125
Hinches, Dashwood v Hinches, Re [1921] 1 Ch 475, 19 TC 521 .... Vol I p 515
Hinton v Madden and Ireland Ltd 38 TC 391, [1959] 3 All ER 356, 1 WLR 875 .... Vol II p 602, Vol III pp 113, 120
Hitchcock v Post Office [1980] ICR 100 .... Vol IV p 45
Hochstrasser v Mayes 38 TC 673, [1958] 3 WLR 215, [1959] Ch 22, [1960] AC 376 .... Vol II p 452, Vol IV p 407
Hodgins, JT (Inspector of Taxes) v Plunder & Pollak (Ireland) Ltd 3 ITC 135, [1957] IR 58 .... Vol II pp 382 500, 515, 602, Vol III p 65
Hoechst Finance Ltd v Gumbrell [1983] STC 150 .... Vol III p 95 .... Vol V p 496, 680, Vol VI p 158
Hoeper v Tax Commission of Wisconsin [1931] 284 US 206 .... Vol V p 615
Holland v Hodgson [1872] LR 7 CP 328 .... Vol III p 332
Holroyd v Wyatt 1 de G & S 125 .... Vol II p 332

Holt v Inland Revenue Commissioners [1953] 1 WLR 1488 .... Vol V p 295, 577, Vol VI p 203
Hood Barrs v Commissioners of Inland Revenue 27 TC 385, [1945] 1 All ER 500 (on appeal [1946] 2 All ER 768) .... Vol II p 82
Hope-Edwards v Blackburne [1901] 1 Ch 419 .... Vol I p 487
Horsfall, exp [1827] 108 ER 820 .... Vol IV p 332
Houghland v RR Low (Luxury Coaches) Ltd [1962] .... Vol III p 253
Howe (Earl) v Commissioners of Inland Revenue 7 TC 289 .... Vol V p 108
Howe, ex p Brett, Re [1871] 6 Ch App 838 .... Vol III p 265
Howth Estate Co v WJ Davis (Inspector of Taxes) 2 ITC 74, [1936] ILTR 79 .... Vol II p 429
HT Ltd, Re (in Liq) [1984] ILRM 583 .... Vol III p 523
Hudson Bay Co Ltd v Stevens 101 LT 96, 25 TLR 709, 5 TC 424 .... Vol I pp 1, 474
Hudson v Wrightson 26 TC 55 .... Vol III p 9
Hughes v Metropolitan Railway Co [1877] 2 AC 439 .... Vol V p 589
Hughes v Utting and Co Ltd 23 TC 174, [1940] AC 463 .... Vol II p 472
Hughes, HPC (Inspector of Taxes) v Miss Gretta Smyth (Sister Mary Bernard) 1 ITC 418, [1933] IR 253 .... Vol II p 82
Humble v Humble 12 Beav 43 .... Vol II p 332
Humphrey v Peare 6 TC 201, [1913] 2 IR 462 .... Vol I p 1, 155
Huntington v Attrill [1893] AC 150 .... Vol V p 45
Huntley v Gaskell [1906] AC 56 .... Vol I p 259
Hutton v The West Cork Railway Co [1883] 23 Ch D 654 .... Vol III p 706, ... Vol IV p 247
Hyam v Commissioners of Inland Revenue [1929] SC 384, 14 TC 479, [1929] SC LT 361 .... Vol II p 32

I

Iannelli v Meroni [1977] ECR 557 .... Vol VI p 472
Iarnród Éireann v Ireland (28 April 1995) .... Vol V p 213
Igote Ltd v Badsey Ltd (18 July 2000) .... Vol VI p 454
Imperial Chemical Industries of Australia & New Zealand Ltd v Federal Commissioner of Taxation [1970] 120 CLR 396, 1 ATR 450 .... Vol IV p 68
Imperial Tobacco Co Ltd v Kelly 25 TC 292, [1943] 1 All ER 431, [1943] 2 All ER 119 .... Vol II p 281
Income Tax Commissioners of Bihar and Orissa Singh [1942] 1 All ER 362 .... Vol II p 500
India (Government of), Ministry of Finance (Revenue Division) v Taylor [1955] AC 491 .... Vol VI p 21
India (Republic of) v Indian Steamship Co (No 2) [1998] AC 878 .... Vol VI p 386
Industrie en Handelsonderreming Vreugdenhil BV v Commission (Case 282/90) [1992] ECR 1937 .... Vol VI p 21
Indyka v Indyka [1966] 3 All ER 583 (CA), [1967] 2 All ER 689, [1969] 1 AC 33 .... Vol IV p 437
Ingram v Inland Revenue Commissioners [1986] Ch 585, [1986] 2 WLR 598 .... Vol III p 683
Ingram, JG & Son Ltd v Callaghan 45 TC 151 .... Vol III p 363
Inland Revenue Commissioners v Blott [1921] 2 AD 171 .... Vol IV p 135

Inland Revenue Commissioners v Broadway Cottages Trust [1955] CJ 20; [1954] 3 WLR 438; [1954] 3 All ER 120; 98 SJ 588; 47 R & IT 574 35 TC 577 .... Vol V p 37
Inland Revenue Commissioners v Burmah Oil Co Ltd [1981] 54 TC 200, [1982] STC 30 .... Vol III p 683
Inland Revenue Commissioners v City of Glasgow Police Athletic Association 34 TC 76, [1953] AC 380 .... Vol II p 393
Inland Revenue Commissioners v Clay [1914] 3 KB 466 .... Vol V p 577
Inland Revenue Commissioners v Cock Russell 29 TC 387, 28 ATC 393, [1949] 2 All ER 889 .... Vol II p 419
Inland Revenue Commissioners v Crossman [1937] AC 26 .... Vol V p 577
Inland Revenue Commissioners v Doorley [1933] IR 750 .... Vol II p 25, 195, 326 .... Vol III p 683, Vol IV p 22, 91, 2006 p 82
Inland Revenue Commissioners v Duke of Westminster [1936] AC 1, [1935] 104 LJ (KB) 383, 153 LT 223, 51 TLR 467, 19 TC 490 .... Vol II p 464, Vol III p 683, Vol V p 163
Inland Revenue Commissioners v Duke of Westminster [1979] 3 All ER 775 .... Vol V p 6
Inland Revenue Commissioners v Europa Oil (NZ) Ltd [1971] AC 760, [1971] 2 WLR 55 .... Vol III p 683
Inland Revenue Commissioners v Falkirk Temperance Cafe 11 TC 353, [1927] SC 261 .... Vol I p 387
Inland Revenue Commissioners v Frere [1965] AC 402 .... Vol III p 403
Inland Revenue Commissioners v Metrolands Property Finance Ltd [1981] STC 195 .... Vol V p 347
Inland Revenue Commissioners v N 101 ILTR 197 .... Vol III p 319
Inland Revenue Commissioners v National Federation of Self Employed and Small Businesses Ltd [1982] AC 617 .... Vol IV p 229
Inland Revenue Commissioners v Newcastle Breweries Ltd 12 TC 927, 42 TLR 609 .... Vol I p 207
Inland Revenue Commissioners v Paterson 9 TC 163 .... Vol III p 484
Inland Revenue Commissioners v Plummer [1935] All ER 295 .... Vol V p 6
Inland Revenue Commissioners v Plummer [1980] AC 896, [1979] 3 WLR 689, [1979] 3 All ER 775, [1979] 54 TC 1, [1979] STC 793 .... Vol III p 683, Vol V p 108
Inland Revenue Commissioners v Ramsey (1935) 20 TC 70 .... Vol V p 108
Inland Revenue Commissioners v Reid's Trustees [1949] AC 361 .... Vol III p 56
Inland Revenue Commissioners v Rossminster [1980] AC 952 .... Vol VI p 142
Inland Revenue Commissioners v Scottish & Newcastle Breweries Ltd [1981] STC 50, [1982] STC 296 .... Vol IV pp 68, 284, 425
Inland Revenue Commissioners v Strong 15 SLR 704 .... Vol I p 155, 427
Inland Revenue Commissioners v The Duke of Westminster [1936] AC 19 & 24 .... Vol II p 175, 2006 p 82
Inland Revenue Commissioners v Thompson [1937] 1 KB 290 .... Vol III p 553
Inland Revenue Commissioners v Wesleyan and General Assurance Society [1946] 2 All ER 749, [1946] 62 TLR 741 (CA), [1948] 1 All ER 555, [1948] 64 TLR 173, 30 TC 11 (HL) .... Vol II p 464, Vol III p 683
Inland Revenue Commissioners v Wolfson [1949] WN 190 .... Vol II p 175
Inspector of Taxes v Kiernan [1981] IR 117, III ITR 19 .... Vol VI p 132, 580, 588, 699

Intercommunale Voor Zeewatercontziltung (INZO) v Belgian State [1996] ECR 1-857 (Case 110/94)....Vol VI p 824
International Fishing Vessels Ltd v Minister for the Marine [1989] IR 149 ....Vol IV p 485
Inverclyde (Lord)'s Trustees v Millar 9 TC 14, [1924] SC 14 ....Vol II p 25, 195 Vol III p 246
Inverclyde, Re [1924] SC 18 ....Vol II p 326
Inwards v Baker [1965] 2 QB 29 ....Vol V p 589
Ioannides v Republic of Cyprus (6 November 1978)....Vol V p 615
Irish Agricultural Machinery Ltd v Ó Culacháin (Inspector of Taxes) [1987] IR 458, [1990] IR 535 ....Vol IV pp 35, 125, 361, 533 ....Vol V p 22, Vol VI p 524
Irish Creamery Milk Suppliers Association v The Government of Ireland ....Vol III p 73
Irish Permanent Building Society v Registrar of Building Societies, Irish Life Building Society [1981] ILRM 242 ....Vol III p 28
Irish Provident Assurance Co Ltd (In Liquidation) v Kavanagh (Inspector of Taxes) 1 ITC 52, [1930] IR 231 ....Vol I p 318
Irish Shell and BP Ltd v Costello [1981] ILRM 66 ....Vol IV p 269 ....Vol V p 108, 515
Irvine and Fullerton Property Investment Society v Cuthbertson 43 SC LR 17 ....Vol II p 25

J

James, Ex p [1874] 8 Ch App 609 ....Vol V p 615
Jarrold v John Good & Sons Ltd 40 TC 681....Vol III p 219, Vol IV p 68, Vol V p 200
Jefferson Ltd v Bhetcha [1979] 1 WLR 898, [1979] 2 All ER 1108 ....Vol VI p 784
Jeffrey v Rolls-Royce Ltd 40 TC 443, [1960] 2 All ER 640 ....Vol II p 602
Jenkins Productions Ltd v Commissioners of Inland Revenue 29 TC 142, EPT Leaflet No 21 [1944] 1 All ER 610 ....Vol II p 130
Jennings v Kinder 38 TC 673, [1959] Ch 22, [1958] 3 WLR 215....Vol II p 452
Jennings v Middlesborough Corporation 34 TC 447....Vol III p 253
Johnson v New Jersey [1966] 384 US 719 ....Vol V p 615
Jones v Commissioners of Inland Revenue 7 TC 310 ....Vol V p 108, 1998 p 184
Jones v Cwmmorthin Slate Co 1 TC 267....Vol II p 382
Jones v Flint 19 Ad & E 753....Vol II p 636
Jones v Leeming [1930] AC 415....Vol II p 204
Jones v Nuttall 10 TC 349....Vol III p 319
Jones v The Mersey Docks 11 HL Ca 480....Vol II p 211
Jones v The South West Lancashire Coal Owners' Association Ltd [1927] AC 827 ....Vol II p 211
Jones v Wright 13 TC 221, 44 TLR 128, 139 LTR 43....Vol I p 601
Jones, Re [1933] Ch 842 ....Vol V p 565
Jones, Re 26 Ch D 736....Vol V p 526
Jones, Samuel & Co (Devondale) Ltd v Commissioners of Inland Revenue 32 TC 513, [1952] SLT 144....Vol II p 267, Vol III p 65
Jordan and Harrison v MacDonald and Evans [1952] ITLR 101 ....Vol IV p 45
Joyce, Re [1946] IR 277....Vol III p 572
Julius v The Bishop of Oxford 5 AC 214 p 222....Vol I p 104

K

K Co v Hogan (Inspector of Taxes) [1985] ILRM 200 .... Vol IV p 547
Kahn v Shevin [1974] 416 US 351 .... Vol V p 615
Kealy, JB (Inspector of Taxes) v O'Mara (Limerick) Ltd 2 ITC 265,
[1942] IR 616 .... Vol II pp 25, 45, 222, 500, 602
Kearns v Dillon [1997] 3 IR 287 .... Vol VI p 636
Keenan Brothers Ltd [1985] ILRM 641 .... Vol III p 548, Vol V p 108
Keenan v Shield Insurance Company Ltd [1988] IR 89 .... 2006 p 56
Keir v Gillespie 7 TC 473, 478 .... Vol III p 319
Kelly, Peter (Estate of), Re [1908] .... Vol II p 332
Kellystown Co v Hogan [1985] ILRM 200 Vol V p 515
Kelsall Parsons & Co v Commissioners of Inland Revenue 21 TC 608,
[1938] SC 238 .... Vol II p 515
Kemp (as Hawkins' Executor) v Evans 20 TC 14 .... Vol II p 393
Kenmir Ltd v Frizzell (1968) 1 WLR 329 .... Vol VI p 618
Kennard Davis v Commissioners of Inland Revenue 8 TC 341 .... Vol II p 326
.... Vol III pp 229, 403
Kennedy (Inspector of Taxes) v The Rattoo Co-operative Dairy Society Ltd
1 ITC 282 .... Vol III p 533
Kennedy v Ireland [1987] IR 587 .... Vol VI p 68
Kenny v Attorney General 11 LR IR 253 .... Vol V p 539
Kenny v Harrison [1902] 2 KB 168 .... Vol III p 661
Kensington Income Tax Commissioners v Aramayo 6 TC 279 & 613,
[1916] 1 AC 215 .... Vol II p 291
Kent v Sussex Sawmills Ltd (1947) IR 177 .... Vol V p 108
Keogh v Criminal Assets Bureau [2004] ILRM 481, VI ITR 641 .... Vol VI p 720, 800
Kidston v Aspinall [1963] 41 TC 371 .... Vol II p 627, Vol IV p 187
Kiely v Minister for Social Welfare (No 2) [1977] IR 267 .... Vol VI p 68, 720
Kilmarnock Equitable Co-operative Society Ltd, Re 42 TC 675 .... Vol III p 65, 304
Kilroy v Parker [1966] IR 309 .... Vol V p 37
Kinemas (H & G) Ltd v Cooke 18 TC 116 .... Vol III p 178
King v Attorney General [1981] IR 233 .... Vol III p 127, Vol VI p 386
King v Foxwell 3 Ch D 518 .... Vol I p 259
King, The v British Columbia Fir and Cedar Timber Co Ltd [1932] AC 441 .... Vol I p 164
King, The v Earl Cadogan [1915] 3 KB 485 .... Vol II p 464
Kinsela v Russell Kinsela Property in Liquidation [1986] 4 NSWLR 722 .... Vol IV p 247
Kirby (Inspector of Taxes) v Thorn EMI Plc (1987) STC 621 .... Vol VI p 454
Kiriri Cotton Co Ltd v Dewani [1960] AC 192 .... Vol V p 615
Kirke's Trustees v Commissioners of Inland Revenue (Supra) 11 TC 323,
[1927] SC HL 56, 136 LT 582 .... Vol II p 115
Kirkness v John Hudson & Co Ltd 36 TC 28 .... Vol III p 477
Kleinwort Benson Ltd v Lincoln City Council [1999] 2 AC 349 .... Vol VI p 840
Knetsch v US [1960] 364 US 361 .... Vol III p 683
Knight v Calder Grove Estates 35 TC 447 .... Vol II p 382
Knight's, Re 5 Coke Rep 54B .... Vol II p 222
Knowlton v Moore [1900] 178 US 41 .... Vol V p 615
Knox v Guidea 11th ILR 482 .... Vol I p 583

L

Lands Allotment, Re [1894] 1 Ch 616\1986 4 NSWLR 722 .... Vol IV p 247
Langford v Mahoney (1843) 51 I Eq R 569 .... Vol VI p 442
Larkins v National Union of Mineworkers [1985] IR 671 .... Vol V p 45
Larner v London County Council [1949] 2 KB 683 .... Vol V p 615
Latchford and Sons Ltd v Minister for Industry [1950] IR 33 .... Vol VI p 636
Lauderdale Peerage, Re 10 AC 692 .... Vol I p 259
Law Shipping Co Ltd v Commissioners of Inland Revenue 12 TC 621, [1924] SC 74 .... Vol II p 267
Lawrie, Wmp v Commissioners of Inland Revenue 34 TC 20, [1952] SLT 413 .... Vol II p 360, Vol IV p 425
Laycock v Freeman Hardy and Willis Ltd 22 TC 288, [1939] 2 KB 1 .... Vol II p 315
Leach v Pogson 40 TC 585 .... Vol III p 253
Lean and Dickson v Ball 10 TC 345, 655 .... Vol III p 319
Lee v Dangar Grant & Co .... Vol III p 387
Leeder v Counsel [1942] 1 KB 264 .... Vol II p 204
Leeds Permanent Building Society v Proctor [1982] STC 821, [1982] 3 All ER 925 .... Vol IV pp 68, 284
Lehnhausen v Lake Shore Auto Parts Co [1973] 410 US 356 .... Vol V p 615
Leicestershire County Council v Faraday [1941] 2 KB 205 .... Vol IV p 332, Vol V p 266
Leigh v Dickson 15 QBD 85 .... Vol I p 601
Leigh v Inland Revenue Commissioners 11 TC 590, [1928] 1 KB 73 .... Vol III p 484
Leigh v Taylor .... Vol III p 332
Leitch v Emmott 14 TC 633, [1929] 2 KB 236 .... Vol I p 563, Vol IV p 1
Levene v Inland Revenue Commissioners 13 TC 486, [1928] AC 217 .... Vol I pp 259, 375, 387
Lewis Merthyr Consolidated Collieries Ltd [1929] 1 Ch 498 ..... Vol IV p 107, Vol V p 388
Lewis, ex p, 21 QBD 191 .... Vol I p 221
Lincoln Wagon and Engine Co Ltd v Commissioners of Inland Revenue 12 TC 494 .... Vol II p 429
Linkletter v Walker [1965] 381 US 618 Vol V p 615
Lismore RDC v O'Malley 36 ILTR 54, 56 .... Vol II p 241
Liverpool & London & Globe Insurance Co v Bennett [1911] 2 KB 577, [1913] AC 610, 6 TC 327 .... Vol I p 447, Vol III pp 633, 644
Lloyd v Sulley 21 SC LR 482, 2 TC 37 .... Vol I p 259
Lomax v Newton 24 TC 558, 216 LT 419, [1953] 1 WLR 1123, [1953] 2 All ER 801 .... Vol II pp 366, 460
London and Northern Estates Co v Harris 21 TC 197, [1937] 3 All ER 252, 106 LJKB 823 .... Vol II p 429
London Contract Corporation v Styles [1887] 2 TC 239 .... Vol II p 515
London County Council v Attorney General 4 TC 265, [1901] AC 26 .... Vol II pp 222, 332, 393
London County Freehold and Leasehold Properties Ltd v Sweet 24 TC 412, [1942] 2 All ER 212, 58 TLR 281 .... Vol II p 429, Vol V p 496
London Export Corporation Ltd v Jubilee Coffee Roasting Co Ltd [1958] 1 Lloyd's Rep 367 .... 2006 p 56
London Investment & Mortgage Co v Worthington 38 TC 86 .... Vol III p 165
London Library v Carter 2 TC 594 .... Vol II p 661

London Real Property Co Ltd v Jones 15 TC 266, [1930] AC 432............Vol I pp 487, 515
London School Board v Northcraft [1889] 2 Hudsons BC 4 Ed 147................Vol IV p 332
Lord Advocate v Jaffrey [1921] 1 AC 146 ....Vol IV p 437
Lothian Chemical Co Ltd v Rogers (1926) 11 TC 508 .... Vol IV p 135, Vol VI p 158
Louisville Gas and Electric Co v Coleman [1928] 277 US 32.........................Vol III p 127
Loveridge, Drayton v Loveridge, Re [1902] 2 CH 865...Vol I p 427
Lowe v Inland Revenue Commissioners [1983] STC 816................................Vol IV p 135
Lowndes v de Courcy (7 April 1960) SC ....Vol V p 589
Lucas and Chesterfield Gas & Water Board, Re [1909] 1 KB 16 ....Vol III p 298
Luipaard's Vlei Estate and Gold Mining Co Ltd v Inland Revenue Commissioners
15 TC 573, [1930] 1 KB 593 .... Vol I pp 487, 583, Vol II p 332, Vol III p 229
Luke v Inland Revenue Commissioners [1963] AC 557 ....Vol IV p 162
Lumsden v Inland Revenue Commissioners [1914] AC 877.............................Vol V p 539
Lupton v Cadogan Gardens Developments 47 TC 1, [1971] 3 All ER 460....... Vol III p 253
Lupton v RA and AB Ltd [1968] 2 All ER 1042..Vol III p 253
Lupton v SA and AB 47 TC 598 ....Vol V p 61
Lurcott v Wakely and Wheeler [1911] 1KB 905 ....Vol II p 267
Lynham v Butler (No 2) [1933] IR 74, [1932] 67 ILTR 75, [1932] LJ IR 72
....Vol III p 533
Lyons, J & Co Ltd v Attorney General [1944] Ch D 281, 1 All ER 477,
[1944] Cr 287 .... Vol III p 219, Vol IV p 68, Vol V p 200
Lysaght v Commissioners of Inland Revenue 13 TC 511, [1928] AC 234
....Vol I pp 249, 387

M

M v An Bord Uchtála [1975] IR 140, [1977] IR 287 .... Vol V p 615, 696
MacAuley v The Minister for Post and Telegraphs [1966] IR 345.................... Vol III p 533
MacCarthaigh (Inspector of Taxes) v Cablelink Ltd VI ITR 599......................Vol VI p 618
Macduff, Re 13 TC 846, [1896] Second Chancery p 466 and 467.......................Vol I p 542
MacKeown (Inspector of Taxes) v Patrick J Roe 1 ITC 206,
[1928] IR 195 ....Vol I p 618
MacLaine & Co v Eccott [1926] AC 424, 10 TC 481 ....Vol I pp 330, 571
Maclaine v Gatty [1921] 1 AC 376...Vol V p 615
MacLennan, Re [1939] 1 Ch 750..Vol V p 565
Macsaga Investments Co Ltd v Lupton 44 TC 659 ....Vol III p 253
Madgett and Baldwin v Commissioners of Customs and Excise
[1998] STC 1189..Vol VI p 597
Madigan PJ & p Madigan v Attorney General, The Revenue Commissioners
[1986] ILRM 136 ....Vol IV p 323
Maher and Nugent's Contract, Re [1910] IR 167 ....Vol V p 560
Maher v The Attorney General [1973] IR 140 ....Vol V p 615, Vol VI p 720
Mahoney's, Re [1910] 2 IR 741 ....Vol I p 221
Maire v Wood [1958] SLT 326 ....Vol III p 467
Malcolm v Lockhart 7 TC 99, [1919] AC 463 ....Vol I p 496, Vol II p 315
Mallalieu v Drurnmond (Inspector of Taxes) [1983] STC 665 ....Vol VI p 328
Mallandin Investments Ltd v Shadbolt 23 TC 367 ....Vol I p 164
Mallett v Stavely Coal & Iron Co Ltd [1928] 2 KB 405, 13 TC 772 ....Vol II p 222, 515
Malone v Harrison [1979] 1 WLR 1353...Vol V p 615
Malone v Manton 131 LTR 144...Vol II p 222

Mann Crossman & Paulin Ltd v Compton [1947] 1 All ER 742, 28 TC 410..... Vol II p 515
Mann v Edinburgh Northern Tramway Co [1893] AC 69 .... Vol VI p 442
Mara (Inspector of Taxes) v GG (Hummingbird) Ltd [1982] ILRM 421
.... Vol III pp 9, 43, 178, 211, 219, 253, 373, 441, 496, 644
.... Vol IV pp 117, 125, 233, 269, 284, 349
.... Vol V p 6, 22, 98, 139, 201, 239
.... Vol VI p 328, 454, 524, 580, 597, 618, 674, 691, 757, 2006 p 64
Marbridge Mines Ltd v The Minister for National Revenue
71 DTC 5231 .... Vol VI p 524
Marbury v Madison [1803] 5 US 49 .... Vol V p 615
Margerison v Tyre Soles Ltd 25 TC 59 .... Vol II p 515
Margrett v Lowestoft Water and Gas Co 19 TC 481 .... Vol II p 267
Mark Fishing Co v United Fishermen and Allied Workers Union 24 DLR
(3rd ed) p 585 .... Vol III p 467, Vol VI p 373
Market Investigations Ltd v Minister for Social Security [1968] 2 All ER 732,
[1969] 2 QB 173 .... Vol III p 43, Voll IV p 45
.... Vol V p 239, Vol VI p 757
Marleasing SA v La Commercial Internacional de Alimentacionsia
[1990] 1 ECR 4135 .... Vol VI p 21
Marron v Cootehill (No 2) Rural District Council [1915] AC 792 .... Vol V p 539
Marsden & Sons Ltd v Commissioners of Inland Revenue 12 TC 217 .... Vol I p 642
Marshall (Inspector of Taxes) v Kerr [1983] STC 360 .... Vol V p 347
Marshall v Crutwell [1875] LR 20 Eq 328, 44 LJ Ch 504, 39 JP 775 .... Vol V p 272
Martin v Lowry [1926] 1 KB 550, [1927] AC 312, 41 TLR 574,
11 TC 297 .... Vol I pp 155, 629
Mason v New South Wales [1959] 102 CLR 108 .... Vol V p 615
Massey (Lord) v Commissioners of Inland Revenue [1918] 2 KB 584 .... Vol V p 108
Massey v Crown Life Insurance [1978] 2 All ER 576 .... Vol V p 239, Vol VI p 758
Mathews v Cork County Council 5 TC 545, [1910] 2 IR 521 .... Vol I p 45
Matthews v Chicory Marketing Board (1938) 60 CLR 263 .... Vol III p 73
Maudslay, Sons & Field, Re (1900) 1 Ch 1002 .... Vol VI p 386
Maxwell v McLure 6 Jur NS 407, 8 WR 370 .... Vol I p 259
Mayfair Property Co, Re [1898] 2 CH 28 .... Vol II p 326
Mayo Perrott v Mayo Perrott [1958] IR 336, [1958] 93 ILTR 195 .... Vol IV p 437
McC v KED [1985] IR 697, [1987] ILRM 189 .... Vol IV p 437
McCall v Bradish-Ellames [1950] IJR 16, 84 LTR 78 .... Vol IV p 367
McCann, Charles Ltd v S Ó Culacháin (Inspector of Taxes) [1985] IR 298,
[1986] IR 196 .... Vol III pp 441, 611
.... Vol IV p 35, 361, 466, 526, 533, 547
.... Vol V p 21, 515, Vol VI p 132, 524, 691, 699, 2006 p 82
McCarthy v Keane & Others (16 December 2004, unreported) SC .... 2006 p 56
McCausland, Samuel v Ministry of Commerce [1956] NILR 36
.... Vol III pp 304, 441, 611, Vol IV p 35, 533
.... Vol V p 22, Vol VI p 524, 69, 2006 p 82
McClean, Re [1950] IR 180 .... Vol VI p 422
McConnells Trustees Commissioners of Inland Revenue [1927] SLT 14
.... Vol V p 295, 532
McDermott v Loy (July 1982) HC .... Vol VI p 758

McDonald v Bord Na gCon [1964] IR 350, [1965] IR 217............ Vol III pp 387, 577, 590
....Vol V p 288, 615, 696, Vol VI p 68, 386
McDonald v Shand 39 TLR 444, 8 TC 420..Vol I p 214
McDougall v Smith [1918] 7 TC 134 ....Vol II p 596
McEnery, Re [1941] IR 323 Vol V p 37
McEvoy v Belfast Banking Co [1935] Ac 24, [1834] NI 67; [1933] 68 ILTR 3, [1934] All ER 800, [1934] 103 LJPC 137, 151 LT 501, 40 Com Cas 1
.... Vol V p 272, 1998 p 169
McGarry (Inspector of Taxes) v Limerick Gas Committee 1 ITC 405, [1932] IR 125 ....Vol II pp 500, 515, Vol VI p 329
McGee v The Attorney General [1974] IR 284.. Vol V p 615
McGlinchey v Wren [1982] IR 154, [1983] ILRM 169 .... Vol III p 533
McGrath v McDermott (Inspector of Taxes) [1988] IR 258, III ITR 683
....Vol III p 271, Vol IV pp 91, 547
.... Vol V pp 6, 108, 163, 295, 472, 515
....Vol VI p 132, 329, 422, 580, 588, 636, 2006 p 82
McGuinness v Armstrong Patents Ltd [1980] IR 289 .... Vol VI p 422
McIntosh v Lord Advocate [2001] 2 All ER 638 .... Vol VI p 386
McIntyre v Commissioners of Inland Revenue 12 TC 1006 .... Vol III p 211
McKenna v Eaton Turner 20 TC 566, [1937] AC 162..Vol II p 68
McKenna v Herlihy [1920] 7 TC 620...Vol II p 636
McKinlay v HT Jenkins & Son Ltd 10 TC 372 ....Vol II p 281
McKinley v Minister for Defence [1992] 2 IR 333 .... Vol IV p 437
McLaren v Needham 39 TC 37 ....Vol II p 515
McLaughlin v Mrs Blanche Bailey 7 TC 508, [1920] IR 310 & 316.................Vol I p 496,
....Vol II p 315
McLellan Rawson and Co Ltd v Newall 36 TC 117.. Vol III p 1
McLoughlin, Edward and Thomas Marie Tuite v The Revenue Commissioners and Attorney General [1986] IR 235, [1986] ILRM 304, [1990] IR 83
....Vol III p 533, 641, Vol IV p 395, Vol VI p 386, 446
McMahon v The Attorney General [1972] IR 69 .... Vol V p 615
McMillan v Guest [1941] 1 KB 258, [1942] AC 561, 24 TC 190........................Vol II p 68
McNally, Daniel v O Maoldhomhniagh.....................................Vol IV p 547, Vol V p 515
McPhail v Doulton [1971] AC 424; [1970] 2 WLR 1110; [1970] 2 All ER 228 114 SJ 375 .... Vol V p 37
McRae v Commissioners of Inland Revenue [1960] 34 Tax Court of US Reports 20 .... Vol III p 683
McStay v Assicurazioni Generali SpA [1991] ILRM 237 ....2006 p 56
McTaggart v Strump 10 TC 17, [1925] SC 599 ....Vol II p 464
Meenaghan v Dublin County Council [1984] ILRM 616.................................. Vol IV p 485
Meijer v Dept of Trade [1979] ECR 1387 .... Vol VI p 472
Melling v Ó Mathghamhna [1962] IR 1 ....Vol III p 387, Vol IV p 395, Vol VI p 386
Mersey Docks and Harbour Board v Lucas 2 TC 25, [1903] 8 AC 891
....Vol I pp 387, 601, 656, Vol II pp 154, 211, 592
....Vol III p 484, Vol V p 539
Mersey Docks v Cameron 11 HL Ca 443 ....Vol II p 211
Mesco Properties Ltd, Re [1979] 1 WLR 558 .... Vol III p 523
Mesurier, Le v Le Mesurier [1985] AC 517 .... Vol IV p 437

Michelham, Re [1921] 1 Ch 705 .... Vol II p 332
Middlesex Justices 2 QBD 510 .... Vol I p 221
Mikrommatis v Republic of Cyprus [1961] 2 RSCC 125 .... Vol V p 615
Miley v Rooney 4 TC 344, [1918] 1 IR 455 .... Vol I p 542
Millheim v Barewa Oil & Mining Co NL [1971] WAR 65 .... Vol V p 226
Milnes v J Beam Group Ltd 50 TC 675 .... Vol III p 340
Minister for Agriculture v Norgo Ltd [1980] IR 155 .... Vol V p 691
Minister for Fisheries v Sealy [1939] IR 21 .... Vol V p 221
Minister for Industry and Commerce v Hale [1967] IR 50 .... Vol III p 43
Minister for Justice v Siúcre Éireann [1992] IR 215 .... Vol V p 226
Minister for Labour, The v PMPA Insurance Co Ltd (under administration) [1990] IR 284 .... Vol IV p 391
Minister for Social Welfare v John Griffiths [1992] ILRM 667 .... Vol VI p 373
Minister of Finance v Smith [1927] AC 193 .... Vol I p 195
Minister of National Revenue v Anaconda American Brass Ltd [1956] 1 All ER 20, [1956] AC 85 .... Vol II p 515, Vol III p 198, Vol IV p 135
Mitchell v B W Noble Ltd 43 TLR 102, [1927] 1 KB 719, 137 LTR 33, 11 TC 372 .... Vol I p 375, Vol II p 500, 515
Mitchell v Commissioners of Inland Revenue 25 TC 380, [1943] SC 541 .... Vol II p 636
Mitchell v Egyptian Hotels Ltd [1915] AC 1022; 6 TC 542 .... Vol I p 183
Mitchell v Ross 40 TC 11 .... Vol III p 43
Mogul of Ireland v Tipperary (NR) CC [1976] IR 260 .... Vol V p 272
Mohanlal Hargovino of Jubbulpore v Commissioners of Income Tax [1949] AC 521 28 ATC 287 .... Vol II p 515
Montreal Coke and Manufacturing Co v Minister for National Revenue [1944] 1 All ER 743 .... Vol VI p 329
Mooney (Inspector of Taxes) v McSweeney V ITR 163, [1997] IR 424 .... Vol VI p 203
Mooney v Ó Coindealbháin (No 2) [1992] 2 IR 23 .... Vol V p 326
Mooney, TB v EP Ó Coindealbháin & The Revenue Commissioners .... Vol V p 326
Moore & Co v Hare [1915] Sess Cas 91, 52 SC LR 59, 6 TC 572 .... Vol II p 45, 500
Moore & Co v Hare 6 TC 572, [1915] SC 91 .... Vol II p 32, 515
Moorhouse v Lord 10 HC Cas 272 .... Vol I p 259
Morant v Wheal Grenville Mining Co 3 TC 298 .... Vol II p 382
Morgan v Tate and Lyle 35 TC 367, [1953] Ch 601, [1955] AC 21 .... Vol II p 500, 515, Vol VI p 329
Morgan, Re 24 Ch D 114 .... Vol V p 526
Morice v The Bishop of Durham 10 TC 86 p 539, [1925] 10 Vesey 522 .... Vol I p 542
Morrow v Carty [1957] NI 174 .... Vol V p 589
Morse v Stedeford 18 TC 457 .... Vol II p 515
Moses v Macferlan [1760] 2 Burr 1005 .... Vol IV p 247, Vol V p 615
Mostyn (Lord) v London 3 TC 294, [1895] 1 QB 170 .... Vol I p 515
Moville District Board Of Conservators v D Ua Clothasaigh (Inspector of Taxes) 3 ITC 1, [1950] IR 301 .... Vol II p 154
Mowleim, Re 43 LJ CH 354 .... Vol I p 427
Moynihan v Greensmyth [1977] IR 55 .... Vol V p 615
Muckley, Bernard and Anne Muckley v Ireland, The Attorney General and The Inland Revenue Commissioners [1985] IR 472, [1986] ILRM 364 .... Vol III p 188
Mullingar RDC v Rowles 6 TC 85, [1913] 2 IR 44 .... Vol I pp 1, 427

Mulloy v Minister for Education [1975] IR 88 .... Vol III p 127
Multipar Syndicate Ltd v Davitt (Inspector of Taxes) [1945] 1 All ER 298 ..... Vol IV p 505
Munby v Furlong 50 TC 491 .... Vol III pp 113, 120
Municipal Mutual Insurance Ltd v Hills Vol XVI TC p 448 .... Vol II p 211
Murph's Restaurants, Re [1979] ILRM 141 .... Vol V p 226
Murphy v Attorney General [1982] IR 241 .... Vol III pp 127, 188
.... Vol V p 424, Vol VI p 514, 840
Murphy v Dublin Corporation [1972] IR 215, [1972] 107 ILTR 65 .... Vol III p 533
Murphy v Minster for Industry and Commerce [1987] IR 295 .... Vol IV p 378
Murphy v Roche [1987] IR 106 .... Vol V p 696
Murray v Ireland & Attorney General [1985] IR 532, [1985] ILRM 542 .... Vol IV p 437
Murtagh Properties Ltd v Cleary [1972] IR 330 .... Vol III p 127
.... Vol IV p 323, Vol V p 615
Musker v English Electric Co Ltd 41 TC 556, (Ch D) 106 SJ 511 .... Vol II p 602

N

Narich Property Ltd v Commissioner of Payroll Tax [1984] ICR 286 .... Vol IV p 45
.... 2006 p 64
Nashville, Chattanooga & St Louis Railway v Browning [1940] 310 US 362 ... Vol V p 615
Nathan, Re 12 QBD 461 .... Vol I p 221
National Bank of Scotland v The Lord Advocate 30 SL Rep 579 .... Vol V p 560
National Bank of Wales, Re [1897] 1 Ch 298 .... Vol II p 175
National Bank v Baker 17 TC 381, [1932] 1 KB 668 .... Vol I pp 474, 503
National Irish Bank Ltd (No 1), Re [1999] 3 IR 145 .... Vol VI p 784
National Irish Banks Ltd v Radio Telefís Éireann (20 March 1998) SC .... Vol VI p 68
National Provident Institution v Brown 8 TC 57, [1921] 2 AC 222 .... Vol I p 515
National Provincial Bank of England v Jackson 33 Ch D 1 .... Vol V p 560
Naval Colliery Co Ltd v Commissioners of Inland Revenue 12 TC 1017 .... Vol III p 95
Neale v City of Birmingham Tramways Co [1910] 2 Ch 464 .... Vol II p 175
Nesbitt v Mitchell 11 TC 211 .... Vol II p 115
Nestor v Murphy [1979] IR 326 .... Vol IV p 162, Vol VI p 386
Nevile Reid & Co Ltd v Commissioners of Inland Revenue 12 TC 545
.... Vol I p 130, Vol III p 611
New York Life Assurance Co v Styles 2 TC 460 [1914] 14 AC 381 .... Vol I p 387
Newcastle City Council v Royal Newcastle Hospital [1959] AC 248 .... Vol II p 636
Newman Manufacturing Co v Marrable [1931] 2 KB 297 .... Vol V p 539
Nicholls v Gibson [1996] STC 1008 .... Vol VI p 686
Nicoll v Austin 19 TC 531 .... Vol II p 452
Nixon v Commissioner of Valuation [1980] IR 340 .... Vol III p 319
Noble, BW Ltd v Inland Revenue Commissioners 12 TC 923 .... Vol II p 175
Nokes v Doncaster Amalgamated Collieries Ltd (1940) AC 1014 .... Vol VI p 454
Nolder v Walters 15 TC 380 .... Vol II p 366
Nord Getreide v Haupdzolla MT Hamburg-Jones [1985] ECR 3127 .... Vol VI p 21
Norris v Attorney General [1984] IR 36 .... Vol IV p 437, Vol VI p 68
North Australian Cement Ltd v Federal Commission of Taxation 89 ATC 4765
.... Vol VI p 524
Northend v White & Leonard [1975] 1 WLR 1037 .... Vol III p 633
Northern Association Co v Russell 26 SLR 330, 2 TC 551 .... Vol I p 474
Northern Bank Finance Co Ltd v Quinn [1979] ILRM 221 .... Vol V p 226

Northern Insurance Co v Russell 2 TC 571 .... Vol III p 373
Norton v Shelby County [1886] 118 US 425 .... Vol V p 615
Nova Media Services v Minister for Posts and Telegraphs [1984] ILRM 161
.... Vol VI p 636
Nugent-Head v Jacob 30 TC 83, [1947] 1 KB 17 .... Vol II p 75

O

Ó Coindealbháin (Inspector of Taxes) v Breda O'Carroll [1989] IR 229,
IV ITR 221 .... Vol V p 472, Vol VI p 60
Ó Coindealbháin (Inspector of Taxes) v TB Mooney [1990] IR 422
.... Vol V p 239, 323, 326, 2006 p 64
Ó Cualacháin v McMullen Bros Ltd [1955] 2 IR 217, IV ITR 284, V ITR 200
.... Vol VI p 525, 597, 618, 699
Ó Culacháin (Inspector of Taxes) v McMullan Brothers Ltd [1955] 2 IR 217
IV ITR 284, V ITR 20 .... Vol IV p 425, Vol V p 200, 317, 482
.... Vol VI p 525, 618, 699
Ó Culacháin, S (Inspector of Taxes) v Hunter Advertising Ltd IV ITR 35
.... Vol IV p 466, 533, Vol V p 22, 376,Vol VI p 48
Ó Laochdha v Johnson & Johnson (Ireland) Ltd [1991] 2 IR 287, IV ITR 361
.... Vol VI p 691
Ó Srianain (Inspector of Taxes) v Lakeview Ltd .... Vol IV pp 68, 284, Vol V p 317
O'B v S [1984] ILRM 86 .... Vol IV pp 415, 437
O'Brien v Bord na Mona [1983] IR 255, [1983] ILRM 314 .... Vol III pp 533, 590
.... Vol IV p 512
O'Brien v Commissioner for Tipperary (South Riding) Board of Health
[1938] IR 761 .... Vol III p 43
O'Brien v Keogh [1972] IR 144 .... Vol III p 127, Vol V p 615
O'Brien v Manufacturing Engineering Co Ltd [1973] IR 334, 108 ILTR 105
.... Vol III p 127, Vol V p 615
O'Byrne v Minister for Finance [1959] IR 1, 94 ILTR 11 .... Vol III p 127, Vol V p 615
O'C, JB v PCD and A Bank 3 ITR 153 .... Vol V p 347
O'Connell (Inspector of Taxes) v Tara Mines Ltd VI ITR 523 .... Vol VI p 699
O'Croinin and Quinn v Brennan [1939] IR 274 .... Vol III p 387, Vol VI p 386
O'Dwyer (Inspector of Taxes) & Inland Revenue Commissioners v Irish
Exporters and Importers Ltd (In Liquidation) 2 ITC 251, [1943] IR 176 .... Vol II p 82
O'Farrell & Another, Re [1960] IR 239, [1958] 95 ILTR 167 .... Vol III p 533
O'Flaherty v Browne [1907] 2 IR 416 .... Vol V p 272
O'G, T v Attorney General [1985] ILRM 61 .... Vol IV p 437
O'Grady v Bullcroft Main Collieries 17 TC 93 .... Vol III p 65, Vol IV p 425
O'Kane, J & R & Co v Commissioners of Inland Revenue 12 TC 303, HL
126 LT707, 56 ILTR 57 .... Vol I p 1
O'Keeffe v An Bord Pleanála [1992] ILRM 69 .... Vol IV pp 170, 512
O'Keeffe v Ferris [1993] 3 IR 165 .... Vol VI p 386
O'Loan, HA (Inspector of Taxes) v Messrs M J Noone & Co 2 ITC 430,
[1949] IR 171 .... Vol III p 178
O'R v O'R [1985] IR 367 .... Vol III p 533, Vol VI p 561
O'Rourke v Revenue Commissioners [1996] 2 IR 1, V ITR 321
.... Vol VI p 514, 588, 840

O'Shea (Inspector of Taxes) v Coole Parkview Service Station Ltd
(25 May 2000) HC .... Vol VI p 618
O'Sullivan (Inspector of Taxes) v P Ltd 3 ITC 355 .... Vol III p 683
.... Vol V p 295, Vol VI p 618, 2006 p 82
Oakey Abattoir Pty Ltd v Federal Commissioner of Taxation 84 ATC 4718 .... Vol III p 683
Oakthorpe Holdings Ltd, In Re [1989] ILRM 62 .... Vol V p 388
Odeon Associated Theatres Ltd v Jones 48 TC 257, [1971] 1 WLR 422,
[1972] 2 All ER 407, ITR Vol III p 198 .... Vol IV pp 135, 304
Odhams Press Ltd v Cook 56 TLR 704, [1938] 2 All ER 312, 4 All ER 545,
23 TC 233 .... Vol I p 642
Ogilvie v Kitton [1908] Sess Cas 1003, 5 TC 338 .... Vol I p 183
Old Battersea and District Building Society v The Commissioners of Inland Revenue
[1898] 2 QBD 294 .... Vol IV p 296
Old Bushmills Distillery Co Ltd, Exp Brydon, Exp Bank of Ireland
[1896] 1 IR 301 .... Vol I p 28
Olive & Partington Ltd v Rose 14 TC 701 .... Vol II p 115
Oppenheim v Tobacco Securities Trust Co Ltd [1951] AC 297; [1951] 1 All ER 31
[1951] 1 TLR 118 .... Vol V p 37
Oriental Inland Steam Co, Re [1874] Ch App 557 .... Vol IV p 247
Ormond Investment Co Ltd v Betts 13 TC 400, [1927] 2 KB 326, [1928] AC 143
138 LT 600 .... Vol I p 447, Vol II p 429, 482, Vol VI p 8
Ormonde (Marchioness of) v Brown 17 TC 333 .... Vol II p 491
Osler v Hall & Co [1923] 1 KB 720, 17 TC 68 .... Vol II p 55
Ostime v Australian Mutual Provident Society 39 TC 492,
[1959] 3 All ER 245 .... Vol III p 246
Oughtred v Inland Revenue Commissioners [1959] 3 WLR 906 .... Vol IV pp 187, 367
Ounsworth v Vickers Ltd 6 TC 671, [1915] 3 KB 267 .... Vol I pp 91, 642
.... Vol II p 32, 45, 515, Vol IV p 425
Overseers of the Savoy v Art Union of London 12 TC 798, [1894] 2 QB 62
.... Vol I p 542
Owen v Sassoon 32 TC 101 .... Vol III p 633
Owens v Greene and Freeley v Greene [1932] IR 225, [1932] 67 ILTR 161
.... Vol V p 272
Oxford Benefit Building & Investment Society [1896] 35 Ch 502 .... Vol V p 186, 195

P

Paddington Burial Board v Commissioners of Inland Revenue 13 QBD 9 .... Vol II p 211
Page Boy Couriers Ltd, Re [1983] ILRM 510 .... Vol VI p 191
Page v The International Agency & Industrial Trust Ltd [1893] 62 LJ Ch 610
.... Vol V p 186, 195
Palmer v Johnson 13 QBD 351 .... Vol V p 539
Palser v Grinling Property Holding Co Ltd [1948] AC 291 .... Vol V p 686
Panama, New Zealand and Australian Royal Mail Co, Re 5 Ch App 318 .... Vol III p 661
Paperlink v Attorney General [1984] ILRM 373 .... Vol IV p 323
Parchim [1918] AC 157 .... Vol I p 130
Parish of Brighton, Guardians of [1891] 2 QN 157 .... Vol II p 175
Parke v Daily News [1962] 2 All ER 929 .... Vol III p 706, Vol IV p 247
Parke v Walker (1961) SLT 251 .... Vol VI p 373
Parker & Cooper Ltd v Reading [1926] 1 Ch 975 .... Vol V p 226

Parker v Chapman 13 TC 677 .... Vol III p 484
Parker v Great Western Railroad Co [1856] .... Vol III p 441
Parker v Walker [1961] SCT 252 .... Vol III p 467
Parsons v Attorney General [1943] Ch 12 .... Vol V p 600
Parsons v Kavanagh [1990] ILRM 560 .... Vol IV p 323
Partington v Attorney General [1869] LR 4 HL 100 .... Vol I p 601, Vol II p 332
.... Vol III p 683, Vol V p 163, 539, Vol VI p 422, 636
Partington, ex p, 6 QB 649 .... Vol II p 130
Partridge v Mullandaine 2 TC 179, [1886] 18 QBD 276 .... Vol I pp 155, 195
.... Vol III p 484
Paterson, John (Motors) Ltd v Commissioners of Inland Revenue 52 TC 39
.... Vol III p 559
Patrick v Broadstone Mills [1954] 1 All ER 163, [1954] 1 WLR 158, 35 TC 44
.... Vol II p 515, Vol IV p 135
Patterson v Marine Midland Ltd [1981] STC 540 .... Vol V p 139
Pattinson Deceased, Re, Graham v Pattinson [1885] 1 TLR 216 .... Vol V p 272
Pattison v Marine Midland Ltd [1984] 2 WLR 11 .... Vol V p 139
Pavey and Matthews Proprietary Ltd v Paul (1987) 162 CLR 221 .... Vol VI p 514
Pearse v Woodall-Duckham Ltd [1978] STC 372 .... Vol IV p 135
Pearson v Inland Revenue Commissioners [1980] 2 WLR 871 .... Vol III p 104
Peel v London North Western Rly [1907] 1 Ch D 5 .... Vol II p 241
Peisch v Ware 4 Cranch 347 .... Vol VI p 386
Penrose v Penrose [1933] Ch 793 .... Vol V p 600
People (Attorney General) v Bell [1969] IR 24 .... Vol V p 221
Perkins Executor v Inland Revenue Commissioners 13 TC 851 .... Vol III p 484
Perrin v Dickson 14 TC 608, [1929] 2 KB 85, [1930] 1 KB 107 .... Vol II p 464
.... Vol V p 10, 1998 p 184
Perry v Astor [1943] 1 KB 260, 19 TC 255, [1935] AC .... Vol II p 82
Persse (Estate of), Re (1888) Land Judges Court .... Vol II p 332
Pesca SCA Valentina v The Minister for Fisheries [1985] IR 193 .... Vol VI p 422, 636
Peter Dodson 77 Cr App Reps 1983 .... Vol III p 153
Peter Merchant Ltd v Stedeford 30 TC 496 .... Vol II p 515
Petrotim Securities Ltd v Ayres [1964] 1 All ER 269, 41 TC 389
.... Vol III p 253, 340, 373
Philips v Bourne 27 TC 498, [1947] 1 KB 533 .... Vol III p 19, 319
Phillips (Inspector of Taxes) v Keane 1 ITC 69, [1925] 2 IR 48 .... Vol II p 460
Phillips v United Kingdom (5 July 2001), HC .... Vol VI p 386
Phillips v Whieldon Sanitary Potteries Ltd 65 TLR 712, 33 TC 213 .... Vol II pp 267, 360
Pickford v Quirke 13 TC 251 .... Vol III p 253
Pickles v Foulsham 9 TC 261, [1923] 2 KB 413, [1925] AC 458 .... Vol I p 259
.... Vol II p 68
Pigs and Marketing Board v Donnelly (Dublin) Ltd [1939] IR 413 .... Vol III p 127
.... Vol IV p 162
Pilcher v Logan [1914] 15 SR NSW 24 .... Vol III p 484
Platt v Attorney General of New South Wales 3 AC 336 .... Vol I p 259
PMPA Garages Ltd, Re [1992] IR 332 .... Vol V p 323, Vol VI p 514
Pooley, Re 40 Ch D 1 .... Vol I p 601

Port Sudan Cotton Co v Govindaswamy Chettiar & Sons [1971] 1 Lloyd's Rep 166 ....2006 p 56
Potts' Exeuctors v Inland Revenue Commissioners [1951] AC 443, [1951] 1 All ER 76, [1951] 1 TLR 152, [1950] 32 TC 211 .... Vol III p 683
Power Lane Manufacturing Co v Putnan [1931] 2 KB 309 .... Vol V p 540
Power Securities Limited v Daly (27 February 1984, unreported) HC ....2006 p 56
Poynting v Faulkner 5 TC 145, 93 LT 367 ....Vol I p 155
Pratt v Swanmore Builders Ltd and Baker [1980] 2 Lloyd's Rep 504 ....2006 p 56
Premier Periclase v Valuation Tribunal (24 June 1999, unreported) HC ....2006 p 64
Prestcold (Central) Ltd v Minister of Labour [1969] 1 All ER 69 .... Vol III p 611
Preston, Re [1985] 2 WLR 836 .... Vol III p 356
Pretore di Cento v A person or persons unknown (Case 110/76) [1977] ECR 851 .... Vol VI p 21
Pretoria-Pietersburg Railway Co Ltd v Elwood 95 LT 468, 98 LT 741, 6 TC 508 ....Vol I p 427
Prince v Mapp (Inspector of Taxes) [1970] 1 WLR 260 .... Vol VI p 329
Private Motorists Provident Society Ltd (in liquidation), Re (23 June 1995), 1995 ITR 159 .... Vol V p 195
Proprietary Articles Trade Association v AG of Canada [1931] AC 310 .... Vol VI p 386
Pryce v Monmouthshire Canal Co 4 AC 197 .... Vol V p 540
Psalms and Hymns (Trustees of) v Whitwell 7 TLR 164, 3 TC 7 ....Vol I p 387
Punjab Co-Operative Bank Ltd Amritsar v Income Tax Commissioner Lahore [1940] AC 1055 .... Vol III p 373
Punton v Ministry of Pensions and National Insurance [1963] 1 All ER 275 ....Vol II p 491
Pyrah v Annis 37 TC 163, [1956] 2 AE 858, [1957] 1 All ER 186 ....Vol II p 515

Q

Queen v Bishop of Oxford 4 QBD 245 ....Vol II p 108
Queen v Commissioners of Customs and Excise , ex p EMU Tabac [1988] ECR 1–1605 ....Vol VI p 472
Queen v The Pharmaceutical Society of Ireland [1896] 2 IR 384 ....Vol I p 542
Queensland Stations Property Ltd v Federal Commr of Taxation (1945) 70 CLR 539 .... Vol V p 239, 2006 p 64
Quinn v Leathen [1901] AC 495 ....Vol II p 500
Quinn's Supermarket v Attorney General [1972] IR 1 .... Vol III p 127 ....Vol IV pp 323, 437, Vol V p 615, Vol VI p 721

R

R (County Councils North Riding and South Riding County Tipperary) v Considine [1917] 2 IR 1 ....Vol I p 221
R v Buttle 39 LJ MC 115 ....Vol II p 175
R v Chartered Accountants of England and Wales, ex p Brindle [1994] BCC 297 ....Vol VI p 784
R v Chief Metropolitan Magistrate ex p Secretary of State for the Home Department [1989] 1 All ER 151 .... Vol VI p 21
R v Commissioners for Special Purposes of Income Tax 2 TC 332, 21 QBD 313 ....Vol I p 221

R v Commissioners for Special Purposes of Income Tax 7 TC 646, [1920] 1 KB 26 .... Vol I p 221
R v Commissioners of Income Tax for the City of London 91 LTR 94 .... Vol I p 221
R v Cotham [1898] 1 QB 802 .... Vol III p 290
R v Crawshaw Bell C C 303, 8 Cox 375 .... Vol I p 195
R v Criminal Injuries Compensation Board, ex p Lain [1967] 2 QB 864, [1967] 3 WLR 348, [1967] 2 All ER 770 .... Vol III p 290
R v General Income Tax Commissioners for Offlow 27 TLR 353 .... Vol I p 221
R v Governor of Pentonville Prison ex p Khubchandani (1980) 71 Crim App R 241 .... Vol VI p 21
R v Gregory 5 B and AD 555 .... Vol I p 195
R v Inland Revenue Commissioners ex p Unilever Plc (1996) STC 681 .... Vol V p 418
R v National Insurance Commissioner; ex p Hudson [1972] AC 944 .... Vol V p 615
R v Panel on Takeovers and Mergers, ex p Fayed [1992] BCLC 938 .... Vol VI p 784
R v Peters [1886] 16 QBD 636 .... Vol III p 19
R v R [1984] IR 296, [1985] ILRM 631 .... Vol III p 533, 590, Vol VI p 561
R v Waller [1910] 1 KB 364 .... Vol V p 691
R v Walton, General Commissioners, ex p Walton [1983] FTC 464 .... Vol VI p 686
R v Woodhouse [1906] 2 KB 501 .... Vol III p 290
Rabbitt v Grant [1940] IR 323 .... Vol II p 32
Radcliffe v Bartholomew (1892) 1 QB 161 .... Vol VI p 422
Radio Pictures Ltd v Commissioners of Inland Revenue 22 TC 106 .... Vol II p 281
Rahill v Brady [1971] IR 69 .... Vol III p 19
Ramsay Ltd v Inland Revenue Commissioners [1982] AC 300, [1981] 2 WLR 449, [1981] 1 All ER 865, [1981] 54 TC 101, [1981] STC 174 .... Vol III p 104, 683
.... Vol IV p 547, Vol V p 3, 108, 164, 295, 515,
.... Vol VI p 203, 2006 p 82
Ramsey v Liverpool Royal Infirmary [1930] AC 588 .... Vol III p 572
Ranelaugh (Earl) v Hayes [1683] 1 Vern 189 .... Vol III p 265
Ransom v Higgs [1973] 2 All ER 657, [1974] 1 WLR 1594, [1974] 3 All ER 949, [1974] 50 TC 1 .... Vol II p 614, Vol III pp 572, 683
Reade v Brearley 17 TC 687 .... Vol I p 656
Readymix (Éire) Ltd v Dublin County Council and the Minister for Local Government (30 July 1974) SC .... Vol V p 357
Readymix Concrete v Commissioner of Taxation (Australia) .... Vol III p 441
Readymix Concrete v Minister for Pensions [1968] 1 All ER 433, [1968] 2 QB 497 .... Vol IV p 45, Vol V p 239, Vol VI p 758, 2006 p 64
Reed v Cattermole 21 TC 35, [1937] 1 KB 613 .... Vol II p 452
Reed v Seymour 11 TC 625, [1906] 2 KB 594, [1926] 1 KB 588, 42 TLR 514, 135 LTR 259 .... Vol I p 155, 618
Rees Roturbo Development Syndicate Ltd v Ducker (Commissioners of Inland Revenue) 13 TC 366 .... Vol I p 474, 629
Reg v Bow Road Justices, ex p Adedigba [1968] 2 QB 572 .... Vol III p 19
Reg v Commissioners of Woods and Forests 15 QB 767 .... Vol I p 221
Reg v Galsworthy [1892] 1 QB 348 .... Vol II p 241
Reg v Inland Revenue Commissioners, ex p Fed of Self-Employed [1982] AC 617 .... Vol IV p 170
Reg v Labourchere 12 QBD 328 .... Vol I p 427

Reg v Lords of the Treasury 16 QB 357 .... Vol I p 221
Regent Oil Co Ltd v Strick [1966] AC 295 .... Vol V p 139
Regina and Jones [1978] 1 WLR 195 .... Vol III p 153
Regina v Inspector of Taxes ex p Clarke [1974] 1 QB 220 .... Vol III p 159
Reid, re [1921] 64 DLR 598, 50 OLR 595 .... Vol V p 272
Reid's Trustees v Dawson (1915) SC (HL) 47 .... Vol V p 540
Reids Trustees v Commissioners of Inland Revenue [1929] 14 TC 512 .... Vol III p 477
Reilly v McEntee [1984] ILRM 572 .... Vol V p 366
Religious Tract and Book Society of Scotland v Forbes 33 SLR 289, 3 TC 415 .... Vol I p 387
Rellim Ltd v Vise 32 TC 254 .... Vol III p 1
Revenue Commissioners, The v HI .... Vol V p 393
Revenue Commissioners, The v Switzer Ltd 2 ITC 290, [1945] IR 378 .... Vol II p 130
Rex (Waterford County Council) v Local Government Board [1902] 2 IR 349 .... Vol III p 590
Rex v BC Fir and Cedar Lumber Co Ltd 17 TC 564, 147 LT 1 .... Vol I p 427
Rex v Dibdin [1910] p 57 .... Vol II p 130
Rex v General Commissioners of Income Tax for the City of London (ex p Gibbs) [1940] 2 KB 242, [1942] AC 402, 24 TC 221 .... Vol II p 55
Rex v James Whitney 1 Moody 3 .... Vol III p 19
Rex v Sarah Chapple [1804] Russell & Ryan 77 .... Vol III p 19
Rex v Special Commissioners of Income Tax 20 TC 381, (ex p Elmhirst [1936] 1 KB 487) .... Vol I p 571
Rex v Williams [1942] AC 541 .... Vol VI p 818
Reynolds Australia Alumina Ltd v Federal Commissioner of Taxation (31 March 1987), Fed Court of Aus, (1987) 77 ALR 543 .... Vol VI p 525
Reynolds v Times Newspapers [1998] 3 All ER 961 .... Vol VI p 196
Rhodesia Railways Ltd v Collector of Income Tax, Bechuanaland Portectorate [1933] AC 368 .... Vol II p 32, 267
Rhymney Iron Co Ltd v Fowler [1896] 2 QB 79 .... Vol I p 164
Richardson, Re 50 LJ Ch 488 .... Vol I p 130
Richmond's Trustees v Richmond [1935] SC 585 .... Vol V p 565
Ricketts v Colquhoun 10 TC 118, KBD [1924] 2 KB 347, CA [1925] 1 KB 725, HL, [1926] AC 1 .... Vol I p 64, Vol II p 366, 460
Ridge Securities Ltd v Commissioners of Inland Revenue 44 TC 373 .... Vol III p 253, 373
Right Hon Earl of Iveagh, The v Inland Revenue Commissioners 1 ITC 316, [1930] IR 386, 431 .... Vol I p 375, 387
River Estates Ltd v Director General of Inland Revenue [1984] STC 60 .... Vol III p 178
Roache v Newsgroup Newspapers Ltd [1998] EMLR 161 .... Vol VI p 196
Roberts v Williamson 26 TC 201, [1944] 60 TLR 561 .... Vol II p 241
Robertson v MacDonagh [1880] 6 LR IR 433 .... Vol III p 484
Robinson v Corry 18 TC 411, [1934] 1 KB 240 .... Vol II p 452
Robinson v Scott Bader Co Ltd 54 TC 757 .... Vol IV p 73
Robinson, WA, t/a James Pim & Son v JD Dolan (Inspector of Taxes) 2 ITC 25, [1935] IR 509 .... Vol III p 165
Roche v Kelly & Co Ltd [1969] IR 100 .... Vol IV p 45, Vol V p 239

Roche v Minister for Industry & Commerce [1978] IR 149 .... Vol V p 696
Rodgers v ITGWU [1978] ILRM 51 .... Vol IV p 323
Rogers v Booth [1937] 2 All ER 751 .... Vol VI p 771
Rogers v Inland Revenue 16 SC LR 682, 1 TC 225 .... Vol I p 259
Rolled Steel Ltd v British Steel Corporation [1986] 1 Ch 246 .... Vol IV p 247
Rolls v Miller [1884] 27 Ch D 71 .... Vol V p 686
Rolls-Royce Ltd v Jeffrey 40 TC 443, [1962] 1 All ER 801 .... Vol II p 602
Rompelman v Minister Van Financien, case 268/83 .... Vol V p 76, Vol VI p 824
Rondel v Worsley [1969] 1 AC 191 .... Vol III p 484
Roper v Ward [1981] ILRM 408 .... Vol IV p 247
Rorke v Commissioners of Inland Revenue [1960] 1 WLR 1132,
39 TC 194 .... Vol II p 515
Rosyth Building and Estates Co Ltd v p Rogers (Surveyor of Taxes)
[1921] Sess Cas 372, 58 SLR 363, 8 TC 11 .... Vol I p 447, 515
Routledge & Co Ltd [1904] 2 Ch 474 .... Vol II p 130
Rowan's Trustees v Rowan [1940] SC 30 .... Vol V p 565
Rownson, Drew & Clydesdale Ltd v Commissioners of Inland Revenue
16 TC 595 .... Vol I pp 164, 427
Rowntree & Co v Curtis 8 TC 678, [1925] 1 KB 328 .... Vol II p 32
Royal Bank of Canada v Inland Revenue Commissioners
[1972] 1 Ch 665 .... Vol III p 356
Royal Bank of Ireland & O'Shea [1943] 77 ILTR .... Vol V p 1
Royal College of Surgeons of England v Commissioners of Inland Revenue
4 TC 344, [1899] 1 QB 871 .... Vol I p 542
Royal Crown Derby Porcelain Co Ltd v Russell [1949] 2 KB 417 .... Vol III p 19, 533
Royal Insurance Co Ltd v Stephen 14 TC 22, 44 TLR 630 .... Vol I p 503, Vol III p 373
Royal Insurance Co Ltd v Stephen 44 TLR 630, 14 TC 22 .... Vol I p 474, Vol II p 419
Royal Liver Friendly Society [1870] LR 5 Exch 78 .... Vol IV p 296
Royal Trust Co v Attorney General for Alberta [1930] AC 144 .... Vol VI p 818
Royster Guano Co v Virginia [1920] 253 US 412 .... Vol III p 127
Russell v Aberdeen Town and County Bank 2 TC 321, 13 AC 418 .... Vol II p 515
Russell v Russell [1985] 315 .... Vol IV p 437
Russell v Scott [1936] 55 CLR 440, [1936] 36 SR NSW 454, 53 NSWWN 178
.... Vol V p 272
Russell v Scott [1948] AC 422 .... Vol III p 56
Russell v Wakefield Waterworks Co [1875] LR 20 Eq 474 .... Vol IV p 247
Russian Petroleum Co Ltd [1907] 2 Ch 540 .... Vol II p 130
Rustproof Metal Window Co Ltd v Commissioners of Inland Revenue 29 TC 243,
177 LT 657 .... Vol II p 602
Ryall v Hoare 8 TC 521, [1923] KB 447 .... Vol I p 155, 474
Ryanair v The Labour Court (14 October 2005, unreported) HC .... 2006 p 64
Ryan v Asia Mill 32 TC 275 .... Vol II p 515
Ryan v Oceanic Steam Navigation Co Ltd [1914] 3 KB 731 .... Vol I p 330
Ryan v The Attorney General [1965] IR 294 .... Vol V p 615
Ryans Car Hire v Attorney General [1965] IR 642 .... Vol V p 272
Ryle Brehon Airlines v Ming (1995) 3 WLR 64 .... Vol V p 412

S

S v S [1983] IR 68 .... Vol IV p 437
SA Roquette Freres v French State (Case 145/79) [1980] ECR 3333 .... Vol VI p 21
Salisbury House Estate Ltd v Fry [1930] 1 KB 304, [1930] AC 432,
15 TC 266 .... Vol I pp 447, 487, 515, Vol II p 315, Vol III p 95, Vol IV p 1
Salvesen's Trustee's v Commissioners of Inland Revenue [1930] SLT 387
.... Vol V p 532, 577
San Paulo (Brazilian) Railway Co v Carter 73 LT 538, 3 TC 407 .... Vol I p 183
Sargeant (Inspector of Taxes) v Eayers 48 TC 573 .... Vol V p 496, Vol VI p 158
Sargood Bros v The Commonwealth [1910] 11 CLR 258 .... Vol V p 615
Saunders (GL) (in liquidation), Re [1986] 1 WLR 215 .... Vol V p 387
Saunders v Dixon 40 TC 329 .... Vol II p 515
Saunders, GL Ltd (in liquidation), Re [1986] 1 WLR 215, [1985] 130 SJ 166,
[1985] 83 LS Gaz 779 .... Vol IV p 107
Saxone Lilley and Skinner Holdings Ltd v Commissioners of Inland Revenue
44 TC 122 .... Vol III p 65
Scales v George Thompson & Co Ltd 13 TC 83 .... Vol III p 178
Schofield v Hall 49 TC 538, [1975] STC 353 .... Vol III pp 113, 120, 219
.... Vol IV pp 68, 284, 425
Scoble v Secretary of State for India 4 TC 618 .... Vol V p 108, 1998 p 184
Scottish Co-operative Wholesale Society v Meyer [1958] 3 All ER 66 .... Vol III p 423
Scottish Golf Club [1913] 3 KB 75 .... Vol I p 515
Scottish Investment Trust Co v Forbes 3 TC 231 .... Vol I p 474, Vol II p 419
.... Vol III p 373
Scottish Provident Institution v Farmer [1912] Sess Case 452, 6 TC 34 .... Vol I p 1
Scottish Widows Fund Life Assurance Society Ltd v Farmer 5 TC 502 .... Vol III p 484
Seaham Harbour Dock Co v Crook 16 TC 333 .... Vol III p 165
Sebel Products Ltd v Commissioners of Customs and Excise [1949] Ch 409
.... Vol V p 615
Sebright, Re [1944] 1 Ch 287 .... Vol II p 332
Secretan v Hart 45 TC 701 .... Vol IV p 135
Secretary of State for India v Scoble 4 TC 618, [1903] AC 299 .... Vol II p 464
Severn Fishery Board v O'May [1919] 2 KB 484, 7 TC 194 .... Vol II p 154, 204
.... Vol IV p 73
Shadford v H Fairweather and Co Ltd 43 TC 291 .... Vol III p 1
Sharkey v Wernher 36 TC 275, [1954] 2 All ER 753, [1955] 3 All ER 493 .... Vol II p 315
.... Vol III p 253, 340
Shaw v Lawless 5 Cl & F 129 .... Vol I p 601
Shell-Mex v Manchester Garages [1971] 1 WLR 612 .... Vol IV p 269
Shepherd v Harrison LR 5 HL 116 .... Vol I p 130
Sherdley v Sherdley [1987] STC 217 .... Vol III p 683
Sherry Re .... Vol III p 387
Shilton v Wilmhurst [1991] STC 88 .... Vol VI p 203
Sillar, Re [1956] IR 344 .... Vol III p 572
Simpson v Tate 9 TC 314 .... Vol II p 366
Simpson v The Grange Trust Ltd 19 TC 231, [1934] 2 KB 317,
50 TLR 389 (HL) .... Vol I p 447

Simpson v The Grange Trust Ltd 19 TC 231, 51 TLR 320,
[1934] 2 KB 317 .... Vol II p 429
Sinclair v Brougham [1914] AC 415 .... Vol IV p 247
Sinclair v Cadbury Brothers 18 TC 157 .... Vol III p 65
Singer v Williams [1918] 2 KB 432, [1921] 1 AC 41, 7 TC 419
.... Vol I p 583, Vol II pp 82, 491
Small v Easson 12 TC 351, [1920] SC 758 .... Vol II p 500
Smart v Lincolnshire Sugar Co Ltd 20 TC 643 .... Vol III p 165
Smidth and Co v Greenwood 8 TC 193, [1920] 3 KB 275, [1921] 3 KB 583,
[1922] 1 AC 417 .... Vol I p 330
Smith v Incorporated Council of Law Reporting for England and Wales
6 TC 477, [1914] 3 KB 674 .... Vol II p 32, 393, 515
Smith v Lion Brewery Co Ltd 5 TC 568, [1911] AC 155 .... Vol I p 515, 642
Smith v The Law Guarantee and Trust Society Ltd [1904] Ch 569 .... Vol I p 45
Smith, John & Son v Moore 12 TC 266, [1921] 2 AC 13 .... Vol II p 515
Smyth v Revenue Commissioners [1931] IR 643 .... Vol V p 577
Smyth v Stretton 20 TLR 443, 5 TC 41 .... Vol I p 155
Society of the Writers to the Signet v Commissioners of Inland Revenue
2 TC 257, [1886] 14 Sess Cas 34 .... Vol I p 542
Solamon v Solamon & Co Ltd [1897] AC 22 .... Vol IV p 247
Soleil, Le Ltd v Minister of National Revenue 73 DTC 5093 .... Vol IV p 466
Solicitors Act 1954, Re [1960] IR 239 .... Vol III p 577
Solomon v Commissioners of Customs and Excise 2 QB 116 .... Vol III p 246
Somerville v Somerville 5 Ves 750, 758 .... Vol I p 259
Sother Smith v Clancy 24 TC 1 Vol V p 108, ... 1998 p 184
South Australia v The Commonwealth [1941] 65 CLR 373 .... Vol V p 615
South Behar Railway Co v Inland Revenue Commissioners 12 TC 657,
[1925] AC 485 .... Vol I p 108, 318
South East Sheffield Citizens' Advice Bureau v Grayson [2004] ICR 1138
.... Vol VI p 771
Southampton & Itchen Bridge Co v Southampton Local Board .... Vol II p 241
Southern Railway of Peru v Owen 36 TC 602, [1957] AC 334 .... Vol II p 515
Southern v Aldwych Property Trust Ltd 23 TC 707, [1940] 2 KB 266,
56 TLR 808 .... Vol II pp 95, 429, Vol V p 680
Southern v Borax Consolidated Ltd 23 TC 597 [1940] 4 All ER 412,
[1941] 1 KB 111 .... Vol II pp 45, 267, 500, 515
Southwell v Savill Bros 4 TC 430, [1901] 2 KB 349 .... Vol II pp 32, 45, 515
.... Vol VI p 158
Spaight v Dundon [1961] IR 201 .... Vol IV p 437
Spanish Prospecting Co Ltd [1911] 1 Ch 92 .... Vol I p 1
Spencer v McGarry 2 ITC 297, [1946] IR 11 .... Vol II p 241
Spencer v Metropolitan Board of Works LR 22 Ch Div 149 .... Vol V p 570
Spencer, Re, Spencer v Harte (1881) 51 LJ Ch 271 .... Vol VI p 442
Spikers v Benedik Abbatoir CV (1986) ECR 1119 .... Vol VI p 618
Spurway v Spurway [1894] 1 IR 385, Sel and 28 ILTR 2 .... Vol I p 259
Spyer v Phillipson [1931] 2 Ch 183 .... Vol III p 332
St Andrew's Hospital (Northampton) v Shearsmith 2 TC 219, 19 QBD 624 .... Vol I p 387
St John's School Mount Ford & Knibbs v Ward 49 TC 523 .... Vol V p 201

St Johns School v Ward 49 TC 524 .... Vol III p 219
St Lucia Usines and Estates Co Ltd v Colonial Treasurer of St Lucia 131 LT 267, [1924] AC 508 .... Vol I p 214
Stainers Executors v Purchase 32 TC 408 .... Vol IV p 135
Standing v Bowring [1885] 31 Ch D 282, 55 LJ Ch 218, 54 LT 191, 34 WR 204, 2 TLR 202 .... Vol V p 272
Stanley v Gramaphone and Typewriter Ltd 5 TC 358, [1908] 2 KB 89-95 .... Vol I p 28
State (at the prosecution of Brookfield Securities Ltd) v The Collector Customs and Excise .... Vol IV p 419
State (Calcul International Ltd and Solatrex International Ltd) v the Appeal Commissioners and the Revenue Commissioners (18 December 1986) HC .... Vol VI p 784
State (Carmody), The v De Burca (1970) HC .... Vol V p 691
State (Creedon) v Criminal Injuries Compensation Tribunal [1988] IR 51 .... Vol IV p 485
State (Daly) v Minister for Agriculture [1987] IR 1965 .... Vol IV p 485
State (Elm Developments Ltd) v An Bord Pleanala [1981] ILRM 108 .... Vol IV p 505
State (Gettins) v Judge Fawsitt [1945] IR 183 .... Vol VI p 386
State (Healy) v Donoghue [1976] IR 325 .... Vol IV p 478, Vol V p 615
State (Hully) v Hynes 100 ILTR 145 .... Vol VI p 21
State (Keegan and Lysaght) v Stardust Victims Compensation Tribunal [1986] IR 642 .... Vol IV p 170, Vol IV p 512
State (Keller) v Galway County Council and Another [1958] IR 142 .... Vol III p 290
State (McFadden) v The Governor of Mountjoy Prison [1981] ILRM 113 .... Vol VI p 21
State (Multiprint Label System Ltd) v President of Circuit Court [1984] ILRM 545 .... Vol IV p 505
State (Nicolaou) v An Bord Uchtála [1966] IR 567, [1966] 102 ILTR 1 .... Vol III p 127 .... Vol IV p 437, Vol V p 615
State (O'Duffy) v Bennet [1935] IR 70 .... Vol V p 691
State (O'Rourke) v Kelly [1983] IR 58 .... Vol IV p 278, Vol VI p 386
State (Quinn) v Ryan [1965] IR 70 .... Vol VI p 68
State (Ryan) v Inland Revenue Commissioners [1934] IR 13 .... Vol I p 563 .... Vol II p 326
State (Sherrin) v Kennedy [1966] IR 379 .... Vol V p 615, Vol VI p 68
State (Walsh) v An Bord Pleanála [1981] ILRM 535 .... Vol IV p 505
State Board of Tax Commissioners v Jackson [1931] 283 US 527 .... Vol III p 127
State v Sealy [1939] IR 21 .... Vol IV p 401
State, The (at the prosecution of Patrick J Whelan) v Michael Smidic (Special Commissioners of Income Tax) 2 ITC 188, [1938] IR 626 .... Vol II p 374
Stedeford v Beloe 16 TC 505, [1931] 2 KB 610, [1932] AC 388 .... Vol I p 618, Vol II p 393
Steer, Re 3 H & N 599 .... Vol I p 259
Stephen Court Ltd v JA Browne (Inspector of Taxes) (1984) ILRM 231, V ITR 680 .... Vol V p 496, Vol VI p 158
Stephenson Jordan and Harrison Ltd v Mcdonald and Evans [1952] ITR 191 .... Vol VI p 37
Stevens (Inspector of Taxes) v Tirard [1940] 23 TC 321 .... Vol IV p 221
Stockport Schools [1898] 2 Ch 687 .... Vol IV p 296
Stonegate Securities Ltd v Gregory [1980] IR 241 .... Vol VI p 191

Stovall v Denno [1967] 388 US 293 .... Vol V p 615
Strick v Regent Oil Co 43 TC 1, [1964] AC 295, [1966] 1 All ER 585 .... Vol II p 515,
.... Vol IV p 135
Strong and Company of Romsey Ltd v Woodfield 5 TC 215, [1906] AC 448
.... Vol VI p 329
Stubart Investments Ltd v The Queen [1984] CTC 294, 84 DTC 6305 .... Vol III p 683
Styles v The New York Life Insurance Co LR 14 AC 381 .... Vol II p 211
Sudeley (Lord), Re .... Vol III p 477
Sulley v Attorney General 29 LJ Ex 464, 2 TC 149 .... Vol I pp 183, 330
Sulley v Royal College of Surgeons Edinburgh 29 SC LR 620, [1892] 3 TC 173
.... Vol I p 542
Sun Insurance Officer v Clark 6 TC 59, [1912] AC 443 .... Vol II pp 211, 515
.... Vol IV p 135
Sun Life Assurance Society v Davidson 37 TC 330 .... Vol III p 95
.... Vol V p 496, 680, Vol VI p 158
Sun Newspapers v Federal Commissioner of Taxation [1938] 61 CLR 337
.... Vol II p 515
Sunday Tribune Ltd (in liq), Re [1984] IR 505 .... Vol V p 239
Superwood Holdings v Sun Alliance Insce Group [1995] .... Vol V p 226
Sutherland v Commissioners of Inland Revenue 12 TC 63, 55 SC LR 674, EPD Leaflet No 9 .... Vol I p 1, Vol III p 253
Swaine (Inspector of Taxes) v VE 3 ITC 387, [1964] IR 423, 100 ILTR 21
.... Vol III p 1, 9
Swan Brewery Co Ltd (No 2) ACLR 168 .... Vol V p 226
Swedish Central Railway Co Ltd v Thompson 9 TC 342, [1925] AC 495 .... Vol II p 68
Swire, Re 30 Ch D 239 .... Vol III p 340
Switzer v Commissioners of Valuation [1902] 2 IR 275 .... Vol II p 241
Symons v Weeks [1983] STC 195 .... Vol IV p 135

T

T v T [1983] IR 29, [1982] ILRM 217 .... Vol IV p 437
T v T [2002] 3 IR 334 .... Vol VI p 764
Tara Prospecting Ltd v Minister for Energy [1993] ILRM 771 .... Vol VI p 637, 721
Tasker, W & Sons Ltd [1905] 1 Ch 283 .... Vol II p 130
Taylor Clarke International Ltd v Lewis (Inspector of Taxes) 1997 STC 499 .... Vol V p 164
.... Vol VI p 203
Tebrau (Johore) Rubber Syndicate Ltd v Farmer [1910] SC 906, 47 SLR 816, 5 TC 658 .... Vol I pp 1, 474
Tempany v Hynes [1976] IR 101 .... Vol IV p 304, 367, Vol VI p 203
Temperley v Visibell Ltd 49 TC 129 .... Vol IV p 1
Tennant v Smith 3 TC 158, [1892] AC 150 .... Vol II p 452, Vol V p 540, Vol VI p 637
Texaco (Ireland) Ltd v Murphy (Inspector of Taxes) [1991] 2 IR 449, IV ITR 91
.... Vol V p 323, Vol VI p 588, 637, 744
Texaco Ireland Ltd v S Murphy (Inspector of Taxes) [1989] IR 496, [1991] 2 IR 449
.... Vol V p 376
Thomas Merthyr Colliery Co Ltd v Davis [1933] 1 KB 349 .... Vol I p 164
Thomas v Richard Evans & Co Ltd 11 TC 790 .... Vol I p 164
Thomas, Re [1982] 4 All ER 814 .... Vol V p 45
Thomas, Weatherall v Thomas, Re [1900] 1 Ch 319 .... Vol II p 32

Thompson Magnesium Elektron Ltd [1944] 1 All ER 126, 26 TC 1 .... Vol II p 515
Thomson Hill Ltd v Comptroller of Income Tax [1984] STC 251 .... Vol IV p 135
Thomson v Bensted 7 TC 137, [1919] Sess Cas 8 .... Vol I p 259
Thomson v Goold & Co [1910] AC 409 .... Vol VI p 21
Thomson v St Catherines College, Cambridge [1919] AC 468 .... Vol V p 615
Thorley, Re [1891] 2 Ch 613 .... Vol I p 601
Thyateira (Archbishop of) v Hubert 168 LT 190, 25 TC 249 .... Vol II p 68
Tierney v An Post [2000] 1 IR 536 .... 2006 p 64
Tilley v Wales [1943] AC 386 .... Vol IV p 407
Tillmans and SS Knutsford [1908] 2 KB 385 .... Vol IV p 296
Tilson, Re [1951] IR 1 .... Vol V p 615
Timpson's Executors v Yerberry 20 TC 155 .... Vol II p 592
Tinker v Tinker [1970] p 136 .... 1998 p 169
Todd v Egyptian Delta Land & Investment Co Ltd 14 TC 119, [1929] AC 1
.... Vol II p 68
Tollemach Settled Estates (Trustees of) v Coughtrie 30 TC 454, [1961] AC 880
.... Vol II p 491
Tomadini v Administrazione delle Finanze dello Steto [1979] EC Vol II 1814
.... Vol IV p 492
Tool Metal Manufacturing Co Ltd v Tungsten Electric Co Ltd [1955] 1 WLR 761
.... Vol V p 589
Tormey v Ireland & Attorney General [1985] IR 289, [1985] ILRM 375
.... Vol III p 577, Vol IV p 437, Vol VI p 561
Trans-Prairie Pipelines Ltd v Minister for National Revenue 70 DTC 6351
.... Vol VI p 329
Travers v Holley [1953] p 246, [1953] 3 WLR 507, [1953] 2 All ER 794 .... Vol IV p 437
Trevor v Whitworth [1887] 12 Appeal Cases 414 .... Vol IV p 247
Trinidad Petroleum Development Co v Inland Revenue Commissioners 21 TC 1,
[1937] 1 KB 408 .... Vol II p 332, Vol III p 229
Tryka Ltd v Newall 41 TC 146 .... Vol III p 363
Tuck & Sons v Priester [1887] 19 QBD 629, 638 .... Vol III p 19
Tucker (Inspector of Taxes) v Granada Motorway Services Ltd (1979) STC 393
.... Vol V p 496
Turner v Cuxson 2 TC 422, 22 QBD 150 .... Vol I p 155
Turner v Last 42 TC 517 .... Vol III p 1
Turton v Cooper 5 TC 138, 92 LTR 863, [1907] 2 KB 694 .... Vol I p 155, 618
Tyler, In Re [1907] 1 KB 865 .... Vol V p 615
Tzu Tsai Cheng v The Governor of Pentonville Prison [1973] AC 931 .... Vol VI p 21

U

Ua Clothasaigh, D (Inspector of Taxes) v Patrick McCartan 2 ITC 367,
[1948] IR 219 .... Vol V p 615
Udny V Udny LR 1 SC Appeals 441 .... Vol I p 259, Vol V p 481
Ulster Investment Bank Ltd v Euro Estates & Drumkill Ltd [1982] ILRM 57
.... Vol V p 226
Union Cold Storage Co v Jones 8 TC 725, 129 LTR 512 .... Vol I p 642, Vol II p 500
United Bars Ltd (Receivership), Walkinstown Inn Ltd (Receivership) and Raymond
Jackson v The Inland Revenue Commissioners [1991] IR 396 .... Vol V p 388

United Collieries Ltd v The Commissioners of the Inland Revenue
12 TC 1248 .... Vol II p 382
United States v Bagakaiiam 524 US 321 .... Vol VI p 386
United States v Inkley [1989] 1 QB 255 .... Vol V p 45
United States v Peltier [1975] 422 US 531 .... Vol V p 615
United States v Ursery 518 US 267 .... Vol VI p 386
United Steel Companies Ltd v Cullington (No 1) 23 TC 71, 162 LT 23 .... Vol II p 515
University of London Press Ltd v University Tutorial Press Ltd [1916] 2 Ch 601,
[1916] WN 321 .... Vol III p 496
Unwin v Hanson [1891] 2 QB 115 .... Vol III p 19
Urquhart, D (Decd) & Revenue Commissioners v AIB Ltd, Re [1979] IR 197
.... Vol V p 366
Usher's Wiltshire Brewerey Ltd v Bruce [1915] AC 433, 6 TC 399, [1919] 1 KB 25
.... Vol I pp 91, 642, Vol II p 222, 267, 500, 515
.... Vol III p 198, Vol IV p 135

V

Vacuum Oil Co Proprietaries v Comrs of Taxation (25 February 1964) .... Vol II p 515
Vale, JB (Inspector Of Taxes) v Martin Mahony & Brothers Ltd 2 ITC 331,
[1947] IR 30 .... Vol II p 267, 360, 515
Vallambrosa Rubber Co Ltd v Farmer 5 TC 529, [1910] SC 519 .... Vol I pp 91, 642
.... Vol II p 32, 382, 515, Vol IV p 425
Van Den Berghs Ltd v Clark [1935] AC 431, 19 TC 390 .... Vol I p 642
.... Vol II pp 32, 222, 515
Van Hool McArdle Ltd (in liquidation), Re, Inland Revenue Commissioners
v Donnelly [1983] ILRM 329 .... Vol III p 523
Vestey v Inland Revenue Commissioners (1962) 2 WLR 221 .... Vol V p 108
Vestey (Lord)'s Executors and Vestey v Inland Revenue Commissioners [1951] Ch 209,
[1950] 2 All ER 891 (HL), [1949] 1 All ER 1108, [1949] 31 TC 1 (CA)
.... Vol III p 683
VIEK Investments Ltd v The Inland Revenue Commissioners [1991] 2 IR 520
.... Vol III p 9, Vol IV pp 323, 437
Vionnet, Madeleine et Cie v Wills [1940] 1 KB 72 .... Vol II p 281
Vodafone Cellular Ltd v Shaw (Inspector of Taxes) [1997] STC 734 .... Vol VI p 329
.... Vol II p 25, 195, 326, Vol III p 683, Vol IV p 22, 91
.... Vol V p 108, 376, Vol VI p 48, 422, 580, 588, 637, 700, 744
Von Colson v Landnordhein-Westfalen Case 14/83 [1984] ECR 1891 .... Vol VI p 21

W

W Ltd v Wilson (Inspector of Taxes) .... Vol IV p 187
W v W [1993] 2 IR 476 .... Vol V p 482
Wagner Miret v Fondo de Grantia Salaril case [1993] ECR I 6911 .... Vol VI p 21
Waldie & Sons Ltd v Commissioners of IR [1919] Sess Cas 697, 12 TC 113
.... Vol I p 447
Wales v Graham 24 TC 75 .... Vol II p 366
Wales v Tilley [1943] AC 386 .... Vol IV p 407
Walker v Boyd [1932] LJ 402 .... Vol II p 32
Walker v Giles [1848] 6 CB 662 .... Vol IV p 296
Wandesforde's 1 ITC 248, (23 May 1928) .... Vol I p 259

Ward v Kinahan Electrical Ltd [1984] IR 292 .... Vol VI p 561
Warrender v Warrender [1835] 2 C & F 488 .... Vol IV p 437
Waterford Glass (Group Services) Ltd v The Revenue Commissioners
[1990]1 IR 334 .... Vol IV p 187, Vol IV p 367, Vol V 181
Watkins v US (1956) 354 US 178 .... Vol VI p 68
Watson v Everitt v Blunden 18 TC 402 .... Vol I p 601
Watson v Hornby 24 TC 506, [1942] 2 All ER 506 .... Vol II p 315
Watson v Rowles 95 LJKB 959, 42 TLR 379, 11 TC 171 .... Vol II p 68
Webb v Ireland [1988] IR 353 .... Vol IV p 170, 492, Vol VI p 637
Wedick v Osmond and Co [1935] IR 838 p 845 .... Vol I p 542
Welbeck Securities v Powlson [1986] STC, [1987] STC 468 .... Vol IV p 547
.... Vol V p 515
Wellaway v Courtier [1918] 1 KB 200 .... Vol II p 636
Wemyss v Wemyss Trustee [1921] SC 40 .... Vol I p 259
Werle & Co v Colquhoun 2 TC 402, 20 QBD 753 .... Vol I p 28, 387
West Mercia Safetyware Ltd (In Liq) v Dodd [1988] Butterworths Company
Law Cases 250 .... Vol IV p 247
West v Phillips 38 TC 203 .... Vol III p 1, 373
Westcombe v Hadnock Quarries Ltd 16 TC 137 .... Vol III p 165
Westcott v Woolcombes Ltd [1987] STC 600 .... Vol VI p 203
Westminister Bank Ltd v Osler 17 TC 381, 146 LTR 441, 148 LTR 41
.... Vol I p 474, 503, Vol II p 419, Vol III p 373
Westminster (Duke of) v Commissioners of Inland Revenue 151 LTR 489,
51 TLR 467, 19 TC 490, [1936] AC 1 .... Vol I pp 601, 618, 629
.... Vol II pp 222, 515
Westminster Bank Executor and Trustee Co (Channel Islands) Ltd v National Bank of
Greece SA 46 TC 472 .... Vol VI p 818
Westminster Bank Ltd v Riches 28 TC 159 .... Vol II p 332
Westminster v Commissioners of Inland Revenue 19 TC 490, [1936] AC 1 .... Vol I p 515
Weston v Hearn 25 TC 425, [1943] 2 All ER 421 .... Vol II p 452
Westwinds Holdings Co Ltd (21 May 1974) .... Vol III p 423
Whelan, Norah v Patrick Madigan (18 July 1978) HC .... Vol III p 332
Whicker v Hume 7 HLC p 160 .... Vol I p 259
Whimster & Co v Commissioners of Inland Revenue 12 TC 813 .... Vol IV p 135
.... Vol II p 419, Vol III p 198
White, Re [1892] 2 Ch 217 .... Vol I p 601
Whiteley Ltd, William v The King [1909] 101 LT 741 .... Vol V p 615
Wiley v Revenue Commissioners [1989] IR 350 .... Vol VI p 637
Wiley v Revenue Commissioners [1994] 2 IR 160 .... Vol VI p 637
Wilks v Heeley [1832] 1 Cr & M 249 .... Vol III p 265
William's Executors v Commissioners of Inland Revenue 26 TC 23 .... Vol I p 164
Williams v Burgess (1840)10 LG, QB 11 .... Vol VI p 422
Williams v Corbet 8 Sim 349 .... Vol I p 601
Williams v Grundy's Trustees 18 TC 271, [1934] 1 KB 524 .... Vol II p 627
Williams v Singer 7 TC 387, [1921] 1 AC 65 .... Vol III p 477
Williams v Wallis and Cox [1914] 2 KB 478 .... 2006 p 56
Wilson Box (Foreign Rights) Ltd v Brice 20 TC 736 .... Vol III p 1
Wilson v John Lane .... Vol III p 441

Wilson v West Sussex Co Council [1963] 2 QB 764 .... Vol V p 357
Wimpey International Ltd v Warland, Associated Restaurants Ltd v Warland [1987] Simons Tax Intelligence [1988] STC 149, [1989] STC 273 .... Vol IV p 284, Vol V p 201
Winans v Attorney General [1904] AC 287 .... Vol I p 259
Wing v O'Connell (Inspector of Taxes) 1 ITC 170, [1927] IR 84 .... Vol I p 155, Vol I p 427, 618, Vol II p 261, Vol III p 165
Winget Ltd: Burn v The Company, Re [1924] 1 Ch p 550 .... Vol II p 108
Winsconsin v Pelican Insurance Co [1887] 127 US 265 .... Vol V p 45
Wisdom v Chamberlain [1969] 1 All ER 332, 45 TC 92 .... Vol III p 253, Vol V p 6
Wolmershausen v Gullick .... Vol III p 265
Woolwich Building Society v Inland Revenue Commissioners [1993] AC 70, V ITR 321 .... Vol V p 323, Vol VI p 514, 840

X

Xenos v Wickham LR 2 HL 296 .... Vol V p 560
XX Ltd v Ó hArgain (20 June 1975) .... Vol III p 1

Y

Yarmouth v France [1880] 19 QBD 646, [1887] 19 QBD 647 .... Vol II p 602 .... Vol III pp 113, 120, 219, Vol IV pp 68, 425, Vol V p 201, 317
Yates (Inspector of Taxes) v Starkey (1951) Ch 465 .... Vol V p 472
Yates v Starkey 32 TC 38, [1951 Ch 465 .... Vol IV p 221
Young v Inland Revenue Commissioners 12 TC 827, [1926] SC 30 .... Vol I p 240
Young v Racecourse Betting Control Board 38 TC 426 .... Vol IV p 73
Young v Robertson 4 Macq HL 314 .... Vol V p 540
Young v Sealey [1949] Ch 278, [1949] 1 All ER 92, [1949] LJR 529, [1948] 93 SJ 58 .... Vol V p 272
Young's Estate, Re [1918] 1 IR 30 .... Vol II p 332
Yuill v Wilson STC 1980 .... Vol III p 340

Z

Zita Modes Sàrl v Administrationde l'enregistrement et des domaines (Case C–497/01) (27 November 2003) ECJ .... Vol VI p 618

Statutes considered

Adaptation of Enactments Act 1922
.... Vol VI p 68
Adoption Act 1952
.... Vol V p 696
s 4 .... Vol IV p 415
s 26(2) .... Vol IV p 415
Arbitration Act 1954
ss 38, 41 .... 2006 p 56
Acquisition of Land (Assessment of Compensation) Act 1919
.... Vol IV p 485
s 2 .... Vol III p 298
Attorneys and Solicitors Act 1870
8 .... Vol VI p 441
Bankers Books of Evidence Acts 1879–1959 .... Vol VI p 561
Capital Acquisition Tax Act 1976
s 2 .... Vol III p 104
s 15–18 .... Vol V p 295, 680
s 21 .... Vol V p 200
s 39(4) .... Vol V p 295
s 52(2) .... Vol V p 295
s 56. .... Vol IV p 340
s 58(3) .... Vol V p 221
s 146 .... Vol V p 138
Sch 2 Pt 1 para 9 .... Vol V p 686
Central Bank Act 1971
s 2 .... Vol III p 559, 664
ss 7 to 31 .... Vol III p 559, 664
s 58 .... Vol III p 559, 664
Capital Gains Tax Act 1975
s 3 .... Vol IV p 515, 547
s 8 .... Vol IV p 515, 547
(2) .... Vol IV p 543
(5) .... Vol IV p 217
s 11 .... Vol VI p 203
s 12 .... Vol III p 683, Vol V p 163
s 19 .... Vol III p 559, 664
s 28 .... Vol IV p 1
s 33 .... Vol II p 683
s 46 .... Vol V p 163, Vol VI p 203
s 47 .... Vol IV p 515, 547
s 49(1) .... Vol IV p 125
Sch 2 para 2 .... Vol VI p 203
Sch 4 paras 6, 7, 11(4) .... Vol IV p 217

Capital Gains Tax Act 1975 (contd)
Sch 4 para 8(2)(b) .... Vol IV p 125
Sch 4 para 11(1), (6) .... Vol IV p 543
Common Law Procedure (Ireland) Act 1854
.... Vol V p 70
Companies (Consolidation) Act 1908
s 69 .... Vol V p 532
s 82(2) .... Vol V p 532
s 107 .... Vol II p 108
s 209 .... Vol II p 108
Companies Act 1963
s 8 .... Vol IV p 247
s 89 .... Vol V p 226
s 98 .... Vol III p 548, Vol IV p 91, Vol V p 388
s 147 .... Vol IV p 247
s 150 .... Vol IV p 247
s 201(3) .... Vol IV p 82
s 202 .... Vol IV p 82
s 205 .... Vol III p 423
s 214 .... Vol VI p 191
s 225 .... Vol V p 186
s 230 .... Vol V p 186
s 231(e) .... Vol VI p 191
s 235 .... Vol V p 186
s 244 .... Vol III p 120
s 281 .... Vol III p 523
s 285 .... Vol III p 120, 509, 548
.... Vol IV p 82, Vol V p 388
s 297 .... Vol VI p 386
Companies Act 1990
s 8 .... Vol V p 226
s 14 .... Vol V p 226
s 19 .... 2000 p 261
s 21 .... 2000 p 261
s 134 .... Vol V p 388
s 227 .... Vol V p 226
Constitution of Ireland 1937
.... Vol V p 70
Article 6 .... Vol VI p 68
Article 15 .... Vol VI p 68
Article 18 .... Vol VI p 68
Article 28 .... Vol VI p 68
Article 29.3 .... Vol VI p 386
Article 30 .... Vol VI p 68
Article 34 .... Vol V p 70, Vol VI p 125
Article 34.1 .... Vol III p 590
Article 34.3.4 .... Vol III p 419

Constitution of Ireland 1937 (contd)
Article 37 .... Vol VI p 125
Article 38 .... Vol VI p 386
Article 38.1 .... Vol III p 387, 419
Article 38.2 .... Vol III p 419
Article 38.5 .... Vol III p 419
Article 40 .... Vol V p 70, 614, Vol VI p 68, 125
Article 40.1 .... Vol III p 188, Vol IV p 437, Vol V p 481, Vol VI p 386
Article 40.3 .... Vol III p 188, 590
.... Vol IV p 437
Article 41 .... Vol III p 188, Vol IV p 437
.... Vol V p 614
Article 43 .... Vol V p 70, Vol VI p 386
Article 50 .... Vol V p 481, Vol VI p 68

Conveyancing Act 1881
s 14.......... Vol V p 589

Conveyancing Act 1891
s 7.......... Vol V p 181

Copyright Act 1963
s 1.......... Vol IV p 314
s 17.......... Vol IV p 314

Corporation Tax Act 1976
.... Vol III p 611
s 1.......... Vol III p 53
(1).......... Vol V p 107
s 2.......... Vol IV p 415
s 4.......... Vol III p 670
s 6.......... Vol III p 553, Vol V p 107,
s 8.......... Vol I p 330
(1).......... Vol IV p 12
(2).......... Vol IV p 12
s 9 (1).......... Vol V p 107
s 10.......... Vol V p 10
s 11.......... Vol III p 553
(i).......... Vol V p 107
(iii) .... Vol V p 107
s 13.......... Vol V p 107
s 15.......... Vol I p 447, Vol II p 429, Vol V p 680
(1) .... Vol VI p 158
(6) .... Vol VI p 158
s 16(1).......... Vol III p 363
(2).......... Vol III p 340
s 21.......... Vol IV p 91, Vol V p 200
s 25.......... Vol I p 86, Vol III p 340
s 27(1).......... Vol III p 363
s 28.......... Vol III p 430
s 37.......... Vol IV p 475

Corporation Tax Act 1976 (contd)

s 52 ..... Vol IV p 401
s 54 ..... Vol III p 304
s 58 ..... Vol IV p 633, 2001 p 80, Vol VI p 524
(3) ..... Vol III p 229, Vol V p 221
s 59 ..... Vol IV p 633
s 78 ..... Vol III p 304
s 83 ..... Vol III p 246
s 84 ..... Vol III p 246
(1) ..... Vol III p 517
s 87(8) ..... Vol III p 246
s 100 ..... Vol III p 517
s 101 ..... Vol III p 517
s 107 ..... 2000 p 76
s 131 ..... Vol III p 373
s 140 ..... Vol III p 533
s 142 ..... Vol III p 553
s 143 ..... Vol III p 120
s 145 ..... Vol VI p 132, 579
s 146 ..... Vol III p 559, 644, Vol V p 138
s 147 ..... Vol III p 553
s 151 ..... Vol III p 246
s 155 ..... Vol IV p 12, Vol III p 246
..... Vol V p 226
s 156 ..... Vol V p 226
(1)(*b*) ..... Vol III p 246
s 162 ..... Vol III p 211
s 182 ..... Vol III p 363
s 184 ..... Vol III p 363
s 307 ..... Vol III p 253
Sch 1 para 10 ..... Vol IV p 91
Sch 3 s 164 ..... Vol III p 56

Courts of Justice Act 1936

s 38 ..... Vol V p 322
s 65 ..... Vol V p 195

Courts (Supplemental Provisions) Act 1961

..... Vol III p 641, Vol IV p 395
s 52 ..... Vol V p 221

Courts Acts 1924–1981

..... Vol III p 641

Courts Act 1981

s 22 ..... Vol III p 403
(1) ..... Vol V p 322, Vol VI p 588

Court Officers Act 1926

..... Vol V p 186, 195

Courts of Justice Act 1924
s 38(3) .... Vol IV p 437
s 94 .... Vol III p 387
Courts of Justice Act 1936
s 38 .... Vol V p 322
s 65 .... Vol V p 186, 195
s 76 .... Vol IV p 278
Courts of Justice Act 1961
.... Vol V p 221
Criminal Assets Bureau Act 1996
.... Vol VI p 386, 502, 561
s 3 .... Vol VI p 561
s 4 .... Vol VI p 422, 561, 720, 800
s 5 .... Vol VI p 561, 720, 800
s 7 .... Vol VI p 561
s 8 .... Vol VI p 125, 561, 800
(1) .... Vol VI p 422
(8) .... Vol VI p 441
s 10 .... Vol VI p 422, 441, 561, 720, 800
Criminal Justice Act 1988 (UK)
s 71 .... Vol V p 45
s 77(8) .... Vol V p 45
Criminal Justice Act 1994
s 63 .... Vol VI p 561
Criminal Justice (Theft and Fraud Offences) Act 2001
s 3(2) .... Vol VI p 711
Customs Consolidation Act 1876
.... Vol VI p 386
s 42 .... Vol VI p 472
s 186 .... Vol IV p 395, Vol VI p 472
s 204 .... Vol IV p 386
s 205 .... Vol VI p 142
Customs and Inland Revenue Regulation Act 1890
s 30 .... Vol IV p 386
Customs Act 1956
.... Vol V p 348
s 2 .... Vol VI p 472
Customs (Temporary Provisions) Act 1948
.... Vol VI p 386
Customs and Excise (Miscellaneous Provisions) Act 1988
s 5(1) .... Vol VI p 142
Debtors (Ireland) Act 1840
s 26 .... Vol V p 322, Vol VI p 588

Domicile and Recognition of Foreign Divorces Act 1986
.... Vol IV p 437
Enforcement of Court Orders Act 1926
s 2 .... Vol IV p 86
s 13 .... Vol IV p 86
Ethics in Public Office Act 1995
.... Vol VI p 68
European Arrest Warrant Act 2003 .... Vol VI p 711
Excise Management Act 1827
s 86 .... Vol IV p 278
s 90 .... Vol IV p 278
Excise Collection and Management Act 1841(4 & 5 Vict c 20)
s 24 .... Vol III p 265
Executive Power (Consequential Provisions) Act 1937
.... Vol VI p 68
Extradition Act 1965
s 42(2) .... Vol VI p 667
s 47 .... Vol VI p 667
s 50 .... 1998 p 76, Vol VI p 667
Extradition (European Union Convention) Act 2001
s 26 .... Vol VI p 667
Farm Tax Act 1985
.... Vol III p 229
s 3 .... Vol V p 288
s 9 .... Vol V p 288
Finance Act 1894
s 1 .... Vol V p 600
s 2(1)(a) .... Vol V p 600
s 5(3) .... Vol V p 526
s 7(5) .... Vol V p 294, 532, 577
s 10 .... Vol V p 577
s 22(2)(a) .... Vol V p 600
Finance (1909–1910) Act 1910
s 59(2) .... Vol V p 589
s 74(5) .... Vol IV p 187
Finance Act 1910 Pt V
ss 73–75 .... Vol V p 570
Finance Act 1915
s 21(2) .... Vol VI p 158
s 41(1) .... Vol VI p 158
Finance Act (No 2) 1915
s 45(5) .... Vol I p 1
Sch IV Pt I rule 1 .... Vol I p 240
Sch IV Pt III .... Vol I p 34

Finance Act 1918
s 33 .... Vol VI p 158
s 35 .... Vol I p 28
Finance Act 1920
s 16 .... Vol II p 596
s 17 .... Vol V p 539
s 52 .... Vol III p 56
(2) .... Vol I p 70, 108
(I) .... Vol I p 359
(a) .... Vol I p 108, 119
(b) .... Vol I p 330
s 53 .... Vol I p 629, Vol II p 382
.... Vol III p 56
(2)(b) .... Vol II p 412
(h) .... Vol II p 195
s 54(1) .... Vol II p 130
Pt V .... Vol I p 627
Finance Act 1921
s 21 .... Vol IV p 386
s 30(1)(*c*) .... Vol I p 383
s 53 .... Vol I p 315, Vol II p 195
Sch 2 Pt II
rule 1 .... Vol I p 130
Finance Act 1922
s 18 .... Vol II pp 393, 452
s 20 .... Vol II p 82
(1) .... Vol II p 352
(1)(*c*) .... Vol I p 411
Finance Act 1923
s 17 .... Vol V p 539
Finance Act 1924
s 10 .... Vol I p 656
Finance Act 1925
s 11 .... Vol V p 565
s 12 .... Vol I pp 249, 259
Finance Act 1926
s 24(*a*) .... Vol IV p 395
s 25(1) .... Vol IV p 395
Sch 1 Pt II .... Vol II p 491
s 1(3) .... Vol II p 304
s 2(2) .... Vol II p 304
Finance Act 1929
s 5 .... Vol I p 571
s 8(1) .... Vol I p 146

Finance Act 1929 (contd)
s 9 .... Vol II p 515
(2) .... Vol I p 146
s 10 .... Vol I p 563, Vol II p 304
.... Vol III p 568
s 11 .... Vol I pp 563, Vol II p 393
.... Vol II pp 304, 464, 491
s 12 .... Vol II pp 55, 115
s 14 .... Vol II p 482
s 17 .... Vol I p 618
s 18 .... Vol II p 304
s 33(1)(*d*) .... Vol II p 25
Sch 1 Pt II .... Vol I p 393, Vol II p 61
Sch 2 para (3) .... Vol II p 304
Finance Act 1932
s 3(4) .... Vol V p 565
s 4 .... Vol I p 393
s 46 .... Vol V p 539
Finance Act 1935
s 6 .... Vol I p 583
(1) .... Vol II p 472
s 21 .... Vol V p 696
(8) .... Vol IV p 162
Finance Act 1937
s 2 .... Vol II p 82
(1) .... Vol II p 352
Finance Act 1939
s 3 .... Vol V p 565
s 7 .... Vol II p 315
Finance Act 1940
s 3 .... Vol V p 393
s 18 .... Vol IV p 386
Finance Act 1941
s 32 .... Vol V p 589
s 36(4) .... Vol II p 175
s 39 .... Vol II p 19
Finance Act 1944
s 14 .... Vol II p 175
Finance Act 1946
s 24 .... Vol II p 195
Finance Act (No 2) 1947
s 13(1) .... 1998 p 169
(4) .... 1998 p 169
(5) .... 1998 p 169
s 23 .... Vol V p 570

Finance Act 1956
Pt V .... Vol II p 602
Finance Act 1958
s 23 .... Vol IV p 323
s 24 .... Vol IV p 323
s 25 .... Vol IV p 323
s 26 .... Vol IV p 323
Finance Act (No 2) 1959
.... Vol IV p 82
s 13(1) .... Vol II p 588
Finance Act 1962
s 22 .... Vol IV p 162
Finance Act 1963
s 34(4)(*d*)(i) .... Vol III p 419
(iii) .... Vol III p 419
Finance Act 1964
s 26 .... Vol III p 56
Finance Act 1965
s 23 .... Vol VI p 203
Finance Act 1967
s 9 .... Vol VI p 524
s 12 .... Vol V p 393
s 138–143 .... Vol V p 393
s 153 .... Vol V p 393
s 241 .... Vol V p 317
s 439 .... Vol V p 393
Finance Act 1968
s 7 .... Vol III p 590
s 8 .... Vol III p 590, Vol VI p 1
s 11 .... Vol VI p 1
s 14 .... Vol IV p 91
s 43(1) .... Vol IV p 170
Finance Act 1969
s 2 .... Vol III p 496, Vol V p 98
s 3 .... Vol V p 393
s 65(1) .... Vol III p 533
Finance Act 1970
s 17 .... Vol IV p 269, 304
s 20 .... Vol III p 484
s 24 .... Vol IV p 187
s 26 .... Vol IV p 68
Finance Act 1971
s 22 .... Vol IV p 22
s 25 .... Vol IV p 22
s 26 .... Vol V p 200

Finance Act 1972
ss 14–25 .... Vol IV p 340
Sch 1 .... Vol IV p 340

Finance Act 1973
s 34 .... Vol III p 670

Finance Act 1974
s 8 .... Vol V p 393
s 13 .... Vol IV p 1
(1) .... Vol III p 319
s 15 .... Vol IV p 1
s 17 .... Vol IV p 1
s 21 .... Vol IV p 1
s 22 .... Vol V p 680
s 31 .... Vol III p 246
s 59 .... Vol III p 356

Finance Act 1975
s 12 .... Vol IV p 1
s 25 .... Vol V p 348
s 31 .... Vol I p 130, Vol III pp 51, 178
(1) .... Vol IV p 304
(2) .... Vol IV p 135

Finance Act 1976
s 21 .... Vol IV p 269
s 26 .... Vol III p 51
s 30 .... Vol IV pp 62, 91
(4) .... Vol V p 322
s 41 .... 2000 p 59
s 46 .... Vol IV p 162, Vol V p 696

Finance Act 1977
s 43 .... Vol III p 611
Pt V Sch 1 .... Vol III p 611

Finance Act 1978
.... Vol V p 322
s 46 .... Vol IV p 91
ss 138–142 .... Vol V p 614

Finance Act 1980
s 1 .... Vol V p 393
s 2 .... Vol V p 393
s 8 .... Vol V p 129
s 18 .... Vol V p 129
s 21 .... Vol III p 188
s 38–51 .... Vol V p 226
s 39 .... Vol III p 611, Vol IV p 35
.... Vol IV pp 361, 526, Vol VI p 579
(1), (2) and (5) .... Vol VI p 132

Finance Act 1980 (contd)
s 41(2) .... Vol III p 304, Vol IV p 35
.... Vol IV p 466
(4) .... Vol IV p 466
(8) .... Vol V p 376, 1998 p 99
s 42 .... Vol IV p 361, Vol V p 221
s 50 .... Vol VI p 524
s 57 .... Vol IV p 478
s 79 .... Vol III p 73
Pt I Ch VI .... Vol III p 441, Vol V p 21
Finance Act 1982
Sch 2 .... Vol IV p 35
s 4 .... Vol IV p 323
s 26 .... Vol IV p 35
s 69(1) .... Vol IV p 395
Finance Act 1983
s 3 .... Vol IV p 437
s 9 .... Vol III p 533
s 18 .... Vol III p 153, Vol V p 348
s 19 .... Vol I p 195, Vol II p 291, Vol V p 424
s 56 .... Vol III p 120
s 60(11) .... Vol VI p 743
s 85 .... Vol VI p 513
s 94 .... Vol III p 387, Vol IV p 395
(2) .... Vol IV p 478, Vol VI p 783
(4) .... Vol IV p 478
(9) .... Vol IV p 478
s 95 .... Vol III p 127
Finance Act 1985
s 51 .... Vol VI p 596
Finance Act 1986
s 46 .... Vol III p 253
s 48(2) .... Vol V p 210
s 91 .... Vol VI p 596
s 96(1) .... Vol IV p 187
Finance Act 1987
s 14 .... Vol V p 213
s 15 .... Vol V p 213
s 17–19 .... Vol V p 213
s 53 .... Vol IV p 278
Finance Act 1988
s 1 .... Vol V p 424
s 7 .... Vol V p 424
s 13 .... Vol VI p 720
s 15 .... Vol VI p 720
s 16 .... Vol V p 210

Finance Act 1988 (contd)
s 17 .... Vol VI p 422, 720
s 73 .... Vol V p 70
Finance Act 1989
s 86 .... Vol V p 6, 2006 p 82
s 92 .... 2000 p 55
Finance Act 1990
s 14 .... Vol V p 213
s 26 .... Vol V p 213
s 41 .... Vol VI p 579
(1) .... Vol V p 376, Vol VI p 48
(5) .... 1999 p 72, Vol VI p 132
Finance Act 1991
s 6 .... Vol VI p 498
s 86, 87 .... Vol VI p 596
Finance Act 1992
s 15 .... Vol V p 472
s 242 .... Vol IV p 419
Finance Act 1995
s 10 .... Vol V p 472
s 104 .... Vol VI p 743
s 105(3) .... Vol VI p 743
Finance Act 1998
s 15(2) .... Vol VI p 422
Finance Act (Miscellaneous Provisions) 1956
.... Vol VI p 524
s 13(3) .... Vol III p 452
Finance (Profits of Certain Mines) (Temporary Relief from Taxation) Act 1956
.... Vol VI p 524
Finance Act (Miscellaneous Provisions) 1968
s 17 .... Vol II p 667, Vol III p 9
s 18 .... Vol III p 271
(2) .... Vol III p 198
Finance (Excise Duties) (Vehicles) Act 1952
.... Vol IV p 170
Finance (Taxation of Profits of Certain Mines) Act 1974
.... Vol IV p 91, Vol VI p 524
Fraudulent Conveyances Act 1635
.... Vol III p 706
Family Law Act 1995
s 16 .... Vol VI p 764
Garda Síochána Pension Order 1981
.... 1998 p 113

Holidays (Employees) Act 1973
.... Vol III p 505
Imposition of Duties Act 1957
.... Vol IV p 162
Industrial Development Act 1969
s 33 .... Vol IV p 22
Interpretation Act 1937
s 11 .... Vol III pp 559, 644
Income Tax Act 1843
.... 1998 p 183
Income Tax Act 1918
Sch B .... Vol II p 636
rule 8 .... Vol II p 1, Vol II p 241
Sch D .... Vol I p 330, 474, 496, 515
.... Vol II p 32, 45, 140, 164
.... 360, 374, 419
Sch D Case I .... Vol I p 427, 629
.... Vol II p 211, 291, 315, 500,
rule 3 & 6 602
Sch D Cases I & II .... Vol I p 86
rule 1(1) .... Vol I p 642
rule 2 .... Vol II p 382
rule 3 .... Vol I p 375, 642, Vol II p 515
(*a*) .... Vol II p 222
(*d*) and (g) .... Vol II p 267
rule 4 .... Vol II p 115
rule 7 .... Vol I p 43 rule 11
.... Vol II p 55
Sch D Cases II & VI .... Vol I p 195
Sch D Case III .... Vol I pp 45, 393, 491
.... Vol II pp 15, 393, 464, 568, 592
rule 2 (s 17) .... Vol II p 304
rule 4 .... Vol III p 19
rule 5 .... Vol II p 222
Sch D Case IV
rule 2(*a*) .... Vol I p 259
Sch D Case V
rule 3 .... Vol I p 249
Sch D Case VI .... Vol II p 204, 261
Sch E .... Vol I p 155, 601
.... Vol II p 68, 452
rule 1 .... Vol I p 214, 618
rule 5 .... Vol I p 214
rule 7 .... Vol II p 261
rule 9 .... Vol I p 64, Vol II pp 366, 460

Income Tax Act 1918 (contd)
Case VI........Vol II p 154
rule 16........Vol I pp 115, 563, Vol II p 75
rule 21........Vol I p 487
s 5........Vol I p 231
s 16........Vol V p 565
s 25........Vol I p 221
s 29........Vol V p 565
s 30 (1)........Vol VI p 386
s 33 (1)........Vol I p 447, Vol II p 429
s 100(2)........Vol I p 642
s 133........Vol I p 571
s 137........Vol I p 571
s 149........Vol I p 1, 571, 656
(1)(*e*)........Vol II p 60
s 186........Vol II p 1, 241
s 187........Vol II pp 1, 241
s 202........Vol I p 221
s 209........Vol I p 642, Vol II p 515
Sch 1........Vol III p 56
Income Tax Assessment Act 1936–1938
s 78........Vol VI p 524
Income Tax Act 1967
........Vol II pp 366, 460, Vol III p 1, Vol VI p 524
Sch E........Vol III p 467
s 1........Vol III p 559, 644
........Vol IV p 73
s 4........Vol V p 108, 1998 p 183
s 7(*a*)........Vol III p 533
s 10........Vol VI p 203
s 11........Vol III p 9
(1)........Vol V p 496
s 12........Vol III p 9
s 17........Vol II p 641
s 25........Vol II p 393
s 52........Vol V p 108, 1998 p 183
s 53........Vol I pp 1, 28, 45, 115, 119, 207, 231, 231
........Vol I pp 318, 427, 474, 629
........Vol II pp 60, 164, 204, 304, 393, 491, 592, 614
........Vol III pp 165, 484, 568, Vol IV pp 45, 73, 135, Vol VI p 817
........Vol V p 108
(1)........Vol III pp 559, 644
s 54........Vol V p 21
s 57........Vol I p 130
s 58........Vol I p 146
........Vol I p 91

Income Tax Act 1967 (contd)
s 61 .... Vol I pp 104, 375, 503, 642
.... Vol II pp 32, 45, 267, 281, 360
.... Vol II pp 382, 500, 515, 602
.... Vol IV p 187, 425, Vol V p 496
.... Vol VI p 328
s 61(*a*) .... Vol IV p 22
(*e*) .... Vol V p 138
(*f*) .... Vol V p 138
s 62(2) .... Vol IV p 304
s 76 .... Vol I pp 249, 259, Vol II p 304, Vol V p 481,Vol VI p 817
s 80 .... Vol IV p 187
s 81 .... Vol IV p 187
(5)(*d*) .... Vol III p 95, Vol V p 680
(6)(a)(i) .... Vol V p 680
s 83 .... Vol IV p 187
s 91 .... Vol IV p 187
s 105 .... Vol III p 477, 553
s 109 .... 1998 p 113
s 110 .... Vol I pp 214, 601, 656, Vol II pp 261, 452
.... Vol III p 43, 505, Vol IV p 45
.... Vol IV p 221, 391, 407, Vol VI p 203, 498
s 111 .... Vol IV p 221
s 114 .... Vol I p 618, Vol IV pp 233, 407
.... Vol V p 134
s 115 .... Vol IV p 221
(1)(*a*) .... Vol V p 134
s 117 .... Vol II p 452, Vol IV p 323
s 118 .... Vol IV p 323
s 119 .... Vol IV p 323
s 120 .... Vol IV p 323
s 126 .... Vol III p 590, Vol V p 322
s 127 .... Vol II p 641
s 128 .... Vol II p 641
s 129 .... Vol III p 590
s 131 .... Vol III p 590
s 133(1) .... Vol II p 588
s 138 .... Vol V p 129, 614
s 146 .... Vol V p 496
s 161(1) .... Vol III p 670
s 162 .... Vol III p 290, 298
s 169 .... Vol V p 348
(4) .... Vol III p 387
s 172 .... Vol IV p 478
(4) .... Vol V p 348
s 174(1) .... Vol IV p 332
(*a*) .... Vol V p 265
s 176 .... Vol IV p 221

Income Tax Act 1967 (contd)

s 178(1) .... Vol III p 387
s 184 .... Vol VI p 125, 720
(2) .... Vol III p 533
s 186 .... Vol I p 34, Vol II p 627
.... Vol IV p 187
s 192 .... Vol IV p 188, Vol V p 129, 614
s 193 .... Vol I p 115
s 194 .... Vol I p 563, Vol II p 75
.... Vol V p 424
s 195 .... Vol V p 424, 614
(1) .... Vol V p 129
s 196 .... Vol V p 614
s 197 .... Vol V p 614
s 198 .... Vol V p 614
s 200 .... Vol I p 183
s 207 .... Vol III p 553
s 212 .... Vol III p 553
s 220(5) .... Vol II p 661
s 224 .... 1998 p 113
s 238 .... Vol III p 387
s 239 .... Vol V p 108, 1998 p 183
s 240 .... Vol III p 387
s 241 .... Vol III p 113, 219
.... Vol IV p 68, 425, Vol V p 6
(1) .... Vol V p 200
(5) .... Vol III p 253
s 244 .... Vol IV p 91
s 245 .... Vol IV p 91
s 252 .... Vol III p 253
s 254 .... Vol III p 65
s 255 .... Vol III p 65, 661, 2000 p 56
(1)(d) .... Vol V p 357
s 282 .... Vol III p 253
s 296 .... Vol III p 253, 387
s 300 .... Vol VI p 386
s 307 .... Vol III p 332
s 333 .... Vol I p 542, Vol VI p 8
s 334 .... Vol I p 383, Vol VI p 8
s 348 .... Vol I p 538
s 349 .... Vol III p 28
s 361 .... Vol III p 246
s 416 .... Vol I p 221, 571, 618, 629
.... Vol II p 55, Vol III pp 332, 577
.... Vol IV pp 62, 73, 91, 125, 187, Vol VI p 125, 636, 720
s 416(1) .... Vol VI p 422
(6) .... Vol III p 533, Vol V p 210

Income Tax Act 1967 (contd)

s 428 .... Vol III p 159, 198, 611, 1998 p 111
.... Vol IV p 401, 505
.... Vol V p 54, 76, 163, 221, 481, 496,
.... Vol VI p 60, 132, 203, 579, 596, 618
s 428(*b*) .... Vol III p 340
(9) .... Vol IV p 91, Vol V p 322
s 429 .... Vol II p 374, Vol III p 219
.... Vol IV pp 125, 401, 407, 505
s 430 .... Vol I p 487, Vol II p 332
.... Vol III pp 159, 198, 496, 559, 611, 644
.... Vol IV pp 62, 125, 401, 425, 505
.... Vol V p 54, 138, 221, 481
s 438 .... Vol I p 411
s 439 .... Vol III p 242
s 440 .... Vol II p 82
s 443 .... Vol II p 352
.... Vol IV p 221
s 448 .... Vol II p 82
s 478 .... Vol V p 424
s 485 .... Vol III p 533, 590, Vol VI p 720
s 488 .... Vol III p 577
s 496 .... Vol III p 559, 644
s 498 .... Vol V p 322
s 500 .... Vol III p 387, 641
.... Vol IV p 395, 478
s 501 .... Vol III p 577, Vol IV p 478
s 502 .... Vol IV p 478
s 503 .... Vol IV p 395
s 506 .... Vol IV p 478
s 507 .... Vol IV p 478
s 508 .... Vol III p 387
s 527 .... Vol IV p 73
s 542(2) .... Vol V p 348
s 550 .... Vol V p 322
(1) .... Vol IV p 91
(2A)(*c*) .... Vol IV p 62
Pt XXVI .... Vol III p 577
Sch 2 para 3 .... Vol I p 64

Income Tax Act 1970 (UK)

s 130(*f*) .... Vol V p 138

Inland Revenue Regulations Act 1890

s 21 .... Vol V p 691

Interpretation Act 1937
s 11(h) .... Vol VI p 422
s 18 .... Vol VI p 422
Labour Exchange Act 1909
.... Vol III p 253, Vol IV p 45
Limited Partnerships Act 1907
.... Vol III p 253
Local Government (Planning and Development) Act 1963
s 5 .... Vol V p 357
s 528(6) .... Vol V p 357
Local Government (Planning and Development) Act 1976
.... Vol IV p 543
Local Government (Planning and Development) Act 1982
.... Vol IV p 543
Minerals Development Act 1940
s 14 .... Vol V p 696
Offences against the State (Amendment) Act 1985
.... Vol VI p 386
Partnership Act 1890
.... Vol III p 253
Petty Sessions (Ireland) Act 1851
s 22 .... Vol IV p 278
s 42 .... Vol IV p 278
Police Property Act 1897 .... Vol VI p 636
Poor Law Act 1834 (4 & 5 Wm 4 c 76)
s 86 .... Vol V p 560
Poor Relief (Ireland) Act 1838 (1 & 2 Vict c 56)
s 96 .... Vol V p 560
Preferential Payments in Bankruptcy (Ireland) Act 1889
.... Vol VI p 1
Proceeds of Crime Act 1996
.... Vol VI p 636
s 2 .... Vol VI p 386, 502
s 3, 4, ... Vol VI p 386
s 6 .... Vol VI p 502
s 7, 8, 9 .... Vol VI p 386
Prosecution of Offences Act 1974
.... Vol III p 641
s 3 .... Vol IV p 395, Vol V p 691
Racing Board and Racecourses Act 1945
s 4 .... Vol IV p 73
ss 14–16 .... Vol IV p 73
s 27(1) .... Vol IV p 73

Revenue Act 1898 (61 & 62 Vict c 46)
s 13 .... Vol V p 560
Revenue Act 1911
s 15 .... Vol V p 570
Roads Act 1993 .... 2000 p 287
Road Traffic Act 1961
s 49 .... Vol VI p 720
Road Traffic Act 1988 (UK)
s 157 .... 2000 p 65
Road Transport Act 1932
s 2, 7, 8, 10, 11, 12 .... Vol VI p 743
Road Transport Act 1933
s 66 .... Vol VI p 743
Sale of goods Act 1893
.... Vol V p 21
Scrap Iron (Control of Exhaust) Act 1938 .... Vol VI p 386
Sea Fisheries Protection Act 1933
s 9 .... Vol IV p 401
Settled Land Act 1882
.... Vol V p 526, 600
Social Welfare Act 1952
s 27(2) .... Vol V p 472
Social Welfare Act 1976
s 18(1) .... Vol V p 472
Social Welfare (Consolidation) Act 1981
.... Vol IV p 113
s 2 .... Vol V p 472
(4) .... Vol IV p 378
s 5(1) .... Vol IV p 378
s 9 .... Vol III p 509
(1),(2) .... Vol IV p 378
s 10 .... Vol III p 509, Vol VI p 1
(1),(3) .... Vol IV p 378
s 92 .... Vol IV p 221, Vol V p 472, Vol VI p 60
s 94 .... Vol IV p 221, Vol VI p 60
s 95 .... Vol V p 472, Vol VI p 60
s 111 .... Vol V p 239
s 114 .... Vol IV p 391
s 298 .... Vol V p 239
s 299 .... Vol III p 436, Vol V p 239
Social Welfare Act 1982
s 2 .... Vol V p 472

Social Welfare (Consolidation) Act 1993
.... Vol V p 95
s 16
(1) .... Vol VI p 1
(2) .... Vol VI p 1
s 247 .... Vol VI p 771
s 263 .... Vol VI p 674, 2006 p 62
s 271 .... Vol VI p 373, 674, 2006 p 62
s 301 .... Vol VI p 1
Social Welfare (No 2) 1993
Part III .... Vol VI p 373
Solicitors Act 1954
s 68 .... Vol VI p 793
Solicitors (Amendment) Act 1960
s 32 .... Vol VI p 793
Stamp Duties (Ireland) Act 1842
s 38 .... Vol V p 539, Vol VI p 743
Stamp Duties Act 1854
s 1 .... Vol V p 570
Stamp Act 1870
s 17 .... Vol V p 1
ss 96–99 .... Vol V p 570
Stamp Duties Management Act 1891 (54 & 55 Vict c 38)
s 10 .... Vol V p 560
Stamp Act 1891
s 1 .... Vol IV p 187
s 3 .... Vol IV p 187
s 12 .... Vol V p 570
s 13 .... Vol IV p 367, Vol V p 181
s 14 .... Vol V p 363
(4) .... Vol V p 1
s 23 .... Vol V p 570
s 54 .... Vol IV p 187, 367
ss 59–61 .... Vol V p 570
ss 175–78 .... Vol V p 570
Succession Act 1965
.... Vol III p 559
s 9(2) .... Vol V p 600
s 10 .... Vol V p 367
s 67(1) .... Vol V p 367
s 111 .... Vol V p 600
(1) .... Vol V p 367
s 115 .... Vol V p 367, 600

Succession Act 1965 (contd)
s 120 .... Vol V p 367
Pt VIII .... Vol V p 271
Succession Duty Act 1853
s 18 .... Vol V p 539
Taxes Consolidation Act 1997
s 15 .... Vol VI p 793
s 58 .... Vol VI p 441, 502
s 86(i) .... Vol VI p 636
s 112 .... Vol VI p 686
s 128 .... Vol VI p 686
s 268 .... Vol VI p 699
s 443 .... Vol VI p 691
s 811 .... 2006 p 82
s 851 .... Vol VI p 561
s 877 .... Vol VI p 800
s 879 .... Vol VI p 800
s 919 .... Vol VI p 561
s 922 .... Vol VI p 502, 561, 636
s 933 .... Vol VI p 125, 422, 446, 502, 561, 636, 720, 800
s 941 .... Vol VI p 513, 686, 691, 699, 743, 793, 817
(9) .... Vol VI p 588
s 950 .... Vol VI p 686, 800
s 951 .... Vol VI p 561, 800
s 952 .... Vol VI p 561
s 954 .... Vol VI p 561, 720
s 955(2)(a) .... Vol VI p 125
s 957 .... Vol VI p 561, 720, 783, 800
(2) .... Vol VI p 502
s 958 .... Vol VI p 561
s 961 .... Vol VI p 561, 800
s 962 .... Vol VI p 561, 800
s 963 .... Vol VI p 561
s 964 .... Vol VI p 561
s 966 .... Vol VI p 422, 561, 720
(5)(a) .... Vol VI p 125, 446
s 967 .... Vol VI p 561
s 983 .... Vol VI p 686
s 984 .... Vol VI p 686
s 998 .... Vol VI p 561
s 1002 .... Vol VI p 800
s 1017 .... 2000 p 58
s 1025 .... Vol VI p 764
s 1030 .... Vol VI p 764
s 1078 .... Vol VI p 636, 667
s 1080 .... Vol VI p 720
s 1082 .... Vol VI p 636, 800

Taxes Consolidation Act 1997 (contd)
s 1084 .... Vol VI p 636, 686
s 1086 .... Vol VI p 636
s 1097 .... Vol VI p 125
s 1100 .... Vol VI p 561
Taxes Management Act 1880
s 59 .... Vol I p 1
Tribunal of Inquiry (Evidence) Act 1921
.... Vol VI p 68
Tribunal of Inquiry (Evidence) (Amendment) Act 1979
.... Vol VI p 68
Unemployment Assistance Act 1933
.... Vol III p 253, Vol IV p 45
Unfair Dismissals Act 1977
.... Vol V p 239
Value Added Tax Act 1972 (No 22)
.... Vol VI p 484
Sch 1(12) .... Vol III p 680
Sch 4 .... Vol IV p 117
Sch 6 .... Vol IV p 349
s 1(1) .... Vol III p 611
s 2 .... Vol IV p 117, 314, 2003 p 77, Vol VI p 561
s 3 .... Vol VI p 561
(1)(*f*) .... Vol V p 76
(5) .... Vol VI p 618
s 4(3A) .... 2006 p 55
(4) .... Vol V p 76
s 5 .... Vol IV p 117, 314, Vol VI p 561
s 6 .... Vol VI p 561
s 8 .... Vol V p 61
s 9 .... Vol V p 61
s 10 .... Vol III p 332, Vol V p 418
(9) .... Vol V p 76
s 10(10) .... Vol V p 76
s 11 .... Vol IV p 117, Vol V p 418
s 12 .... Vol V p 76, 412
s 16 .... Vol V p 412
s 17 .... Vol VI p 561
s 19 .... Vol V p 412, Vol VI p 561
s 20(1) .... Vol V p 412
s 22 .... Vol VI p 561
s 23 .... Vol VI p 561
s 24 .... Vol VI p 561
s 25 .... Vol III p 332, 2002 p 135
.... Vol V p 76
(2) .... Vol VI p 596, 618

Value Added Tax Act 1972 (contd)
s 26 .... Vol IV p 478
s 27 .... Vol IV p 386, 478
s 32 .... Vol V p 76
s 43 .... Vol V p 418
Value Added Tax Act (Amendment) Act 1978 (No 34)
s 3 .... Vol IV p 314
Value Added Tax Act (UK) 1983
s 39(3) .... Vol V p 45
Value Added Tax Act 1994 (UK)
s 72 .... Vol VI p 667
Waiver of Certain Tax, Interest & Penalties Act 1993
s 2 .... Vol V p 210
(2) .... Vol VI p 125
s 3 .... Vol V p 210
(6) .... Vol VI p 125
Wills Act 1837
.... Vol V p 271

Regulations and Statutory Instruments

Agricultural Levies (Export Control) Regulations 1983 (UK)
.... Vol VI p 20
Backing of Warrants (Republic of Ireland) (Rule of Speciality) Order 1924 (UK) .... Vol VI p 667
Double Taxation Relief (Taxes on Income and Capital Gains) [UK]
Order 1976 (SI 319/1976) .... Vol V p 129
Article 15 .... Vol V p 54
Article 18(2) .... Vol V p 54
EC Council Directive No 77/388/EEC
.... Vol V p 76
EC Council Directive No 81/77/EEC
.... Vol VI p 20
EC Council Directive No 83/182/EEC of 28 March 1983
.... Vol IV p 512
EC Council Directive 92/12/EEC .... Vol VI p 472
EEC Regulations
804/68 and 2682/72 .... Vol IV p 492
EEC Council Regulations
729/1970, 974/1971 and 667/85 .... Vol VI p 20
European Communities (Companies) Regulations 1973
SI 163/1973 .... Vol V p 226
European Communities (Exemption from Import Charges of
Certain Vehicles etc Temporarily Imported) Regulations 1983
SI 422/1983 .... Vol IV p 512
Farm Tax (Adjusted Acreage) Regulations
SI 321/1986 .... Vol V p 288
Farm Tax Regulations 1986
SI 237/1986 .... Vol V p 288
Finance Act 1966
SI 152/1970 .... Vol III p 73
SI 160/1979 .... Vol III p 73
Hydrocarbon Oil (Rebated Oil) Regulations 1961 Article 8,
SI 28/1960 .... Vol IV p 113
Hydrocarbon (Heavy) Oil Regulations 1991, Regulation 12 .... Vol VI p 472
Imposition of Duties Order 1975
SI 221/1975 .... Vol IV p 162, Vol V p 696
Imposition of Duties (No 221) (Excise Duties) Order 1975
SI 307/75, art 12 .... Vol VI p 74
Imposition of Duties (No 236) (Excise Duties on Motor Vehicles etc) 1979
SI 57/1979 para 12 .... Vol IV pp 170, 512
SI 353/1984 .... Vol IV p 512
Article 12 .... Vol VI p 636
Income Tax (Employments) Regulations 1960
SI No 28/1960. .... Vol II p 588, Vol III p 590, Vol V p 322
rule 2 .... Vol IV p 113
reg 21 .... Vol VI p 686

Social Welfare (Collection of Employment Contributions by the Collector General) Regulations 1979
SI 77/1979 .... Vol III p 467, 509
Social Welfare (Collection of Employment Contributions) Regulations 1989
SI 302/1989. .... Vol IV p 378
Solicitors Professional Practice, Conduct and Discipline Regulation 1986 (SI 405/1986)
reg 5, 6, 7 .... Vol VI p 79
Superior Court Rules
SI 15/1986
Order 56
r 41 .... 2006 p 55
Order 84
r 20(4) .... Vol V p 363
r 25(5) .... Vol V p 363
Order 99
r 1 .... Vol VI p 196
Order 122
r 10 .... Vol VI p 422
Supreme Court & High Court (Fees) Order 1984
SI 19/1984 as amended by SI 36/1985 .... Vol III p 530
Treaty of Rome
Article 28 .... Vol VI p 472
Article 30 .... Vol VI p 472
Article 38 .... Vol VI p 20
Article 39 .... Vol VI p 20
Article 90 .... Vol VI p 472
Article 93 .... Vol VI p 472
Article 95 .... Vol VI p 472
Article 177 .... Vol III p 73
Article 235 .... Vol VI p 20
VAT Regulations 1979
SI 63/1979 .... Vol V p 76, 2006 p 55
VAT (Refund of Tax)(No 13) Order 1980
SI 263/1980 .... Vol IV p 170
VAT (Special Provisions) Order 1981
.... Vol VI p 618
VAT (Exported Goods) Regulations 1992
(SI 438/1992) .... Vol V p 412
VAT Registration Regulation 1993
SI 30/1993 .... Vol V p 61

Destination Table (Taxes Consolidation Act 1997)

This table may be used to trace the present location of older legislation as re-enacted in the Taxes Consolidation Act, 1997.

Former Enactment			Destination in TCA 1997
Finance Act 1928 (1928 No 11)			
s 34	(2)		s 872(1)
Income Tax Act 1967 (1967 No 7)			
Pt I			
s 1		Definitions of "assurance company", "commencement of this Act", "municipal rate", "National Debt Commissioners" and "repealed enactments" in ITA 1967 s 1(1) unnecessary (obsolete)	ss 2(1), 3(1)
	(2)	Unnecessary (construction)	
	(3)	Unnecessary (interpretation)	
	(4)	Unnecessary (interpretation)	
	(5)	Rep by CTA 1976 s 164 and Sch 3 Pt II	
	(6)	Unnecessary (obsolete)	
2			s 3(2), (3)
3			s 1(2)
4			s 12
5			s 14(2)
6			s 14(1)
7		Rep by FA 1972 s 46(1) and Sch 4 Pt I	
8			s 1087
Pt II			
ss 9-42		Rep by FA 1969 s 65(1) and Sch 5 Pt I	
43		Rep by FA 1996 s 132(2) and Sch 5 Pt II	
44		Rep by FA 1969 s 65(1) and Sch 5 Pt I	
45		Rep by FA 1969 s 65(1) and Sch 5 Pt I	
46		Rep by FA 1997s 146(2) and Sch 9 Pt II	
Pt III			
s 47			s 17(1)
48			s 33
49	(1), (2)		s 34
49	(3)	Rep by DR&IA 1967 s 4 and Sch 6	
50			s 35
51			ss 17(2), 32
Pt IV			
s 52			s 18(1), (3)
53			s 18(2), (3)
54	(1)		s 654
	(2)(a)		s 655(3)
	(2)(b),(3), (4)	Rep by FA 1969 s 65(1) and Sch 5 Pt I	
55			s 54
56	(1)-(3)		s 56
	(4)-(6)	Rep by FA 1969 s 65(1) and Sch 5 Pt I	
57			s 81(1)
58	(1)		s 65(1)
	(2)-(4)		s 66
	(5), (6)		s 67

Former Enactment		*Destination in TCA 1997*
Income Tax Act 1967 (1967 No 7) (contd)		
s 58A	(s 58A inserted by FA 1995 s 19)	s 68
59		s 69
60		s 65(2)-(4)
61		s 81(2)
62 (1)(a), (b)		s 89(2)
(b)(proviso)		s 656(2)
(2)		s 89(1)(a), (c)
63		s 84
64	Rep by CTA 1976 s 164 and Sch 3 Pt I	
65	Unnecessary (spent)	
66	Rep by FA 1969 s 65(1) and Sch 5 Pt I	
67 (1)-(3A)		s 85
(4)	Rep by FA 1969 s 31	
68 (1)		s 108
(2)	Rep by FA 1997	ss 146(2) and Sch 9 Pt II
69 (1), (2)	Definition of "capital allowance" rep by FA 1975 s 33 and Sch 1 Pt II	s 1007(1), (2)
69 (3)		ss 880(3), 1007(3)
70 (1)-(3A)		s 880(2)-(6)
(3B)		s 900(3)
(4)		s 1052(4)(a), (c), (e)
(5)		s 880(1)
71 (1)		s 1008(1)
(2)(a), (b)		s 1008(2)
(c)	Unnecessary (spent)	
(3)-(5)		s 1008(3)-(5)
72		s 1010
73		s 1012
74		s 1011
75		s 70(1)
76 (1)		s 71(1)
(2)(a)		s 71(2)
(b)	Rep by CTA 1976 s 164 and Sch 3 Pt I	
(3)		s 71(3)
(4)	Rep by FA 1994 s 157(1)	
(5), (6)		s 71(5), (6)
(7), (8)	Rep by CTA 1976 s 164 and Sch 3 Pt I	
77 (1)		s 70(2)
(2)		s 70(3)
(3), (4)	Ceased by FA 1990 s 17(2)	
(5)		s 70(4)
78	Rep by FA 1969 s 65(1) and Sch 5 Pt I	
79		s 74
80 (1)		ss 96(1), 888(1)
(2)		s 96(2)
(3)	Unnecessary (obsolete)	
(4), (5)		s 96(3), (4)
81 (1)		ss 75(1), 96(1)
(2)		s 75(2)

Former Enactment	*Destination in TCA 1997*
Income Tax Act 1967 (1967 No 7) (contd)	
s 81 (3)(a)	s 75(3)
(b), (c) . . Ceased by FA 1990 s 18(2)	
(4)-(8)	s 97
(9), (10) . . . Unnecessary (spent)	
82 . . . . Rep by FA 1997 s 146(2) and Sch 9 Pt II	
83	s 98
84	s 99
85	s 100
86	s 75(4)
87 . . . . Rep by FA 1969 s 65(1) and Sch 5 Pt I	
88 (1)	s 918(4)
(2), (3) . . . . Rep by FA 1969 s 65(1) and Sch 5 Pt I	
89	s 384
89A . . . . Rep by FA 1996 s 132(2) and Sch 5 Pt II. (s 89A inserted by F(MP)A 1968 s 7)	
90	s 101
91	s 102
92	s 103
93 (1), (2)	s 104
(3)	s 1087(2)
94	s 888
95 . . . . Rep by FA 1969 s 65(1) and Sch 5 Pt I	
96-103 . . . . Unnecessary (obsolete)	
104 . . . . Rep by FA 1969 s 65(1) and Sch 5 Pt I	
105	s 52
106 . . . . Rep by FA 1997 s 146(2) and Sch 9 Pt II	
107	s 107
108 . . . . Rep by CTA 1976 s 164 and Sch 3 Pt I	
Pt V	
s 109	s 19(1)
110	s 112
111 . . . . Deleted by FA 1990 s 19(b) with saver for enactments which refer to s 111	
112	s 113
113	s 948
114(1)-(5)	s 123(1)-(5)
(6) . . . . Unnecessary (spent)	
(7)	s 123(6)
115(1)	s 201(2)
(1A)(a)	s 201(3)
(b). . . . Unnecessary (operative date)	
(2)-(4)	s 201(4)-(6)
(5)-(7)	s 201(1)
(8)	s 201(7)
116	s 117
117	s 118
118(1), (2)	s 119(1), (2)
(3) . . . . Deleted by FA 1969 s 32(a)	
(4)	s 119(3), (4)
(5) . . . . Deleted by FA 1969 s 32(a)	

Former Enactment		*Destination in TCA 1997*
Income Tax Act 1967 (1967 No 7) (contd)		
s 119(1), (2)		s 116(1)
(3), (4)		s 116(3), (4)
120(1)		s 897(6)
(2)		s 897(7)
(3)	Unnecessary (duplication)	
121	Rep by FA 1973 s 42	
(1), (3)		s 116(1)
122(2)		s 116(2)
123		s 120
124		s 983
125		s 984(1), (2)
126		s 985
127(1)(a)-(f),		s 986(1)(a)-(j), (g), (h)
(ff)	Deleted by FA 1974 s 11 and Sch 1 Pt II	
(2)		s 986(2)
(3)(a)(i)		s 986(3)(a)
(ii)	Deleted by FA 1974 s 11 and Sch 1 Pt II	
(b)		s 986(3)(b)
(c)	Deleted by FA 1974 s 11 and Sch 1 Pt II	
(4)-(5A)		s 986(4)-(6)
(6)	Unnecessary (spent)	
(7)		s 986(7)
127A	(s 127A inserted by FA 1992 s 233)	s 903
128(1),(1A),(2)		s 987(1)-(3)
(3)	Deleted by FA 1982 s 60(2)	
(4)		s 987(4)
129		s 991(1)
130	Ceased by FA 1974 s 71(a)	
131		s 993(1)-(4)
132		s 994
133		s 997
Pt VI		
s 134-136	Rep by FA 1974 s 86 and Sch 2 Pt I	
137		s 458
138		s 461
138A(1)-(6)	(s 138A inserted by FA 1980 s 3. and substituted by FA 1985 s 4)	s 462
(7)	Rep by FA 1996 s 132(2) and Sch 5 Pt II	
138B	(s 138B inserted by FA 1980 s 3)	s 472
139	Ceased by FA 1982 s 2(3) and Sch 1	
140	Ceased by FA 1982 s 2(3) and Sch 1	
141(1)-(6)		s 465
(7)	Rep by FA 1996 s 132(2) and Sch 5 Pt II	
142		s 466
142A	(s 142A inserted by FA 1982 s 5(1))	s 473
143	Ceased by FA 1992 s 4(a)	
144	Rep by FA 1979 s 32(1)	
145(1)-(3)		s 470(1)-(3)
(3A)	Rep by FA 1996 s 132(2) and Sch 5 Pt II	
(4)		s 470(4)
(5)	Rep by FA 1996 s 132(2) and Sch 5 Pt II	
146		s 459(1)

Former Enactment		*Destination in TCA 1997*
Income Tax Act 1967 (1967 No 7) (contd)		
s 147	Rep by FA 1969 s 65(1) and Sch 5 Pt I	
148	Rep by FA 1969 s 65(1) and Sch 5 Pt I	
149		s 459(2)
150	Rep by FA 1969 s 65(1) and Sch 5 Pt I	
151	Ceased by FA 1992 s 4(a)	
152	Ceased by FA 1992 s 4(a)	
153		s 1032
154		s 1016, Sch 32, para 21(1)
Pt VII		
s 155		s 849
156		s 850
157		s 853
158		s 854
159		s 855
160		s 856(1), (2)
161		s 852(1), (2)
162		s 851
163		s 857(1)-(3)
164		s 860
165		s 861(1)
166(1)	Unnecessary (continuity)	
(2)		s 862
Pt VIII		
s 167	Rep by F(MP)A 1968 s 6(1)	
168	Rep by F(MP)A 1968 s 6(1)	
169(1)(a)	Rep by FA 1969 s 65(1) and Sch 5 Pt I	
(b)-(4)		s 877
170		s 878
171	Rep by F(MP)A 1968 s 6(1)	
172(1), (2), (4), (6)		s 879(1)-(4)
(3)	Rep by F(MP)A 1968 s 6(1)	
(5)		s 1052(4)(a), (c), (e)
173(1)-(7), (9)		s 889(10)
173(8)	Deleted by FA 1982 s 60(2)(b)(ii)	
174		s 900(1), (2), (4)
175		s 891
176		s 890
177	Rep by FA 1997 s 146(2) and Sch 9 Pt II	
178		s 897(1)-(5)
179	Rep by F(MP)A 1968 s 6(1)	
180	Rep by FA 1969 s 65(1) and Sch 5 Pt I	
181		s 918(1)-(3)
182		s 920
183(1)(a)		s 921(2)
(b)	Rep by FA 1969 s 65(1) and Sch 5 Pt I	
(2)-(5)(a)		s 921(3)-(6)
183(5)(b)	Rep by FA 1969 s 65(1) and Sch 5 Pt I	
(6)	Rep by FA 1969 s 65(1) and Sch 5 Pt I	
(7)		s 921(1)
184		s 922
185		s 923

Former Enactment	*Destination in TCA 1997*
Income Tax Act 1967 (1967 No 7) (contd)	
s 186	s 924
187(1)	s 928(1)
(2) Rep by FA 1996 s 132(2) and Sch 5 Pt II	
(3)	s 964(2)
188(1)	s 863
(2) Rep by FA 1974 s 86 and Sch 2 Pt I	
189	s 867
190	s 929
191(1)-(5)	s 930
(6) Deleted by FA 1995 s 15(c)	
Pt IX	
s 192	s 1015
193	s 1016
194	s 1017
195	s 1018
195A(1)-(6) (s 195A inserted by FA 1983 s 6)	s 1020
(7) Unnecessary (commencement)	
195B (s 195B inserted by FA 1993 s 10(1))	s 1019
195C (s 195C inserted by FA 1993 s 10(1))	s 1021
196	s 1022
197	s 1023
198	s 1024
199 Rep by FA 1994 s 157(1)	
200	s 1034
201	s 1035
202	s 1036
203	s 1037
204	s 1038
205	s 1039
206 Rep by FA 1994 s 157(1)	
207	s 1044
208	s 1045
209	s 1046(1), (2)
210(1), (2)	s 1047
(3) Rep by FA 1969 s 65(1) and Sch 5 Pt I	
211(1)-(3)	s 1048
(4) Deleted by FA 1973 s 6	
212	s 1049
213	s 1050
Pt X	
ss 214-217 Rep by CTA 1976 s 164 and Sch 3 Pt I	
Pt XI	
218 Definition of "capital allowance" rep by FA 1975 s 33 and Sch 1 Pt II	s 698
219(1)	s 699(1)
(2) Rep by CTA 1976 s 164 and Sch 3 Pt I	
(3) Unnecessary (transitional)	
(4)(a) Unnecessary (spent)	
(b), (c)	s 699(2)
220(1)-(5), (7) Rep by FA 1978 s 52(1) and Sch 3 Pt I	
(6) Rep by CTA 1976 s 164 and Sch 3 Pt I	
221 Rep by CTA 197 s 164 and Sch 3 Pt I 6	

Former Enactment		*Destination in TCA 1997*
Income Tax Act 1967 (1967 No 7) (contd)		
Pt XII		
s 222	Rep by FA 1972 s 46(2) and Sch 4 Pt II	
223	Rep by FA 1972 s 46(1) and Sch 4 Pt I	
224(1), (2), (4)		s 126(1), (2)
(3), (5), (6)	Rep by FA 1979 s 6	
225		s 790
226	Rep by FA 1972 s 46(2) and Sch 4 Pt II with saver in FA 1972 Sch 1 Pt III para 4 (substituted by FA 1997 s 146(1) and Sch 9 para 5(3)) for enactments which refer to ITA 1967 Pt XII Ch II	
227	Rep by FA 1972 s 46(2) and Sch 4 Pt II with saver in FA 1972 Sch 1 Pt III para 4 (substituted by FA 1997 s 146(1) and Sch 9 para 5(3)) for enactments which refer to ITA 1967 Pt XII Ch II	
228	Rep by FA 1972 s 46(2) and Sch 4 Pt II with saver in FA 1972 Sch 1 Pt III para 4 (substituted by FA 1997 s 146(1) and Sch 9 para 5(3)) for enactments which refer to ITA 1967 Pt XII Ch II	
229	Rep by FA 1972 s 46(2) and Sch 4 Pt II with saver in FA 1972 Sch 1 Pt III para 4 (substituted by FA 1997 s 146(1) and Sch 9 para 5(3)) for enactments which refer to ITA 1967 Pt XII Ch II	
230	Rep by FA 1972 s 46(2) and Sch 4 Pt II with saver in FA 1972 Sch 1 Pt III para 4 (substituted by FA 1997 s 146(1) and Sch 9 para 5(3)) for enactments which refer to ITA 1967 Pt XII Ch II	
231	Rep by s 46(2) and Sch 4 Pt II FA 1972 with saver in FA 1972 Sch 1 Pt III para 4 (substituted by FA 1997 s 146(1) and Sch 9 para 5(3)) for enactments which refer to ITA 1967 Pt XII Ch II	
232	Rep by FA 1972 s 46(2) and Sch 4 Pt II with saver in FA 1972 Sch 1 Pt III para 4 (substituted by FA 1997 s 146(1) and Sch 9 para 5(3)) for enactments which refer to ITA 1967 Pt XII Ch II	
233	Rep by FA 1972 s 46(2) and Sch 4 Pt II with saver in FA 1972 Sch 1 Pt III para (substituted by FA 1997 s 146(1) and Sch 9 para 5(3)) for enactments which refer to ITA 1967 Pt XII Ch II	
234	Rep by FA 1972 s 46(2) and Sch 4 Pt II with saver in FA 1972 Sch 1 Pt III para 4 (substituted by FA 1997 s 146(1) and Sch 9 para 5(3)) for enactments which refer to ITA 1967 Pt XII Ch II	
235(1)-(5)		s 784(1)-(5)
(6)		s 783(4)
(7)(a)-(c)		s 783(3)
(d)	Rep by FA 1996 s 132(2) and Sch 5 Pt II	
(8)		s 783(2)
(9)		s 783(1)(a), (c)
(10)		s 784(6)

Former Enactment	*Destination in TCA 1997*
Income Tax Act 1967 (1967 No 7) (contd)	
s 235A(1)-(6) . . . (s 235A inserted by FA 1974 s 66)	s 785
(7). . . . . . . Unnecessary (transitional)	
236(1)	s 787(6)
(1A)-(2B)	s 787(8)-(12)
(2C) . . . . . . Unnecessary (transitional)	
(3)-(7)	s 787(1)-(5)
(8)	s 787(13)
(9)	s 787(14)
(10). . . . . . . Rep by FA 1974 s 86 and Sch 1 Pt I	
(11)	s 787(7)
237 . . . . Rep by CTA 1976 s 164 and Sch 3 Pt I	
238(1), (2)	s 787(15), (16)
(3), (4)	s 783(5), (6)
239	s 788
240	s 789
241(1)(a)	s 284(1)
(b)	s 284(2)(a), (3)
(c)	s 300(1)
proviso	s 284(2)(b)
(1A) . . . . . . Unnecessary (obsolete)	
(2)	s 299(1)
(3)	s 304(4)
(4)	s 304(2)
(5)	s 298(1)
(6)	s 284(4)
(6A)	s 284(5)
(7)-(9). . . . . Rep by FA 1996 s 132(2) and Sch 5 Pt II	
(9A)(a)	s 316(1)(a)
(b)	s 316(2)
(10)	ss 284(6), 301(1)
(11)(a)	s 284(7)
(b)	s 406
241A(1), (2) . . . (s 241A inserted by FA 1994 s 24(a))	s 291
(3)	s 301(1)
242 . . . . Rep by FA 1996 s 132(2) and Sch 5 Pt II	
243 . . . . Rep by FA 1996 s 132(2) and Sch 5 Pt II	
Pt XIV	
s 244(1)	s 763(2)
(2),(2A)	s 764
(3)-(7)	s 765
(8), (9)	s 763(5), (6)
245	s 670
246 . . . . Unnecessary (obsolete)	
247 . . . . Unnecessary (obsolete)	
248 . . . . Unnecessary (obsolete)	
249 . . . . Rep by FA 1996 s 132(2) and Sch 5 Pt II	
250 . . . . Unnecessary (obsolete)	

Former Enactment	Destination in TCA 1997
Income Tax Act 1967 (1967 No 7) (contd)	
Pt XV	
s 251(1)	ss 283(2), 300(1)
(2)	s 316(3)
(3) .... Unnecessary (operative date)	
(4) (a),(b), (bb)(i),(bbb), (c) Unnecessary (spent)	
(bb)(ii), (d)	s 283(3)
(5)	s 304(3)(b)
(6)	s 283(1)
(7)	s 283(6)
252	ss 298(1), 299(1), 304(4)
253	ss 301(2), 304(6)(b)
254(1)(a), (b)	s 271(2), (4)
(c)	ss 271(1), 320(1)
(d), (e)	ss 278(1), (2), (6), 305
(2) .... Unnecessary (spent)	
(2A)	s 271(4)
(2B)...... Unnecessary (spent)	
(3)	s 271(6)
(3A)...... Deleted by FA 1994 s 22(1)	
(4)(a)	s 316(3)
(b)	s 317(2)
(5)	s 304(4)
(6)	s 304(2), (3)(a)
(7)	s 271(5)
255(1)-(5)	s 268(1)-(3), (5)-(8)
(6)	s 320(2)
256	s 270
257	s 268(4)
258 .... Unnecessary (operative date)	
259 .... Rep by FA 1996 s 132(2) and Sch 5 Pt II	
260	s 316(1)(a)
261	s 316(2)
262 .... Rep by FA 1996 s 132(2) and Sch 5 Pt II	
263(1) .... Unnecessary (interpretation)	
(2), (3)	s 282
(4)	ss 270, 268(4)
264	s 272
265	s 274(1), (3), (4), (5), (8)
266	s 277
267	s 278(1), (3), (4), (5), (6)
268	s 269
269	s 281
270	s 280
271......... Definitions of "initial allowance" "wear and tear allowance" unnecessary	s 288(4)(a)
272(1)-(3)	s 288(1)-(3)
(4)	s 288(4)(b)

Former Enactment	*Destination in TCA 1997*
Income Tax Act 1967 (1967 No 7) (contd)	
s 272(5)(a), (b)	s 288(5)
(c) ..... Unnecessary (spent)	
(6)	s 288(6)
273(1)	s 290
(2)........ Rep by FA 1996 s 132(2) and Sch 5 Pt II	
274	s 292
275	s 293
276	s 294
277	s 289
278	s 295
279	s 296
280	s 297
281	s 298(2)
282	s 300
283(1)	s 301(1)
(2)........ Rep by FA 1969 s 65(1) and Sch 5 Pt I	
284	s 754
285	s 755
286	s 756
287 .... Unnecessary (obsolete)	
288	s 757
289 .... Unnecessary (obsolete)	
290(1)-(3)	s 758
(4)........ Unnecessary (obsolete)	
291	s 759
292	s 761
293	s 760
294(1)-(5)	s 303(1)-(5)
(6)	s 302(1)
(7)	s 303(6)
(8)	s 302(2)
(9)	s 303(7)
(10)	s 302(1)
(11), (12)	s 303(8), (9)
295	s 304(2), (4), (5), (6)(a)
296(1)	s 305(1)
(2)........ Unnecessary (obsolete)	
(3)-(5)	s 305(2)-(4)
297	s 306
298	s 311
299(1)-(3)	s 312(2)-(4)
(4)(a), ... s 312(5) (b),(i), (b)(ii)	
(b)(iii)	s 762(2)(a)
(5)	s 312(6)
(6)	s 312(1)
300	s 313
301	s 314
302	s 315

Former Enactment		*Destination in TCA 1997*
Income Tax Act 1967 (1967 No 7) (contd)		
s 303(1)		ss 316(1), 762(2)(b)
(2)		s 316(2)
(3)		s 317(2)
304(1)		ss 318, 320(1)
(2)-(6)		s 320(2)-(6)
305		s 769
306	Rep by FA 1996 s 132(2) and Sch 5 Pt II	
(1)		s 381(1)
(1A)	Rep by FA 1997 s 146(2) and Sch 9 Pt II	
(1AA)	Ceased by FA 1990 s 27(2)(a)	
(1AAA)-(6)		s 381(2)-(7)
307(1)		s 381(1)
(1A)	Repealed by FA 1997 s 146(2) and Sch 9 Pt II	
(1AA)	Ceased by FA 1990 s 27(2)	
(1AAA)-(6)		381(2)-(7)
308	Unnecessary (spent)	
309(1), (2)		s 382(1), (2)
(3)	Rep by FA 1969 s 65(1) and Sch 5 Pt I	
310		s 383
311		s 385
312		s 386
313(1), (2)		s 387
(3)	Unnecessary (spent)	
314(1)		s 388
(2)	Rep by FA 1975 s 33 and Sch 1 Pt II	
315		s 389
316		s 390(1), (3)
317(1)	Definition of "capital allowances" deleted by FA 1975 s 33 and Sch 1 Pt II	s 391(1)
(2)(a) from "In paragraph (a)"to end	Rep by FA 1997 s 146(2) and Sch 9 Pt II	
(b)-(d)		s 391(2)
318		s 392
319		s 393
320		s 394
321		s 395
322		s 391(3)
323-328	Rep by CTA 1976 s 164 and Sch 3 Pt I	
329-332	Ceased by FA 1983 s 7	
333		s 207(1), (2)
334(1) (a), (c)		s 208(2)
(b)	Rep by FA 1969 s 65(1) and Sch 5 Pt I	
(2)	Rep by FA 1969 s 65(1) and Sch 5 Pt I	
(2A)		s 208(3)
(3)		s 208(1)
335		s 211(1)-(4)
336		s 213(1), (2)
337	Ceased by FA 1993 s 43(1)	
338		s 206

Former Enactment		*Destination in TCA 1997*
Income Tax Act 1967 (1967 No 7) (contd)		
339 (1)	Rep by F(MP)A 1968 s 3(5) and Sch Pt IV	
(2)		ss 207(3), 211(5), 213(3)
(3)	Rep by F(MP)A 1968 s 3(5) and Sch Pt IV	
(4)		ss 207(4), 211(6), 213(4)
340(1)		s 204(2)
(2)(a)-(c)		s 204(1)
(d), (ff), (g)	Rep by FA 1983 s 120 and Sch 4	
(e), (f)	Rep by FA 1997 s 146(2) and Sch 9 Pt II	
(3)	Rep by FA 1983 s 120 and Sch 4	
341	Rep by DR&IA 1967 s 4 and Sch 6	
342	Rep by DR&IA 1967 s 4 and Sch 6	
343	Rep by FA 1997 s 62(2)	
344	Rep by FA 1996 s 132(2) and Sch 5 Pt II	
345		s 199
346	Rep by FA 1996 s 132(2) and Sch 5 Pt II	
347	Rep by CTA 1976 s 164 and Sch 3 Pt I	
348		s 215
349		s 235
350		s 216
351-352	Rep by FA 1969 s 65(1) and Sch 5 Pt I	
353		s 193 Sch 32, para 2
354		s 194
Pt XXII		
s 355	Rep by FA 1977 s 54(1)(a) and Sch 2 Pt I	
356	Rep by FA 1977 s 54(1)(b) and Sch 2 Pt II	
357	Rep by FA 1977 s 54(1)(a) and Sch 2 Pt I	
358(1)	Unnecessary (saver for FA 1950 s 12)	
(2), (3)		s 833
359		s 834
360	Rep by FA 1996 s 132(2) and Sch 5 Pt II	
361(1)-(7)		s 826(1)-(7)
(8)		s 826(9)
362	Rep by FA 1987 s 23 with saver	
363	Rep by CTA 1976 s 166 and Sch 4 Pt II	
364	Rep by CTA 1976 s 166 and Sch 4 Pt II	
365	Rep by FA 1977 s 146(2) and Sch 9 Pt II	
366	Rep by FA 1977 s 146(2) and Sch 9 Pt II	
Pt XXIII		
s 367		s 748
368		s 749
369(1)		s 750
369(2)	Rep by FA 1977 s 54(1)(a) and Sch 2 Pt I	
370		s 751
Pt XXIV		
s 371		s 752
372		s 753
Pt XXV		
s 373	Rep by CTA 1976 s 164 and Sch 3 Pt I	
374 - 414	Rep by CTA 1976 s 164 and Sch 3 Pt I	
415		s 932
(1)-(7)(f)		s 933(1)-(7)(f)
(7)(g)	Unnecessary (obsolete)	
(8)		s 933(8)

Former Enactment		*Destination in TCA 1997*
Income Tax Act 1967 (1967 No 7) (contd)		
s 415(8A)	Deleted by FA 1983 s 9(a)(i)(IV)	
(9)		s 933(9)
(10)		s 942(9)
(11)	Rep by FA 1974 s 86 and Sch 2 Pt I	
416		s 933(1)-(7)(f)
417	Ceased by FA 1976 s 30(8)	
418	Ceased by FA 1971 s 17(3)	
419	Rep by FA 1997 s 146(2) and Sch 9 Pt II	
420	Deleted by FA 1983 s 9(b)	
421		s 934
422		s 935
423		s 936
424		s 937
425		s 938
426		s 939
427		s 940
428		s 941
429		s 942(1)-(8), (10)
430		s 943
431		s 944
432 (1)		ss 864(1), 949(1)
(2)-(4)		s 949(2)-(4)
Pt XXVII		
s 433		s 237
434 (1)-(5A)		s 238(1)-(6)
(6)	Unnecessary (obsolete)	
(7)	Unnecessary (spent)	
(8)		s 238(7)
435	Rep by CTA 1976 s 164 and Sch 3 Pt I	
436-437	Rep by FA 1969 s 65(1) and Sch 5 Pt I	
Pt XXVIII		
s 438		s 791(2)-(4)
439		s 792(1)-(4)
440	Ceased by FA 1995 s 12(3)	
441		s 793
442		s 791(1)
443(1)		s 795
443(2), (3)		s 794(2), (3)
(4)	Ceased by FA 1995 s 12(3)	
(5)		s 794(4)
444		s 796(1), (2)(a), (b), (c)
445		s 794(5)
446		s 797
447	Definition of "child" rep by FA 1996 s 132(2) and Sch 5 Pt II, definition of "minor" unnecessary (duplication)	s 794(1)s 794(1)
448(1), (3), (4)		s 798(1)-(3)
(2)	Rep by FA 1996 s 132(2) and Sch 5 Pt II	
449		s 812 (1), (2), (4)
Pt XXIX		
s 450		s 799

Former Enactment		*Destination in TCA 1997*
Income Tax Act 1967 (1967 No 7) (contd)		
s 451		s 800
452		s 801(1)-(8)
453		s 802
454		s 803
455		s 804
Pt XXX		
s 456	Rep by CTA 1976 s 164 and Sch 3 Pt I	
457	Rep by CTA 1976 s 164 and Sch 3 Pt I	
458		s 1091
Pt XXXI		
s 459		s 60
460		s 61
461		s 62
462		s 63
462A	(s 462A inserted by FA 1994 s 15)	s 64
463		s 42
464		s 43
465		s 45(1)
466		s 36
467-468(2)	Rep by FA 1997 s 146(2) and Sch 9 Pt II	
468(3)		s 47
469	Rep by FA 1997 s 146(2) and Sch 9 Pt II	
470		s 50
471	Rep by FA 1997 s 146(2) and Sch 9 Pt II	
472(1)		Sch 32, para 1(1)
(2)	Rep by FA 1997 s 146(2) and Sch 9 Pt II	
473	Rep by FA 1997 s 146(2) and Sch 9 Pt II	
474		s 49, Sch 32 para 1(2)
475		s 51
476	Rep by FA 1996 s 132(2) and Sch 5 Pt II	
477 (1)		s 960
(2), (3)	Rep by FA 1996 s 132(2) and Sch 5 Pt II	
478		s 961
479	Rep by FA 1996 s 132(2) and Sch 5 Pt II	
480	Rep by FA 1996 s 132(2) and Sch 5 Pt II	
481	Rep by FA 1969 s 65(1) and Sch 5 Pt I	
482(1), (2)		s 971
(3)	Rep by FA 1996 s 132(2) and Sch 5 Pt II	
483	Rep by IT(A)A 1967 s 1	
484(1)-(4)		s 972(1)-(4)
(5)	Unnecessary (obsolete)	
(6), (7)		s 972(5), (6)
485(1), (2)		s 962(1), (2)
(3), (4)	Rep by FA 1974 s 86 and Sch 2 Pt I	
(5)		s 962(3)
485(6)	Unnecessary (spent)	
486(1), (2), (4)		s 963
(3)	Rep by FA 1997 s 146(2) and Sch 9 Pt II	
487		s 964(1)
488		s 966
489		s 965
490	Rep by FA 1967 s 25 and Sch 3 Pt I	

Former Enactment	*Destination in TCA 1997*
Income Tax Act 1967 (1967 No 7) (contd)	
s 491	s 998
492	s 968
493	s 969
494 (1)	s 970
(2) .... Rep by FA 1996 s 132(2) and Sch 5 Pt II	
495 .... Rep by FA 1996 s 132(2) and Sch 5 Pt II	
496 .... Rep by FA 1997 s 146(2) and Sch 9 Pt II	
497	s 460
498	s 865
499 .... Unnecessary (operative date)	
500(1)-(3)	s 1052(1)-(3)
(4)	s 1052(4)(a)-(e)
501	s 1053(1)-(4)
502	s 1053(5)-(7)
503	s 1054(2)-(4)
504	s 1060
505	s 1055
506	s 1069(2)
507	s 1068
508	s 1061
509	ss 1054(1), 1069(1)(a)
510	s 1062
511	s 1063
512	s 1065
513	s 1059
514	s 1070
515	s 1057
516	s 1056
517	s 1064
518	s 1066
519	s 874
520	s 1058
521	s 1067
522-524 ...... Rep by FA 1974 s 86 and Sch 2 Pt I	
525	s 127(1)-(5)
526-527 ...... Rep by FA 1974 s 86 and Sch 2 Pt I	
528	s 926
529 .... Ceased by FA 1971 s 17(3)	
530-531 ...... Rep by CTA 1976 s 164 and Sch 3 Pt I	
532 .... Rep by FA 1974 s 86 and Sch 2 Pt I	
533	s 866
534	s 1090
535	s 1088
536	s 868
537	s 870
538	s 875
539	s 901
540 .... Rep by FA 1996 s 132(2) and Sch 5 Pt II	
541	s 873

Former Enactment *Destination in TCA 1997*

Income Tax Act 1967 (1967 No 7) (contd)

s 542(1)........Rep by F(MP)A 1968 s 3(5) and Sch Pt IV
(2)...s 869(1)
(3)........Deleted by FA 1975 s 29
(4)-(7)...s 869(2)-(5)
543..........Rep by FA 1996 s 132(2) and Sch 5 Pt II
544 (1)...s 837
(2)........Rep by FA 1969 s 65(1) and Sch 5
545 (1)...s 1096
(2)........Rep by FA 1969 s 65(1) and Sch 5 Pt I
546..........Ceased by FA 1990 s 27(2)(a)
547...s 483(1)-(3)
548..........Rep by FA 1969 s 65(1) and Sch 5 Pt I
549...s 1004
550 (1)...s 1080(1)
(2)........Ceased by FA 1990 s 24
(2A)......Rep by FA 1997 s 146(2) and Sch 9 Pt II
(3)-(5)...s 1080(2)-(4)
551(1), (2)(a)......................................s 1081
(2)(b).....Rep by FA 1974 s 86 and Sch 2 Pt I
552..........Unnecessary (commencement)
553...s 111

Pt XXXVIII
s 554..........Unnecessary (commencement and repeals)
555..........Unnecessary (obsolete)
556..........Unnecessary (savings in relation to ITA 1967)
557..........Rep by FA 1996 s 132(2) and Sch 5 Pt II
558..........Rep by FA 1996 s 132(2) and Sch 5 Pt II
559..........Unnecessary (continuity and construction)
560..........Unnecessary (continuity)
561..........Unnecessary (short title)

Sch 1...Sch 2
Pt I..Pt 2
Pt II..........Rep by FA 1997 s 146(2) and Sch 9 Pt II.
Pts III-V...Pts 3-5
Pt VI...Pt 1

Sch 2
Rule 1(1), (2)......................................s 925
(3).......Rep by FA 1996 s 132(2) and Sch 5 Pt II
2...s 19(2)
3...s 114
4...s 115
5-7.......Rep by FA 1976 s 81 and Sch 5 Pt I

Sch 3
para1-11..Sch 3
12, 13..s 201(1)(a)
14..Sch 3

Sch 4
para1(1)..s 459(3)
(2), (3)....Rep by F(MP)A 1968 s 3(5) and Sch Pt IV
2(1),(3),(4),(5)....................................s 459(4)
(2)........Rep by F(MP)A 1968 s 3(5) and Sch Pt IV
3.........Rep by F(MP)A 1968 s 3(5) and Sch Pt IV
Sch 5..........Deleted by FA 1996 s 13(b)

Former Enactment	*Destination in TCA 1997*
Income Tax Act 1967 (1967 No 7) (contd)	
Sch 6	
Pt I .... Rep by FA 1977 s 54 and Sch 2 Pt I	
II .... Rep by FA 1977 s 54 and Sch 2 Pt I	
III,para 1	s 73
para 2-5 ... Rep by FA 1977 s 54 and Sch 2 Pt I	
Sch 7 .... Rep by FA 1977 s 54 and Sch 2 Pt I	
Sch 8	Sch 25
Sch 9 .... Unnecessary (obsolete)	
Sch 10	Sch 24
para 1-4	para 1-4(1)
5, 6	para 5, 6
7 .... Rep by CTA 1976 s 166(2) and Sch 4 Pt II	
8-14	para 7-13
Sch 11	Sch 21
Sch 12	Sch 22
Sch 13 .... Rep by FA 1996 s 132(2) and Sch 5 Pt II	
Sch 14 .... Rep by FA 1967 s 25 and Sch 3	
Sch 15	Sch 29
Sch 16 .... Rep by CTA 1976 s 164 and Sch 3 Pt I	
Sch 17	Sch 27
Sch 18	Sch 28
para I .... Rep by FA 1969 s 65(1) and Sch 5 Pt I	
II-IX	paras 1-8
Sch 19 .... Unnecessary (repeals)	
Income Tax (Amendment) Act 1967 (1967 No 7)	
Preamble ..... Unnecessary (obsolete)	
s 1 .... Unnecessary (cesser of ITA 1967 ss 480(2), (3), 483)	
2 .... Unnecessary (short title)	
Finance Act 1967 (1967 No 17)	
s 1 .... Unnecessary (spent)	
2 .... Insertion of ITA 1967 s 139(5)	
3 .... Amendment of ITA 1967 s 141(1)	s 465
4 .... Amendment of ITA 1967 s 142(1)	s 466
5 .... Substitution of ITA 1967 s 251(4)	ss 283(2), 300(1)
6 (1) .... Substitution of ITA 1967 s 254(1)	s 271(2), (4)
(2) .... Insertion of ITA 1967 s 262(4)	s 316(2)
7 .... Amendment of ITA 1967 s 335	s 211(1)-(4)
8 .... Amendment of ITA 1967 s 344	
9 (1)........ Amendment of ITA 1967 ss 383, 386(2)	s 963
(2)(a) ..... Amendment of ITA 1967 s 386	s 963
(b) ..... Amendment of ITA 1967 s 387	s 964(1)
(c) ..... Amendment of ITA 1967 s 389	
10 .... Substitution of ITA 1967 s 523	
11 (1),(2),(2A)	s 285(1), (2), (3)
(3)	s 299(2)
(4)	s 285(8)
12 (1)	s 469(1)
proviso to definition of "dependant"	s 469(4)
(2)(a), (c)	s 469(2)
(b)..... Deleted by FA 1972 s 9	
(3)	s 469(3)

Former Enactment			*Destination in TCA 1997*
Finance Act 1967 (1967 No 17) (contd)			
s 12	(4)		s 469(5)
	(5)		s 469(6)
	(6)	Amendment of ITA 1967s 153(1)(d)	s 1032
	(7)	Amendment of ITA 1967 s 193	s 1016
Pt V			
s 25		Unnecessary (application of schedule)	
26		Unnecessary (care and management)	
27(2), (6)		Unnecessary (construction and commencement)	
Sch 3, Pt I		Repeal of ITA 1967 s 490 and Sch 14	
Finance (Miscellaneous Provisions) Act 1968 (1968 No 7)			
s 1	(1)	Substitution of ITA 1967 s 156(1)	s 850
	(2)	Unnecessary (obsolete)	
2		Insertion of ITA 1967 s 181(3)	s 918(1)-(3)
3	(1)	Amendment of ITA 1967 ss 164(2), 416(5), 418(6), 422(3), 429(3)	ss 860, 933(1)-(7)(f), 935, 942(1)-(8), (10)
	(2)-(5)	Unnecessary (application of schedules)	
	(6)	Amendment of SR&O No 48 of 1928 and SIs Nos 152 of 195, 28 of 1960 and 231 of 1961	
4	(1)	Substitution of ITA 1967 s 186(2)	s 920
	(2)	Unnecessary (spent)	
	(3)	Amendment of ITA 1967 s 211	s 1048
	(4)	Substitution of ITA 1967 s 526(6)	
	(5)(a)	Amendment of ITA 1967 s 498	s 865
	(b)	Unnecessary (spent)	
5	(1)		s 876
	(2)	Amendment of ITA 1967 Sch 15	Sch 29
6	(1)	Repeal of ITA 1967 ss 167, 168, 171, 172(3), 179	
	(2)	Amendment of ITA 1967 s 169(1)	s 877
	(3)	Amendment of ITA 1967 s 169(4)	s 877
	(4)	Amendment of ITA 1967 s 170(1)	s 878
	(5)	Amendment of ITA 1967 s 176(1)	s 890
	(6)	Amendment of ITA 1967 s 177	
	(7)	Amendment of ITA 1967s 211(3)	s 1048
7	(1)	Insertion of ITA 1967 s 81(4)(f), s 89A	s 97
	(2)	Unnecessary (spent).	
8		Amendment of ITA 1967 Sch 15	Sch 29
9	(1), (2)		s 200(1)
	(3)	Unnecessary (commencement)	
13		Rep by CTA 1976 s 164 and Sch 3 Pt II	
14		Unnecessary (obsolete)	
15		Rep by CTA 1976 s 164 and Sch 3 Pt II	
Pt IV			
16	(1),(2),(4)	Definition of "control" unnecessary (obsolete)	s 639
	(3)	Ceased by FA 1996 s 131(9)(b)	
17			s 640
18			s 641
19			s 642
20	(1)(a)	Unnecessary (operative date)	
	(b)-(17)		s 643
21			s 644
22			s 645

Former Enactment		*Destination in TCA 1997*
Finance (Miscellaneous Provisions) Act 1968 (1968 No 7)		
s 23 (1)-(3),(5)		s 646
(4)	Rep by FA 1974 s 86 and Sch 2 Pt I	
24 (1)	Unnecessary (commencement)	
(2)	Unnecessary (obsolete)	
Pt V		
27		s 999
29 (2)	Unnecessary (construction)	
Sch Pt I	Amendment of ITA 1967 ss 1(1), 13(1), 37(1)(f)(ii), 38, 41(3), 50(3)(4), 54(4), 60(3), 73(3), 76(5)(6), 81(6), 82(2)(a), 90(2)(3), 113(1)(2), 120(1)(c)(2), 156(2)(3)(4), 164(2), 190(1), 191(4)(5), 194(2)(c), 195(3)(a), 203(1)-(3), 204, 214(2), 228(3), 238(1)(2), 240(1), 241(1), 245(14), 259, 296(3)(4), 301(1), 307(5)(6), 315(1)(2), 367(3), 371(7)(c), 379(1), 382(2), 397, 413(1), 414, 416(1)-(9), 417, 418(1)(2)(3)(6), 421(2), 422(1)(2), 424, 425(1), 426(1), 427(a), 428(1)(9), 429(1)(2), 430(1), 431(1)(2), 432(1)-(4), 437(1)(2), 441(2), 446(2), 462(3)(4), 501(1)(c), 506, 529, 537(2), 542(6), 549(5), 553(2), Sch 6 Pt III para 1(2), 3(2)(3), 4(1)(2), Sch 10 para 13(1), Sch 11 para 3(4), Sch 12 para 2(1)(2), 3(2),(5), Sch 16 paras 1-3, 10	ss 2(1), 3(1), 35, 84, 1012, 71(5)-(6),73, 97, 101, 948, 897(6), 850, 860, 929, 930, 1017, 1018, 1037, 1038, 787(15)-(16),789,284(1), 670, 305(2)-(4), 314, 381(2)-(7), 389, 748, 752, 933(1)-(7)(f),934, 935, 937, 938, 939,940, 941,942(1)-(8)(10), 943, 944,864(1),949(1)-(4), 793, 797, 1053(1)-(4), 1069(2), 870, 869(2)-(5), 1004,111,Sch 21,Sch 22, Sch 24 paras 7-13
Sch Pt II	Amendment of ITA 1967 ss 49(1), 152(6), 181(1)(a), 460(a), 484(3), 530(1), 531(1)-(3), Sch 1 Pt I para 3, 4, Sch1 Pt II para 1, 3, Sch 1 Pt III para 1, 2, Sch 1 Pt IV para 3, 9, Sch 2 para 6(1)(2), Sch 6 Pt II para (3), Sch 16 para 4, 5, 7, 8, 11, Sch 16 para 10	ss 34, 918(1)-(3), 61, 972(1)-(4), Sch 2 Pt 2, Sch 2 Pts 3-5 Sch 2 Pt 1,
Sch Pt III	Amendment of ITA 1967 ss 36(2), 152(4)(b), 163(2), 339(2), 530(5), 536(1), Sch 1 Pt I para 4, 5, Sch 4 para 1(1), 2(3), Sch 17 Pt I,	ss 857(1)-(3); 207(3), 211(5),213(3);1054(2)-(4); 868; Sch 2 Pt 2; 459(4); Sch 27, 459(3),
Sch Pt IV	Repeal of ITA 1967 ss 22(2), 153(3), 339(1)(3), 542(1), Sch 4 para 1(2)(3), 2(2), 3	
	Amendment of ITA 1967 ss 29(1), 30, 35, 36(1), 214(1)(2), 329(1), 332(1), 451(5), 496(1), 530(4), 536(2), 544(2), 553(1)(2), Sch 1 Pt I para 5, Sch 1 Pt IV par1(1), Sch 4 para 2(1), Sch 6 Pt II para (1)	ss 800, 868, 111 Sch 2 Pt 2, Sch 2 Pt 1
Finance Act 1968 (1968 No 33)		
s 1	Unnecessary (spent)	
2		s 768
3		s 480
4	Rep by FA 1996 s 132(2) and Sch 5 Pt II	
5	Rep by FA 1969 s 65(1) and Sch 5	
6 (1)-(5)		s 886
(6)	Amendment of ITA 1967 s 508(1)	s 1061
7 (1), (2)		s 989(2), (3)
(3)	Rep by FA 1974 s 71	
(4), (5)		s 989(4), (5)
(6)	Unnecessary (duplication)	
(7)	Unnecessary (duplication)	

Former Enactment		*Destination in TCA 1997*
Finance Act 1968 (1968 No 33) (contd)		
s 7 (8)	Definition of "income tax month" unnecessary (duplication)	s 989(1)
8 (1),(2) (4)		s 990
(3)	Rep by FA 1974 s 71	
9 (a)		s 991(2)(a)
proviso	Rep by FA 1974 s 71	
(b)		s 991(2)(b)
10		s 992
11		s 1000
12	Amendment of ITA 1967 s 138(1)	s 461
13	Rep by FA 1983 s 17(1)	
14	Amendment of ITA 1967 s 244	s 126(1), (2)
15	Insertion of ITA 1967 s 416(8A)	s 933(1)-(7)(f)
16	Amendment of ITA 1967 s 421(3)	s 944
17	Amendment of ITA 1967 s 523(1)(b)	
27-30	Rep by CTA 1976 s 164 and Sch 3 Pt II	
Pt VIII		
s 34	Rep by CTA 1976 s 164 and Sch 3 Pt III	
35	Rep by CTA 1976 s 166 and Sch 4 Pt II	
36	Rep by CTA 1976 s 164 and Sch 3 Pt III	
37 (1)		ss 203(1), 109(1)
37 (2)		s 203(2)
37 (3)-(7)		s 109(2)-(6)
37 (8)	Unnecessary (duplication)	
37 (9)	Unnecessary (operative date)	
38	Substitution of ITA 1967 s 251(4)	s 283(3)
39	Amendment of ITA 1967 s 254(2)	s 271
41	Rep by Trustee Savings Banks Act 1989	
47	Unnecessary (care and management).	
48 (2), (5)	Unnecessary (construction and commencement)	
Finance (No 2) Act 1968 (1968 No 37)		
s 1	Unnecessary (interpretation)	
8		s 46
10	Unnecessary (care and management)	
11 (4)	Unnecessary (construction)	
Finance Act 1969 (1969 No 21)		
s 1	Unnecessary (spent)	
2		s 195(1)-(11)
3 (1),(2),(4)		s 467
(3)	Rep by FA 1996 s 132(2) and Sch 5 Pt II	
(5)	Amendment of ITA 1967 s 153(1)(d)	s 1032
(6)	Rep by FA 1980 s 19 and Sch 1 Pt III	
(7)	Amendment of ITA 1967 s 497	s 460
(8)	Rep by FA 1980 s 19 and Sch 1 Pt III	
4	Rep by FA 1996 s 132(2) and Sch 5 Pt II	
5	Rep by FA 1996 s 132(2) and Sch 5 Pt II	
6	Unnecessary (obsolete)	
7	Amendment of FA 1967 s 12(2)	s 469(2)
8	Amendment of ITA 1967 s 125(a)	s 984(1), (2)
9	Amendment of ITA 1967 s 138	s 461
10	Amendment of ITA 1967 s 141	s 465
11	Amendment of ITA 1967 s 142(1)	s 466
12	Substitution of ITA 1967 s 157(c)	s 853
13	Insertion of ITA 1967 s 193(2A)	s 1016
14	Insertion of ITA 1967 s 246(1A)	

Former Enactment		*Destination in TCA 1997*
Finance Act 1969 (1969 No 21) (contd)		
s 15	Amendment of ITA 1967 s 374(2)	
16	Amendment of ITA 1967 s 402	
17	Insertion of ITA 1967 s 523(5)	
18 (1)	Definition of "farming" rep by FA 1996 s 132(2) and Sch 5 Pt II	s 232(1)
(2)(a)	Rep by FA 1974 s 14	
(b)		s 231
(c)		s 232(2)
19		s 53
20	Rep by CTA 1976 s 164 and Sch 3 Pt I	
21	Amendment of ITA 1967 Sch 6 Pt III para 1	s 73
22	Substitution of ITA 1967 s 81	ss 75, 96, 97
23	Substitution of ITA 1967 s 82	
24	Substitution of ITA 1967 s 89	s 384
25		s 1041
26 (1)-(4)		s 106
(5)	Unnecessary (duplication)	
(6)	Unnecessary (operative date)	
27	Amendment of ITA 1967 s 80	ss 96, 882
28	Substitution of ITA 1967 s 90	s 101
29	Substitution of ITA 1967 s 93	s 103
30	Amendment of ITA 1967 s 65	
31	Amendment of ITA 1967 s 67	s 85
32	Amendment of ITA 1967 s 118	s 119
33 (1)	Unnecessary (application of schedule)	
51-54	Rep by CTA 1976 s 164 and Sch 3 Pt II	
63 (1)		s 48(2)
(2)		s 48(1)(a)
64 (1), (2)	Amendment of ITA 1967 s 255	s 790
(3), (4)		s 274(6), (7)
(5)	Unnecessary (operative date)	
65	Unnecessary (repeals)	
66	Unnecessary (care and management)	
67 (2), (7)	Unnecessary (construction and commencement)	
Sch 4, Pt I	Amendment of ITA 1967 ss 53(1), 83, 84(1), 86, 89A, 92(1), 94, 162(3)(a), 183(1), 184(1), 214(3), 267(5)(a), 307(1), 316(2), 334(1), 335, 336, 433, 434, Sch 18 and F(MP)A 1967 s 18(2)(g)	ss 18(2)(3), 75(4), 98, 99, 103, 888, 851, 921, 922, 278(1)(3)-(6), 381(1),390 (1)(3), 208(2), 211(1)-(4), 213(1),(2),237,238(1)-(6), Sch 28, 641
Sch 5, Pt I	Repeal of ITA 1967 ss 2(2)(d), 9-42, 44, 45, 54(3)(4), 56(4)(5)(6), 66, 75(2)(ii), 78, 87, 88(2)(3), 95, 104, 106(2), 147, 148, 150, 169(1)(a), 180, 183(1)(b), (5)(b)(6), 210(3), 243(3), 244(6)(b), 245(8)(a), 267(5)(6), 283(2), 309(3), 334(1)(b)(2), 351, 352, 385(2), 436, 437, 477(2)(a), (b), 480(6), 481, 524(3)(a), 545(2),548, Sch 18 para 1 and FA 1968 s 5	
	Amendment of ITA 1967 ss 1(1), 2(1)(c), 4, 52(1)(b), 53(1), 54(2), 60(1), 61(c), 86, 107(1), 169(2), 183(1), 186(1), 219(1), 235(7)(c),251(1),322, 333(1)(a),388, 416(1), 480(1), 485, 533, 544(1), Sch 15	ss 2(1), 3(1); 3(2)(3); 12; 18(1)(3); 18(2)(3); 655(3); 65(2)-(4); 81(2); 75(4); 107;877;921(2);924; 699(1);784(1)-(5); 283(2), 300(1);391(3); 208(2); 933(1)-(7)(f); 866; 837 962(1)(2); Sch 29
Sch 5, Pt III	Repeal of ITA 1967 s 404(7), (8)	

Former Enactment		*Destination in TCA 1997*
Finance Act 1970 (1970 No 14)		
s 1	Unnecessary (spent).	
2 (1), (2)	Ceased by FA 1971 s 2	
(3)	Insertion of ITA 1967 s 153(1)(dd)	s 1032
(4)	Amendment of ITA 1967 s 193(6)	s 1015
2 (5)	Amendment of ITA 1967 s 497	s 460
3 (1)	Amendment of ITA 1967 s 6	s 14(1)
(2)	Unnecessary (operative date)	
4	Amendment of FA 1967 s 11(1) and FA 1969 s 4(1)	s 285(1)-(3)
5	Insertion of ITA 1967 s 127(1)(ff)	
6	Amendment of ITA 1967 s 134	
7	Amendment of ITA 1967 s 135(1)	
8	Amendment of ITA 1967 s 136	
9	Amendment of ITA 1967 s 138(3)	s 461
10	Amendment of ITA 1967 s 141(1A)(a)	s 465
11	Amendment of ITA 1967 s 142(1)	s 466
12	Amendment of ITA 1967 s 221(2)(h)(i)	
13	Amendment of ITA 1967 s 236(1) and Sch 5	s 787(6)
14 (1),(2),(3)		s 287
(4)		s 301(1)
(5)	Amendment of ITA 1967 s 241(7)	
15	Amendment of ITA 1967 s 331(3)	
16	Amendment of ITA 1967 s 332(8)	
17(1)	Definitions of "construction contract", construction paymentscard" and "construction tax deduction card" deleted by FA 1992 s 28(a)(ii)	ss 530(1), 531(11)(c)
(2),(2A),(3) (4),(5), (6), (6A), (6B)		s 531(1), (3), (4), (5), (6), (8), (9), (10)
(7)(a), (b)		s 531(11)(a), (b)
(c)	Deleted by FA 1992 s 28(e)(iii)	
(8), (9), (10)		s 531(12), (13), (14),
(10A),(10B) (11)(12)		(15), (16), (7), (2)
(13)		s 530(2)
(14),(15),(16), (17),(19),(20)	s 531(17), (18)	
17A	(s 17A inserted by FA 1992 s 233)	904
18		s 197
19(1), (2), (2A)		s 279
(3)	Unnecessary (construction)	
(4)	Unnecessary (operative date)	
(5)	Unnecessary (operative date)	
20(1)		s 91(3)
(2)		s 91(1)
(3)(a)-(d)		s 91(2)
(e)	Unnecessary (operative date)	
(4)		s 91(4)
(5)(a)	Rep by FA 1975 s 33 and Sch 1 Pt II	
(b), (c)(d)		s 91(5)
21		s 95
22		s 92

Former Enactment		*Destination in TCA 1997*
Finance Act 1970 (1970 No 14) (contd)		
s 23 (1), (2), (3)		s 90(1)-(3)
(4) s 89(1)(b)		
(5)		s 90(4)
(6)	Unnecessary (operative date)	
24 (1), (2)(a)		s 87
(2)(b)	Rep by CTA 1976 s 164 and Sch 3 Pt II	
24 (3)	Unnecessary (operative date)	
25		s 93
26 (1)-(4)		s 94
(5)	Unnecessary (operative date)	
Pt VI		
s 57 (1)	Unnecessary (duplication)	
(2)-(4)		s 829
(5)	Unnecessary (obsolete)	
58	Amendment of FA 1968 s 35(3)(b)	
59 (1),(2),(3)		ss 38, 48(1)(b)
(5)	Amendment of ITA 1967 s 474(1)	
(6)		s 48(2)
61	Unnecessary (care and management)	
62 (2), (7)	Unnecessary (construction and commencement)	
Finance (No 2) Act 1970 (1970 No 25)		
s 1	Ceased by FA 1972 s 10	
7	Unnecessary (care and management)	
8 (2), (5)	Unnecessary (construction and commencement)	
Finance Act 1971 (1971 No 23)		
Pt I		
s 1	Unnecessary (obsolete)	
2	Unnecessary (cesser of FA 1970 s 2)	
3	Amendment of ITA 1967 s 58 (amendment ceased by FA 1990 s 14(2)	
4 (1)-(4),(6)		s 72
(5)	Unnecessary (operative date)	
5		s 86
6	Amendment of ITA 1967 s 134	
7	Amendment of ITA 1967 s 135	
8	Amendment of ITA 1967 s 136	
9	Insertion of ITA 1967 s 139(6)	
10	Amendment of ITA 1967 s 142(1)	s 466
11 (1), (2)		s 468
(3)	Deleted by FA 1980 s 5	
(4)	Rep by FA 1996 s 132(2) and Sch 5 Pt II	
(5)	Amendment of ITA 1967 s 153(1)(d)	s 1032
(6)	Deleted by FA 1980 s 5	
(7)	Amendment of ITA 1967 s 497	s 460
(8)	Deleted by FA 1980 s 5	
12	Amendment of ITA 1967 s 244	ss 763-765
13	Amendment of ITA 1967 s 251(4)(c)	ss 283(2), 300(1)
14	Amendment of ITA 1967 s 254(2)	
15	Amendment of ITA 1967 s 336	s 213(1), (2)
16 (1)(a), (b)	Amendment of ITA 1967 s 443	
(c)	Amendment of ITA 1967 s 444	
(2), (3)		s 796(2)(d), (e), (f)
17 (1), (2)(a)	Amendment of ITA 1967 s 550	s 1080(1)
(2)(b)	Unnecessary (operative date)	
(3)	Unnecessary (cesser of ITA 1967 ss 418, 529)	

Former Enactment		*Destination in TCA 1997*
Finance Act 1971 (1971 No 23) (contd)		
s 18	Amendment of ITA 1967 s 419	
19	Amendment of ITA 1967 ss 428, 429,	ss 941, 942(1)-(8)(10)
20 (1)-(4), (6)		s 1082
(5)	Unnecessary (operative date)	
21 (1)(a)	Insertion of FA 1970 s 17(2)(aa)	
(b),(c),(d)	Unnecessary (obsolete)	
(2)	Insertion FA 1970 s 17(6A), (6B), (6C)	s 531(5)(6)(8)(9)(10)
(3)	Unnecessary (obsolete)	
22	Unnecessary (spent)	
23	Unnecessary (obsolete)	
24	Unnecessary (obsolete)	
25	Unnecessary (obsolete)	
26 (1),(2),(2A)		s 285(1), (2), (3)
(3)		s 299(2)
(4)		s 285(8)
(5)	Amendment of FA 1970 s 14(1)	s 287
Pt VI		
s 54	Unnecessary (care and management)	
55 (2), (6)	Unnecessary (construction and commencement)	
Finance Act 1972 (1972 No 19)		
Pt I		
s 1 (1)	Rep by FA 1974 s 86 and Sch 2 Pt I	
(2)	Amendment of ITA 1967 s 522	
2	Amendment of ITA 1967 ss 127(1), 128(1)	ss 986(1)(a)-(j), 987(1)-(3)
3	Amendment of ITA 1967 s 135	
4	Amendment of ITA 1967 s 138	s 461
5	Amendment of ITA 1967 s 141	s 465
6	Amendment of ITA 1967 s 142(1)	s 466
7	Amendment of ITA 1967 s 485(5)	s 962(1), (2)
8	Amendment of ITA 1967 s 486	s 963
9	Amendment of FA 1967 s 12(2)	s 469(2)
10	Unnecessary (cesser of F(No 2)A 1970 s 1)	
11	Rep by FA 1997 s 146(2) and Sch 5 Pt II	
12	Unnecessary (repeals)	
13 (1), (2), (4)	Definitions of "ordinary share capital", "proprietary director" and "proprietary employee" rep by FA 1975 s 86 and Sch 2 Pt III, definition of "Revenue Commissioners" unnecessary	s 770
(3)	Rep by FA 1974 s 86 and Sch 2 Pt II	
14		s 771
15 (1)		s 772(1)
(2)(a)-(e),(g)		s 772(2)
(2)(f)	Rep by FA 1974 s 64	
(3)		s 772(3)
(4)	The matter from "In applying this subsection" to end rep by FA 1996 s 132(2) and Sch 5 Pt II	s 772(4)
(5)-(7)		s 772(5)-(7)
15 (8)	Unnecessary (operative date)	
16 (1), (2), (3)		s 774(1), (3), (5)
(4)		s 774(6), Sch 32 para 26
(5)		s 774(7)
(6)	Rep by FA 1996 s 132(2) and Sch 5 Pt II	

Former Enactment		*Destination in TCA 1997*
Finance Act 1972 (1972 No 19) (contd)		
s 16 (7)		s 774(2)
16A	(s 16A inserted by FA 1997 s 41)	s 775
17 (1), (2)		s 776
(3)	Rep by FA 1996 s 132(2) and Sch 5 Pt II	
(4)	Unnecessary (operative date)	
18 (1)(a), (2)-(5)		s 772
(b)	Rep by FA 1996 s 132(2) and Sch 5 Pt II	
(6)	Insertion of ITA 1967 s 2(2)(cc)	s 3(2), (3)
(7)	Unnecessary (operative date)	
19		s 778
20		s 779
21 (1)-(4), (5)(a), (6), (7)	s 780	
(5)(b)	Unnecessary (operative date)	
22 (1)-(4)		s 781
(5)	Unnecessary (operative date)	
23		s 782
24	Rep by FA 1996 s 132(2) and Sch 5 Pt II	
25	Rep by FA 1996 s 132(2) and Sch 5 Pt II	
Pt V		
s 42 (1)	Amendment of ITA 1967 s 251(4)	
(2)	Amendment of ITA 1967 s 246(1)	
43		s 212
46	Unnecessary (repeals)	
47	Unnecessary (care and management)	
48 (2), (5)	Unnecessary (construction and commencement)	
Sch 1, Pt I		Sch 23, Pt I,
para1, 2		para 1, 2
3(1)-(3)		para 3
(4)	Unnecessary (operative date)	
4, 5		para 4, 5
Sch 1, Pt II	Unnecessary (obsolete)	
Sch 1, Pt III		
para 1	Amendment of ITA 1967 s 63	s 84
2	Amendment of ITA 1967 s 115(1)	s 201(2)
3	Amendment of ITA 1967 Sch 15	Sch 29
4	Saver for enactments which contain reference to ITA 1967 Pt XII Ch II (substituted by FA 1997 s 146(1) and Sch 9 para 5(3))	
Sch 1, Pt IV	Rep by FA 1996 s 132(2) and Sch 5 Pt II	
Sch 1, Pt V	Rep by FA 1996 s 132(2) and Sch 5 Pt II	
Sch 1, Pt VI		
paras 1-4	Sch 23, Pt 2, paras 6-9	
5	Insertion of ITA 1967 s 2(2)(dd)	s 3(2), (3)
Sch 3	Amendment of ITA 1967 ss 1(1), 8(1), (2)	ss 2(1), 3(1), s 1087
Sch 4	Repeal of ITA 1967 ss 7, 63(a), (b), (c) and proviso, 152(5), 222, 223, Pt XII Ch II	
Finance Act 1973 (1973 No 19)		
s 1 (1)	Amendment of ITA 1967 s 129	s 991(1)
(2)	Unnecessary (operative date)	
2	Amendment of ITA 1967 s 138(3)	s 461
3	Amendment of ITA 1967 s 141	s 465
4	Amendment of ITA 1967 s 142(1)	s 466
5		Sch 32, para 21(2)
6	Unnecessary (deletion of ITA 1967 s 211(4))	

Former Enactment | *Destination in TCA 1997*

Finance Act 1973 (1973 No 19) (contd)

Former Enactment		Destination in TCA 1997
s 7	Amendment of ITA 1967 s 229(1)(i)	
8	Amendment of ITA 1967 s 246	
9 (1)	Amendment of ITA 1967 s 251(4)(d)	s 283(3)
(2)		s 283(7)
proviso	Unnecessary (operative date)	
10	Amendment of ITA 1967 s 254(2)	s 316(3)
11	Amendment of ITA 1967 s 272	s 288
12	Amendment of ITA 1967 s 336	s 213(1), (2)
13	Amendment of ITA 1967 s 357(3)	
14	Insertion of ITA 1967 s 387(4)	
15	Insertion of ITA 1967 s 439(1)(ii)(a)	s 792(1)-(4)
16	Amendment of FA 1971 s 22(2)	
17	Amendment of FA 1971 s 26(1)	s 285(1), (2), (3)
18	Amendment of FA 1972 s 21	s 780
19 (1), (2)		s 192
(3)	Unnecessary (operative date)	
20		s 209
21		s 767
22		s 993(5)
23	Deleted by FA 1992 s 4	
24	Rep by FA 1982 s 20(7)	
25		ss 373(2)(a), 374
26		ss 373(2)(a), 375
27		ss 373(2)(a), 377
28		ss 373(2)(a), 378
29		ss 373(2)(a), 379
30 (1), (5), (6)		s 373(1), (2)(a), (3)
(2), (3), (4)		s 380
31	Unnecessary (spent)	
32	Rep by FA 1977 s 54 and Sch 2 Pt I	
33 (1)(a),(b),(c)		s 13(1)
(d)	Unnecessary (duplication)	
(2), (3), (4), (5), (7)	s 13(2)-(6)	
(6)	Unnecessary (commencement)	
34 (1), (2)		s 234(1), (2)(a)
(2A)-(7)		s 234(3)-(8)
35		s 1089(1)
39	Rep by CTA 1976 s 164 and Sch 3 Pt III	
40 (1)-(5)		s 275
(6)	Unnecessary (obsolete)	
(7)	Unnecessary (construction and operative date)	
41	Insertion of ITA 1967 s 117(7), (8)	s 118
42	Unnecessary (cesser of ITA 1967 s 121)	
43	Amendment of ITA 1967 s 128	s 987
44	Insertion of ITA 1967 s 335(2), (3), (4)	s 211(1)-(4)
45	Amendment of ITA 1967 s 413(2)	
46	Amendment of ITA 1967 s 503(2)	s 1054(2)-(4)
92 (1)		ss 39(1), 48(1)(c)
(2)(a)		s 39(2)
(b)		s 48(2)
(4)	Amendment of ITA 1967 s 474(1)	s 49, Sch 32 para 1(2)
97	Unnecessary (care and management)	
98(2), (6)	Unnecessary (construction and commencement)	
Sch 1	Deleted by FA 1992 s 4(b)	

Former Enactment		*Destination in TCA 1997*
Finance Act 1973 (1973 No 19) (contd)		
Sch 2	Rep by FA 1977 s 54 and Sch 2 Pt I	
Sch 3		
paras1, 3-5,7,8		Sch 1
2	Amendment of ITA 1967 Sch 15	Sch 29
6	Unnecessary (obsolete)	
Sch 4	Rep by FA 1977 s 54 and Sch 2 Pt I	
Sch 5	Deleted by FA 1996 s 13(b)	
Pt I		
para1-5		Sch 9, para 1to 5
6(a),(c)- (e)		Sch 9, para 6(a)-(d)
(b)	Unnecessary (duplication)	
7, 9		Sch 9 para 7, 8
8, 10	Rep by CTA 1976s 164 and Sch 3	
Pt II	Unnecessary (duplication)	
Finance (Taxation of Profits of Certain Mines) Act 1974 (1974 No 17)		
s 1 (1)	Definition of "tax" unnecessary (duplication)	s 672(1)
(2),(6),(7)		s 672(2), (3), (4)
(3)-(5)	Unnecessary (construction)	
2 (1)		s 673(1)
proviso	Deleted by FA 1990 s 93(a)	
(2)	Unnecessary (spent)	
(3)	Unnecessary (obsolete)	
(4)		s 673(3)
3 (1)	Unnecessary (spent)	
(2)-(5)		s 674(1)(a), (2), (3), (4)
4		s 675
5		s 676
6		s 677
7 (1), (3), (4)		s 678
(2)	Unnecessary (spent)	
7A	(s 7A inserted by FA 1990 s 39(d))	s 679(1)(a),(2)-(5)
8		s 680
8A(1)-(9)	(s 8A inserted by FA 1996 s 34)	s 681
8A (10)	Unnecessary (obsolete)	
9	Rep by CTA 1976 s 164 and Sch 3 Pt II	
10		s 682(1)-(3)
11		s 683
12	Rep by CTA 1976 s 164 and Sch 3 Pt II	
13-15	Rep by CTA 1976 s 164 and Sch 3 Pt I	
16-17	Rep by CTA 1976 s 164 and Sch 3 Pt II	
18	Unnecessary (short title, construction and commencement)	
Finance Act 1974 (1974 No 27)		
Pt I		
s 1	Amendment of ITA 1967 s 1(1)	
2	Amendment of ITA 1967 s 4	
3	Unnecessary (obsolete)	
4		s 59
5 (1)		s 237(1)(b), (2)
proviso	Rep by CTA 1976 s 164 and Sch 3 Pt 1	
(2), (3)		s 16
6	Unnecessary (obsolete)	
7	Amendment of ITA 1967 s 142(1)	

Former Enactment		*Destination in TCA 1997*
Finance Act 1974 (1974 No 27) (contd)		
s 8 (1)		s 464
(2)	Rep by FA 1996 s 132(2) and Sch 5 Pt II	
9	Substitution of ITA 1967 s 152(1)	
10	Unnecessary (cesser of charge to sur-tax)	
11	Unnecessary (supplementary)	
12	Unnecessary (commencement)	
13 (1)		s 654
(2), (3)	Rep by FA 1983 s 120 and Sch 4	
14	Unnecessary (repeal of FA 1969 s 18(2)(a))	
15		s 655(1), (2)
16 (1)		s 657(1)
(2)		s 657(2)
(3)	Deleted by FA 1976s 14(1)(c)	
(4)		s 657(3)
(5)		s 657(1)
17-19	Rep by FA 1983 s 120 and Sch 4	
20	Ceased by FA 1983 s 24	
20A	Unnecessary (spent)	
20B(1)	(s 20B inserted by FA 1981 s 10)	s 657(4)
(2)		s 657(5)
proviso	Unnecessary (obsolete)	
(3)		s 657(6)
(4)		s 657(7)
(5)		s 657(8)
(6)		s 657(9)
(7)		s 657(10)
(8)		s 657(11)
(9)		s 657(12)
21	Ceased by FA 1980 s 24	
Finance Act 1974 (1974 No 27)		
s22(1)	Section 658 is applied on a modified basis by Sch 32 para 23 to reflect the application of FA 1974 s 22 in relation to certain old expenditure	s 658(1)
(2)		s 658(2)(a)
proviso		s 658(2)(b)
(2A)		s 658(3)
(2B)		s 658(4)
(2C)	Deleted by FA 1994 s 23	
(3)		s 658(5)
(4)	Deleted by FA 1982 s 16	
(5)		s 658(6)
(6)		s 658(7)
(7)		s 658(8)
(8)		s 658(9)
proviso		s 658(10)
(9)		s 658(11)
(10)		s 658(12)
(11)		s 658(13)
23	Rep by CTA 1976 s 164 and Sch 3 Pt I	
24	Unnecessary (obsolete)	

Former Enactment		Destination in TCA 1997
Finance Act 1974 (1974 No 27) (contd)		
s 25		s 660
26	Amendment of ITA 1967 s 307	s 381(1)
27 (1)-(6)	Definitions of "basis year" unnecessary (obsolete) and "market gardening" unnecessary (duplication)	s 662
(7)	Rep by CTA 1976 s 164 and Sch 3 Pt II	
28	Rep by FA 1983 s 120 and Sch 4	
29	Substitution of ITA 1967 s 496	
30	Rep by FA 1996 s 132(2) and Sch 5 Pt II	
31 (1), (2), (4)		s 246(1), (2), (4)
(3)(a)	Rep by FA 1996 s 132(2) and Sch 5 Pt II	
(3)(b)-(g)		s 246(3)
32		s 245
33		s 247(1)-(3)
34		s 248(1)-(3)
35(1)-(3)		s 249
35(4), (5)		ss 247(4), (5), 248(4), (5)
36		s 253
37		s 254
38	Rep by FA 1997 s 146(2) and Sch 9 Pt II	
39		s 255
40	Rep by FA 1996 s 132 (2) and Sch 5 Pt II	
41 (1)-(6)		s 813
(7)	Unnecessary (obsolete)	
42 (1)	Amendment of ITA 1967 s 61(l)	s 82(2)
(2)	Unnecessary (commencement)	
43	Insertion of ITA 1967 s 75(3), (4)	s 70(1)
44	Rep by FA 1997 s 146(2) and Sch 9 Pt II	
45	Amendment of ITA 1967 s 77(3)	
46		s 71(4)
47	Substitution of ITA 1967 s 219(1)	s 699(1)
48	Amendment of ITA 1967 s 221(2)	
49	Amendment of ITA 1967 ss 231(4)(a), 232(2), 233(2)(a)	
50	Rep by FA 1996 s 132(2) and Sch 5 Pt II	
51 (1)	Amendment of ITA 1967 s 535(1)(b)	s 1088
(2)	Unnecessary (operative date)	
52	Rep by FA 1997 s 146(2) and Sch 9 Pt II	
54	Rep by FA 1997 s 146(2) and Sch 9 Pt II	
55		s 814
56 (1), (2), (3)(b), (c), (4)		s 816
(3)(a)	Rep by CTA 1976 s 164 and Sch 3 Pt II	
57 preamble, (1)-(7) and (8)(a)-(c),(e),(f)		s 806
(d)	Unnecessary (obsolete)	
(9)	Unnecessary (operative date)	
58		s 807
59(1)-(5)		s 808
(6)	Amendment of ITA 1967 Sch 15	Sch 29
60		s 809
61		s 810
62(1), (2)		s 105
(3)	Unnecessary (obsolete)	

Former Enactment		*Destination in TCA 1997*
Finance Act 1974 (1974 No 27) (contd)		
s 63	Amendment of F(MP)A 1968 s 20	s 643
64(1)	Unnecessary (cesser of FA 1972 s 115(2)(f) and ITA 1967 Sch 3 proviso para 4)	
(2)	Substitution of FA 1972 Sch 1 Pt III para 4	
65	Amendment of ITA 1967 s 235	ss 783-784
66	Insertion of ITA 1967 s 235A	s 785
67	Amendment of ITA 1967 s 236 and Sch 5	s 787
69	Amendment of ITA 1967 s 429	s 942(1)-(8), (10)
70	Amendment of ITA 1967 s 489(1)	s 965
71	Unnecessary (cesser of ITA 1967 s 130, FA 1969 ss 7(3), 8(3) and 9(a)(proviso)	
72		s 988
73 (1)-(4)		s 898
(5)	Amendment of ITA 1967 Sch 15	Sch 29
74		s 671
Pt IV		
s 86	Unnecessary (application of schedule)	
87	Unnecessary (care and management)	
88(2), (5)	Unnecessary (construction and commencement)	
Sch 1, Pt I	Amendment of ITA 1967 ss 137-141, 143, 146, 149, 153, 193, FA 1969 s 3, FA 1971 s 11	ss 193, 458, 459(1)-(2), 460, 461, 462, 465, 467, 468, 472, 1032, 1032
Sch 1, Pt II	Amendment of ITA 1967 ss 115(1)(b), 127, 133(1), 195, 233(2), 406(5), 434(1), 435(1), 451(5), 488, 497, 525(1), 528, 530, 543, Sch 1 Pt I para 1(c), Sch 1 Pt II para 1(b), Sch 16 para 8, 9, FA 1967 s 12(2), FA 1968 ss 3, 34(6)	ss 201(2), 986, 997 1018, 238(1)-(6), 800, 966, 460, 127(1)-(5), 926, Sch 2, 469(2), 480
Sch 2, Pt I	Repeal of ITA 1967 ss 134, 135, 136, 144(3), 188(2), 198, 236(10), s 387(4)(c), 396(4), 410(4) , 416(11), 485(3)(4), 522, 523, 524, 526, 527, 532, 551(2)(b), Sch 10 para 5(1)(b) and proviso, F(MP)A 1968 ss 3(6)(a)(b) (c)(i)(c)(vi), 23(4), FA 1972 s 1(1)	
	Amendment of ITA 1967 ss 2(2)(c), 3, 70(1)(c), 116(1), 117(1), 145(1), 162(2), 172(1)(c), 187(1), 191(2), (3), 192(1), 194(1)(a), 196, 231(2)(3), 288(2), 291, 293, 329(1)(b), 332(1)(b), 344(4), 345, 356, 361, 365, 336(b), 387(3)(a), 419, 420, 441(1), 446(1), 465, 486(1), 489(1), 491(1), 492(1), 493, 501(1)(c), 502(2), 505, 511, 521, 539(1), 547(3), 549(1), 550, 552(2), 554(4), 555, 556(1), 559(1), Sch 6 Pt II para 1, 10 Pt III para (3)(1), Sch para 1(1), 5(1)(a), Sch 15, IT(A)A 1967 preamble para 2, FA 1968 ss 6(2)(a), 37(6), 48(2), F(No 2)A 1968 ss 8, 11(4), FA 1969 ss 63(1), 67(2), FA 1970 ss 19(5), 62(2), FA 1971 s 20(2), FA 1972 s 48(2), FA 1973 ss 33(1)(d), (6), 98(2)	ss 1(2), 3(2)(3), 45(1), 48(2), 117, 118, 199, 470(1)-(3),483(1)-(3), 757, 759, 760, 793, 797, 826(1)-(7)(9), 851, 879(1)-(4), 880(2)-(6), 886, 901, 928(1), 930, 963,965, 968, 969, 998, 1000,1004, 1015, 1017, 1022, 1053(1)-(4),1054(2)-(4), 1055, 1063, 1067, 1080(1), 1082, Sch 24 paras 1(1), 6, Sch 29
Sch 2, Pt II	Repeal of definitions of "ordinary share capital", "proprietary director", "proprietary employee" in FA 1972 s 13(1), (3)	
Sch 3	Repealed by FA 1983 s 120 and Sch 4	

Former Enactment		*Destination in TCA 1997*
Finance Act 1975 (1975 No 6)		
s 1	Amendment of ITA 1967 s 142(1)	s 466
2	Amendment of ITA 1967 s 143(3)(b)	
3	Amendment of ITA 1967 s 251(4)(d)	ss 283(2), 300(1)
4	Insertion of ITA 1967 s 254(2A)	s 271(4)
5	Amendment of ITA 1967 s 264	s 272
6	Amendment of FA 1971 s 22(2)	
7	Amendment of FA 1971 s 26(1)	s 285(1)-(3)
8	Amendment of FA 1973 s 8	
9	Amendment of FA 1973 s 19	s 192
10	Amendment of FA 1974 s 3	
11 (1)	Substitution of FA 1974 s 6(1)	
s 11 (2)	Unnecessary (application of schedule)	
12	Substitution of FA 1974 s 13(1)	s 654
13	Amendment of FA 1974 s 15(3)	s 655(1), (2)
14 (1)	Amendment of FA 1974 s 16	s 657(1)
(2)	Unnecessary (operative date)	
15	Amendment of FA 1974 s 17(4)	
16	Amendment of FA 1974 s 20(1)	
17	Amendment of FA 1974 s 21(1)	
18	Amendment of FA 1974 s 22	s 658
19	Amendment of ITA 1967 s 80	ss 96, 888(1)
20	Amendment of ITA 1967 s 83	s 98
21 (1)-(7)		s 947
(8)	Rep by CTA 1976 s 164 and Sch 3 Pt II	
22	Unnecessary (application of schedule)	
25	Amendment of ITA 1967 s 542	s 869
26	Amendment of FA 1968 s 9(b)	s 991(2)(b)
27	Amendment of FA 1973 s 35	s 1089(1)
28	Unnecessary (obsolete)	
29		s 319
30	Rep by CTA 1976 s 164 and Sch 3 Pt I.	
31	Rep by FA 1996 s 132(2) and Sch 5 Pt II	
31A	Rep by FA 1996 s 132(2) and Sch 5 Pt II	
32	Amendment of FA 1974 s 41(7)	
33 (1)		s 2(1)
(2)	Unnecessary (application of schedule)	
34 (1)	Amendment of ITA 1967 s 255(1)	s 268(1)-(3),(5)-(8)
(2)(a)(i)		s 271(4)(b)
(ii)		s 272(3)(b)
(iii)		ss 272(4)(b), 274(1)(b)(ii)
(b)	Unnecessary (spent)	
(3)	Unnecessary (operative date)	
35	Unnecessary (application of schedule)	
56	Unnecessary (care and management)	
57(2), (5)	Unnecessary (construction and commencement)	
Sch 1		
Pt I	Amendment of ITA 1967 ss 138, 139, 140, 141, FA 1969 s 3 FA 1971 s 11, FA 1974 s 8	ss 460,461, 464-466, 467, 1032
Pt II	Amendment of ITA 1967 ss 69(1), 218, 317(1), 236(3), 314, FA 1970 s 20(5)(a), FA 1971 s 22, FA 1973 39(1)(b), (7), FA 1974 s 27(1)	ss 1007(1)-(2), 698,) 391(1), 787(6), 662
Pt III	Amendment of ITA 1967 s 288(2), F(TPCM)A 1974 ss 1, 7(4), 11(2)	ss 757, 59
Sch 2		
Pt I	Unnecessary (obsolete)	
Pt II	Amendment of ITA 1967 Sch 15	Sch 29

Former Enactment		*Destination in TCA 1997*
Finance Act 1975 (1975 No 6) (contd)		
Pt III	Amendment of ITA 1967 ss 81(3), 91(1)(b), 92(2)	
Sch 3	Rep by FA 1996 s 132(2) and Sch 5 Pt II	
Sch 5	Rep by FA 1996 s 132(2) and Sch 5 Pt II	
Finance (No 2) Act 1975 (1975 No 19)		
s 1	Unnecessary (obsolete)	
3	Unnecessary (care and management)	
4	Unnecessary (short title, construction and commencement)	
Capital Gains Tax Act 1975 (1975 No 20)		
s 1	Unnecessary (short title)	
2 (1)(3)(4)		s 5
(2)	Rep by FA 1996 s 132(2) and Sch 5 Pt II	
(5)		s 3(4)
(6)	Unnecessary (construction)	
(7)	Unnecessary (construction)	
(8)	Unnecessary (construction)	
3 (1)-(3)		s 28
(4)	Deleted by FA 1992 s 60(1)(b)	
4(1)-(4)(6)-(8)		s 29(1)-(7)
(2) proviso	Rep by FA 1977 s 54 and Sch 2 Pt I	
(5)		s 30
5 (1)		s 31
(2)		s 979
(3)		s 1042
6	Rep by CGT(A)A 1978 s 17 and Sch 2	
7(1)		s 532(1)
(2)		ss 545(1), 546(1)
8 (1)		s 534
(2)		s 535(2)
(3)		s 567(2)
(4), (5), (6)		s 537
(7)		s 535(1)
9		s 547
10 (1)		s 542(1)
(2)		s 539
(3)		s 542(2)
11		s 545(2), (3)
12 (1)		s 546(2)
(2)		s 546(3)
(3), (4), (5)		s 538
(6)		s 546(4)
(7)		s 546(5)
13		s 1028
14		s 573
15 (1), (9), (11)		s 574
(2)		s 575
(3), (8)		s 576
(4)-(5A)(6)(12)		s 577
(7)		s 578
(10)		s 567(1)

Former Enactment		*Destination in TCA 1997*
Capital Gains Tax Act 1975 (1975 No 20) (contd)		
s 16		s 601(1), (2), (4), (5)
17		s 602
18		s 603
19 (1)		s 607(1)(a), (b), (c), (d), (f)
(2)		s 607(2)
20		s 593
20A	(s 20A inserted by FA 1993 s 24)	s 594
20B	(s 20B inserted by FA 1994 s 58)	s 595
21		s 608(2)-(4)
22		s 609
23		s 610, Sch 15, Pt I
24		s 613
25		s 604
26(1)-(6)		s 598
(7)	Rep by CGT(A)A 1978 s 17 and Sch 2	
27(1)(a)-(c), (2)-(4)		s 599
(d)	Rep by FA 1996 s 132(2) and Sch 5 Pt II	
28		s 597
29(1)-(3), (5)		s 536
(4)	Rep by CGT(A)A 1978 s 17 and Sch 2	
30		s 612
31 (1)-(4), (6)		s 731(1)-(5)(a)
(5)		Sch 32, para 25
32		s 732
33 (1)-(6)		s 549
(7)	Ceased by FA 1996 s 131(9)(a)	
(8)	Rep by FA 1996 s 132(2) and Sch 5 Pt II	
34		s 550
35 (1)-(3), (5)		s 589
35 (4)	Deleted by CTA 1976 s 140(2) and Sch 2 Pt II, para 3(2)	
36		s 590(1)-(9)
37		s 579
38		s 828(1)-(3)
39		s 611
40		s 569
41		s 570
42		s 572
43		s 1005
44 (1)		s 981
(2)		s 563(1)
45		s 543
46 (1)-(6)		s 541(1)-(6)
(7)(a)-(d)		s 541(7)(a), (b), (c), (g)
47(1)-(6)(8)-(11)		s 540
(7)	Rep by CGT(A)A 1978 s 17 and Sch 2	
48		s 533
49 (1)-(6)		s 548(1)-(6)
(7)	Rep by FA 1997 s 146(2) and Sch 5 Pt II	

Former Enactment		*Destination in TCA 1997*
Capital Gains Tax Act 1975 (1975 No 20) (contd)		
s 50 (1)	Amendment of PCTA 1927 s 1	
(2)	Amendment of IRRA 1890 s 39	
s 51 (1)	For leases only, otherwise unnecessary (application of schedules)	s 566
(2)		s 544(8)
Sch 1, Pt I		
para1		s 544(1)-(6)
Sch 1, Pt I		
para 2		s 551
3(1)-(5)		s 552
(6)		s 828(4)
(7)		s 565
4		s 554
5(1), (2), (4)		s 555
(3)		s 544(1)
6		s 557
7		s 559
8		s 560(1), (2)
9		s 560(3), (4), (5)
10		s 561
11		s 562
12		s 564
13	Rep by CGT(A)A 1978 s 17 and Sch 2	
14(1)-(5)		s 581
(6)	Rep by CGT(A)A 1978 s 17 and Sch 2	
15		s 596
Sch 1, Pt II	Rep by CGT(A)A 1978 s 17 and Sch 2	
Sch 2		
para1		s 583
2(1)-(7)(9)		s 584
(8)	Rep by CGT(A)A 1978 s 17 and Sch 2	
2A	(para 2A inserted by FA 1990 s 87)	s 733
3		s 585
4		s 586(1), (2)
5		s 587(1)-(3)
5A	(para 5A inserted by FA 1997 s 70)	s 588
6		s 600(1)-(5)
Sch 3		Sch 14
para1		para 2
2		para 3
3		para 4(1)-(6)
4		para 5
5		para 6
6		para 7
7		para 8
8		para 9
9		para 10
10		para 1

Former Enactment	*Destination in TCA 1997*
Capital Gains Tax Act 1975 (1975 No 20) (contd)	
Sch 4	
para1(1)	s 849(1), (2)
(2)	s 931(1)
(3)	ss 851, 976(1)
Sch 4	
para2(1)	ss 931(2), 976(2)
(2)	ss 29(8), (9), 567(3), (4), 849(3)-(6), 861(1), 863, 864, 865, 869, 870, 875, 931(3), 949, 976(3), 999, 1043, 1051, 1083, Sch 1
3(1)(3)-(5)	s 913(1), (3)-(5), (7)
(2)	ss 874, 913(2), 1077(1)
(6)	s 1077(2)
para 4	s 914
5	s 915
6	s 916
7	s 917
8(1)	s 945
(2)(a)-(i),(k)	
(2)(j) .... Rep by CGT(A)A 1978 s 17 and Sch 2	
9	s 946
10(1)	s 913(8)
(2)	s 1029
11(1)-(10A)	s 980
(11) .... Unnecessary (operative date)	
12	s 568
13	s 544(7)
14	s 911
15	s 982
16	s 871
17	s 977
18	s 978
19	s 913(6)
Corporation Tax Act 1976 (1976 No 7)	
Pt I	
s 1 (1), (2), (3)	s 21
(4) .... Unnecessary (cesser of corporation profits tax)	
(5)	s 4(1)
2	s 129
3	s 24
4	s 864(2)
5	s 152(1), (2)
Pt II	
6 (1), (2), (3)	s 26(1), (2), (3)
(4) .... Rep by FA 1997s 146(2) and Sch 9 Pt II	
(5)	s 849
(6) .... Amendment of PCTA 1927 s 1	
(7) .... Amendment of IRRA 1890 s 39	
7	s 919(6)

Former Enactment		*Destination in TCA 1997*
Corporation Tax Act 1976 (1976 No 7) (contd)		
s 8 (1), (2), (3)		s 25
(4)		ss 1040, 1046(3)
9		s 27
10		s 243(1), (2), (4)-(9)
10A(1)(a), (b)(ii)	(s 10A inserted by FA 1992 s 46(1)(a))	s 454(1)
(b)(i)	Unnecessary (obsolete)	
(2), (3)		s 454(2), (3)
11 (1), (2)(b), (3)-(8)		s 76
(2)(a)	Unnecessary (obsolete)	
12 (1) to(7)		s 77
(8)	Rep by FA 1996 s 132(2) and Sch 5 Pt II	
12A	(s 12A inserted by FA 1994 s 95(a))	s 79
13 (1)		s 78(1)
(1A)	Matter from “and section 132(2) shall have effect” to the end. Unnecessary (obsolete)	s 78(2)
(1B)		s 78(3)(a), (b)
(1C), (2)		s 78(4), (5)
13 (3)(a), (c)		s 78(6)
(b)	Rep by CGT(A)A 1978 s 17 and Sch 2	
(4), (5)		s 78(7), (8)
14(1), (2)		s 307
(3)-(8)		s 308
14A	(s 14A inserted by FA 1994 s 56(b))	s 402
15		s 83
16 (1)-(8)(10)		s 396
(9)	Ceased by FA 1983 s 51	
16A	(s 16A inserted by FA 1992 s 46(1)(c))	s 455
17 (1)	Definitions of “farming” and “market gardening” unnecessary (duplication)	s 663(1)
(2)-(4)		s 663(2)-(4)
(5)	Matter from “In this subsection” to “section 157” unnecessary (obsolete)	s 663(5)
18 (1)-(3)		s 397
(4)	Ceased by FA 1983 s 51	
19		s 399
20		s 400
21 (1)	Unnecessary (application of income tax provisions for purposes of corporation tax)	
(2)	Unnecessary (non-application of income tax provisions)	
(3)	Unnecessary (obsolete).	
(4)		s 309
22 (1)		s 827
(2)		s 826(8)
23 (1)		ss 826(1)-(7), (9), 827
(2)-(4)-(5)		Sch 24, para 4(2)
24		s 156

Former Enactment		*Destination in TCA 1997*
Corporation Tax Act 1976 (1976 No 7) (contd)		
s 25 (1)-(7)		s 157
(8)	Ceased by FA 1983 s 51	
26 (1)-(3), (3) proviso para (a), (4)-(6)		s 158
(3) proviso para (b)	Ceased by FA 1983 s 51	
27 (1)-(7)		s 401
(8)	Unnecessary (obsolete)	
Pt III		
s 28	Ceased by FA 1988 s 33(2)	
28A(1)	(s 28A inserted by FA 1996 s 44)	s 22(1)(a)
(2)-(8)		s 22(2)-(8)
(9)	Unnecessary (obsolete)	
28A(10)		s 457
29		s 844
30 (1)	Unnecessary (interpretation)	
(2)-(4)		s 700
(5)(a)	Amendment of ITA 1967 s 219	s 699(1)
(b)	Unnecessary (obsolete)	
31 (1)-(3)	Ceased by FA 1986 s 34(a)	
(4)	Unnecessary (obsolete)	
(5)		s 702(2)
(6)	Ceased by FA 1986 s 34(a)	
(7)	Unnecessary (obsolete)	
(8)		s 702(1)
(9)	Rep by FA 1992 s 43(4)	
(10)	Unnecessary (spent)	
32 (1), (2)		s 1009(2), (3)
(3)(a)-(d)		s 1009(4)
(c)(proviso)	Unnecessary (spent)	
(4)		s 1009(5)
(5)		s 1009(1)
33 (1)-(1B)(2)		s 707
(3)		s 728
33A(1)-(5), (7), (8)	(s 33A inserted by FA 1992 s 44)	s 708
(6)	Unnecessary (spent)	
33B	(s 33B inserted by FA 1993 s 11(c))	s 712
34		s 709
35		s 710(1)-(5)
35A	(s 35A inserted by FA 1993 s 11(d))	s 711
36		s 713(1)-(6)
36A(1)-(6)(8)	(s 36A inserted by FA 1993 s 11(f))	s 723
(7)		s 706(4)
36B	(s 36B inserted by FA 1993 s 11(f))	s 724
36C	(s 36C inserted by FA 1993 s 11(f))	s 725
37	Deleted by FA 1982 s 42	
38		s 714
39		s 715
40		s 716
41		s 717(1), (3)-(6)
42(1)-(5), (8)		s 718
(6), (7)	Rep by FA 1977 s 54 and Sch 2 Pt I	
43		s 726

Former Enactment		*Destination in TCA 1997*
Corporation Tax Act 1976 (1976 No 7) (contd)		
s 44		s 727
45		s 729(1)-(6)
46		s 730
46A	(s 46A inserted by FA 1992 s 44(d)) Definitions of "collective investment undertaking", "market value", "trading company" and "units" deleted by FA 1993 s 11(j)(i)	s 719
46B(1)	(s 46B inserted by FA 1992 s 44(d))	s 720(1)
(proviso)		s 720(2)
paras (iii)-(v) (proviso) para (i), (ii)	Unnecessary (spent)	
(2)-(4)		s 720(3)-(5)
47	Deleted by FA 1992 s 44(e)	
48		s 721
49		s 722
50 (1)	Unnecessary (declaratory)	
(2)-(4)		s 706(1)-(3)
51(1)-(3)(a) (4)-(6)		s 845
(3)(b), (c)	Rep by FA 1996 s 132(2) and Sch 5 Pt II	
52 (1)-(4)(6)		s 846
52 (5)	Rep by FA 1996 s 132(2) and Sch 5 Pt II	
Pt IV		
s 53-63	Unnecessary (spent)	
64		s 145(1), (2)(a), (3)-(10)
65		s 146
66	Ceased by CTA 1976 s 66A(3)	
66A(1)(2)(a)	(s 66A inserted by FA 1992 s 35(a)) Definitions of "the adjusted average relieved distribution", "the average relieved distribution" and "the relieved distribution". Unnecessary (spent)	s 145(11)(a)(b)
(2)(b)	Unnecessary (redundant)	
(3)	Unnecessary (cesser of CTA 1976 ss 66 and 67)	
(proviso)	Rep by FA 1997 s 146(2) and Sch 9 Pt II	
(4)	Rep by FA 1997 s 146(2) and Sch 9 Pt II	
67	Ceased by CTA 1976 s 66A(3)	
68	Rep by FA 1996 s 132(2) and Sch 5 Pt II	
69-75	Unnecessary (spent)	
76(1),(2)(a)(ii), (2)(b),(3)-(8)		s 144
(2)(a)(i)	Unnecessary (obsolete)	
76A(1)	Unnecessary (obsolete) (s 76A inserted by FA 1992 s 35(b))	
(2)	Unnecessary (cesser of CTA 1976 s 76(2)(a)(i))	
(proviso)	Rep by FA 1997 s 146(2) and Sch 9 Pt II	
(3)	Rep by FA 1997 s 146(2) and Sch 9 Pt II	
77	Unnecessary (spent)	
Pt VI		
s 78	Unnecessary (spent)	
Pt VII		
s 79	Ceased by FA 1988 s 33(2)	
80	Rep by FA 1997 s 61(2)	

Former Enactment		*Destination in TCA 1997*
Corporation Tax Act 1976 (1976 No 7) (contd)		
Pt VIII		
s 81		s 142
82		s 143
Pt IX		
s 83 (1)	Unnecessary (declaratory)	
(2), (3)		s 20
83 (4)		s 153(1)
(5)		s 152(3)
84		s 130
84A(1)	Section 84A as inserted by FA 1984 s 41 was substituted by FA 1989 s 21(1) but FA 1989 s 21(2) saved provisions of s 84A as it existed before the substitution in respect of certain types of loans. Section 134 of the Bill reflects those provisions while s 133 of the Bill reflects provisions of s 84A as substituted by FA 1989 s 21(1) and as subsequently amended	s 134(3)
(2)		s 134(5)
(3)		ss 134(1)(a), 133(7)
(3A)(a)		s 133(8)(b)
(proviso)	Unnecessary (spent)	
(b)		s 133(8)(c)
(c)		s 133(8)(d)
(d)		s 133(8)(e)
(e)		s 133(8)(a)
(3B)(a)	(s 84A(3B) was substituted by FA 1992 s 40(b) as respects certain loans advanced after 20.12.91; accordingly the original s 84A(3B) (inserted by FA 1991 s 28(a)) still applies for loans advanced before that date)	s 133(9)(a)
(proviso)		133(9)(b)
(3B)(b)		ss 133(9)(c),
(proviso)		s 133(11)
(a)	These three references relate to s 84A(3B) as substituted by FA 1992 s 40(b)	s 133(10)(a)
(b)		s 133(10)(b))
(b)(proviso)		s 133(11))
(4)		s 134(1)(b)
(4A)(a)		s 133(13)(b)
(b)	(s 84A(4A)(b) proviso (para (a) is spent)	s 133(13)(c)
(4A)(c)		s 133(13)(a)
(5)		s 134(1)(a), (c)
(6)		s 134(1)(a)
(7)-(8)	Unnecessary (spent)	
(9)		s 134(4)
(10)		s 134(6)
(9)		s 133(1)(d)
(10)		s 133(4)
85		s 131

Former Enactment		*Destination in TCA 1997*
Corporation Tax Act 1976 (1976 No 7) (contd)		
s 86		s 132
87		s 135
88		s 136
89		s 137
90	Ceased by FA 1983 s 51	
91	Ceased by FA 1983 s 51	
s 92	Unnecessary (spent)	
93		s 140
Pt X		
s 94		s 430
95		s 431
96		s 436
97		s 437
98 (1)-(7), (9)		s 438
(8)	Unnecessary (spent)	
99 (1), (2), (4)		s 439
(3)	Unnecessary (spent)	
100	Section 100(4) definition of "distributable income" para (b). Unnecessary (spent)	s 434
101		s 440
102		s 432
103		s 433
104		s 435
Pt XI		
s 105		s 410
106	Rep by FA 1992 s 50	
107		s 411
108		s 412
109		s 413
110		s 414
111		s 415
112		s 416
113		s 417
114		s 418
115		s 419
116		s 420
116A(1)(a), (b),(ii),(2)-(4)	(s 116A inserted by FA 1988 s 34)	s 456
(b), (5) (b)(i), (4)(a)	Unnecessary (spent)	
117(1)-(3)(a), (b), (d), (4)		s 421
(3)(c)	Unnecessary (spent)	
118		s 422
119		s 423
120	Definition of "connected person" in s 120(5) unnecessary (obsolete)	s 424.
121		s 425
122(1)-(5)		s 426
(6)	Unnecessary (obsolete)	

Former Enactment		*Destination in TCA 1997*
Corporation Tax Act 1976 (1976 No 7) (contd)		
s 123		s 427
124		s 428
125		s 429
Pt XII		
126		s 614
127		s 615
128		s 553
129(1)-(6)(b)		s 616
129(6)(c)(7)		s 590(11)
130		s 617
131		s 618
132		s 619
133		s 620
134		s 626
135		s 623
136		s 624
137		s 625
138		s 621
139(1)-(6)	The matter from "and section 157" to end in s 139(6) unnecessary (obsolete)	s 622
Pt XIII		
s 140(1)	Unnecessary (application of schedule)	
(2)	Unnecessary (application of schedule)	
(3)	Unnecessary (construction)	
Pt XIV		
s 141(1)-(1B)(3)		s 882(2)-(5)
(2)		s 1073
142(1)		s 883
(proviso)	Unnecessary (obsolete)	
(2)		s 1074
143(1)-(6), (7)(a),(b),(d)		s 884
(7)(c), (8)		s 1071
(9)-(11)		s 1072
(12)(a)		s 930
(b)		s 861(2)
(c)		ss 861(2), 884
144		s 919(1)-(5)
145(1), (2)		s 973
145(3)		s 1080
(4)		s 1082
(5)		s 974
146(1)		s 864, Pt 40 Ch I, s 949
(2)		s 856(3)
147(1), (2)		ss 207(3), (4), 211(5), (6), 213(3), (4), 483(1)-(3), 860, 861(1), 862, 863, 865, 868, 869, 870, 873, 874, 875, 886,

Former Enactment		*Destination in TCA 1997*
Corporation Tax Act 1976 (1976 No 7) (contd)		
s 142(1), (2) (contd)		898, 901, 928(1), 929, 947, 998, 1004, 1049, 1055, 1056, 1057, 1058, 1066, 1067, 1068, 1069, 1070, 1081(1)
(3), (4)		ss 1059, 1060, 1061, 1062, 1063, 1065, 1076(2)
147(5)		s 857(4)
148		s 1064
149		s 1075
150		s 647
s 151(1)-(13)		s 239
(14)	Amendment of ITA 1967 s 434	s 238(1)-(6)
152		s 240
153	Rep by FA 1996 s 132(2) and Sch 5 Pt II	
154		ss 882(1), 1076(1)
Pt XV		
s 155(1), (2)		s 1(2)
(3), (4)		s 2(2), (3)
(5)		ss 2(1), 4(1)
(6)-(8)	Unnecessary (construction)	
(9)-(13)		s 4(2)-(6)
156		s 9
157	Ceased by FA 1996 s 131	
158		s 11
159		s 590(10)
160		s 1033
161		s 927
162(1)-(6)		s 441
(7)	Unnecessary (obsolete)	
163		s 830
164	Unnecessary (application of schedule)	
165	Unnecessary (non-application of FA 1924 s 38 for corporation tax)	
166	Unnecessary (application of schedule)	
167	Ceased by FA 1983 s 51(2)	
168	Ceased by FA 1983 s 51(2)	
169	Unnecessary (obsolete)	
170	(s 170(3A)(a) (proviso) is spent)	s 141
171		s 2(4)
172	Unnecessary (relates to introduction of corporation tax)	
Pt XVI		
s 173	Unnecessary (relates to commencement of corporation tax)	
174	Unnecessary (relates to winding up of corporation profits tax)	
174(3)(proviso)		Sch 32, para 18(2)
175		Sch 32, para 19
176	Unnecessary (spent)	
177		Sch 32, para 8
178		s 139
179	Unnecessary (spent)	
180	Unnecessary (commencement)	
181	Unnecessary (spent)	
182(1)-(3), (3)(proviso)		
para (a),(bb),		

Former Enactment		*Destination in TCA 1997*
Corporation Tax Act 1976 (1976 No 7) (contd)		
s 182(4)		Sch 32, para 16(1)-(4)
(3)(proviso) para (b),(c)	Unnecessary (obsolete)	
183		Sch 32, para 17
184(1)		Sch 32, para 18(1)
(2)		Sch 32, para 18(3)
184(3)		Sch 32, para 18(4)(a), (b)
(proviso) para (iiA)		Sch 32, para 18(4)(c)
(proviso) para (i)-(iii)	Unnecessary (obsolete)	
(4)		Sch 32, para 18(5)
185	Unnecessary (spent)	
186	Unnecessary (application of schedule)	
187	Unnecessary (obsolete)	
188	Unnecessary (short title and construction)	
Sch 1		
para 1	Definition of "tax" in para 1(3) unnecessary (duplication)	s 321(1)-(7)
2		s 321(8)
3		s 321(9)
4	Unnecessary (obsolete)	
5	Unnecessary (obsolete)	
6	Substitution of ITA 1967 s 241	s 284
7	Substitution of ITA 1967 s 242	
8	Substitution of ITA 1967 s 243	
9	Substitution of ITA 1967 s 244	s 763(2)
10	Substitution of ITA 1967 s 245	s 670
11	Substitution of ITA 1967 s 246	
12	Substitution of ITA 1967 s 247	
13	Substitution of ITA 1967 s 248	
14	Substitution of ITA 1967 s 249	
15	Substitution of ITA 1967 s 251	ss 283(2), 300(1), 316(3)
16	Substitution of ITA 1967 s 252	ss 298(1), 299(1), 304(4)
17	Substitution of ITA 1967 s 254	ss 271(1), (2), (4), 278(1), (2), (6), 305, 320(1)
18	Substitution of ITA 1967 s 256	s 270
19	Substitution of ITA 1967 s 258	
20	Substitution of ITA 1967 s 259	
21	Substitution of ITA 1967 s 260	s 316(1)(a)
22	Substitution of ITA 1967 s 262	
23	Substitution of ITA 1967 s 264	s 272
24	Substitution of ITA 1967 s 265	s 274(1), (3), (4), (5), (8)
25	Substitution of ITA 1967 s 266	s 277
26	Substitution of ITA 1967 s 267	s 278(1), (3), (4), (5), (6)
27	Substitution of ITA 1967 s 270	s 280
28	Substitution of ITA 1967 s 271	s 288(4)(a)
29	Substitution of ITA 1967 s 272	s 288
30	Substitution of ITA 1967 s 274	s 292
31	Substitution of ITA 1967 s 275	s 293
32	Substitution of ITA 1967 s 279	s 296
33	Substitution of ITA 1967 s 280	s 297
34	Substitution of ITA 1967 s 282	s 300
Sch 1		
para 35	Substitution of ITA 1967 s 284	s 754
36	Substitution of ITA 1967 s 285	s 755
37	Substitution of ITA 1967 s 286	s 756
38	Substitution of ITA 1967 s 288	s 757
39	Substitution of ITA 1967 s 290	s 758

Former Enactment		*Destination in TCA 1997*
Corporation Tax Act 1976 (1976 No 7) (contd)		
Sch 1 (contd)		
para 40	Substitution of ITA 1967 s 291	s 759
41	Substitution of ITA 1967 s 292	s 761
42	Substitution of ITA 1967 s 293	s 760
43	Substitution of ITA 1967 s 294	ss 302, 303
44	Substitution of ITA 1967 s 295	s 304(2),(4)-(6)(a)
45	Substitution of ITA 1967 s 297	s 306
46	Substitution of ITA 1967 s 299	ss 312, 762
47	Substitution of ITA 1967 s 301	s 314
48	Substitution of ITA 1967 s 302	s 315
49	Substitution of ITA 1967 s 303	ss 316(1)(2), 317(2), 762(2)(b)
50	Substitution of ITA 1967 s 304	ss 318, 320(1), (2), (6)
51	Substitution of ITA 1967 s 305	s 769
52	Substitution of ITA 1967 s 306	s 381
53	Substitution of FA 1967 s 11	s 285(1), (2), (3), (8), 299(2)
54	Substitution of FA 1968 s 4	
55	Substitution of FA 1969 s 4	
56	Substitution of FA 1970 s 14	ss 287, 301(1)
57	Substitution of FA 1971 s 22	
58	Substitution of FA 1971 s 23	
59	Substitution of FA 1971 s 24	
60	Substitution of FA 1971 s 26	ss 285(1), (2), (3), (8), 288, 299(2)
61	Substitution of FA 1973 s 9(2)	s 283(7)
62	Substitution of FA 1973 s 25	ss 373(2)(a), 374
63	Substitution of F(TPCM)A 1974 s 1	s 672
64	Substitution of F(TPCM)A 1974 s 2	s 673
65	Substitution of F(TPCM)A 1974 s 3	
66	Substitution of F(TPCM)A 1974 s 4	s 675
67	Substitution of F(TPCM)A 1974 s 5	s 676
68	Substitution of F(TPCM)A 1974 s 6	s 677
69	Substitution of F(TPCM)A 1974 s 7	s 678
70	Substitution of FA 1974 s 22	s 658
71	Substitution of FA 1974 s 25	s 660
72	Substitution of FA 1975 s 34	s 248(1)-(3)
Sch 2, Pt I		
para 1	Amendment of ITA 1967 s 1	ss 2(1), 3(1)
2	Amendment of ITA 1967 s 8	s 1087
3	Amendment of ITA 1967 s 83	s 98
4	Amendment of ITA 1967 s 169	s 877
5	Amendment of ITA 1967 s 181(1)	s 918(1)-(3)
6	Amendment of ITA 1967 s 183(1)	s 921
7	Amendment of ITA 1967 s 184(2)(a)	s 922
8	Amendment of ITA 1967 s 186(1)	s 924
9	Amendment of ITA 1967 s 239(6)	
10	Amendment of ITA 1967 s 329	
11	Amendment of ITA 1967 s 331	
12	Amendment of ITA 1967 s 332	
Sch 2, Pt I		
para13	Amendment of ITA 1967 s 333(1)(b)	s 207(1), (2)
14	Amendment of ITA 1967 s 335(1)	s 211(1)-(4)
15	Amendment of ITA 1967 s 336	s 213(1), (2)
16	Amendment of ITA 1967 s 337(2)	
17	Amendment of ITA 1967 s 367(7)	
18	Amendment of ITA 1967 s 369(1)	s 750
19	Amendment of ITA 1967 s 370	s 751
20	Amendment of ITA 1967 s 371	s 752

Former Enactment		*Destination in TCA 1997*
Corporation Tax Act 1976 (1976 No 7) (contd)		
Sch 2 Pt I (contd)		
para 21	Amendment of ITA 1967 s 372	s 753
(1)	Amendment of ITA 1967 s 449(1)	s 812 (1), (2), (4)
(2)		s 812(3)
23	Amendment of ITA 1967 s 450(2)(d)	s 799
24		s 801(9)
25	Amendment of ITA 1967 s 458(1)	s 1091
26		s 51
27		s 483(4)
28	Amendment of ITA 1967 Sch 12	Sch 22
29	Unnecessary (obsolete)	
30		s 109
31		Sch 32, para 26
32	Amendment of FA 1973 s 24	
33		s 375
34		s 23
35		s 234(2)(b)
36(1), (3)		Sch 1, para 1, 2, 5
(2)	Unnecessary (obsolete)	
37	Amendment of F(TPCM)A 1974 s 8(1)	s 680
38		s 682(4)
39	Substitution of F(TPCM)A 1974 s 11	s 682(1)-(3)
40	Amendment of F(TPCM)A 1974 s 18(2)	
41	Amendment of FA 1974 s 4(b)	s 59
42	Amendment of FA 1974 s 31(3)(f)	s 246(1), (2), (4
43	Amendment of FA 1974 s 33(1)	s 247(1)-(3)
44	Amendment of FA 1974 s 38(2)	
45		s 813
46	Amendment of FA 1974 s 54	
47(1)		s 814
(2)	Amendment of FA 1974 s 55	s 814
48		s 671
49	Unnecessary (obsolete)	
50	Unnecessary (spent)	
Sch 2, Pt II		
para 1	Amendment of CGTA 1975 s 2(1)	s 5
2	Amendment of CGTA 1975 s 33(7)(b)	
3	Amendment of CGTA 1975 s 35	s 589
4	Amendment of CGTA 1975 s 36(1), (8)	s 590(1)-(9)
5	Amendment of CGTA 1975 s 36(4)(d)	s 590(1)-(9)
6		ss 563(2), 975(2)
7		s 548(7)
8	Amendment of CGTA 1975 Sch 1 par 2(1)	s 551
9	Amendment of CGTA 1975 Sch 1 par 3(3)(a)(ii), (iii)	s 552
Sch 3, Pt II		
para10	Amendment of CGTA 1975 Sch 1 para 22(1)(a)	
11		Sch 14, para 4(7)
12		s 975(1)
13	Unnecessary (spent)	
Sch 3, Pt I	Repeal of ITA 1967 ss 64, 76(7), (8), 108, Pt X, ss 219(2), 220(6), 221, 237, Pt XIX Ch III, s 347, Pt XXV, s 435, Pt XXX Ch I, Pt XXXVI Ch II, Sch 16, FA 1969 s 20, FA 1973 ss 11, 24(2),	

Former Enactment		*Destination in TCA 1997*
Corporation Tax Act 1976 (1976 No 7) (contd)		
Sch 3, Pt I (contd)	F(TPCM)A 1974 ss 13, 14, 15, 16, FA 1974 ss 4 proviso, 23, 54(4), FA 1975 ss 5, 18, 30	
	Amendment of ITA 1967 ss 1(1), 75(2), 76(2), 316(2), 371(7)(c), 432(3)(a), 543, FA 1972 s 16(4), FA 1973 ss 24(8), 26, FA 1974 s 5(1)	ss 2(1), 3(1); 70(1); 71(2); 390(1), (3); 752 949(2)-(4); s 774(6), Sch 32 para 26; 373(2)(a), 375; s 237(1)(b), (2)
Sch 3, Pt II	Repeal of ITA 1967 s 1(5), FA 1967 s 21, F(MP)A 1968 ss 13, 15, FA 1968 Pt IV, s 48(4), FA 1969 Pt VI, FA 1970 s 24(2)(b), FA 1971 ss 46, 49, 50, FA 1972 s 43 (insofar as it relates to corporation tax), FA 1973 s 37, F(TPCM)A 1974 ss 12, 17, FA 1974 ss 27(7), 53, 56(3)(a), FA 1975 s 21(8)	
	Amendment of ITA 1967 ss 555(1)(e),556, 559(1), FA 1969 s 63 , FA 1970 s 21, FA 1973 ss 30, 33, 34(2), 35, 98(2), Sch 3 para 7, F(TPCM)A 1974 s 10, FA 1974 ss 41(2), 74, FA 1975 s 28, Sch 2	ss 48, 95, 373, 13(1), 234(1)(2)(a), 1089(1), Sch 1, 682(1)-(3), 813, 671, 75(1), 96(1), 97, 102, 103, Sch 29
Sch 3, Pt III	Repeal of FA 1968 ss 34, 36, FA 1973 s 39, FA 1974 s 68	
Sch 4, Pt I	Amendment of ITA 1967 ss 355, 361(1), Sch 10, FA 1970 s 57	s 826(1)-(7), Sch 24, 829
Sch 4, Pt II	Repeal of ITA 1967 ss 363, 364, Sch 10 para 3(1), 7, FA 1968 s 35Sch 24 paras 7-13	
	Amendment of ITA 1967 Sch 10 para 8(3)(c)	Sch 24 paras 7-13
Sch 5	Unnecessary (spent)	
Finance Act 1976 (1976 No 16)		
Pt I		
s 1	Amendment of ITA 1967 s 128(4)	s 987(4)
2	Amendment of ITA 1967 s 142(1)	s 466
3	Amendment of ITA 1967 s 174	s 900(1), (2), (4)
4	Insertion of ITA 1967 s 197(1A)	s 1023
5	Amendment of ITA 1967 s 316(2)	s 390(1), (3)
6 (1)	Amendment of ITA 1967 s 477	s 960
(2)	Amendment of FA 1971 s 20(2)	s 1082
7	Amendment of ITA 1967 s 497	s 460
8	Amendment of ITA 1967 s 525(1)	s 127(1)-(5)
9	Amendment of F(No 2)A 1975 s 1	
10	Unnecessary (obsolete)	
11 (1)-(3)		s 881
(4)	Amendment of ITA 1967 Sch 15	Sch 29
(5)	Amendment of ITA 1967 s 169(1)	s 877
12	Rep by FA 1996 s 132(2) and Sch 5 Pt II	
13		s 805
14	Substitution of FA 1968 s 11	
15	Rep by FA 1996 s 132(2) and Sch 5 Pt II	
16	Rep by FA 1996 s 132(2) and Sch 5 Pt II	
17(1)-(3)(a)(4)(b)		s 996
(3)(b), (4)(a)	Unnecessary (obsolete)	
18	Amendment of FA 1974 s 21	
19	Rep by FA 1983 s 120 and Sch 4	
20	Amendment of FA 1970 s 17	ss 530, 531
21	Substitution of FA 1970 s 17	ss 530, 531
22		s 57
23	Rep by FA 1978 s 5	
24	Amendment of FA 1973 ss 31, 37	

Former Enactment		*Destination in TCA 1997*
Finance Act 1976 (1976 No 16) (contd)		
s 25	Rep by FA 1997 s 146(2) and Sch 9 Pt II	
26	Amendment of FA 1975 s 31(1), insertion of FA 1975 s 31A and Sch 5	
27	Insertion of CTA 1976 s 54(4)	
28	Unnecessary (obsolete)	
29		s 1089(2)
30	Rep by FA 1997 s 146(2) and Sch 9 Pt II	
31		s 373(2)(b)
32		s 376
33	Rep by FA 1978 s 52(1) and Sch 4 Pt I	
34		s 905
Pt VI		
s 81 (1), (3)(a)	Unnecessary (application of schedule)	
82	Unnecessary (care and management)	
83 (2), (6)	Unnecessary (construction and commencement)	
Sch 1, Pt I	Amendment of ITA 1967 ss 138, 141(1A)	ss 458, 465
Sch 5, Pt I	Repeal of ITA 1967 s 125(a) and Sch 2 Rules 5, 6, 7	
	Amendment of ITA 1967 ss 157(c), 557	s 853
Finance Act 1977 (1977 No 18)		
s 1	Amendment of ITA 1967 s 142	s 466
2 (1)	Amendment of ITA 1967 s 236	s 787
(2)	Unnecessary (application of schedule)	
3	Amendment of FA 1974 s 59(3)	s 808
4	Amendment of ITA 1967 s 477(1), (2) and FA 1976 s 6(2)(b)	ss 960, 1082
5 (1)	Unnecessary (obsolete)	
(2)	Unnecessary (application of schedule)	
6 (1), (2)	Unnecessary (obsolete)	
(3)	Unnecessary (application of schedule)	
7	Rep by FA 1980 s 2	
8	Substitution of FA 1974 s 54	
9	Amendment of FA 1974 s 15(3)	s 655(1), (2)
10	Amendment of FA 1974 s 16(1)	s 657(1)
11	Substitution of FA 1974 s 19	
12 (a)	Amendment of FA 1974 s 21	
(b)	Insertion of FA 1974 s 21	
13	Unnecessary (obsolete)	
14		Sch 32, para 23(2)
15	Ceased by FA 1982 s 26(1)	
16 (1), (2)	Amendment of CTA 1976 ss 13, 37	s 78
(3)	Ceased by FA 1982 s 31(2)	
17	Amendment of FA 1982 s 28	
18	Ceased by FA 1982 s 26(1)	
19 (1), (2)	Unnecessary (spent)	
(3)	Rep by FA 1982 s 26(2) and Sch 2	
20-32	Unnecessary (obsolete)	
33	Amendment of CGTA 1975 s 3(3)	s 28
34	Amendment of CGTA 1975 s 31	s 731(1)-(5)(a), Sch 32 para 25
35	Substitution of CGTA 1975 s 32	s 732
36		s 6
37	Unnecessary (spent)	
38	Amendment of FA 1973 s 8(1)	

Former Enactment		*Destination in TCA 1997*
Finance Act 1977 (1977 No 18) (contd)		
s 39 (1)-(5)	Definition of "the former Agreements" unnecessary (obsolete)	s 832
(2)	Unnecessary (spent)	
(4)(b) proviso	Rep by FA 1996 s 132(2) and Sch 5 Pt II	
40	Unnecessary (spent)	
41 (1)	Amendment of CTA 1976 s 171	s 2(4)
(2)	Unnecessary (operative date)	
42	Unnecessary (application of schedule)	
43	Unnecessary (application of schedule)	
53		s 825
54 (1)	Unnecessary (application of schedule)	
55	Unnecessary (care and management)	
56 (2), (7)	Unnecessary (construction and commencement)	
Sch 1, Pt I	Amendment of ITA 1967 Sch 5	
Sch 1, Pt II	Amendment of ITA 1967 ss 1(1), 153(1), 497, 525(1), CTA 1976 ss 66(3)(b), 82(6)	ss 2(1), 3(1); 1032; 460; 127(1)-(5); 143
Sch 1, Pt III	Amendment of ITA 1967 s 138(1), (2)	s 461
Sch 1, Pt IV	Amendment of CTA 1976 ss 58(10), 109(1), 176(6)(a), Sch 5 para 1(6), FA 1968 s 37(4), FA 1972 s16(4), FA 1973 ss 24(9), 26, FA 1974 s 55(4)	s 413; 109(2)-(6); 774(6); Sch 32 para 26; 373(2)(a), 375; 814
Sch 1, Pt V	Amendment of FA 1975 ss 31, 31A, Sch 3, Sch 5, and FA 1976 s 12	
Sch 2, Pt I	Repeal of ITA 1967 ss 355, 357, 369(2), Sch 6 Pts I, II, and III, paras 2, 3, 4, 5, Sch 7, FA 1973 ss 32, 38, and Sch 2, 4, CGTA 1975 s 4(2) proviso, CTA 1976 s 42(6), (7), SI No 143 of 1975 Amendment of FA 1968s 35(2)	
Pt II	Repeal of s 356	
Finance Act 1978 (1978 No 21)		
s 1	Amendment of ITA 1967 s 142	s 466
2	Substitution of ITA 1967 s 143(3)	
3	Amendment of ITA 1967 s 193	s 1016
4 (1)	Amendment of ITA 1967 s 236	s 787
(2)	Unnecessary (application of schedule)	
5	Unnecessary (cesser of FA 1976 s 23)	
6	Unnecessary (obsolete)	
7	Substitution of FA 1973 s 19	s 192
8		s 250
9	Rep by FA 1996 s 132(2) and Sch 5 Pt II	
10 (1)-(6)	Unnecessary (obsolete)	
(7)	Amendment of ITA 1967 s 193(2)	s 1016
11 (1)	Substitution of ITA 1967 s 211(2)	s 1048
(2)	Substitution of ITA 1967 s 504(2)	s 1060
12 (1)	Amendment of FA 1974 s 13	s 654
(2)	Insertion of FA 1974 Sch 3	
13	Amendment of FA 1974 s 15	s 655(1), (2)
14	Amendment of FA 1974 Pt I Ch II	
15 (1), (2)		s 661
(3)	Unnecessary (duplication)	
16 (1)	Amendment of ITA 1967 s 477	s 960
(2)	Unnecessary (obsolete)	
17	Unnecessary (spent)	
18	Unnecessary (obsolete)	
19	Substitution of ITA 1967 s 30	
20	Amendment of FA 1977 Pt I Ch IV	
21	Amendment of CTA 1976 s 28	
22	Amendment of FA 1971 s 26(1)	s 285(1), (2), (3)

Former Enactment		*Destination in TCA 1997*
Finance Act 1978 (1978 No 21) (contd)		
s 23	Amendment of FA 1973 s 8(1)	
24	Amendment of FA 1977 s 40(1)	
25 (1)		s 273(1)
(2)		s 273(2)
(2A)		s 273(3)
(3)		s 273(8)
26		s 310
27 (1)	Amendment of FA 1975 s 31A	
(2)	Amendment of FA 1976 s 12	
28 (1)	Unnecessary (obsolete)	
(2)	Unnecessary (obsolete)	
(3)	Amendment of CTA 1976 s 45	s 729(1)-(6)
(4)	Amendment of CTA 1976 s 64(3)(c)(ii)	s 145(1), (2)(a), (3)-(10)
(5)	Amendment of CTA 1976 s 79(6)	
(6)	Amendment of CTA 1976 s 178(1)	
(7)	Unnecessary (spent)	
46	Amendment of ITA 1967 ss 129, 550, FA 1970 s 17(6A), FA 1971 s 20(2) , CTA 1976 ss 145, 152	ss 991(1); 1080(1); 531(5)(6)(8)(9); 1082; 973, 974, 1080, 1082; 240
47		s 1092
s 52 (1)	Unnecessary (application of schedule)	
53	Unnecessary (care and management)	
54 (2), (8)	Unnecessary (construction and commencement)	
Sch 1		
Pt I	Amendment of ITA 1967 Sch 5	
Pt II	Amendment of ITA 1967 s 138	ss 461, s 464 and FA 1974 s 8
Pt III	Rep by FA 1996 s 132(2) and Sch 5 Pt II	
Pt IV	Insertion of FA 1974 Sch 3	
Sch 2	Unnecessary (obsolete)	
Sch 4	Repeal of ITA 1967 s 220 (in so far as it is unrep) and FA 1976 s 33	
Capital Gains Tax (Amendment) Act 1978 (1978 No 33)		
s 1 (1)		s 1(2)
(2)	Unnecessary (interpretation)	
(3)-(5)	Unnecessary (construction)	
2	Substitution of CGTA 1975 s 3(3)	s 28
3 (1)-(7)		s 556(1)-(7)
4	Ceased by FA 1982 s 30(2)	
5		s 605
6 (1)	Substitution of CGTA 1975 s 14(1)	s 573
(2)	Unnecessary (operative date)	
7 (1)	Substitution of CGTA 1975 s 15(4)(b)	s 577
(2)	Unnecessary (operative date)	
8	Substitution of CGTA 1975 s 27	s 599
9	Insertion of CGTA 1975 s 28(2A)	s 597
10	Substitution of CGTA 1975 s 39(1)	s 611
11	Amendment of CTA 1976 ss 13, 37	s 78
12	Amendment of CTA 1976 s 90	
13	Amendment of CTA 1976 s 127(1)	s 615
14	Amendment of CTA 1976 s 132(2)	s 619
15	Amendment of CGTA 1975 Sch 4	ss 29(8)(9), 544(7), 567 (3)(4), 568, 849(1)(2), 849 (3)-(6), 851, 861(1), 863-865, 869-871, 874, 875, 911, 913-917, 931, 945, 946, 949, 976, 977, 978, 980, 982, 999,

Former Enactment		*Destination in TCA 1997*
Capital Gains Tax (Amendment) Act 1978 (1978 No 33) (contd)		
s 15 (contd)		Sch 1, 1029, 1043, 1051, 1077(1), 1077(2), 1083
16	Unnecessary (application of schedule)	
17	Unnecessary (application of schedule)	
18	Unnecessary (short title, construction and commencement)	
Sch 1		
para 1		s 556(8), (9)
2	Unnecessary (obsolete)	
3	The matter from "and section 4" to the end is unnecessary (obsolete)	s 582
4		s 580
5	Substitution of CGTA 1975 Sch 2 para 2(3)	s 584
6	Unnecessary (obsolete)	
7		s 546(6)
8		s 601(3)
9	Substitution of CGTA 1975 s 32(3)	s 732
10		s 558
Sch 2	Repeal of CGTA 1975 ss 6, 26(7), 29(4), 47(7), Sch 1 Pt I para 13, 14(6) and PtII, Sch 2 para 2(8), Sch 4 para 8(2)(j), CTA 1976 s 13(3)(b)	
	Amendment of CGTA 1975 ss 11(1), (2),16(4), 51(2), Sch 4 para 13, FA 1977 s 16(3)	ss 545(2)(3), 601(1)(2)(4)(5) 544(8), 544(7)
Finance Act 1979 (1979 No 11)		
s 1	Substitution of ITA 1967 s 142(1A)	s 466
2 (1)	Amendment of FA 1977 s 5	
(2)	Unnecessary (application of schedule)	
3 (1), (2)	Unnecessary (obsolete)	
(3)	Unnecessary (application of schedule)	
4	Insertion of ITA 1967 s 138A	s 462
5	Rep by FA 1996 s 132(2) and Sch 5 Pt II	
6	Unnecessary (cesser of ITA 1967 s 224(3), (5), (6), otherwise obsolete)	
7	Unnecessary (spent)	
8 (1		ss 125(1), 471(1)
(2)(a)		s 471(2)
(b)	Rep by FA 1996 s 132(2) and Sch 5 Pt II	
(3)		s 471(3)
(4)		s 125(3)
(4A)		s 125(4)
(5)	Unnecessary (operative date)	
(6)		s 125(2)
9	Amendment of ITA 1967 s 496(2)(b), FA 1974 ss 38(1), 44, 52(b), FA 1978 s 8(2)	s 250
10	Rep by FA 1982 s 8(8)	
11	Rep by FA 1980 s 16	
12	Amendment of ITA 1967 s 488(5)	s 966
13	Amendment of FA 1974 ss 15, 19	s 655(1), (2)
14	Unnecessary (spent)	
15	Amendment of FA 1974 s 20	
16	Amendment of FA 1974 s 21(1)	
17	Amendment of ITA 1967 s 307	s 381(1)
18	Amendment of ITA 1967 s 308	

Former Enactment | *Destination in TCA 1997*

Finance Act 1979 (1979 No 11) (contd)

s 19		Substitution of ITA 1967 s 318(1)	s 392
20		Substitution of ITA 1967 s 319(1)	s 393
21		Amendment of CTA 1976 ss 10(6), 169, FA 1978 s 18(5) proviso	s 243(1), (2), (4)-(9)
22		Insertion of FA 1977 s 25A	
23		Amendment of FA 1975 s 31A and FA 1976 s 12	
24		Amendment of FA 1971 s 22	
25		Amendment of FA 1978 s 25(1)	s 273(1)
26		Unnecessary (obsolete)	
27		Substitution of FA 1976 s 25	
28	(1)-(3)		s 786
	(4)	Amendment of ITA 1967 s 239(8)	s 788
	(5)	Amendment of CTA 1976 s 50(4)(a)	s 706(1)-(3)
29		Amendment of ITA 1967 s 517 and CTA 1976 s 148	s 1064
30		Insertion of ITA 1967 s 70(3A), (3B)	ss 880(2)-(6), 900(3)
31		s 902	
32	(1)	Unnecessary (repeal of ITA 1967 s 144)	
	(2)	Unnecessary (declaratory)	
	(3)	Unnecessary (obsolete)	
33		Insertion of ITA 1967 s 439(1A)	s 791(2)-(4)
34		Amendment of ITA 1967 Sch 12	Sch 22
35		Insertion of CGTA 1975 s 25(9A)	s 604
36		Amendment of CGTA 1975 s 27(1) s 599	
37	(1)	Unnecessary (CGTA 1975 cesser of s 31(4))	
	(2)	Amendment of CGTA 1975 s 31(5)	
58		Unnecessary (care and management)	
59	(2), (6)	Unnecessary (construction and commencement)	
Sch 1			
Pt 1		Amendment of ITA 1967 ss 1(1), 153(1)(dd), 497, 525(1)	ss 2(1), 3(1), 1032, 460, 127(1)-(5)
Pt II		Amendment of ITA 1967 s 138, FA 1974 s 8	ss 461, 464
Sch 2		Unnecessary (obsolete)	

Finance Act 1980 (1980 No 14)

Pt I			
s 1			s 187
2	(1)-(4),(6),(7)		s 188
	(5)	Unnecessary (cesser of FA 1977 s 7)	
s 3		Substitution of ITA 1967 ss 138, 138A Insertion of ITA 1967 138B	ss 461, 462, 472
4	(1), (2)	Unnecessary (obsolete)	
	(3)	Unnecessary (application of schedule)	
5		Amendment of FA 1971 s 11	s 468
6		Amendment of ITA 1967 ss 143, 152(1)	
7		Rep by FA 1997 s 146(2) and Sch 9 Pt II	
8		Unnecessary (obsolete)	
9		Amendment of ITA 1967 s 3	s 1(2)
10		Amendment of ITA 1967 s 115 and Sch 3	s 201, Sch 3
11		Amendment of ITA 1967 s 336	s 213(1), (2)
12		Amendment of ITA 1967 s 340(2)	s 204(1)
13		Substitution of ITA 1967 s 344(1), (2)	
14		Amendment of ITA 1967 s 447 and FA 1971 s 20(2)	ss 794(1), 1082
15		Amendment of FA 1979 s 7(1) and Sch 2	
16		Unnecessary (FA 1979 cesser of s 11)	

Former Enactment		*Destination in TCA 1997*
Finance Act 1980 (1980 No 14) (contd)		
s 17	Amendment of ITA 1967 ss 58, 72, 77, 241, 244, 245, 296	ss 65(1); 1010; 70(2); 284, 300(1); 763-735; 670; 305(1)
18	Substitution of ITA 1967 Pt IX Ch I	
19	Unnecessary (application of schedule)	
20	Unnecessary (obsolete)	
21	Unnecessary (obsolete)	
22	Amendment of FA 1974 ss 15, 19	s 655(1), (2)
23	Unnecessary (obsolete)	
24	Unnecessary (FA 1974 cesser of ss 20, 21)	
25	Rep by FA 1983 s 120 and Sch 4	
26	Ceased by FA 1988 s 52(3)	
27	Substitution of FA 1974 s 22(2)	s 658(2)(a)
28	Rep by FA 1996 s 132(2) and Sch 5 Pt II	
37	Amendment of FA 1977 Pt I Ch I	
38		s 442(1)
39		s 443
39A(1)-(7)(10)	Definition of "EEC Treaty" unnecessary (obsolete)	s 445
(2) proviso	Deleted by FA 1988 s 35	
(8), (9)	Deleted by FA 1989 s 23	
39B(1)-(7)(a), (b),(8)-(10)		s 446(1)-(12)
(7)(c)	Rep by FA 1988 s 36(1)	
39C		s 449
39D		s 450
40		s 442(2)
41 (1)		s 448(1)
(2)		s 448(2)(a)
(3)-(5)(8)(9)		s 448(3)-(7)
(6), (7)	Unnecessary (obsolete)	
42 (1)-(4)	Unnecessary (obsolete)	
(5)	Substitution of CTA 1976 s 58(10)	
(6)	Amendment of CTA 1976 s 64	s 145(1), (2)(a), (3)-(10)
43	Unnecessary (obsolete)	
44		s 453
45 (1)-(3), (5)-(8)		s 147, Sch 32 para 4
(1A) 1st proviso para (a)	Unnecessary (obsolete)	
(4)	Unnecessary (obsolete)	
46		s 148
47 (1)	Amendment of CTA 1976 s 182	Sch 32, para 16(1)-(4)
(2)		Sch 32, para 5(2)
48 (1)	Amendment of CTA 1976 s 184	Sch 32, para 18
(2)		Sch 32, para 6(2)
49		s 149
50		s 444
51		ss 151, 447
52	Amendment of FA 1977 s 40(1)	
53 (1)	Amendment of FA 1975 s 31A	
(2)	Amendment of FA 1976 s 12	
(3)-(6)	Unnecessary (obsolete)	
54	Amendment of ITA 1967 ss 416(5), 421	ss 933(1)-(7)(f), 934
55	Substitution of ITA 1967 s 4	s 12
56	Amendment of FA 1973 s 24	

Former Enactment		*Destination in TCA 1997*
Finance Act 1980 (1980 No 14) (contd)		
s 57	Amendment of ITA 1967 ss 448(5), 500	ss 798(1)-(3), 1052
58	Amendment of ITA 1967 s 265(4)	s 274(1), (3), (4), (5), (8)
59	Substitution of ITA 1967 s 516	s 1056
60	Substitution of FA 1976 s 34(2)	s 905
61	Amendment of CGTA 1975 ss 2(3), 13(4). 25(9A)(b), Sch 4 para 10(2)	ss 5, 1028, 604, 1029
62	Amendment of CGTA 1975 ss 7(1), 46	ss 532(1), 541
Pt VI		
89	Substitution of FA 1978 s 47(1)	s 1092
95	Unnecessary (care and management)	
96 (2), (7)	Unnecessary (construction and commencement)	
Sch 1		
Pt I	Amendment of ITA 1967 s 141(1A), FA 1969 s 3	ss 465, 467
Pt II	Substitution of ITA 1967 Sch 3	s 201(1)(a), Sch 3
Pt III	Amendment of ITA 1967 ss 82(3), 139, 145(2), 183(7), 307(2)(a)(i), Sch 15, FA 1967 s 12, FA 1969 s 3(1)(a), FA 1974 ss 8(1), 28(6), FA 1976 s 11(3) Repeal of FA 1969 ss 3(6), (8), FA 1978 s 3, FA 1979 s 7(2)(b)	ss 470(1)-(3), 921(1) 381(2)-(7), Sch 29, 469(1), 467, 464, 881
Finance Act 1981 (1981 No 16)		
1	Amendment of FA 1980 ss 1, 2	ss 187, 188
2 (1), (2)	Unnecessary (obsolete)	
(3)	Unnecessary (application of Schedule)	
3	Amendment of FA 1980 s 8	
4	Amendment of ITA 1967 s 128	s 987(1)-(3)
5	Amendment of ITA 1967 s 198(1)	s 1024
6	Rep by FA 1997 s 146(2) and Sch 9 Pt II	
7	Amendment of FA 1970 s 17(2)	s 531(1), (3), (4)
8 (a)	Amendment of FA 1979 s 7	
(b)	Amendment of FA 1979 Sch 2	
9	Amendment of ITA 1967 ss 81(3),111(1)(b). 553(2), FA 1970 s 23(2), F(TPCM)A 1974 s 11(1), (2)	ss 75(3); 111, 90(1)-(3), 683
10	Insertion of FA 1974 s 20B	s 683
11	Insertion of ITA 1967 s 334(2A)	s 208(3)
12	Amendment of ITA 1967 s 477(2)	
13	Rep by FA 1996 s 132(2) and Sch 5 Pt II	
15 (1)	Amendment of CTA 1976 s 6(4)	
(2), (3)	Unnecessary (obsolete)	
16	Substitution of CTA 1976 s 143(1), (2)	s 884
17 (a)	Insertion of FA 1980 s 39(1A)-(1D)	s 443
(b)	Insertion of FA 1980 s 39A	s 445
18	Rep by FA 1997 s 146(2) and Sch 9 Pt II	
19	Amendment of FA 1973 s 34(3)	s 234(3)-(8)
20 (1)	Amendment of FA 1975 s 31A	
(2)	Amendment of FA 1976 s 12	
(3), (5), (6)	Unnecessary (obsolete). There is no s 20(4)	
21	Unnecessary (obsolete)	
22	Insertion of CTA 1976 s 152(4)	s 240
23 (1)(a)		ss 325(1), 326(1), 327(1), 329(1), (2)
(b)		s 329(7)
(c)		s 329(9)(a)
(1)(d)	Unnecessary (obsolete)	

Former Enactment	*Destination in TCA 1997*
Finance Act 1981 (1981 No 16) (contd)	
s 23 (2)	ss 325(2), 326(4), 327(2)
proviso	ss 325(3), 326(5), 327(3)
(3)(a)	ss 325(4), 326(6), 327(4)
(b), (c)	s 329(8)
(4)	s 329(6)
(5)	ss 325(5), 326(7), 327(5)
(6)(a)	ss 325(6)(a), 326(8), 327(7)
(b)	s 325(6)(b)
(7)(a)	ss 325(7)(a), 326(9), 327(7)
(b)	s 325(7)(b)
(8)	s 329(3)
(9)(a)	s 329(4)(a)
(b)	s 329(5)
(10)	s 329(11)
(11)	s 329(12)
23 .... Sch 32, para 14 .. Sch 32, para 14 of the Bill saves the provisions of s 23 FA 1981 (in so far as that section applied to areas other than the Custom House Docks Area)	
24 (1)	s 326(1)
(2)(a)	s 326(1)
(b)	s 326(1)
(c) ..... Unnecessary (obsolete)	
(d) ..... Unnecessary (obsolete)	
s 24 (2) (e)	s 326(8), (9)
(f)	s 326(9)
(g)	s 329(4)(b)
(3)	s 326(10)
24 .... Sch 32, para 14. . Sch 32, para 14 of the Bill saves the provision of FA 1981 s 24 (in so far as that section applied to areas other than the Custom House Docks Area)	
25	Sch 32, para 9
26	Sch 32, para 10
27 .... Amendment of ITA 1967 s 254(1)	s 271
28 .... Substitution of F(MP)A 1968 s 17(1)	s 640
29 (1) .... Unnecessary (declaratory)	
(2)(a) ..... Substitution of F(MP)A 1968 s 18	s 641
(b) ..... Unnecessary (obsolete)	
(3) .... Substitution of F(MP)A 1968 ss 20, 21, 22	ss 643-645
(4) .... Amendment of ITA 1967 Sch 15	Sch 29
52	s 1093
53 .... Unnecessary (care and management)	
54 (2), (7) .... Unnecessary (construction and commencement)	
Sch 1 .... Amendment of ITA 1967 ss 138A, 138B(1), 141(1A), FA 1969 s 3(1), FA 1971 s 11(2)	ss 462, 472, 465, 467, 468
Finance Act 1982 (1982 No 14)	
s 1 .... Amendment of FA 1980 ss 1(2), 2(6)	ss 187, 188
2 (1), (2) .... Unnecessary (obsolete)	
(3) .... Unnecessary (application of schedule)	
3 .... Amendment of FA 1980 s 8	
4 (1) .... Unnecessary (commencement)	

Former Enactment		*Destination in TCA 1997*
Finance Act 1982 (1982 No 14) (contd)		
s 4 (2)-(6), (9)		s 121
(7)	Amendment of ITA 1967 s 178(1)	s 897(1)-(5)
(8)	Amendment of ITA 1967 Sch 15	Sch 29
5 (1)	Insertion of ITA 1967 s 142A	s 473
(2)	Amendment of ITA 1967 s 198(1)(a)	s 1024, Sch 29 and Sch 15
6	Rep by FA 1996 s 132(2) and Sch 5 Pt II	
7	Insertion of ITA 1967 s 152(1A)	
8 (1)-(5), (7), (9)		s 122
(6)	Amendment of ITA 1967 s 178(1)	s 897(1)-(5)
(8)	Unnecessary (cesser of FA 1979 s 10)	
9 (1), (2)		s 205
(3)	Unnecessary (commencement)	
10	Amendment of ITA 1967 s 485(5)	s 962(3)
11	Amendment of ITA 1967 s 486	s 963
12	Amendment of FA 1979 s 7(1) and Sch 2	
13	Rep by FA 1996 s 132(2) and Sch 5 Pt II	
14	Amendment of ITA 1967 s 477(2)	s 960
15	Amendment of FA 1974 s 21A(1)	
16	Amendment of FA 1974 s 22	s 658(1)
18		s 225
19 (1)-(2A),		s 482(1)-(4),
(3)-(4A)(5)		(5), (6), (7)
(6)		s 482(10)
20 (1)-(6), (8)		s 840
(7)	Unnecessary (cesser of FA 1973 s 24)	
21	Rep by FA 1997 s 146(2) and Sch 9 Pt II	
22	Rep by FA 1997 s 146(2) and Sch 9 Pt II	
23	Unnecessary (obsolete)	
24 (1)	Amendment of FA 1975 s 31A	
(2)	Amendment of FA 1976 s 12	
25	Unnecessary (obsolete)	
26 (1)(a)	Unnecessary (cesser of FA 1977 ss 15, 17(1)(a), 18)	
(b)	Unnecessary (obsolete)	
(2)	Unnecessary (application of schedule)	
27 (1)	Amendment of CTA 1976 s 6(4)	
(2)	Unnecessary (obsolete)	
(3)	Unnecessary (obsolete)	
(4)	Amendment of ITA 1967 s 550	s 1080(1)
28	Unnecessary (spent)	
29	Unnecessary (interpretation)	
30 (1)	Amendment of CGTA 1975 s 3	s 28
(2)	Unnecessary (cesser of CGT(A)A 1978 s 4)	
(3)	Unnecessary (obsolete)	
31 (1)	Amendment of CTA 1976 s 13	s 78
(2)	Unnecessary (cesser of FA 1977 s 16(3))	
32	Amendment of CGTA 1975 ss 13(4), 16 and CGT(A)A 1978 Sch 1	ss 546(6), 556(8)(9), 558, 580, 582, 584, 601, 732, 1028,
33	Insertion of CGTA 1975 s 5(3)	s 1042
34 (1)	Substitution of CGTA 1975 Sch 4 para 11(5)	s 980
(2), (3)	Unnecessary (obsolete)	
35	Amendment of CTA 1976 s 90(4)	
36 (1)		s 648
(2)-(3A)	Deleted by FA 1992 s 60(2)	
(4)-(6)		s 649
(7)	Deleted by FA 1992 s 68(b)	
37		s 650

Former Enactment		*Destination in TCA 1997*
Finance Act 1982 (1982 No 14) (contd)		
s 38		s 651
39		s 652
40 (1), (2)		s 653
(3)	Insertion of CTA 1976 s 25(8)	
(a)		s 607(1)(e)
(b)	Ceased by FA 1992 s 24(2)	
42 (a)	Substitution of CTA 1976 s 36(3)(a)	s 713(1)-(6)
(b)	Deletion of CTA 1976 s 37	
43	Unnecessary (spent)	
44	Unnecessary (spent)	
45	Unnecessary (spent)	
46	Unnecessary (spent)	
47	Unnecessary (spent)	
48	Unnecessary (spent)	
49	Unnecessary (spent)	
50	Definition of "ordinary share capital" unnecessary (duplication)	s 509
51 (1)-(7)		s 510
(8)	Amendment of ITA 1967 Sch 15	Sch 29
52		s 511
53		s 512
54		s 513
55		s 514
56		s 515
57		s 516
58		s 517
58A	(s 58A inserted by FA 1997 s 50)	s 518
59		s 1082
60	Amendment of ITA 1967 ss 128, 173(6), 426(3), 500, FA 1968 s 6(5), CTA 1976 s 64(9), FA 1976 s 34(4), FA 1979 s 31(5), FA 1980 s 45(8)	ss 987(1)-(3), 889(10) 939, 1052, 886, s 145(1), (2)(a), (3)-(10), 905, 902, s 147, Sch 32 para 4
61	Amendment of ITA 1967 s 371	s 752
62	Insertion of CGTA 1975 s 9(3), (4)	s 547
63		ss 586(3), 587(4)
104	Unnecessary (care and management)	
105(2), (7)	Unnecessary (construction and commencement)	
Sch 1	Amendment of ITA 1967 ss 138, 138A, 141(1A), 142(1), FA 1969 s 3(1), FA 1971 s 11(2), FA 1974 s 8(1). Cesser of ITA 1967 ss 139, 140	ss 461, 462, 464-468
Sch 2, Pt I		
para 1	Unnecessary (cesser of FA 1977 s 19(3))	
2, 3	Unnecessary (spent)	
Sch 2, Pt II		
para 1	Amendment of FA 1980 s 41(2)	s 448(2)(a)
2	Unnecessary (spent)	
3	Amendment of FA 1980 ss 47(2), 48(2)	Sch 32, paras 5(2), 6(2)
4	Unnecessary (spent)	
Sch 3		Sch 11
Finance Act 1983 (1983 No 15)		
Pt I		
s 1	Amendment of FA 1980 s 1(2)	s 187
2	Amendment of FA 1980 s 8	
3		s 1025

Former Enactment		*Destination in TCA 1997*
Finance Act 1983 (1983 No 15) (contd)		
s 4		s 1026(1), (2)
5	Amendment of FA 1982 s 6	
6	Insertion of ITA 1967 s 195A	s 1020
7	Unnecessary (cesser of ITA 1967 Pt XX)	
8	Amendment of ITA 1967 s 344	
9	Amendment of ITA 1967 ss 416, 421, 428, 429, 430, deletion of s 420	ss 933(1)-(7)(f), 934, 941, 942(1)-(8), (10), 943
10	Amendment of ITA 1967 s 496(2A)	
11	Substitution of FA 1974 s 15	s 655(1), (2)
12	Amendment of FA 1974 s 20A	
13	Amendment of FA 1982 s 13(1)	
14	Substitution of ITA 1967 s 307(1A)	
15	Amendment of FA 1974 s 22	s 658
16	Unnecessary (spent)	
17 Preamble	Unnecessary (declaratory).	
(1)	Unnecessary (cesser of FA 1968 s 13)	
(2)	Amendment of ITA 1967 s 175	s 891
18		s 908
19 (1), (2)		s 58
(3)	Unnecessary (duplication)	
(4)	Unnecessary (operative date)	
19A	(s 19A inserted by DCITPA 1996 s 12)	s 859
20		s 909
21 (1), (2)		s 892
(3)	Amendment of ITA 1967 Sch 15	Sch 29
22 (1), (2)		s 885
(3)	Amendment of ITA 1967 Sch 15	Sch 29
23		s 1086
24	Amendment of FA 1982 s 58(1).	s 517
25	Substitution of FA 1982 ss 21(3), 23(3)	
26 (1)	Amendment of FA 1975 s 31A	
(2)	Amendment of FA 1976 s 12	
(3), (4)	Unnecessary (obsolete)	
27	Unnecessary (spent)	
28 (1)	Unnecessary (cesser of FA 1978 s 28(1))	
(2)	Unnecessary (obsolete)	
(3)	Unnecessary (obsolete)	
29	Unnecessary (spent)	
30	Unnecessary (spent)	
31	Amendment of FA 1982 ss 43, 44, 45, 46	
32		s 220
33	Amendment of CTA 1976 s 56(1)	
34	Amendment of FA 1978 Sch 2	
35	Insertion of CTA 1976 s 98(9)	s 438
36	Substitution of CTA 1976 s 143(7)	s 1071
37	Substitution of CTA 1976 s 146(1)	s 864, Pt 40 Ch I, s 949
38		s 159
39		s 160
40		s 161
41		s 162
42 (1)		s 163
(2)	Unnecessary (obsolete)	
43		s 164
44		s 165
45		s 166

Former Enactment		*Destination in TCA 1997*
Finance Act 1983 (1983 No 15) (contd)		
s 46 (1)-(8)		s 167
(9)	Unnecessary (spent)	
47 (1)-(3)		s 168
(4)	Amendment of ITA 1967 s 361(1)	s 826(1)-(7)
47A	(s 47A inserted by FA 1995 s 37)	s 169
48 (1),(2)(a), (3)(4)		s 170
(2)(b)	Unnecessary (spent)	
49	Unnecessary (spent)	
50 (1)-(10), (11)(a)-(d) (12), (13)		s 171
(11)(e)	Rep by FA 1997 s 146(2) and Sch 9 Pt II	
51	Unnecessary (cesser of CTA 1976 ss 16(9), 18(4), 25(8), 26(3) proviso para (b), 90, 91, 167, 168)	
52	Unnecessary (spent)	
53		s 172
54	Rep by FA 1988 s 70(2)	
55	Amendment of CGTA 1975 Sch 4 para 8	s 945
56 (1)	Unnecessary (operative date)	
(2)-(10)		s 571
Pt V		
s 94		s 1078
Pt VII		
s 120	Unnecessary (application of schedule)	
121	Unnecessary (care and management).	
122(2), (6)	Unnecessary (construction and commencement)	
Sch 4	Repeal of ITA 1967 s 340(2)(d)(ff)(g), (3), FA 1974 ss 13(2)(3), 17, 18, 19, 21A, 28, Sch 3, FA 1976 s 19, FA 1980 s 25	
	Amendment of FA 1974 ss 13(1), 20B(3)(b), FA 1978 s 15(2)	ss 654, 657(6), 661
Finance Act 1984 (1984 No 9)		
s 1	Amendment of FA 1980 ss 1(2), 2(6)	ss 187, 188
2	Unnecessary (obsolete)	
3 (1), (2)	Unnecessary (obsolete)	
(3)	Unnecessary (application of schedule)	
4	Amendment of FA 1982 s 6(2)	
5	Amendment of ITA 1967 s 142A(2)(a)(i)	s 473
6	Amendment of ITA 1967 s 432(1)	ss 864(1), 949(1)
7	Unnecessary (cesser of FA 1968 s 41(9))	
8	Amendment of FA 1969 s 3(1)	s 467
9	Substitution of ITA 1967 s 349	s 235
10	Amendment of FA 1983 s 16	
11(1)(3)(4)		s 488(1)-(3)
(2)	Unnecessary (obsolete)	
12 (1)		s 489(1)
1st proviso	Deleted by FA 1991 s 15(1)(a)	
2nd proviso		s 489(2)
(2), (7)		s 488(1)
(3)		s 489(3), (6)
1st proviso		s 489(4)
2nd proviso		s 489(5)

Former Enactment		*Destination in TCA 1997*
Finance Act 1984 (1984 No 9) (contd)		
s 12 (4)		s 489(7)
(5)		s 489(8)
(6)		s 489(9)
(6A)		s 489(10)
(8)		s 489(11)
(9)	Rep by FA 1996 s 132(2) and Sch 5 Pt II	
(10)		s 489(12)
(10A)		s 489(13)
(11)		s 489(15)
proviso	Deleted by FA 1996 s 17(c)(ii)	
13 (1)-(2C)		s 490
(2) proviso	Deleted by s 25(c)(i) FA 1993	
(3)	Amendment of ITA 1967 s 198(1)	s 1024
13A	(s 13A inserted by FA 1989 s 9)	s 491
13B	(s 13B inserted by FA 1996 s 20)	s 492
14		s 493
14A	(s 14A inserted by FA 1995 s 17(1)(d))	s 494
15 (1)-(12)		s 495
(13)	Deleted by FA 1991 s 15(d)	
16 (1)-(3)		s 496
(2)(a)(iii)	Deleted by FA 1991 s 15(e)(i)	
(4)		s 488(4)
16A	(s 16A inserted by FA 1995 s17(1)(g))	s 497
17		s 498
18		s 499
19		s 500
20		s 501
21		s 502
22		s 503
23		s 504
24 (1)-(8)		s 505
(9)	Amendment of ITA 1967 Sch 15	Sch 29
25		s 506
26 (1)-(4)		s 507
(1A)	Deleted by FA 1991 s 15(1)(f)	
27		s 508
28 (1)		ss 45(2), 48(3)
(2)		ss 45(3), 48(4)
(3)		ss 45(4), 48(5)
29 (1)	Definition of "tax" unnecessary (duplication)	s 815(1)
(2)		s 815(2)
(2A)		s 815(3)
(3)(a)		s 815(4)
(b)	Unnecessary (obsolete)	
(4), (5)		s 815(5), (6)
29 (6)	Amendment of ITA 1967 Sch 15	Sch 29
(7)	Unnecessary (operative date)	
30	Amendment of FA 1976 s 30	
31	Amendment of FA 1982 ss 56(1), (2), 58(1) and Sch 3	ss 515, 517, Sch 11
32		s 484
33	Rep by FA 1996 s 132(2) and Sch 5 Pt II	

Former Enactment		*Destination in TCA 1997*
Finance Act 1984 (1984 No 9) (contd)		
s 34	Unnecessary (spent)	
35	Amendment of ITA 1967 ss 251(4)(d), 254(2A)(a), 264(1) proviso para (ii), (3) proviso para (ii), 265(1) proviso para (ii)	ss 271(4), 272, 274(1)(3)-(5),(8)
36		s 268(1)(a)(ii), (9)(a)
37	Amendment of FA 1981 s 23 Sch 32, para 14	ss 325, 326, 327, 329
38	Amendment of FA 1981 s 25	Sch 32, para 9
39	Amendment of FA 1981 s 26(1)	Sch 32, para 10
40 (1)-(10)(a)		s 403
(10)(b)	Unnecessary (obsolete)	
(11)	Unnecessary (obsolete)	
41	Insertion of CTA 1976 s 84A	ss 134, 134(1)(4)
42 (1), (2), (3)		s 138
(4), (5)	Unnecessary (obsolete)	
43	Amendment of FA 1978 Sch 2 Pt I	
44	Amendment of FA 1982 ss 43, 44, 45, 46	
45 (a)	Amendment of FA 1980 s 38	s 442(1)
(b)	Amendment of FA 1980s 39	s 443
46	Amendment of FA 1983s 51(2)	
47	Amendment of FA 1983s 52	
48-65	Rep by FA 1996 s 132(2) and Sch 5 Pt II	
66 (a)		s 607
(b)	Ceased by FA 1988 s 70(2)(b)	
67	Insertion of CGTA 1975 s 25(10A)	s 604
Pt VI		
s 115	Unnecessary (care and management)	
116(2), (7)	Unnecessary (construction and commencement)	
Sch 1		
Pt I	Amendment of ITA 1967 ss 1(1), 153(1)(dd),497, 525(1)	ss 2(1), 3(1), 1032, 460 127(1)-(5)
Pt II	Amendment of ITA 1967 ss 138, 138A	ss 461, 462
Sch 2		Sch 10
Finance Act 1985 (1985 No 10)		
s 1	Amendment of FA 1980 ss 1(2), 2(6),	ss 187, 188
2	Amendment of FA 1984 s 2	
3 (1), (2)	Unnecessary (obsolete)	
(3)	Unnecessary (application of schedule)	
4	Substitution of ITA 1967 s 138A	s 462
5	Amendment of FA 1982 s 6	
6 (1)	Substitution of ITA 1967 s 125	s 984(1), (2)
(2)		s 984(3)
7	Amendment of ITA 1967 s 142A(2)	s 473
8	Amendment of ITA 1967 s 344	
9	Amendment of FA 1968 ss 7(5), 8	ss 989(4), (5), 990
10 (1)(a)		s 664(1)(a)
(b)	Unnecessary (obsolete)	
(2)-(6)		s 664(2)-(6)
11	Amendment of FA 1983 s 16	
12	Amendment of ITA 1967 s 550(4)	s 1080(2)-(4)
13	Amendment of FA 1984 ss 11(1), 12(4), 15(7)(b), 26, 27(8)	ss 488(1)-(3), 489(7) 495, 507, 508
14 (1)	Substitution of FA 1969 s 18(2)(b)	
(2)	Unnecessary (operative date)	
15	Substitution of FA 1973 s 21	s 767
16	Unnecessary (spent)	

Former Enactment		*Destination in TCA 1997*
Finance Act 1985 (1985 No 10) (contd)		
s 17 (1)	Amendment of FA 1975 s 31A	
(2)	Amendment of FA 1976 s 12	
(3)	Unnecessary (application)	
18	Amendment of FA 1984 ss 49, 51	
19	Unnecessary (spent)	
20	Amendment of ITA 1967 ss 251(4)(d), 254(2A)(a), 264(1) proviso para (ii), 264(3) proviso para (ii), 265(1) proviso para (iii)	ss 283(3), 271(4) 272, 274(1)(3)-(5)(8)
21	Sch 32, para 11. . Sch 32 para 14 of the Bill saves the provisions of FA 1985 s 21 (in so far as that section applied to areas other than the Custom House Docks Area)	
(1)(a)		s 327(1)(a)
(b)	Unnecessary (construction)	
(2)(a)(i)		s 327(1)
(ii)		s 327(3)(a)(ii)
(iii)	Unnecessary (spent)	
(iv)		s 327(1)
(v)	Unnecessary (obsolete)	
(vi)		s 327(1)
(vii)		s 329(9)(b)
(viii)		s 327(4)
(ix)		s 327(6), (7)
(x)		s 327(7)
(xi)		s 329(4)(b)
(xii)		s 329(12)
(b)	Unnecessary (obsolete)	
(3)		s 327(8)
(4)		s 327(9)
(5)		s 329(10)
22 (1)		ss 326(1), 329(1)
(2)		s 326(2)
(3)		s 326(3)
(4)	Unnecessary (spent)	
(5)		s 329(10)
22	Sch 32, para 11. . Sch 32, para 14 of the Bill saves the provisions of FA 1985 s 22 (in so far as that section applied to areas other than the Custom House Docks Areas)	
23 (1)	Substitution of CTA 1976 s 6(4)	
(2)	Unnecessary (spent)	
24		s 218
25	Amendment of FA 1983 s 52	
Pt V		
s 60	Amendment of ITA 1967 s 143(5)	
Pt VI		
s 69		s 44
70	Unnecessary (care and management)	
71 (2), (7)	Unnecessary (construction and commencement)	

Former Enactment		*Destination in TCA 1997*
Finance Act 1985 (1985 No 10) (contd)		
Sch 1	Amendment of ITA 1967 ss 138, 141(1A),	ss 461, 465, 467, 468 FA 1969 s 3(1), FA 1971 s 11(2)
Finance Act 1986 (1986 No 13)		
s 1	Amendment of FA 1980 s 2(6)	s 188
2	Amendment of FA 1984 s 2	
3 (1), (2)	Unnecessary (obsolete)	
(3)	Unnecessary (application of schedule)	
4	Substitution of ITA 1967 s 141	s 465
5	Amendment of FA 1967 s 12(1)	s 469(1)
6	Amendment of FA 1982 s 6	
7	Insertion of FA 1979 s 8(6)	s 125(2)
8	Rep by FA 1997 s 146(2) and Sch 9 Pt II	
9 (1)(a), (b)(i), (iii)		s 128(1)
(b)(ii)	Unnecessary (obsolete)	
(2)-(11)(a)		s 128(2)-(11)
(11)(b)	Amendment of ITA 1967 Sch 15	Sch 29
10 (1), (2)(a)(b), (6)	Rep by FA 1992 s 12 for share options granted on or after 29.1.92. Section 10 still applies to share options granted before that date	Sch 32, para 7
(2)(c), (3)-(5)	Unnecessary (obsolete)	
11	Substitution of FA 1982 s 52(7), (8)	s 511
12 (1)-(8)	Definitions of "full-time director" and "full-time employee" deleted by FA 1996 s 12 and definition of "ordinary share capital" unnecessary (duplication)	s 479
(9)	Deleted by FA 1996 s 132(2) and Sch 5 Pt II	
13	Amendment of FA 1984 s 12(11)	s 489(15)
14	Ceased by FA 1992 s 13	
15 (1)	Amendment of FA 1975 s 31A	
(2)	Amendment of FA 1976 s 12	
(3)	Unnecessary (application)	
16	Unnecessary (obsolete)	
17-30	Rep by FA 1997 s 146(2) and Sch 9 Pt II	
31	Definition of "operative date" unnecessary (spent)	s 256
32		s 257
33 (1)-(9), (a)-(d), (10)		s 258
(9)(e)	Rep by FA 1997 s 146(2) and Sch 9 Pt II	
33A(1),(2), (2) proviso para (b),(3),(4)	(s 33A inserted by FA 1996 s 42)	s 260
(2) proviso para (a)	Unnecessary (obsolete)	
34 (a)	Unnecessary (cesser of CTA 1976 s 31(1), (2), (3), (6))	
(b)	Amendment of CTA 1976 s 31(4), (9)	
35 (1)(a)-(cc)		s 261
(d), (e)	Deleted by FA 1992 s 22(1)(b)(ii)	
(2)-(4)	Unnecessary (obsolete)	
(5)	Unnecessary (cesser of ITA 1967 s 344)	
36		s 262

Former Enactment		*Destination in TCA 1997*
Finance Act 1986 (1986 No 13) (contd)		
s 37(1)		s 263
(1) proviso para (ii),(2)		
(1) proviso para (i) (3), (4)	Unnecessary (obsolete)	
37A	(s 37A inserted by FA 1992 s 22(1)(c))	s 264
37B	(s 37B inserted by FA 1992 s 22(1)(c))	s 265
38		s 266
39		s 267
40 (1)	Amendment of ITA 1967 Sch 15	Sch 29
(2)	Amendment of FA 1983 s 94(2)	s 1078
41 (1), (2)	Definition of "designated area" unnecessary (obsolete)	s 322(1)
(3)		s 322(4)
42	Sch 32, para 11 of the Bill saves the provisions of FA 1986 s 42 (in so far as that section applied to areas other than the Custom House Docks Area)	Sch 32, para 11
(1)	Definitions of "multi-storey car-park", "qualifying period" and "the relevant local authority" unnecessary (obsolete)	s 323(1)
(2)		s 323(2)(a), (3)(a)
1st proviso		s 323(2)(b)
2nd proviso		s 323(4)
(3)	Deleted by FA 1991 s 22(2)	
(4)	Unnecessary (obsolete)	
(4)proviso		s 323(3)(b)
(5), (6), (8), (9)	Unnecessary (obsolete)	
(7)		s 323(5)
43	Deleted by FA 1994 s 35(1)(b)	
44	Sch 32, para 12 of the Bill saves the provisions of FA 1986 s 44 (in so far as that section applied to areas other than the Custom House Docks Area)	Sch 32, para 12
(1)(a)(b)	Definition of "qualifying period" and "the relevant local authority" unnecessary (obsolete)	s 328(1)
(b) proviso	Deleted by FA 1995 s 32(1)(c)	
44 (1)(c)(f)(g)	Unnecessary (obsolete)	
(d)		s 329(9)(b)
(e)		s 328(3)
(2)		s 328(2)
(3)		s 329(12)
(4)	Rep by FA 1996 s 132(2) and Sch 5 Pt II	
(5)	Amendment of ITA 1967 s 198(1)	s 1024
45	Sch 32, para 13 of the Bill saves the provisions of FA 1986 s 45 (in so far as that section applied to areas other than the Custom House Docks Area)	Sch 32, para 13
(1)(a)(c)		s 324(1)
(b)	Unnecessary (obsolete)	
(2)		s 324(2)
1st proviso para (a)	Unnecessary (obsolete)	
1st proviso para (b)		s 324(3)
2nd proviso	Unnecessary (obsolete)	

Former Enactment		*Destination in TCA 1997*
Finance Act 1986 (1986 No 13) (contd)		
s 46 (1)-(3)		s 1013(1)-(3)
(4)	Rep by FA 1997 s 146(2) and Sch 9 Pt II	
(5)	Unnecessary (obsolete)	
(6)		s 1013(4)(b)
47	Amendment of FA 1985 s 16(1)(b)(i)	
48 (1)-(4)	Definitions of "specified date" (obsolete) and "tax" (duplication) unnecessary	s 1084(1)-(4)
49	Amendment of FA 1976 s 30(1)	
50 (1)		s 373(2)(c)
(2)	Amendment of FA 1976 s 32	s 376
51	Amendment of FA 1981 s 25(1)	Sch 32, para 9
52 (1)		s 317(3)
(2)	Insertion of ITA 1967 s 264(3A)	s 272
53	Amendment of FA 1984 s 40	s 403
54	Insertion of CTA 1976 s 84A(10)	s 133(4)
55 (1)	Amendment of CTA 1976 ss 25(5), 26(4)	ss 157, 158
(2)	Unnecessary (operative date)	
56 (1)	Amendment of CTA 1976 s 70	
(2)	Amendment of CTA 1976 s 39A	
57 (1)	Substitution of CTA 1976 s 155(10)	s 4(2)-(6)
(2)	Unnecessary (operative date)	
58	Unnecessary (spent)	
59 (a)	Insertion of CTA 1976 s 33(1A), (1B)	s 707
(b)	Insertion of CTA 1976 s 39(4A)	s 715
(c)	Insertion of CTA 1976 s 40(1A)	s 716
(d)	Amendment of CTA 1976 s 50	s 706(1)-(3)
60	Amendment of CGTA 1975 s 3(3)	s 28
61	Unnecessary (spent)	
Pt VI		
112(1), (2)		s 7
(3)	Unnecessary (operative date)	
113(1)-(3)	Definition of "tax" in s 113(1) unnecessary (duplication)	s 887
(4)	Unnecessary (cesser)	
(5)		s 928(2), (3)
(6)		s 967
114(1)	Amendment of ITA 1967 s 429	s 942(1)-(8), (10)
(2)	Amendment FA 1976 s 30	
(3)	Amendment of FA 1983 s 107	
(4)	Unnecessary (operative date)	
115		s 1001
116(1)	Substitution of ITA 1967 s 161	s 852(1), (2)
(2)		s 852(3)
117	Unnecessary (care and management)	
118(2), (7), (8)	Unnecessary (construction and commencement)	
Sch 1	Amendment of ITA 1967 ss 138, 138A(2), 138B(1), FA 1974 s 8(1)	ss 461, 462 472, 464
Sch 2	Rep by FA 1992 s 12	
Sch 3	Unnecessary (obsolete)	
Sch 4		
Pt I, II		Sch 5
Pts III, IV, V, VI, VII	Unnecessary (obsolete)	
Income Tax (Amendment) Act 1986 (1986 No 34)		
s 1	Substitution of ITA 1967 s 110	s 112
2	Unnecessary (short title and construction)	

Former Enactment			Destination in TCA 1997
Finance Act 1987 (1987 No 10)			
Pt I			
s 1		Amendment of FA 1982 s 6	
2	(1)	Unnecessary (duplication)	
	(2)		s 664(1)(a)
	proviso		s 664(1)(b)(i)
3		Amendment of FA 1986 s 16	
4		Rep by FA 1994 s 157(1)	
5		Amendment of FA 1986 s 14	
6		Rep by FA 1997 s 146(2) and Sch 9 Pt II	
7	(1)-(4)		s 259
	(5)	Unnecessary (construction)	
8		Amendment of FA 1984s 12	ss 488, 489
9		Insertion of FA 1984 s 13(2A), (2B), (2C)	s 490
10		Insertion of FA 1984 s 15(3A), (13)	s 495
11		Amendment of FA 1984 s 16	ss 488(4), 496
12		Insertion of FA 1984 s 26(1A) and substitution of Sch 2 para 1	Sch 10
13			s 520
14			s 521
14A		(s 14A inserted by FA 1988 s 8(c))	s 522
15			s 523
16			s 524
17			s 525
18			s 526
19			s 527
20			s 528
21			s 529
22	(1)	Amendment of FA 1975 s 31A	
	(2)	Amendment of FA 1976 s 12	s 77
	(3)	Unnecessary (application)	
23	(1)	Unnecessary (repeal of ITA 1967 s 362)	
	(2)		s 835
24			s 286
25	(1)		s 317(1)
	(2)		s 317(4)
26		Amendment of FA 1984 s 40(10)(a)	s 403
27	(1)(a)	Unnecessary (obsolete)	
	(1)(b)		s 322(2)
	(2)		s 322(3)
28	(1)	Par (iv) of definition of "qualifying ship" deleted by FA 1990 s 42(1)	s 407(1)
	(2)		s 407(3)
	(3)	Insertion of FA 1980 s 39(1CC1)	s 443
	(4)		s 407(4)
	(5)(a)		s 407(6)
	(b)		ss 133(1)(d), 134(1)(d)
29		Insertion of FA 1980 s 39(1CC2)	s 443
30		Insertion of FA 1980 s 39B	s 446(1)-(12)
31		Insertion of FA 1980 s 39(1CC3)	s 443
32		Unnecessary (spent)	
33		Amendment of CTA 1976 s 79	
34			s 220

Former Enactment		*Destination in TCA 1997*
Finance Act 1987 (1987 No 10) (contd)		
s 35 (1)-(20)		s 481, Sch 32 para 22
(21)	Unnecessary (obsolete)	
(22)	Rep by FA 1997 s 146(2) and Sch 9 Pt II	
Pt VI		
52	Amendment of ITA 1967 s 162(3)	s 851
54	Unnecessary (care and management)	
55(2), (7)	Unnecessary (construction and commencement)	
Finance Act 1988 (1988 No 12)		
Pt I		
s 1	Amendment of FA 1980 ss 1(2), 2(6)	ss 187, 188
2	Amendment of FA 1986 s 2	
3 (1), (2)	Unnecessary (obsolete)	
(3)	Unnecessary (application of schedule)	
4	Amendment of FA 1982 s 6	
5 (1)	Unnecessary (spent)	
(2)	Unnecessary (construction)	
6	Amendment of FA 1986 Sch 2	
7	Amendment of FA 1984 s 16(2)(a)	
8	Amendment of FA 1987 Pt I Ch III	
9 (1)	Definition of "relevant chargeable period" obsolete except for purposes of s 955(5)	ss 950(1), 955(5)(a)
(2), (3)		s 950(2), (3)
(4)	Deleted by FA 1991 s 45(b)	
10 (1)-(12)	(s 10(12) also provided for the amendment of ITA 1967 Sch 15)	s 951
11		s 952
12		s 953
13		s 954
14 (1), (2)		s 955(1), (2)(a)
(2) proviso para (a)-(e)		s 955(2)(b)
para (f)	Unnecessary (obsolete)	
(3), (4)		s 955(3), (4)
(5)		s 955(5)(b)(i)
15		s 956
16		s 1084(1), (5)
17		s 957
18 (1)-(3), (3)1st proviso		s 958(2)-(5)
(3) 2nd proviso		
paras (a),(b)		s 958(6)(a), (b)
para (c)	Unnecessary (spent)	
(3A)-(6)		s 958(7)-(10)
(7)		s 958(1)
19 (1)	Rep by FA 1997 s 146(2) and Sch 9 Pt II	
(2)	Amendment of ITA 1967 s 550	s 1080(1)
20 (1) to(4)	Ceased by FA 1990 s 27(2)(b)	
(5)	(The cesser of FA 1988 s 20 by FA 1990 s 27 does not effect the provision of s 20(5))	s 959(7)
21 (1)		s 959(1)
(2)		s 1069(1)(b)
(3), (4), (5)		s 959(2), (3), (4)

Former Enactment			*Destination in TCA 1997*
Finance Act 1988 (1988 No 12) (contd)			
s 21	(6)	Rep by FA 1997 s 146(2) and Sch 9 Pt II	
	(7), (8)		s 959(5), (6)
22		Rep by FA 1997 s 146(2) and Sch 9 Pt II	
23	(1)	Amendment of FA 1975 s 31A	
	(2)	Amendment of FA 1976 s 12	
	(3)	Unnecessary (application)	
24	(1)		s 373(2)(d)
	(2)	Unnecessary (obsolete)	
25		Amendment of FA 1986 s 44(1)(a)	s 328(1)
26		Unnecessary (spent)	
27		Amendment of FA 1981 s 23	ss 325(1), 326(1), 327(1), 329(1)(2)
28		Amendment of FA 1985 s 21	ss 326, 327, 329, Sch 32, para 11
29		Amendment of FA 1985 s 22	Sch 32, para 11
30	(1)		ss 774(4)(a), 608(1)(a), 717(2)(a)
	(2)(a)		s 774(4)(b)
	(b)		s 608(1)(b)
	(c)		s 717(2)(b)
31	(1)	Unnecessary (obsolete)	
	(2)	Unnecessary (application of schedule)	
32	(1)	Amendment of FA 1980 s 45	s 147, Sch 32 para 4
	(2)	Unnecessary (obsolete)	
	(3)	Unnecessary (application of schedule)	
33	(1)	Substitution of CTA 1976 s 1(1)	s 21
	(2)	Unnecessary (cesser of CTA 1976 ss 28, 79)	
	(3)	Unnecessary (application of schedule)	
34		Insertion of CTA 1976 s 116A	s 456
35		Amendment of FA 1980 s 39A(2)	s 445
36	(1)	Rep FA 1980 s 39B(7)(c)	
	(2)	Unnecessary (obsolete)	
	(3)	Amendment of FA 1980 s 39B(6)	s 446(1)-(12)
	(4)		s 451
37			s 452
38		Insertion of FA 1974 s 31(3)(cc)	s 246(3)
39			s 217
40	(1)	Amendment of FA 1987 s 28(1)	s 407(1)
	(2)	Unnecessary (obsolete)	
	(3)	Amendment of FA 1987 s 28(4)(c)	s 407(4)
41			s 222
42			Sch 32, para 3
43		Amendment of ITA 1967 s 251	ss 283(2)(3)(6), 300(1), 304(3)(b), 316(3)
44		Insertion of ITA 1967 s 254(7)	ss 271(1)(2)(4)-(6), 278(1), (2), (6), 304(2)(3)(a)(4), 305, 316(3), 317(2), 320(1)
45		Amendment of ITA 1967 s 265	s 274(1), (3)-(5), (8)
46		Substitution of FA 1967 s 11(2)	s 285(1), (2), (3)
47		Substitution of FA 1971 s 26(2)	s 285(1), (2), (3)
48		Substitution of FA 1978 s 25(2)	s 273(2)
49		Amendment of FA 1981 s 25(1)	Sch 32, para 9
50		Amendment of ITA 1967 ss 254(2A)(a), 264(1) proviso para (ii), 264(3) proviso para (ii), 265(1) proviso para (iii)	s 271(4), 272, 274(1)(3)-(5)(8)

Former Enactment		*Destination in TCA 1997*
Finance Act 1988 (1988 No 12) (contd)		
s 51 (1)(a)		ss 271(3)(a), 273(5)(a), 283(4)(a), 285(5)(a)
(b)	Unnecessary (obsolete)	
(c)		ss 273(5)(b), 285(5)(b)
(cc)		ss 271(3)(b), 273(5)(c), 285(5)(c)
proviso		ss 271(3)(b), 273(5)(c), 283(4)(b), 285(5)(c)
(d)		ss 274(2), 285(5)(d)
(2)(a),(c),(d)		s 283(3)(a)
(b)	Unnecessary (obsolete)	
(3)		s 285(4)
(4)(a)		s 271(4)(a)
(b)		s 273(4)
(5)		s 274(2)
(6)		ss 271(1), 273(1), 283(1), 285(1)
52 (1)	Amendment of FA 1974 s 22	s 658(1)
(2)	Amendment of FA 1977 s 14(1)	Sch 32, para 23(2)
(3)	Cesser of FA 1980 s 26 (unnecessary)	
70 (1)(a)	Insertion of ITA 1967 s 467A	
(b)	Amendment of ITA 1967 s 474(1)	s 49, Sch 32 para 1(2)
(2)(a)		s 607(1)(d)
(b)	Unnecessary (cesser of FA 1983 s 54 and FA 1984 s 66(6) (in so far as it relates to Bord Telecom Eireann))	
71 (1), (2)(a)		s 1006
(2)(b)	Unnecessary (obsolete)	
72 (1)-(6)	Unnecessary (obsolete)	
(7)	Amendment of FA 1983 s 23(4)	s 1086
73 (1)-(16), (18)		s 1002
(17)	Deleted by FA 1992 s 241(e)	
74 (1), (2)		s 8
(3)	Unnecessary (commencement)	
76	Unnecessary (care and management)	
77 (2), (7), (8)	Unnecessary (construction and commencement)	
Sch 1	Amendment of ITA 1967 ss 138, 138A(2), 138B(1)	ss 461, 462, 472
Sch 2	Unnecessary (obsolete)	
Sch 3	Unnecessary (obsolete)	
Finance Act 1989 (1989 No 10)		
s 1	Amendment of FA 1980 ss 1, 2	ss 187, 188
2	Amendment of FA 1984 s 2	
3	Amendment of FA 1982 s 6	
4 (1)-(6)		Sch 32, para 20
(7)	Rep by FA 1996 s 132(2) and Sch 5 Pt II	
4 (8)	Amendment of ITA 1967 s 198(1)	s 1024
5	Insertion of FA 1969 s 2(5A)-(5D)	s 195(1)-(11)
6	Amendment of FA 1982 s 8(1)(a)	s 122
7	Rep by FA 1997 s 146(2) and Sch 9 Pt II	
8	Ceased by FA 1992 s 4	
9	Amendment of FA 1984 ss 12(1), 16(2)(2A), 17, insertion of s 13A	s 489(1)(2), 493, 496, 498,
10		s 995

Former Enactment		Destination in TCA 1997
Finance Act 1989 (1989 No 10) (contd)		
s 11 (1)	Amendment of FA 1975 s 31A	
(2)	Amendment of FA 1976 s 12	
(3)	Unnecessary (spent)	
(4)	Unnecessary (application)	
12 (1)		s 373(2)(e)
(2)	Amendment of FA 1976 s 32	s 376
13	Substitution of ITA 1967 s 251(7)	
14	Substitution of ITA 1967 s 254(7)	s 271(5)
15	Amendment of FA 1974 s 22(2)	s 658(2)(a)
16	Insertion of FA 1978 s 25(3)	s 273(8)
17	Amendment of FA 1981 s 26	Sch 32, para 10
18 (1)		s 734(1)(a), (c)
(2)-(9), (11),(11A),(12)		s 734(2)-(12)
(10)	Deleted by FA 1993 s 20(b)	
19 (1), (2), (3)		s 893
(4)	Amendment of ITA 1967 Sch 15	Sch 29
20	Substitution of CTA 1976 s 36(2)	s 713(1)-(6)
21 (1)	Substitution of CTA 1976s 84A	s 134(3)
(2)(a)		ss 133(3), 134(2)
(2)(b)	Unnecessary (spent)	
22	Amendment of FA 1980 ss 38, 39(1CC)	ss 442(1), 443
23	Deletion of FA 1980 s 39A(8), (9)	
24	Amendment of FA 1980 s 45	s 147, Sch 32 para 4
25 (1)-(3)		s 154(1)-(3)
(4)		s 154(6)
26	Substitution of FA 1984 s 42(1)	s 138
27 (1)	Amendment of CTA 1976 s 100(3)(h)	s 434
(2)	Amendment of FA 1980 s 41(1)	s 448(1)
(3)	Unnecessary (operative date)	
28	Amendment of FA 1987 s 35	s 481, Sch 32, para 22
29	Amendment of CGTA 1975 Sch 4 para 11	s 980
30	Amendment of FA 1986 s 61(1)	
31 (1)	Amendment of FA 1988 s 70(2)	s 607(1)(d)
(2)	Unnecessary (operative date)	
32	Amendment of CGTA 1975 s 19	s 607(1)(a)-(d)(f), (2)
33		s 610, Sch 15, Pt I
Pt VI		
86		s 811
87	Insertion of CGTA 1975 s 33(5A)	s 549
88 (1)-(7)		s 817
(8)	Unnecessary (operative date)	
89 (1)	Amendment of ITA 1967 s 433(1)	s 237
(2)		s 242
Pt VII		
95 (1)(a)	Insertion of ITA 1967 s 467B	
(b)	Amendment of ITA 1967 s 474(1)	s 49, Sch 32 para 1(2)
(2)	Amendment of CGTA 1975 s 19(d)	s 607
98 (1)	Amendment of FA 1973 s 92(1)	ss 39(1), 48(1)(c)
(2)	Amendment of FA 1984 s 66(a)	s 607
99	Unnecessary (care and management)	
100(2), (7), (8)	Unnecessary (construction and commencement)	

Former Enactment		*Destination in TCA 1997*
Finance Act 1989 (1989 No 10) (contd)		
Sch 1 para 1(1)-(6), (7)(a)-(d), (8)	Sch 1 para 1(7)(e) rep by FA 1997 s 146(2) and Sch 9 Pt II	Sch 18 para 1
para 2		para 2
para 3	Amendment of ITA 1967 Sch 15, FA 1983 s 94(2)	Sch 29
Judicial Separation and Family Law Reform Act 1989 (1989 No 6)		
s 26		s 1027(a)
Finance Act 1990 (1990 No 10)		
s 1	Amendment of FA 1980 ss 1, 2	ss 187, 188
2	Amendment of FA 1984 s 2	
3	Amendment of FA 1982 s 6	
4	Amendment of FA 1969 s 3(1)	s 467
5 (1), (2)		s 189
(3)	Unnecessary (commencement)	
6	Amendment of FA 1989 s 8	
7		s 190
8	Amendment of FA 1976 s 13(2)	s 805
9	Amendment of FA 1980 s 28(3)	
10	Amendment of FA 1984 ss 11(1), 12, 16	s 488(1)-(3), 489(1), 496
11		s 251
12	Amendment of ITA 1967 Sch 3	s 201(1)(a), Sch 3
13 (1), (3), (4)		s 214
(2)	Unnecessary (commencement)	
14 (1)	Amendment of ITA 1967 s 58	ss 65(1), 66, 67
(2)	Unnecessary (cesser of FA 1971 s 3)	
15	Substitution of ITA 1967 s 60	s 65(2)-(4)
16	Unnecessary (spent)	
17 (1)(a)	Amendment of ITA 1967 Pt IV Ch IV	
(b)	Amendment of ITA 1967 Sch 6	s 73
(2)	Unnecessary (cesser of ITA 1967 s 77(3)(4))	
18 (1)	Amendment of ITA 1967 ss 81(3), 89	ss 75(3), 384
(2)	Unnecessary (cesser of ITA 1967 s 81(3)(b)(c))	
19 (a)	Substitution of ITA 1967 s 110	s 112
(b)	Unnecessary (deletion of ITA 1967 s 111 with saver for any enactment which refers to ITA 1967 s 111)	
20 (1)	Amendment of ITA 1967 Sch 18	Sch 28
(2)	Amendment of FA 1974 s 20B	s 657(4)(5)
(3)	Unnecessary (cesser of FA 1980 s 17 Table Pt I para (a), (b) and FA 1981s 9(a), (b))	
(4)	Unnecessary (spent)	
21	Unnecessary (spent)	
22 (1)	Amendment of ITA 1967 ss 262(2), 297(2)	s 306
(2)	Amendment of FA 1974 s 22(2A)(c)	s 658(3)
23 (1)	Amendment of ITA 1967 s 70	ss 880(1)-(6), 900(3), 1052(4)(a)(c)(e)
(2)	Amendment of ITA 1967 s 172	ss 879(1)-(4), 1052(4)(a)(c)(e)
(3)	Amendment of FA 1988 ss 9, 10	ss 950, 951, 955(5)(a).
(4)	Unnecessary (spent)	
(5)	Unnecessary (commencement)	
24 (a)	Amendment of ITA 1967 s 477(1)	s 960
(b)	Unnecessary (cesser of ITA 1967 s 550(2) and FA 1982 s 27(4))	
(c)	Amendment of CTA 1976 s 6(4)	
(d)	Amendment of FA 1988 s 18	s 958

Former Enactment		*Destination in TCA 1997*
Finance Act 1990 (1990 No 10) (contd)		
s 25 (1)	Amendment of FA 1986 s 48	s 1084(1)-(4)
(2)	Unnecessary (operative date)	
(3)	Unnecessary (spent)	
26 (1)	Unnecessary (invalid)	
(2)	Unnecessary (spent)	
(3)	Unnecessary (spent)	
27 (1)	Amendment of ITA 1967 s 236(11)	s 787(7)
(2)	Unnecessary (cesser of ITA 1967 ss 307(1AA), 546 and FA 1988 s 20)	
28	Substitution of ITA 1967 s 421(2)	s 934
29 (1)(2)(5)(6)		s 1014
(3)	Amendment of CGTA 1975 s 2(1)	s 5
(4)	Amendment of CTA 1976 s 1(5)	s 4(1)
(7)	Unnecessary (operative date)	
30 (1)	Amendment of FA 1986 ss 42(1), 44(1)(a), 45(1)(a)	Sch 32 paras 11, 12, 13
(2)	Amendment of FA 1989 s 4(1)(a)	Sch 32 para 20
31	Amendment of FA 1987 s 27(1)(a)(ii)	
32	Amendment of FA 1986 s 45(2)	Sch 32 para 13
33 (1)		ss 324(4)(b), 333(4)(b), 345(8)(b), 354(5)(b), 370(8)(b)
(2)(a)	Definition of "qualifying premises" unnecessary (duplication),	ss 324(4)(a), 333(4)(a), 345(8)(a), 354(5)(a), 370(8)(a)
33 (2)(b)	Unnecessary (obsolete)	
34 (1)(a)		ss 155(1), 489(14)(a)
(b)(i)	Unnecessary (obsolete)	
(1)(b)(ii)		ss 155(2)(c), 489(14)(b)
(2)		ss 155(2)(a), 489(14)(c)(d)
(3)		s 155(3)
(4)		s 489(14)(e)
(5), (6)		s 155(4), (5)
35 (1), (2)		s 735
(3)	Unnecessary (operative date)	
36	Unnecessary (obsolete)	
37	Unnecessary (obsolete)	
38	Amendment of FA 1989 s 25(3)(a)	s 154(1)-(3)
39 (a)-(c)	Amendment of F(TPCM)A 1974 ss 2(1), 3(2), 4(1)	ss 673(1), 674(1)(a)(2)-(4), 675
(d)	Insertion of F(TPCM)A 1974 s 7A	s 678
40	Amendment of FA 1980 s 38	s 442(1)
41 (1)	Amendment of FA 1980 s 39	s 443
(2)	Unnecessary (spent)	
(3)	Unnecessary (obsolete)	
(4)(a)		s 133(1)(e)
(b)	Unnecessary (duplication)	
(5)		s 403(9)(a)
(6)		s 442(1)
42 (1)	Amendment of FA 1987 s 28(1)	s 407(1)
(2)	Unnecessary (obsolete)	
43	Substitution of CTA 1976 s 10(4)	s 243(1), (2), (4)-(9)
44 (1)	Insertion of CTA 1976 s 116(10)	s 420
(2)	Unnecessary (spent)	
45	Unnecessary (spent)	

Former Enactment		*Destination in TCA 1997*
Finance Act 1990 (1990 No 10) (contd)		
s 46	Amendment of CTA 1976 s 84A	ss 133, 134
47	Amendment of CTA 1976 s 101	s 440
48	Amendment of CTA 1976 s 162	s 441
49	Amendment of CTA 1976 s 151	ss 238(1)-(6), 239
50	Insertion of CTA 1976 s 152(4)	s 240
51 (1), (2)		s 241
(3)	Substitution of ITA 1967 s 434(5A)	s 238
(4)	Unnecessary (operative date)	
52	Amendment of FA 1980 s 41(1)	s 448(1)
53	Amendment of CTA 1976 s 58(10)	
54	Substitution of CTA 1976 s 143(1)	s 884
55	Amendment of FA 1983 s 50	s 171
56	Substitution of FA 1983 s 24	s 517
57		s 703
58	Amendment of CTA 1976 s 129(2)	s 616
59		s 704
60		s 705
61	Amendment of ITA 1967 s 337	
62		s 740
63		s 741
64		s 742
65		s 743
66		s 744
67		s 745
68		s 746
69 (1)-(7)		s 747
(8)	Unnecessary (obsolete)	
70	Amendment of ITA 1967 s 241(1)	s 284(1)(2)(a)(b),(3), 300(1)
71	Amendment of FA 1967 s 11	s 285(1), (2), (3)
72	Amendment of FA 1971 s 26	ss 285(1)(2)(3)(8), 287, 299(2)
73	Amendment of ITA 1967 s 251	ss 283(2), 300(1), 316(3)
74	Amendment of ITA 1967 s 254	ss 271(1)(4)(6), 278(1)(2)(6), 305, 320
75	Insertion of FA 1970 s 19(2A)	s 279
76	Amendment of FA 1978 s 25	s 273(1)(2)(3)(8)
77	Amendment of FA 1974 s 22	s 658
78	Amendment of ITA 1967 s 265(1)	s 274(1)(3)-(5)(8)
79	Amendment of ITA 1967 s 276	s 294
80	Substitution of FA 1988 s 51(2), (3), (4)	ss 283(3)(a), 285(4), 271(4)(a), 273(4)
81 (1)(a)		ss 271(3)(c), 273(7)(a)(i), 283(5), 285(7)(a)(i)
(b)		s 273(7)(a)(ii)
(c)		s 285(7)(a)(ii)
(1) proviso		ss 273(7)(b), 285(7)(b)
(2)(a), (b)		s 283(3)(b)
(c)	Unnecessary (obsolete)	
(3)		s 285(6)
(4)		s 271(4)(a)
(5)		s 273(6)
82	Amendment of CGTA 1975 s 3(3)	s 28
83	Amendment of CGTA 1975 s 36	s 590(1)-(9)
84	Amendment of CGTA 1975 s 26	s 598
85	Amendment of CGTA 1975 s 27(3)	s 599

Former Enactment		*Destination in TCA 1997*
Finance Act 1990 (1990 No 10) (contd)		
s 86	Amendment of CGTA 1975 Sch 1 para 15(3)	s 596
87	Insertion of CGTA 1975 Sch 2 para 2A	s 733
Pt VII		
s 131	Insertion of FA 1970 s 17(14)-(17)	s 531(17), (18)
136	Insertion of FA 1982 Sch 3 para 4A	Sch 11
137	Insertion of FA 1986 Sch 2 para 15	
138(1)		ss 45(3),(4)(a), 48(4)(a),(5)(a)
(2)	Amendment of FA 1984 s 28	ss 45(2)-(4), 48(3)-(5)
139	Unnecessary (care and management)	
140(2), (8)	Unnecessary (construction and commencement)	
Sch 1	Unnecessary (obsolete)	
Sch 2	Unnecessary (obsolete)	
Sch 3		Sch 16
Sch 4		Sch 17
Sch 5		Sch 19
Sch 6		Sch 20
Finance Act 1991 (1991 No 13)		
Pt I		
s 1	Amendment of FA 1980 ss 1, 2	ss 187, 188
2 (1), (2)		s 15
(3)	Unnecessary (application of schedule)	
3 (1), (2)	Unnecessary (obsolete)	
(3)	Unnecessary (application of schedule)	
4 (1), (2)		s 463
(3)	Rep by FA 1996 s 132(2) and Sch 5 Pt II	
(4)	Unnecessary (commencement)	
5	Amendment of FA 1989 s 8	
6	Amendment of ITA 1967 s 110	s 112
7	Insertion of ITA 1967 s 138B(3)	s 472
8	Substitution of ITA 1967 s 142A(2)(b)	s 473
9	Amendment of FA 1982 s 6	
10 (1)	Unnecessary (interpretation)	
(2)		s 664(1)(a), (b)(ii)
11	Amendment of FA 1986 s 31(1)	s 256.
12		s 773
13		s 210
14	Amendment of FA 1984 ss 12, 13	ss 488(1), 489, 490, 1024
15 (1)	Amendment of FA 1984 ss 12, 13, 13A, 15, 16, 26	ss 488(1)(4), 489, 490, 491, 495, 496, 507, 1024,
(2)	Amendment of FA 1984 Sch 2 para 1	Sch 10
16	Unnecessary (obsolete)	
17 (1)	Amendment of FA 1984 s 13	s 490
(2)	Amendment of FA 1984 s 15(2)	s 495
(3)(a)	Unnecessary (obsolete)	
(b)	Ceased by FA 1994 s 17	
(4)	Unnecessary (interpretation)	
18 (1)	Amendment of FA 1975 s 31A	
(2)	Amendment of FA 1976 s 12	
(3)	Amendment of FA 1980 s 28	
(4)	Unnecessary (application)	
19 (1)	Amendment of FA 1989 s 18(1)	s 734
(2)		s 734(1)(b)
(3)	Unnecessary (obsolete)	
20 (1), (3)		s 230
(2)		s 610, Sch 15, Pt I

Finance Act 1991 (1991 No 13) (contd)

Former Enactment		*Destination in TCA 1997*
s 21 (1)	Amendment of FA 1986 s 45	Sch 32, para 13
(2)	Unnecessary (operative date)	
22 (1)		s 271(4)(a)
(2)(a)	Unnecessary (cesser of FA 1986 s 42(3))	
(b)	Unnecessary (operative date)	
23	Amendment of FA 1970 s 19	s 279
24		s 408
25	Amendment of FA 1974 s 22	s 658
26		s 276
27	Amendment of FA 1984 s 29	s 815(1)(2)
28	Amendment of CTA 1976 s 84A	ss 133(7)(13), 134(1)(4)-(6)
29	Insertion of CTA 1976 s 87(4)(e)	s 135
30 (1)	Amendment of CTA 1976 s 35	s 710(1)-(5)
(2)		s 710(6)
31		s 110
32 (1)	Amendment of FA 1980 s 39(3)(a)	s 443
(2)	Unnecessary (operative date)	
33	Amendment of FA 1980 s 39A	s 445
34	Amendment of FA 1980 s 39B(2)	s 446(1)-(12)
35	Amendment of FA 1990 s 41(6)	s 442(1)
36		s 831
37	Unnecessary (obsolete)	
38	Substitution of FA 1988 s 30(1)	ss 774(4)(a), 608(1)(a), 717(2)(a)
39	Amendment of FA 1990 s 45(2)(a)	
40	Amendment of FA 1988 s 41(1)(a)	s 222
41		s 220
42	Amendment of CGTA 1975 s 26	s 598
43 (1), (2)		s 606
(3)	Unnecessary (operative date)	
44	Amendment of FA 1989 s 33(2)	s 610, Sch 15, Pt I
45	Amendment of FA 1988 s 9	ss 950(1)-(3), 955(5)(a).
46	Amendment of FA 1988 s 10	s 951
47	Amendment of FA 1988 s 12	s 953
48	Insertion of FA 1988 s 13(7)	s 954
49	Amendment of FA 1988 s 14(5)	s 955(5)(b)(i)
50	Amendment of FA 1988 s 15(1)	s 956
51	Amendment of FA 1988 s 17(1)	s 957
52	Amendment of FA 1988 s 18	s 958(2)-(5)
53	Amendment of FA 1988 s 21	s 959(1)
54-55	Rep by FA 1997 s 156(1)(a)	
56 (1)(a)(i)		s 325(1)
(ii)	Unnecessary (spent)	
(iii)	Rep by FA 1997 s 156(1)(b)	
(iv)	Unnecessary (spent)	
(b)		s 325(1)
(bb)	Unnecessary (obsolete)	
(c)	Unnecessary (obsolete)	
(2)		s 325(2)
proviso	Rep by FA 1997 s 156(1)(b)	
57 (1)(a)	Rep by FA 1997 s 156(1)(c)	
(b)(i)		s 327(1)
(ii),(iii)	Unnecessary (obsolete)	
(2)	Rep by s 156(1)(c)	
(3)(a)(i)		s 327(1)
(ii)	Unnecessary (obsolete)	
(aa)		s 327(1)
(b)	Unnecessary (obsolete)	

Former Enactment		*Destination in TCA 1997*
Finance Act 1991 (1991 No 13) (contd)		
s 57 (3)(bb)	Unnecessary (obsolete)	
(c)	Unnecessary (obsolete)	
58 (1)(a)	Rep by FA 1997 s 156(1)(d)	
(b)(i)		s 326(1)
(ii)(iii)	Unnecessary (obsolete)	
(2)	Rep by FA 1997 s 156(1)(d)	
(3)(a)		s 326(1)
(b)	Unnecessary (obsolete)	
(c)	Unnecessary (obsolete)	
59	Definitions of “the Act of 1975”, “the Act of 1976” unnecessary (duplication) and “relevant day” unnecessary (operative date)	s 173
60		s 174
60A	(s 60A inserted by FA 1997 s 39(b))	s 175
61		s 176
62		s 177
63		s 178
64		s 179
65		s 180
66		s 181
67		s 182
68 (1)-(3)		s 183
(4)	Amendment of ITA 1967 Sch 15	Sch 29
69	Insertion of FA 1983 ss 45(9), 47(1)(c)	ss 166, 168I
70		s 184
71		s 185
72		s 186
Pt VII		
s 126	Amendment of ITA 1967 s 141(4)	s 465
128	Amendment of FA 1970 s 17(5)(a)	s 531(5)(6)(8)(9),
130(1)	Amendment of FA 1988 s 73(1)	s 1002
(2)	Unnecessary (operative date)	
131	Unnecessary (care and management)	
132(2), (8)	Unnecessary (construction and commencement)	
Sch 1, Pt I	Amendment of ITA 1967 s 1(1), FA 1974 s 3(1), and cesser of FA 1974 s 3	ss 2(1), 3(1)
Sch 1, Pt II	Amendment of ITA 1967 ss 138, 138A(2)	ss 461, 462
Sch 2		Sch 6
Oireachtas (Allowance to Members) and Ministerial and Parliamentary Offices (Amendment) Act 1992 (1992 No 3)		
s 4		s 836
Finance Act 1992 (1992 No 9)		
s 1	Amendment of FA 1980 ss 1, 2	ss 187, 188
2 (1)(a)	Amendment of FA 1991 s 2	
(b)	Unnecessary (obsolete)	
(2)(a)	Amendment of ITA 1967 s 198	s 1024
(b)	Unnecessary (spent)	
3	Amendment of FA 1982 s 6	
4	Unnecessary (cesser of ITA 1967 ss 143, 151, 152, FA 1973 s 23 and Sch 1, FA 1989 s 8)	
5	Amendment of ITA 1967 s 432(1)	ss 864(1), 949(1)
6	Amendment of FA 1972 ss 15(3), 21(2), 22	ss 772(3), 780, 781

Former Enactment | *Destination in TCA 1997*

Finance Act 1992 (1992 No 9) (contd)

Section	Subsection	Former Enactment	Destination in TCA 1997
s 7	(1)	Insertion of FA 1979 s 8(4A)	s 125(3)
	(2)	Unnecessary (operative date)	
8		Amendment of FA 1982 s 4	ss 121, 897(1)-(5), Sch 29
9		Amendment of FA 1982 s 8(1)	s 122
10		Amendment of FA 1987 s 13(1)	s 520
11		Amendment of FA 1987 s 14	s 521
12		Cesser of FA 1986 s 10 and Sch 2, but only as respects share options granted on or after 29 January 1992	Sch 32, para 7(1)
13		Unnecessary (cesser of FA 1986 s 14)	
14	(1)-(3)		s 252
	(4)	Insertion of FA 1974 s 34(3)	s 248(1)-(3)
15	(1)		s 126(3)(a)
	(2)		s 126(3)(b)
	proviso		s 126(4)
	(3)		s 126(6)
	(4)		s 126(7)
16		Amendment of FA 1977 s 36(a)	s 6
s 17	(1)	Amendment of FA 1982 s 56 and Sch 3 para 1(4)	s 515, Sch 11
	(2)	Unnecessary (spent)	
18	(1)	Substitution of ITA 1967 s 525	s 127(1)-(5)
	(2)	Substitution of ITA 1967 s 115(1)(b)	s 201(2)
	(3)		s 127(6)
19	(1)	Insertion of FA 1973 s 34(2A)	s 234(3)-(8)
	(2)	Amendment of CTA 1976 s 170	s 141
20		Amendment of FA 1980 s 28(3)	
21	(1)		s 373(2)(f)
	(2)	Amendment of FA 1976 s 32	s 376
22	(1)	Amendment of FA 1986 ss 31, 35, insertion of ss 37A, 37B	ss 256, 261, 264, 265
	(2)	Unnecessary (operative date)	
23	(1)	Amendment of FA 1986 s 46(2)	s 1013(1)-(3)
	(2)(a)	Unnecessary (operative date)	
	(b)		s 1013(5)(a)
23	(3)		s 1013(5)(b)
24	(1)(a)	Insertion of ITA 1967 s 467C	
	(b)	Amendment of ITA 1967 s 474(1)	s 49, Sch 32 para 1(2)
	(2)(a)	Amendment of CGTA 1975 s 19(d)	s 607
	(b)	Unnecessary (cesser of FA 1982 s 41 in so far as it relates to Bord Gais Eireann)	
25			s 405
26	(1)-(3), (5)	Rep by FA 1996 s 132(2) and Sch 5 Pt II	
	(4)	Insertion of ITA 1967 s 241(6A)	s 284(5)
27	(1)	Amendment of ITA 1967 s 255(1)(bb)	s 268(1)-(3), (5)-(8)
	(2)	Unnecessary (operative date)	
28		Amendment of FA 1970 s 17	ss 530(1)(2), 531
29		Amendment of FA 1986 ss 41(2), 42, 44(1)(a), 45(1)(a)	ss 322(1), s 323(1), 324(1), 328(1), Sch 32, para 11
30		Amendment of FA 1987 s 27(1)(a)(ii)	
31		Amendment of FA 1989 s 4(1)	Sch 32, para 20
32		Amendment of FA 1988 s 18(3)(b)	s 958(2)-(5)
33	(1)	Amendment of FA 1988 s 21	ss 959, 1069(1)(b)
	(2)	Unnecessary (operative date)	
34		Amendment of FA 1991 ss 56(1)(a), 57, 58	s 325(1)
35		Insertion of CTA 1976 ss 66A, 76A	s 145(11)(a), (b)
36			s 736

Former Enactment		*Destination in TCA 1997*
Finance Act 1992 (1992 No 9) (contd)		
s 37 (1)		s 154(3)(a), (4)
(2)		s 154(5)
38 (1)	Substitution of CTA 1976 s 83(4)	s 153(1)
(2)		s 153(2)
39	Definition of "the definition of scientific research" unnecessary (obsolete)	s 763(1)(3)(4)
40	Amendment of CTA 1976 s 84A	ss 133, 134
41	Substitution of FA 1989 s 21(2)	ss 133(3), 134(2)
(1)	Amendment of ITA 1967 ss 464, 470, 474(2)	ss 45(1), 49, 50, Sch 32 para 1(2)
42 (2)		s 398(1)
(3)(a)	Unnecessary (spent)	
(b)		s 398(2)
proviso	Unnecessary (spent)	
(4)	Unnecessary (obsolete)	
43 (1)-(3)	Unnecessary (spent)	
43 (4)	Unnecessary (repeal of CTA 1976 s 31(9))	
44 (a), (b)	Amendment of CTA 1976 s 33	ss 707, 728
(c), (d)	Insertion of CTA 1976 ss 33A, 46A, 46B	ss 708, 719, 720
(e)	Unnecessary (deletion of CTA 1976 s 47)	
(f)	Amendment of CTA 1976 s 50(1)	
45		s 487
46 (1)(a)	Insertion of CTA 1976 s 10A	s 454
(b)	Amendment of CTA 1976 s 16(1)	s 396
(c)	Insertion of CTA 1976 s 16A	s 455
(2)	Amendment of CTA 1976 s 116A	s 456
47	Amendment of FA 1980 s 39	s 443
48	Unnecessary (spent)	
49 (1)	Insertion of CTA 1976 s 25(5A)	s 157
(2)	Insertion of CTA 1976 s 26(4A)	s 158
50 (1)	Amendment of CTA 1976 s 105	s 410
(2)	Unnecessary (repeal of CTA 1976 s 106)	
(3)	Unnecessary (operative date)	
51 (1)	Amendment of FA 1983 s 44	s 165
(2)	Unnecessary (operative date)	
52	Amendment of FA 1980 s 39A	s 445
53	Amendment of FA 1980 s 39B	s 446(1)-(12)
54	Substitution of FA 1980 s 41(1)	s 448(1)
55 (1), (2)		s 1085(1), (2)
(3)	Unnecessary (operative date)	
56		s 88
57	Amendment of FA 1988 s 39	s 217
58	Amendment of FA 1987 s 35(1)	s 481, Sch 32, para 22
59	Amendment of CGTA 1975 ss 13(4), 16(1)(2), CGT(A)A 1978 Sch 1 para 8	s 655(1)(2), 601(3)
60 (1)	Substitution of CGTA 1975 s 3(3)	ss 283(2), 300(1)
(2)	Unnecessary (deletion of FA 1982 s 36(2), (3), (3A))	
61		s 600(6)
62 (1)	Insertion of CGTA 1975 s 9(5)	s 272
(2)	Unnecessary (operative date)	
63	Amendment of CGTA 1975 s 47	
64		s 630
65		s 631
66		s 632
67		s 633
68	Amendment of FA 1982 s 36	s 648

Former Enactment		*Destination in TCA 1997*
Finance Act 1992 (1992 No 9) (contd)		
s 69		s 634
70		s 635
71		s 636
72		s 637
73	Amendment of CTA 1976 s 132(2).	s 619
74		s 638
75		s 684
76		s 685
77		s 686
78		s 687
79		s 688
80 (1), (2)		s 689
(3)	Unnecessary (operative date)	
81 (1)-(5), (7)		s 690
(6)	Unnecessary (obsolete)	
82		s 691
83		s 692
84		s 693
85		s 694
86		s 695
87		s 696
88		s 697
226	Definition of "relevant chargeable period" unnecessary (obsolete). ITA 1967 s 226(7) also provided for the amendment of Sch 15	s 894
227	Amendment of ITA 1967 ss 94, 173, 176	ss 888, s 889(10), 890
228		s 899
229	Amendment of FA 1989 s 19	s 893
230(1)-(6)	Definition of relevant chargeable period" unnecessary (obsolete).	s 895
(7)	Unnecessary (operative date)	
230A	(s 230A inserted by FA 1995 s 41)	s 896
231	Substitution of FA 1986 s 6	
232	Substitution of FA 1976 s 34	s 905
233	Insertion of ITA 1967 s 127A	s 903
234	Amendment of ITA 1967 s 128(1)	s 987(1)-(3)
235	Insertion of FA 1970 s 17A	s 904
236		s 906
237		s 912
238	Amendment of FA 1979 s 31	s 902
239	Amendment of FA 1983 s 20	s 909
240	Amendment of FA 1983 s 23	s 1086
241	Amendment of FA 1988 s 73	s 1002
242		s 1094
243(a)(i), (b)	Amendment of FA 1983 s 94	s 1078
(ii)	Rep by FA 1996 s 132(2) and Sch 5 Pt II	
244	Amendment of FA 1988 s 9(1)	ss 950(1)-(3), 955(5)(a).
245	Insertion of FA 1986 s 48(3)	s 1084(1)-(4)
246	Insertion of CGTA 1975 Sch 4 para 3(4A)	s 913(1), (3)-(5), (7)
247	Amendment of CTA 1976 s 143	ss 861(2), 884, 930, 973, 974, 1071, 1072, 1080, 1082

Former Enactment		*Destination in TCA 1997*
Finance Act 1992 (1992 No 9) (contd)		
s 248	Amendment of ITA 1967 ss 128(1A), 173(6), 426(3), 500(1)(2), FA 1979 s 31(5), FA 1980 s 45(8), FA 1983 s 112(1)(a)(3)	s 987(1)-(3), 889(10), 939, 1052(1)-(3), 902, 147, Sch 32 para 4
253	Unnecessary (care and management)	
254(2), (8), (9)	Unnecessary (construction and commencement)	
Sch 1	Substitution of Table to FA 1982 s 4(4)	s 121
Sch 2		Sch 13
Finance (No 2) Act 1992 (1992 No 28)		
s 1	Insertion of FA 1980 s 41(9)	s 448(3)-(7)
2	Amendment of FA 1980 s 45(3).	s 147, Sch 32 para 4
3	Amendment of FA 1986 ss 31(1), 37A(1), 37B(1)	s 256, 256, 265
29	Unnecessary (care and management)	
30 (2)	Unnecessary (construction and commencement)	
Finance Act 1993 (1993 No 13)		
Pt I		
s 1	Amendment of FA 1980 ss 1, 2	ss 187, 188
2 (1)	Amendment of FA 1991 s 2	s 15
(2)	Unnecessary (application of schedule)	
3 (1), (2)	Unnecessary (obsolete)	
(3)	Unnecessary (application of schedule)	
4	Amendment of FA 1982 s 6	
5	Rep by FA 1997 s 146(2) and Sch 9 Pt II	
6	Substitution of FA 1990 s 11	
7 (1)	Insertion of ITA 1967 s 115(1A)	s 201(3)
(2)		s 124
8 (a)	Amendment of ITA 1967 s 115	s 201(2)
(b)	Amendment of ITA 1967 Sch 3	s 201(1)(a), Sch 3
9	Unnecessary (spent)	
10	Insertion of ITA 1967 ss 195B, 195C,	ss 1019, 1021
11	Amendment of CTA 1976 ss 33, 36, 38, 43, 46A, 50, substitution of s 46, insertion of ss 33B, 35A, 36A, 36B, 36C	s 706(1)-(3), 707, 711, 712, 713(1)-(6), 714, 719, 726, 724, 725
12 (1)	Unnecessary (spent)	
(2)(a)	Unnecessary (spent)	
(b)		Sch 32, para 24
13		s 737
14 (1)-(3)		s 838(1)-(3)
(4)(a)-(c), (d)-(f)		s 838(4)
(c)proviso	Unnecessary (operative date)	
(5)		s 838(5)
(6)(a), (c)		s 838(6)
(b)	Unnecessary (operative date)	
(7)		s 838(7)
15 (1)	Amendment of FA 1986 ss 31(1),35(1),37A	s 256, 261, 264
(2)	Unnecessary (spent)	
16		s 839
17		s 738
18		s 739
19	Amendment of CGTA 1975 s 31(4)	
20	Amendment of FA 1989 s 18	s 734
21	Amendment of FA 1984 s 29(2A)(b)	s 980
22	Amendment of CTA 1976 s 16(5)	s 396
23	Amendment of CTA 1976 s 33A(1)	s 708
24	Insertion of CGTA 1975 s 20A	s 594

Former Enactment			*Destination in TCA 1997*
Finance Act 1993 (1993 No 13) (contd)			
s 25		Amendment of FA 1984 ss 11, 12, 13, 13A, 14, 15, 16, 22, 23	s 488(1)(2)(3), 489, 490, 493, 495, 496, 503 503, 1024,
26		Amendment of FA 1986 s 12(2)	s 479
27	(1)-(3)	Definitions of "full-time working officer or employee" and "personal company" deleted by FA 1995 s 74	s 591(1)-(4)
	(4)(a)(b)(i), (iv)		s 591(5)
	(4)(ii)(iii)	Deleted by FA 1995 s 74	
	(5)		s 591(6)
	proviso	Unnecessary (spent)	
	(6)-(13)		s 591(7)-(14)
	(14)	Unnecessary (obsolete)	
	(15)	Unnecessary (operative date)	
28		Rep by FA 1996 s 132(2) and Sch 5 Pt II	
29	(1)		s 482(1)(a)
	(2)		s 482(9)
30	(1)	Amendment of FA 1986 ss 42, 44(1), 45	s 328(1), Sch 32 paras 11, 13
	(2)	Unnecessary (operative date)	
31		Amendment of FA 1989 s 4(1)	Sch 32, para 20
32		Amendment of FA 1991 ss 56(1)(a), 57, 58	s 325(1), 326(1), 327(1),
33	(1)	Substitution of FA 1988 s 51(1)(a)	ss 271(3)(a), 273(5)(a), 283(4)(a)(5)(a)
	(2)	Unnecessary (operative date)	
34	(1)	Substitution of ITA 1967 ss 254(4)(b),	s 317(2), 317(2), 769 303(3), 305(2)(b)
	(2)	Substitution of FA 1974 s 22(11)	s 658(1)
	(3)	Substitution of FA 1986 s 52(1)(a)(i)	s 317(3)
	(4)	Unnecessary (operative date)	
35	(1)(a), (2)-(6)		s 701
	(b)	Unnecessary (obsolete)	
36		Amendment of FA 1974 s 56	s 816
37			s 223
38		Rep by FA 1997 s 146(2) and Sch 9 Pt II	
39	(1)	Amendment of CTA 1976 s 6(4)	s 26(1), (2), (3)
	(2)	Unnecessary (operative date)	
40		Amendment of FA 1988 s 18	s 958
41		Amendment of FA 1993 s 50(6)	
42	(1)	Amendment of CTA 1976 s 1(5)	s 4(1)
	(2)	Unnecessary (operative date)	
43		Unnecessary (cesser of ITA 1967 s 337)	
44	(1)	Amendment of FA 1980 s 39	s 443
	(2)	Unnecessary (operative date)	
45	(1)	Amendment of CTA 1976 s 84A	s 134(3)
	(2)	Unnecessary (operative date)	
46	(1), (2)		s 150
	(3), (4)	Unnecessary (spent)	
	(5)	Amendment of FA 1980 s 45(7)	s 147, Sch 32 para 4
	(6)	Unnecessary (operative date)	
47	(1), (2)		s 80
	(3)	Insertion of FA 1980 s 39(1CC10)	s 443
	(4)	Unnecessary (commencement)	
48		Amendment of FA 1987 s 35	s 481, Sch 32 para 22
49		Rep by FA 1997 s 146(2) and Sch 9 Pt II	
50		Amendment of CTA 1976 s 10A	s 454(1)
51			s 486
140		Amendment of FA 1992 s 242	s 1094
142		Unnecessary (care and management)	

Former Enactment		*Destination in TCA 1997*
Finance Act 1993 (1993 No 13) (contd)		
s 143(2), (8)	Unnecessary (construction and commencement)	
Sch 1	Amendment of ITA 1967 ss 1(1),138, 38A(2)	ss 2(1), 3(1), 461, 462
Waiver of Certain Tax, Interest and Penalties Act 1993 (1993 No 24)		
s 10	Amendment of ITA 1967 s 512(1)	s 1065
11	Substitution of ITA 1967 s 516	s 1056
12	Amendment of ITA 1967 Sch 15	Sch 29
13		s 907
Finance Act 1994 (1994 No 13)		
Pt I		
s 1	Amendment of FA 1980 ss 1, 2	ss 187,188
2	Amendment of FA 1991 s 2 and FA 1993 Sch 1	ss 2(1), 3(1), 15, 461, 462
3 (1), (2)	Unnecessary (obsolete)	
(3)	Unnecessary (application of schedule)	
4	Insertion of ITA 1967 s 138B(2A)	s 472
5	Amendment of FA 1982 s 6	
6	Rep by FA 1997 s 146(2) and Sch 9 Pt II	
7	Insertion of ITA 1967 s 145(3A)	s 470(1)-(3)
8	Amendment of FA 1967 s 12(2)	s 469(1)
9	Amendment of FA 1982 s 8(1)	s 122
10	Unnecessary (spent)	
11	Amendment of FA 1992 Sch 2	Sch 13
12 (1)	Amendment of FA 1986 ss 35(1), 37A(1)	s 261, 264
(2)	Amendment of FA 1993 s 14(1)(c)	s 838(1)-(3)
13	Amendment of FA 1988 s 18(3)(b)	s 958
14 (1)	Unnecessary (interpretation)	
(2)-(5)		s 195(12)-(15)
15	Insertion of ITA 1967 s 462A	
16 (1)	Amendment of FA 1984 ss 11(1), 14(7A)(a), 16(2)(a)	s 488(1)-(3), 493
(2)	Unnecessary (operative date)	
17	Unnecessary (cesser of FA 1991 s 17(3)(b))	
18 (1)	Substitution of FA 1982 s 19(2)	s 482(1), (2), (3), (4)
(2)		s 482(8)
19 (1)-(6)		s 236
(7)	Unnecessary (commencement)	
20 (1)	Amendment of FA 1987 s 35	s 481, Sch 32 para 22
(2)	Unnecessary (operative date)	
21 (1)		s 373(2)(g)
(2)	Amendment of FA 1976 s 32	s 376
22 (1)	Amendment of ITA 1967 ss 254, 256, 264, 265	s 271, 278(1)(2)(6), 304(4), 305, 316(3), 317(2)
(2)	Unnecessary (operative date)	
23 (1)	Amendment of FA 1974 s 22	s 658
(2)	Unnecessary (operative date)	
24	Insertion of ITA 1967 s 241A, amendment of ss 272(1), 304(1)	ss 288(1)-(3), 291, 301(1), 314
25 (1)	Amendment of FA 1989 s 18	s 734
(2)	Unnecessary (commencement)	
26	Amendment of FA 1984 s 29(2A)	s 815(3)
27	Amendment of CTA 1976 ss 83, 88	ss 20, s 152(3), 153(1)
28	Amendment of FA 1973 s 34(1)	s 234(1), (2)(a)
29 (1)	Insertion of FA 1986 s 46(6)	s 1013(4)(b)
(2)(a)	Unnecessary (operative date)	
(b)		s 1013(4)(c)
30 (1)-(5), (7)		s 404
(6)	Unnecessary (obsolete)	

Former Enactment		*Destination in TCA 1997*
Finance Act 1994 (1994 No 13) (contd)		
s 31	Amendment of FA 1993 s 49(1)(a)	
32 (1)-(4)		s 227
(5)		s 610, Sch 15 Pt I
33	Amendment of CTA 1976 s 36A(2)	s 723
34	Amendment of FA 1993 ss 13, 14, 16.	ss 256, 261, 264, 737, 838
35 (1)	Amendment of FA 1986 ss 42, 44, 45, deletion of s 43	s 323, 324, 328(1)-(3), 329(9)(b)(12), 1024, Sch 32 paras 11,12,13
(2)	Unnecessary (operative date)	
36	Amendment of FA 1987 s 27(1)	s 322(2)
37 (1)	Amendment of FA 1991 ss 55, 56, 57, 58.	s 325(1)(2), 326(1), 327(1)
(2)	Unnecessary (operative date)	
38 (1), (3), (4)		s 339
(2)	Unnecessary (obsolete)	
39		s 340
40		s 341
41		s 342
41A	(s 41A inserted by FA 1995 s 35(1)(e))	s 343
41B	(s 41B inserted by FA 1995 s 35(1)(f))	s 344
42 (1)-(7)		s 345(1)-(7)
(8)	Amendment of FA 1990 s 33	ss 324(4)(b), 333(4)(b), 345(8)(b), 354(5)(b), 370(8)(b)
43		s 346
44		s 347
45		s 348
46 (1)-(4), (7)	Proviso to definition of "qualifying premises" deleted by FA 1995 s 35(1)	s 349
(5)	Rep by FA 1996 s 132(2) and Sch 5 Pt II	
(6)	Amendment of ITA 1967 s 198(1)(a)	s 1024
47		s 350
48 (1), (2)	Amendment of FA 1980 s 39(1A)	s 443
(2)	Amendment of FA 1990 s 41	s 443
49	Amendment of FA 1988 s 37	s 452
50 (1)	Amendment of CTA 1976 s 84A	s 134(3)
(2)		s 133(12)(a)-(d)
(3)	Unnecessary (operative date)	
proviso(i)		s 133(12)(e)
proviso(ii)	Unnecessary (operative date)	
51	Amendment of FA 1992 s 56(2)	s 88
52 (1)		s 221(1)
(2)		s 221(2)(a)(b)
53	Amendment of FA 1980 s 39B(6)	s 446(1)-(12)
54	Insertion of s 39C, amendment of FA 1980 s 41(1)	s 448(1)
55	Insertion of FA 1983 s 44(8)	s 165
56	Insertion of CTA 1976 ss 12A, 14A	s 79
57	Amendment of FA 1993 ss 17, 18.	ss 738, 739
58	Insertion of CGTA 1975 s 20B	s 595
59	Substitution of FA 1989 s 25(1)	s 154(1)-(3)
60	Amendment of CTA 1976 s 35(1A)	s 710(1)-(5)
61	Amendment of FA 1984 s 40	s 403
62	Amendment of FA 1987 s 28(1)	s 407(1)
63 (1)	Amendment of CGTA 1975 Sch 4	29(8)(9), 544(7), 567(3)(4), 568, 849(1)(2), 849(3)-(6), 851, 861(1), 863-865,

Former Enactment		*Destination in TCA 1997*
Finance Act 1994 (1994 No 13) (contd)		
s 63 (1)		869-871, 874, 875, 911, 913-917, 931, 945, 946, 949, 976, 977, 978, 980, 982, 999, Sch 1, 1029, 1043, 1051, 1077(1), 1077(2), 1083
(2)	Unnecessary (operative date)	
64 (1), (2)	Amendment of CGTA 1975	s 31731(1)-(5)(a), Sch 32 para 25
(3)		s 731(7)
65	Amendment of FA 1993 s 27	s 591(1)-(4)
66 (1)-(8)		s 592
(8A)	Rep by FA 1997 s 146(2) and Sch 9 Pt II	
(9)	Unnecessary (operative date)	
Pt VII		
s 149		s 818
150		s 819
151		s 820
152		s 821
153		s 822
154		s 823
155	Amendment of ITA 1967 s 153	s 1032
156		s 824
157(1)	Unnecessary (repeal of ITA 1967 ss 76(4), 199, 206, FA 1987 s 4)	
(2)	Unnecessary (spent)	
158	Unnecessary (commencement)	
161(1)		ss 40(1), 48(1)(d)
(2)(a)		s 40(2)
(2)(b)		s 48(1)(d)
(3)	Amendment of ITA 1967 s 474(1)	s 49, Sch 32 para 1(2)
(5)	Amendment of FA 1984 s 66	s 607
162(1)	Substitution of ITA 1967 s 486(1), (2)	s 963
(2)	Unnecessary (operative date)	
(2)	Unnecessary (spent)	
(3)	Unnecessary (operative date)	
164		s 196
165	Unnecessary (care and management)	
166(2), (8)	Unnecessary (construction and commencement)	
Sch 1	Amendment of ITA 1967 ss 138, 138A(2),	ss 461, 462
Sch 2		Sch 4
Finance Act 1995 (1995 No 8)		
Pt I		
s 1	Amendment of FA 1980 ss 1, 2	ss 187,188
2	Amendment of FA 1991 s 2	
3 (1), (2)	Unnecessary (obsolete)	s 15
(3)	Unnecessary (application of schedule)	
4	Amendment of FA 1982 s 6	
5	Amendment of ITA 1967 s 142A	s 473
6 (1)-(5)		s 474
(6)	Rep by FA 1996 s 132(2) and Sch 5 Pt II	
(7)	Amendment of ITA 1967 s 198(1)(a)	s 1024
7 (1)-(8)		s 477
(9)(a)	Amendment of ITA 1967 s 198(1)(a)	s 1024
(b)	Amendment of ITA 1967 Sch 15	Sch 29

Former Enactment			*Destination in TCA 1997*
Finance Act 1995 (1995 No 8) (contd)			
s 7	(10)	Rep by FA 1996 s 132(2) and Sch 5 Pt II	
8	(1)(a)(c)		s 848(1)
	(b)	Unnecessary (obsolete)	
	(2)-(5)(a)		s 848(2)-(5)
	(5)(b)		s 848(1)(a)
	(6), (7)		s 848(6), (7)
9		Amendment of FA 1982 s 8(1)	s 122
10	(1)	Substitution of FA 1992 s 15(2)	ss 126(3)(b)
	(2)	Amendment of FA 1994 s 10	
11	(1)	Amendment of FA 1986 s 31(1)	s 256
	(2)	Amendment of FA 1993 s 14(3)	s 838(1)-(3)
12	(1)	Amendment of ITA 1967 ss 443, 444, 445, 447	ss 794(1)-(5), 795
	(2)	Unnecessary (operative date)	
	(3)	Unnecessary (cesser of ITA 1967 ss 440, 443(4))	
13	(1)(a)	Insertion of ITA 1967 s 439(1A)	s 792(1)-(4)
	(b)	Unnecessary (operative date)	
	(2)	Amendment of ITA 1967 s 439	s 792(1)-(4)
13	(3)		Sch 32, para 27
14	(1)	Insertion of ITA 1967 s 94(e)	s 888
	(2)	Amendment of FA 1992 ss 226(1), 228(1)	ss 894, 899
	(3)	Unnecessary (operative date)	
15		Amendment of ITA 1967 s 191	s 930
16		Amendment of FA 1982 s 56 and Sch 3	s 515, Sch 11
17	(1)	Amendment of FA 1984 ss 11(1), 12, 13, 15, 16, 22, 23, insertion of ss 14A, 16A,	ss 488, 489, 490, 494, 495, 496, 498, 503, 504
	(2)	Unnecessary (operative dates)	
18	(1)	Amendment of FA 1970 s 17	ss 530(1), 531(11)
	(2)	Unnecessary (operative date)	
19		Insertion of ITA 1967 s 58A	s 68
20		Amendment of FA 1982 s 19	s 482
21		Rep by FA 1996 s 132(2) and Sch 5 Pt II	
22		Rep by FA 1996 s 132(2) and Sch 5 Pt II	
23	(1)		s 373(2)(g)
	(2)	Amendment of FA 1976 s 32	s 376
24	(1)	Amendment of ITA 1967 s 265(1)(c)	s 274(1), (3), (4), (5), (8)
	(2)	Unnecessary (operative date and cesser of FA 1994 s 22(1)(d)(i))	
25	(1)	Amendment of ITA 1967 s 272	s 288(1)-(3)
	(2)	Unnecessary (operative date)	
26		Amendment of FA 1988s 51(1)	ss 271(3)(a), 273(5)(a), 283(4)(a), 285(5)(a)
27		Substitution of FA 1990 s 81(1)	ss 273(7)(b), 285(7)(b)
28		Amendment of FA 1994 s 49(1)	s 452
29			s 847
30	(1)	Amendment of FA 1986 s 48(2)	s 1084(1)-(4)
	(2)	Unnecessary (operative date)	
31		Amendment of FA 1988 s 18	s 958
32	(1)	Amendment of FA 1986 ss 41, 42, 44	s 322(1), 323, Sch 32 paras 11, 12
	(2)	Unnecessary (operative date)	
33		Amendment of FA 1987 s 27(1)(b)	s 322(2)-(3)
34	(1)	Amendment of FA 1991 ss 54(3), 55, 56, 57(2), 58(2)	s 325(1)(2)
	(2)	Unnecessary (operative date)	

Former Enactment		*Destination in TCA 1997*
Finance Act 1995 (1995 No 8) (contd)		
s 35 (1)	Amendment of FA 1994 ss 38(1), 39, 40, 41, 42(1), 43(1), 46(1), insertion of ss 41A, 41B	s 339, 340, 341, 342, 343, 344, 345(1)-(7), 346, 349
(2)	Unnecessary (operative date)	
36 (1)	Amendment of FA 1987 s 35	s 481, Sch 32 para 22
(2)	Unnecessary (operative date)	
37	Insertion of FA 1983 s 47A	s 169
38	Amendment of FA 1989 s 18(1)	s 734(1)(a), (c)
39	Amendment of FA 1994 s 27	ss 20, s 152(3), 153(1)
40		s 198
41	Insertion of FA 1992 s 230A	s 896
42	Amendment of FA 1992 ss 75(1), 77(1)	ss 684, 686
43		s 224
44 (1), (2)		s 220
(3)		s 610, Sch 15 Pt I
45 (1)	Unnecessary (obsolete)	
(2)	Unnecessary (application of schedule)	
46 (1)		s 351
(2)	Unnecessary (obsolete)	
47		s 352
48		s 353
49 (1)-(4)		s 354(1)-(4)
(5)	Amendment of FA 1990 s 33	ss 324(4)(b), 333(4)(b), 345(8)(b), 354(5)(b), 370(8)(b)
49A	(s 49A inserted by FA 1996 s 30)	s 355
50		s 356
51		s 357
52		s 358
53		s 359
54 (1)	Substitution of CTA 1976 s 1(1)	s 21
(2)	Unnecessary (application of schedule)	
55 (1)	Amendment of CTA 1976 s 162(4)	s 441
(2)	Unnecessary (operative date)	
proviso	Unnecessary (obsolete)	
56	Amendment of FA 1992 s 45(1)(a)	s 487
57 (1)		s 221(1)
(2)		s 221(2)(c)(d)
58	Amendment of CTA 1976 s 141	ss 882(2)-(5), 1073
59 (1)-(4)		s 766
(5)	Unnecessary (obsolete)	
60	Amendment of CTA 1976 s 23	ss 826(1)-(7), (9), 827, Sch 24, para 4(2)
61	Amendment of FA 1980 s 41(1)(b)	s 448(1)
62	Insertion of FA 1980 s 39D	s 446(1)-(12)
63	Amendment of FA 1980 s 39C	s 449
64	Insertion of CTA 1976 s 43(2A)	s 726
65	Substitution of FA 1980 s 39B(6)(c)(iiia)	s 446(1)-(12)
66 (1), (2)		s 1085(3), (4)
(3)	Unnecessary (operative date)	
67	Amendment of FA 1993 s 51	s 486
68	Insertion of CGTA 1975 s 20A(4)	s 594
69	Amendment of CTA 1976 s 46B(1)	s 720(1)(2)
70 (1)	Amendment of CGTA 1975 Sch 4 para 4(1)	s 914
(2)	Unnecessary (operative date)	

Former Enactment		*Destination in TCA 1997*
Finance Act 1995 (1995 No 8) (contd)		
s 71 (1)	Amendment of CGTA 1975 s 26	s 598
(2)	Unnecessary (operative date)	
72 (1)	Amendment of CGTA 1975 s 27(4)(a)	s 599
(2)	Unnecessary (operative date)	
73 (1)	Insertion of FA 1982 s 39(4), (5)	s 652
(2)	Unnecessary (operative date)	
74 (1)	Amendment of FA 1993 s 27	s 591
(2)	Unnecessary (operative date)	
75	Amendment of FA 1995 s 66	s 1085(3), (4)
76	Amendment of CGTA 1975 Sch 4 para 11	s 980
Pt VII		
s 167	Amendment of FA 1986 ss 31(1), 37(1)	ss 256, 263
168	Amendment of ITA 1967 s 175(4)	s 891
169	Amendment of FA 1994 s 152(1)	s 821
170	Amendment of FA 1994 s 154(2)	s 823
172		s 1079
173(1)	Amendment of ITA 1967 ss 416, 421, 422, 423, 424, 427, 428, 429, 432	ss 864(1), 933(1)-(7)(f), 934, 935,936, 937, 940, 941, 942(1)-(8), (10), 949(1)-(4)
(2)	Substitution of FA 1969 s 2(5B)	s 195(1)-(11)
(3)	Unnecessary (application).	
173 (4)	Unnecessary (operative date)	
174	Amendment of FA 1986 s 115	
175		s 910
176		s 1003
177(1)-(6)		s 1095
(7)	Unnecessary (operative date)	
178	Unnecessary (care and management)	
179(2), (8), (9)	Unnecessary (construction and commencement)	
Sch 1	Amendment of ITA 1967 ss 138, 138A(2)	s 461, s 462
Sch 2	Unnecessary (obsolete)	
Sch 3		Sch 8
Sch 4	Unnecessary (obsolete)	
Family Law Act 1995 (1995 No 26)		
s 49	Amendment of FA 1983 s 4	s 1026(1), (2)
Finance Act 1996 (1996 No 9)		
Pt I		
s 1	Amendment of FA 1980 ss 1, 2.	ss 187, 188
2	Amendment of FA 1991 s 2	s 15
3 (1), (2)	Unnecessary (obsolete)	
(3)	Unnecessary (application of schedule)	
4	Unnecessary (obsolete)	
5		s 478
6	Amendment of FA 1982 s 4	s 121
7 (1)	Substitution of ITA 1967 s 145(1)	s 470(1)-(3)
(2)	Unnecessary (operative date)	
8 (1)	Amendment of FA 1992 Sch 2	
(2)	Unnecessary (operative date)	
9		s 191
10		s 664(1)(a), (b)(iii)
11 (1)		s 656(1)
(2)	Amendment of ITA 1967 s 62(1)(b)	s 89(2)
12	Amendment of FA 1986 s 12	s 479
13 (a)	Substitution of ITA 1967 s 236(1A)	s 787(8)-(12)
(b)	Unnecessary (deletion of ITA 1967 Sch 5)	

Former Enactment | *Destination in TCA 1997*

Finance Act 1996 (1996 No 9) (contd)

Former Enactment			Destination in TCA 1997
s 14		Amendment of FA 1969 s 2(2)(a)	s 195(1)-(11)
15	(1)-(5), (8)		s 475
	(6)	Rep by FA 1997 s 146(2) and Sch 9 Pt II	
	(7)	Amendment of ITA 1967 s 198(1)(a)	s 1023
16		Amendment of FA 1984 s 11(1)	s 488(1), (2), (3)
17		Amendment of FA 1984 s 12	ss 488(1), 489
18		Amendment of FA 1984 s 13	s 490
19		Amendment of FA 1984 s 13A	s 491
20		Insertion of FA 1984 s 13B	s 492
21		Unnecessary (obsolete)	
22		Insertion of FA 1984 s 15(3C)	s 495
23		Amendment of FA 1984 s 16	s 496
24		Amendment of FA 1984 s 16A	s 497
25	(1), (2)		s 233
	(3)	Amendment of CTA 1976 s 93(1)	s 140
	(4)	Unnecessary (operative date)	
26	(1)	Amendment of FA 1984 s 41B(1)	
26	(2)	Unnecessary (operative date)	
27		Amendment of FA 1991 s 22	s 271(4)(a)
28		Amendment of ITA 1967 ss 264, 265	s 272, s 274(1),(3)-(5),(8)
29		Amendment of ITA 1967 s 255(1)	s 268(1)-(3), (5)-(8)
30		Insertion of FA 1995 s 49A	s 355
31	(1)	Substitution of FA 1987 s 35	s 481, Sch 32, para 22
	(2)(a),(3),(4)		Sch 32, para 22(1)-(4)
	(b)	Unnecessary (obsolete)	
	(1)	Amendment of FA 1973 s 34(1)	s 234(1), (2)(a)
	(2)	Amendment of CTA 1976 s 170	s 141
	(3)	Unnecessary (operative date)	
33	(1)	Substitution of FA 1974 s 31(3)(cc)	
	(2)	Unnecessary (operative date)	
34		Insertion of F(TPCM)A 1974 s 8A	s 681
35	(1)	Amendment of FA 1989 s 18(1)	s 734
	(2)	Unnecessary (operative date)	
36	(1)	Insertion of FA 1993 s 13(8)(bb)	s 737
	(2)	Unnecessary (operative date)	
37	(1)	Amendment of FA 1993 s 14	s 838
	(2)	Unnecessary (operative date)	
38	(1)	Amendment of FA 1993 s 17	s 738
	(2)	Unnecessary (operative date)	
39	(1)		ss 41, 228, 610
	(2)		s 228
	(3)		s 41
	(4)	Amendment of ITA 1967 s 474(1)	s 49, Sch 32 para 1(2)
	(5)	Amendment of CGTA 1975 s 19(1)	s 607(1)(a), (b), (c), (d), (f)
	(6)		s 610, Sch 15 PtI
39	(7)	Unnecessary (repeal of Securitisation (Proceeds of Certain Mortgages) Act, 1995 s 14)	
	(8)	Unnecessary (operative date)	
40	(1), (2)		s 226
	(3)	Unnecessary (operative date)	
41		Amendment of FA 1970 s 17	ss 530(1), 531(11)
42		Insertion of FA 1986 s 33A	s 260
43	(1)	Amendment of FA 1988 s 51(1)(a)	ss 271(3)(a), 273(5)(a), 283(4)(a), 285(5)(a)
	(2)	Unnecessary (operative date)	
44		Insertion of CTA 1976 s 28A	s 22
45	(1)	Amendment of CTA 1976 s 12A	s 79
	(2)	Unnecessary (operative date)	

Former Enactment		*Destination in TCA 1997*
Finance Act 1996 (1996 No 9) (contd)		
s 46	Amendment of CTA 1976 s 33A(1)	s 708
47 (1)	Insertion of CTA 1976 s 35A(1A)	s 711
(2)	Unnecessary (operative date)	
48 (1)	Amendment of CTA 1976 s 36(2)	s 713(1)-(6)
(2)	Unnecessary (operative date)	
49 (1)	Amendment of CTA 1976 s 36A(6)	s 723
(2)	Unnecessary (operative date)	
50 (1)	Insertion of CTA 1976 s 46B(4)	s 720(3)-(5)
(2)	Unnecessary (operative date)	
51	Amendment of CTA 1976 s 135	s 623
52 (1)	Amendment of CTA 1976 s 162(4)	s 441
(2)	Unnecessary (operative date)	
proviso	Unnecessary (obsolete)	
53	Amendment of FA 1980 s 39A(6)(c)	s 445
54 (1)	Amendment of FA 1987 s 28	ss 133(1)(d), 134(1)(d), 407(1)(3)(4)(6), 443
(2), (5)		s 407(5)
(3)(a), (4)		s 407(1)
(b)		s 407(2)
55 (1)	Amendment of FA 1991 s 31	s 110
(2)	Unnecessary (operative date)	
56	Amendment of FA 1992 s 56	s 88
57 (1)	Amendment of FA 1995 s 59	s 766
(2)	Unnecessary (operative date)	
58 (1)	Amendment of FA 1983 ss 44(5), 47(1)	ss 165, 168
(2)	Unnecessary (operative date)	
59	Amendment of CGTA 1975 Sch 4 para 11	s 980
60 (1)	Amendment of CGTA 1975 s 26(6)(a)	s 598
(2)	Unnecessary (operative date)	
61 (1)	Insertion of CGTA 1975 s 46(7)	s 541(7)(a)-(c), (g)
(2)	Unnecessary (operative date)	
62 (1)	Insertion of FA 1993 s 27(2A)	s 591(1)-(4)
(2)	Unnecessary (operative date)	
63 (1)	Amendment of FA 1994 s 66	s 592
(2)	Unnecessary (operative date)	
64		s 610, Sch 15
65		s 360
66		s 361
67		s 362
68		s 363
69 (1)-(3), (5)		s 364
(4)	Amendment of ITA 1967 s 198(1)(a)	s 1024
70		s 365
Pt VI		
s 130		s 872(2)
131(1)-(8)		s 10
(9)(a)	Unnecessary (obsolete)	
(b)	Unnecessary (cesser of F(MP)A 1968 s 16(3), CGTA 1975 s 33(7), CTA 1976 s 157)	
132(1), (2)	Unnecessary (application of schedules)	
(3)	Unnecessary (construction)	
133	Definition of "farming" and "tax" unnecessary (duplication)	s 665
134		s 666
135		s 667
136		s 668

Former Enactment		*Destination in TCA 1997*
Finance Act 1996 (1996 No 9) (contd)		
s 137		s 669
Pt VII		
s 139	Amendment of FA 1995 s 176(2)	s 1003
142	Unnecessary (care and management)	
143(2), (7), (8)	Unnecessary (construction and commencement)	
Sch 1	Amendment of ITA 1967 ss 138, 138A(2), 141(1), FA 1969 s 3(1), FA 1971 s 11(2)	ss 461, 462, 465, 467, 468
Sch 5		
Pt I	Amendment of ITA 1967 ss 2, 79, 145, 146, 149, 153, 195A, 235(7), 239, 241, 297, 299, 312(2), 316, 433(1), 434(1), 468(2), 471(2), 497	ss 3(2)(3), 74, 237, 238(1)(6), 306, 312, 386, 390(1)(3), 459(1)(2), 460, 762(2)(a), 470(1)-(4), 783(3), 788, 1020, 1032, Sch 32, para 1(1)
	Substitution of ITA 1967 ss 137, 321	s 458, 395
	Amendment of FA 1967 s 11, FA 1968 s 6, FA 1969 s 19 , FA 1971 s 26, FA 1972 Sch 1, FA 1973 s 34, F(TPCM)A 1974 s 1, FA 1974 s 62, CTA 1976 ss 6, 50, 102(1), 147(2), FA 1978 s 25, FA 1980 s 2, FA 1983 ss 3, 94(2), FA 1985 s 10, FA 1986 s 12, FA 1987 s 24, FA 1991 s 4 , FA 1992 s 83, FA 1995 s 177	ss 207(3)(4), 211(5)(6), 213(3)(4), 234, 26(1)-(3), 273, 273(1)-(3)(8), 285(1)-(3)(8), 286, 287, 299(2), 432, 463, 479, 483(1)-(3), 53, 664(1)(a), 672(1), 692, 706(1)-(3), 863, 865, 868, 869, 870, 849, 860, 861(1), 862, 873, 874, 875, 877, 886, 898, 901, 928(1), 929, 947, 998, 1004, 1025, 1049, 105, 1055, 1056, 1057, 1058, 1066, 1067, 1068, 1069, 1070, 1078, 1081(1), 1095, Sch 23 Pt I paras 1-5
Pt II	Repeal of ITA 1967 ss 43, 89A, 138A(7), 141(7), 145(3A)(5), 241(7)(8)(9), 242, 243, 244(4)(e), 247(3), 249, 259, 262, 273(2), 306, 344, 346, 360, 448(2), 476, 477(2), (3), 479, 480, 482(3), 494(2), 495, 540, 543, 557, 558, Sch 2 rule 1(3), Sch 13, FA 1967 s 12(5)(c), FA 1968 s 4, FA 1969 ss 3(3), 4, 5, FA 1971 s 11(4), FA 1972 ss 16(6), 17(3), 18(1)(b), 24, 25, Sch 1 Pt II para 1(2), Sch 1 Pts IV, V, FA 1974 ss 4(c), 8(2), 30, 40, 50, FA 1975 ss 31, 31A, Sch, 3, Sch 5, CGTA 1975 ss 2(2), 27(1)(d), 33(8), CTA 1976 ss 12(8), 51(3)(b)(c), 52(5), 68, 153, FA 1976 ss 12, 15, 16, FA 1977 s 39(4)(b) proviso, FA 1978 s 9, Sch 1 Pt III, FA 1979 ss 5, 8(2)(b), FA 1980 s 28, FA 1981 s 13, FA 1982 ss 6, 13, FA 1983 s 94(1)(ee), FA 1984 ss 12(9), 33, Pt I Ch VIII, IX, FA 1986 ss 12(9), 44(4), FA 1989 s 4(7), FA 1991 s 4(3), FA 1992 ss 26(1)(2)(3)(5), 243(a)(ii), FA 1993 s 28, FA 1994 s 46(5), FA 1995 ss 6(6), 7(10), 21, 22	
	Amendment of ITA 1967 ss 58(5), 186(3), 187(1), 235(7), 244(5)(b)(6), 245(7), 300(1), 309, 441, 442, 447, 478, 484(3), 496(1)(c), Sch 2 rule 3, FA 1969 s 18(1), FA 1972 s 15(4), FA 1974 ss 4(b)(e), 27(2), 31(3), FA 1975 Sch 2 Pt I para 2, CGTA 1975 s 27(3), CTA 1976 ss 11(6), 39(2)(b), 43(5)(a), 147(2)	ss 59, 67, 76, 114, 207(3)(4), 211(5)(6), 213(3)(4), 232(1), 246(3), 313, 382(1)(2), 483(1)-(3), 599, 662, 670, 715, 726, 765, 772(4), 783(3), 791(1), 793, 794(1), 860, 861(1), 862, 863, 865, 868, 869, 870, 873, 874, 875, 886, 898, 901, 924, 928(1), 929, 947, 961,

Former Enactment		Destination in TCA 1997
Finance Act 1996 (1996 No 9) (contd)		
Pt II (contd)		964(2), 972(1)-(4), 998, 1004, 1049, 1055, 1056, 1057, 1058, 1066, 1067, 1068, 1069, 1070, 1081(1)
Disclosure of Certain Information for Taxation and Other Purposes Act 1996 (1996 No 25)		
s 5	Insertion of ITA 1967 s 184(3)	s 922
6	Substitution of CTA 1976 s 144(4)	s 919(1)-(5)
10	Insertion of FA 1983 s 18(4A)	s 908
11	Substitution of FA 1983 s 19(2)	s 58
12	Insertion of FA 1983 s 19A	s 859
Criminal Assets Bureau Act 1996 (1996 No 31)		
s 23	Substitution of FA 1983 s 19A(3)(a)	s 859
24 (1)	Substitution of ITA 1967 s 184(3)	s 922
(2)	Substitution of CTA 1976 s 144(4)(b)	s 919(1)-(5)
Family Law (Divorce) Act 1996 (1997 No 33)		
s 31		s 1027(b)
32	Amendment of FA 1983 s 4	s 1026(1), (2)
35		s 1031
Finance Act 1997 (1997 No 22)		
Pt I		
s 1	Amendment of FA 1980 ss 1, 2	ss 187, 188
2	Amendment of FA 1991 s 2	s 15
3 (1), (2)	Unnecessary (duplication)	
3 (3)	Unnecessary (application of schedule)	
4 (1)	Amendment of FA 1992 s 15(2)	s 126(3)(b)(4)
(2)		s 126(8)
5 (a)	Insertion of FA 1983 s 4(3)	s 1026(1), (2)
(b)	Unnecessary (repeal of Family Law Act 1995 s 49 and Family Law (Divorce) Act 1996 s 32	
6 (1)	Insertion of ITA 1967 s 127(5A)	s 986(4)-(6)
(2)	Unnecessary (operative date)	
7	Amendment of FA 1996 s 15	s 475
8 (1)-(7), (10),(11)		s 476
(8)	Amendment of ITA 1967 s 137	s 458
(9)	Amendment of ITA 1967 s 198(1)(a)	s 1024
9	Amendment of FA 1984 ss 11, 14A, 16, 16A	ss 488(1)-(4), 494, 496, 497
10	Amendment of FA 1992 s 14	ss 248(1)-(3), 252
11 (1)	Amendment of ITA 1967 s 353	s 193 Sch 32, para 2
(2)	Unnecessary (operative date).	
(3)	Unnecessary (spent)	
(4)	Amendment of ITA 1967 s 178(1)	s 897(1)-(5)
12	Amendment of ITA 1967 s 115(1A)	s 201(3)
13 (1)	Amendment of FA 1970 s 17	ss 530(1), 531(11)
(2)	Amendment of ITA 1967 Sch 15	Sch 29
14		s 202
15	Insertion of FA 1971 s 4(6)	s 72
16		s 485
17 (1)	Amendment of FA 1982 s 19	s 482
(2)	Amendment of FA 1993 s 29(1)	s 482(1)(a)
(3)	Unnecessary (operative date)	
18	Amendment of FA 1996 s 134	s 666
19	Amendment of FA 1996 s 135(1)(b)	s 667
20 (1)-(13)		s 659
(14)	Amendment of FA 1975 s 29	s 319

Former Enactment			*Destination in TCA 1997*
Finance Act 1997 (1997 No 22) (contd)			
s 21	(1)		s 373(2)(i)
	(2)	Amendment of FA 1976 s 32	s 1009
22		Amendment of ITA 1967 s 241	ss 284, 298(1), 299(1), 301(1), 304(2)(4), 316(1)(a)(2), 406
23	(1)	Amendment of ITA 1967 ss 265, 266,	ss 274(1) (3)-(5)(8), 277
	(2)	Unnecessary (operative date)	
24			s 409
25	(1)-(5), (7)		s 843
	(6)	Unnecessary (operative date)	
26		Amendment of FA 1994 ss 38, 39, 42	ss 339, 340, 324(4)(b), 333(4)(b), 345(8)(b), 354(5)(b), 370(8)(b)
27		Amendment of FA 1986 s 45(2), FA 1994 s 42(3), FA 1995 s 49(3)	ss 324(2), 346, 354(1)-(4)
28		Insertion of FA 1980 s 39B(10)	s 446(1)-(12)
29	(1)		s 82(2)
	(2)		s 243(3)(b)
	(3)		s 390(2)(b)
	(4)		s 82(3)
	(5)		ss 82(4), 243(3)(c), 390(2)(c)
	(6)		ss 82(1), 243(3)(a), 390(2)(a)
30	(1)	Amendment of FA 1987 s 35	s 481, Sch 32 para 22
	(2)		Sch 32, para 22(6)-(8)
31	(1)	Amendment of FA 1993 s 14	s 838(1)-(4)
	(2)	Unnecessary (operative date)	
32		Amendment of FA 1989 s 18(1)	s 734(1)(a), (c)
33			s 55
34		Amendment of FA 1990 s 138(1)	ss 45(3)(4)(a), 48(4)(a),(5)(a)
35		Substitution of FA 1993 s 17(4)(a)	s 738
36		Amendment of FA 1974 s 31	s 246(1)-(4)
37	(1)		ss 4(1), 136(2),139(1), 143(2)(7), 145(2)(a), (11)(a), 729(5)
	(2)	Unnecessary (application of schedule)	
38		Amendment of FA 1992 s 37(1)	s 154(3)(a)(4)(5)
39	(1)(a)	Amendment of FA 1991 s 59	s 173
	(b)	Insertion of FA 1991 s 60A	s 175
	(2)	Unnecessary (operative date)	
40	(1)	Amendment of FA 1996 s 40(2)	s 226
	(2)	Unnecessary (operative date)	
41	(1)(a)	Amendment of FA 1972 s 16	s 774(1)-(3)(5)-(7), Sch 32 para 26
	(b)	Insertion of FA 1972 s 16A	s 775
	(2)	Amendment of CTA 1976 Sch 2 Pt I para 31	Sch 32 para 26
	(3)	Unnecessary (commencement)	
42			s 627
43			s 628
44			s 629
45	(1)	Amendment of ITA 1967 s 464	s 43
	(2)	Unnecessary (operative date)	
46	(1)	Amendment of ITA 1967 s 470(1)(b)	s 50
	(2)	Unnecessary (operative date)	
47	(1)	Amendment of ITA 1967 s 474(2)	s 49, Sch 32 para 1(2)
	(2)	Unnecessary (operative date)	

Former Enactment	*Destination in TCA 1997*
Finance Act 1997 (1997 No 22) (contd)	
s 48 (1), (2)	s 842
(3) .... Unnecessary (operative date)	
49 (1), (2)	s 220
(3)	s 610, Sch 15 Pt I
(4)	Sch 32, para 3
50 (a) .... Amendment of FA 1982 s 52	s 511
(b) .... Insertion of FA 1982 s 58A	s 518
(c) .... Amendment of FA 1982 Sch 3	Sch 11
51	s 519
52	s 366
53	s 367
54	s 368
55	s 369
56	s 370(1)-(7)
(8) .... Amendment of FA 1990 s 33	ss 324(4)(a)(b), 333(4)(a)(b), 345(8)(b), 354(5)(b), 370(8)(b)
57 (1)-(3), (5)	s 371
(4) .... Amendment of ITA 1967 s 137	s 458
58	s 372
59 (1) .... Substitution of CTA 1976 s 1(1)	s 21
(2) .... Unnecessary (application of schedule)	
60 (1) .... Amendment of CTA 1976 s 28A	s 22(1)(a), (2)-(8)
(2) .... s 22(1)(b)	
(3) .... Unnecessary (operative date)	
61 (1), (3), (4)	s 841
(2) .... Unnecessary (repeal of CTA 1976 s 80)	
62(1), (3)-(5)	s 229
(2) .... Unnecessary (repeal of ITA 1967 s 343)	
63	s 219
64 .... Amendment of FA 1992 s 56	s 88
65 .... Amendment of FA 1993 s 51	s 454(1)
66 (1) .... Amendment of FA 1988 s 36(4)(a)	s 451
(2) .... Unnecessary (operative date)	
67 (1) .... Insertion of CTA 1976 s 35(1B)	s 710(1)-(5)
(2) .... Unnecessary (operative date)	
68 (1) .... Amendment of CTA 1976 s 36	s 713(1)-(6)
(2) .... Unnecessary (operative date)	
69 (1) .... Substitution of CTA 1976 s 46A(3)(a)	s 719
(2) .... Unnecessary (operative date)	
70 (1) .... Insertion of CGTA 1975 Sch 2 para 5A	s 588
(2) .... Unnecessary (operative date)	
71 (1)-(3)	s 1031
(4) .... Unnecessary (repeal of s 35 Family Law (Divorce) Act, 1996)	
(5) .... Unnecessary (operative date)	
72 (1)-(3)	s 1030
(4) .... Unnecessary (repeal of Family Law Act 1995 s 52)	
(5) .... Unnecessary (operative date)	
73 (1) .... Insertion of CGTA 1975 s 15(5A)	s 577
(2) .... Unnecessary (operative date)	
74 (1) .... Amendment of CGTA 1975 s 20A	s 594
(2) .... Unnecessary (operative date)	
75 (1) .... Amendment of FA 1993 s 27	s 591(1)-(5)
(2) .... Unnecessary (operative date)	

Former Enactment		*Destination in TCA 1997*
Finance Act 1997 (1997 No 22) (contd)		
s 76	Amendment of FA 1994 s 66	s 592
77 (1)	Insertion of FA 1982 s 39(3A)	s 652
(2)	Unnecessary (operative date)	
78 (1)	Amendment of CGTA 1975 s 46(7)	s 541(7)(a), (b), (c), (g)
(2)		s 541(8)
Pt VII		
s 144		s 37
145		s 244
146(1), (2)	Unnecessary (application of schedule)	
(3)	Unnecessary (interpretation)	
147		s 330
148		s 331
149		s 332
150(1)-(3)		s 333(1)-(3)
(4)	Amendment of FA 1990 s 33	ss 324(4)(b), 333(4)(b), 345(8)(b), 354(5)(b), 370(8)(b)
150(5)		s 333(5)
151		s 334
152		s 335
153		s 336
154		s 337
155		s 338
156(1)	Repeal of FA 1991 ss 54, 55, 56(1)(a)(iii), (2) proviso, 57(1)(a), (2), 58(1)(a), (2)	
(2)	Amendment of ITA 1967 s 137	s 458
(3)	Amendment of CTA 1976 s 33A(1)	s 708
(4)	Amendment of FA 1991 s 56(1)(c)	
157	Amendment of ITA 1967 s 162(3)	s 851
158	Substitution of FA 1983 s 23(2), (3)	s 1086
159		s 858
160(1)	Amendment of FA 1992 s 242(1)	s 1094
165	Unnecessary (care and management)	
166(2), (8), (9)	Unnecessary (construction and commencement)	
Sch 1	Amendment of ITA 1967 ss 138, 138A(2) and FA 1974 s 8(1)	ss 461, 462, 464
Sch 2		
para 1		ss 4(1), 136(2), 139(1), 143(2), (7), 145(2)(a), (11)(a), 729(5)
2		s 729(7)
3 (1)	Unnecessary (operative date)	
(2)	Unnecessary (cesser of FA 1978 s 28(7), FA 1983 s 28(3), FA 1988 Sch 2 Pt I para 4, FA 1990 Sch 1 para 3, FA 1995 Sch 2 para 3)	
(3)		s 145(2)(b)
Sch 3		Sch 12
Sch 4		s 659 Table
Sch 5		Sch 26

Former Enactment		*Destination in TCA 1997*
Finance Act 1997 (1997 No 22) (contd)		
Sch 6, Pt I		
para 1		ss 26(4), 78(3)(c)
2(1)		Sch 32, para 16(5), 18(6)(a)
(2)		Sch 32, para 18(6)(b)
(3)		Sch 32, para 16(3)(b), 18(4)(b)
Pt II		
para 1(1)		s 448(2)(b)
(2)	Amendment of FA 1980 s 41(2)	s 448(2)(a)
(1)	Amendment of FA 1980 ss 47(2), 48(2)	Sch 32 paras 5(2), 6(2)
2(2)		Sch 32 para 5(3), 6(3)
Sch 9		
Pt I	Amendment of ITA 1967 ss 1(1), 58(1), 61, 76(1)(c), 77(5), 81(5)(b), 89(2), 137, 138B, 142(1)(b), 183, 197, 198, 225, 239(4), 241(1)(b)(i), 241A, 256, 284(3), 304, 309(2), 310(3), 318(1), 319(1), 349, 429(4), 441(1), 446(1), 450(2), 466(3)(b), 474(1), 484, 492(1)(d), 525(5)(a), Sch 6 Pt III Par 1(2), FA 1967 s 12(1), F(MP)A 1968 s 9, FA 1970 ss 14(2), 19(2A), 59(1), FA 1972 ss 15, 18(5), Sch 1 Pt III para 4, FA 1973 ss 25(1), 34(3), F(TPCM)A 1974 ss 7(4), CGTA 1975 ss 2(1), 25(9A)(a), 38(1), CTA 1976 ss 76, 84A, 93(7), 101(6), 103(3), 124(6), 145(3), 160, 162(5), 170(7), FA 1980 ss 39(1CC), 45(1)(a), FA 1982 ss 8, 58(3), FA 1984 ss 12(7)(b), 13A(1A), 13B(1), 14(1)(a), 15(3C)(b), FA 1986 s 33A(3), FA 1988 s 12, FA 1992 ss 45(1)(a), 84(11), FA 1993 s 14, 35(1)(a), FA 1994 ss 14(3)(b)(i), 45(2), 66(7)(a), FA 1995 s 48(5), FA 1996 s 68(2) s 194, 225	ss 3(1), 5, 38, 48(1)(b), 49, 65(1),70(4), 71(1), 73, 81(2), 97, 122, 127(1)-(5), 134(3), 140, 141, 144, 147 195(12)-(15), 2(1), 200(1), 234(3)-(8), 235, 245, 260, 270, 279, 284, 287, 291, 301(1), 316, 318, 320(1), 348, 353, 36, 363, 373(2)(a), 374, 382(1)(2), 383, 384, 392, 393, 406, 428, 433,440, 441, 443, 458, 466, 469(1), 472, 487, 488(1), 491, 492, 493, 495, 517, 592, 604,678, 681, 693, 701, 754, 772,772, 788, 790, 793, 797, 799, 808, 828(1)-(3), 838, 921, 942(1)-(8)(10), 953, 968, 972, 973, 1023, 1024, 1033, Sch 32 paras 1(2), para 4
	Substitution of ITA 1967 s 354, FA 1982 s 18	
Pt II	Repeal of ITA 1967 ss 46, 68(2), 82, 106, 177, 307(1A), 340(2)(e)(f), 365, 366, 419, 467, 467A, 467B, 467C, 468(1)(2), 469, 471, 472(2), 473, 484(5), 486(3), 496, 550(2A), Sch 1 Pt II, Sch 18 para VIII(1), FA 1972 s11, FA 1974 ss 38, 44, 52, 54, CGTA 1975 s 49(7), CTA 1976 ss 6(4), 66A(3) proviso, 66A(4), 76A(2) proviso, (3), FA 1976 ss 25, 30, FA 1980 s 7, FA 1981 ss 6, 18, FA 1982 ss 21, 22, FA 1986 s 8, Pt I Ch III, ss 33(9)(e), 46(4), FA 1987 ss 6, 35(22), FA 1988 ss 19(1), 21(6), 22, FA 1993 s 7, Sch 1 para 1(7)(e), FA 1994 ss 5, 38, 49, FA 1995 s 6, 66(8A), FA 1996 s 15(6).	
	Amendment of ITA 1967 ss 1(1), 307(1), 317(2), FA 1974 s 16(5), CGTA 1975 s 32(4)(b), CTA 1976 ss 76(6), 152(3), FA 1983 s 50(11), FA 1986 s 33(9)(d), FA 1989 Sch 1 para 1(7)(d)	ss 2(1), 3(1), 381(1), 144, 171, 240, 258, 657(1), 732, Sch 18 para 1
Sch 10		Sch 7

Index

A

Abandonment

of an option within the meaning of CGTA 1975 s 47(3) *TA Dilleen (Inspector of Taxes) v Edward J Kearns* Vol IV p 547

Absent

landowner returns to take on active farming *EP Ó Coindealbháin (Inspector of Taxes) v KN Price* Vol IV p 1

Absolute interest

discretionary trust, when absolute interest passes *BKJ v The Revenue Commissioners* Vol III p 104

Accountants

working papers, whether the inspector of taxes is entitled to call for production of a taxpayer's nominal ledger, whether the nominal ledger formed part of the accountant's working papers *JJ Quigley (Inspector of Taxes) v Maurice Burke* Vol IV p 332, Vol V p 265

Accounting

method of accounting for tax purposes, whether replacement cost basis is acceptable or whether historical cost accounting is the only method of commercial accountancy, *Carroll Industries Plc (formerly PJ Carroll & Co Ltd) and PJ Carroll & Co Ltd v S O'Culacháin (Inspector of Taxes)* Vol IV p 135

Accounting period

accounts made up half-yearly, whether Revenue required to determine accounting period *The Revenue Commissioners v R Hilliard & Sons Ltd* Vol II p 130

Acquisition of Land (Assessment of Compensation) Act 1919

section 2 *Peter C Heron & Others v The Minister for Communications* Vol III p 298

Additional assessments

whether the inspector of taxes had made a "discovery" on finding that inadmissible deductions had been allowed in the computation of the company's tax liability for certain years and whether he was entitled to raise additional assessments for those years *W Ltd v Wilson (Inspector of Taxes)* Vol 11 p 627, *Hammond Lane Metal Co Ltd v S O'Culacháin (Inspector of Taxes)* Vol III p 197

Administration

procedures of Revenue Commissioners, whether unfair and unconstitutional, enforcement order issue to city sheriff after payment of tax, defamation of plaintiff *Giles J Kennedy v E G Hearne, The Attorney General & Others* Vol III p 590

Admissibility

of evidence of illegality *Daniel Collins and Michael Byrne, Daniel Collins and Redmond Power as Executor of the Will of Michael Byrne, deceased and Daniel Collins v J D Mulvey (Inspector of Taxes)* Vol II p 291

Adopted children

whether "issue" included adopted children *In the matter of John Stamp deceased Patrick Stamp v Noel Redmond & Ors* Vol IV p 415

Adoption Act 1952

ss 4, 26(2), adoption heavily qualified, whether permissible to adopt paying provisions of ITA 1967 into corporation tax code while ignoring charging provisions *Wayte (Holdings) Ltd (In Receivership) Alex Burns v E N Hearne* Vol III p 553

Advance payment

received on foot of obligation with bank, whether income from trade *JG Kerrane (Inspector of Taxes) v N Hanlon (Ireland) Ltd* Vol III p 633

Advertising

agency, whether a profession for the purposes of corporation tax surcharge *Mac Giolla Mhaith (Inspector of Taxes) v Cronin & Associates Ltd* Vol III p 211

company producing materials for use in advertising, whether manufacture *S Ó Culacháin (Inspector of Taxes) v Hunter Advertising Ltd* Vol IV p 35

newspaper publisher, newspapers are "goods" for the purpose of manufacturing relief, whether advertising income is from a separate trade and qualifies for such relief *L McGurrin (Inspector of Taxes) v The Champion Publications Ltd* Vol IV p 466

Agreement

whether an agreement between the taxpayer and the inspector of taxes in relation to an assessment under appeal is binding and conclusive *The Hammond Lane Metal Co Ltd v S Ó Culacháin (Inspector of Taxes)* Vol IV p 197

construction of documents and transactions *B McCabe (Inspector of Taxes) v South City & County Investment Co Ltd* Vol V p 107, 1998 p 183

Agricultural Society

definition of *The Trustees of The Ward Union Hunt Races v Hughes (Inspector of Taxes)* Vol I p 538

Allowable loss

capital gains tax used for avoidance of tax, whether allowable *Patrick McGrath & Others v JE McDermott (Inspector of Taxes)* Vol III p 683

Allowances

UK resident working in Ireland, wife working in UK, whether he is entitled to married allowance and rate bands *S Fennessy (Inspector of Taxes) v John Mc Connellogue* Vol V p 129

Amnesty

1993, whether applies *Liam J Irwin (Collector General) v Michael Grimes* Vol V p 209, *Crimianl Assets Bureau v Gerard Hutch* Vol VI p 125

Annual charge

on rental income left to beneficiary provided he continued to manage the property whether remuneration under Schedule E *Gerald O'Reilly v WJ Casey (Inspector of Taxes)* Vol 1 p 601

Annual profits or gains

veterinary body corporate performing Statutory functions, surplus of receipts over expenditure whether liable to tax *The Veterinary Council v F Corr (Inspector of Taxes)* Vol II p 204

Annuity

payable tax free from a trust, the trust is accountable to the Revenue Commissioners for the tax, where such tax is refunded by the Revenue Commissioners to the annuitant is the annuitant accountable to the trust for the tax so refunded *In re Swan, Deceased; The Hibernian Bank Ltd v Munro & Ors* Vol V p 565

paid between group companies, whether capital or revenue *B Mc Cabe (Inspector of Taxes) v South City & County Investment Co Ltd* Vol V p 107

Appeal Commissioners

appeal against findings of fact of an Appeal Commissioner *Ó Culacháin (Inspector of Taxes) v Stylo Barrett Shoes Ltd* Vol VI p 617

grounds for setting aside findings of fact by Appeal Commissioners *Mara v GC (Hummingbird) Ltd* Vol II p 687

nature of powers and functions limited or unlimited, determination of tax liability by High Court and Appeal Commissioners whether mutually exclusive *The State (Calcul International Ltd and Solatrex International Ltd) v The Appeal Commissioners and The Revenue Commissioners* Vol III p 577

power and function of Appeal Commissioners *CG v The Appeal Commissioners and Others* Vol VI p 783

whether findings by an Appeal Commissioner were law or fact *DA MacCarthaigh, Inspector of Taxes v Cablelink Ltd, Cablelink Waterford Ltd and Galway Cable Vision Ltd* Vol VI p 595

whether Inspector of Taxes was correct in law in holding that interest earned on client monies was not income of the respondents and accordingly was taxable at the standard rate of income tax *PO Cahill (Inspector of Taxes) v Patrick O'Driscoll, Michael O'Driscoll and William F O'Driscoll* Vol VI p 793

Appeals

against assessment to tax by Criminal Assets Bureau *CG v The Appeal Commissioners and Others* Vol VI p 783

against 'freezing order' granted to CAB by the High Court *Criminal Assets Bureau v John Kelly* Vol VI p 501

against a decision of the High Court to refuse on a judicial review application to quash three convictions with six months imprisonment for each offence imposed in the District Court on the appellant for failure to make income tax returns *Thomas O'Callaghan v JP Clifford & Others* Vol IV p 478

computation of appeal period *Criminal Assets Bureau v P McS* Vol VI p 421

duty to provide appeal information to taxpayer, legitimate expectation *Terence Keogh v Criminal Assets Bureau, Revenue Commissioners and the Attorney General* Vol VI p 635

new grounds, appellants right to introduce *Boland's Ltd v The Commissioners of Inland Revenue* Vol 1 p 34

whether appeal should be adjourned pending outcome of criminal proceedings *CG v The Appeal Commissioners and Others* Vol VI p 783

Appeals (contd)

right to a late appeal *Criminal Assets Bureau v P McS* Vol VI p 421, *Criminal Assets Bureau v D(K)* Vol VI p 445

summonses served in respect of tax liabilities the subject matter of earlier appeals whether Circuit Court judge has discretion to accept late filing of notice and fee, whether dissatisfaction expressed at the Circuit Court appeal hearings, whether dissatisfaction must be expressed immediately after determination by the Circuit Court, whether notice to county registrar must be lodged within 21 days together with the £20 fee, whether payment of tax denies access to the courts, whether requirements are directory or mandatory, whether tax must be paid before the case stated is determined, whether time lapse after expression of dissatisfaction is fatal *Michael A Bairead v Martin C Carr* Vol IV p 505

time for notice of appeal meaning of "immediately" *The State (Multiprint Label Systems Ltd) v The Hon Justice Thomas Neylon* Vol III p 159

to Circuit Court, whether Circuit Court Judge has authority to award costs in tax appeal hearings *The Revenue Commissioners v Arida Ltd* Vol IV p 401, Vol V p 221

to High Court by way of case stated from decision of Circuit Judge, failure to notify the respondent the fact that a case has been stated *A & B v WJ Davis (Inspector of Taxes)* Vol II p 60

Appeals procedures

prerequisites to a valid appeal not optional and can only be circumscribed in limited circumstances, date for commencement of appeal period not open ended *Terence Keogh v Criminal Assets Bureau, Revenue Commissioners* Vol VI p 635

Appellant

company's accounts, based on current cost accounting convention (ie replacement cost) *Carroll Industries Plc (formerly PJ Carroll & Co Ltd) and PJ Carroll & Co Ltd v S Ó Culacháin (Inspector of Taxes)* Vol IV p 135

right of, to introduce new grounds of appeal *Boland's Ltd v The Commissioners of Inland Revenue* Vol 1 p 34

Arbitration

value added tax, whether arbitrator's award should be set aside on basis of misconduct *Campus Stadium Ireland Development Ltd v Dublin Waterworld Ltd* 2006 p 55

compulsory acquisition of land, whether property arbitrator obliged to give breakdown of his award, whether breakdown required for capital gains tax purposes, whether failure by applicant to request an apportionment of the award rules out any further relief, whether applicant can appeal without the breakdown for the award, whether failure to advance further arguments of unfairness amounted to acceptance of the normal practice, *Manning, J v Shackleton, J & Cork Co Council* Vol IV p 485

Artistic exemption

exemption of earnings from original and creative works of artistic or cultural merit, whether journalism qualifies *John Healy v SI Breathnach (Inspector of Taxes)* Vol III p 496

Artistic exemption (contd)

legal text books, refusal by inspector of taxes to grant exemption from income tax under FA 1969 s 2, exemption granted if the books are original and creative works which are generally recognised as having cultural or artistic merit. *Michael Forde Decision* Vol IV p 348

Assessment

basis of assessment under Case III *O'Conaill (Inspector of Taxes) v R* Vol II p 304

basis of, commencement and cessation within a year, whether assessment for the previous year can be reviewed *AB v JD Mulvey (Inspector of Taxes)* Vol II p 55

builder's profits *The State (at the prosecution of Patrick J Whelan) v Michael Smidic (Special Commissioners of Income Tax) and Edward Connolly v AG Birch (Inspector of Taxes)* Vol I p 583

confirmed, allowability of expenses *The King (Harris Stein) v The Special Commissioners* Vol I p 62

joint, whether husband is liable on wife's income, *Gilligan v Criminal Assets Bureau, Galvin, Lanigan & Revenue Commissioners* Vol V p 424

made in the absence of returns, *Criminal Assets Bureau v Gerard Hutch* Vol VI p 125

of remuneration paid in year after for work done in earlier year *Bedford (Collector-General) v H* Vol II p 588

when assessments became final and conclusive *Terence Keogh v Criminal Assets Bureau, Revenue Commissioners and the Attorney General* Vol VI p 635

whether arbitrary and unreasonable *Criminal Assets Bureau v Sean and Rosaleen Hunt* Vol VI p 559

whether can be reopened *Boland's Ltd v The Commissioners of Inland Revenue* Vol I p 34

Assigned

personal pension and other assets assigned to company pension continued to be paid to pensioner, whether pensioner liable to tax on pension *Cronin (Inspector of Taxes) v C* Vol II p 592

Associated company

whether a company, resident and trading in Northern Ireland was an associated company of a company resident and trading in the State for the purposes of CTA 1976 s 28 (ie reduced rate of corporation tax for small companies) *MA Bairead (Inspector of Taxes) v Maxwells of Donegal Ltd* Vol III p 430

Auctioneer's commission

whether revenue or capital management expense *Stephen Court Ltd v JA Browne (Inspector of Taxes)* Vol V p 680

Avoidance

dealing in and developing land *O'Connlain (Inspector of Taxes) v Belvedere Estates Ltd* Vol III p 271

sports club, whether set up for tax avoidance or bona fide purposes *Revenue v ORMG* Vol III p 28

whether tax avoidance valid *McGrath v McDermott* Vol III p 683

B

Bad debts

recovered by executor but allowed during lifetime of deceased, whether executor carrying on a trade, whether such bad debts recovered are taxable *CD v J MO' Sullivan* Vol II p 140

Banana ripening

whether qualified for manufacturing relief *PJ O'Connell (Inspector of Taxes) v Fyffes Banana Processing Ltd* Vol VI p 131

Bank

confidentiality between banks and customers *JB O'C v PCD and A Bank* Vol III p 153

government stocks purchased to comply with Central Bank requirements, whether carrying on trade of dealing in securities, whether liable as profits under Schedule

or exempt capital gains on Government stocks *JA Browne (Inspector of Taxes) v Bank of Ireland Finance Ltd* Vol III p 644

whether personal liability of members is unlimited) *CIR v The Governor and Company of The Bank of Ireland* Vol I p 70

whether Inspector of Taxes entitled to a Court Order *In the Matter of GO'C & AO'C (Application of Liam Liston)* Vol V p 346

Bank account

application by Revenue for court order for bank to furnish details of accounts to taxpayers *In re G O'C & A O'C (Application of Liam Liston (Inspector of Taxes))* Vol V p 346

Barrister's fees

due prior to his appointment to the bench, fees refused but could be paid to a family company if solicitors so wished *EP Ó Coindealbháin (Inspector of Taxes) v The Honourable Mr Justice Sean Gannon* Vol III p 484

Basis of assessment

commencement and cessation within a year, whether assessment for the previous year can be reviewed *AB v JD Mulvey (Inspector of Taxes)* Vol II p 55

under Case III *O'Conaill (Inspector of Taxes) v R* Vol II p 304

Beneficial owner

personal pension and other assets assigned to company pension continued to be paid to pensioner, whether pensioner liable to tax on pension *Cronin (Inspector of Taxes) v C* Vol II p 592

whether director controlled a company and whether managing director was the beneficial owner of, or able to control more than 5% of its ordinary shares *Associated properties Ltd v The Revenue Commissioners* Vol II p 175

Benefit in kind

cars, whether charge to benefit in kind on sales representatives is constitutional *Paul Browne & Others v The Revenue Commissioners & Others* Vol IV p 323

rent paid for employee *Connolly (Inspector of Taxes) v Denis McNamara* Vol II p 452

Bloodstock

animal bought in course of trade, sent to stud after successful racing career and subsequently sold to a syndicate whether amount realised on syndication a trading receipt *Mac Giolla Riogh (Inspector of Taxes) v G Ltd* Vol II p 315

Board of Conservators

surplus revenue, whether annual profits or gains *Moville District Board of Conservators v D Ua Clothasaigh (Inspector of Taxes)* Vol II p 75

Bookmaker

bookmaker convicted and fined in the District Court of offences under the Betting Acts penal warrant for imprisonment, whether constitutional, *John B Murphy v District Justice Brendan Wallace & Others* Vol IV p 278

levies on course betting, whether taxable a income or profits of a trade *The Racing Board v S Ó Culacháin* Vol IV p 73

profits of a bookmaker from transactions in Irish Hospital Sweepstakes tickets, whether receipts assessable to tax under Schedule D *HH v MJ Forbes (Inspector of Taxes)* Vol II p 164

betting duty, whether necessary for Revenue Commissioners to comply with Regulations Act 1890 before proceedings can commence for failure to pay duty on bets *DPP v Michael Cunningham* Vol V p 691

Books

barrister's books, whether plant *Breathnach (Inspector of Taxes) v MC* Vol III p 113

Breach

customs regulations, seizure by the Revenue Commissioners of an oil tanker *McCrystal Oil Co Ltd v The Revenue Commissioners & Others* Vol IV p 386

Brewery

trade or business, whether liability in respect of transactions under DORA requisition orders *Arthur Guinness Son & Co Ltd v Commissioners of Inland Revenue* Vol I p 1

Builder's profits

assessment of *The State (at the prosecution of Patrick J Whelan) v Michael Smidic (Special Commissioners of Income Tax)* Vol I p 571 and *Edward Connolly v AG Birch (Inspector of Taxes)* Vol I p 583

capitalised value of ground rents and fines, whether liable to tax *Birch (Inspector of Taxes) v Denis Delaney* Vol I p 515 and *Edward Connolly v AG Birch (Inspector of Taxes)* and *Swaine (Inspector of Taxes) v VE* Vol I p 583

Building societies

company lending money to non-members to purchase property, whether trading as a building society *Property Loan & Investment Co Ltd v The Revenue Commissioners* Vol II p 25

instruments relating to the internal affairs of a society were exempt from stamp duty, whether this exemption extended to a transfer of a premises to a society to conduct its business *Irish Nationwide Building Society v Revenue Commissioners* Vol IV p 296

Business

carried on abroad *The Executors and Trustees of A C Ferguson (deceased) v Donovan (Inspector of Taxes)* Vol I p 183

C

Cable television system

whether liable to value added tax on sales to customers *TJ Brosnan (Inspector of Taxes) v Cork Communications Ltd* Vol IV p 349

Capital acquisitions tax

whether succession under Act is automatic or must be claimed *In the Matter of the Estates of Cummins (Decd); O'Dwyer & Ors v Keegan & Ors* Vol V p 367

COMPETENT TO DISPOSE

whether surviving spouse competent to dispose of statutory share in estate *In Re the Estate of Urquhart, D (decd) & Revenue Commissioners v AIB Ltd* Vol V p 600

FAVOURITE NEPHEW RELIEF

gift of farm to niece – whether niece worked substantially full time on the farm *AE v The Revenue Commissioners* Vol V p 686

valuation of shares in private non-trading company *Revenue Commissioners v Henry Young* Vol V p 294

Capital allowances

barrister's books, whether plant *Breathnach (Inspector of Taxes) v MC* Vol III p 113

expenditure on installation of suspended ceiling in supermarket, whether plant qualifying for capital allowances *Dunnes Stores (Oakville) Ltd v MC Cronin (Inspector of Taxes)* Vol IV p 68

in designated area, whether plant used exclusively in designated area, whether allowance extends to plant used under a hire contract *Daniel McNally v S O Maoldhomhniagh* Vol IV p 22

holiday cottages, whether qualifying for capital allowances *McMahon, T & Ors v Rt Hon Lord Mayor Alderman & Burgess of Dublin* Vol V p 357

industrial building structure for dock undertaking, whether bonded transit sheds used as clearing house and not for storage qualify *Patrick Monahan (Drogheda) Ltd v O'Connell (Inspector of Taxes)* Vol III p 661

poultry house, whether plant and machinery *O'Srianain (Inspector of Taxes) v Lakeview Ltd* Vol III p 219

racecourse stand, *O'Grady (Inspector of Taxes) v Roscommon Race Committee* Vol V p 317

share of, on leasing transaction, involving a purported limited partnership, against his personal income tax liability. *DA MacCarthaigh (Inspector of Taxes) v Francis Daly* Vol III p 253

whether a building which housed offices, a showroom, a canteen, computer department and utilities qualified for industrial building allowance under ITA 1967 s 255 *O'Conaill (Inspector of Taxes) v JJ Ltd* Vol III p 65

whether capital allowances apportioned in accordance with ITA 1967 s 220(5), should be confined to the allowances outlined in Part XVI of that Act *SW Ltd v McDermott (Inspector of Taxes)* Vol II p 661

Capital allowances (contd)

whether mining operation qualifies for ESR or capital allowances *Patrick J O'Connell (Inspector of Taxes) v Tara Mines Ltd* Vol VI p 523

Capitalised

builder's profits capitalised value of ground rents and fines, whether liable to tax *Birch (Inspector of Taxes) v Denis Delaney* Vol I p 515 and *Edward Connolly v A G Birch (Inspector of Taxes)* Vol I p 583 and *Swaine (Inspector of Taxes) v VE* Vol II p 472

Capital expenditure

whether annual interest on loan to redeem preference shares is a deductible expense *Seán MacAonghusa (Inspector of Taxes) v Ringmahon Company* Vol VI p 327

Capital gains tax

ACCOUNTABLE PERSON

disposal of property by mortgagee as nominee for mortgagor, accountable person for capital gains tax purposes, repayment of 15% deducted by purchaser in the absence of tax clearance certificate *Bank of Ireland Finance Ltd v The Revenue Commissioners* Vol IV p 217

ALLOWABLE LOSS

capital gains tax used for avoidance of tax, whether allowable *Patrick McGrath & Others v JE McDermott (Inspector of Taxes)* Vol III p 683

valuation of lands as at 6 April 1974 *J McMahon (Inspector of Taxes) v Albert Noel Murphy* Vol IV p 125

CAPITAL GAINS TAX

on sale of lands *EP Ó Coindealbháin (Inspector of Taxes) v KN Price* Vol IV p 1

sale of whiskey in a bond by a publican, whether liable to capital gains tax *McCall (deceased) v Commissioners of Inland Revenue* Vol I p 28

CAPITAL LOSS

loss on realisation of *investments The Alliance & Dublin Consumers' Gas Co v Davis (Inspector of Taxes)* Vol I p 207

CLEARANCE CERTIFICATE

on sale of bonds, whether applicant ordinarily resident in the state is entitled to a clearance certificate *The State (FIC Ltd) v O'Ceallaigh* Vol III p 124

whether absence of a clearance certificate prohibited the Revenue Commissioners from repaying tax deducted by purchaser *Bank of Ireland Finance Ltd v The Revenue Commissioners* Vol IV p 217

COMPULSORY ACQUISITION

of land, whether property arbitrator obliged to give breakdown of his award, whether breakdown required for capital gains tax purposes, whether failure by applicant to request an apportionment of the award rules out any further relief, whether applicant can appeal without the breakdown for the award, whether failure to advance further arguments of unfairness amounted to acceptance of the normal practice, *David Manning v John R Shackleton & Cork County Council* Vol IV p 485

Capital gains tax (contd)

COMPULSORY PURCHASE

compensation determined without regard to tax arising on disposal *Peter C Heron & Others v The Minister For Communications* Vol III p 298

of land, whether property arbitrator obliged to give breakdown of his award, whether breakdown required for capital gains tax purposes, whether failure by applicant to request an apportionment of the award rules out any further relief, whether applicant can appeal without the breakdown for the award, whether failure to advance further arguments of unfairness amounted to acceptance of the normal practice *David Manning v John R Shackleton & Cork County Council* Vol IV p 485

CONSIDERATION

whether money received under a non-competition agreement could constitute consideration for the disposal of shares *Patrick J O'Connell (Inspector of Taxes) v John Fleming* Vol VI p 453

DEBT

whether loan notes are a simple debt or a debt on a security *Patrick J O'Connell (Inspector of Taxes) v Thomas Keleghan* Vol VI p 201

whether a loan with conversion rights constitutes a debt within the meaning of CGTA 1975 s 46(1) *Mooney (Inspector of Taxes) v McSweeney* Vol V p 163

VALUATION OF LAND

agricultural land, appeal against market value at 6 April 1974 as determined by Circuit Court, whether agricultural value the sole determining factor, whether development potential attached on 6 April 1974, whether subsequent planning permission for milk processing plant relevant *J McMahon (Inspector of Taxes) v Albert Noel Murphy* Vol IV p 125

whether CGT chargeable on redemption of loan notes for cash *Patrick J O'Connell (Inspector of Taxes) v Thomas Keleghan* Vol VI p 201

Capital or revenue

annuity paid between group companies *B Mc Cabe (Inspector of Taxes) v South City & County Investment Co Ltd* Vol V p 107

auctioneer's commission *Stephen Court Ltd v Browne (Inspector of Taxes)* Vol V p 680

compensation for loss of profits *The Alliance and Dublin Consumers' Gas Co v McWilliams (Inspector of Taxes)* Vol I p 104

dividends from sales of capital assets, whether liable to corporation profits tax *K Co v Hogan (Inspector of Taxes)* Vol III p 56

exchange losson foreign currency loans, whether capital or revenue *TG Brosnan (Inspector of Taxes) v Mutual Enterprises Ltd* Vol V p 138

interest on loan following redemption of share capital, whether allowable against trading income *Sean MacAonghusa v Ringmahon Co* Vol VI p 327

lump sum paid on the execution of a lease *W Flynn (Inspector of Taxes) v John Noone Ltd* and *W Flynn (Inspector of Taxes) v Blackwood & Co (Sligo) Ltd* Vol II p 222

management expenses, whether allowable *Hibernian Insurance Co Ltd v MacUimis (Inspector of Taxes)* Vol VI p 157

Capital or revenue (contd)

payment in advance on the signing of a lease, whether capital *O'Sullivan (Inspector of Taxes) v P Ltd* Vol II p 464

racecourse stand, whether deductible repairs or non deductible capital expenditure or expenditure qualifying as plant *Michael O'Grady (Inspector of Taxes) v Roscommon Race Committee* Vol IV p 425

removing top-soil from surface of quarry *Milverton Quarries Ltd v The Revenue Commissioners* Vol II p 382

solicitor's fees – payable by investment company *Stephen Court Ltd v Browne (Inspector of Taxes)* Vol V p 680

training grants, whether capital or revenue receipt *O'Cleirigh (Inspector of Taxes) v Jacobs International Ltd Incorporated* Vol III p 165

whether capital expenditure *Airspace Investments Ltd v M Moore (Inspector of Taxes)* Vol V p 3

whether expenditure incurred by petrol marketing company under exclusivity agreements with retailers is revenue or capital *Dolan (Inspector of Taxes) v AB Co Ltd* Vol II p 515

Carry forward

of losses *Molmac Ltd v MacGiolla Riogh (Inspector of Taxes)* Vol II p 482

Cars

whether charge to benefit in kind on sales representatives is constitutional *Paul Browne & Others v The Revenue Commissioners & Others* Vol IV p 323

Case stated

request for, by taxpayer *The King (Harris Stein) v The Special Commissioners* Vol I p 62

time for notice of appeal meaning of "immediately" *The State (Multiprint Label Systems v Thomas Neylon* Vol III p 159

Cattledealer

whether the taxpayer was a "dealer in cattle" within the meaning of ITA 1918 Sch D Case III rule 4 and ITA 1967 s 78. *De Brun (Inspector of Taxes) v K* Vol III p 19

Ceilings

expenditure on installation of suspended ceiling in supermarket, whether plant qualifying for capital *allowances Dunnes Stores (Oakville) Ltd v M C Cronin (Inspector of Taxes)* Vol IV p 68

Certiorari

whether applicant was entitled to order of certiorari where decision is confirmed and enacted *C Mc Daid v His Honour Judge Sheehy & Ors* Vol V p 696

Cessation of business

assessment of builders profits *The State (at the prosecution of Patrick J Whelan) v Michael Smidic (Special Commissioners of Income Tax)* and *The State (at the prosecution of Patrick J Whelan) v Michael Smidic (Special Commissioners of Income Tax)* Vol I p 571

basis of assessment, commencement and cessation within a year, whether assessment for the previous year can be reviewed *AB v JD Mulvey (Inspector of Taxes)* Vol II p 55

Cessation of business (contd)

deduction of corporation profits tax and excess corporation profits tax in computing profits for income tax purposes *JM O'Dwyer (Inspector of Taxes) v The Dublin United Transport Co Ltd* Vol II p 115

losses forward *Cronin (Inspector of Taxes) v Lunham Brothers Ltd* Vol III p 363

phasing down of business, whether constituted trading, whether collection of debts constituted trading *The City of Dublin Steampacket Co v Revenue Commissioners* Vol I p 108

Change of ownership

losses forward *M Cronin (Inspector of Taxes) v Lunham Brothers Ltd* Vol III p 363

Charge card

scheme, the meaning of paid, *The Diners Club Ltd v The Revenue and The Minister for Finance* Vol III p 680

Chargeable person

joint assessment, whether husband is liable for both incomes *Gilligan v Criminal Assets Bureau, Galvin, Lanigan & Revenue Commissioners* Vol V p 424

whether applicant was a chargeable person and, accordingly, was obliged to submit tax returns for relevant years *AS v Criminal Assets Bureau* Vol VI p 799

Charges

on book debts by deed of mortgage, whether fixed or floating charge *AH Masser Ltd (in receivership) & Others v The Revenue Commissioners* Vol III p 548

Charitable bequest

whether it had to be expended in Ireland *The Revenue Commissioners v The Most Reverend Edward Doorley* Vol V p 539

Charity

income from securities and from school, whether for charitable purposes *The Pharmaceutical Society of Ireland v The Revenue Commissioners* Vol I p 542

nun, whether assessable on income from employment which she gives to her order *JD Dolan (Inspector of Taxes) v "K" National School Teacher* Vol I p 656

trade carried on by beneficiary of charity, whether exempt *Beirne (Inspector of Taxes) v St Vincent De Paul Society (Wexford Conference)* Vol I p 383

whether a charity "established" in Ireland *Revenue Commissioners v Sister of Charity of the Incarnate Word* Vol VI p 7

Children

children's pension, whether income of parent for income tax purposes *Ó Coindealbháin (Inspector of Taxes) v Breda O'Carroll* Vol IV p 221

father taking his elder children and his mother-in-law into partnership, subsequent assignment of mother-in-law's interest to his younger children whether income of children to be deemed to be income of father *JM O'Dwyer (Inspector of Taxes) v Cafolla & Co* Vol II p 82

increase in widows contributory pension in respect of dependent children, whether taxable on parent *Sean Ó Síocháin (Inspector of Taxes) v Bridget Neenan* Vol V p 472

Children (contd)

settlement of income, deed of appointment by parent in favour of child *E G v Mac Shamhrain, (Inspector of Taxes)* Vol II p 352

whether "issue" included adopted children *In the matter of John Stamp deceased Patrick Stamp v Noel Redmond & Others* Vol IV p 415

Circuit Court

appeal hearings, whether Circuit Court Judge has authority to award costs in tax appeal hearings *The Revenue Commissioners v Arida Ltd* Vol IV p 401, Vol V p 221

summonses served in respect of tax liabilities the subject matter of earlier appeals whether Circuit Court judge has discretion to accept late filing of notice and fee, whether dissatisfaction expressed at the Circuit Court appeal hearings, whether dissatisfaction must be expressed immediately after determination by the Circuit Court, whether notice to county registrar must be lodged within 21 days together with the £20 fee, whether payment of tax denies access to the courts, whether requirements are directory or mandatory, whether tax must be paid before the case stated is determined, whether time lapse after expression of dissatisfaction is fatal *Michael A Bairead v Martin C Carr* Vol IV p 505

whether a Circuit Court Judge hearing an appeal pursuant to ITA 1967 s 429 has jurisdiction to award costs *The Revenue Commissioners v Arida Ltd* Vol IV p 401, Vol V p 221

Club

to promote athletics or amateur games or sports, whether bona fide or tax avoidance *Revenue v ORMG* Vol III p 28

Coal mining

trading as fuel merchants, whether new trade of coal mining was set up or commenced *H A O'Loan (Inspector of Taxes) v Messrs MJ Noone & Co* Vol II p 146

Collector

of vintage motor cars *Karl Keller v The Revenue Commissioners & Others Commencement* Vol IV p 512

College/Schools

whether operated for charitable purposes *The Pharmaceutical Society of Ireland v The Revenue Commissioners* Vol I p 542

Commencement

and cessation within a year, whether assessment for the previous year can be reviewed *AB v JD Mulvey (Inspector of Taxes)* Vol II p 55

fuel merchants, whether new trade of coal mining was set up or commenced *H A O'Loan (Inspector of Taxes) v Messrs M J Noone & Co* Vol II p 146

Company

definition of, within the meaning of FA 1920 s 52(3) *CIR v The Governor and Company of The Bank of Ireland* Vol I p 70

in receivership preferential claim *The Attorney-General, Informant v Irish Steel Ltd and Vincent Crowley, Defendants* Vol II p 108

Company (contd)

meetings, whether they took place, whether resolution was passed, whether share issue invalid *In re Sugar Distributors Ltd* Vol V p 225

non-resident *The Cunard Steam Ship Co Ltd v Herlihy (Inspector of Taxes), and The Cunard Steam Ship Co Ltd v Revenue Commissioners* Vol I p 330

Company secretary

role of *Wayte (Holdings) Ltd (In Receivership) Alex Burns v Edward N Hearne* Vol III p 553

Compensation

ex gratia payments, by British government for malicious damage to property or personal injury sustained, whether trading receipt *WA Robinson T/A James Pim & Son v J D Dolan (Inspector of Taxes)* Vol I p 427

for compulsory purchase, determined without regard to tax arising on disposal *Peter C Heron & Others v The Minister For Communications* Vol III p 298

for loss of profits, whether income or capital receipt *The Alliance and Dublin Consumers' Gas Co v McWilliams (Inspector of Taxes)* Vol I p 207 and *F Corr (Inspector of Taxes) v F E Larkin* Vol II p 164

Compulsory sale

to Minister for Finance, in return for sterling equivalents, of dollar balances consisting of income from securities, etc, in the USA whether moneys so received assessable *J M O'Sullivan (Inspector of Taxes) v Julia O'Connor, as Administratrix of Evelyn H O'Brien, Deceased* Vol II p 61

Confidentiality

between banks and customers *JB O'C v PCD and A Bank* Vol III p 153

Inspector of Taxes entitled to Court Order *In the Matter of GO'C & AO'C (Application of Liam Liston (Inspector of Taxes))* Vol V 346

Confirmation of assessment

allowance of expenses where assessment has been confirmed *The King (Harris Stein) v The Special Commissioners* Vol I p 62

Conflict

in terms of deed *AH Masser Ltd (in receivership) & Others v The Revenue Commissioners* Vol III p 548

Constitutional rights

constitution validity of taxing statute applicable to married persons *Bernard Muckley & Anne Muckley v Ireland, Attorney General and Revenue Commissioners* Vol III p 188

to have recourse to High Court denied *Michael Deighan v Edward N Hearn & Others* Vol III p 533

whether charge to benefit in kind on sales representatives is constitutional *Paul Browne & Others v The Revenue Commissioners & Others* Vol IV p 323

whether common law rule of dependant domicile of a wife whether constitutional *JW v JW* Vol IV p 437

whether constitutional right to earn a livelihood infringed – whether legislation requires amendment *James G Orange v The Revenue Commissioners* Vol V p 70

Constitutional rights (contd)

whether Imposition of Duties Act 1957 s 1 is constitutional *C Mc Daid v His Honour Judge Sheehy & Ors* Vol V p 696

whether method of granting credit for Professional services withholding tax is constitutional *Michael Daly v The Revenue Commissioners* Vol V p 213

whether rights to privacy and fair procedures infringed *Charles J Haughey and Others v Moriarty and Others* Vol VI p 67

whether rights to fair trial and silence had been violated and privilege against self-incrimination interfered with *CG v The Appeal Commissioners and Others* Vol VI p 783

whether undertaking by the State under Article 41.3 to guard the institution of marriage infringed, whether imposition of higher taxes or married couples repugnant to the Constitution *Francis & Mary Murphy v The Attorney General* Vol V p 613

Construction contracts

whether lorry owners carrying sand and gravel were engaged as subcontractors under a construction contract, whether the lorry owners became the proprietors of the quarry materials *O'Grady v Laragan Quarries Ltd* Vol IV p 269

Contract

availability of remedy of specific performance where VAT not paid pursuant to contract *Cyril Forbes v John Tobin And Janet Tobin* Vol VI p 483

Contract for sale

of legal estate, whether a contract for sale of property *Waterford Glass (Group Services) Ltd v The Revenue Commissioners* Vol IV p 187

stamp duties, amount chargeable, contracts and consideration structured to minimise stamp duty *VIEK Investments Ltd v The Revenue Commissioners* Vol IV p 367

Contract of service or contract for services

branch manager of local Employment Office of Dept of Social Welfare *Ó Coindealbháin (Inspector of Taxes) v TB Mooney* Vol IV p 45

demonstrator of food products at supermarket *H Denny & Sons (Irl) Ltd v Minister for Social Welfare* Vol V p 238

members of fishing vessel *Minister for Social Welfare v John Griffiths* Vol IV p 378

temporary employee engaged through an employment agency *The Minister for Labour v PMPA Insurance Co Ltd (under administration)* Vol III p 505

whether a trade union official was performing services under a contract of service or a contract for service *Philip Kirwan v Technical Engineering and Electrical Union* Vol VI p 771

wholesale distributor of newspapers *Tony McAuliffe v Minister for Social Welfare* Vol V p 94

winding up, preferential payments, tests applicable *In the Matter of Sunday Tribune* 1998 p 177

Control

by trustees *The Executors and Trustees of AC Ferguson (deceased) v Donovan (Inspector of Taxes)* Vol I p 183

Control (contd)

interest paid by a company to a person having controlling interest in the company *The Revenue Commissioners v Associated properties Ltd* Vol II p 412

whether director controlled a company and whether managing director was the beneficial owner of, or able to control more than 5% of its ordinary shares *Associated properties Ltd v The Revenue Commissioners* Vol II p 175

Conveyance for sale

what constitutes a conveyance for sale under Stamp Act of 1891 *Waterford Glass (Group Services) Ltd v The Revenue Commissioners* Vol IV p 187

Co-operative

surplus of from dealing with members, whether trading profits, whether exempt *Kennedy (Inspector of Taxes) v The Rattoo Co-operative Dairy Society Ltd* Vol I p 315

Copyright

whether corporate body exploiting copyrights supplying service within meaning of VATA – Copyright Act 1963 *Phonographic Performance (Ireland) Ltd v J Somers (Inspector of Taxes)* Vol IV p 314

Corporation profits tax

accounting period, whether Revenue Commissioners are required to determine *The Revenue Commissioners v R Hilliard & Sons Ltd* Vol II p 130

company lending money to non-members to purchase property, whether trading as a building society *Property Loan & Investment Co Ltd v The Revenue Commissioners* Vol II p 25

foreign company trading in Ireland provision for devaluation of foreign currency not allowed as deduction from profits *The Revenue Commissioners v L & Co* Vol II p 281

liability to *Commissioners of Inland Revenue v The Governor & Company of The Bank of Ireland* Vol I p 70

paid by a company to a person having controlling interest in that company *The Revenue Commissioners v Associated Properties Ltd* Vol II p 412

surplus of co-op from dealing with members, whether trading profits, whether exempt *Kennedy (Inspector of Taxes) v Rattoo Co-operative Dairy Society Ltd* Vol 1 p 315

whether collection of rents and dividends and distribution of dividends constituted trading *The Commissioners of Inland Revenue v The Dublin and Kingstown Railway Co* Vol I p 119 and *The Great Southern Railways Co v The Revenue Commissioners* Vol I p 359

whether excess corporation profits tax is exigible for accounting periods in respect of which no corporation profits tax (other than excess corporation profits tax) is payable *The Revenue Commissioners v Orwell Ltd* Vol II p 326

whether phasing down of business constituted trading *The City of Dublin Steampacket Co v Revenue Commissioners* Vol I p 108

Corporation tax

application of income tax provisions to corporation tax *Wayte (Holdings) Ltd (In receivership) Alex Burns v Edward N Hearne* Vol III p 553

Corporation tax (contd)

deduction of management expenses of investment company *Hibernian Insurance Company Limited v MacUimis (Inspector of Taxes)* Vol VI p 157

distribution of assets, Schedule F, statutory interpretation of general avoidance provision *The Revenue Commissioners v O'Flynn Construction Ltd, John and Michael O'Flynn* 2006 p 81

industrial buildings allowance *Kevin McGarry (Inspector of Taxes) v Harding (Lord Edward Street) Properties Ltd* Vol VI p 699

manufacturing relief for film production, whether relief applies to short advertising films produced for television, whether relief applies for accounting periods prior to FA 1990 *Saatchi & Saatchi Advertising Limited v Kevin McGarry (Inspector of Taxes)* Vol VI p 47

manufacturing relief for recycling wastepaper into new paper products, whether there was a significant change in raw materials and whether raw materials were acquired in bulk *P O'Muircheasa (Inspector of Taxes) v Bailey Wastepaper Limited* Vol VI p 579

manufacturing relief for timber harvesting *Sean Neeson (Inspector of Taxes) v Longford Timber Contractors Ltd* Vol VI p 691

manufacturing relief production of materials for use in advertising, whether manufacture *S Ó Culacháin (Inspector of Taxes) v Hunter Advertising Ltd* Vol IV p 35

surcharge, whether an advertising agency provides professional services for the purposes of corporation tax surcharge *Mac Giolla Mhaith (Inspector of Taxes) v Cronin & Associates Ltd* Vol III p 211

whether annual interest on loan to redeem preference shares is a deductible expense *Seán MacAonghusa (Inspector of Taxes) v Ringmahon Company* Vol VI p 327

whether operation is manufacturing or mining *Patrick J O'Connell (Inspector of Taxes) v Tara Mines Ltd* Vol VI p 523

Cost accounting

method of accounting for tax purposes, whether replacement cost basis is acceptable or whether historical cost accounting is the only method of commercial accountancy *Carroll Industries Plc (formerly PJ Carroll & Co Ltd) and PJ Carroll & Co Ltd v S Ó Culacháin (Inspector of Taxes)* Vol IV p 135

Costs

whether a Circuit Court Judge hearing an appeal pursuant to ITA 1967 s 429 has jurisdiction to award costs *Revenue v Arida Ltd* Vol IV p 401, Vol V p 221

Court fees

amount on which court fees are chargeable in liquidation *In re Private Motorists Provident Society Ltd (In Liqdtn) & W J Horgan v Minister for Justice* Vol V p 186, *In re Hibernian Transport Companies Ltd* Vol V p 194

Court order

whether Irish bank account is subject to UK court order restraining taxpayer from accessing funds *Governor & Co of the Bank of Ireland v Michael John Meeneghan & Ors* Vol V p 44

Covenants

to covenantees in Third World countries, whether covenantors entitled to relief under ITA 1967 s 439(1) and whether covenantees entitled to exemption limits under FA 1980 s 1 *Action Aid Ltd v Revenue Commissioners* Vol V p 392

whether an individual was entitled to repayment of tax deducted from payments made under an indenture of covenant pursuant to ITA 1967 s 439(1)(iv) *The Revenue Commissioners v HI* Vol III p 242

Crime

non-payment of excise duty payable on bets entered into by the defendant a registered bookmaker, whether recovery of an excise penalty a criminal matter *The Director of Public Prosecutions v Seamus Boyle* Vol IV p 395

proceeds liable to tax, *Criminal Assets Bureau v Gerard Hutch* Vol VI p 125

Crime and criminal earnings

Proceeds of Crime Act 1996 *John Gilligan v Criminal Assets Bureau, Revenue Commissioners & Others* Vol VI p 383

recovery of unpaid tax not limited to assets which are the proceeds of crime where the assessment is based on criminal activity *AS v Criminal Assets Bureau* Vol VI p 799

Criminal Assets Bureau

and assessments for income tax *The Criminal Assets Bureau v John Kelly* Vol VI p 501

anonymity of CAB officers *Criminal Assets Bureau v P McS* Vol VI p 421

not confined to issuing proceedings where assets were derived from criminal activity *Criminal Assets Bureau v Sean and Rosaleen Hunt* Vol VI p 559

whether assessments were arbitrary and unreasonable *AS v Criminal Assets Bureau* Vol VI p 799

whether CAB entitled to execute a judgement *Criminal Assets Bureau v H(S) and H(R)* Vol VI p 441

whether Mareva Injunction proceedings can be brought by plenary summons *The Criminal Assets Bureau v Patrick A McSweeney* Vol VI p 421

Currency

compulsory sale of, to Minister for Finance, in return for sterling equivalents, of dollar balances consisting of income from securities, etc, in the USA whether moneys so received assessable *J M O'Sullivan (Inspector of Taxes) v Julia O'Connor, as Administratrix of Evelyn H O'Brien, Deceased* Vol II p 61

Customs and excise duties

milk products, whether a whey or skimmed milk product, whether export refunds on consignments from EC countries to non EC countries, whether re-classification renders products liable for repayment of export refunds, whether Revenue Commissioners responsible for classification whether Revenue Commissioners and state chemist negligent and in breach of duty whether Minister entitled to counterclaim against plaintiff *Carbery Milk Products Ltd v The Minister for Agriculture & Others* Vol IV p 492

whether unconstitutional for applicant to be convicted and fined for keeping hydrocarbon oil in his motor vehicle on which custom and excise duty had not been paid, whether delegation of powers under Imposition of Duties Act 1957 is permissible *Charles McDaid v Hon Judge David Sheehy, DPP & Ors* Vol IV p 162, Vol V p 696

Customs duties

locus standi evasion of customs duties on specified goods *Gerard Curtis and Brendan Geough v The Attorney General and The Revenue Commissioners* Vol III p 419

seizure of oil tanker and contents for breach of regulations *McCrystal Oil Co Ltd v The Revenue Commissioners & Others* Vol IV p 386

Customs Law

validity of warrants grounding searches and seizures by Customs Officers *Simple Imports Limited and Another v Revenue Commissioners and Others* Vol VI p 141

D

Damages

for detinue and conversion arising from seizure by Revenue Commissioners of oil tanker *McCrystal Oil Co Ltd v The Revenue Commissioners & Others* Vol IV p 386

Dealing in or developing land

building contractors, whether lands the subject matter of a contract for sale entered into during an accounting period constitute trading stock for the year ending in that accounting period, whether inclusion of the lands in the accounts in accordance with good accounting procedure was evidence of the commercial reality of the transaction, whether absence of possession, conveyance of legal estate and planning permission relevant to taxpayer's claim for relief *Murnaghan Brothers Ltd v S O'Maoldhomhnaigh* Vol IV p 304

interest in land acquired and disposed of within one accounting period *M Cronin (Inspector of Taxes) v Cork & County Property Co Ltd* Vol III p 198

property company, farm land, letting to partners on conacre, area zoned for development, land transferred to new company, whether land trading stock of company *L O hArgain (Inspector of Taxes) v B Ltd* Vol III p 9

property company, whether ordinary principles of commercial accounting apply or whether artificial method of valuation pursuant to F(MP)A 1968 s 18(2) prevails *M Cronin (Inspector of Taxes) v Cork & County Property Co Ltd* Vol III p 198

whether the surplus from the sale of property was profit of a trade of dealing in or developing land, or the profit of a business which was deemed by F(MP)A 1968 s 17, to be such a trade *Mara (Inspector of Taxes) v GG (Hummingbird) Ltd* Vol II p 667

Debenture stock

whether loan notes constitute debenture stock *Patrick J O'Connell (Inspector of Taxes) v Thomas Keleghan* Vol VI p 201

Debts

determining restriction in prevention of charging, assigning or otherwise disposing of book debts and other debts *AH Masser Ltd (in receivership) & Others v The Revenue Commissioners* Vol III p 548

on securities, loan notes, liability to capital gains tax *PJ O'Connell (Inspector of Taxes) v T Keleghan* Vol VI p 201

Debts (contd)

whether a loan with conversion rights constitutes a debt within the meaning of CGTA 1975 s 46(1) *Mooney (Inspector of Taxes) v McSweeney* Vol V p 163

whether *situs* of a speciality debt is the country where the deed is situate *PV Murtagh (Inspector of Taxes) v Samuel Rusk* Vol VI p 817

Deductions

MANAGEMENT EXPENSES

by investment company *Howth Estate Co v WJ Davis (Inspector of Taxes)* Vol I p 447

losses in holding company, whether notional management fees deductible Corporation tax *Belville Holdings Ltd (in receivership and liquidation) v Cronin (Inspector of Taxes)* Vol III p 340

SCHEDULE D CASE I AND II

compensation paid to tenants of adjoining premises for interference with light and air, whether allowable Case I deduction *WJ Davis (Inspector of Taxes) v X Ltd* Vol II p 45

cost of replacement of weighbridge house *JT Hodgins (Inspector of Taxes) v Plunder & Pollak (Ireland) Ltd* Vol II p 267

deduction from excess profits duty for replacement of capital items *Boland's Ltd v The Commissioners of Inland Revenue* Vol I p 34

deduction of corporation profits tax and excess corporation profits tax in computing profits for income tax purposes *J M O'Dwyer (Inspector of Taxes) v The Dublin United Transport Co Ltd* Vol II p 115

deduction of management expenses of investment company *Hibernian Insurance Company Limited v MacUimis (Inspector of Taxes)* Vol VI p 157

expenditure on mill *sanitation JB Vale (Inspector of Taxes) v Martin Mahony & Brothers Ltd* Vol II p 32

expenditure on temporary *premises Martin Fitzgerald v Commissioners of Inland Revenue* Vol I p 91

expenses of promoting Bill in Parliament *McGarry (Inspector of Taxes) v Limerick Gas Committee* Vol I p 375

foreign company trading in Ireland provision for devaluation of foreign currency not allowed as deduction from profits. *The Revenue Commissioners v L & Co* Vol II p 281

formation expenses, whether allowable against trading profits *JB Kealy (Inspector of Taxes) v O'Mara (Limerick) Ltd* Vol I p 642

inadmissible, whether the inspector of taxes had made a "discovery" on finding that inadmissible deductions had been allowed in the computation of the company's tax liability for certain years and whether he was entitled to raise additional assessments for those years *W Ltd v Wilson (Inspector of Taxes)* Vol II p 627

incidental expenses, whether a deduction should be allowed under ITA 1967 Schedule 2 para 3, in respect of incidental expenses *MacDaibheid (Inspector of Taxes) v SD* Vol III p 1

legal fees in defending action in High Court for balance alleged to be due to a building contractor in respect of the construction of cinema, whether allowable Case I deduction *Casey (Inspector of Taxes) v AB Ltd* Vol II p 500

Deductions (contd)

on rebuilding of business premises, whether portion thereof deductible in computing profits *Curtin (Inspector of Taxes) v M Ltd* Vol II p 360

removing top-soil from surface of quarry *Milverton Quarries Ltd v The Revenue Commissioners* Vol II p 382

whether expenditure incurred by petrol marketing company under exclusivity agreements with retailers is revenue or capital *Dolan (Inspector of Taxes) v AB Co Ltd* Vol II p 515

whether expenses of management or by management *Hibernian Insurance Co Ltd v MasUimis (Inspector of Taxes)* Vol V p 495, Vol VI p 157

woodlands, whether purchasing and planting of trees is allowable deduction from farming profits *Connolly (Inspector of Taxes) v WW* Vol II p 657

SCHEDULE D CASE III

interest *Phillips (Inspector of Taxes) v Limerick County Council* Vol I p 66

SCHEDULE D CASE V

whether letting fees and legal expenses incurred by the company in respect of first lettings of property qualified as deductions under ITA 1967 s 81(5)(*d*) *GH Ltd v Browne (Inspector of Taxes)* Vol III p 95

SCHEDULE E

travelling expenses *Phillips (Inspector of Taxes) v Keane* Vol I p 64, *SP O'Broin (Inspector of Taxes) v Mac Giolla Meidhre/Finbar Pigott* Vol II p 366 and *HF Kelly (Inspector of Taxes) v H* Vol II p 460

Delegation of powers

by Government to Customs and Excise department whether unconstitutional *Charles McDaid v His Honour Judge David Sheehy, the Director of Public Prosecutions & Others* Vol IV p 162, Vol V p 696

Deposit

company engaged in manufacture and erection of prefabricated buildings deposit of 15 per cent of total cost paid on execution of contract, whether payment on account of trading stock or security for contracts *O'Laoghaire (Inspector of Taxes) v CD Ltd* Vol III p 51

company engaged in manufacture and export of ambulances, deposit received on foot of obligation with bank, whether income from trade *JG Kerrane (Inspector of Taxes) v N Hanlon (Ireland) Ltd* Vol III p 633

whether expenses of management or by management *Hibernian Insurance Co Ltd v MacUimis (Inspector of Taxes)* Vol V p 495, Vol VI p 157

Designated areas

capital allowances, whether plant used exclusively in designated area, whether allowance extends to plant used under a hire contract *Daniel McNally v S O Maoldhomhniagh* Vol IV p 22

Determination of an appeal

assessment of builders profits *The State (at the prosecution of Patrick J Whelan) v Michael Smidic (Special Commissioners of Income Tax)* Vol I p 571

Determination of an appeal (contd)

statutory provision requiring person to express dissatisfaction with the determination of a point of law "immediately after the determination" *The State (Multiprint Label Systems Ltd) v The Honourable Justice Thomas Neylon* Vol III p 159

Development of land

trading property company, farm land, letting to partners on conacre, area zoned for development, land transferred to new company, whether land trading stock of company *L Ó hArgáin (Inspector of Taxes) v B Ltd* Vol III p 9

whether the surplus from the sale of property was profit of a trade of dealing in or developing land, or the profit of a business which was deemed by F(MP)A 1968 s 17, to be such a trade *Mara (Inspector of Taxes) v GG (Hummingbird) Ltd* Vol II p 667

Development land

valuation agricultural land, appeal against market value at 6 April 1974 as determined by Circuit Court, whether agricultural value the sole determining factor, whether development potential attached on 6 April 1974, whether subsequent planning permission for milk processing plant relevant *J McMahon (Inspector of Taxes) v Albert Noel Murphy* Vol IV p 125

Director

resident abroad, of a company incorporated in the State but managed and controlled abroad. whether Schedule E *employment WJ Tipping (Inspector of Taxes) v Louis Jeancard* Vol II p 68

Disabled persons

redundancy payments to disabled employees, whether exempt from income tax, whether distinction to be made between disabled employees whose jobs continued and disabled employees whose jobs ceased *P O Cahill (Inspector of Taxes) v Albert Harding & Others* Vol IV p 233

to what extent must disabled persons be disabled to import goods eg motor vehicle free of excise duty *Michael Wiley v The Revenue Commissioners* Vol IV p 170

Discontinuance

of trade *Boland's Ltd v Davis (Inspector of Taxes)* Vol I p 86

Discovery

right to reopen assessment of Inspectors of Taxes *Hammond Lane Metal Co Ltd v S O'Culacháin (Inspector of Taxes)* Vol IV p 197 *W Ltd v Wilson (Inspector of Taxes)* Vol II p 627

Discretionary trust

discretionary powers of trustees, meaning of dependents *Crowe Engineering Ltd v Phyllis Lynch and Others* Vol IV p 340

interpretation of residuary bequest, whether bequest failed for uncertainty, whether bequest infringed rule against perpetual trusts *In the Matter of the Estate of Mary Davoren, Deceased; Thomas O'Byrne v Michael Davoren and Anne Coughlan* Vol V p 36

when absolute interest passes *BKJ v The Revenue Commissioners* Vol III p 104

Disposal

of assets at an undervalue by a company *Kill Inn Motel Ltd (In Liquidation) v The Companies Acts 1963/1983* Vol III p 706

Disposal (contd)

of property by mortgagee as nominee for mortgagor, accountable person for capital gains tax purposes, repayment of 15% deducted by purchaser in the absence of tax clearance certificate *Bank of Ireland Finance Ltd v The Revenue Commissioners* Vol IV p 217

paper for paper transaction, capital gains tax implications *PJ O'Connell v T Keleghan* Vol VI p 201

Disposition of income

deed of appointment by parent in favour of child *EG v Mac Shamhrain, (Inspector of Taxes)* Vol II p 352

deed of trust in favour of charitable objects with provision for re-vestment of income in settlor in certain contingencies, whether income of settlor or trustees *HPC Hughes (Inspector of Taxes) v Miss Gretta Smyth (Sister Mary Bernard) & Others* Vol I p 411

in favour of children *JM O'Dwyer (Inspector of Taxes) v Cafolla & Co* Vol II p 82

Distance trades

Boland's Ltd v Davis (Inspector of Taxes) Vol I p 86

Distributions

interest paid by Irish subsidiary to Japanese parent company on loan from parent company whether tax should be deducted at source under Double Tax Treaty or

whether the payment should be treated as distribution under Schedule F *Murphy (Inspector of Taxes) v Asahi Synthetic Fibres (Ireland) Ltd* Vol III p 246

Dividends

from sales of capital assets whether liable to corporation profits tax *K Co v Hogan (Inspector of Taxes)* Vol III p 56

payment of, whether payment through inter-company account was sufficient evidence of actual payment, whether payment of cheque required, whether making of accounting entry a mere record of underlying transaction, whether a dividend declared on 11 December 1980 was received by related company not later than 12 December 1980, whether making of journal entries after 23 December 1980 material evidence *Sean Murphy (Inspector of Taxes) v The Borden Co Ltd* Vol III p 559

whether dividends paid represented profit earning capacity of a company, *E A Smyth v The Revenue Commissioners* Vol V p 532

Doctrines of res judicata and equitable estoppel

Boland's Ltd v The Commissioners of Inland Revenue Vol I p 34

Domicile

Captain R H Prior-Wandesforde v The Revenue Commissioners Vol I p 249, *The Right Hon Earl of Iveagh v The Revenue Commissioners* Vol I p 259, *In the Goods of Bernard Louis Rowan, Deceased Joseph Rowan v Vera Agnes Rowan & Others* Vol III p 572, *Proes v The Revenue Commissioners* Vol V p 481

common law rule that wife takes domicile of dependence of her husband, whether constitutional *JW v JW* Vol IV p 437

DORA requisition orders

liability in respect of transactions under *Arthur Guinness Son & Co Ltd v Commissioners of Inland Revenue* Vol I p 1

Double taxation

Ireland United Kingdom Double Taxation Agreement *PV Murtagh (Inspector of Taxes) v Samuel Rusk* Vol VI p 817

Double taxation relief

wife's remuneration taxed in Northern Ireland – whether appellant entitled to double taxation relief in Ireland *John Travers v Sean Ó Siocháin (Inspector of Taxes)* Vol V p 54

E

Earned income

income from the leasing of premises, whether leasing constitutes trading whether earned income *Pairceir (Inspector of Taxes) v EM* Vol II p 596

Ejusdem generis rule

as applied in interpretation of statutes *M Cronin (Inspector of Taxes) v Lunham Brothers Ltd* Vol III p 370

Emoluments

of office, grant to a President of a college on retirement *JD Mulvey (Inspector of Taxes) v Denis J Coffey* Vol I p 618

of employment, rent paid for employee *Connolly (Inspector of Taxes) v Denis McNamara* Vol II p 452

professional services rendered without prior agreement as regards remuneration payment on termination of services whether chargeable as income *WS McGarry (Inspector of Taxes) v E F* Vol II p 261

Employee

branch manager of local Employment Office of Dept of Social Welfare *Ó Coindealbháin (Inspector of Taxes) v TB Mooney* Vol IV p 45

demonstrator of food products at supermarket, whether an employee or self-employed *H Denny & Sons (Irl) Ltd v Minister for Social Welfare* Vol V p 238

whether a member of the crew of a fishing vessel can be an "employee", whether there can be an "employee" without there being a corresponding employer, whether Social Welfare (Consolidation) Act 1981 applies to self employed persons, whether scheme of Act and regulations is limited to employer/employee circumstances whether Minister has unlimited power to make regulations enabling any person to be treated as an employee *The Minister for Social Welfare v John Griffiths* Vol IV p 378

whether director became employee of company *Patrick J O'Connell (Inspector of Taxes) v Thomas Keleghan* Vol VI p 201

whether share fishermen employed on contract of service or engaged in a joint venture with boat owner *Francis Griffin v Minister for Social, Community and Family Affairs* Vol VI p 371

wholesale distributors of newspapers *Tony McAuliffe v Minister for Social Welfare* Vol V p 94

Employer's obligations

to deduct PAYE and PRSI from employee's emoluments *EN Hearne (Inspector of Taxes) v O'Cionna & Others T/A J A Kenny & Partners* Vol IV p 113

Employments

appeal as to whether a contract of services or a contract for services – wholesale distributor of newspapers, *Tony McAuliffe v The Minister for Social Welfare* Vol V p 94

branch manager of local Employment Office of Dept of Social Welfare whether the taxpayer was engaged under a contract of service or a contract for services *Ó Coindealbháin (Inspector of Taxes) v TB Mooney* Vol IV p 45

contract of service or contract for services, temporary employee engaged through an employment agency *The Minister for Labour v PMPA Insurance Co Ltd (under administration)* Vol III p 505

demonstrator of food products at supermarket, whether an employee or self-employed *H Denny & Sons (Irl) Ltd v Minister for Social Welfare* Vol V p 238

director resident abroad, of a company incorporated in the State but managed and controlled abroad. whether Schedule E employment *WJ Tipping (Inspector of Taxes) v Louis Jeancard* Vol II p 68

whether contract for services between skipper of fishing vessel and crew members, *Director of Public Prosecutions v Martin McLoughlin* Vol III p 467

whether dockers working under a pooling arrangement can receive unemployment benefit when they are not occupied unloading ships, whether dockers had a contract of employment with their Association, separate contracts on each occasion of their employment, whether level of earnings material to question of employment *James Louth & Others v Minister for Social Welfare* Vol IV p 391

whether the taxpayer was engaged under a contract of service or a contract for services *McDermott (Inspector of Taxes) v BC* Vol III p 43

Whether a trade union official was performing services under a contract of service or a contract for service *Philip Kirwan v Technical Engineering and Electrical Union* Vol VI p 771

Enforcement of Revenue Debts

Governor & Co of Bank of Ireland v Michael John Meeneghan and Others Vol V p 44 *In the Matter of the Extradition Acts John Oliver Byrne v Noel Conroy* Vol VI p 19

Errors

inadmissible deductions, whether the inspector of taxes had made a "discovery" on finding that inadmissible deductions had been allowed in the computation of the company's tax liability for certain years and whether he was entitled to raise additional assessments for those years *W Ltd v Wilson (Inspector of Taxes)* Vol II p 627

Estate company

expenses of management, company whose business consists mainly in the making of investments *Casey (Inspector of Taxes) v The Monteagle Estate* Co Vol II p 429

Estate duty

charitable bequest, whether it had to be expended in Ireland *The Revenue Commissioners v The Most Reverend Edward Doorley* Vol V p 539

whether conveyancing form determines liability *The Attorney General v Power & Anor* Vol V p 525

Estate duty (contd)

whether due when consideration is stated in receipt clause of deed but payment is not pursued by the disponer *Revenue v Daniel Anthony Moroney & Ors* Vol V p 589

whether surviving spouse competent to dispose of statutory share in estate *In Re the Estate of Urquhart, D (Decd) & Revenue Commissioners v AIB Ltd* Vol V p 600

Estoppel

whether stamped conveyance invalid *Parkes (Roberta) v David Parkes* 1998 p 169

Evasion

locus standi evasion of customs duties on specified goods *Gerard Curtis and Brendan Geough v The Attorney General and The Revenue Commissioners* Vol III p 419

Evidence

secondary evidence that beneficial interest in securities had been transferred not admissible *Gilbert Hewson v JB Kealy (Inspector of Taxes)* Vol II p 15

Ex gratia payments

by British government for malicious damage to property or personal injury sustained, whether trading receipt *WA Robinson T/A James Pim & Son v JD Dolan (Inspector of Taxes)* Vol I p 427

Excess corporation profits tax

whether excess corporation profits tax is exigible for accounting periods in respect of which no corporation profits tax (other than excess corporation profits tax) is payable *The Revenue Commissioners v Orwell Ltd* Vol II p 326

Excess profits duty

accounting period, whether Revenue Commissioners are required to determine *The Revenue Commissioners v R Hilliard & Sons Ltd* Vol II p 130

brewery, whether liability in respect of transactions under DORA requisition orders *Arthur Guinness Son & Co Ltd v Commissioners of Inland Revenue* Vol I p 1

deductions from, expenditure on temporary premises *Martin Fitzgerald v Commissioners of Inland Revenue* Vol I p 91

notional loss in trade from decrease in value of stock not allowed *The Revenue Commissioners v Latchford & Sons Ltd* Vol I p 240

profits, whether ascertained by actual or standard percentage *Boland's Ltd v The Commissioners of Inland Revenue* Vol I p 34

stock relief, definition of trading stock in hand *Green & Co (Cork) Ltd v The Revenue Commissioners* Vol I p 130

whiskey in bond sold by publican *McCall (deceased) v Commissioners of Inland Revenue* Vol I p 28

Exchange loss

on foreign currency loans, whether capital or revenue *TG Brosnan (Inspector of Taxes) v Mutual Enterprises Ltd* Vol V p 138

Excise duty

and the importation of kerosene containing the colour marker coumarin vis a vis Article 28 of the Treaty of Rome and Council Directive 92/12/EEC *Oliver Masterson v Director of Public Prosecutions* Vol VI p 471

Excise duty (contd)

availability of excise duty rebate on fuel purchased in the State but combusted outside the State *The Revenue Commissioners v Bus Éireann* Vol VI p 743

bookmaker convicted and fined in the District Court of offences under the Betting Acts penal warrant for imprisonment, whether constitutional *John B Murphy v District Justice Brendan Wallace & Others* Vol IV p 278

imposed on proprietors of slaughter houses and exporters of live animals, whether ultra vires and void *Doyle & Others v An Taoiseach & Others* Vol III p 73

non-payment of excise duty payable on bets entered into by the defendant a registered bookmaker, whether recovery of an excise penalty a criminal matter *The Director of Public Prosecutions v Seamus Boyle* Vol IV p 395

publican's licence, whether new licence obtainable, whether application within six year period, meaning of year immediately preceding *Peter Connolly v The Collector of Customs and Excise* Vol IV p 419

to what extent must disabled persons be disabled to import goods eg motor vehicle free of excise duty *Michael Wiley v The Revenue Commissioners* Vol IV p 170

whether creditor to resort to securities received from principal before proceeding against surety *The Attorney General v Sun Alliance and London Insurance Ltd* Vol III p 265

whether Imposition of Duties Act 1957 s 1 is constitutional *C Mc Daid v His Honour Judge Sheehy & Ors* Vol V p 696

whether rebate available on fuel combusted outside the State and whether Road Transport Act 1932 has extra-territorial effect *The Revenue Commissioners v Bus Éireann* Vol VI p 743

whether zero rated for VAT purposes, *DH Burke & Sons Ltd v The Revenue Commissioners, Ireland and The Attorney General* Vol V p 418

Exclusivity agreements

whether expenditure incurred by petrol marketing company under exclusivity agreements with retailers is revenue or capital *Dolan (Inspector of Taxes) v AB Co Ltd* Vol II p 515

Executor

carrying on trade, recovery by executor of debts allowed as bad debts in lifetime of deceased, whether a trading receipt *CD v JM O'Sullivan (Inspector of Taxes)* Vol II p 140

Exemptions

AGRICULTURAL SOCIETY

definition of *The Trustees of The Ward Union Hunt Races v Hughes (Inspector of Taxes)* Vol I p 538

ARTISTIC

exemption of earnings from original and creative works of artistic or cultural merit, whether journalism qualifies *John Healy v SI Breathnach (Inspector of Taxes)* Vol III p 496

legal text books, refusal by inspector of taxes to grant exemption from income tax under FA 1969 s 2, Exemption granted if the books are original and creative works which are generally recognised as having cultural or artistic merit *Michael Forde Decision* Vol IV p 348

Exemptions (contd)

BUILDING SOCIETIES

instruments relating to the internal affairs of a society were exempt from stamp duty, whether this exemption extended to a transfer of a premises to a society to conduct its business *Irish Nationwide Building Society v Revenue Commissioners* Vol IV p 296

CHARITIES

trade carried on by beneficiary of charity, whether exempt *Beirne (Inspector of Taxes) v St Vincent De Paul Society (Wexford Conference)* Vol I p 383

INDUSTRIAL AND PROVIDENT SOCIETIES

surplus of co-op from dealing with members, whether trading profits, whether exempt *Kennedy (Inspector of Taxes) v The Rattoo Co-operative Dairy Society Ltd* Vol I p 315

ORIGINAL AND CREATIVE

writing, school textbooks – whether within the meaning of FA 1969 s 2 *The Revenue Commissioners v Colm O'Loinsigh* Vol V p 98

Expenditure

loan interest payable after redemption of share capital whether allowable trading expense, *Sean MacAonghusa v Ringmahon* Vol VI p 327

on installation of suspended ceiling in supermarket whether plant qualifying for capital allowances *Dunnes Stores (Oakville) Ltd v MC Cronin (Inspector of Taxes)* Vol IV p 68

on mill sanitation *JB Vale (Inspector Of Taxes) v Martin Mahony & Brothers Ltd* Vol II p 32

on racecourse stand, whether deductible as repairs *Michael O'Grady (Inspector of Taxes) v Roscommon Race Committee* Vol IV p 425

on rebuilding of business premises whether portion thereof deductible in computing profits *Curtin (Inspector of Taxes) v M Ltd* Vol II p 360

on temporary premises *Martin Fitzgerald v Commissioners of Inland Revenue* Vol I p 91

Expenses

allowance of, where assessment has been confirmed *The King (Harris Stein) v The Special Commissioners* Vol 1 p 62

compensation paid to tenants of adjoining premises for interference with light and air, whether allowable Case I deduction *WJ Davis (Inspector of Taxes) v X Ltd* Vol II p 45

deduction of expenses of management by investment company *Howth Estate Co v W J Davis (Inspector of Taxes)* Vol I p 447

formation expenses, whether allowable against trading profits *JB Kealy (Inspector of Taxes) v O'Mara (Limerick) Ltd* Vol I p 642

from Schedule E *SP O'Broin (Inspector of Taxes) v Mac Giolla Meidhre/Finbar Pigott* Vol II p 366 and *HF Kelly (Inspector of Taxes) v H* Vol II p 460

incidental expenses, whether a deduction should be allowed under ITA 1967 Sch 2 para 3 *MacDaibheid (Inspector of Taxes) v SD* Vol III p 1

of management, company whose business consists mainly in the making of investments *Casey (Inspector of Taxes) v The Monteagle Estate Co* Vol II p 429

Expenses (contd)

of management, investment appraisal expenditure whether allowable as management expense *Hibernian Insurance Co Ltd v MacUimis (Inspector of Taxes)* Vol VI p 157

of management, whether tax deductible, meaning of *Hibernian Insurance Company Limited v MacUimis (Inspector of Taxes)* Vol V p 495, Vol VI p 157

of management, whether auctioneer's/solicitors fees are revenue or capital – *Stephen Court Ltd v JA Browne (Inspector of Taxes)* Vol V p 680

of promoting bill in Parliament *McGarry (Inspector of Taxes) v Limerick Gas Committee* Vol I p 375

of removing top soil from surface of quarry whether capital or revenue expenditure *Milverton Quarries Ltd v The Revenue Commissioners* Vol II p 382

Exported Live Stock (Insurance) Board

statutory body, whether carrying on a trade *The Exported Live Stock (Insurance) Board v T J Carroll (Inspector of Taxes)* Vol II p 211

Export sales relief

ambulances manufactured in the State and exported *JG Kerrane (Inspector of Taxes) v N Hanlon (Ireland) Ltd* Vol III p 633

sale of meat into intervention, exporter need not be owner at time of export *Cronin (Inspector of Taxes) v IMP Midleton Ltd* Vol III p 452

whether mining operation qualifies for ESR or capital allowances *Patrick J O'Connell (Inspector of Taxes) v Tara Mines Ltd* Vol VI p 523

Export refunds

milk products, whether a whey or skimmed milk product, whether export refunds on consignments from EC countries to non EC countries, whether re-classification renders products liable for repayment of export refunds, whether Revenue Commissioners responsible for classification whether Revenue Commissioners and state chemist negligent and in breach of duty whether Minister entitled to counterclaim against plaintiff *Carbery Milk Products Ltd v The Minister for Agriculture & Others* Vol IV p 492

Extension

of period for making distribution of dividends *Rahinstown Estates Co v M Hughes (Inspector of Taxes)* Vol III p 517

Extradition Order

appeal on grounds of a revenue offence, whether EEC levies constitute a tax *John Oliver Byrne v Noel Conroy* Vol VI p 19

order of rendition, appeal, test for corresponding offence, revenue offence exception, whether offence of cheating the public revenue exists in Ireland *The Attorney General v Anthony Karl Frank Baird Hilton* 2004 p 109

order of rendition, corresponding offence, revenue offence, additional sentences of imprisonment *The Attorney General v Charles Ashleigh Nicholson and Ruth Ellen Ashleigh Nicholson* Vol VI p 667

F

Fair Procedures

constitutional right to fair procedures *Charles J Haughey & Others v Moriarty & Others* Vol VI p 67

Farm tax

whether implementation of Farm Tax Act constituted unfair procedures, effect of repeal of that Act, consequences of absence of amending legislation *Purcell v Attorney General* Vol IV p 229, Vol V p 288

Farming

BLOODSTOCK

animal bought in course of trade, sent to stud after successful racing career and subsequently sold to a syndicate whether amount realised on syndication a trading receipt *Mac Giolla Riogh (Inspector of Taxes) v G Ltd* Vol II p 315

CATTLEDEALER

whether the taxpayer was a "dealer in cattle" within the meaning of ITA 1918 Sch D Case III rule 4 and ITA 1967 s 78 *De Brun (Inspector of Taxes) v K* Vol III p 19

MARKET GARDENING

valuation of land occupied for market gardening *L v WS McGarry (Inspector of Taxes)* Vol II p 241

OCCUPATION OF LANDS

whether the appellant company was in occupation of lands, forming part of a military establishment, for the purposes of ITA 1918 Sch B or ITA 1967 *O Conaill (Inspector of Taxes) v Z Ltd* Vol II p 636

PIG REARING

whether the activity of intensive pig rearing constituted farming for the purposes of FA 1974 s 13(1) *Knockhall Piggeries v JG Kerrane (Inspector of Taxes)* Vol III p 319

WOODLANDS

whether purchasing and planting of trees is allowable deduction from farming profits *Connolly (Inspector of Taxes) v WW* Vol II p 657

Fees

due to a barrister prior to his appointment to the bench, fees refused but could be paid to a family company if solicitors so wished *EP Ó Coindealbháin (Inspector of Taxes) v The Honourable Mr Justice Sean Gannon* Vol III p 484

High Court fees on funds realised by liquidator in course of liquidation, whether applicable to secured creditors or to proceeds of sale of property subject to a fixed charge *Michael Orr (Kilternan) Ltd v The Companies Acts 1963-1983, and Thornberry Construction (Irl) Ltd v The Companies Acts 1963-1983* Vol III p 530

Film production

whether accounting periods prior to FA 1990 qualify for relief *Saatchi & Saatchi Advertising Ltd v Kevin McGarry (Inspector of Taxes)* Vol V p 376

Finality

of Special Commissioners' decision *The King (Evelyn Spain) v The Special Commissioners* Vol I p 221

Finance company

dealing in stocks and shares, whether investments should be valued at cost or market value *AB Ltd v Mac Giolla Riogh (Inspector of Taxes)* Vol II p 419

Fixtures

installation of fixtures subject to low rate of value added tax, whether or not television aerials attached to roof of a house are fixtures *John Maye v The Revenue Commissioners* Vol III p 332

Foreign company

director resident abroad, of a company incorporated in the State but managed and controlled abroad. whether Schedule E employment *WJ Tipping (Inspector of Taxes) v Louis Jeancard* Vol II p 68

foreign company trading in Ireland provision for devaluation of foreign currency not allowed as deduction from profits. *The Revenue Commissioners v L & Co* Vol II p 281

Foreign currency loans

whether exchange loss is capital or revenue *TG Brosnan (Inspector of Taxes) v Mutual Enterprises Ltd* Vol V p 138

Foreign pension

pension received by Irish resident from British company, whether income from foreign possession *McHugh (Inspector of Taxes) v A* Vol II p 393 and *Forbes (Inspector of Taxes) v GHD* Vol II p 491

Foreign property

claim for relief under ITA 1918 Case V rule 3, question of residence and domicile *Captain R H Prior-Wandesforde v the Revenue* Commissioners Vol I p 249 and *The Right Hon The Earl of Iveagh v The Revenue Commissioners* Vol I p 259

Foreign Revenue Debt

UK vat, *Governor & Co of the Bank of Ireland v Meenaghan & Ors* Vol V p 44

Foreign tax

whether recoverable in Ireland *Governor & Co of the Bank of Ireland v Michael John Meeneghan & Ors* Vol V p 44

Foreign trades

basis of assessment under Case III *O'Conaill (Inspector of Taxes) v R* Vol II p 304

Formation expenses

whether allowable against trading profits *JB Kealy (Inspector of Taxes) v O'Mara (Limerick) Ltd* Vol I p 642

Forward purchase contracts

fall in market value of goods before delivery, *The Revenue Commissioners v Latchford & Sons Ltd* Vol I p 240

Fraudulent Conveyances Act 1634 (10 Charles 1)

Kill Inn Motel Ltd (In Liquidation) v The Companies Acts 1963/1983 Vol III p 706

Fuel merchants

whether new trade of coal mining was set up or commenced *HA O'Loan (Inspector of Taxes) v Messrs MJ Noone & Co* Vol II p 146

Functions of courts

and legislature *McGrath & Or v JE McDermott (Inspector of Taxes)* Vol III p 683

Funds in court

whether general rules applicable Schedules A, B, C, D and E apply to the court when paying interest on debts out of funds in court and whether tax deductible from income accrued to funds in court for years prior to 1922/23 *Colclough v Colclough* Vol II p 332

G

Gifts

consider orders and CAB powers to execute *Criminal Assets Bureau v H(S) and H(R)* Vol VI p 441

made by a company *Kill Inn Motel Ltd (In Liquidation) v The Companies Acts 1963/1983* Vol III p 706

whether gift arises when consideration is stated in receipt clause of deed but payment is not pursued by the disponer *The Revenue Commissioners v Daniel Anthony Moroney & Ors* Vol V p 589

whether "marriage gratuity" received on resignation was a retirement payment under ITA 1967 s 114 or was a perquisite of her office under ITA 1967 s 110 *Sean Ó Síocháin (Inspector of Taxes v Thomas Morrissey Eleanor Morrissey* Vol IV p 407

whether present from employer taxable as gift, or emolument under Schedule E *Wing v O'Connell (Inspector of Taxes)* Vol I p 155

Goods

distinguished from services *Dunnes Stores (Oakville) Ltd v MC Cronin (Inspector of Taxes)* Vol IV p 68

Government stocks

purchased to comply with Central Bank requirements, whether carrying on trade of dealing in securities, whether liable as profits under Schedule D or exempt capital gains on Government stocks *JA Browne (Inspector of Taxes) v Bank of Ireland Finance Ltd* Vol III p 644

Ground rents

whether fines and capitalised value of ground rents are assessable to tax *Birch (Inspector of Taxes) v Denis Delaney* Vol I p 515

Group relief

whether the expression "total income means income before or after the deduction of group relief *Cronin (Inspector of Taxes) v Youghal Carpets (Yarns) Ltd* Vol III p 229

Group companies

recovery of outstanding taxes from a group of companies, whether Revenue Commissioners may appropriate payments between separate companies within the group, whether insolvency of a company is relevant to gratuitous alienation of assets *Frederick Inns Ltd, The Rendezvous Ltd, The Graduate Ltd, Motels Ltd (In Liquidation) v The Companies Acts 1963-1986* Vol IV p 247

H

Hauliers

whether lorry owners carrying sand and gravel were engaged as subcontractors under a construction contract, whether the lorry owners became the proprietors of the quarry materials *O'Grady v Laragan Quarries Ltd* Vol IV p 269

High Court

powers of determination of tax liability by High Court and Appeal Commissioners whether mutually exclusive, nature of powers and functions of Appeal Commissioners limited or unlimited *The State (Calcul International Ltd and Solatrex International Ltd) v The Appeal Commissioners and The Revenue Commissioners* Vol III p 530

whether the High Court retains an inherent jurisdiction to determine a person's liability to tax *Criminal Assets Bureau v Sean and Rosaleen Hunt* Vol VI p 559

High Court fees

on funds realised by liquidator in course of liquidation, whether applicable to secured creditors or to proceeds of sale of property subject to a fixed charge *Michael Orr (Kilternan) Ltd v The Companies Acts 1963-1983, and Thornberry Construction (Irl) Ltd v The Companies Acts 1963-1983* Vol III p 530

Historical cost accounting

method of accounting for tax purposes, whether replacement cost basis is acceptable or whether historical cost accounting is the only method of commercial accountancy *Carroll Industries Plc (formerly PJ Carroll & Co Ltd) and PJ Carroll & Co Ltd v S Ó Culacháin (Inspector of Taxes)* Vol IV p 135

Holiday cottages

whether qualifying for capital allowances *McMahon, T & Ors v Rt Hon Lord Mayor Alderman & Burgess of Dublin* Vol V p 357

Holidays (Employees) Act 1973

The Minister for Labour v PMPA Insurance Co Ltd (under administration) Vol III p 505

Hospital

whether carrying on a trade *RG Davis (Inspector of Taxes) v The Superioress Mater Misericordiae Hospital, Dublin* Vol I p 387

Hotel-keeping

whether hostel qualified as 'trade of hotel-keeping' *Kevin McGarry (Inspector of Taxes) v Harding (Lord Edward Street) Properties Ltd* Vol VI p 699

Husband

and wife, living apart *Donovan (Inspector Of Taxes) v CG Crofts* Vol I p 115

and wife, living together *Ua Clothasaigh (Inspector of Taxes) v McCartan* Vol II p 75

tax paid by a married couple in excess of the amounts payable by a husband and wife if taxed as separate persons, *Francis & Mary Murphy v Attorney General* Vol V p 613

Husband (contd)

wife's income from securities assessed on husband in first year of wife's income from securities *JD Mulvey (Inspector of Taxes) v RM Kieran* Vol I p 563

I

Illegal trades

not assessable to tax *C Hayes (Inspector of Taxes) v RJ Duggan* Vol I p 195

Immediately

statutory provision requiring person to express dissatisfaction with the determination of a point of law "immediately after the determination" *The State (Multiprint Label Systems Ltd) v The Honourable Justice Thomas Neylon* Vol III p 159

Immovable goods

valuation of interest in immovable property subject to an arbitrator's award *Campus Stadium Ireland Development Ltd v Dublin Waterworld Ltd* 2006 p 55

whether connection/reconnection at premises was integral to the provision of telecommunication signals and whether it consisted of work on immovable goods *DA MacCarthaigh, Inspector of Taxes v Cablelink Ltd, Cablelink Waterford Ltd and Galway Cable Vision Ltd* Vol VI p 595

Importation

of used motor vehicles from a Member State *Karl Keller v The Revenue Commissioners & Others* Vol IV p 512

Imprisonment

bookmaker convicted and fined in the District Court of offences under the Betting Acts penal warrant for imprisonment, whether constitutional *John B Murphy v District Justice Brendan Wallace & Others* Vol IV p 278

return of income, failure to make, appeal against a decision of the High Court to refuse on a judicial review application to quash three convictions with six months imprisonment for each offence imposed in the District Court on the appellant for failure to make income tax returns *Thomas O'Callaghan v JP Clifford & Others* Vol IV p 478

Incidental expenses

whether a deduction should be allowed under ITA 1967 Sch 2 para 3, in respect of incidental expenses *MacDaibheid (Inspector of Taxes) v SD* Vol III p 1

Income

accumulated for minor, benefit taken by way of capital *The King (Evelyn Spain) v The Special Commissioners* Vol I p 221

father taking his elder children and his mother-in-law into partnership, subsequent assignment of mother-in-law's interest to his younger children whether income of children to be deemed to be income of father *JM O'Dwyer (Inspector of Taxes) v Cafolla & Co* Vol II p 82

from the leasing of premises, whether earned income *Pairceir (Inspector of Taxes) v EM* Vol II p 596

not "immediately derived" from a trade of business *JG Kerrane (Inspector of Taxes) v N Hanlon (Ireland) Ltd* Vol III p 633

Income (contd)

on estate in course of administration *Moloney (Inspector of Taxes) v Allied Irish Banks Ltd as executors of the estate of Francis J Doherty deceased* Vol III p 477

payment for maintenance of residence not part of total income *The Most Honourable Frances Elizabeth Sarah Marchioness Conyngham v The Revenue Commissioners* Vol I p 231

personal pension and other assets assigned to company pension continued to be paid to pensioner, whether pensioner liable to tax on pension *Cronin (Inspector of Taxes) v C* Vol II p 592

professional services rendered without prior agreement as regards remuneration payment on termination of services whether chargeable as income *WS McGarry (Inspector of Taxes) v EF* Vol II p 261

received on foot of an obligation with bank *JG Kerrane (Inspector of Taxes) v N Hanlon (Ireland) Ltd* Vol III p 633

trust in favour of charitable objects with provision for re-vestment of income in settlor in certain contingencies, whether income of settlor or trustees *HPC Hughes (Inspector of Taxes) v Miss Gretta Smyth (Sister Mary Bernard) & Others* Vol I p 411

whether children's pension is treated as income of the parent or income of the children for income tax purposes *EP Ó Coindealbháin (Inspector of Taxes) v Breda O'Carroll* Vol IV p 221

whether increase in widows contributory pension for children is taxable income of parent *Sean Ó Síocháin (Inspector of Taxes) v Bridget Neenan* Vol V p 472

Income tax

Acts *Michael Deighan v Edward N Hearne & Others* Vol III p 533

appeal to High Court by way of case stated from decision of Circuit Judge, failure to notify the respondent the fact that a case has been stated *A & B v WJ Davis (Inspector of Taxes)* Vol II p 60

application of provisions to corporation tax *Wayte (Holdings) Ltd (In Receivership) Alex Burns v Edward N Hearne* Vol III p 553

assessable profits, not received in the year of assessment *MacKeown (Inspector of Taxes) v Patrick J Roe* Vol I p 214

difference between contracts of and for service *Patrick J O'Connell (Inspector of Taxes) v Thomas Keleghan* Vol VI p 201

domicile and ordinary residence *Captain R H Prior-Wandesforde v the Revenue Commissioners* Vol I p 249 and *The Right Hon The Earl of Iveagh v The Revenue Commissioners* Vol I p 259

exclusions, whether impugned transaction was tax avoidance pursuant to TCA 1997, s 811 *The Revenue Commissioners v O'Flynn Construction Ltd, John and Michael O'Flynn* 2006 p 81

exemption for agricultural societies *The Trustees of The Ward Union Hunt Races v Hughes (Inspector of Taxes)* Vol I p 538

husband and wife living apart, wife's income assessed on husband *Donovan (Inspector of Taxes) v CG Crofts* Vol I p 115

husband and wife living together *D Ua Clothasaigh (Inspector of Taxes) v Patrick McCartan* Vol II p 75

Income tax (contd)

rate applicable to interest earned on clients' funds held by solicitors' firms *PO Cahill (Inspector of Taxes) v Patrick O'Driscoll, Michael O'Driscoll and William F O'Driscoll* Vol VI p 793

residence of company *The Cunard Steam Ship Co Ltd v Herlihy (Inspector of Taxes), and The Cunard Steam Ship Co Ltd v Revenue Commissioners* Vol I p 330

school/colleges whether operated for charitable purposes *The Pharmaceutical Society of Ireland v The Revenue Commissioners* Vol I p 542

trust in favour of charitable objects with provision for re-vestment of income in settlor in certain contingencies, whether income of settlor or trustees *HPC Hughes (Inspector of Taxes) v Miss Smyth (Sister Mary Bernard) & Others* Vol I p 411

veterinary, body corporate performing statutory functions, whether profits liable to tax *The Veterinary Council v F Corr (Inspector of Taxes)* Vol II p 204

wife's income from securities assessed on husband in first year of wife's income from securities *JD Mulvey (Inspector of Taxes) v RM Kieran* Vol I p 563

whether a trade union official had a contractual relationship with a trade union *Philip Kirwan v Technical Engineering and Electrical Union* Vol VI p 771

RETURNS

of income, what constitutes a proper return of income for the assessment of income tax *MA Bairead v M McDonald* Vol IV p 475

SCHEDULE A

income tax paid, whether further balance due *Estate Of Teresa Downing (Owner)* Vol I p 487

SCHEDULE B

profits from stallion fees, whether liable to tax under Schedule B or Schedule D income tax paid, whether further balance due *Cloghran Stud Farm v AG Birch (Inspector of Taxes)* Vol I p 496

occupation of lands, whether the appellant company was in occupation of lands, forming part of a military establishment, for the purposes of ITA 1918 Schedule B or ITA 1967 *O Conaill (Inspector of Taxes) v Z Ltd* Vol II p 636

valuation of land occupied for market gardening *L v WS McGarry (Inspector of Taxes)* Vol II p 241

SCHEDULE D

assessment of builders profits *The State (at the prosecution of Patrick J Whelan) v Michael Smidic (Special Commissioners of Income Tax)* Vol I p 571 and *Edward Connolly v AG Birch (Inspector of Taxes)* Vol I p 583

change in nature of trade or new trade, trading as fuel merchants, whether new trade of coal mining was set up or commenced *HA O'Loan (Inspector of Taxes) v Messrs MJ Noone & Co* Vol II p 146

cost of replacement of weighbridge house, whether allowable deduction *JT Hodgins (Inspector of Taxes) v Plunder & Pollak (Ireland) Ltd* Vol II p 267

ex gratia payments, by British government for malicious damage to property or personal injury sustained, whether trading receipt *WA Robinson T/A James Pim & Son v JD Dolan (Inspector of Taxes)* Vol I p 427

management expenses, deduction of, by investment company *Howth Estate Co v WJ Davis (Inspector of Taxes)* Vol I p 447

Income tax (contd)

nurseries and market gardens, assessment of income by reference to annual profits estimated according to the rules of Schedule D *WS McGarry (Inspector of Taxes) v JA Spencer* Vol II p 1

obsolescence of assets *Evans & Co v Phillips (Inspector of Taxes)* Vol I p 43

payment in advance on the signing of a lease, whether capital *O'Sullivan (Inspector of Taxes) v p Ltd* Vol II p 464

personal pension assigned to company but continued to be paid to pensioner, whether pensioner liable to tax *Cronin (Inspector of Taxes) v C* Vol II p 592

profits from stallion fees, whether liable to tax under Schedule B or Schedule D income tax paid, whether further balance due *Cloghran Stud Farm v AG Birch (Inspector of Taxes)* Vol I p 496

profits of a bookmaker from transactions in Irish Hospital Sweepstakes tickets, whether receipts assessable to tax under Schedule D *HH v MJ Forbes (Inspector of Taxes)* Vol II p 614

trade or business, brewery, whether liability in respect of transactions under DORA requisition orders *Arthur Guinness Son & Co Ltd v Commissioners of Inland Revenue* Vol I p 1

SCHEDULE D, CASE I & II

an obsolescence of assets *Evans & Co v Phillips (Inspector of Taxes)* Vol I p 43

assessment of wife's first years income on husband *JD Mulvey (Inspector of Taxes) v RM Kieran* Vol I p 563

bad debts recovered *Bourke (Inspector of Taxes) v Lyster & Sons Ltd* Vol II p 374

basis of assessment *JD Mulvey (Inspector of Taxes) v RM Kieran* Vol I p 563

basis of assessment, commencement and cessation within a year, whether assessment for the previous year can be reviewed *AB v JD Mulvey (Inspector of Taxes)* Vol II p 55

bloodstock, animal bought in course of trade, sent to stud after successful racing career and subsequently sold to a syndicate whether amount realised on syndication a trading receipt *Mac Giolla Riogh (Inspector of Taxes) v G Ltd* Vol II p 315

builder's profits, capitalised value of ground rents and fines, whether liable to tax *Birch (Inspector of Taxes) v Denis Delaney* Vol I p 515 and *Edward Connolly v AG Birch (Inspector of Taxes)* Vol I p 583 and *Swaine (Inspector of Taxes) v VE* Vol II p 472

compensation for loss of profits, whether income or capital receipt *The Alliance and Dublin Consumers' Gas Co v McWilliams (Inspector of Taxes)* Vol I p 207

compensation for loss of profits, whether trading receipt *F Corr (Inspector of Taxes) v FE Larkin* Vol II p 164

compensation paid to tenants of adjoining premises for interference with light and air, whether allowable Case I deduction *WJ Davis (Inspector of Taxes) v X Ltd* Vol II p 45

compulsory sale to Minister for Finance, in return for sterling equivalents, of dollar balances consisting of income from securities etc, in the USA whether moneys so received assessable *JM O'Sullivan (Inspector of Taxes) v Julia O'Connor, as Administratrix of Evelyn H O'Brien, Deceased* Vol II p 61

deduction for expenses of promoting bill in Parliament *McGarry (Inspector of Taxes) v Limerick Gas Committee* Vol I p 375

Income tax (contd)

deduction for interest paid *Phillips (Inspector of Taxes) v Limerick County Council* Vol I p 66

deduction of corporation profits tax and excess corporation profits tax in computing profits for income tax purposes *JM O'Dwyer (Inspector of Taxes) v The Dublin United Transport Co Ltd* Vol II p 115

deduction of loss on realisation of investments *The Alliance & Dublin Consumers' Gas Co v Davis (Inspector of Taxes)* Vol I p 104

deduction, legal fees in defending action in High Court for balance alleged to be due to a building contractor in respect of the construction of cinema, whether allowable Case I deduction *Casey (Inspector of Taxes) v AB Ltd* Vol II p 500

discontinuance of trade, set off of losses *Boland's Ltd v Davis (Inspector of Taxes)* Vol I p 86

ex gratia payments, by British government for malicious damage to property or personal injury sustained, whether trading receipt *WA Robinson T/A James Pim & Son v JD Dolan (Inspector of Taxes)* Vol I p 427

execution of document under seal of the Isle of Man, Secondary evidence that beneficial interest in securities had been transferred not admissible *Gilbert Hewson v JB Kealy (Inspector of Taxes)* Vol II p 15

formation expenses, whether allowable against trading profits *JB Kealy (Inspector of Taxes) v O'Mara (Limerick) Ltd* Vol I p 642

hospital and private nursing home whether carrying on a trade *RG Davis (Inspector of Taxes) v The Superioress, Mater Misericordiae Hospital, Dublin* Vol I p 387

illegal trades, not assessable to tax *C Hayes (Inspector of Taxes) v RJ Duggan Vol I p 195* and *Daniel Collins and Michael Byrne Daniel Collins and Redmond Power as Executor of the Will of Michael Byrne, deceased and Daniel Collins v JD Mulvey (Inspector of Taxes)* Vol II p 291

income from the leasing of premises, whether leasing constitutes trading whether earned income *Pairceir (Inspector of Taxes) v EM* Vol I p 596

Industrial and Provident Societies, trading with both members and non-members, investments and property purchased out of trading profits, whether the dividends and rents form part of the profits of the trade *The Revenue Commissioners v Y Ltd* Vol II p 195

losses forward *Molmac Ltd v MacGiolla Riogh (Inspector of Taxes)* Vol II p 482

lump sum paid on execution of lease, whether capital payment or rent paid in advance, whether liable under Case I and II or Case III *W Flynn (Inspector of Taxes) v John Noone Ltd, and W Flynn (Inspector of Taxes) v Blackwood & Co (Sligo) Ltd* Vol II p 222

on rebuilding of business premises, whether portion thereof deductible in computing profits *Curtin (Inspector of Taxes) v M Ltd* Vol II p 360

profit on realisation of investments, whether trading profit *Agricultural Credit Corporation Ltd v JB Vale (Inspector of Taxes)* Vol I p 474 and *Davis (Inspector of Taxes) v Hibernian Bank Ltd* Vol I p 503

removing top-soil from surface of quarry *Milverton Quarries Ltd v The Revenue Commissioners* Vol II p 382

statutory body, whether carrying on a trade *The Exported Live Stock (Insurance) Board v TJ Carroll (Inspector of Taxes)* Vol II p 211

Income tax (contd)

trade carried on by beneficiary of charity, whether exempt, *Beirne (Inspector of Taxes) v St Vincent De Paul Society (Wexford Conference)* Vol I p 383

whether expenditure incurred by petrol marketing company under exclusivity agreements with retailers is revenue or capital *Dolan (Inspector of Taxes) v AB Co Ltd* Vol II p 515

SCHEDULE D, CASE III

foreign trades, basis of assessment under Case III *O'Conaill (Inspector of Taxes) v R* Vol II p 304

interest received *Irish Provident Assurance Co Ltd (In Liquidation) v Kavanagh (Inspector of Taxes)* Vol I p 45

ITA 1918 rule 7 *Evans & Co v Phillips (Inspector of Taxes)* Vol I p 43

liability to, business carried on abroad *The Executors and Trustees of AC Ferguson (deceased) v Donovan (Inspector of Taxes)* Vol I p 183

lump sum paid on execution of lease, whether capital payment or rent paid in advance, whether liable under Case I & II or Case III *W Flynn (Inspector of Taxes) v John Noone Ltd, and W Flynn (Inspector of Taxes) v Blackwood & Co (Sligo) Ltd* Vol II p 222

pension received by Irish resident from British company, whether income from foreign possession *McHugh (Inspector of Taxes) v A* Vol I p 393 and *Forbes (Inspector of Taxes) v GHD* Vol II p 491

settlement of income, deed of appointment by parent in favour of child *EG v Mac Shamhrain, (Inspector of Taxes)* Vol II p 352

SCHEDULE D, CASE IV

illegal trades, not assessable to tax under Case IV *C Hayes (Inspector of Taxes) v RJ Duggan* Vol I p 195

lump sum paid on execution of lease, whether capital payment or rent paid in advance, whether liable under Case I & II or Case III *W Flynn (Inspector of Taxes) v John Noone Ltd; W Flynn (Inspector of Taxes) v Blackwood & Co (Sligo) Ltd* Vol II p 222

professional services rendered without prior agreement as regards remuneration payment on termination of services whether chargeable as income *W S McGarry (Inspector of Taxes) v EF* Vol II p 261

SCHEDULE D, CASE V

domicile and ordinary residence *Captain RH Prior-Wandesforde v the Revenue Commissioners* Vol I p 249 and *The Right Hon The Earl of Iveagh v The Revenue Commissioners* Vol I p 259

SCHEDULE E

benefit in kind, rent paid for employee *Connolly (Inspector of Taxes) v Denis McNamara* Vol II p 452

branch manager of local Employment Office of Dept of Social Welfare whether the taxpayer was engaged under a contract of service or a contract for services *Ó Coindealbháin (Inspector of Taxes) v TB Mooney* Vol IV p 45

calculation of PAYE due in respect of remuneration paid in year following that in which work was done, method of assessment *Bedford (Collector-General) v H* Vol II p 588

deductions *Phillips (Inspector of Taxes) v Keane* Vol I p 64

Income tax (contd)

deductions *SP O'Broin (Inspector of Taxes) v Mac Giolla Meidhre/Finbar Pigott* Vol II p 366 and *HF Kelly (Inspector of Taxes) v H* Vol II p 460

director resident abroad, of a company incorporated in the State but managed and controlled abroad. whether Schedule E employment *WJ Tipping (Inspector of Taxes) v Louis Jeancard* Vol II p 68

interest due on overpayment of PAYE *O'Rourke v Revenue Commissioners* Vol V p 321

nun, whether assessable on earnings which are given to her order *JD Dolan (Inspector of Taxes) v "K" National School Teacher* Vol I p 656

present from employer, whether taxable as gift or emolument *Wing v O'Connell (Inspector of Taxes)* Vol I p 155

remuneration charging section provision in will charging rental income from estate with annual amount payable to beneficiary provided he continued to manage the property *Gerald O'Reilly v WJ Casey (Inspector of Taxes)* Vol I p 601

remuneration of office, grant to a President of a college on retirement *JD Mulvey (Inspector of Taxes) v Denis J Coffey* Vol I p 618

whether contract for services between skipper of fishing vessel and crew members *Director of Public Prosecutions v Martin McLoughlin* Vol III p 467

whether the taxpayer was engaged under a contract of service or a contract for services *McDermott (Inspector of Taxes) v BC* Vol III p 43

SCHEDULE F

interest paid by Irish subsidiary to Japanese parent company on loan from parent company whether tax should be deducted at source under Double Tax Treaty or whether the payment should be treated as distribution under Schedule F *Murphy (Inspector of Taxes) v Asahi Synthetic Fibres (Ireland) Ltd* Vol III p 246

Income tax and corporation profits tax

company in receivership preferential claim *The Attorney-General v Irish Steel Ltd and Vincent Crowley* Vol II p 108

Inducement payments

whether liable to income tax *PJ O'Connell (Inspector of Taxes) v T Keleghan* Vol VI p 201

profit/trading receipts *O'Dwyer (Inspector of Taxes) and the Revenue Commissioners v Irish Exporters and Importers Ltd (In Liquidation)* Vol I p 629

Industrial and Provident Societies

surplus of co-op from dealing with members, whether trading profits, whether exempt *Kennedy (Inspector of Taxes) v The Rattoo Co-op Dairy Society Ltd* Vol I p 315

trading with both members and non-members, investments and property purchased out of trading profits, whether the dividends and rents form part of the profits of the trade *The Revenue Commissioners v Y Ltd* Vol II p 195

Industrial building

structure for dock undertaking, whether bonded transit sheds used as clearing house and not for storage qualify *Patrick Monahan (Drogheda) Ltd v O'Connell (Inspector of Taxes)* Vol III p 661

Industrial building (contd)

whether a building which housed offices, a showroom, a canteen, computer department and utilities qualified for industrial building allowance under ITA 1967 s 255 *O'Conaill (Inspector of Taxes) v JJ Ltd* Vol III p 65

Information

available to Revenue Commissioners, accountants working papers, whether the inspector of taxes is entitled to call for production of a taxpayer's nominal ledger, whether the nominal ledger formed part of the accountant's working papers *JJ Quigley (Inspector of Taxes) v Maurice Burke* Vol IV p 332, Vol V p 265

transfer of assets to offshore tax havens, whether accountants could be requested to furnish relevant particulars in respect of all their clients *Warnock & Others practising as Stokes Kennedy Crowley & Co v The Revenue Commissioners* Vol III p 356

Inspector of Taxes

empowered to require of an individual by notice a return of income *Thomas O'Callaghan v JP Clifford & Others* Vol IV p 478

entitlement to recompute standard percentage basis of profits for excess profits duty *Boland's Ltd v The Commissioners of Inland Revenue* Vol I p 34

whether Inspector of Taxes was correct in law in holding that interest earned on client monies was not income of the respondents and accordingly was taxable at the standard rate of income tax *PO Cahill (Inspector of Taxes) v Patrick O'Driscoll, Michael O'Driscoll and William F O'Driscoll* Vol VI p 793

Interest

deduction for interest paid from interest received *Phillips (Inspector of Taxes) v Limerick County Council* Vol I 66

earned by non-resident company manufacturing through a branch in the State, tax free profits from branch paid into foreign bank account, whether interest earned on foreign bank account is taxable in Ireland *Murphy (Inspector of Taxes) v Dataproducts (Dublin) Ltd* Vol IV p 12

earned on deposit interest after date of liquidation *A Noyek & Sons Ltd (in voluntary liquidation), Alex Burns v Edward N Hearne* Vol III p 523

in possession, whether conveyancing form determines liability to estate duty *The Attorney General v Power & Anor* Vol V p 525

on loan after redemption of share capital, whether allowable as trade expense *Sean MacAonghusa v Ringmahon* Vol VI p 327

on overpaid income tax, whether appeal of assessments under wrong Schedule rules out interest on overpayments of tax, whether appeal to nil assessments to tax rules out interest on overpayments on tax *Ó Coindealbháin (Inspector of Taxes) v TB Mooney* Vol IV p 45

on overpaid PAYE, whether due or not, *O'Rourke v Revenue Commissioners* Vol V p 321

on repayment of tax *Navan Carpets Ltd v Ó Culacháin (Inspector of Taxes)* Vol III p 403

paid by a company to a person having controlling interest in that company *The Revenue Commissioners v Associated Properties Ltd* Vol II p 412

Interest (contd)

paid by Irish subsidiary to Japanese parent company on loan from parent company whether tax should be deducted at source under Double Tax Treaty or treated as distribution under Schedule F *Murphy (Inspector of Taxes) v Asahi Synthetic Fibres (Ireland) Ltd* Vol III p 246

paid on foreign securities in the form of loan stock *PV Murtagh (Inspector of Taxes) v Samuel Rusk* Vol VI p 817

rate applicable to interest on VAT repayments by Revenue Commissioners and whether 'performance rate' is a rate of interest *Bank of Ireland Trust Services Limited v The Revenue Commissioners* Vol VI p 513

repayment of interest on tax paid in mistake of law, common law right to restitution, rate of interest according to Courts of Justice Acts *O'Rourke v Revenue Commissioners* Vol V p 321

stamp duties, new interest and penalty provisions introduced by FA 1991 s 100 came into effect on 1 November 1991 and previous provision for interest and penalties under Stamp Act 1891 s 15 were repealed on 29 May 1991, the date of the passing of FA 1991, whether interest and penalties applied between 29 May 1991 and 1 November 1991 *Edward O'Leary v The Revenue Commissioners* Vol IV p 357 *Terence Byrne v The Revenue Commissioners* Vol V p 560

whether annual interest on loan to redeem preference shares is a deductible expense *Seán MacAonghusa (Inspector of Taxes) v Ringmahon Company* Vol VI p 327

whether repayments of VAT should carry interest *Bank of Ireland Trust Services Limited v The Revenue Commissioners* Vol VI p 513

Interest and income from securities and possessions

execution of document under seal of the Isle of Man, secondary evidence that beneficial interest in securities had been transferred, not admissible *Gilbert Hewson v JB Kealy (Inspector of Taxes)* Vol II p 15

Interpretation of documents

Court entitled to look at reality of what has been done *Waterford Glass (Group Services) Ltd v The Revenue Commissioners* Vol IV p 194, *B McCabe (Inspector of Taxes) v South City & County Investment Co Ltd* Vol V p 119, 1998 p 183

Interpretation of statutes

of excise duties payable under SI 422/1983 and EC Directive *Karl Keller v The Revenue Commissioners & Others* Vol IV p 512

of statutes, absurdity *K Company v Hogan* Vol III p 56

of statutes, ambiguity *McNally v Maoldhomnaigh* Vol IV p 22

of statutes, ejusdem generis rule *M Cronin v Lunham Brothers Ltd* Vol III p 370

of statutes, exemption *The Revenue Commissioners v Doorley* Vol V p 539

of statutes, mandatory *The Revenue Commissioners v Henry Young* Vol V p 294

of statutes, relief *Texaco Ireland Ltd v Murphy* Vol IV p 91 *Ó Coindealbháin v Gannon* Vol III p 484, *McCann v Ó Culacháin* Vol III p 304 *Ó Culacháin v McMullan Bros* Vol IV p 284, Vol V p 200, *O'Sullivan v The Revenue Commissioners* Vol V p 570

of statutes, rules of construction *De Brun (Inspector of Taxes) v Kiernan* Vol III p 19, *McGrath v McDermott* Vol III p 683

Interpretation of statutes (contd)

of taxing act *EP Ó Coindealbháin (Inspector of Taxes) v The Honourable Mr Justice Sean Gannon* Vol III p 484

of the TCA 1997, ss 933(4) and 934(6) *Robert Harris v JJ Quigley and Liam Irwin* Vol VI p 839

of the TCA 1997, s1002 *AS v Criminal Assets Bureau* Vol VI p 799

Investments

finance company, dealing in stocks and shares, whether investments should be valued at cost or market value *AB Ltd v Mac Giolla Riogh (Inspector of Taxes)* Vol II p 419

investment incurred for the purpose of intended economic activity *Brendan Crawford (Inspector of Taxes) v Centime Ltd* Vol VI p 823

profits on realisation of whether trading profits *The Agricultural Credit Corporation Ltd v JB Vale (Inspector of Taxes)* Vol I p 474 and *The Alliance & Dublin Consumers' Gas Co v Davis (Inspector of Taxes)* Vol I p 104 and *Davis (Inspector of Taxes) v Hibernian Bank Ltd* Vol I p 503

Investment company

deduction of expenses of management *Howth Estate Co v WJ Davis (Inspector of Taxes)* Vol I p 447, *Hibernian Insurance Company Limited v MacUimis (Inspector of Taxes)* Vol VI p 157 and *Casey (Inspector of Taxes) v The Monteagle Estate Co* Vol II p 429

Issue

whether "issue" included adopted children *In the matter of John Stamp deceased Patrick Stamp v Noel Redmond & Others* Vol IV p 415

J

Joint ownership

whether survivor entitled, whether resulting trust *M Lynch v M Burke & AIB plc* Vol V p 271

Joint assessment

whether husband is liable for wife's income *Gilligan v Criminal Assets Bureau, Galvin, Lanigan & Revenue Commissioners* Vol V p 424

Journalism

exemption of earnings from original and creative works of artistic or cultural merit, whether journalism qualifies *John Healy v SI Breathnach (Inspector of Taxes)* Vol III p 496

Judicial function

exercise of by Inspector of Taxes *Michael Deighan v Edward N Hearne & Others* Vol III p 533

exercise of by Appeal Commissioners *The State (Calcul International and Solatrex International Ltd) v The Appeal Commissioners and The Revenue Commissioners* Vol III p 577

Judicial review

appeal for judicial review re income tax *CG v The Appeal Commissioners and Others* Vol VI p 783

appeal for judicial review re income tax *AS v Criminal Assets Bureau* Vol VI p 799

application for, re stamp duty *Kenny J v Revenue Commissioners, Goodman & Gemon Ltd (Notice Parties)* Vol V p 363

application re VAT *DH Burke & Sons Ltd v The Revenue Commissioners and Others* Vol V 418, *Taxback Ltd v The Revenue Commissioners* Vol V 412

Jurisdiction

of High Court relating to Social Welfare appeals *Albert Kinghan v The Minister for Social Welfare* Vol III p 436

L

Land

dealing in and developing *O'Connlain (Inspector of Taxes) v Belvedere Estates Ltd* Vol III p 271

whether the surplus from the sale of property was profit of a trade of dealing in or developing land, or the profit of a business which was deemed by F(MP)A 1968 s 17, to be such a trade *Mara (Inspector of Taxes) v GG (Hummingbird) Ltd* Vol II p 667

Land Purchase Acts

arrears of jointure tax paid under Schedule A, whether further balance due *Estate Of Teresa Downing (Owner)* Vol I p 487

Lease

lump sum paid on execution of lease, whether capital payment or rent paid in advance *W Flynn (Inspector of Taxes) v John Noone Ltd, and W Flynn (Inspector of Taxes) v Blackwood & Co (Sligo) Ltd* Vol II p 222

payment in advance on the signing of a lease, whether capital *O'Sullivan (Inspector of Taxes) v p Ltd* Vol II p 464

Leasing

income from the leasing of premises, whether leasing constitutes trading, whether earned income *Pairceir (Inspector of Taxes) v EM* Vol II p 596

Legal costs

whether a Circuit Court Judge hearing an appeal pursuant to ITA 1967 s 429 has jurisdiction to award costs *The Revenue Commissioners v Arida Ltd* Vol IV p 401, Vol V p 221

Legal fees

in defending action in High Court for balance alleged to be due to a building contractor in respect of the construction of cinema, whether allowable Case I deduction *Casey (Inspector of Taxes) v AB Ltd* Vol II p 500

whether letting fees and legal expenses incurred by the company in respect of first lettings of property qualified as deductions under ITA 1967 s 81(5)(*d*) *GH Ltd v Browne (Inspector of Taxes)* Vol III p 95

Letting expenses

whether letting fees and legal expenses incurred by the company in respect of first lettings of property qualified as deductions under ITA 1967 s 81(5)(*d*) *GH Ltd v Browne (Inspector of Taxes)* Vol III p 95

Lessors

trade carried on *The Great Southern Railways Co v The Revenue Commissioners* Vol I p 359

Liability

of liquidator to employer's contribution of PRSI in respect of "reckonable earnings" of employees, when payable preferential status *The Companies Act 1963-1983 v Castlemahon Poultry Products Ltd* Vol III p 509

of personal representatives *Moloney (Inspector of Taxes) v Allied Irish Banks Ltd as executors of the estate of Francis J Doherty deceased* Vol III p 477

of receiver, to corporation tax *Wayte (Holdings) Ltd (In receivership) Alex Burns v Edward N Hearne* Vol III p 553

personal, of members of bank, whether unlimited *CIR v The Governor & Company of The Bank of Ireland* Vol I p 70

Limited

partnership, share of capital allowances on leasing transaction, involving a purported limited partnership, against his personal income tax liability *DA MacCarthaigh (Inspector of Taxes) v Francis Daly* Vol III p 253

Liquidation

court fees, amount on which court fees are chargeable in a liquidation *In re Private Motorists Provident Society ltd (In Liqdtn) & W J Horgan v Minister for Justice* Vol V p 186, *In re Hibernian Transport Companies Limited* Vol V p 194

deferral of revenue debts pending completion of contracts by company *The Companies Act 1963-1983 and MFN Construction Co Ltd (in liquidation) on the application of Patrick Tuffy (liquidator)* Vol IV p 82

whether a sum which arose to the company on the liquidation of a wholly owned subsidiary was part of its trading profits *Guinness & Mahon Ltd v Browne (Inspector of Taxes)* Vol III p 373

whether deposit interest earned on monies held by the official liquidator liable to tax *In Re HT Ltd (in Liquidation) & Others* Vol III p 120

whether assessments of PRSI entitled to super preferential priority *Re Coombe Importers Ltd (In Liq) and Re the Companies Acts 1963-1990* Vol VI p 1

Liquidator

liability of, to employer's contribution of PRSI in respect of "reckonable earnings" of employees, when payable preferential status *The Companies Act 1963-1983 v Castlemahon Poultry Products Ltd* Vol III p 509; *Re Coombe Importers Ltd (In Liq) and Re the Companies Acts 1963-1990* Vol VI p 1

Loan interest

payable follwoing redemption of share capital whether allowable *Sean Mac Aonghusa v Ringmahon* Vol VI p 327

Loan notes

whether capital gains tax deferred pending redemption of, *PJ O'Connell v T Keleghan* Vol VI p 201

whether consideration by way of loan note should give rise to Schedule E assessment *Patrick J O'Connell (Inspector of Taxes) v Thomas Keleghan* Vol VI p 497

whether loan notes are debenture stock or shares *Patrick J O'Connell (Inspector of Taxes) v Thomas Keleghan* Vol VI p 201

whether income arising from loan notes is chargeable to Irish tax *PV Murtagh (Inspector of Taxes) v Samuel Rusk* Vol VI p 817

Loan stock

loan stock certificates and related instruments issued under seal *PV Murtagh (Inspector of Taxes) v Samuel Rusk* Vol VI p 817

Losses

carry forward of losses *Molmac Ltd v MacGiolla Riogh (Inspector of Taxes)* Vol II p 482 and *M Cronin (Inspector of Taxes) v Lunham Brothers Ltd* Vol III p 363

discontinuance of trade, set off of losses *Boland's Ltd v Davis (Inspector of Taxes)* Vol I p 86

in trade, notional, from fall in market value of goods before delivery *The Revenue Commissioners v Latchford & Sons Ltd* Vol I p 240

Lump sum

paid on execution of lease, whether capital payment or rent paid in advance *W Flynn (Inspector of Taxes) v John Noone Ltd, and W Flynn (Inspector of Taxes) v Blackwood & Co (Sligo) Ltd* Vol II p 222

redundancy payments to disabled employees, whether exempt from income tax, whether distinction to be made between disabled employees whose jobs continued and disabled employees whose jobs ceased *PO Cahill (Inspector of Taxes) v Albert Harding & Others* Vol IV p 233

whether paid on account of retirement or due to ill health *BD O'Shea (Inspector of Taxes) v Michael Mulqueen* Vol V p 134

M

Market gardening

valuation of land occupied for market gardening *L v WS McGarry (Inspector of Taxes)* Vol II p 241

Market value

of shares in a private trading company, *EA Smyth v The Revenue Commissioners* Vol V p 532, *In the estate of Thomas McNamee & Others v The Revenue Commissioners* Vol V p 577

Management

expenses, deduction of, by investment company *Howth Estate Co v WJ Davis (Inspector of Taxes)* Vol I p 447 and *Casey (Inspector of Taxes) v The Monteagle Estate Co* Vol II p 429, *Hibernian Insurance Company Limited v MacUimis (Inspector of Taxes)* Vol V p 495, Vol VI p 157, *Stephen Court Ltd v JA Browne (Inspector of Taxes)* Vol V p 680

Management (contd)

losses in holding company, whether notional management fees deductible Corporation tax *Belville Holdings Ltd (in receivership and liquidation) v Cronin (Inspector of Taxes)* Vol III p 340

Mandamus

finality of Special Commissioners' decision *The King (Evelyn Spain) v The Special Commissioners* Vol I p 221

order for mandamus – clearance certificate *The State (Melbarian enterprises Ltd) v The Revenue Commissioners* Vol III p 291

Manufacturing relief

assembly of agricultural machinery whether manufacturing *Irish Agricultural Machinery Ltd v S Ó Culacháin (Inspector of Taxes)* Vol III p 661

film production, whether relief given for accounting periods prior to FA 1990 *Saatchi & Saatchi Advertising Ltd v Kevin McGarry (Inspector of Taxes)* Vol V p 376, Vol VI p 47

newspaper publisher, newspapers are "goods" for the purpose of manufacturing relief, whether advertising income is from a separate trade and qualifies for such relief *L McGurrin (Inspector of Taxes) v The Champion Publications Ltd* Vol IV p 466

process of ripening bananas whether constituted manufacturing *Charles McCann Ltd v S Ó Culacháin (Inspector of Taxes)* Vol III p 304, *PJ O'Connell v Fyffes Banana Processing Ltd* Vol VI p 131

processing of and sale of milk produced by the company, whether constituted the manufacture of goods for the purposes of the reduction in corporation tax provided for in FA 1980 Pt I Ch VI *Cronin (Inspector of Taxes) v Strand Dairy Ltd* Vol III p 441

production of day old chicks, whether day old chicks are goods within the meaning of FA 1980, whether process constitutes manufacturing, whether use of extensive plant machinery and skilled workers constitute a process of manufacturing *JF Kelly (Inspector of Taxes) v Cobb Straffan Ireland Ltd* Vol IV p 526, *TG Brosnan (Inspector of Taxes) v Leeside Nurseries Ltd* Vol V p 21

production of films for use in advertising, whether manufacture *S Ó Culacháin (Inspector of Taxes) v Hunter Advertising Ltd* Vol IV p 35

whether business that recycles wastepaper into new paper products qualifies for manufacturing relief *P O'Muircheasa (Inspector of Taxes) v Bailey Wastepaper Limited* Vol VI p 579

whether production of J Cloths and nappy liners from bales of fabric is a manufacturing process *D O Laochdha (Inspector of Taxes) v Johnson & Johnson (Ireland) Ltd* Vol IV p 361

whether proper construction of words of s 41 brought advertisements within definition of goods *L McGurrin (Inspector of Taxes) v The Champion Publications Ltd* Vol IV p 466

whether sophisticated system of growth of plants within glasshouses constitute a manufacturing process *TG Brosnan (Inspector of Taxes) v Leeside Nurseries Ltd* Vol V p 21

Manufacturing relief (contd)

wholesaler of beers and stouts, also conditions bottled stout, whether conditioning of bottled Guinness constitutes manufacturing process, whether plant and equipment sufficiently sophisticated *J Hussey (Inspector of Taxes) v MJ Gleeson & Co Ltd* Vol IV p 533

Mareva injunction

obligation on party obtaining interim injunction to prosecute proceedings promptly *Criminal Assets Bureau v PS and PS* Vol VI p 465

whether action to freeze person's assets can be brought by plenary summons *The Criminal Assets Bureau v Patrick A McSweeney* Vol VI p 421

Marriage gratuity

whether "marriage gratuity" received on resignation was a retirement payment under ITA 1967 s 114 or was a perquisite of her office under ITA 1967 s 110 *Sean Ó Siocháin (Inspector of Taxes) v Thomas Morrissey* Vol IV p 407

Married persons

aggregation of incomes of married persons unconstitutional *Francis Murphy & Partner v Attorney General* Vol V p 613

aggregation of earned income of married persons unconstitutional *Bernard Muckley and Anne Muckley v Ireland, The Attorney General and The Revenue Commissioners* Vol III p 188

joint assessment whether husband is liable for tax on both incomes *Gilligan v Criminal Assets Bureau, Galvin, Lanigan & Revenue Commissioners* Vol V p 424

living apart *Donovan (Inspector of Taxes) v CG Crofts* Vol I p 115

living together *D Ua Clothasaigh (Inspector of Taxes) v Patrick McCartan* Vol II p 75

wife's income from securities assessed on husband in first year of wife's income from securities *JD Mulvey (Inspector of Taxes) v RM Kieran* Vol I p 563

UK resident working in Ireland, wife working in UK, whether he is entitled to married allowance and rate bands *S Fennessy (Inspector of Taxes) v John Mc Connellogue* Vol V p 129

Meetings

of companies, whether they took place, whether resolution was passed, whether share issue invalid *In re Sugar Distributors Ltd* Vol V p 225

Mill

expenditure on mill *sanitation JB Vale (Inspector of Taxes) v Martin Mahony & Brothers Ltd* Vol II p 32

Mining

whether operation is mining or manufacturing *Patrick J O'Connell (Inspector of Taxes) v Tara Mines Ltd* Vol VI p 523

Mistake

whether monies paid in mistake of law recoverable, whether a common law right to repayment *O'Rourke v Revenue Commissioners* Vol V p 321

N

Newspaper publisher

newspapers are "goods" for the purpose of manufacturing relief, whether advertising income is from a separate trade and qualifies for such relief *L McGurrin (Inspector of Taxes) v The Champion Publications Ltd* Vol IV p 466

Non-resident company

manufacturing through a branch in the State, tax free profits from branch paid into foreign bank account, whether interest earned on foreign bank account is taxable in Ireland *S Murphy (Inspector of Taxes) v Dataproducts (Dublin) Ltd* Vol IV p 12

Non-residents – EU

whether entitled to VAT refunds through refunding agencies *Taxback Limited v The Revenue Commissioners* Vol V p 412

Nuns

whether assessable on income from employment which is given to the order *JD Dolan (Inspector of Taxes) v "K" National School Teacher* Vol I p 656

Nurseries and market gardens

assessment of income by reference to annual profits estimated according to the rules of Schedule D *WS McGarry (Inspector of Taxes) v JA Spencer* Vol II p 1

Nursing home

profits derived from hospital and associated private nursing home, whether trade carried on *RG Davis (Inspector of Taxes) v The Superioress Mater Misericordiae Hospital, Dublin* Vol I p 387

O

Obsolescence of assets

Evans & Co v Phillips (Inspector of Taxes) Vol I p 43

Occupation of lands

whether the appellant company was in occupation of lands, forming part of a military establishment, for the purposes of ITA 1918 Sch B or ITA 1967 *O Conaill (Inspector of Taxes) v Z Ltd* Vol II p 636

Option

deed of release, whether release constitutes a sale for stamp duty purposes *In re Cherrycourt v The Revenue Commissioners* Vol V p 180

Original

document not produced, secondary evidence that beneficial interest in securities had been transferred not admissible *Hewson v JB Kealy (Inspector of Taxes)* Vol II p 15

P

Paid

the meaning of, whether charge/credit cards mean paid for *The Diners Club Ltd v The Revenue and The Minister for Finance* Vol III p 680

Partnership

as distinguished form employment *Francis Griffin v Minister for Social, Community and Family Affairs* Vol VI p 371

father taking his children into partnership, whether income of children is deemed to be income of father *JM O'Dwyer (Inspector of Taxes) v Cafolla & Co* Vol II p 82

share of capital allowances on leasing transaction, involving a purported limited partnership, against his personal income tax liability *DA MacCarthaigh (Inspector of Taxes) v Francis Daly* Vol III p 253

sole trader admitted partner at beginning of year, during the year the business is sold to limited company, whether sole traders previous year's assessment can be revised *AB v JD Mulvey (Inspector of Taxes)* Vol II p 55

whether capital investment necessary for partnership *Francis Griffin v Minister for Social, Community and Family Affairs* Vol VI p 371

Patent rights

whether income from patent rights disregarded for income tax purposes, where payable to non residents, whether tax avoidance scheme *Pandion Haliaetus Ltd & Ors v The Revenue Commissioners* Vol III p 670

PAYE

due in respect of remuneration paid in year following that in which work was done, assessment *Bedford (Collector-General) v H* Vol II p 588

employer's obligations to deduct PAYE and PRSI from employee's emoluments *EN Hearne (Inspector of Taxes) v O'Cionna & Ors T/A JA Kenny & Ptnrs* Vol IV p 113

PAYE regulations

whether procedures unfair and unconstitutional, enforcement order issue to city sheriff after payment of tax, defamation of plaintiff *Giles J Kennedy v EG Hearne, the Attorney General & Others* Vol III p 590

Payment

of dividends, whether payment through inter-company account was sufficient evidence of actual payment, whether payment of cheque required, whether making of accounting entry a mere record of underlying transaction, whether a dividend declared on 11 December 1980 was received by related company not later than 12 December 1980, whether making of journal entries after 23 December 1980 material evidence *Sean Murphy (Inspector of Taxes) v The Borden Co Ltd* Vol II p 559

payment of excise duty deferred *The Attorney General v Sun Alliance and London Insurance Ltd* Vol III p 265

Penalties

non-payment of excise duty payable on bets entered into by the defendant a registered bookmaker, whether recovery of an excise penalty a criminal matter, *The Director of Public Prosecutions v Seamus Boyle* Vol IV p 395

prosecution for payment of a Revenue penalty, whether criminal or civil proceedings *Director of Public Prosecutions v Robert Downes* Vol III p 641

Penalties (contd)

whether penalties for failure to make returns are unconstitutional *Edward McLoughlin and Thomas Marie Tuite v The Revenue Commissioners and The Attorney General* Vol III p 387

Pension

personal pension and other assets assigned to company pension continued to be paid to pensioner, whether pensioner liable to tax on pension *Cronin (Inspector of Taxes) v C* Vol II p 64

social welfare (Consolidation Act 1951 s 299), whether entitled to old age contributory pension, meaning of entry into insurance, definition of contribution year, whether issue open to appeal *Albert Kinghan v The Minister for Social Welfare* Vol III p 436

Personal representatives

liability of personal representatives *Moloney (Inspector of Taxes) v Allied Irish Banks Ltd as executors of the estate of Francis J Doherty deceased* Vol III p 477

Personal rights

of citizen violated *Michael Deighan v Edward N Hearne & Others* Vol III p 533

of citizens *Bernard Muckley and Anne Muckley v Ireland, The Attorney General and The Revenue Commissioners* Vol III p 188

Petrol canopies

whether forecourt canopies at petrol filling stations constitute plant for tax purposes *S Ó Culacháin v McMullan Brothers* Vol IV p 284, Vol V p 200

Petrol marketing company

whether expenditure incurred under exclusivity agreements with retailers is revenue or capital *Dolan (Inspector of Taxes) v AB Co Ltd* Vol II p 515

Petroleum exploration

whether constitutes scientific research, whether such scientific research qualifies for tax relief by way of an allowance under ITA 1967 s 244 *Texaco Ireland Ltd v S Murphy (Inspector of Taxes)* Vol IV p 91

Pig rearing

whether the activity of intensive pig rearing constituted farming for the purposes of FA 1974 s 13(1) *Knockhall Piggeries v Kerrane (Inspector of Taxes)* Vol III p 319

Plant

barrister's books, whether plant *Breathnach (Inspector of Taxes) v MC* Vol III p 113

expenditure on installation of suspended ceiling in supermarket whether plant qualifying for capital allowances *Dunnes Stores (Oakville) Ltd v MC Cronin (Inspector of Taxes)* Vol IV p 68

poultry house, whether plant and machinery qualifying for capital allowances *O'Srianain (Inspector of Taxes) v Lakeview Ltd* Vol III p 219

racecourse stand, whether deductible repairs or non deductible capital expenditure or expenditure qualifying as plant *Michael O'Grady (Inspector of Taxes) v Roscommon Race Committee* Vol IV p 425, Vol V p 317

whether forecourt canopies at petrol filling stations constitute plant for tax purposes *S Ó Culacháin v McMullan Brothers* Vol IV p 284, Vol V p 200

Poultry house

whether plant and machinery qualifying for capital allowances *O'Srianain (Inspector of Taxes) v Lakeview Ltd* Vol III p 219

Power of revocation

settlement of income, deed of appointment by parent in favour of child *EG v Mac Shamhrain (Inspector of Taxes)* Vol II p 352

Precedent

whether High Court decisions are binding on Appeals Officers *Francis Griffin v Minister for Social, Community and Family Affairs* Vol VI p 371

Preferential claim

in receivership, income and corporation profits tax *The Attorney-General v Irish Steel Ltd and Vincent Crowley* Vol III p 265 and *In Re HT Ltd (in Liquidation) & Others* Vol III p 120

in receivership and liquidation *In the Matter of H Williams (Tallaght) (In Receivership & Liquidation) and the Companies Act 1963-1990* Vol V p 388

preferential creditors priority in receivership *United Bars Ltd (In Receivership), Walkinstown Inn Ltd (In Receivership) and Raymond Jackson v The Revenue Commissioners* Vol IV p 107

status under Companies Act 1963 s 285 *The Companies Act 1963-1983 v Castlemahon Poultry Products Ltd* Vol III p 509

whether assessemnts of PRSI entitled to super preferential priorty *Re Coombe Importers Ltd (In Liq) and Re the Companies Acts 1963-1990* Vol VI p 1

Preference shareholders

whether entitled to participate in capital distribution whether entitled to a portion of issue of new ordinary shares *Williams Group Tullamore Ltd v Companies Act 1963 to 1983* Vol III p 423

Premium

on lease payable by instalments, whether allowable under ITA 1967 s 91 *The Hammond Lane Metal Co Ltd v S Ó Culacháin (Inspector of Taxes)* Vol IV p 197

Printing

and processing in UK, whether manufacturing *S Ó Culacháin (Inspector of Taxes) v Hunter Advertising Ltd* Vol IV p 35

Privacy

right to privacy *Charles J Haughey v Moriarty and Others* Vol VI p 67

Proceeds of crime

recovery of unpaid tax not limited to assets which are the proceeds of crime where the assessment is based on criminal activity *AS v Criminal Assets Bureau* Vol VI p 799

Proceeds of Crime Act 1996

constitutional and non-constitutional issues regarding provisions relating to proceeds derived from criminal activity *John Gilligan v Criminal Assets Bureau, Revenue Commissioners & Others* Vol VI p 383

Proceeds of Crime Act 1996 (contd)

jurisdiction of High Court to impose orders under the legislation *John Gilligan v Criminal Assets Bureau, Revenue Commissioners & Others* Vol VI p 383

Processes

in form of loannotes, capital gains tax implications *PJ O'Connell v T Keleghan* Vol VI p 201

Professional services withholding tax

whether method of granting credit for same is constitutional *Michael Daly v The Revenue Commissioners* Vol V p 213

Profits

FROM ILLEGAL TRADE

Daniel Collins and Michael Byrne, Daniel Collins and Redmond Power as Executor of the will of Michael Byrne, deceased and Daniel Collins v JD Mulvey (Inspector of Taxes) Vol II p 291

FROM STALLION FEES

whether liable to tax under Schedule B or Schedule D income tax paid, whether further balance due *Cloghran Stud Farm v AG Birch (Inspector of Taxes)* Vol I p 496

NOT RECEIVED IN THE YEAR OF ASSESSMENT

MacKeown (Inspector of Taxes) v Patrick J Roe Vol I p 214

OF A TRADE

bad debts recovered, *Bourke (Inspector of Taxes) v Lyster & Sons Ltd* Vol II p 374

compensation for loss of profits, whether income or capital receipt *The Alliance and Dublin Consumers' Gas Co v McWilliams (Inspector of Taxes)* Vol I p 207

derived from hospital and associated private nursing home, whether trade carried on *RG Davis (Inspector of Taxes) v The Superioress, Mater Misericordiae Hospital, Dublin* Vol I p 387

profit/trading receipts *O'Dwyer (Inspector of Taxes) and the Revenue Commissioners v Irish Exporters and Importers Ltd (In Liquidation)* Vol I p 629

ON REALISATION OF INVESTMENTS

whether trading profits, *The Agricultural Credit Corporation Ltd v JB Vale (Inspector of Taxes)* Vol I p 474 and *The Alliance & Dublin Consumers' Gas Co v Davis (Inspector of Taxes)* Vol I p 104 and *Davis (Inspector of Taxes) v Hibernian Bank Ltd* Vol I p 503

ON SWEEPSTAKES

C Hayes (Inspector of Taxes) v R J Duggan Vol I p 195

Prosecution

for payment of a Revenue penalty *DPP v Robert Downes* Vol III p 641

PRSI

employer's contribution in respect of "reckonable earnings" of employees, when payable, liability of liquidator preferential status *The Companies Act 1963-1983 v Castlemahon Poultry Products Ltd* Vol III p 509

employer's obligations to deduct PAYE and PRSI from employee's emoluments *EN Hearne (Inspector of Taxes) v O'Cionna & Ors t/a JA Kenny & Ptnrs* Vol IV p 113

PRSI (contd)

whether share fishermen liable to PRSI as self-employed *Francis Griffin v Minister for Social, Community and Family Affairs* Vol VI p 371

Publican's licence

excise duty, whether new licence obtainable, whether application within six year period, meaning of year immediately preceding *Peter Connolly v The Collector of Customs and Excise* Vol IV p 419

purchase of, in a bond, by a publican whether trading transaction *McCall (deceased) v Commissioners of Inland Revenue* Vol I p 28

Publishers

newspaper publisher, newspapers are "goods" for the purpose of manufacturing relief, whether advertising income is from a separate trade and qualifies for such relief *L McGurrin (Inspector of Taxes) v Champion Publications Ltd* Vol IV p 466

Q

Quarry

removing top-soil from surface of quarry *Milverton Quarries Ltd v The Revenue Commissioners* Vol II p 382

R

Racing and Racecourses Act 1945

sections 4, 15, 27 *The Racing Board v S Ó Culacháin* Vol IV p 73

Racecourse stand

whether deductible repairs or non deductible capital expenditure or expenditure qualifying as plant *Michael O'Grady (Inspector of Taxes) v Roscommon Race Committee* Vol IV p 425, Vol V p 317

Racing bodies

whether exemption for Agricultural Societies apply *to The Trustees of The Ward Union Hunt Races v Hughes (Inspector of Taxes)* Vol I p 538

Railways

lines leased to another company at an annual rent *The Commissioners of Inland Revenue and The Dublin and Kingstown Railway Co* Vol I p 119

lessors of railway line, whether a railway undertaking *The Great Southern Railways Co v The Revenue Commissioners* Vol I p 359

Realisation

of assets, meaning of, *In re Private Motorists Provident Society ltd (In Liqdtn) & WJ Horgan v Minister for Justice* Vol V p 186, *In re Hibernian Transport Companies Limited* Vol V p 194

Receiver

company in receivership preferential claim *The Attorney-General v Irish Steel Ltd and Vincent Crowley* Vol II p 108

liability to corporation tax *Wayte (Holdings) Ltd (In Receivership) Alex Burns v Edward N Hearne* Vol III p 553

Receivership

preferential creditors priority in receivership *United Bars Ltd (In Receivership), Walkinstown Inn Ltd (In Receivership) and Raymond Jackson v The Revenue Commissioners* Vol IV p 107

Recovery of tax

from a group of companies, whether Revenue Commissioners may appropriate payments between separate companies within the group, whether insolvency of a company is relevant to gratuitous alienation of assets *Frederick Inns Ltd, The Rendezvous Ltd, The Graduate Ltd, Motels Ltd (In Liquidation) v The Companies Acts 1963-1986* Vol IV p 247

Redundancy payments

whether lump sum payments to disabled employees exempt from income tax *O Cahill (Inspector of Taxes) v Albert Harding & Others* Vol IV p 233, *BD O'Shea (Inspector of Taxes) v Michael Mulqueen* Vol V p 134

Refunding agencies – VAT

whether VAT refunds obtainable through refunding agencies *Taxback Limited v The Revenue Commissioners* Vol V p 412

Regulations

betting duty, whether necessary for Revenue Commissioners to comply with Regulations Act 1890 before proceedings can commence for failure to pay duty on bets *DPP v MichaelCunningham* Vol V p 691

Release

deed of, whether release of an option is a sale *In re Cherrycourt v The Revenue Commissioners* Vol V p 180

Religious orders

whether entitled to repayment of tax deducted from payments made under an indenture of covenant pursuant to ITA 1967 s 439(1)(iv) *The Revenue Commissioners v HI* Vol III p 242

Remuneration

calculation of PAYE due in respect of remuneration paid in year following that in which work was done, method of assessment *Bedford (Collector-General) v H* Vol II p 588

charging section provision in will charging rental income from estate with annual amount payable to beneficiary provided he continued to manage the property *Gerald O'Reilly v WJ Casey (Inspector of Taxes)* Vol I p 601

of office, grant to a President of a college on retirement *JD Mulvey (Inspector of Taxes) v Denis J Coffey* Vol I p 618

professional services rendered without prior agreement as regards remuneration payment on termination of services whether chargeable as income *W S McGarry (Inspector of Taxes) v EF* Vol II p 261

Rent

lump sum paid on execution of lease, whether capital payment or rent paid in advance *W Flynn (Inspector of Taxes) v John Noone Ltd, and W Flynn (Inspector of Taxes) v Blackwood & Co (Sligo) Ltd* Vol II p 222

Rent (contd)

paid by employing company for house occupied voluntarily by employee *Connolly (Inspector of Taxes) v Denis McNamara* Vol II p 452

payment in advance on the signing of a lease, whether capital *O'Sullivan (Inspector of Taxes) v P Ltd* Vol II p 464

Repairs

allowability of *Martin Fitzgerald v Commissioners of Inland Revenue* Vol I p 91

expenditure on roof, whether deductible repairs or non deductible capital expenditure *Michael O'Grady (Inspector of Taxes) v Roscommon Race Committee* Vol IV p 425

new bar and extension to old bar, whether non-deductible capital improvements *Michael O'Grady (Inspector of Taxes) v Roscommon Race Committee* Vol IV p 425

racecourse stand, whether deductible repairs or non deductible capital expenditure or expenditure qualifying as plant *Michael O'Grady (Inspector of Taxes) v Roscommon Race Committee* Vol IV p 425, Vol V p 317

re-design or lower terracing, whether an improvement *Michael O'Grady (Inspector of Taxes) v Roscommon Race Committee* Vol IV p 425

work done to walls whether deductible repairs or non deductible capital expenditure *Michael O'Grady (Inspector of Taxes) v Roscommon Race Committee* Vol IV p 425

Repayments

provision for interest on repayments of tax *Navan Carpets Ltd v S Ó Culacháin (Inspector of Taxes)* Vol III p 403

stamp duty inadverently paid, whether repayment due, *Terence Byrne v The Revenue Commissioners* Vol V p 560

whether Revenue can withhold VAT repayments *Taxback Limited v The Revenue Commissioners* Vol V p 412

whether taxpayer entitled to repayment of overpaid tax pending outcome of case stated *Robert Harris v JJ Quigley and Liam Irwin* Vol VI p 839

Repealed legislation

effect of repeal of Farm Tax Act, consequences of absence of amending legislation *Purcell v Attorney General* Vol IV p 229, Vol V p 288

Replacement cost accounting

method of accounting for tax purposes, whether replacement cost basis is acceptable or whether historical cost accounting is the only method of commercial accountancy *Carroll Industries Plc (formerly PJ Carroll & Co Ltd) and PJ Carroll & Co Ltd v S Ó Culacháin (Inspector of Taxes)* Vol IV p 135

Residence

of company *The Cunard Steam Ship Co Ltd v Herlihy (Inspector of Taxes), and The Cunard Steam Ship Co Ltd v Revenue Commissioners* Vol I p 330

ordinary residence and domicile, Income tax, Sch D, Case V *Captain RH Prior-Wandesforde v the Revenue Commissioners* Vol I p 249 and *The Right Hon The Earl of Iveagh v The Revenue Commissioners* Vol I p 259

Residence (contd)

UK resident working in Ireland, wife working in UK, whether he is entitled to married allowance and rate bands *S Fennessy (Inspector of Taxes) v John Mc Connellogue* Vol V p 129

whether individual is resident *LJ Irwin (Collector General) v M Grimes* Vol V p 209

whether long term residence determines domicile *Proes v The Revenue Commissioners* Vol V 481

Residential property tax

residential property tax, whether unconstitutional *PJ Madigan & p Madigan v The Attorney General, The Revenue Commissioners & Others* Vol III p 127

Restoration

of destroyed premises under covenant to repair *Martin Fitzgerald v Commissioners of Inland Revenue* Vol I p 91

Retailers Scheme for VAT

interpretation of scheme, *DH Burke & Sons Ltd v The Revenue Commissioners, Ireland and the Attorney General* Vol V p 418

Retirement payments

whether "marriage gratuity" received on resignation was a retirement payment under ITA 1967 s 114 or was a perquisite of her office under ITA 1967 s 110 *Sean Ó Síocháin (Inspector of Taxes) v Thomas Morrissey* Vol IV p 407

whether lump sum was paid on account of retirement or due to ill health *B D O'Shea (Inspector of Taxes) v Michael Mulqueen* Vol V p 134

Return

of income, what constitutes a proper return of income for the assessment of income tax *MA Bairead v M McDonald* Vol IV p 475; *In the Matter of G O'C & A O'C (Application of Liam Liston (Inspector of Taxes))* Vol V p 346

of income, failure to make, appeal against a decision of the High Court to refuse on a judicial review application to quash three convictions with six months imprisonment for each offence imposed in the District Court on the appellant for failure to make income tax returns *Thomas O'Callaghan v JP Clifford & Others* Vol IV p 478

whether wife obliged to prepare and deliver a separate return of income *Gilligan v Criminal Assets Bureau & Others* Vol V p 424

Roll over relief

proceeds of sale reinvested in acquisition of further lands, whether rollover relief on transfer of a trade applies *EP Ó Coindealbháin (Inspector of Taxes) v KN Price* Vol IV p 1

S

Sanitation

expenditure on mill sanitation, whether allowable deduction from trade *profits JB Vale (Inspector of Taxes) v Martin Mahony & Brothers Ltd* Vol II p 32

Sale

of meat into intervention within the EEC *Cronin (Inspector of Taxes) v IMP Middleton Ltd* Vol III p 452

meaning of sale for stamp duty purposes, whether release of an option is a sale *In re Cherrycourt v The Revenue Commissioners* Vol V p 180

Schedule E

gifts, whether present from employer taxable as gift, or emolument under Schedule E *Wing v O'Connell (Inspector of Taxes)* Vol I p 155

School/colleges

whether operated for charitable purposes *The Pharmaceutical Society of Ireland v The Revenue Commissioners* Vol I p 542

Scientific research

whether petroleum exploration constitutes scientific research, whether such scientific research qualifies for tax relief by way of an allowance under ITA 1967 s 244 *Texaco Ireland Ltd v S Murphy (Inspector of Taxes)* Vol IV p 91

Search warrants

Requirement for Customs Officer to have reasonable grounds for suspicion that goods were on premises *Simple Imports Limited and Another v Revenue Commissioners and Others* Vol VI p 141

Validity thereof *Simple Imports Limited and Another v Revenue Commissioners and Others* Vol VI p 141

Secondary evidence

not admissible *Gilbert Hewson v J B Kealy (Inspector of Taxes)* Vol II p 15

Seizure

interpleader summons arose out of the seizure by the applicant in his role as Revenue sheriff of goods and chattels claimed to be the property of the claimant in the action *Patrick Cusack v Evelyn O'Reilly & The Honourable Mr Justice Frank Roe & Others* Vol IV p 86

of oil tanker by the Revenue Commissioners *McCrystal Oil Co Ltd v The Revenue Commissioners & Others* Vol IV p 386

Series of transactions

through a chain of companies including the abandonment by the respondent and his wife of their respective options *TA Dilleen (Inspector of Taxes) v Edward J Kearns* Vol IV p 547

with associated companies *O'Connlain (Inspector of Taxes) v Belvedere Estates Ltd* Vol III p 271

Services

supply of, for value added tax purposes, by a solicitor to a non resident, not established in the state but resident in EU, where services deemed to be supplied *JJ Bourke (Inspector of Taxes) v WG Bradley & Sons* Vol IV p 117

whether a contract of services or a contract for services *Henry Denny & Sons (Ir) Ltd v Minister for Social Welfare* Vol V p 238, *Ó Coindeabháin v Mooney* Vol III p 45

Services (contd)

whether package of services was a single supply or two separate services *DA MacCarthaigh, Inspector of Taxes v Cablelink Ltd, Cablelink Waterford Ltd and Galway Cable Vision Ltd* Vol VI p 595

Settlement of legal action

compensation paid to tenants of adjoining premises for interference with light and air, whether allowable Case I deduction *Davis (Inspector of Taxes) v X Ltd* Vol II p 45

Settlement of income

deed of appointment by parent in favour of child *EG v Mac Shamhrain (Inspector of Taxes)* Vol II p 352

Shares

finance company, dealing in stocks and shares, whether investments should be valued at cost or market value *AB Ltd v Mac Giolla Riogh (Inspector of Taxes)* Vol II p 419

whether loan notes are treated as shares *Patrick J O'Connell (Inspector of Taxes) v Thomas Keleghan* Vol VI p 201

Shareholders

whether preference shareholders are entitled to participate in capital distribution whether entitled to a portion of issue of new ordinary shares whether opposition of minority shareholders *Williams Group Tullamore Ltd v Companies Act 1963 to 1983* Vol III p 423

Slaughter houses

excise duty imposed on proprietors of slaughter houses and exporters of live animals, whether ultra vires and void *Doyle & Others v An Taoiseach & Others* Vol III p 73

Single source

foreign trades, basis of assessment under Case III *O'Conaill (Inspector of Taxes) v R* Vol II p 304

Social welfare

contract meter reader, whether the meter reader performed services under a contract of service or a contract for services, whether appeals officer was entitled to conclude that a contract of service existed *Electricity Supply Board v The Minister for Social Community and Family Affairs and others* 2006 p 63

employee, whether a member of the crew of a fishing vessel can be an "employee", whether there can be an "employee" without there being a corresponding employer, whether Social Welfare (Consolidation) Act 1981 applies to self employed persons, whether scheme of Act and regulations is limited to employer/ employee circumstances whether Minister has unlimited power to make regulations enabling any person to be treated as an employee. *The Minister for Social Welfare v John Griffiths* Vol IV p 378

employer's contribution of PRSI in respect of "reckonable earnings" of employees, when payable, liability of liquidator preferential status *The Companies Act 1963-1983 v Castlemahon Poultry Products Ltd* Vol III p 509

Social welfare (contd)

meaning of entry into insurance, definition of contribution year, whether entitled to old age contributory pension, whether issue open to appeal *Albert Kinghan v The Minister for Social Welfare* Vol III p 436

whether dockers working under a pooling arrangement can receive unemployment benefit when they are not occupied unloading ships, whether dockers had a contract of employment with their Association, separate contracts on each occasion of their employment, whether level of earnings material to question of employment *James Louth & Others v Minister for Social Welfare* Vol IV p 391

whether a wholesale distributor of newspapers a self employed person *Tony McAuliffe v Minister for Social Welfare* Vol V p 94

widows contributory pension, whether increase for dependent children liable to tax on parent, *Sean Ó Síocháin (Inspector of Taxes) v Bridget Neenan* Vol V p 472. 1998 p 111

Solicitors fees

whether allowable as management expense, *Stephen Court Ltd v JA Browne (Inspector of Taxes)* Vol V p 680

Special Commissioners

whether facts found by can be re-opened *McCall (deceased) v Commissioners of Inland Revenue* Vol I p 28

Speciality debts

whether *situs* of a speciality debt is the country where the deed is situate *PV Murtagh (Inspector of Taxes) v Samuel Rusk* Vol VI p 817

Sports

club, whether set up for tax avoidance or *bona fide* purposes *Revenue v ORMG* Vol III p 28

Stallion fees

profits from, whether liable to tax under Schedule B or Schedule D income tax paid, whether further balance due *Cloghran Stud Farm v AG Birch (Inspector of Taxes)* Vol I p 496

Stamp duties

agreement for sale granting immediate possession on payment of deposit followed by agreement for sale of residual interest, whether the transfer of the residual interest stampable on the value of the residual interest or on the value of the entire property whether *Waterford Glass (Group Services) Ltd v Revenue* Vol IV p 187

charitable bequest, whether it had to be expended in Ireland for to qualify for exemption under SD (Ire) Act 1842 s 38 *The Revenue Commissioners v The Most Reverend Edward Doorley* Vol V p 539

deed inadvertently stamped, whether repayment due, *Terence Byrne v The Revenue Commissioners* Vol V p 560

instruments relating to the internal affairs of a society were exempt from stamp duty, whether this exemption extended to a transfer of a premises to a society to conduct its business *Irish Nationwide Building Society v Revenue Commissioners* Vol IV p 296

Stamp duties (contd)

new interest and penalty provisions introduced by FA 1991 s 100 came into effect on 1 November 1991 and previous provision for interest and penalties under Stamp Act 1891 s 15 were repealed on 29 May 1991, the date of the passing of FA 1991, whether interest and penalties applied between 29 May 1991 and 1 November 1991 *Edward O'Leary v The Revenue Commissioners* Vol IV p 357

substance of transactions, amount chargeable on a deed of transfer, contracts and consideration structured to minimise stamp duty *VIEK Investments Ltd v The Revenue Commissioners* Vol IV p 367

whether doubt in a Stamp Act construed in favour of the taxpayer, whether a lease as a conveyance for sale, *JF O'Sullivan v The Revenue Commissioners* Vol V p 570

whether deeds not properly stamped were admissible in evidence *AIB plc v James Bolger & Joan Bolger* Vol V p 1; *Kenny, J v Revenue Commissioners, Goodman & Gemon Ltd (Notice Parties)* Vol V p 362

Stamping

whether subsequent stamping of a document can displace what the documents says on its face, in the absence of fraud, sham or other vitiating circumstance *Patrick J O'Connell (Inspector of Taxes) v John Fleming* Vol VI p 453

Statutory body

whether carrying on a trade *The Exported Live Stock (Insurance) Board v TJ Carroll (Inspector of Taxes)* Vol II p 211

Stock

IN TRADE

building contractors, whether lands the subject matter of a contract for sale entered into during an accounting period constitute trading stock for the year ending in that accounting period, whether inclusion of the lands in the accounts in accordance with good accounting procedure was evidence of the commercial reality of the transaction, whether absence of possession, conveyance of legal estate and planning permission relevant to taxpayer's claim for relief *Murnaghan Brothers Ltd v S O'Maoldhomhnaigh* Vol IV p 304

cost of, development company *O'Connlain (Inspector of Taxes) v Belvedere Estates Ltd* Vol III p 271

notional loss from decrease in value of goods before delivery *The Revenue Commissioners v Latchford & Sons Ltd* Vol I p 240

trading property company, farm land, letting to partners on conacre, area zoned for development, land transferred to new company, whether land trading stock of company *L O hArgain (Inspector of Taxes) v B Ltd* Vol III p 9

Stock relief

building contractors, whether lands the subject matter of a contract for sale entered into during an accounting period constitute trading stock for the year ending in that accounting period, whether inclusion of the lands in the accounts in accordance with good accounting procedure was evidence of the commercial reality of the transaction, whether absence of possession, conveyance of legal estate and planning permission relevant to taxpayer's claim for relief *Murnaghan Brothers Ltd v S O'Maoldhomhnaigh* Vol IV p 304

Stock relief (contd)

company engaged in manufacture and erection of prefabricated buildings deposit of 15 per cent of total cost paid on execution of contract, whether payment on account of trading stock or security for contracts, whether deposit should be deducted from value of stock for stock relief purposes *Ó Laoghaire (Inspector of Taxes) v CD Ltd* Vol III p 51

definition of trading stock in hand *Green & Co (Cork) Ltd v The Revenue Commissioners* Vol I p 130

under FA 1975 s 31, sales must be direct to farmers, assembly not understood as manufacturing by well informed laymen *Irish Agricultural Machinery Ltd v S Ó Culacháin (Inspector of Taxes)* Vol III p 611

Stocks

change therein, causing reduction in value, whether trading profit *Davis (Inspector of Taxes) v Hibernian Bank Ltd* Vol I p 503

finance company, dealing in stocks and shares, whether investments should be valued at cost or market value *AB Ltd v Mac Giolla Riogh (Inspector of Taxes)* Vol II p 419

Shares

change therein, causing reduction in value, whether trading profit *Davis (Inspector of Taxes) v Hibernian Bank Ltd* Vol I p 503

Subrogation agreements

whether third party bound by terms of original agreement *The Companies Act 1963-1983 v MFN Construction Co Ltd (in liquidation) on the application of Patrick Tuffy (liquidator)* Vol IV p 82

Subcontractors

whether lorry owners carrying sand and gravel were engaged as subcontractors under a construction contract, whether the lorry owners became the proprietors of the quarry materials *O'Grady v Laragan Quarries Ltd* Vol IV p 269

Subsidiary

whether a "post-appointed day company" was a subsidiary of the appellant company *Associated Properties Ltd v The Revenue Commissioners* Vol II p 175

Substance of transactions

stamp duties, amount chargeable on a deed of transfer, contracts and consideration structured to minimise stamp duty *VIEK Investments Ltd v The Revenue Commissioners* Vol IV p 367

Succession

joint ownership whether survivor entitled, whether resulting trust *M Lynch v M Burke & AIB plc* Vol V p 271

whether surviving spouse must exercise right under Succession Act *In the Matter of the Estates of Cummins (Decd): O'Dwyer & Ors v Keegan & Ors* Vol V p 367

Summons

served in respect of tax liabilities the subject matter of earlier appeals whether Circuit Court judge has discretion to accept late filing of notice and fee, whether dissatisfaction expressed at the Circuit Court appeal hearings, whether dissatisfaction must be expressed immediately after determination by the Circuit Court, whether notice to county registrar must be lodged within 21 days together with the £20 fee, whether payment of tax denies access to the courts, whether requirements are directory or mandatory, whether tax must be paid before the case stated is determined, whether time lapse after expression of dissatisfaction is fatal *Michael A Bairead v Martin C Carr* Vol IV p 505

Superannuation scheme

whether trustees have absolute discretion on the distribution of the fund following the death of a member, whether a separated wife, a common law wife and children are entitled to be considered as beneficiaries, whether renunciation under a separation deed rules out entitlement, whether trustees are bound by a direction in the member's will *Crowe Engineering Ltd v Phyllis Lynch & Others* Vol IV p 340

Surety

whether creditor to resort to securities received from principal before proceeding against surety *Attorney General v Sun Alliance & London Insurance Ltd* Vol III p 265

Surcharge

corporation tax, advertising agency, whether a profession for the purposes of corporation tax surcharge *Mac Giolla Mhaith (Inspector of Taxes) v Cronin & Associates Ltd* Vol III p 211

undistributed income of close company *Rahinstown Estates Co v M Hughes (Inspector of Taxes)* Vol III p 517

T

Tax amnesty

inducement to evade tax *Beverly Cooper-Flynn v RTE, Charlie Bird and James Howard* Vol VI p 195

Tax avoidance

dealing in and developing land *O'Connlain (Inspector of Taxes) v Belvedere Estates Ltd* Vol III p 271

no general anti-avoidance legislation, allowable losses for capital gains tax used for avoidance of tax, whether allowable *Patrick McGrath & Others v JE McDermott (Inspector of Taxes)* Vol III p 683

patent rights paid to non-residents, scheme within *Furniss v Dawson* principle *Pandion Haliaetus Ltd, Ospreycare Ltd, Osprey Systems Design Ltd v The Revenue Commissioners* Vol III p 670

premium on lease payable by instalments, whether allowable under ITA 1967 s 91 or whether tax avoidance scheme *The Hammond Lane Metal Co Ltd v S Ó Culacháin (Inspector of Taxes)* Vol IV p 197

sports club, whether set up for tax avoidance or bona fide purposes *Revenue v ORMG* Vol III p 28

Tax avoidance (contd)

stamp duties, substance of transactions, amount chargeable on a deed of transfer, contracts and consideration structured to minimise stamp duty *VIEK Investments Ltd v The Revenue Commissioners* Vol IV p 367

transfer of assets to offshore tax havens, whether accountants could be requested to furnish relevant particulars in respect of all their clients *Warnock & Others practising as Stokes Kennedy Crowley and Co v The Revenue Commissioners* Vol III p 356

whether tax avoidance scheme under ITA 1967 Ch VI effective *The Hammond Lane Metal Co Ltd v S Ó Culacháin (Inspector of Taxes)* Vol IV p 197

whether a tax avoidance scheme *Airspace Investments Ltd v M Moore (Inspector of Taxes)* Vol V p 3

whether a tax avoidance scheme valid *Revenue Commissioners v Henry Young* Vol V p 295

Tax clearance certificate

capital gains tax, on sale of bonds, whether applicant ordinarily resident in the state is entitled to a clearance certificate *The State (FIC Ltd) v O'Ceallaigh* Vol III p 124

for Government contracts, whether Revenue Commissioners can have regard to tax default of previous "connected" company *The State (Melbarian Enterprises Ltd) v The Revenue Commissioners* Vol III p 290

whether absence of a clearance certificate prohibited the Revenue Commissioners from repaying tax deducted by purchaser *Bank of Ireland Finance Ltd v The Revenue Commissioners* Vol IV p 217

Tax deducted from annuity

payable under a trust, where such tax is refunded by the Revenue Commissioners to the annuitant, is the annuitant accountable to the trust for the tax so refunded *In re Swan , Deceased; The Hibernian Bank Ltd v Munro & Ors* Vol V p 565

Tax evasion

Inducement to evade tax *Beverly Cooper-Flynn v RTE, Charlie Bird and James Howard* Vol VI p 195

Tax havens

transfer of assets to offshore tax havens, whether accountants could be requested to furnish relevant particulars in respect of all their clients *Warnock & Others practising as Stokes Kennedy Crowley and Co v The Revenue Commissioners* Vol III p 356

Taxable person

whether respondent was taxable person pursuant to Value Added Tax Act 1972 *Brendan Crawford (Inspector of Taxes) v Centime Ltd* Vol VI p 823

Taxpayer's Charter of Rights

application and enforcement of the terms of the Taxpayer's Charter of Rights is subject to the operation of the Tax Code *Terence Keogh v Criminal Assets Bureau, Revenue Commissioners* Vol VI p 635

Tax returns

return of income, what constitutes a proper return of income for the assessment of income tax *MA Bairead v M McDonald* Vol IV p 475

Technical information

payments made under an agreement for the supply of *S Ltd v O'Sullivan* Vol II p 602

Temporary employee

engaged through employment agency *The Minister for Labour v PMPA Insurance Co Ltd (under administration)* Vol III p 505

Time limit

for claiming repayment of stamp duty, whether expired, *Terence Byrne v The Revenue Commissioners* Vol V p 560

30-day period for filing returns prescribed by TCA 1997, s 933 *AS v Criminal Assets Bureau* Vol VI p 799

Total income

payment for maintenance and upkeep of residence not part of total income *The Most Honourable Frances Elizabeth Sarah Marchioness Conyngham v The Revenue Commissioners* Vol I p 231

whether the expression "total income means income before or after the deduction of group relief *Cronin (Inspector of Taxes) v Youghal Carpets Ltd* Vol III p 229

Trade

bad debts recovered, liability to tax *Bourke (Inspector of Taxes) v Lyster and Sons Ltd* Vol II p 374

brewery, whether liability in respect of transactions under DORA requisition orders *Arthur Guinness Son & Co Ltd v CIR*

carried on *Arthur Guinness Son & Co Ltd v CIR* Vol I p 1

carried on wholly in England *O'Conaill (Inspector of Taxes) v R* Vol II p 304

collection of rents and dividends and distribution of dividends, whether constituted trading *The Commissioners of Inland Revenue and The Dublin and Kingstown Railway Co* Vol I p 119

collection of, debts whether constituted trading *The City of Dublin Steampacket Co v Revenue Commissioners* Vol I p 108

executor carrying on trade, recovery by executor of debts allowed as bad debts in lifetime of deceased, whether a trading receipt *CD v JM O'Sullivan (Inspector of Taxes)* Vol II p 140

exercised in the State *The Cunard Steam Ship Co Ltd v Herlihy (Inspector of Taxes), and The Cunard Steam Ship Co Ltd v Revenue Commissioners* Vol I p 330

formation expenses, whether allowable against trading profits *JB Kealy (Inspector of Taxes) v O'Mara (Limerick) Ltd* Vol I p 642

income from the leasing of premises, whether leasing constitutes trading whether earned income *Pairceir (Inspector of Taxes) v EM* Vol II p 596

income school and exam fees whether trading income *The Pharmaceutical Society of Ireland v The Revenue Commissioners* Vol I p 542

Trade (contd)

Industrial and Provident Societies, trading with both members and non-members, investments and property purchased out of trading profits, whether the dividends and rents form part of the profits of the trade *The Revenue Commissioners v Y Ltd* Vol II p 195

levies on course betting, whether taxable a income or profits of a trade *The Racing Board v S Ó Culacháin* Vol IV p 73

payments on foot of earlier debt where profit arose, whether constituted trading *The City of Dublin Steampacket Co v Revenue Commissioners* Vol I p 108

profits/receipts *O'Dwyer (Inspector of Taxes) and the Revenue Commissioners v Irish Exporters and Importers Ltd (In Liquidation)* Vol I p 629

sale at cost plus interest, whether constituted trading *McCall (deceased) v Commissioners of Inland Revenue* Vol I p 28

statutory body, whether carrying on a trade *The Exported Live Stock (Insurance) Board v T J Carroll (Inspector of Taxes)* Vol II p 211

surplus of co-op from dealing with members, whether trading profits, whether exempt *Kennedy (Inspector of Taxes) v The Rattoo Co-op Dairy Society Ltd* Vol I p 315

trade consisting of the manufacturing of goods or sale of machinery or plant to farmers *Irish Agricultural Machinery Ltd v S Ó Culacháin (Inspector of Taxes)* Vol III p 611

whether a sum which arose to the company on the liquidation of a wholly owned subsidiary was part of its trading profits *Guinness & Mahon Ltd v Browne (Inspector of Taxes)* Vol III p 373

whiskey in bond sold by publican, whether trading transaction *McCall (deceased) v Commissioners of Inland Revenue* Vol I p 28

Trading stock

building contractors, whether lands the subject matter of a contract for sale entered into during an accounting period constitute trading stock for the year ending in that accounting period, whether inclusion of the lands in the accounts in accordance with good accounting procedure was evidence of the commercial reality of the transaction, whether absence of possession, conveyance of legal estate and planning permission relevant to taxpayer's claim for relief *Murnaghan Brothers Ltd v S O'Maoldhomhnaigh* Vol IV p 304

in hand, definition, for stock relief purposes *Green & Co (Cork) Ltd v The Revenue Commissioners* Vol I p 130

property company, farm land, letting to partners on conacre, area zoned for development, land transferred to new company, whether land trading stock of company *L O hArgain (Inspector of Taxes) v B Ltd* Vol III p 9

Training grants

whether capital or revenue receipt *O'Cleirigh (Inspector of Taxes) v Jacobs International Ltd Incorporated* Vol III p 165

Transfer

of a business, whether the exemption under s 3(5)(b)(iii) of the Value Added Tax Act 1972 applies where there is a transfer of a business or part thereof or the 'benefit' of the business is transferred *Ó Culacháin, Inspector of Taxes v Stylo Barratt Shoes Ltd* Vol VI p 617

of assets to offshore tax havens *Warnock & Others practising as Stokes Kennedy Crowley and Co v The Revenue Commissioners* Vol III p 356

of land property company, farm land, letting to partners on conacre, area zoned for development, land transferred to new company, whether land trading stock of company *L O hArgain (Inspector of Taxes) v B Ltd* Vol III p 9

Travelling expenses

Schedule E deductions *Phillips (Inspector of Taxes) v Keane* Vol I p 64

Trees

whether purchasing and planting of trees is allowable deduction from farming profits *Connolly (Inspector of Taxes) v WW* Vol II p 657

Tribunal

of inquiry, whether Tribunal of Inquiry Evidence Act 1921 applies, whether a Tribunal constitutionally valid *Charles Haughey & Other v Attorney General and Others* Vol VI p 67

Trusts

business carried on abroad controlled by resident trustees *The Executors and Trustees of A C Ferguson (deceased) v Donovan (Inspector of Taxes)* Vol I p 183

joint ownership whether survivor entitled, whether resulting trust *M Lynch v M Burke & AIB plc* Vol V p 271

payment under, for maintenance of residence not part of total income *The Most Hon Frances Elizabeth Sarah Marchioness Conyngham v The Revenue Commissioners* Vol I p 231

trust in favour of charitable objects with provision for re-vestment of income in settlor in certain contingencies whether income of settlor or trustees *HPC Hughes (Inspector of Taxes) v Miss Gretta Smyth (Sister Mary Bernard) & Others* Vol I p 411

whether respondents were acting in fiduciary capacity, solicitor's duty to account *PO Cahill (Inspector of Taxes) v Patrick O'Driscoll, Michael O'Driscoll and William F O'Driscoll* Vol VI p 793

Trustees

powers of, superannuation scheme whether trustees have absolute discretion on the distribution of the fund following the death of a member, whether a separated wife, a common law wife and children are entitled to be considered as beneficiaries, whether renunciation under a separation deed rules out entitlement, whether trustees are bound by a direction in the member's will *Crowe Engineering Ltd v Phyllis Lynch & Others* Vol IV p 340

under Succession Act 1965 *Moloney (Inspector of Taxes) v Allied Irish Banks Ltd as executors of the estate of Francis J Doherty deceased* Vol III p 477

U

Unconstitutional

aggregation of earned income of married persons unconstitutional *Bernard Muckley and Anne Muckley v Ireland, The Attorney General and The Revenue Commissioners* Vol III p 188

bookmaker convicted and fined in the District Court of offences under the Betting Acts penal warrant for imprisonment, whether constitutional *John B Murphy v District Justice Brendan Wallace & Others* Vol IV p 278

residential property tax, whether unconstitutional *PJ Madigan & p Madigan v The Attorney General, The Revenue Commissioners & Others* Vol III p 127

whether penalties for failure to make returns are unconstitutional *Edward McLoughlin and Thomas Marie Tuite v The Revenue Commissioners and The Attorney General* Vol III p 387

whether unconstitutional for applicant to be convicted and fined for keeping hydrocarbon oil in his motor vehicle on which custom and excise duty had not been paid, whether delegation of powers under Imposition of Duties Act 1957 is permissible *Charles McDaid v His Honour Judge David Sheehy, the Director of Public Prosecutions & Others* Vol IV p 162, Vol V p 696

Unjust enrichment

whether Revenue Commissioners were unjustly enriched as a result of the retention of overpaid tax *Robert Harris v JJ Quigley and Liam Irwin* Vol VI p 839

Unjust enrichment of the State

whether a common law right to restitution *O'Rourke v Revenue Commissioners* Vol V p 321

V

Valuation

agreement for sale granting immediate possession on payment of deposit followed by agreement for sale of residual interest, whether the transfer of the residual interest stampable on the value of the residual interest or on the value of the entire property whether *Waterford Glass (Group Services) Ltd v The Revenue Commissioners* Vol IV p 187

agricultural land, appeal against market value at 6 April 1974 as determined by Circuit Court, whether agricultural value the sole determining factor, whether development potential attached on 6 April 1974, whether subsequent planning permission for milk processing plant relevant *J McMahon (Inspector of Taxes) v Albert Noel Murphy* Vol IV p 125

of land under F(MP)A 1968 s 18, development company *Ó Connlain (Inspector of Taxes) v Belvedere Estates Ltd* Vol III p 271

of land occupied for market gardening *L v McGarry (Inspector of Taxes)* Vol II p 241

of shares in a private trading company, *E A Smyth v Revenue Commissioners* Vol V p 532, *In the estate of Thomas McNAmee & Other v The Revenue Commissioners* Vol V p 577

of shares in a private non-trading company *Revenue Commissioners v Henry Young* Vol V p 294

Valuation (contd)

finance company, dealing in stocks and shares, whether investments should be valued at cost or market value *AB Ltd v Mac Giolla Riogh (Inspector of Taxes)* Vol II p 419

Value added tax

arbitrator's award, whether arbitrator misconducted himself in valuating property which was the subject of an award *Campus Stadium Ireland Development Ltd v Dublin Waterworld Ltd* 2006 p 55

cable television system whether liable to value added tax on sales to customers *TJ Brosnan (Inspector of Taxes) v Cork Communications Ltd* Vol IV p 349

excise duty, whether zero rated *DH Burke & Sons Ltd v The Revenue Commissioners, Ireland and The Attorney General* Vol V p 418

installation of fixtures subject to low rate of value added tax, whether or not television aerials attached to roof of a house are fixtures *John Maye v The Revenue Commissioners* Vol III p 332

interpretation of when a transaction involves the sale of a business *Cyril Forbes v John Tobin And Janet Tobin* Vol VI p 483

meaning of development property *Cyril Forbes v John Tobin And Janet Tobin* Vol VI p 483

Property Unit Trust – whether VAT credits allowable on all expenses at pre lease and post lease stages – special VAT provisions *Erin Executor and Trustee Co Ltd v The Revenue Commissioners* Vol V p 76

refunds to non-EU residents, whether refunds obtainable through refunding agencies, whether revenue justified in withholding repayments, *Taxback Limited v The Revenue Commissioners* Vol V p 412

scheme for retailers, interpretation of, whether based on purchases or sales, *DH Burke & Sons Ltd v The Revenue Commissioners, Ireland and The Attorney General* Vol V p 418

supply of services by a solicitor to a non resident, not established in the state but resident in EU, where services deemed to be supplied *JJ Bourke (Inspector of Taxes) v WG Bradley & Sons* Vol IV p 117

whether agreement to purchase retail premises and fixtures and fittings was chargeable to VAT *Ó Culacháin, Inspector of Taxes v Stylo Barratt Shoes Ltd* Vol VI p 617

whether non resident company registered in the State entitled to be registered for value added tax *WLD Worldwide Leather Diffusion Ltd v The Revenue Commissioners* Vol V p 61

whether corporate body exploiting copyrights supplying service within meaning of VATA – Copyright Act 1963 *Phonographic Performance (Ireland) Ltd v J Somers (Inspector of Taxes)* Vol IV p 314

whether repayments of VAT should carry interest *Bank of Ireland Trust Services Limited v The Revenue Commissioners* Vol VI p 513

whether respondent was taxable person pursuant to Value Added Tax Act 1972 *Brendan Crawford (Inspector of Taxes) v Centime Ltd* Vol VI p 823

whether respondents engaged in the supply of two separate services with two separate VAT rates *DA MacCarthaigh, Inspector of Taxes v Cablelink Ltd, Cablelink Waterford Ltd and Galway Cable Vision Ltd* Vol VI p 595

Value added tax (contd)

whether value added tax is subject to laws of the European Union *Governor & Co of the Bank of Ireland v Michael John Meeneghan & Ors* Vol V p 44

Veterinary

body corporate performing statutory functions whether profits liable to tax *The Veterinary Council v F Corr (Inspector of Taxes)* Vol II p 204

Vocation

professional jockey *Wing v O'Connell (Inspector of Taxes)* Vol I p 155

Voluntary liquidator

whether liability of voluntary liquidator is different than that of court liquidator *A Noyek & Sons Ltd (in voluntary liquidation), Alex Burns v EN Hearne* Vol III p 523

W

Widows

contributory pension and children contributory pensions granted pension payable to the widow whereas children's pension payable to widow for children *E Ó Coindealbháin (Inspector of Taxes) v Breda O'Carroll* Vol IV p 221

whether increases in widow's contributory social welfare pension by resson of dependent children constitutes taxable income received by and assessable on the widow *Sean Ó Síocháin (Inspector of Taxes) v Bridget Neenan* Vol VI p 59

Wife

separate domicile *JW v JW* Vol IV p 437

Winding up

deferred by reason of scheme of arrangement approved by High Court *The Companies Act 1963-1983 and MFN Construction Co Ltd (in liquidation) on the application of Patrick Tuffy (liquidator)* Vol IV p 82

preferential payments, whether employee engaged under a contract of service or contract for services *In the matter of The Sunday Tribune Limited (in Liquidation)* 1998 p 177

shorter period allowed for making distributions of share capital in a winding up *Rahinstown Estates Co v M Hughes (Inspector of Taxes)* Vol III p 517

whether assessments of PRSI entitled to super preferential priority *Re Coombe Importers Ltd (In Liq) and Re the Companies Acts 1963-1990* Vol VI p 1

Winding Up Petition

Meaning of substantial and reasonable defence to Revenue petition to wind up company for unpaid taxes *In the Matter of Millhouse Taverns Ltd and the Companies Act 1963-1999*Vol VI p 191

Withholding tax

on professional services, whether method of granting credit for same is constitutional *Michael Daly v The Revenue Commissioners* Vol V p 213

Woodlands

whether purchasing and planting of trees is allowable deduction from farming profits *Connolly (Inspector of Taxes) v WW* Vol II p 657